A powerful Online Learning Center accompanies *Writing Today*, Second Edition:

**www.mhhe.com/writingtoday**

The site features all the resources of Catalyst 2.0, the premier online tool for writing, research, and editing.

To access premium Catalyst content, please use the following code:

G8JR-Y9P7-TTEH-9487-THW4

Catalyst 2.0 features interactive tutorials on document design and visual rhetoric, guides for avoiding plagiarism and evaluating sources, electronic writing tutors for composing a range of essays and more than 4,500 exercises with feedback in grammar, usage, and punctuation.

Throughout Writing Today you will find **More Options Online** boxes directing you to specific Catalyst 2.0 resources that provide further help on the topic at hand.

Visit **www.mhhe.com/writingtoday** to access a wealth of online writing resources.

# Writing Today

*Book title*

## Contexts and Options for the Real World

*subtitle – optional*

### SECOND EDITION

*not title*

**DONALD PHARR**
*Saint Leo University*

**SANTI V. BUSCEMI**
*Middlesex County College*

*Editors Keep in this order*

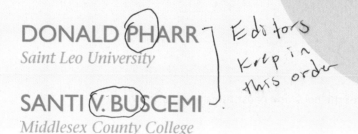

*use 1st city listed* — *publishin company*

**Mc Graw Hill** **Higher Education**

Boston   Burr Ridge, IL   Dubuque, IA   New York   San Francisco   St. Louis
Bangkok   Bogotá   Caracas   Kuala Lumpur   Lisbon   London   Madrid   Mexico City
Milan   Montreal   New Delhi   Santiago   Seoul   Singapore   Sydney   Taipei   Toronto

# Higher Education

*Writing Today*
*Contexts and Options for the Real World*

This book is printed on acid-free paper.

2 3 4 5 6 7 8 9 0 DOC DOC 0 9

*only year*

ISBN: 978-0-07-353322-3
MHID: 0-07-353322-X

Vice president and Editor-in-chief: *Michael Ryan*
Publisher: *David S. Patterson*
Senior sponsoring editor: *Christopher Bennem*
Director of development: *Carla Kay Samodulski*
Marketing manager: *Allison Jones*
Editorial coordinator: *Jesse Hassenger*
Senior media producer: *Todd Vaccaro*
Production editors: *Melissa Williams/Bonnie Briggle, Lachina Publishing Services*
Lead production supervisor: *Randy Hurst*
Interior designer: *Glenda King*
Cover designer: *Laurie Entringer*
Compositor: *Lachina Publishing Services*
Typeface: *9.5/12 Stone Serif*
Printer and binder: *RR Donnelley & Sons, Inc.*

Text credits appear on page C-1 at the end of the book and constitute an extension of the copyright page.

**Library of Congress Cataloging-in-Publication Data**
Pharr, Donald.
    Writing today : contexts and options for the real world / Donald Pharr, Santi Buscemi.—2nd ed.
      p. cm.
      Includes index.
    ISBN-13: 978-0-07-353322-3
    ISBN-10: 0-07-353322-X
    1. English language—Rhetoric. 2. Report writing. 3. English language—
    Grammar—Problems, exercises, etc. I. Buscemi, Santi V. II. Title.
PE1408.P46 2008
808'.042—dc22
                                                                        2007068455

www.mhhe.com

*This book is dedicated to*

*Mary F. Pharr and*

*Elaine Buscemi*

*for their support, love,*

*and—above all—patience.*

# ABOUT THE AUTHORS

## DONALD PHARR

Donald Pharr received his bachelor's degree from Indiana State University and his master's and doctorate from the University of Georgia. He is the co-author (with Gerald J. Schiffhorst) of *The Short Handbook for Writers*, second edition. He taught for many years in the Florida community college system, where he specialized in applied composition: business, technical, and science writing. As well, he has spent almost two decades consulting as a technical writer and editor. Dr. Pharr is currently associate professor of English at Saint Leo University. He lives in Lakeland, Florida, with his wife, Mary.

## SANTI V. BUSCEMI

Santi V. Buscemi teaches reading, composition, and literature at Middlesex County College in Edison, New Jersey, where he was chair of the Department of English for twenty-eight years. He is the author of *A Reader for College Writers*, sixth edition, *75 Readings*, ninth edition, *75 Readings Plus*, seventh edition, *The Basics*, fourth edition, and the writing software *AllWrite!* He has lectured on freshman composition and developmental education at regional and national conferences in the United States and South Africa. He also served as a business and technical writing consultant/trainer for the Altria Group, Horizon Blue Cross/Blue Shield, the Port Authority of New York and New Jersey, and Bristol-Myers Squibb. He has also translated *C'era Una Volta,* the fairy tales of Luigi Capuana, from the Italian. Professor Buscemi is past president of the New Jersey College English Association and the New Jersey Association for Developmental Education, and he served on the NADE Adjunct Task Force.

# CONTENTS

# PART 2
# STRUCTURES

CHAPTER 10

CHAPTER 11

CHAPTER 12

## PART 4
# GRAMMAR AND MECHANICS

# PREFACE

The careers that today's students aspire to, and the preparation that they need for those careers, are different from what they were only ten years ago. Much of this change, of course, can be attributed to the electronic revolution in communications, which presents students with increasingly sophisticated tools for researching, writing, revising, and communicating with others. Consequently, in recent years, the English composition course, already essential in a complete and well-planned college curriculum, has also been changing in new and challenging ways.

As composition instructors with sixty years of experience between us, we have learned that today's college students need and want a curriculum that challenges them in the classroom, provides them with skills they can use in other college courses, and, most important, prepares them to communicate effectively in the professional and business worlds. Our goal in the first edition of *Writing Today* was to give students realistic, practical reasons to master college reading and writing because success in writing is a prerequisite to achieving continued success in college and in their careers. Therefore, we decided to write a text that would focus on both academic and professional contexts for writing. *Writing Today* addresses the skepticism of students who see English composition classes as just another hurdle on their way to a degree. *Writing Today* helps them use reading and writing as tools for continued intellectual growth that they can employ in any writing context they confront, long after having completed even their most advanced degrees.

In the second edition of *Writing Today*, we are moving forward. Our emphasis is even more practical, helping students realize the writing challenges that lie before them and giving them still more tools with which to meet those challenges.

## WELCOME TO THE SECOND EDITION!

We have thoroughly revised *Writing Today* in order to address the changing needs of its users. This revision strengthens existing components of the original text while also adding new and very valuable sections throughout the text:

## INTRODUCTION

We have added an introductory chapter, "Achieving Student Success," to help students with the transition to the college environment. In our experience, when students fail a college course, it is rarely because of a lack of ability; instead, these students are not using their abilities in a way that matches the requirements of the course. Traditional-age students who enroll in college are facing a major transition in their lives, one that requires much more from them than they might realize at first glance. As well, people in their thirties or forties who are returning to college—or attending for the first time—find that they must deal with a new and complex set of responsibilities added to their already busy lives. This chapter helps all new and newly returning students by focusing on attitude, information access, preparation and organization, classroom decorum, study habits, and time management.

## PART 1: APPROACHES

- Part 1 has been revised to strengthen its emphasis on the relation of college writing to writing contexts that students will face after they graduate.
- We have combined the first edition's chapters 4 and 5 into one chapter on revision: "Reshaping Your Essay: Global Revision, Editing, and Proofreading." This comprehensive approach allows students to develop a more holistic sense of this crucial stage in the writing process.
- The second edition of *Writing Today* recognizes the increasing importance of visual literacy in today's world. We have increased our coverage of this issue throughout the book, and in Part 1 we have added a new section to each of the four chapters: "Responding to Visuals." This section alerts students to the importance of visual literacy and prepares them for the more complex visual literacy assignments that they will find in Part 2.

## PART 2: STRUCTURES

- In response to the demand for more coverage of visual literacy, we have added two important components to each chapter in Part 2: a visual representation analysis assignment and a section called "Responding to an Image." Each relates the chapter's coverage—narration, definition, process analysis, and so on—to images from our modern commercial and popular culture as well as images from our history. These sections give students wide opportunities to expand their visual literacy and hone their essay-writing skills.
- A major part of the college experience today is the oral presentation. After each of the professional essays in chapters 5–14, we have added oral presentation assignments that reflect the themes and ideas of the essay. We have also linked these to the new Chapter 18: "Group Projects and Oral Presentations."

## PART 3: APPLICATIONS

- Part 3 has been substantially expanded and thoroughly reorganized.
- New Chapter 15 ("Writing Proposals") covers a crucial type of applied writing, the proposal. People working in almost any type of business or profession need to know how to develop effective proposals, and this chapter covers the subject in depth.
- New Chapter 16 ("Writing Critiques") examines not only critiques of literary and artistic works but also those addressing more practical subjects. This chapter includes four critiques by professional writers.
- New Chapter 18 ("Group Projects and Oral Presentations") addresses two crucial areas for college students: working with a team and developing effective presentations. Increasingly, college faculty are making the group project a standard assignment in many courses, and the same faculty often require oral presentations as well. The chapter covers these two subjects, along with their synthesis—the group oral presentation—and how to develop effective visual aids, including slide shows.

- Part 3's new organization presents a more logical sequencing of its chapters: writing proposals, writing critiques, business formats, group projects and oral presentations, essay examinations, the research process, the research paper, and writing about literature. The first edition's Chapter 18 ("Quoting Text") is now the final section of Chapter 20 ("The Research Process").

## PART 4: GRAMMAR AND MECHANICS

- Part 4 has been revised for a stronger focus on identifying and correcting common errors.

## OPTIONS WITHIN DIFFERENT WRITING CONTEXTS

In today's high-tech-dominated world, students are confronted with an exciting, and often bewildering, array of choices in how to write, when to write, and what to write about. A writer's decisions don't happen in a vacuum, of course. As much as possible, we offer scenarios related to the world of writing both inside and outside college. In fact, the chapters in Part 2, "Structures," begin with brief vignettes in which writing and challenges associated with writing play a part in solving problems found in typical business and professional environments. These scenarios help students connect their own daily concerns and their academic and future goals with what the text offers.

In addition, each chapter in Part 2 offers a job-related writing prompt at the end of the chapter along with two sections that ask students to respond to, analyze, or otherwise discuss visual images that carry an intriguing message about our history and culture. Other prompts ask them to explore questions by researching Internet sources. In all cases, the text encourages students to focus on specific questions that allow them to apply the techniques and strategies discussed and illustrated in the chapter. Several chapters in Part 3 also emphasize the notion that effective writing makes use of well-defined contexts. For example, the chapter on business formats suggests a variety of scenarios to which students can respond by writing e-mails, letters, and memoranda, including the all-important context of a job search.

## PRACTICAL OPTIONS THAT MAKE STUDENTS EFFECTIVE WRITERS

In addition to the many years we have spent teaching English composition, we have both worked closely with corporate executives and government officials who need to communicate better with employees, customers, and the public; we have both designed and delivered corporate training programs; we have written and edited reports, letters, and even speeches for major corporations; and we have taught both business and technical communication in college. Our experience as professional writers in both academia and in the business world has taught us that learning rules and principles, albeit important, will supply only about a third of what it takes to become an effective writer. The rest depends on the writer's own good judgment and hard work. In any context, writers must constantly make choices among the variety of options that are available to them, from which technique to use to explore their ideas, through which pattern or patterns to use to support their main point, to which suggestions from fellow students or co-workers to follow in revising a draft. That is why we decided to focus on the importance of the writer's responsibility for choosing and to provide as much guidance as possible regarding the process by which writers exercise judgment.

Indeed, the theme of identifying, choosing among, and exercising options runs throughout the text, with "Consider Your Options" notes in the margin that stress the need to make choices. In addition, student writing through much of the first three parts of the text demonstrates how students can employ a spectrum of rhetorical techniques and choices, and annotated first drafts of student essays at the end of each chapter in Part 2 show students in the process of exercising specific rhetorical and linguistic options as they revise their writing. Our experience in field testing the ideas in this text clearly points to the benefits of allowing students to make informed choices as they work their way through the writing process. Doing so simply makes them more responsible and, therefore, more effective writers.

## OPTIONS FOR USING TECHNOLOGY

Today, a writer's contexts almost always include some form of technology. In keeping with this reality, we have thoroughly integrated *Writing Today,* second edition, with *Catalyst*, the most complete electronic resource for research and writing available. "More Options Online" notes in the margin tell students when they can go online to find additional advice, online writing tutors, help with research, diagnostic tests, over 3,000 practice exercises, and more. In addition, the text includes explanations of the use of word processors, the Internet, databases, and other tools generated by the electronic revolution, along with helpful hints for using electronic resources for researching, drafting, and editing.

## A FOUR-IN-ONE TEXT OPTION

As a guide to the writing process—with a reader and visual texts integrated into this guide—a guide to research, and a handbook for editing student work, *Writing Today* offers a complete text for the first-year writing course.

### A Guide to the Writing Process

**A Practical Introduction to the Process.** The four chapters in Part 1, "Approaches," are a thorough and well-illustrated discussion of the writing process. Chapter 1 provides a definition of the essay and explains its importance as an academic tool and as a way to learn skills that can be applied in the types of writing more often seen in business and professional settings. Through the numerous student and professional examples in the next three chapters, readers easily trace various steps and strategies from which to choose when writing an essay. Again, we emphasize the notion of options for writers and the importance of exercising one's judgment in a particular context.

**Patterns Presented as Options.** Part 2, "Structures," includes nine chapters that are devoted to discussions of the rhetorical options, or patterns, from description to argument. The tenth chapter, Chapter 14, covers essays that use more than one pattern and explains how to draw on a variety of strategies to address complex questions. Each chapter in Part 2 contains three professional essays, complete with introductory materials and questions for writing and discussion. At the end of each chapter, the final and first drafts of a student essay written using the option covered in that chapter show the process of revision in action.

**An Emphasis on Making Choices in Revision.** The guidelines for writing an essay in each chapter end by suggesting the kinds of questions a writer must ask and answer as he or she reviews an essay during the revision stage.

**Plenty of Options for Writing Topics.** Each chapter in Part 2 concludes with a series of suggested assignments, including assignments based on visual images, Internet research, and the workplace.

**Readings, Cartoons, and Photographs.** The reading selections in *Writing Today* offer students examples of writers facing different contexts and choosing among options, and the visuals help introduce the rhetorical options and give students ideas for their own writing.

**Selections from a Variety of Fine Authors.** Integrated into each chapter in Part 2, the diverse selection of professional readings includes essays by Bharati Mukherjee, Barbara Ehrenreich, Sandra Cisneros, Thomas McGuane, Maxine Hong Kingston, Fran Lebowitz, Umberto Eco, David Sedaris, and Lynda Barry, as well as time-tested classics such as "Why I Want a Wife" by Judy Brady and "Just Walk on By" by Brent Staples. The essays, on engaging topics such as personal technology, student employment, and rock lyrics as well as such provocative issues as immigration, violence, and the media, are enjoyable to read, provide plenty of opportunity for discussion, and serve as strong models.

**A Strong Connection Between Reading and Writing.** Two complementary sections in each of the chapters in Part 2 are designed to help students make the most of the connection between reading and writing: "Reading with a Writer's Eye" and "Writing with a Reader's Eye." The first section encourages students to engage the text so that they understand the choices professional writers make, the techniques and strategies they employ, and the purposes and contexts they address. Again, our purpose here is to stress the importance of using one's judgment and exercising appropriate options when creating any piece of writing. The next part of each chapter offers suggestions for every step in the writing process and a part-by-part analysis of a student's essay in the drafting stage. Called "Writing with a Reader's Eye," this section stresses that students need to see themselves as their intended readers and to consider how such an audience might envision, interpret, and react to what they have written.

**Visuals That Help Make the Rhetorical Options Real for Students.** Engaging cartoons, many of them work-related, open the chapters on rhetorical options in Part 2. At the end of each chapter, two sections ask students to analyze and respond to images that reveal more meaning than initially meets the eye.

## A Guide to Research and More

**Writing in College and Professional Contexts.** Part 3, "Applications," covers a number of specialized projects and skills common to college and professional writing. Chapter 15, a new addition to *Writing Today*, offers thorough coverage of proposal writing. Chapter 16, also new to this edition, discusses how critiques work and offers examples by four professional writers. Chapter 17 discusses business formats, including appropriate practices for e-mailing in business contexts as well as writing more traditional correspondence. The coverage of writing résumés and letters of application will be especially useful to students seeking employment. Chapter 19 provides excellent advice on taking various types of examinations, especially the essay exam. Chapter 22, on writing about literature, contains two student essays that analyze works of fiction and poetry included in the text.

**Unique Coverage of Using Quotations.** The final section of Chapter 20 offers extensive advice on using quoted material in a paper according to the Modern Language Association (MLA) and the American Psychological Association (APA) formats. As such, this chapter prepares students for the types of writing covered in  Chapter 21 ("The Research Paper") and Chapter 22 ("Writing About Literature").

**Thorough Coverage of Writing and Documenting Research Papers.** Chapter 20 provides suggestions on finding and using library and electronic resources. Chapter 21 introduces both the MLA and the APA styles of documentation and contains a complete student research paper in MLA format. Throughout these two chapters, we stress the fact that exercising choice and applying one's judgment are as important when writing a research paper as they are in any other kind of writing. In this regard, we discuss the notion that students are responsible for choosing viable, relevant, and up-to-date sources and that they need to be aware of the many ways in which to incorporate researched material into their work. We discuss the uses of direct quotations, and we explain how and when to paraphrase and to summarize. A complete subsection is devoted to the dangers, as well as the benefits, involved in using the Internet—an unregulated collection of information— as a tool for academic research. Finally, we explain how and why to avoid plagiarism, both intentional and unintentional.

### A Handbook

Part 4, "Grammar and Mechanics," is a comprehensive and thorough college handbook that is easy to read and can be used both in class and as an out-of-class reference. We emphasize practical solutions to the most common problems that students face; provide explanations in familiar, easily understood language; and illustrate principles with numerous appropriate examples. Editing exercises throughout and at the end of each chapter give students plenty of opportunities for practice.

## KEY FEATURES OF *WRITING TODAY*

We designed this text to help students see reading and writing as practical tools both in college and in the world of work. To meet this goal, *Writing Today* includes the following features:

- **A realistic yet humorous approach to writing.** We understand students' concerns and questions about studying English, so we write directly to our readers, helping them understand how and why writing is valuable to them not only in their composition courses but in all of their other classes and throughout their working lives. To help make a subject many of them find forbidding far more inviting, we offer cartoons at the beginning of chapters in Part 2 and practical, often humorous, examples of writing situations and writing pitfalls.

- **An emphasis on student success.** We have devoted the Introduction to this topic, and we have designed the rest of the book to help students move forward with their work, maximize their learning, and get the highest possible grades in their classes.

- **Online resources that support writing instruction.** To prepare students for the many electronic options now available in academic life and the work world, *Writing Today* is accompanied by *Catalyst*, the most complete electronic resource for research and writing available. Accessible either on CD or as part of the text's Web site, this electronic resource gives students and instructors a wealth of additional options, including a bank of more than 3,000 grammar exercises, a diagnostic test, writing tutorials, a tutorial on avoiding plagiarism, Bibliomaker software that automatically formats source information in different documentation styles, and an online handbook. Marginal references to the Web site, titled "More Options Online," appear throughout the text to let students know when additional help is available on *Catalyst*.

- **Plenty of advice on using computers and the Internet.** In keeping with the emphasis on the uses of technology in *Writing Today,* the text offers advice throughout on using the various electronic tools and resources that are available in today's digital writing environment. To make this important advice easy for students to spot, it is identified with an icon.

- **Chapter-opening vignettes from the world of work.** Every chapter in Part 2, "Structures," begins with an often humorous account of an employee using writing to interact with the dreaded Bob, a demanding and sometimes inscrutable supervisor. These scenarios help to make writing real for students by demonstrating how the type of writing they will learn in that chapter has practical applications in the working world. Even more important, they help emphasize the importance of a writer's assessing his or her purpose and audience and of choosing an appropriate strategy for a given writing context.

- **Student writers making choices.** Because student models are so useful to student writers, we offer more than twenty sample student essays. In Part 1 the text follows a student through the process of developing an essay from preliminary activities to final draft. Each chapter in Part 2 includes at least two sample student essays, one in both draft and final form, with comments from the student writer that show how that writer made decisions in moving from the first to the final draft.

- **An extended explanation of and a repeated emphasis on the natural connection between reading and writing.** Through repeated illustration and explanation, we stress that reading and writing are opposite sides of the same coin. As we have noted, each of the ten chapters in Part 2, "Structures," includes two complementary sections to help students make the most of this connection: "Reading with a Writer's Eye" and "Writing with a Reader's Eye." At the same time, these sections impress upon students the importance of evaluating and considering the needs of their audiences and contexts. Finally, the text offers a full range of accessible writing prompts that enable students to draw inspiration from the professional and student essays they have read.

- **Consider Your Options notes.** Throughout the text, these marginal notes prompt students to think about what they already do when they write and what their choices are in a given writing situation. As such, they get students to consider numerous and varied questions about intended audiences, purposes, selection of detail, rhetorical approaches, patterns of organization, word choice, and even sentence structure.

- **An emphasis on choices made in revision.** The process of revising an essay for global concerns as well as for errors in grammar, punctuation, and mechanics is covered in Part 1. The need for revision is then reinforced throughout Part 2. Each chapter includes a list of revision questions that students can use to analyze their own and other students' drafts, along with a revision exercise that provides faulty student essays for students to comment on and revise, giving them meaningful practice in critically reviewing and revising essays.

- **Support for students whose first language is not English.** An icon identifies sections throughout the text that are especially relevant to and useful for students whose first language is not English. The notion of options comes into play here as well. Second-language students often agonize over choosing the correct idiom or finding a word with the appropriate connotation. We keep this in mind whenever we discuss ESL-related concerns, and we provide information that makes the process of choosing easier.

- **A variety of collaborative activities.** Today's student will be called on to collaborate not only with other students in college but also with colleagues at work. *Writing Today* offers numerous collaborative activities throughout, and these activities are identified with an icon that stresses the importance of each individual's contribution to the whole. As well, half of Chapter 18 ("Group Projects and Oral Presentations") is devoted to practical, constructive advice on how to deal with a group's dynamics and maximize the group's performance.

- **A complete introduction to the research process.** Chapters 20 and 21 provide commonsense advice for every stage of the research process, along with guidelines for finding print and online sources, advice on quoting and citing text, models for documenting print and online sources using both the MLA and APA styles, and a sample student research paper.

- **A complete grammar handbook.** In our sixty years in the classroom, we have had plenty of opportunities to observe and analyze the kinds of errors students make; each of us is also the author of a grammar handbook. We apply our combined experience in Part 4, "Grammar and Mechanics," a complete, easily referenced guide to sentence errors, punctuation, and mechanics. It also includes grammar exercises as well as a glossary of usage.

- **A chapter on writing for business.** In keeping with the book's emphasis on writing for the world of work, Chapter 17 offers advice for writing the most common types of business documents students will encounter, including memos, e-mails, letters of application, résumés, and business letters.

- **Chapters on essay examinations and writing about literature.** Chapter 18 offers down-to-earth, practical advice on how students can successfully approach one of the most stressful events in higher education: the essay examination. Chapter 22 offers advice for writing about fiction and poetry, along with two sample student essays and definitions of literary terms.

- **Chapters on writing proposals and critiques.** Chapter 15 explains the increasingly important writing format known as the proposal and shows its applications. Chapter 16 looks at the other side of this issue and discusses critiques of existing works, performances, and documents.

- **An appendix on designing documents.** This appendix gives advice on how to create visual elements to enliven documents and oral presentations.

## HELPFUL SUPPLEMENTS FOR STUDENTS AND INSTRUCTORS

*For Students*

As noted above, *Writing Today* offers students access to the many resources available on *Catalyst*, including diagnostic tests, over 3,000 grammar exercises, an online handbook, writing tutors for each of the rhetorical options covered in Part 2 of the text, a tutorial on avoiding plagiarism, Bibliomaker software, which automatically formats source information in five different documentation styles, and plenty of support for research. McGraw-Hill also offers the following dictionary and vocabulary resources:

- **Random House Webster's College Dictionary (ISBN 0-07-240011-0).** This authoritative dictionary includes over 160,000 entries and 175,000 definitions. The most commonly used definitions are always listed first so students can find what they need quickly.

- **The Merriam-Webster Dictionary (ISBN 0-07-310057-9).** Based on the best-selling *Merriam-Webster's Collegiate Dictionary,* this paperback dictionary contains over 70,000 definitions.

- **The Merriam-Webster Thesaurus (ISBN 0-07-310067-6).** This handy paperback thesaurus contains over 157,000 synonyms, antonyms, related and contrasted words, and idioms.

- **Merriam-Webster's Vocabulary Builder (ISBN 0-07-310069-2).** This handy paperback introduces 3,000 words and includes quizzes to test progress.

- **Merriam-Webster's Notebook Dictionary (ISBN 0-07-299091-0).** An extremely concise reference to the words that form the core of English vocabulary, this popular dictionary, conveniently designed for 3-ring binders, provides words and information at students' fingertips.

- **Merriam-Webster's Notebook Thesaurus (ISBN 0-07-310068-4).** Conveniently designed for 3-ring binders, this thesaurus helps students search for words they might need in a given context.  It provides concise, clear guidance for over 157,000 word choices.

- **Merriam-Webster's Collegiate Dictionary and Thesaurus, Electronic Edition (ISBN 0-07-310070-6).** Available on CD-ROM, this online dictionary contains thousands of new words and meanings from all areas of human endeavor, including electronic technology, the sciences, and popular culture.

### For Instructors

- **Advice on the Web site (www.mhhe.com/writingtoday).** The Instructor's portion of the Web site includes advice for new instructors on a variety of subjects, such as teaching the writing process, assigning and teaching the research paper, responding to student writing, and assigning in-class writing, along with sample syllabi.

- **Teaching Composition Faculty Listserv (www.mhhe.com/tcomp).** Moderated by Chris Anson at North Carolina State University and offered by McGraw-Hill as a service to the composition community, this listserv brings together senior members of the college composition community with newer members—junior faculty, adjuncts, and teaching assistants—through an online newsletter and accompanying discussion group to address issues of pedagogy, both in theory and in practice.

- **PageOut.** McGraw-Hill's own PageOut service is available to help you get your course up and running online in a matter of hours—at no cost. Additional information about the service is available online at **http://www.pageout.net.**

## ACKNOWLEDGMENTS

No text is the product of its authors alone. Therefore, we wish to express our sincere appreciation for the work of Joshua Feldman, our developmental editor, who has spent endless hours reviewing, critiquing, guiding, and revising our work. Together we have worked to make *Writing Today* the most complete, accessible, and effective introduction to college writing available. Throughout the process, Josh has provided the guidance and help so necessary to a project of this magnitude. We were very fortunate to have the services of Melissa Williams to manage the second edition's production and of Bonnie Briggle, of Lachina Publishing Services, who provided a beautiful text. We also cannot forget the efforts of Carla Samodulski, who edited the first edition of *Writing Today*. Thanks also go to Lisa Moore, publisher for the English group, who oversaw the project in its early stages, as well as to Christopher Bennem, sponsoring editor, and Lori DeShazo, marketing manager. Finally, we want to thank our former editor, Tim Julet, who brought us together several years ago to work on this very rewarding project. We also wish to thank Bronwyn Becker, Randee Falk, and Judy Voss, all of whom edited various parts of the first edition; Ben Morrison, who developed the online writing tutor; David Staloch, the project manager; and Kim Menning, the art director. We also need to thank Liana Sutton and Penny Freeman for their help with the preparation of the manuscript. In addition, we want to express our gratitude to the students who have allowed us to use their work in order to show how careful essayists approach the writing process: Kevin Hunkovic, Jennifer Janisz, Noelani Jones, Sam Leininger, Manny Meregildo, Curtis Ray Mosley, Claire Reid, and Valerie Richfield. Our thanks also to Christine Francisco, City College of San Francisco, who reviewed the ESL sections in Part 4, and Debora Person, University of Wyoming Law Library, and Carol Ann Moon, Saint Leo University Cannon Memorial Library, who reviewed the sections on library and Internet research in Chapter 20. Finally, we want to thank our many colleagues from across the country who reviewed the manuscript in various stages of its development and provided so much insight, direction, inspiration, and encouragement:

Judith Anderson, *Johnson and Wales University*
Carole Chapman, *Ivy Technical Community College of Indiana*
Sandy Clark, *University of Wyoming – Laramie*
Anthony Grasso, *King's College*
Donna Henderson-Moore, *Cleveland State University*
Priscilla Litorja, *Northeastern Illinois University*
Kristen Maynard, *Tuskegee University*
Victoria McClure, *South Plains College*
Randall Mueller, *Gateway Technical College*
Jacqueline Neighbours, *Central Connecticut State University*
Catherine Olson, *Tomball College*
Daniel Olson, *North Harris College*
Rebecca Olympia Millan, *South Texas College*
Carissa Pokorny-Golden, *Kutztown University of Pennsylvania*
Karin Russell, *Keiser University*
Eric Sterling, *Auburn University – Montgomery*
Jian Sun, *University of Rio Grande*
Victor Uszerowic, *Miami-Dade College – Wolfson*
Michelle Zollars, *Patrick Henry Community College*

*Reviewers of the First Edition*

Nancy Barrineau, *University of North Carolina at Pembroke*; Mark K. Branson, *Davidson County Community College*; Joyce L. Cherry, *Albany State University*; Laurie Cohen, *Seattle Central Community College*; Avon Crismore, *Indiana University–Purdue University*; Linda A. Dethloff, *Prairie State College*; Betty Dillard, *Forsyth Technical Community College*; Patrick M. Ellingham, *Broward Community College*; Jo N. Farrar, *San Jacinto College Central*; Frederic Giacobazzi, *Kirtland Community College*; Richard A. Greene, *Florida Community College at Jacksonville*; Ashan Hampton, *Morehouse College*; Sarah H. Harrison, *Tyler Junior College*; James E. Hodges, *Thomas University*; Michael Hogan, *Southeast Missouri State University*; Lita Hooper-Simanga, *Georgia Perimeter College*; Clay Holliday, *Valencia Community College*; Michael Hricik, *Westmoreland County Community College*; Richard J. Johnson, *Kirkwood Community College*; Virginia Katzeff, *Lake Land College*; Sandra K. Keneda, *Rose State College*; Sandra G. Lakey, *Pennsylvania College of Technology*; Stephen J. Leone, *Westchester Community College*; Colleen A. Lloyd, *Cuyahoga Community College*; T. Michael Mackey, *Community College of Denver*; Nancy Matte,

*Phoenix College*; Yeno Matuka, *Ball State University*; Vernice McCullough, *Glendale Community College*; Leslie Mohr, *Casper College*; John David Moore, *Eastern Illinois University*; Patrice A. Quarg, *Community College of Baltimore County at Catonsville*; Mark Ristroph, *Augusta Technical Institute*; Rachel Ritter, *Miami-Dade Community College*; Sara E. Selby, *Waycross College*; Annabel Servat, *Southeastern Louisiana University*; Phillip Sipiora, *University of South Florida*; Beverly Stamm, *Columbus State Community College*; James Thomas, *Valencia Community College*; William Wade, *Paducah Community College*; Stephen Wilhoit, *University of Dayton*; Fred Wolven, *Miami-Dade Community College*

**Donald Pharr**
**Santi V. Buscemi**

# INTRODUCTION: ACHIEVING STUDENT SUCCESS

## THE SUCCESSFUL STUDENT

One of the most common misconceptions among students we teach is that intelligence is the sole factor in determining college success or failure. To be sure, intellect is important, but other skills are essential, too. The truth is that oftentimes successful students are not necessarily smarter than students who fail; rather, successful students have mastered a set of essential skills that help them perform well in all their college courses. This introduction will familiarize you with some of these skills. Whatever your particular college goals, the strategies and attitudes described here will help you achieve them.

The majority of college students start school at age eighteen or nineteen, having just finished high school. They are called "traditional-age students." Another group, increasing in size and percentage every year, comprises adult learners, who, having spent some years at work and/or raising a family, are returning to college to complete a degree, upgrade their skills, or work toward a raise in salary. They are sometimes called "nontraditional-age students." The life experiences of the two groups are very different, but their ultimate objective is the same: success in college.

### A Serious Approach to College Life

For students coming from high school, one of the great appeals of going to college is the freedom that this experience brings, as well as the fun that they can expect to have. However, the new freedoms and opportunities of college cause some students to lose focus on their studies. The most well-rounded students are able to balance leisure and enjoyment with the primary reasons to go to college: learning, preparing for a career, achieving a degree. These students have a wonderful time during their college years, but they also graduate high in their class rankings and are ready for the world of career responsibilities.

Keep in mind that however enjoyable college can be, it is ultimately a serious matter. It demands a great commitment of time, money, and effort. Your behavior in class should reflect this. Give the instructor your attention and leave the socializing with friends until after class. You will be rewarded with better understanding of course material, and with better grades. Keep in mind also that instructors notice, and often reprimand, the students who sit together in class talking, disrupting the session and annoying their peers. However, if you take your courses seriously, you'll find other serious people—students and faculty—taking an interest in you and your future.

Whatever your age, take the time to investigate other opportunities that your campus offers. Colleges usually show films—high-quality films that are hard to find—as well as offer theatrical productions, art shows, and guest lectures. These opportunities are rarely found in such concentration outside college campuses. Give them a try. At the least, you'll likely meet some interesting people.

When you begin college, you become a member of the college community. You may choose to minimize the membership role that you play, or you can exploit this role and sample a great deal of what your school has to offer.

*Information Access*

Succeeding in a class is not merely a matter of learning the material covered in the course. It is a matter of taking your learning and using it to meet—and exceed—the requirements of the course. Tests, quizzes, essays, and oral presentations will (a) be scheduled and (b) come with the instructor's expectations for how they should be completed. Each instructor will use various ways to give you information about his or her course:

*The course syllabus.* This document tells you which books to buy, when important projects are due, where the instructor's office is, when he or she can be found there, and how to contact him or her by phone or e-mail. If you lose your syllabus, ask your instructor for another copy. It is the map of the course.

*The Web portal.* Many colleges are using this approach, in which course assignments and information are posted on a Web site known as a "portal." If this is the case at your school, then make it a point to check regularly for updates on your courses. Include this site in your computer's "favorites" or "bookmarks" folder.

*The instructor's Web site or the course's Web site.* As with the portal approach, a dedicated Web site lists information about the course that you are taking. However, it tends to be more specific and frequently more helpful. Some of these sites have resource links that will help you with problems that you might encounter in doing the coursework. Others include chatroom functions that allow you to interact with your instructor with greater convenience than a face-to-face meeting offers. Note that some instructors require students to complete exercises or other activities built into the course Web site. In any case, remember to check this site regularly—as with the Web portal address, it should be in your computer's "favorites" or "bookmarks" folder.

*E-mail.* E-mailing your instructor is a very efficient and thorough means of communication. You have a record of the exchange for future reference. Your instructor has the convenience of replying without having to worry about "reaching you."

*Office hours.* Keep track of your instructors' office hours. They are times when your instructor guarantees to be in his or her office and available for your visit. If you work or have class during an instructor's office hours, ask him or her after class for an appointment during a time that is convenient for both of you.

*Regular class attendance.* Regular attendance will help you prepare for graded assignments. Many instructors will describe the exact format of an upcoming exam and/or post study-preparation questions on the classroom overhead projector. Although your instructor will establish a class schedule and try to keep it, things happen: weather catastrophes, illness, and so on. Or, because of the flow of the individual course, the instructor might get ahead of or behind the posted schedule. If you are in class and attentive, you will learn about changes in the upcoming schedule. There is only one thing worse than missing a class or two, coming to class, and seeing your instructor hand you a test to be completed: it's coming back to class and realizing that you missed the test altogether.

*Keep a day planner.* Your memory may be very good, but as we point out in the "Time Management" section at the end of this chapter, the life of a modern college student—of whatever age—is a very busy one indeed. Keeping a planner is highly advised. The old-fashioned print versions are still readily available at office supply stores, or you can keep your schedule on any number of electronic organizers and communication devices, including some cellular phone models. Having a planner will keep you current each day, provide a place to collect all the relevant dates and other information for your courses, and help you avoid costly surprises.

## EXERCISE 1

Self-Evaluation. After having read this section, evaluate your readiness to use this material. Make a list of (a) your effective approaches to information access for your courses and (b) areas in which you need to improve. Finally, what is the one area in which you would most like to change your habits?

### Preparation and Organization

Merely showing up to class every day is not a guarantee of success. You need to come to each class prepared. If you have read the day's material and are prepared to respond to the instructor and ask questions, you'll learn more. You'll also impress your instructor, who will remember you favorably. Here are some ways to be ready to succeed once class is in session:

*Use the syllabus.* Know what the session's lecture will be about. Read the chapters or complete the assigned activities. Prepare a list of questions about issues that puzzle you.

*Keep your class materials centrally located, organized, and easily accessible.* Use one folder and/or one notebook for each course. Date each page of your notes. Never come to class without your textbook unless instructed to do so—on exam days, for instance. If you use a laptop to take notes and track your classes, back up your files to a thumb drive.

*Update your day planner immediately after each class.* The whole point of a planner is so that you don't have to depend on your memory. As soon as you learn new information about one of your classes, record it.

## EXERCISE 2

Self-Evaluation. Answer the following questions about the last time you attended your freshman composition course:

1. Did you take your textbook to class? If not, why not?
2. Did you have your class folder or notebook with you? If not, why not?
3. If you did bring your folder or notebook, what was inside it? Were any necessary materials missing?
4. Are you using the same folder/notebook for more than one class?

### Classroom Decorum

At the best of times, teaching is hard work. But it is made much, much harder by ringing cell phones, disruptive students high-fiving their friends, late arrivals, early departures . . . the list of instructor complaints can be a long one. But keep in mind that when you engage in such behavior, you make not only teaching more difficult, but also learning for your fellow students. Following the tips below will create a positive environment for you and your peers. Also, many instructors reward students who show respect and courtesy in the classroom.

*Be punctual.* Be in your seat with your class materials ready when class begins. Keep in mind that many instructors track late arrivals and then penalize students by using the syllabus's attendance policy.

*Be civil.* If a peer says something that seems stupid or frivolous, don't rub it in. As well, if you talk during class, pass notes, or otherwise interrupt the class, you're depriving others of the opportunity to learn.

*Ask questions.* Instructors sometimes have the uneasy feeling that they're teaching in a vacuum. If you ask pertinent questions or otherwise stimulate discussion, you will improve that day's class for yourself and for everyone in the room.

*Take careful notes.* The next test might not occur for five or six weeks; you need these notes to jog your memory. Taking notes also helps you focus and keeps your mind engaged on the class material. Also, remember to date each set of notes.

*Don't let your technology be a distraction.* Your cell phone should be turned off unless some emergency situation causes you to need to have it turned on and your instructor has agreed to this situation. Don't listen to headphone music during class. If your class allows the use of a laptop, use it for class-related activities only: taking notes should be the primary function.

## Consider Your Options

Frequently, students get behind in a course, receive low grades, and then decide to withdraw from the course. Thus, they create a "debt": in the future they will have to make up that course ("pay back the debt"), probably with some inconvenience ("and with interest that has accrued"). By keeping on track, you can avoid these future obligations.

### EXERCISE 3

Self-Evaluation. What are you like in the classroom? What are your positive qualities? What personal habits would you like to improve?

### Study Habits

Reading for class, preparing for an exam, drafting an essay, and preparing a speech all fall under the general umbrella of study time. How you arrange and deal with this crucial part of your daily life will have a huge effect on your success in college. There is no "best" way to study. However, students who use their time effectively tend to follow some or all of these guidelines:

*Schedule time each day of the week as study time.* For example, if you designate 4:00 to 7:00 on Monday evenings for study, you're more likely to be prepared on Tuesday than had you not scheduled this time. And once you have made such an arrangement, stick to it. If a friend invites you to do something else on a Monday, say that you'll be free at 7:00. As we mentioned at the beginning of this chapter, you should enjoy your college years. However, the best way to experience this enjoyment is to get your duties behind you first. Also be sure to consider your work and family obligations when deciding when to study.

*Find the best place for you to work.* For some students, this is the library. For others, it's a coffeehouse. For nontraditional-age students, it may be a "private room" at home, reserved so that the adult learner can concentrate on schoolwork without being distracted by household activity.

Many students who live in dormitories try to study there. This approach can cause problems, especially if you live in a noisy part of the dorm or if your roommate's view of the college experience seems to have been shaped by multiple viewings of *Animal House.*

Dorm studying has a dangerous appeal. You're surrounded by your own possessions—the comforts of home, so to speak. But consider the fact that many of today's adult office workers, when faced with the need to catch up on some work on a weekend, will drive thirty miles to their office simply to stay away from the comforts of home. As well, if you're trying to study in your dorm room, you may well be distracted by an acquaintance who needs a friend with whom to party or needs one more warm body to fill the Texas hold-'em table. Even if others leave you alone, the dual appeals of television and sleep make the dorm room a potentially unproductive place in which to study.

*Take advantage of review materials.* Prior to an exam, many instructors offer review sessions, hand out pre-test outlines, or make available main points: the material from which the test will be built. These instructors are trying to help their students learn and succeed. Take advantage of this assistance.

*Form or join a study group.* Study groups offer three very valuable benefits. First is structure. If the group meets at a fixed day and time, then each member is expected to attend and contribute. In other words, social pressure helps enforce good study habits. Second, multiple heads are better than one. You may have a solid understanding of one aspect of a subject but be helped by your peers with other aspects. Third is the ability of group members to quiz one another prior to an exam, perhaps while using some of the review materials discussed above. This is one of the best ways to prepare for a test and sharpen your memory.

## EXERCISE 4

Self-Evaluation. Analyze your approach to studying. What works for you? What doesn't? In what areas do you need to improve? Can you think of a specific example of a time in which your approach to studying for an exam really hurt your chances for success? What went wrong?

### Time Management

As a college student—of whatever age—you may be taking a full load of classes, working at one or more jobs, pursuing a romantic relationship, and fulfilling obligations to your parents or children. However, a week contains only 168 hours. If you don't plan carefully, something will have to give. And even with careful planning, things will go wrong: schedules will clash, others' needs will conflict with yours, and wholly unexpected events will change the anticipated nature of a week or even a month. How can you juggle multiple responsibilities and still succeed in college? There's no sure method, but the following suggestions may help:

*Think about your priorities.* Are you at school to be educated and earn a degree, or to party? Do you want to earn a degree, or win a championship in an intramural sport? Take the long view. If you abandon your Monday night study period in favor of a particularly enticing party, you may well have a great time that evening. However, the daylight hours that week will probably tell a different story. Keep your purpose and your long-term goals in mind; they are what should guide you.

*Work ahead and plan carefully in order to account for the inevitable.* You may have a very difficult and demanding job. You may be caring for children or for an aging parent. You may be used to dealing with very real and very important life events, but such events can play havoc with your ability to complete a college semester. Plan accordingly.

*Learn to say no.* If you are a traditional-age student, declining a party invitation probably won't cause you long-term social problems, but when Frank the pizza manager is on the phone demanding your presence to replace your colleague Ed, who is in jail after an unfortunate altercation with the police, saying no is much harder. If you are a nontraditional-age student, having a workplace colleague ask for your help when you need to complete a school project can be a difficult and awkward moment. Remember that for someone to make a request of your time, that person must be able to contact you, in person or by phone. If you usually study in the library, you'll notice that requests for party attendance will become scarcer. If you pause before answering your phone, or use caller ID, you'll avoid Frank the manager or a panicked colleague. Sometimes the best way to decline a demand on your time is to escape being asked.

*Avoid last-minute work.* The student who routinely finishes assignments seven minutes before they're due, prints them off, and then sprints off to class may get an adrenaline rush, but he or she is playing with fire. First, finishing projects right at their deadline is not the way to do one's best work. Second, printers can malfunction, computers freeze up, and files become corrupted. The sensible approach is to block out your time so that (a) you can give each project the attention it deserves and (b) you do nothing at the last minute. It is sometimes impossible to follow these two pieces of advice. At the same time, the more that you can avoid the last-minute approach, the better your work will become and the less you will be exposed to the danger of relying on technology with no time to spare.

## EXERCISE 5

Self-Evaluation. Do you tend to complete assignments with little time to spare? If so, try the following exercise:

1. The next time that you have an out-of-class assignment, plan to finish the assignment 24 hours before it is due.

2. Write out the approach that you'll need to take to make this happen. For example, how will you change your schedule? How will your leisure time be affected? Finally, what do you plan to do with the 24 hours that have just been freed up?

**The first part of this text discusses** the strategies that you will use to complete the assignments given to you in your English composition courses. The finished essay is the goal, but the various parts—large and small—that go into an essay are essential to making the longer form work effectively.

Chapter 1, "The Essay: Determining Purpose, Audience, and Approach," is an introduction to the type of writing that you will use throughout college. Students sometimes object to the importance given to essay writing, failing to see the practical relevance of this form. So let's make an admission: after you finish college, you might spend the rest of your days without ever writing another essay. However (a big *however*), during the remainder of your college years you will face instructors who expect you to know how to write essays and research papers, often with very little specific guidance on approach and format. Furthermore, after you finish school, you might not write essays, but you will be asked to write in a number of contexts using a variety of skills and techniques that you learned in college. Also, the day of the helpful secretary born with the mysterious literacy gene is gone. The computer will sit on *your* desk, not banished to some support person. And the higher up you go, the better your writing skills will need to be. Most CEOs and leading scientists are also very good writers. Communication in the world of work is not a secondary skill; it is essential.

PART

1

# APPROACHES

Chapter 1 shows how the essay is related to its various cousins used in other writing situations. Indeed, if you can write a standard essay, you can write a research paper—or a memo, a feasibility study, a grant proposal, a sales letter, or a narrative cost analysis. The skills you learn in this course will travel with you as long as you need them.

In Chapter 2, "Shaping Your Essay: Prewriting, Focusing, Organizing, and Drafting," we look at what happens when your instructor gives you an assignment. What is the specific audience for your task—the reader(s) who will gauge your work's effectiveness? What is your exact purpose for taking the approach that you choose? What are some ways to get started, to generate ideas and words related to your tasks? What will your focus be—in other words, what is the controlling idea, or thesis, of your document? How will you gather and organize evidence to back up your thesis? And what is the best way to write an initial draft of your text?

The primary components of the essay are its paragraphs, and Chapter 3, "Developing Strong Paragraphs: Exploring Your Options," discusses the many different kinds of paragraphs that you will need to develop a variety of essays. You may well be surprised by the great range of options that you have when planning and developing these essential "building blocks."

The first half of Chapter 4, "Reshaping Your Essay: Revising, Editing, and Proofreading," explains how to revise larger units: paragraphs and essays. Paragraphs frequently wander off course as the writer works through new thoughts on paper and forgets his or her original purpose. Essays sometimes promise too much in their introductions and then fail to deliver. Sometimes, an essay starts in one direction and ends with a conclusion quite different from the one the writer planned. Or an essay may be unified and structurally sound but still not be adequate to the demands of the assignment because the writer has neglected to determine the purpose and audience for this effort.

The second half of Chapter 4 emphasizes the importance of careful sentence construction and word choice. If paragraphs are the basic components of the essay, then sentences are the elements of paragraphs, and, of course, words make up sentences. Clear communication starts at this level. The chapter includes exercises that ask you to correct the errors in someone else's writing. Once you are comfortable with the concepts explained in this chapter, revising your own text, which is never as easy as working on a stranger's text, will become easier and more natural.

One final note: writing is not an art form; it is a skill. If you want to become a better writer and you are willing to work at it, your writing will improve. Writing is not a mysterious practice, nor should it be one that you dread. It is a step-by-step process, and the more you put into this process, the better your results will be. Sometimes this process can even be enjoyable.  •

# THE ESSAY:

## Determining Purpose, Audience, and Approach

People try to get out of themselves and to escape from the man. This is folly; instead of transforming themselves into angels, they turn themselves into beasts; instead of lifting, they degrade themselves. These transcendental humors frighten me, like lofty and inaccessible heights.

—Michel de Montaigne

• *Consider Your Options*

Very often, sophomores, juniors, and seniors will sigh and then remark, "I wish I had paid more attention in Comp 1." Indeed. Although what you will experience in this course will frequently be rigorous, remember that the more you choose to learn in this course, the better off you'll be in the semesters to come.

THE PASSAGE ON THE PRECEDING PAGE was written four hundred years ago by Michel de Montaigne (mon TANE). Montaigne retired early from his law practice and devoted the rest of his life to observing the world and writing about it: the strangeness of human nature, the behavior of animals, the prospect of eternity. Four centuries later, Montaigne's "second career" still makes remarkably good reading, for he was a brilliant thinker and writer who also happened to invent one of the major literary forms: the essay. Montaigne's *Essais* is a collection of his writings, most of them brief and most on a single subject. The French word *essai* means, literally, "attempt"; figuratively, it means "excursion" or "exploration." An important word in the title of this text, *options,* reflects Montaigne's sense of the essay's possibilities. Each document that you produce during your college years—and beyond—will offer you options, choices to be explored as you work through the steps of the writing process.

The essay is only one form of writing practiced in the academic and business worlds. But writing essays will teach you skills necessary for the increasingly complex writing assignments that you will face later in college and for applications in the world of work.

Nevertheless, many students dread the thought of having to write an essay. They see such an assignment as a needlessly formal, artificially narrow means of judging their writing. However, there are three very good reasons that your instructors hold the ability to write essays in such high regard:

1. Someone who can write solid essays proves that he or she can communicate effectively with educated, adult readers.

2. Essays provide an unparalleled opportunity for readers to judge someone's critical-thinking, organizational, and language skills.

3. The writer of a successful essay has thought through a topic, taken "ownership" of the developed topic, and worked through the stages of the writing process—thereby creating an essay that can be a source of pride.

Essays may be written on all manner of subjects, and they can be long, sometimes approaching 25,000 words. However, the essays that you will write during your college years will be much shorter. You will be asked to choose a topic of an appropriate size, consider the topic, plan your essay, organize it, and develop it by providing examples, experiences, and other information. At the same time, you will be expected to follow the rules of what is sometimes called "received American usage" or "standard written English"—that is, acceptable grammar and mechanics. If all this sounds like a lot of work, you're right. Worthwhile things don't come easy, but the rewards are substantial.

The good news is that there is no single "perfect" way to write an essay. Consider the following situation: a writing instructor has asked her class of twenty-five students to write an in-class essay on one highly specific topic. When the essays are graded, five students receive an *A* for their efforts. The instructor lets you read those five essays. It is very likely that you will be struck by the fact that the five compositions are so *dissimilar:* the five students found their way to a superior result by taking very different approaches.

Writing an essay is not like solving an algebraic equation. Within the limits of traditional mathematics, there is only one answer to $2x + 4 = 8$, and there are only a few approaches that will lead you to the right answer: $x = 2$. However, the five students whose essays you read found very different ways to "solve the problem" of the writing assignment. Looking closer, you see that there are other differences as well. The first essay has beautifully formed phrasing and, interestingly, doesn't show many corrections. Another essay's style is more direct and less elegant, but this essay's strength is its organization. A third essay offers a brilliant analysis of the topic, but a glance at an earlier draft reveals the writer's struggle to communicate: every other word is revised, with arrows and asterisks telling the reader where to look next in a forest of corrections.

The first writer may seem to be "naturally gifted," someone who creates magic as soon as the pen hits the paper, but such a writer is a rare creature. The other two are much more typical. Most *A* writers have *learned* to be *A* writers. Writing isn't an art reserved for the gifted few; it's a *skill,* much like dancing or playing golf or balancing your weekly budget. The purpose of this text is to outline your options, to show you the various strategies, large and small, that will help you learn to be a better writer.

# CHARACTERISTICS OF THE ESSAY

Essays appear in many different forms, but every essay has two features, rhetorical context and rhetorical structure. **Rhetorical context** is the reason that the essay exists: a writer has a purpose and an audience for an essay. **Rhetorical structure** is the way the writer chooses to shape the essay so it best fulfills that purpose and reaches that audience. Note that these two major elements of the essay are also key to *any* document that you might write or read: a business letter, an e-mail, a résumé, or a menu.

## Rhetorical Context

As you plan an essay, here are two essential issues for you to consider. The first is the **purpose** of your essay—that is, what this essay will be and what you hope to accomplish with it. The second is your **audience.** To whom are you writing? What does this person or persons know or need to know? What will it take to impress this audience?

### Defining Your Purpose

"What's gonna be your angle on that kidnapping story, Joe?" said the editor.

"I'll focus on the grieving family—that's the angle as far as I see it right now."

*Angle* is a word that describes the journalist's purpose for writing. When an instructor gives you an essay assignment, you must first determine *your* purpose, *your* goal. Two of your goals are fairly basic and obvious. One is to get the assignment done, and done on time. The second is to receive a high grade. But you must get past this level. Try not to treat the assignment as an obstacle, a task not unlike having to clean up a mess. Too often, students spend a little time planning and organizing, write a first draft as quickly as possible, and then breathe a sigh of relief as the paper disappears into the instructor's growing stack. There may have been a time in your education when you could take this approach and be rewarded, but in the immortal words of Austin Powers, "That train has sailed." Your composition instructor will look for evidence that you have used the process of writing—that you have thought, planned, and found your angle. And trying to get a good grade on an essay written with no specific purpose other than to do well is like trying to walk in total darkness.

Traditionally, four purposes for writing are (1) to express, (2) to inform, (3) to entertain, and (4) to persuade. However, these purposes are just a starting point; they lead you into a world of options that will enable you to decide on a much more specific purpose for the document that you intend to write.

So how can thinking about a specific purpose help shape your essay? Consider the following scenarios:

1.  In response to an assignment that asks you to comment on the fact that young adult citizens of the United States rarely bother to vote in state and federal elections, you plan to argue that young adults are allowing older adults to choose who will be elected, for older people vote at a much higher rate than younger people do. In this case, your purpose is to persuade your audience to agree with you. Will this purpose help guide your choice of language? Will you use bold words and forceful claims, or will your language be descriptive and gentle? Probably the former.

2.  You plan to enter an essay in a local writing contest. Your essay will describe your grandmother's small house located in Colorado's Rocky Mountains. This is a magical memory for you; part of your childhood was spent with your grandmother, and those were the best of your growing-up years. Your purpose is to engage your audience and share vivid memories. Will your words be definitive and bold or descriptive and gentle? Probably the latter.

The choices indicated in the preceding examples reflect the necessary relationship between a writer's purpose and the language and evidence that the writer employs. These examples stem from essay topics; however, note the way that a writer's purpose also affects her approach in the following real-life situation.

Jennifer and Diego work in a large department store. Their area is haphazardly maintained because their immediate manager can't be bothered to establish a safe and orderly work environment. Last Tuesday, July 9, a stack of boxed outdoor grills toppled from the summit of a large display rack, bruising Jennifer's elbow and breaking Diego's wrist. This was not the first such incident. Here is Jennifer's e-mail to a friend recounting the incident:

Yesterday I almost got crushed to death. It was crazy!!!! I wasnt hurt

much and I felt rediculus sitting there in a pile of gas cookers and other crap that got carryed down with it. But then I saw Diego, he was white as a ghoste, holding his arm like it was falling off. I ran to get Mr. Wilkins but the creep was gone. The store manager took care of it. You know, this isnt the first time some one got hurt in our area, last month their was that old man who had the lawnchair fall on his sholder.

Here, Jennifer's purpose is to achieve maximum impact, to tell her friend a good story and show how ludicrous her working life is. Twenty-four hours later, however, she must write about the same event in a very different context; the store manager, following company policy, has asked her to fill out an incident report. An incident report has a very narrow purpose: to tell what happened as objectively as possible. Therefore, Jennifer will have to refrain from referring to previous accidents or to her contempt for her immediate supervisor.

On Tuesday, July 9, I was working with Diego Arteche in the outdoor and patio section. We were creating a display underneath the merchandise rack that contains outdoor grills and related products.

At about 2:20 p.m., we heard a noise. I looked up and saw the stacked boxes of gas grills falling toward us. We both tried to scramble out of the way. A box hit me a glancing blow on my left elbow, but several boxes fell on Diego. He was in severe pain with swelling at his wrist and lower forearm.

I ran to get help. I could not find the area manager, Robert Wilkins, but I was able to summon Marie O'Connor, store manager, who called an ambulance. The EMTs arrived at 2:35 and examined me and Diego Arteche. I had only a bruise on my elbow and arm, but Diego's condition was more serious, so he was taken to the emergency room.

At this point Ms. O'Connor pulled extra personnel into Outdoor and Patio to clean up the mess and put everything back in order. I do not know what caused the boxes to fall.

Jennifer Warne

Two weeks later, both Jennifer and Diego have quit their jobs, probably figuring that it's better to take their chances on the open job market than face death by gas grill. Diego, in fact, is filing a lawsuit for workplace negligence. His attorney asks Jennifer to write her preliminary account of what happened at the store in order to help her prepare Diego's case against the company:

On Tuesday, July 9, I was working with Diego Arteche in the outdoor and patio section of the MegalithMart located at 2304 Sanderson Street. We were creating a display underneath the merchandise rack that contains outdoor grills and related products. All the time I have worked at this store, this rack has been consistently overloaded and the boxes stacked unevenly. Both Diego and I had complained about the situation several times to our area manager, Mr. Robert Wilkins, but his response was always to tell us to take care of it when we had time, then assign us another task and tell us to hurry.

At about 2:20 p.m., we heard a noise. I looked up and saw the stacked boxes of gas grills falling toward us. We both tried to scramble out of the way. A box hit me a glancing blow on my left elbow, but several boxes fell on Diego. He was in severe pain with swelling at his wrist and lower forearm.

I ran to get help. I could not find Robert Wilkins, which did not surprise me, since he is frequently unavailable to his subordinates, but I was able to summon Marie O'Connor, store manager, who called an ambulance. The EMTs arrived at 2:35 and examined me and Diego Arteche. I had only a bruise on my elbow and arm, but Diego's condition was more serious, so he was taken to the emergency room.

Diego and I have been working in an unsafe environment for quite a while. In my encounters with our supervisor, Wilkins, it was clear that he simply did not care about such matters as dangerously overloaded shelves and the possibility of employee and/or customer injury. In fact, just a month prior to our incident, an elderly man was injured when a lawn chair fell—from the same rack—onto his shoulders and neck. For some reason, Mr. Wilkins seemed to find this event quite humorous.

• *Consider Your Options*

Have you ever had to write more than one document about the same event or subject? How did the documents differ?

In this document, Jennifer's purpose is to support Diego's efforts by telling the *whole* story, including her opinion of the negligence shown by Robert Wilkins. The attorney will find such a document useful when preparing a civil action.

Jennifer has experienced one event—the workplace accident—but has written three very different documents. Each document serves a different purpose, and Jennifer has let the purpose guide each writing task. Note that Jennifer's purpose affects the following aspects of each of the documents above:

- The type of information given
- The amount of information given
- The tone used to give information
- The level of formality
- The amount of proofreading and revision done

Finding your purpose is a good way to make any writing assignment your own. Let's start with a worst-case scenario. Your instructor assigns you and your class a single topic that seems absolutely dreadful. Your first instinct is to ignore the assignment, but you realize that this would be very dangerous. What should you do? Work as little as possible, completing the assignment in record time with minimal personal involvement? Find a way to let your instructor know how much you dislike this task? Let's be frank: *in adult life, successful people are very good at pretending to care.* Not every situation will attract and hold your interest. In fact, you might someday even have to write in support of an opinion with which you disagree. Whatever the case, you will have to attack this assignment and find a way to make it yours. Later, when you are "surrounded" by the details of your writing process, you may realize that the topic isn't so horrible after all.

## Defining Your Audience

Just as your purpose defines every document that you write, so will your audience. Before you begin an essay, consider these questions:

- Who will read the document that you write?
- Does the reader have specific needs and expectations of which you should be aware?
- Would you characterize your reader(s) as highly skilled text processors or limited in some way?

These questions are part of *audience analysis.* You won't want to "consider" your audience by writing as simply as possible—unless your audience is at the lowest reading level. Instead, you will want to engage your readers at a level that will heighten their experience, allow you to show your level of skill, and help you achieve your purpose.

In the preceding section, Jennifer Warne had to determine her purpose for each of the three documents that she produced. She also had to recognize her audience: her friend, then the MegalithMart corporate offices, and finally Diego's attorney. Notice that the list of aspects affected by Jennifer's audience analysis is the same as the list of aspects affected by her choice of purpose:

- The type of information given
- The amount of information given
- The tone used to give information

- The level of formality
- The amount of proofreading and revision done

On a practical level, knowing your audience can have crucial benefits in any writing situation. For example, technical writers often create user's manuals for various products. Consider what the following "step" in a user's manual tells the reader:

> Plug the electrical cord into the ampulator, plug the other end into the wall, and your ampulator is ready for use.

Now imagine the pool of consumers who seem to function on Homer Simpson's level. As you know, if Homer bothered to read these directions at all, he would find a way to electrocute himself, "ampulate" his toes, or wreak other havoc. A writer more alert to the needs of the *entire* audience might produce a manual with steps like these:

1.  Place the ampulator on a smooth, flat, dry surface.

    DANGER: Do not position the ampulator where it can come into contact with water. A severe shock could result!

2.  Insert end A of the electrical cord into the opening marked "Power In." You should hear a click. (See diagram 4A.)

3.  Insert end B of the electrical cord into a 220-volt grounded wall outlet.

This writer understands that a great proportion of the retail audience doesn't know much about electrical equipment, and the writer has kept this realization in mind while drafting the instructions. The first writer thinks, "This process is simple," but the second writer thinks, "Nothing is simple, and I need to protect the consumer from harm and my company from liability."

Consider a more complex example. You are a civil engineer, and you have been made manager of a wastewater project for the commissioners of Deadzone County, a rural area in the southern part of your state (few people live there; even fewer visit). Part of your responsibilities will involve preparing a feasibility study, a document that will analyze the practicality of the project. This document will be read by the following parties:

1.  Your professional community—the engineers with whom you will work, the Deadzone County engineer, the engineers from the state Environmental Protection Agency (EPA) and federal EPA.

2.  Your boss, a highly skilled engineer who will also be the one to decide whether you get a raise next March.

3.  Your boss's immediate supervisor, one of the company's vice presidents. This person's expertise is cost accounting, not engineering.

4.  The commissioners of Deadzone County, people about whom you know nothing, although you suspect that they were elected because they own businesses or a lot of land. You decide that your best approach to this

important group of readers is to assume that they are intelligent but understand little about civil engineering.

Think of the complexity that your task demands. If you needed to address only your professional peers, your document would be relatively straightforward. However, the presence of the second, the third, and—especially—the fourth group forces you to write a feasibility study that can be read by a very diverse audience. How well you are able to understand the needs of this diverse group will play a large role in the success of your report. Indeed, such a diverse audience will force you to use an entirely different vocabulary—even to provide definitions or add a glossary—than you would if you were writing only for your peers.

That's all very well and good, you might say, but right now I'm taking Comp 1. Isn't my audience just one person, my instructor? Perhaps. But who is that instructor? Try another scenario. Your instructor asks you to write a "how-to" paper, an assignment you see as a virtual gift. You love working with cars, and you decide to write an essay explaining how to tune a carburetor. You approach your fortyish female instructor and announce your intentions. She pushes up her glasses and says, "That's a great idea. I've got a four-barrel Carter in my '71 Mustang, and I've had to tune it up twice in the last eighteen months. What a job!" Did your audience suddenly change for you?

Think further about the idea of audience. For example, your instructor returns your third essay. Along with a grade, he includes these comments: "Your essays so far show careful analysis and strong organization. However, you're still making careless grammatical errors, specifically comma splices and subject-verb agreement errors. Next time, concentrate on polishing your final draft—proofread once more for these errors before you turn in your essay." In this case, your audience—your instructor—has alerted you that his expectations for your next essay have become more specific. The reverse could also happen: "Your essays are very 'clean'; you have a firm grasp of grammar and make a point of avoiding errors. However, you're not giving yourself the freedom to develop your ideas. Loosen up a bit and explore the topic in greater detail." Once again, your instructor has let you know that the expectations of your audience have changed.

In addition to demonstrating how instructors' expectations can vary, these examples also indicate the degree to which purpose and audience are connected. In many ways, audience controls purpose. An instructor who tells you that his or her expectations for your next essay have changed is also telling you to adjust your purpose. More generally, your purpose is sometimes modified by your sense of a need to do something more for your audience.

Learning to write is not like learning to ride a bicycle. In the latter pursuit, people learn to ride competently and safely, and then they stop learning. They reach a plateau. However, there is no plateau in learning to write. Perfection can't be reached, for it doesn't exist. If you keep trying to become a better writer, though, you can only improve. One of your purposes for each writing task will be to build upon the skills that you have already mastered.

*Consider Your Options*

Students sometimes say, "I really love to write and would like to make it a career, but how?" If this statement describes you, consider the growing field of technical writing. What do technical writers do? As an example, think of the user's guide that you receive with virtually every product that you purchase. Someone was paid to write, design, and edit that guide.

## Rhetorical Structures

Unfortunately, many students see the essay as divorced from other forms of real-world writing. The truth is quite different. Almost all writing follows what is sometimes called the "classical pattern." Although it has variations, this pattern always includes an introduction, a body, and a conclusion. Your sense of this rhetorical structure will help you to determine the best way to approach any writing situation—in other words, any rhetorical context.

### The Classical Pattern of Organization

In the classical pattern, the **introduction** welcomes the reader into the chosen topic, then indicates the specific direction that the essay will take while developing the topic. The **body** paragraphs develop the focus, which is the essay's central idea as expressed formally in a thesis statement. The thesis often appears in the essay's introduction. The **conclusion** comments on the implications raised by the body paragraphs and then brings the essay to an appropriate end.

So how does all this relate to writing tasks outside the academic environment? Consider the following memo:

MEMORANDUM

Bindleburg Software

"Where Tomorrow Is But a Day Away"

TO:        All employees
FROM:    Erin McGrath, Human Services Director    *EM*
DATE:     February 10, 2008
SUBJECT: Absence procedure

This memo announces a change in the procedure for filing certificates of absence, effective immediately. If you are absent from work for one or more days, bring your completed certificate of absence to Human Services on the day that you return to work. This office will then process your form and return it to your supervisor. Please call me (ext. 239) if you have any questions.

This document is so brief that you might wonder how a single paragraph could be said to follow any kind of "classical pattern." Well, the first sentence is the introduction; it might seem abrupt, but business documents come to the point quickly. The next two sentences function as the body of the document. They are the reason that the memo needed to be written: to announce a procedural change. The final sentence is the conclusion. Good memos almost always employ the device that you see here, asking the reader to call for clarification if necessary. This way, no one can use the otherwise inevitable "I didn't understand" response if caught violating or ignoring the new procedure.

## Anticipating Rhetorical Options

Part 2 of this text discusses **rhetorical options.** These are the basic patterns that writers use to structure essays. The chapters in Part 2 contain student-written essays that illustrate these options. The Part 2 chapters also contain essays written by professionals, and these writers sometimes "break form." Frequently, their essays aren't so much models as they are examples of how far a pattern of development can be taken.

Part 2 will discuss nine rhetorical options and then illustrate ways that these options can be blended. The ten chapters of Part 2 will examine the following patterns of development:

- Chapter 5: Description (essays that describe a significant person, animal, place, or thing)
- Chapter 6: Narration (essays that tell a story)
- Chapter 7: Exemplification (essays that use examples to prove a point or illustrate an idea)
- Chapter 8: Process analysis (essays that explain how a process unfolds or that tell the reader how to work through a process)
- Chapter 9: Causal analysis (essays that explain why an event happens or explain the effects of an event)
- Chapter 10: Definition (essays that define, explain, and/or illustrate a key idea or term)
- Chapter 11: Classification (essays that analyze a large group of entities by placing them in distinct categories)
- Chapter 12: Comparison and contrast (essays that examine two ideas, people, events, places, or things to show their differences and possible similarities)
- Chapter 13: Argument (essays that support a position on a disputed issue)
- Chapter 14: Blended options (essays that do not depend on a single rhetorical option in their internal development but, instead, use multiple options)

These are the basic patterns of development because they are the ways that mature thinkers make sense of the world around them. A writer uses these rhetorical options when they match his or her purpose and the needs of the audience. For example, if asked to tell how a machine works, a writer would not proceed to **describe** the machine but would instead explain the **process** of its operation. If asked to describe a mountain valley, a writer would tell how it looks, sounds, and smells, not **narrate** the history of events that have taken place there. The standard rhetorical options help writers not only to make sense of the world but also to transmit this understanding to their audience.

# READING WITH A WRITER'S EYE

You make many choices as you plan and write an essay. You can also make choices as you read the essays in this text or any other reading assignments.

## Consider the Writer's Rhetorical Context and Rhetorical Structures

The most basic way to read is merely for information. A more profitable method is sometimes called *critical reading*. However, we prefer the term *active, analytical reading*. In this approach, the reader is aware of not only *what* the writer is saying but also *how* the writer is communicating: the rhetorical structure, the use of transitions, the language level, the freshness of expression. Quite simply, readers who read analytically become better writers because they are conscious of the entire writer-reader connection.

Analytical reading can also help you in some very specific ways. Reading the work of professional writers exposes you to skillfully written and edited English. Good writing is judged by standards developed both by academics and by publishing professionals. Reading *Harper's* or the *New Yorker,* for example, or books published by quality presses will show you *how* language works as well as introduce you to a fascinating world of thought.

## Consider Your Purposes as a Reader

Skilled readers have reasons—purposes—that guide their approach to an essay. For example, they may be reading for entertainment, or they may be studying or doing research. To get the most value from this activity, active, analytical readers use the following strategies as they process an essay:

- Interpret the title. Is it straightforward or perhaps ironic?
- Look for any prefatory information. Is there a headnote, an editor's introduction, or a biographical section?
- Look for any stylistic clues—subheadings, for example—that highlight the essay's organization.
- Annotate the text. Write your responses in the margins or between lines. If a passage is confusing, mark it with an asterisk or question mark. If you don't know a word or phrase, circle it. Come back to these areas later.
- Take notes on a separate piece of paper.
- Reread the passages that caused you trouble. Use a college-level dictionary to look up words that you didn't know.
- Summarize the essay in one paragraph.

As this list illustrates, reading is not a passive process. You *interact* with the text—questioning, agreeing, disagreeing, wondering. And at some point, you will find yourself *evaluating* the writer's output:

- Are the examples sufficient?
- Is the analysis logical?
- Has any information been left out—deliberately or inadvertently—that would have changed the writer's approach had the information been present?
- Is the writer's conclusion warranted?
- Do you *like* what you have read? Does it make you want to learn more about this or other, related subjects?

Read the essay that follows by the professional writer Suzanne Britt, think about it, and then join the discussion that follows.

# Neat People vs. Sloppy People

## SUZANNE BRITT

I've finally figured out the difference between neat people and sloppy people. The distinction is, as always, moral. Neat people are lazier and meaner than sloppy people.

Sloppy people, you see, are not really sloppy. Their sloppiness is merely the unfortunate consequence of their extreme moral rectitude. Sloppy people carry in their mind's eye a heavenly vision, a precise plan, that is so stupendous, so perfect, it can't be achieved in this world or the next.

Sloppy people live in Never-Never Land. Someday is their métier. Someday they are planning to alphabetize all their books and set up home catalogs. Someday they will go through their wardrobes and mark certain items for tentative mending and certain items for passing on to relatives of similar shape and size. Someday sloppy people will make family scrapbooks into which they will put newspaper clippings, postcards, locks of hair, and the dried corsage from their senior prom. Someday they will file everything on the surface of their desks, including the cash receipts from coffee purchases at the snack shop. Someday they will sit down and read all the back issues of *The New Yorker*.

For all these noble reasons and more, sloppy people never get neat. They aim too high and wide. They save everything, planning someday to file, order, and straighten out the world. But while these ambitious plans take clearer and clearer shape in their heads, the books spill from the shelves onto the floor, the clothes pile up in the hamper and closet, the family mementos accumulate in every drawer, the surface of the desk is buried under mounds of paper and the unread magazines threaten to reach the ceiling.

Sloppy people can't bear to part with anything. They give loving attention to every detail. When sloppy people say they're going to tackle the surface of a desk, they really mean it. Not a paper will go unturned; not a rubber band will go unboxed. Four hours or two weeks into the excavation, the desk looks exactly the same, primarily because the sloppy person is meticulously creating new piles of papers with new headings and scrupulously stopping to read all the old book catalogs before he throws them away. A neat person would just bulldoze the desk.

Neat people are bums and clods at heart. They have cavalier attitudes toward possessions, including family heirlooms. Everything is just another dust-catcher to them. If anything collects dust, it's got to go and that's that. Neat people will toy with the idea of throwing the children out of the house just to cut down on the clutter.

Neat people don't care about process. They like results. What they want to do is get the whole thing over with so they can sit down and watch the rasslin' on TV. Neat people operate on two unvarying principles: Never handle any item twice, and throw everything away.

The only thing messy in a neat person's house is the trash can. The minute something comes to a neat person's hand, he will look at it, try to decide if it has immediate use and, finding none, throw it in the trash.

Neat people are especially vicious with mail. They never go through their mail unless they are standing directly over a trash can. If the trash can is beside the mailbox, even better. All ads, catalogs, pleas for charitable contributions, church bulletins and money-saving coupons go straight into the trash can without being opened. All letters from home, postcards from Europe, bills and paychecks are opened, immediately responded to, then dropped in the trash can. Neat people keep their receipts only for tax purposes. That's it. No sentimental salvaging of birthday cards or the last letter a dying relative ever wrote. Into the trash it goes.

Neat people place neatness above everything, even economics. They are incredibly wasteful. Neat people throw away several toys every time they walk through the den. I knew a neat person once who threw away a perfectly good dish drainer because it had mold on it. The drainer was too much trouble to wash. And neat people sell their furniture when they move. They will sell a La-Z-Boy recliner while you are reclining in it.

Neat people are no good to borrow from. Neat people buy everything in expensive little single portions. They get their flour and sugar in two-pound bags. They wouldn't consider clipping a coupon, saving a leftover, reusing plastic nondairy whipped cream containers or rinsing off tin foil and draping it over the unmoldy dish drainer. You can never borrow a neat person's newspaper to see what's playing at the movies. Neat people have the paper all wadded up and in the trash by 7:05 a.m.

Neat people cut a clean swath through the organic as well as the inorganic world. People, animals, and things are all one to them. They are so insensitive. After they've finished with the pantry, the medicine cabinet, and the attic, they will throw out the red geranium (too many leaves), sell the dog (too many fleas), and send the children off to boarding school (too many scuff-marks on the hardwood floors).

## Essay Analysis

As we mentioned, there are two ways to read an essay actively and analytically. One way is to look at the rhetorical context—the writer's purpose, audience, and rhetorical pattern. The second way is to look at the essay's effectiveness—its logic, its evidence, and the impact that it makes upon the reader (you).

### The Essay's Rhetorical Context

"Neat People vs. Sloppy People" is a funny essay; clearly, at least part of Britt's **purpose** was to make us laugh. But good humor is always more than merely funny. Note the opening paragraph:

> I've finally figured out the difference between neat people and
> sloppy people. The distinction is, as always, moral. Neat people are
> lazier and meaner than sloppy people.

Here, Britt states a more serious intent of her essay: to draw a "moral" distinction between neat people and sloppy people. For, as she claims, sloppy people act for "noble reasons" (paragraph 4), whereas neat people "are bums and clods at heart" (paragraph 6). Notice Britt's **thesis statement**—the controlling idea—"Neat people are lazier and meaner than sloppy people." This is the idea she will develop throughout her essay.

Britt strives to turn a common set of assumptions upside down. In our culture, we view neatness as part of a package of virtues: hard work, dedication, punctuality, etc. On the other hand, most of us consider sloppiness to be a sign of "sorry behavior": laziness, shiftlessness, and so on. Britt attacks these assumptions. She argues that neat people are callous, wasteful, and selfish. On the other hand, she believes that sloppy people properly value objects and correspondence, are careful, and take the long view.

Britt has at least three intentions, or purposes: to make us laugh, to get us to see the world in a different way, and to draw a "moral" distinction between two types of people. To illustrate, consider that the incredibly disorganized home office in your uncle's house is perhaps not managed by a slob, but by a closet humanitarian. And perhaps the immaculate household of your friend's mother, reminiscent of the days of June Cleaver (the Beaver's mother), is actually the work of a flinty-eyed monster who tracks you through the house to see where you plan to put down your can of soda.

How about Britt's audience? Part of the appeal of this essay is that it can be read profitably by everyone from intelligent fourth-graders to adults with advanced college degrees. The subject matter is relevant to us all, from the time we are allotted part of a domicile and told "This will be your room." Britt's language, examples, and tone allow this essay to reach such an extended readership.

### The Essay's Rhetorical Structure

Britt compares two classes of people, the neat and the unneat, so her rhetorical option is a logical one: comparison/contrast. As we'll see in Chapter 12, when using this approach, most writers tend to concentrate on contrast, not comparison. Think about how few areas of comparison exist between neat people and sloppy people: both are human beings, and both own stuff. Thus, Britt is correct to concentrate on *differences,* not *similarities.*

Britt uses one of two comparison/contrast strategies. In the subject-by-subject method you see here, the writer discusses the first subject at length, then moves on to the second subject. She discusses the virtues of sloppy people for four paragraphs, then spends seven paragraphs exposing the previously unknown limitations of neat people. Notice the imbalance? Britt's intent is not so much to praise the sloppy as it is to attack the neat; hence, she devotes more "text space" to the latter subject.

"Neat People vs. Sloppy People" breaks some of the guidelines for the standard essay. As you go through the chapters in this text, you will notice the various ways that accomplished writers deviate from the advice offered in this and other writing texts. Sophisticated writers frequently do this, but they always have their reasons, which are inextricably tied to their purpose and audience. Let's evaluate Britt's essay with these thoughts in mind:

1.  The introductory paragraph is very brief. In the essays that you write this term, your instructor will want you to use fully developed introductions, perhaps involving more than one paragraph. In Britt's defense, however, she has little reason to spend her first paragraph defining "sloppy person" and "neat person"—the reader probably has a good grasp of those two concepts. (See pages 53–56 in Chapter 3 for more information on developing introductory paragraphs.)

2.  Britt tends to write in generalizations. She writes about "people"—never her uncle Bob or friend Susan. She is most specific when writing about physical possessions—desks, letters, and so on. This feature of "Neat People vs. Sloppy People" is perhaps its weakest element. In your writing, you will need to go beyond this level and be more specific, "naming names," as it were. (See pages 56–63 and 76–78 in Chapter 3 for more information on using specific evidence.)

3.  Between the "sloppy people" section and the "neat people" section there is an abrupt shift. As mentioned, Britt spends four paragraphs discussing the untidy. She concludes the fourth paragraph with "a neat person would just bulldoze the desk." Her next seven paragraphs discuss neat people and their hidden motivations. This **transition** is abrupt. It works in this essay, but sudden transitions are generally a risky tactic. Your essays will normally include explicit transitions, as we will discuss in Chapter 3 (pages 73–74).

4.  The essay has no concluding paragraph. This is another risky choice by Britt, who must have felt that her essay didn't need a final comment. However, your instructor will expect each of your essays to have an effective conclusion that sums up the development of the essay and provides a graceful ending. At times, students skimp on either the conclusion or the introduction, but they do so at their own peril. (See pages 63–66 in Chapter 3 for more information on developing concluding paragraphs.)

5.  Britt employs a bold **tone** in this essay and, as we discussed above, accompanies this tone with some fairly risky tactics. All told, does she succeed in impressing the reader? We think so. However, for a different angle on this interpretation, try the exercise below.

## EXERCISE 1.1

Using the comparison/contrast, subject-by-subject method, write a new version of "Neat People vs. Sloppy People." However, where Britt uses bold declarations and sweeping generalizations, try another approach: write about a person you know who fits Britt's definition of "neat people" and a person who fits the "sloppy people" definition. Use specific details and examples to contrast the two people. Can you make the same "moral" distinction that Britt does?

# WRITING WITH A READER'S EYE

Being aware of your purpose and audience doesn't mean considering these two issues at the start of the writing process and then forgetting them once you begin to draft. Each sentence that you write and then revise must be a conscious, deliberate gesture toward your audience, reflecting your general purpose and the specific purpose of this particular part of your essay.

The following essay is the final draft that a student named Verlinda wrote in response to a classroom assignment:

> In 550–750 words, describe a person who is more than what first meets the eye.

Verlinda's earlier drafts were unfocused and somewhat "self-absorbed." Read this essay; then answer the questions that follow. Note that the remaining chapters of Part 1 will show this essay in its earlier forms; you will be able to follow its development through the various stages of the writing process.

### A Very Secret Santa

All my years growing up, Betty Wallace was my best friend. I spent a lot of time at her house, and she did the same at mine. Our parents were good friends, and each couple trusted the other implicitly. I grew to see Walter and Leona Wallace as my uncle and aunt.      1

Walter was the more interesting of the two, but not at first glance. An accountant, he seemed to want to fit in. Walter dressed conservatively, which matched his features and size: a black man of middle height, very slightly overweight, with rimless glasses. His only "daring" feature was a neatly trimmed mustache. His personality, at first, also seemed unremarkable. He was quiet, a bit shy, and not really sociable or pleasant. Given his choice, he would sit alone in his big lounge chair and smoke a pipe (an ever-present odor) while watching television. Yet inside Walter Wallace was, if not a heart of gold, then the next best thing: he was the most charitable man I've ever met.      2

I remember the first time I saw an example of Walter's secret side. It was before Christmas, long ago. Betty and I were ten years old and going shopping with Mr. and Mrs. Wallace at the mall. After Walter, swearing under his breath, finally found a parking space, we noticed a commotion a few cars over. A young woman and her seven-year-old      3 were trying to quiet down the three-year-old, who, it seems, had been pulled from the last store they visited without getting what he wanted. The mother looked entirely flustered and was obviously quite poor (the car was dented and covered with rust). The little boy was screaming as if he had been scalded. We walked toward the mall, listening to this drama unfold behind us, and then Walter suddenly disappeared. Mrs. Wallace told us to keep walking, that Walter would catch up. When he did, he said nothing. Confused, I waited until Betty and I were alone to ask for an explanation. "He went back to give that woman some money," Betty explained. "He's done this a thousand times."

At the Wallaces' home there were always six to ten dogs and cats. By some radar, strays knew where to go. Over the objections of Leona, Walter would take them in; carry them to the vet; pay for shots, neutering, and medicine; and keep them if he couldn't convince someone else to take them off his hands. As a child, I remember loving the fact that the Wallace home was full of animals, but I don't think Leona Wallace shared my enjoyment. She didn't like dogs and would freeze in midsentence if a cat jumped in her lap, then launch the cat back towards the floor.

4

Christmastime is wonderful for kids, and Christmases are among my fondest memories. My family and the Wallaces attended Trinity United Methodist, a mostly white church with a middle-class population. However, the arrival of this church's Santa Claus was a great event each year. Walter Wallace as Santa was a complete transformation from Walter Wallace as bespectacled, quiet tax advisor. His voice and laughter boomed through the church as he talked to his small "clients." Walter also took his act on the road; he was a regular fixture at the area hospitals and the children's hospice.

5

Did Walter Wallace have the proverbial heart of gold? Or was he motivated by guilt—a successful man who can't help looking back to a time when he was poor? I don't think either is true. Walter helped young and old, black and white, human and nonhuman only because

6

he couldn't keep himself from doing so. Over the years, Betty told me that her father was miserable if he perceived that he had not done enough in some situation. Betty also told me that Walter's activities caused significant friction in his marriage. But he would not be stopped.

In general, I feel that when someone does something "nice" for another, his or her motives are not altogether altruistic—being nice makes the giver feel good about himself or herself. In the case of Walter Wallace, however, his behavior may well have been involuntary. Does this make Walter any less admirable? I don't think so; I wish the world were full of men like him.

7

## EXERCISE 1.2

Answer the following questions to evaluate the final draft of "A Very Secret Santa."

1. What do you think Verlinda's audience and purpose are? Has she successfully addressed the audience and fulfilled her purpose? Explain.

2. The **thesis** of this essay is stated in the last sentence of the second paragraph: "he was the most charitable man I've ever met." Remember that the thesis is a device used to alert the reader to the essay's purpose. Is this thesis significant enough and specific enough to build an essay around?

3. In paragraph 6, Verlinda considers the mystery of Walter Wallace's motives. Should she have mentioned this mystery in her introduction and thesis?

4. Does Verlinda give enough consideration to the problems that Walter's habits caused for Leona?

5. The writer concludes that Walter acted in the way that he did "because he couldn't keep himself from doing so." Is the evidence that she presents sufficient for this conclusion?

6. This essay follows an **inductive** method. In other words, the writer presents evidence, then uses that evidence to come to a conclusion. However, she could have made a general claim in her thesis—some people are altruistic because they can't keep themselves from being this way—and then proceeded to use the story of Walter as "evidence" for this claim. If the writer had taken this second approach, would her essay be better? Would it gain or lose any charm for the reader?

## The Writing Process

The writer of "A Very Secret Santa," as we have mentioned, did not produce this essay in one step. She employed a series of steps, collectively known as the **writing process.** Here is a brief summary of what this process entails:

- *Planning.* In this stage, you consider the assignment and its requirements. You consider your purpose and your audience, then start to generate ideas.
- *Prewriting.* Some students rush in where angels fear to tread; after the planning stage, they proceed to the drafting stage, producing essays with weak, unfocused structures and poorly developed ideas. However, prewriting allows you to visualize your essay before you begin it. As you cluster, outline, or freewrite (or use some other method of prewriting, as discussed in chapter 2), you generate more ideas and start to see the logical "shape" of your essay.
- *Drafting.* Your first draft may be very rough, but a very rough draft gives you an opportunity to develop your ideas, as we discuss in chapters 2 and 4. If your planning and prewriting have pointed you in the right direction, careful revising will lead you to a polished final essay. Be prepared to write multiple drafts.
- *Revising for content.* After your first draft, you should put the essay aside for a day, if possible. Then go back and read it for its content and its message. Have you written all that you intended, and is what you have written sufficient to meet the assignment's expectations? This revising stage frequently involves **collaboration**, meaning that one or more of your classmates, or readers you recruit on your own, act as your temporary audience. Chapter 4 discusses these issues.
- *Revising for structure.* Is what you have written an essay? Does it produce what its introduction promises? Are all of your paragraphs fully developed around clearly stated topics? See chapters 3 and 4.
- *Revising for grammar and mechanics.* Many students tend to produce as their final draft an essay that sounds very good when read aloud. However, your reading audience will more likely be looking at paper, not listening to a transcript. This stage, sometimes simply referred to as *editing* and *proofreading,* allows you to catch serious errors that can undercut your credibility and also to polish your essay by making final word choices and by fine-tuning your sentences. Chapter 4 covers editing and proofreading.

Chapters 2–4 will take you through these steps of the writing process. Throughout these chapters, we will concentrate on the various **options** that each stage of the writing process offers you. The personal essay is not a boilerplate document; the writer makes choices at every step along the way.

### Responding to Visuals

Visual representations—photographs, paintings, cartoons, and advertisements, for example—can have an effect on us that written texts cannot. It is useful to explore how this mode of communication works and how we can respond to it. All of the chapters in parts 1 and 2 of this book will ask you to examine, analyze, and write about various images taken from our present and our past.

*Dilbert* is an enormously popular cartoon that Scott Adams has published for many years now. It is about the weirdness of the workplace, the contradictory thinking that sometimes gets in the way of honest effort. Examine the accompanying example, and write responses to the questions.

- What does the cartoon accomplish that its "text" (the dialogue in the bubbles) cannot do alone? (Hint: Have someone read you the text without your looking at the cartoon panels.)
- Dogbert is the name of the difficult customer service representative. What is his audience? What does he seem to think about that audience?
- What does Dogbert see as his purpose?
- What does Dogbert's response say about the state of what consumer analyst Clark Howard calls "customer no-service" in the United States?

## Using the Internet

Go to these Web sites to find more tips, techniques, and insights on approaches to the essay:

### The Purdue University Writing Lab

Students can access useful handouts from this online writing lab (OWL). Included are materials on planning a writing project and writing various types of papers (genres): **http://owl.english.purdue.edu**.

### The University of Victoria Hypertext Writer's Guide

This Web site, sponsored by the University of Victoria's English Department, provides ample support for writing several types of essays as well as successful student models. The site also provides good advice on outlining, organizing, and writing introductions and conclusions: **http://web.uvic.ca/wguide**.

### The University of Richmond Writing Center's Writer's Web

This site offers useful suggestions for getting started on a paper and writing thesis statements: **http://writing2.richmond.edu/writing/wweb.html**.

### CHAPTER 2

# SHAPING YOUR ESSAY

## Prewriting, Focusing, Organizing, and Drafting

Before musicians give a concert, they practice and plan. Their audience will not welcome slip-ups. Moreover, the audience has expectations about what music will be performed. If it wants to succeed, a musical group will try to determine those expectations and both meet and surpass them. Similarly, when you write an essay, you want to be proud of it.

THIS ESSAY WILL ALSO EARN A GRADE that will become part of your final course grade and eventually part of your GPA. Why would you do any less than what entertainers do?

**Prewriting, focusing,** and **organizing** are the preliminary steps in writing your first **draft.** Your instructor will likely require you to show evidence of these preliminary activities. Some instructors ask that you turn in all "pieces" of your assignment response: prewriting output, outline, first draft (and any intermediate drafts), and the finished essay. Other instructors may even grade your preliminary activities. But even if your instructor requires that you turn in nothing more than your finished essay, you will be missing a valuable opportunity if you do not plan your approach before you start to write.

Careful planning enables you to write a draft that you can revise without having to scrap whole sections and start over. Yes, professional writers some-times do have to go back to square one, but this problem can usually be avoided by starting out with a plan.

Sometimes, students respond to a discussion of planning by saying, "I just don't have *time* to do all this and write my whole essay." Our response is "You don't have time *not* to plan." Consider this scenario. Next Tuesday at the start of class, your instructor gives you a writing assignment. You have seventy-five minutes, no more, to write an essay. The topic is not given to you until the start of class. This is the type of assignment that most students dread, and with good reason; it's no trip to Maui. The problems here are much like those faced by runners in a short sprint: if they start slowly or stumble along the way, there's not enough time to catch up. On the other hand, students who start by immediately writing their introductory paragraph often find themselves in trouble midway through the essay. They realize that their thesis and focus, which seemed fine early on, are now inappropriate or that the initial approach has yielded one or two acceptable paragraphs but little else. As a result, they struggle to finish—to provide evidence that somehow supports the marginal topic sentences and ideas of those last few paragraphs.

On the other hand, if you spend the first ten minutes putting together an informal "road map," writing a first draft will be dramatically easier. Rather than coming to the end of each body paragraph with the anxious sense that you must now think up something new to say, you can simply refer to your preliminary notes. You will be able to write your entire first draft with confidence because you know where you're going, you know that your ideas are sound, and you have perceived the overall structure of your essay before writing the first word. With a quarter-hour left in the period, while others may still be struggling to finish their first drafts, you are on your second pass, revising and then proofreading. Those ten early minutes have gone a long way toward improving your essay's final quality.

In general, planning also allows you to "test" your topic. Part of the planning process is designed to generate ideas, and during this part of the process, writers often come up with a topic that is superior to their original idea. Such is the nature of writing.

> *Consider Your Options*
>
> What is your current writing process? Does it work for you? What parts of it would you change?

# CHOOSING YOUR TOPIC

Your instructor may assign you a very specific topic, on which you must write within a fairly narrow focus. Or your instructor may give you much more freedom to choose your own topic and approach. Most of the time, instructors' assignments fall between these two ranges, perhaps with a focused topic that leaves the rest of the choices up to you.

## One Writer's Decisions

Chapter 1 contains the finished draft of "A Very Secret Santa," an essay we are using to illustrate the steps of the writing process. This essay was written in response to the following topic:

> In 550-750 words, describe a person who is more than what first meets the eye.

Note that the instructor limits the range of the topic but allows the student writer—Verlinda, in this case—to make the rest of the choices. When approaching this assignment, Verlinda immediately realized that the topic could apply to several people she knew, people whose appearance and general aspect belied their reality. However, some of these people did not seem to offer enough "substance" around which to develop an entire essay:

1.  Amir Goldman, Verlinda's survey of art professor, once mentioned that many years before, he had been a fighter pilot in the Israeli Air Force. This revelation contrasted greatly with Verlinda's early impressions of Dr. Goldman. However, it seemed "anecdotal" and would not provide enough material for an essay.

2.  Angie, a fellow student, had seemed extremely shy when Verlinda knew her in high school. However, "after-school Angie" was a lead ballet dancer of considerable renown, and she expressed her apparently repressed emotions through dance. Verlinda thought about Angie as a topic but then realized that she just didn't know her well enough (she couldn't even remember Angie's last name).

3.  Eduardo Sanchez-Mejiers, whom Verlinda knew through a friend, was planning to transfer to a Bible college at the end of the term; he wanted to become a Baptist minister. Eduardo, a solid citizen, wore hip clothing and drove a Honda coupe with tinted windows and a miniature Puerto Rican flag on the rearview mirror. He was frequently pulled over by the police for what Eduardo called the crime of "driving while brown." The contrast between what Eduardo was really like and how the police perceived him was extreme, but Verlinda rejected this topic as well, for it was *Eduardo's* topic: personal, complicated, and ongoing.

Finally, Verlinda realized that Walter Wallace, a man she had known for a decade, presented the best possibilities for her assignment.

As you can see, Verlinda explored many options before settling on the most promising one. You will have similar choices to make. Time spent wisely at this stage can have substantial benefits. A student who picks the first reasonable-sounding topic, perhaps impatient to get started, may realize—deep into the writing process—that he or she is spending time trying to nurse an inferior topic along. (If you walk onto a car lot and pick the first car that seems desirable, you increase your chances of buying a lemon.) Thinking and choosing carefully at this stage may well help you avoid needless problems later in the day.

## Establishing Your Rhetorical Context

Planning also helps you determine two essential features of your approach:

1. Who is my audience?
2. What is my purpose?

Audience and purpose are inextricably linked. If your instructor asked you to write a process document explaining how to perform a specific computer function, your logical next question would be "For whom?" What if your instructor asked you to write to a group of sixth-graders? What could you assume about the computer skills of this group? What language level would you need to employ? On the other hand, what if your instructor asked you to write this document for a group of retirees? What in your purpose would have to change to meet the needs of this older audience?

Even if your audience is one person—your instructor—you will learn more and more about this person as an audience throughout the semester. Each graded assignment that your instructor returns will contain both explicit and implicit clues about what he or she expects of you on your next attempt. Similarly, the topics and ideas that your instructor brings up in class are a way for him or her to establish an audience for your next essay. If your instructor has been leading up to a classification essay assignment, for example, he or she might mention or hint at certain expectations:

> We've looked at various classification essays and seen how they've worked. We've broken down two of them very carefully to see how they were constructed. By now, you should have a pretty good idea of how to write using this approach. And, while I'm at it, I want, in general, to see more evidence of planning when you turn in your essay.

In this way, your instructor has established the expectations for the new assignment. In effect, your audience has been defined for you.

How about purpose? Your purpose for this new assignment is to try to satisfy the needs of your audience. That sounds simple enough. But look back at the comments and end notes your instructor has written on earlier essays. Shouldn't these, logically, sharpen your sense of purpose?

Of course, you could choose to take the low road. After examining the assignment, you realize that there is an easy way to complete it with minimal effort. This unmotivated approach implies a very *modest* purpose, one not designed for a productive outcome.

Why not consider a more worthy purpose? After examining the assignment, you see that here you have a chance to think through a topic and aim for a more ambitious result. (When this happens, you're not just writing for a grade; you're writing for *yourself.*) Your general purpose, then, will be to write an essay that represents more than the average effort and that affects your reader in the way you want it to, consistent with the goals of the assignment. You may want to explain something so that your reader understands it, or make the reader laugh, or convince the reader to change a view or a behavior. But as you expend more effort than usual while dealing with a more ambitious, complicated topic, you'll find that things can go wrong. Don't let this added difficulty discourage you. Instead, make a mental note to allow more time for revising—checking the structure of your essay, its organization, its logic, its voice. Also, set aside more time for proofreading.

With these ideas in mind, you have a clear purpose for this essay. If the result doesn't quite live up to your hopes, rest assured that your instructor will notice the ambition inherent in your finished essay. Moreover, if you plan carefully and take the steps that you need—in other words, use the writing process to fulfill your purpose—your final draft should be successful, representing a document of which you should rightly be proud.

Establishing purpose and audience in the early stages is extremely important. Notice what happens in the following essay, in which the writer never figured out what he wanted to do and how he wanted to say it.

### A Modern Marvel

The greatest invention of the 20th Century must be computers. The earliest computers were huge, filling up a big room. My friend, Darren, says that "he can't imagine life before computers." I agree.

You see computers everywhere, stores, doctors offices, etc. They're great for word processing. You can write essays, letters and term papers on them and then revise as you need. Printers are great, too. You can choose any font you want and make the type bigger so that it fills up the page.

My dad had a real bad problem with his computer last month. It crashed right when he was in the middle of something, and he couldn't re-boot. He took it to a repair store and they had to send it to the factory. It took three weeks for it to come back, but it's fine now. Other ways computers are used are with accounting and similar stuff.

As you can see, our lives have been much improved by the computer. Everyone should have one. In fact, why doesn't the Federal

Government start a program to give computers to the poor people?

Soon we'll be able to watch real television on our computers as well,

that is a day I look forward to.

Besides a great number of stylistic errors, this essay has no purpose and no structure. It wanders; it contradicts itself. The writer, who has apparently never been told about the Internet, among other developments, barely scratches the surface, piling one random thought upon the next.

The real problem here is that this essay can't be revised; it must be rewritten. The situation is like taking a car in for major repairs; if the estimate reaches a certain level, the owner knows that the best thing to do is simply buy another car.

With careful prewriting and drafting, on the other hand, you will be able to produce a *serviceable* first draft, one you can deal with and improve upon. This chapter works through the steps of the process, starting from the beginning.

# PREWRITING STRATEGIES

Prewriting can help you find a topic and "test" it by seeing how well it holds up under development. It also helps you generate ideas and allows you to see the connections among those ideas. Your choice of prewriting options should be guided by two factors: (1) your rhetorical context (purpose and audience) and (2) your learning style.

## Considering Your Purpose and Audience

On one end of the spectrum is a situation faced daily by people at work: writing a document on a subject that they know intimately, addressed to an audience familiar with the context of the subject. This situation requires only minimal prewriting. On the other end of the spectrum is a complicated document on a subject that the writer is struggling to handle for an audience hostile to the writer's view and needing to be convinced. This document requires a great deal of prewriting, with careful choices made at this stage as well as at the focusing, organizing, and drafting stages. Your sense of your audience and purpose will help you decide both your most promising prewriting options and the extent to which you develop them.

## Considering Your Learning Style

How do you process language and information? Do you tend to hear it (aural learning) or see it (verbal learning)? Or do you tend to "see" information in a different way—in graphic form (visual learning)? Your answers to these questions reflect your preferred *learning style*. Most of us prefer one of the three basic approaches to learning: aural, verbal, or visual. Your preferred learning style will influence your choice of prewriting option(s), although you should always try several prewriting techniques. Even those that aren't really compatible with your learning style can yield results. Here are the various options according to their type:

1. Aural learners:
   - Brainstorming with peers
   - Brainstorming with a recorder

2. Verbal learners:
   - Brainstorming on paper
   - Freewriting
   - Invisible writing
   - Looping

3. Visual learners
   - Clustering
   - Chart making

### Aural Learners: Brainstorming with Peers

The value of brainstorming is that, inevitably, one thought leads to another. In a very short time, a writer can work through his or her cognitive process and have the results on paper.

If you can talk about a topic with your classmates and/or friends, you may get some valuable insights and feedback. (Don't forget to take notes.) You can also do the same for them. One of the interesting features of the writing process is that even if you sit, listen, and don't say a word, you will still learn a great deal about the general topic and your peers' approach to it. In other words, the "shape" of the assignment will become clearer to you. However, it is more likely that you will talk to your classmates, receive their feedback, and vice versa.

## One Writer's Decisions

When Verlinda was brainstorming to generate ideas for her essay, she found that some of her friends were taking an "oddity" approach to the assignment "Describe a person who is more than what first meets the eye." Stories of janitors who were trained violinists, baseball players who could yodel, and so on kept popping up as her friends considered possible topics.

However, Verlinda really didn't want to write about people with unexpected talents. She wanted to write about a person whose hidden qualities held a moral significance. After thinking through various possibilities, Verlinda knew that she had a good example in mind, but she also knew that she needed to approach this project carefully.

Since grade school, Verlinda had had a very close friend named Betty. Verlinda and Betty spent time at each other's houses, and each regarded the other's parents as uncles and aunts, not just friendly adults. Betty's father, Walter, was an accountant. A short, pudgy man with a clipped mustache, Walter was quiet, was not particularly friendly, and was sometimes at the mercy of his temper. Many people were put off by his apparently gruff exterior. Yet in her time with Betty's family, Verlinda had seen Walter give away hundreds of dollars to the poor, pay hundreds more for veterinary care for stray animals, and transform himself annually into an outgoing, exuberant Santa Claus.

However, Verlinda's audience, the class's instructor, Dr. Marshall, had made it clear through his classroom comments that his view of human nature was not rosy. Verlinda brought up her concern to her writing group. Dr. Marshall questioned people's motives constantly, especially those that seemed self-serving. As someone in the group mentioned, he seemed to be a bit cynical. So Verlinda and her fellow group members knew that a "heartwarming" approach might face problems.

But Walter's situation was not a simple story of charity; Betty had told her of the conflict between her parents because of Walter's charitable acts. Also, Walter was racked with guilt when he perceived that he had not done enough. Was there a sort of compulsion here? In fact, it seemed that Walter helped others because he had a great need to do so. This wasn't an issue of simple goodness on his part; he fulfilled others' needs while simultaneously fulfilling his own. "Surely," Verlinda said, "this is an approach that Dr. Marshall will find interesting." The members of her group agreed.

### Aural Learners: Brainstorming with a Recorder

A digital recorder or a computer with voice-recognition software allows you to brainstorm aloud, then play back or read your spoken thoughts. This method is convenient, but it has drawbacks as well as advantages. A recorder can be used in a variety of situations, but eventually you will need to transcribe your thoughts. Voice-recognition software will create a text file that you can save, but this type of software is still evolving, and today's best programs require a great deal of setup before they will work optimally. Moreover, this type of brainstorming is solitary; you won't get the benefit of a peer's feedback. However, some writers prefer such an approach.

### Verbal Learners: Brainstorming on Paper

During brainstorming, no idea is too large or too small. You can use the six questions favored by journalists—*who, what, when, where, how,* and *why*—to generate ideas and details, or you can just jot down thoughts as they occur to you. Remember that you will eventually need specific details in your writing.

Brainstorming is also a time when you should *not* worry about the mechanics of writing. You are compiling a list of ideas, facts, and details. Work quickly; this is no time to let your "internal editor" take over.

## One Writer's Decisions

After she met with her group, Verlinda did the following brainstorming on paper:

for significance (moral), only Walter Wallace

harmless looking man, pass him by in a crowd: short, pudgy, clipped

    mustache, no-rim glasses

accountant, so he wants to fit in

not sociable or talkative—not really pleasant

heart o'gold—but not like some Readers Digest sketch

does he have a heart of gold, or can he just not help helping?

giving money to poor white woman at mall—nonreaction of Mrs. W.

Betty: "happens all the time"

animal adoption business—semipermanent cast of pets, strays taken in
        constantly, fed, vet bills paid, acquaintances strongarmed to adopt
        overflow

Mrs. W. doesn't like animals.

Sometimes Mrs. W. doesn't like Mr. W. because of his tendencies.

Santa Claus—if there were an Olympic Saint Nick competition, Walter
        would win.

Complete transformation

his appeal and help work across gender and color lines—even species

May be compulsive, but the world is a better place with him in it

### Verbal Learners: Freewriting

Freewriting is another version of brainstorming, but instead of writing a list of
ideas and details, you concentrate on writing out your thoughts as they
occur to you. There is no reason to worry about paragraph unity or coherence;
just let go and write. Each sentence doesn't necessarily need to "follow" its
predecessor.

If you wanted to build a building, you'd need materials—bricks, for
instance. Freewriting will help provide you with some of the "bricks" that
you'll need to write your essay. Turn off the internal editor and let yourself go.

## One Writer's Decisions

Verlinda also used freewriting to come up with ideas about Walter. Here is her
response:

No saints here, please, no selfless martyrs—I think Dr. Marshall

has a special red pen to grade those with. Also, no janitors who are

closet violinists, or gardenors who used to be Asian royalty. I don't

know those people, and who cares, anyway?

Walter Wallace, Clark Kent accountant by day, the Charitable Shadow at night. Giving away money, on the quite, like asking a stranger for a cigarette when your suposed to have stopped. $20 here, $10 there. I wish I was close enough to one of those encounters to see the recipients face—shock, awkwardness at this stern looking black man insisting you take money—for your kids, lady, come on.

And that wierd bunch of pets, like discarded pieces of clothing. Cats and dogs lucky as hell, and others fixed, mended, and enoculated and given to protesting friends and family.

Mrs. W, hating animals and fearful of Mr. W's habit—not so much the money but the wierdness. Can't the man help himself? Must be a strain, they've been married over twenty years.

Christmas at church, and a black Santa—kids suprised at first, but swept up by the new Walter, like he'd found a phone booth and changed his personality as well as into the Santa suit. The greatest Santa I've ever seen, a roadshow as well—everyone who needs a free Santa can find one at Walter's house.

Is it charity? Compulsion? One the same as the other? Who knows? A "cure" would make Walter less than what he is, that's for sure. A fascinating man: sitting in that Barcalounger smoking his pipe, watching Monday Night Football, stroking that ancient grey cat.

### Verbal Learners: Invisible Writing

Invisible writing sounds very mysterious, but it's actually an enormously successful prewriting technique for writers afflicted with "internal editor syndrome." These people have trouble with brainstorming on paper or freewriting because they have a compulsion to go back and fix errors; they need things to be right before they move on. If you are one of these perfectionists, try this technique: open a computer file, but before you start to freewrite, turn off the monitor. Then you can work without worrying about errors.

### Verbal Learners: Looping

Looping builds upon any of the five techniques described above. Once you have generated your first set of ideas, go back and list the most important facts/concepts/opinions that you have produced. Then start with this list and

> **Consider Your Options**
>
> What is your learning style—aural, verbal, or visual? How can you use this knowledge to help you in the writing process?

*use your original prewriting technique again.* Looping helps you sharpen your focus. Obviously, you can "loop" more than once as you generate more ideas from your narrowing focus. Looping is a valuable technique to use with particularly difficult assignments and/or with writing situations that are complicated by tricky purpose and audience issues.

### Visual Learners: Clustering and Chart Making

The preliminary prewriting methods that we've looked at so far have been aural or verbal in nature. However, there is another, more graphically oriented set of methods: clustering and chart making. Students who use these methods prefer to "see" the developing essay. In clustering, you write the topic in the center of a piece of paper, then write ideas suggested by the topic around it, connecting these to the topics with lines. Follow the same procedure with your subtopics.

## One Writer's Decisions

Verlinda used a traditional clustering approach when she was trying out various prewriting options:

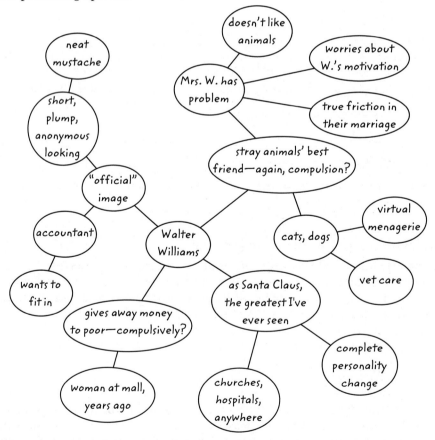

Here is what Verlinda's clustering output would look like if she had used a chart approach:

| | |
|---|---|
| quiet, inconspicuous, not very friendly — maybe self-conscious about needing to fit in as accountant | "daring" mustache may be important, because he transforms into a magnificent Santa Clause — big hit at church, hospitals, everywhere |
| seems very self-contained, cool | but will approach total strangers and give them money when they need it — Why? |
| quite content in suburban home | but home has a farmload of cats and dogs — he always takes in a stray, fixes what's wrong with it, keeps it or finds a home for it — wife is not impressed. In fact, real friction here: she doesn't like animals. |
| compulsive? | saint? |

a little of both?

This approach allows the writer to arrange information uniformly, left to right, centered on a common theme. It works particularly well for the comparison/contrast option, which makes sense when you realize that Verlinda is implicitly contrasting Walter Wallace's appearance with his reality. ............................

As we mentioned earlier, very few students would want to use all of these prewriting approaches for one essay. Rather, you should pick the approaches that work best for you. This way, you will be ready for the next two steps: focusing your topic and developing your essay's organization.

# FOCUSING STRATEGIES

Prewriting helps you think about your ideas and put a range of information and details on paper for future use. By this point, you should have a solid idea of how you will approach your topic. Therefore, now is a good time to determine your **thesis statement**, the guiding idea of your essay.

## Establishing Your Working Thesis

A **thesis** is a sentence or group of sentences that states your controlling idea. A good thesis statement both informs the reader about what will follow and interests the reader in the possibilities that lie ahead. A **working thesis** can be defined as "my thesis right now." It may well change, but it's your starting point, your "road map" for your essay. Later, in the drafting stages, you will want to review your thesis to make sure that it still reflects your developing essay.

To come up with a working thesis, look back to your prewriting. If you've done enough preparation, a thesis statement should already be forming in your mind. If not, do additional prewriting or try out another prewriting technique. (See pages 30–35.)

Chapter 1 explains that the thesis statement appears in the introduction of your essay, normally toward the introduction's end. In business documents, the thesis is the point at which readers decide whether to keep reading. Busy businesspeople need to determine which of the latest e-mail messages is important ("Wait a minute—read on") or garbage ("Is this how they spend their day up there?").

Similarly, your thesis statement will either engage or discourage your reader. Unlike most readers, however, your instructor will keep on reading your essay even if your thesis is boring. Obviously, your aim is to make your reader *want* to read your essay. Note the following thesis:

> If uncontrolled, mosquitoes in swampy areas can produce two negative effects: discomfort and disease.

This thesis does no more than impart information, information that seems obvious when stated in this way. However, notice how the following revision engages the reader:

> Hordes of biting, encephalitis-laden mosquitoes will be swarming all over town unless the swamps are treated this spring.

In this version, the reader can visualize the clouds of pests, hear their buzz, feel their bites, and cringe at the possibility of catching a deadly disease.

A thesis statement generally should *not* be a complicated, self-conscious outlining device, such as the following thesis for an essay on tax policy that is intended for general readers:

> In this essay I will prove that the tax increase being considered will have negative consequences: reduced growth, an overburdened citizenry, and unspecified use of revenues.

Writers want to interest and intrigue readers, not bore them to death. Although taxation is not inherently the most fascinating subject, it tends to engage people because most adults pay taxes. A lively approach is more suitable to the writer's audience and purpose:

> Granting the proposed tax increase will allow the county commissioners to pry from overtaxed residents more dollars that they would have otherwise spent in the private sector, where spending belongs.

The revised thesis avoids the dreadful self-consciousness of the original. In your thesis, as elsewhere, don't refer to your essay as if it were some science fair project. Avoid starting out with "In this essay I will discuss . . ." or "In my paper I will show. . . ." Address your reader in natural, mature, clear language, avoiding a didactic and self-referential tone.

Let's look at some more examples of weak and effective thesis statements:

ORIGINAL      **A 15 percent across-the-board increase in yearly costs will anger returning students.**

REVISED       **Returning students forced to shell out 115 percent of last year's costs for everything from bookstore candy to tuition will probably feel like marching on the president's office.**

ORIGINAL      **My aunt Kaye has had a sad life.**

REVISED       **Losing her husband to a robber, her life savings to a con man, and her eyesight to diabetes, my aunt Kaye has been cheated of a normal, happy life.**

ORIGINAL      **I learned a very good lesson that autumn day.**

REVISED       **On that beautiful autumn day I learned that appearances frequently belie reality, that a soft-spoken, well-dressed man could be the monster that my parents always feared.**

**CATALYST 2.0**

**MORE OPTIONS ONLINE**
For more help with
thesis statements,
go to
www.mhhe.com/
writingtoday.

## EXERCISE 2.1

The following thesis statements are too wordy, self-conscious, flat, and/or boring. Working alone, rewrite them. Be creative, and add details as necessary.

1. The food in my dormitory cafeteria is awful.
2. In this essay I hope to prove that stress, although one of the college student's worst enemies, can be successfully combated.
3. At this point in the semester, my dorm's social life has slowed to a crawl.
4. It is impossible to imagine the effects of open admissions across the state university system.
5. Richter Highway, the city's main thoroughfare, needs to be widened.

## Focusing Your Thesis

A thesis needs to be neither too narrow nor too broad. A thesis that is too narrow will leave you no freedom, and your essay will likely be of little interest to most audiences.

TOO NARROW   **Since my bout with mononucleosis, I've been extremely tired.**

Would you really want to write an essay that is restricted to telling the reader how tired you are? However, note this version:

REVISED    **My recent bout with mononucleosis has acquainted me with the pernicious aftereffects of this common yet underestimated disease: extreme fatigue, dizziness, and lack of energy.**

The topic is still not the most exciting one possible, but you could write a much better essay from the revised thesis than from the original because you have broadened the topic a bit. It could be interesting to people who are at risk of catching mononucleosis, whether or not they know you.

The opposite problem occurs when the thesis is too broad—for example, "The treatment of the homeless in this country is shameful." This is the thesis for a long sociological study of the issue—seven or eight hundred pages might cover the varying approaches and policies used by the many cities, counties, and states to deal with this issue. But in a short essay, you would be reduced to writing a series of generalizations if you used this thesis. Even if you did provide a concrete example of the treatment afforded a single homeless person, your example wouldn't prove anything. One homeless person is (unfortunately) just one example, and his or her situation does not necessarily reflect the lives of all the homeless people in this country.

Note how the revised thesis statement allows the writer enough "room" yet restricts the discussion to a manageable range:

REVISED    **Our city's new vagrancy law has one purpose, to drive the homeless to the next city: out of sight, out of mind.**

This thesis provides the basis for a lively argument that can be handled in 600 words or less.

## Key Elements of an Effective Thesis

An effective thesis (1) indicates your purpose and your controlling idea, (2) provides a general "road map" for your essay, and (3) engages your reader. Here are some ways to ensure that your thesis works:

1.  Phrase your thesis as a complete sentence and not as a title or topic.

    NOT    **Prohibiting talking on cellular telephones while driving.**

    OR     **The dangers of talking on a cellular telephone while driving and the law.**

    BUT    **Talking on a cellular telephone while driving is so dangerous that it should be made illegal.**

2.  State your point outright; do not announce it.

    NOT    **I am going to argue that talking on a cellular telephone while driving is so dangerous that it should be made illegal.**

    OR     **This paper will argue that talking on a cellular telephone while driving is so dangerous that it should be made illegal.**

    BUT    **Talking on a cellular telephone while driving is so dangerous that it should be made illegal.**

3. Don't bother explaining that your thesis is your opinion or what you believe; readers will assume that the idea or opinion you are supporting is your own.

   NOT     It is my opinion that talking on a cellular telephone while driving is so dangerous that it should be made illegal.

   OR     I believe that talking on a cellular telephone while driving is so dangerous that it should be made illegal.

   BUT     Talking on a cellular telephone while driving is so dangerous that it should be made illegal.

4. Make your thesis as specific and pointed as you can.

   NOT     Talking on a cellular telephone while driving is dangerous.

   OR     Talking on a cellular telephone while driving increases the chances of having an accident.

   BUT     Talking on a cellular telephone while driving is so dangerous that it should be made illegal.

## EXERCISE 2.2

Working alone, read the following scenarios. Decide if each thesis is sufficient, too narrow, or too broad for an essay of 500–700 words. Explain your reasoning.

1. Your college has built a new student union. You were familiar with the old one, and you have had just enough time to acquaint yourself with the new one.

   **Topic:** How does the new student union differ from its predecessor?

   **Audience:** Your instructor/fellow students

   **Rhetorical option:** Comparison/contrast

   **Thesis statement:** The new student union is a vast improvement over its predecessor.

2. You work as a math tutor in a computer lab, helping students use the tutorial software. On Wednesday, your supervisor announces that the long-awaited replacement for the aging software has arrived and will be loaded on Friday. She hands you the bulky user's manual, then asks you to write a simplified document to hand out to the students who use the lab.

   **Topic:** How to use the new math tutorial software

   **Audience:** Math students in need of academic support

   **Rhetorical option:** Process analysis

   **Thesis statement:** The new tutorial software has many features and requirements that differ from those of the old software, but following three basic steps will help you find your way through this program.

3.  Your instructor has lectured and led discussions on controversial issues for the past two weeks.

    **Topic:** Argue one side of an issue about which many Americans have strong feelings.

    **Audience:** Your instructor

    **Rhetorical option:** Argument

    **Thesis statement:** Poverty can be eliminated if we all work together to improve education in our nation.

4.  You drive a great deal: to work, at work, to school. Your city is becoming increasingly congested, with more cars each year. Your local newspaper asks readers to write in with their opinions.

    **Topic:** What is a cause or set of causes for local traffic congestion?

    **Audience:** The newspaper's readership

    **Rhetorical option:** Causal analysis

    **Thesis statement:** The real reason for local traffic problems is not congestion but the lack of proper lane-changing procedures by area drivers, leading to unnecessary accidents.

5.  You are an outgoing, gregarious person with many, many friends.

    **Topic:** What types of friends do you have or know about?

    **Audience:** Your instructor

    **Rhetorical option:** Classification

    **Thesis statement:** Friends come in three types: acquaintances, close friends, and lovers.

# ORGANIZATIONAL STRATEGIES

After choosing a topic, establishing audience and purpose, generating ideas, and developing a working thesis, you are now ready for the last step prior to drafting: *structuring* your prewriting so that it can guide you through the rest of the writing process.

## Structuring Your Prewriting

Before you begin to write a draft, you need to establish a structure for your essay. Constructing an **outline** of what you intend to do will help you "see" your essay before you begin. An outline can also reveal gaps—places where you need to do more thinking and prewriting. Three basic types of outlines are informal outlines, sentence outlines, and formal outlines.

### Informal Outlines

**Informal outlines** function as guides, giving writers a path to follow and something to fall back upon if the essay takes a wrong turn. They have the same general structure as formal outlines (discussed on page 42), but they don't need to follow a rigid hierarchy; they are for your use in planning.

The following outline comes from an essay contrasting the "haves" of the United States with the "have-nots":

Thesis: The divide between rich and poor in the United States is insurmountable.

Intro: Richest country on earth, with poor shut out—literally and figuratively—

from this wealth.

Credit

- U.S. wealthy exploit debt rather than vice versa; poor are either denied

   access or brutalized by terms.

Retirement

- The rich invest and can literally plan out the rest of their lives; the poor sur-

   vive day to day, investing in the Lotto if anything.

Residence

- The rich live where they want; the poor live where no one else would dare to.

Conclusion

- Intense separation, which is increasing.

- Rich get richer; poor get much poorer.

This type of outline is very helpful when your time is limited. It is a quick way to structure your thoughts and information while still allowing you to establish a firm plan for your essay.

### Sentence Outlines

The sentence outline is a refinement of the informal outline. In a **sentence outline**, you can include not only the subject of each paragraph but also the topic sentence and any major internal supports that you plan to use. Here is a sentence outline of the essay about the gap between rich people and poor people:

Thesis: The divide between rich and poor in the United States is insurmountable.

**I.**  Credit

 **A.** For the wealthy in the U.S., debt is not a liability; it is an opportunity.

 **B.** The poor, on the other hand, frequently have poor credit or no credit.

**II.**  Retirement

 **A.** Having surplus cash, the rich can invest in their future and for retirement.

 **B.** The poor, however, have no money to "invest"; all their money is used to survive day to day.

**III.** Place of Residence

    **A.** The rich live where they choose to live.

    **B.** The poor, if they have a home at all, live where no one else wants to live.

**IV.** Conclusion

    **A.** There is a separation here that seems to be growing more fixed as time goes by.

    **B.** The rich will get richer, and the poor will slide further into their misery.

### *Formal Outlines*

Your instructor may require you to submit a **formal outline** with your essay. However, formal outlines are not often used in the planning stage; they tend to be constructed *after* a preliminary or final draft has been completed. We discuss the formal outline here because of its obvious relation to the other two outline forms we have included.

Every entry in the formal outline is a complete sentence. Note the standard hierarchy of the formal outline:

**I.** (capitalized roman numeral)

    **A.** (capitalized letter)

        **1.** (Arabic numeral)

This structure will suffice for most short essays; for longer essays, however, you may need to add a fourth level to the hierarchy, using lowercase letters:

**I.** Main idea

    **A.** Second-level idea

        **1.** Third-level idea

            **a.** Detail supporting third-level idea

Because it reveals an essay's structure, the formal outline can be employed as a revision tool. After finishing a draft, a writer may create a formal outline to check the "skeleton" of his or her essay for discrepancies, errors, or gaps that are not apparent in the full essay.

## One Writer's Decisions

Verlinda wrote her formal outline after completing her first draft, partly as a way of locating problems with her draft. (The first draft of Verlinda's essay appears on pages 47–49 at the end of this chapter. The final draft appears in Chapter 1, pages 19–21.)

Thesis: Walter Wallace was the most charitable man I've ever met.

I. Walter practiced "guerilla charity." For example, his convincing the impoverished mother at the mall to take Christmas money for her children was typical of his activities.

II.  Walter believed in helping stray animals.

  A.  No stray was ever turned away.

  B.  His habits caused strain in his marriage.

   1.  Leona did not like animals.

   2.  Walter paid out large amounts to veterinarians.

III.  Walter transformed into an amazing Santa Claus during the holidays. Specifically, he appeared at the family's church, area hospitals, and the children's hospice.

IV.  What are the causes of Walter's "secret side"?

  A.  He didn't seem to be the victim of guilt.

  B.  He seemed compelled to help anyone who needed it.

V.  Whatever the cause, the world is a better place because of Walter Wallace.

# DRAFTING STRATEGIES

At this point, you have organized your ideas and are ready to begin a first draft—but don't expect it to be your final draft. No one is able to write a perfect first draft; even people who write strong first-draft essays realize the need for revision and redrafting. An essay gets stronger as the drafting process continues and the writer also gets more and more invested in the process and its outcome.

Essays tend to be written in two distinct circumstances: (1) supervised writing in class and (2) writing outside of class.

## Drafting In-Class Essays

Writing an essay in class under time constraints is a situation that many students fear. You might not have enough time to do a great deal of planning and prewriting, but as we pointed out earlier, skipping the prewriting stage and moving directly into a draft is a grave mistake. (For more advice on taking essay exams, see Chapter 19.)

After doing as much planning as time will allow—perhaps a quick brainstorming or clustering followed by a rough outline—try to produce the best first draft you can without becoming overly concerned about making it the absolutely best draft you can write. In other words, construct a draft that you can revise. During this process, you may encounter one of the following problems:

1.  **The internal editor.** Some writers can't seem to let a mistake go by, even when they're under time pressure. Rather than stopping, going back, and rewriting or fixing the problem area, simply place an asterisk (*) above it so that the error stands out when you begin to revise. Don't obsess over details in the first draft of an essay; instead, concentrate on completing a serviceable, well-structured text, and revise later.

2.  **Writer's block.** All writers face this problem from time to time. The words won't come, or they come much more slowly than you want them to. What

to do? First, remember that people who don't prewrite have more trouble with writer's block than people who plan and prepare. When you prewrite, thoughts percolate in your brain, generating more mental activity. Second, remember that your prewriting is waiting on paper. If you get stuck, refer to it. Scan through it quickly to get your thoughts moving again.

Have you ever heard of "revisor's block"? Neither have we. Once the first draft has been written, the rest, psychologically speaking, is easier. Our emphasis on prewriting reflects this distinction.

Another issue to consider with writer's block is that your will (in other words, what you want and intend) is not the same as the part of your brain that generates language. Some days, for reasons you may not understand, your will and your language center may not be "in sync"—the words that you write may not match your ideas. This situation is frustrating, and it contributes to writer's block. On difficult days, consider this phenomenon, relax a little, and use the basic steps of the writing process to get yourself going. Sometimes, when writers get past a few minutes of feeling blocked, they find a way into a difficult paragraph or passage and then remember only later that they had been blocked at all.

3.  **Panic.** The panic response is part of our genetic heritage. Thousands of years ago, it was quite useful. Walking around a bend in the trail and coming upon a lion, an early human panicked, leading to flight or a defensive response.

    Unfortunately, neither of these urges will help you much in a college classroom. It is trite to tell people experiencing panic to relax, not to worry so much. A more practical piece of advice is this: concentrate on the steps, not the outcome. To write an essay properly, you will need to achieve a series of objectives. Work on each step; the outcome should take care of itself.

4.  **Stalled introduction.** If you simply can't put your introduction into words, write the balance of your essay first; then come back and write the introduction. Many writers follow this pattern: prewrite, write the body, write the introduction, write the conclusion. Such an approach may seem odd, but it is one effective way to (a) get your first draft done and (b) establish rhetorical unity.

5.  **Bad writing environment.** Classrooms, paradoxically, are sometimes not the best places to work. Try to make yourself as comfortable as possible, and try to ignore distractions—squeaky chairs, talkers, people passing by the door, events outside the window. A distracting environment affects some students more than others; many students are quite comfortable working in an overcrowded room, whereas others get claustrophobic and feel the need for privacy and space.

In the future, students may routinely do in-class writing on computer rather than in longhand. Such a situation will be to the students' advantage. See pages 45–46 of this chapter and pages 86–87 and 97–98 of Chapter 4 for guidelines on using a word processor in the revising stage.

## Drafting Out-of-Class Essays

One of the virtues of out-of-class assignments is the extra time that you have to complete them; another benefit is that you can choose your writing environment. Where a writer chooses to work is a highly personal decision. Some writers try to avoid any external distraction; others can work in a room full of people watching the Super Bowl.

Work where you are comfortable, but if you find yourself becoming distracted, think about moving to a quieter spot. Libraries are great environments for writing; if you've never written an essay in a library, try it.

Having five days or two weeks to produce an essay causes many students to fall into the procrastination trap: "The essay's not due until Tuesday; I'll spend all day Sunday on it." We see two problems here. First, you should try to avoid using a single day to go through all the writing-process steps discussed in this chapter. Your work will improve if you can complete it over two or more days, returning to your writing with a fresh eye (and brain) on each new day. Second, when Sunday rolls around, you might get called in to work, get invited to a wonderful party, or become ill. Putting work off only invites problems, as generations of college students have learned the hard way.

## Drafting with a Computer

Out-of-class essays normally give you the option to compose your essay using a computer's word-processing program; in fact, many assignments require this approach. If you will be using a computer to write your essay, remember that the faster you get your draft into the computer's memory or onto a backup disk, the better your chances of exploiting the capacities of word-processing software.

Composing in longhand may help writers work through the stages of developing an essay, but if the final draft must be typed, then another, possibly avoidable, step must be completed. Many students develop, revise, and polish handwritten essays only to have their efforts complicated when they key their drafts into the computer. These students can avoid a difficult final step by following this strategy: transferring their first draft to a computer file as soon as they have written it. This step allows them to make all revisions in the computer file and eliminates the possibility of introducing errors when a fine, handwritten essay is hastily typed at the last minute.

Here are some specific guidelines for using a computer in the drafting process:

1. **Take advantage of the computer's ability to duplicate your draft.** Here is one student's approach to an assignment requiring a typed essay:

    The essay is the third one of the semester, so all file names start with the label E3. The student has two pieces of prewriting: a freewriting passage and a sentence outline. These two elements are saved in a file called E3P. The student keys in a first draft, named E3A, then copies the file twice under new names: E3B and E3C. Now four files have been saved on the hard drive and on a backup disk or thumb drive. E3B and E3C will be used during revision (see page 86 in Chapter 4), and E3A will be kept as insurance in case the instructor asks to see the first draft or the student is dissatisfied with the revision.

Disaster stories of hard drives crashing or of lost disks that contain the only version of an essay are commonplace. Save your work frequently, and keep it in two different storage locations; this way, you'll have a backup if something goes wrong.

2. **Save everything—forever.** *Save all versions of everything you write, save these materials in more than one location, and keep them forever.* "But won't I fill up my computer?" you might ask. No—text takes up very little memory on a modern PC. Graphics are the items that eat up a computer's memory. If you bought a new computer today and used it only as a word processor, you could save all of your work for fifty years.

3. **Use the printer to your advantage.** By printing out your work at important moments, such as when you are finished working for the day, you will achieve two valuable goals: you will have some more insurance against misadventure, and you will have your writing on paper, which many writers find easier to work with than a monitor's display.

4. **Listen to your text.** If your computer is equipped with Simpletext or a similar program and has speakers, you can actually "hear" your essay. Talking programs are very useful, especially for writers who are auditory learners rather than visual learners.

## Establishing Your Voice

Whether you are writing in class, at home, in longhand, or on a computer, you must determine the voice you will use throughout your essay. Are you planning to write an objective essay, without any references to your feelings and personal impressions? Or are you planning to write about an experience or a person close to you? The answers to these questions will help determine the "voice," or persona, that you create in your essay and will help you resolve a sometimes sticky issue: which pronouns are acceptable in a college-level essay. The following are some frequently asked questions about pronoun use:

1. **Can I use the pronoun *I* to refer to myself in my essay?** The answer is ultimately up to your instructor. For decades, college students were told never to use *I,* but that prohibition rarely stands today. Frequently, your context will determine what you should do. For example, in a technical or legal document, which usually calls for objective writing, *I* is out of place. However, in most of the writing for your composition class, *I* may well be acceptable, especially in essays where you use your own experience as evidence. Once again, check with your instructor.

2. **Can I use the pronoun *you* in my essay?** Be very careful with this issue. *You* is acceptable under only one condition: if the writer is speaking directly to the reader, such as in a letter, a process analysis, or a textbook.

3. **Should I use *one* or *he* or *he or she*?** *One* can sometimes sound absurdly formal ("One can't always tell, can one?"). *He* causes problems unless

you're writing about an all-male population and need to refer to an indefinite example. *He or she* (or *she or he*) is certainly standard today but can cause rhythm problems or general awkwardness. Nine times out of ten, when writers need to refer to a person of either sex, they can rephrase the sentence so that it has a plural context:

AWKWARD    **Every student took his or her seat.**

IMPROVED    **All the students took their seats.**

However, sometimes the plural won't work, as in the following:

> The scholarship winner must complete his or her high school education at least four months prior to matriculating at Parker College.

In this situation, there will be only one winner. (For more information on this subject, consult chapter 27.)

# One Writer's Decisions

Verlinda wrote her first draft after she had generated ideas by prewriting; then she outlined her draft to get a sense of its structure. Her draft includes errors in grammar, spelling, punctuation, and mechanics. (Verlinda's prewriting is on pages 31, 32, 33, 34, and 35. Her formal outline appears on pages 42–43, and her final draft is in chapter 1, pages 19–21.)

*Verlinda's First Draft*

### A Very Secret Santa

All my years growing up; Betty Wallace was my very best friend. I spent a lot of time at her house, she spent a lot of time at my house. Our parents were good friends. Each couple trusted the other implicitly. I grew to see Walter and Leona Wallace as uncle and aunt figures.

Walter was more interesting, but not at first glance. An accountent, he seem to want to fit in. Walter dressed conservatively, which matched his features and size: a black man of middle height, a little over weight, rimless glasses and the only "daring" feature a very neatly trimmed mustache. His personality seemed boring. He was quite, a bit shy, and not really sociable or pleasant. Given his choice, he would sit alone in his big lounge chair and smoke a pipe while watching T.V. Yet Walter Wallace, he was the most charitable man I've ever met.

I remember an example of Walter's secret side. It was before Christmas, years ago, Betty and I were ten years old and going shopping with Mr. and Mrs Wallace at the mall. After Walter finaly found a parking space we noticed a comotion a few cars over. A young woman and her seven-year-old were trying to quiet down the three-year-old. He had been pulled from the last store visited without getting what he wanted. The mother looked entirely flustered and she was obviously quite poor, the little boy was screaming like he had been scalded. We walked toward the mall, listening to this squabble unfold behind us, suddenly Walter disappeared. Mrs. Wallace told us to keep walking, that Walter would catch up. When he did he said nothing.

I waited until Betty and I were alone to ask for an explanation. "He went back to give that woman some money", Betty explained, "He's done this a thousand times".

At the Wallaces' home there was always six to ten dogs and cats. Strays knew where to go. Over the objections of Leona, Walter would take them in, carry them to the vet, pay for shots, nutering, and medicine, and keep them if he couldn't convince some one else to take them off his hands. As a child I remember loving the fact that the Wallace home was full of animals, but I don't think Leona Wallace shared my enjoyment. She didn't like dogs, and would freeze in midsentence if a cat jumped in her lap. Then launching the cat back towards the floor.

Christmastime is wonderful for kids, and it is one of my fondest memories'. My family and the Wallaces attended Trinity United Methodist, a mostly white church with a middle class population. The arrival of Santa Claus was a great event. Walter Wallace as Santa was a complete transformation from Walter Wallace as bespectacled, quiet taxadvisor. His voice and laughter booms through the church as he talks to his small "clients". Walter took his act on the road, at the area hospitals and the children's hospise.

Did Walter Wallace have the proverbeal heart of gold? Or was he motivated by guilt—a successful man who can't help looking back to a time when he was poor? Neither one. Walter helped young and old, black and white, human and nonhuman; only because he couldn't keep himself from doing so. Betty told me that her father was miserable, if he percieved that he had not done enough. She told me that Walter's activities caused signifigant friction in his marriage. But he would not be stopped.

I feel that when people do something "nice" for another that their motives are not altogether altruistic—being nice makes the giver feel good about him or herself. In the case of Walter Wallace however the motive seems to have been more involuntary. Does this make Walter less admirable? I don't think so, I wish the world was full of men like him.

## EXERCISE 2.3

Choose one of the general topics below. Then develop the topic by using the following steps:

1. Identify your purpose and audience.
2. Use a preliminary prewriting method to narrow your topic and generate ideas: either brainstorming/freewriting or clustering/chart making.
3. Decide upon a working thesis.
4. Structure your essay by using an informal outline or a sentence outline.
5. Compose your first draft.

**Topics:**

1. In what ways is your life easier than your parents' or grandparents' lives were when they were about your age? In what ways is it more difficult? Try interviewing a parent, grandparent, or older relative to gather information for this assignment.
2. "First impressions are essential." Agree or disagree.
3. One local, state, or federal law that should be immediately repealed.

4. The strangest person in your extended family.

5. The reasons that students are tempted to cheat on exams or plagiarize papers.

6. Three very different types of physical exercise.

7. An incident in which you were lucky to escape with your life.

8. An anonymous benefactor has given you a restaurant, with the condition that you do not change the nature of the restaurant or sell it to someone else. You must make the restaurant profitable. Unfortunately, the restaurant's name is "Ed's House of Thin Gruel." How will you achieve success?

## *Responding to Visuals*

Frequently, advertising campaigns are memorable because they entertain us and stick in our memory, but the careful observer will note that they don't tell us very much about the company they're supporting. An extremely successful recent campaign features the Gecko, who is the spokeslizard for GEICO, a well-respected U.S. insurance provider. The Gecko has appeared in print, on radio, on television, and online. In speaking roles, the Gecko has a pronounced Australian accent.

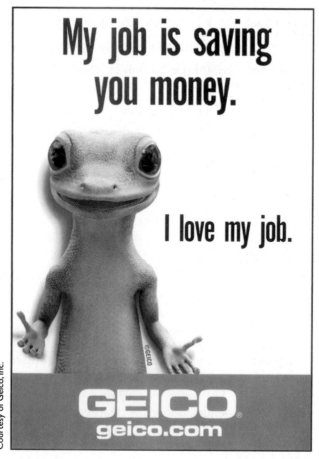

Courtesy of Geico, Inc.

Examine the accompanying ad, which appeared in *Newsweek* magazine, and write responses to the questions.

- What is your overall impression of the visual representation of the Gecko? Is the image appealing? comforting? friendly?
- GEICO is an acronym of the company's original name, the Government Employees Insurance Company. How did a company with that stodgy name end up with a lizard for a spokesbeing? (Do some research on the Internet to help you with that question.)
- What do you think GEICO's overall plan was for placing this ad in *Newsweek*? What is *Newsweek*'s audience? (Again, do some Internet research if needed.)
- In your opinion, is this ad effective? Explain your reasoning.

### Using the Internet

Go to these Web sites to find more tips, techniques, and insights on prewriting and drafting:

#### The University of Richmond Writing Center's Writer's Web

This site offers excellent advice on writing first drafts in various academic disciplines. The section on "focusing and connecting ideas" is also helpful. A topic index and search engine make finding useful material easy, especially in regard to addressing your audience, determining your voice, and deciding on your purpose in various contexts. This Web site also discusses freewriting, brainstorming, clustering, and other prewriting techniques:
**http://writing.richmond.edu/writing/wweb.html**

#### Garbl's Writing Process Links

This site provides an annotated list of several other valuable Web sites (with links) that provide information on the writing process—from overcoming writer's block to planning and drafting to proofreading:
**http://home.comcast.net/~garbl/writing/process.htm**

### CHAPTER 3

# DEVELOPING STRONG PARAGRAPHS

## Exploring Your Options

As we saw in Chapter 1, paragraphs are the building blocks of essays. An essay begins with an introductory paragraph or paragraphs, and this section sets up the rest of the text by leading to the **thesis statement**—the controlling idea of the essay. After the introduction, the body of the essay includes paragraphs that develop and support the thesis statement.

THE CONCLUDING PARAGRAPH OR PARAGRAPHS reflect on the essay and offer final thoughts on the issue being discussed.

Using this structure, a writer might develop an essay as short as three paragraphs (introduction, body, conclusion) or as long as fifty or more paragraphs, with several in the introduction and the conclusion and a great number forming the body. Whatever the length of the essay, however, paragraphs are its building blocks. In essays of the length you will likely be asked to write in this course, a poorly conceived and constructed paragraph will lodge in the reader's memory and override his or her perception of other, better-written parts of your essay. Carefully developed paragraphs are the essential components of effective short essays.

# PARAGRAPHS IN CONTEXT

In this section, we'll concentrate on how to develop the paragraphs that make up the three sections of a classically structured essay.

## Introductory Paragraphs

Whether it consists of one or more than one paragraph, an essay's introduction serves two functions: to provide the background or context of the essay and to indicate the **thesis statement,** the essay's controlling idea.

### Positioning the Thesis

The thesis statement *often* appears at or toward the end of the introduction, as in the following example (the thesis is highlighted):

> I've been dating Scott for about six weeks. During that time we've had "normal" dates—coffee, lunch, movies at the multiplex, movies on his DVD player—but last Wednesday he asked if I would consent to go with him to the last day of a professional golf tournament. I like Scott, I want to see our relationship progress, and I'm a decent actor. Swallowing my horror, I said, "Sure, sounds like fun." What it actually sounded like was unadulterated boredom. **This past Sunday, however, proved that my expectations were completely off base.**

The writer provides us with the necessary background by telling of her relationship with Scott and of her desire to further that relationship. The conflict is brought about by his unexpected invitation to the golf tournament, which leads her to have a set of expectations about the experience. The thesis statement then lets us know that the writer's fears of boredom turned out to be unfounded.

Of course, the thesis statement might also appear in the essay's first sentence. The following revision of the previous example illustrates this approach:

> **This past Sunday I had an experience that showed me how far apart expectations and reality can be.** I've been dating Scott for about six weeks. During that time we've had "normal" dates—coffee, lunch, movies at the multiplex, movies on his DVD player—but last Wednesday he asked if I would consent to go with him to the last day of a professional golf

tournament. I like Scott, I want to see our relationship progress, and I'm a decent actor. Swallowing my horror, I said, "Sure, sounds like fun." What it actually sounded like was unadulterated boredom.

Which approach works better? Probably the original version is preferable in this case. For one thing, starting an essay with a generalization ("This past Sunday I had an experience that showed me how far apart expectations and reality can be") does not interest the reader as much as the lead sentence of the original paragraph ("I've been dating Scott for about six weeks"). Who's Scott? We're curious to learn more. Second, the original version ends the introduction with a clear message that the essay will support the idea that negative expectations can be confounded. In the revised version, the introduction is "leaning" in the wrong direction (toward "unadulterated boredom") as it concludes.

As we mentioned, an essay's introduction does not have to be confined to one paragraph. Note how this writer uses a personal experience in her first paragraph to set up the theme of her essay and its eventual thesis:

Last week in my American history class, Dr. Rodriguez posed an interesting question: "A hundred years ago, what would have been the ways that you could have listened to music?" The answer, of course, is only if someone decided to play or sing live music while you were in hearing range. The idea eventually led me to think of a much quieter, less obtrusive United States in which radio, TV, intercoms, telephones, and all manner of uninvited advertising were not in a person's face during every waking hour.

I also started thinking about another, very prevalent problem today: boredom. I see it all around me. I plan to be a math major, and in my introductory classes I notice students who seem almost stunned by boredom. And why not? **We live in a culture where competing forms of entertainment always try to top previous efforts. We are also so saturated with invasive advertising and entertainment that we are stupefied by any "performer" who doesn't dance and sing.**

Notice that the thesis statement for this essay spans two sentences. The thesis should be as clear and concise as possible. A one-sentence thesis is often preferable, but trying to fit a complicated thesis into one sentence can produce an awkward and/or overly long statement. In some cases you may need two or more sentences to express your thesis.

## Getting Your Reader's Attention

How can you get your reader's attention? Writers use many different techniques. Notice the devices used by the writers of the following introductory paragraphs.

### Using an Engaging Anecdote

Two hurricanes have visited me recently, and except for a few rather hasty observations of my own (which somehow seem presumptuous), all I know about these storms is what I've heard on the radio. I live on the Maine coast, to the east of Penobscot Bay. Formerly, this coast was not in the path of hurricanes, or if it was we didn't seem to know it,

> but times change and we must change with them. My house is equipped
> with three small, old-fashioned radios, two of them battery sets, one a
> tiny plug-in bedside model on which my wife sometimes manages to get
> the Giants after I have turned in. We do not have TV, and because of this
> curious omission we are looked upon as eccentrics, possibly radicals.
>                               —from E. B. White, "The Eye of Edna"

Here, White opens with an anecdote that is alarming in its understatement
("Two hurricanes have visited me lately . . ."), as if mild-mannered acquaintances had dropped in for social visits. The reader is instantly engaged. Furthermore, living through one hurricane would be bad enough, but two?

### Using a Provocative Statement

> If you're a novice in Cyberspace, you may think that buying a computer is a scary and confusing process. But the truth is that if you take a
> little time to learn a few basic principles and some of the technical
> lingo, buying the right computer and getting it to work properly is no
> more complicated than building a nuclear reactor from wristwatch parts
> in a darkened room using only your teeth. So let's get started!
>                     —from Dave Barry, "How to Buy and Set Up a Computer"

Barry opens Chapter 3 of *Dave Barry in Cyberspace* with an intentionally
provocative statement to which the reader instantly reacts. ("A new computer
can't be *that* difficult.") Then Barry continues with an extremely funny account
of the various pitfalls that one can encounter with retail salespeople, "customer
support," and incompatible software.

**Questioning an Assumption**    In the next example, Bill Cosby opens an
essay by questioning, both implicitly and explicitly, one of our most cherished
assumptions—that children are necessary for personal fulfillment:

> So you've decided to have a child. You've decided to give up quiet
> evenings with good books and lazy weekends with good music, intimate
> meals during which you finish whole sentences, sweet private times
> when you've savored the thought that just the two of you and your love
> are all you will ever need. You've decided to turn your sofas into trampolines and to abandon the joys of leisurely contemplating reproductions
> of great art for the joys of frantically coping with reproductions of yourselves. Why?
>                               —from Bill Cosby, "The Baffling Question"

Cosby's essay then goes on to illustrate some of the "joys" of parenthood.

**Using a Quotation**    In *Trials of an Expert Witness,* Dr. Harold L. Klawans
recalls his experiences as a witness in medical malpractice cases. His thesis is
that in a court of law, winning is everything, whether we like this idea or not.
Klawans sees sports as a metaphor for courtroom struggles, and he opens his
first chapter with a quotation from the prominent scholar Jacques Barzun to
illustrate his point:

Jacques Barzun is credited with having proclaimed that "whoever would know the heart and mind of America had better learn baseball." While I will never dispute that axiom, the single action that has come to epitomize much of the American character to me belonged to a figure from an entirely different and much more international sport, namely, basketball. "Red" Auerbach was for many years the coach of the most successful basketball team in the world, the Boston Celtics, who won ten championships in a single eleven-year stretch under his leadership. He was an intense competitor who fought tooth and nail, but as soon as he knew that the game was won, Red relaxed, sat back, and lit a cigar, barely watching either his team or their opponents play out the rest of the game. That act was not one of disdain or arrogance. He had won. He had no more worries. He could relax and enjoy himself. He could sit back and feel the thrill of victory. If his actions increased the agony of defeat, so be it.

—from Harold L. Klawans, *Trials of an Expert Witness*

Note that the quotation is integrated into the text, not just there to be admired, as in the following example:

"When it rains, it pours." Whoever first said that was right on track.

Opening your essay with a quotation can be effective as long as you integrate the quoted text; don't let it "float."

Here are two other methods to capture the reader's attention:

1. Ask a question. For example: *Why is the cafeteria food at this college so uniformly inedible?*

2. Relate compelling statistics. For example: *A recent study by the state human services commission reveals that 15 percent of our children are abused by their twelfth birthday.*

Remember that you are trying to engage your reader's attention, to make that person *want* to continue reading your essay. For this reason, you should *never* use the self-conscious, reflexive approach seen in the work of so many inexperienced writers ("This essay will attempt to prove . . ."). The guideline is simple: don't refer to your essay as an essay while writing it.

## Body Paragraphs

Your choice of body paragraphs will largely be determined by which rhetorical option (description, narration, and so on) you are using to develop your essay. However, since you will often use more than one rhetorical option within an essay, you may need to use several of the following types of paragraphs in one piece of writing.

As we stress in Chapter 1, these approaches to writing are not artificial, theoretical ideas about how you should communicate. Instead, they come from human experience and reality. The approaches that you learn from this book will carry forward into the world of work. Therefore, after the explanation of

**CATALYST 2.0**

**MORE OPTIONS ONLINE**
For more help with thesis statements and introductory paragraphs, go to www.mhhe.com/ writingtoday.

each rhetorical option we have included some examples to show you practical contexts in which people use this approach in their daily working lives.

### Description

In description, the emphasis is on sensory detail—engaging the reader's ability to see, hear, feel, smell, and so on. (For more on sensory detail, see Chapter 5.) Note how the following paragraph from "A Very Secret Santa" focuses on these elements:

> Walter was the more interesting of the two, but not at first glance. An accountant, he seemed to want to fit in. Walter dressed conservatively, which matched his features and size: a black man of middle height, very slightly overweight, with rimless glasses. His only "daring" feature was a neatly trimmed mustache. His personality, at first, also seemed unremarkable. He was quiet, a bit shy, and not really sociable or pleasant. Given his choice, he would sit alone in his big lounge chair and smoke a pipe (an ever-present odor) while watching television. Yet inside Walter Wallace was, if not a heart of gold, then the next best thing: he was the most charitable man I've ever met.

Think about the everyday, real-world uses for description:

- A nurse describing a patient's symptoms
- A patrol officer describing the aftermath of a traffic accident
- A real estate developer describing a promising piece of property to his or her partners

### Narration

The narrative essay, or the narrative paragraph within an essay, tells a story. (For more on narration, see Chapter 6.) Narrative paragraphs use time order, with the writer employing transitions to ensure that the reader can follow the events without losing the "thread" of the story (for a list of transitions, see page 73):

> The game was close, start to finish. With ten seconds left to go, Demetrius fouled out by stopping the Garfield point guard from driving to the basket. The guard made one of the two resulting foul shots, and our enemy had a one-point lead. After a timeout, we had the ball in our forecourt, and guess who was trying to get position on Garfield's very athletic center? Me. It was like a housecat trying to get position on a cougar. We ran a set play, in which our best shooter shot from an angle after our small forward set a pick to block out the defender. Our guard arced the ball toward the basket, and next there was one of those frozen moments while everyone judged the apparent accuracy of the attempt. Then the ball clanged down on the back of the rim and bounced straight up. Robert McAlester leaped up after it, and I followed with my normal tape-delay reaction time.

The writer is trying to accomplish two tasks here. The first is to recount the events of the basketball game by using language that non–basketball fans can understand. The second task is to tell the story of the climactic, exciting final moments. He uses transitions (*next, then*) to good effect here, moving the reader right along with the narrative.

Narration is a powerful rhetorical tool. Consider some of the ways that people use it at work:

- A safety specialist compiling an incident report
- A contractor working up a contractually required progress report for a client
- A paralegal assembling witness testimony for an attorney

### Exemplification

Writers who use the exemplification option are trying to prove a general assertion by providing specific evidence to back it up. (For more on exemplification, see Chapter 7.) Notice how the following paragraph depends on its example:

> We have been preached at for years by the National Safety Council, among others, to obey the posted speed limits. "Speed kills," they tell us. Actually, however, speeding doesn't cause accidents; failure to yield the right-of-way and inability to control a vehicle account for almost all accidents. But excessive speeding can lead to both of these errors. Driving ten miles an hour over the speed limit is the norm for most Americans (including me), but I always shudder when I see someone driving, say, 70 in a 45-mile-per-hour zone. This driver is going so much faster than the surrounding cars that he or she can get in trouble merely due to the other drivers' expectations. Unless a "normal" driver in the traffic is explicitly aware of the high speed of the fastest car, he or she may well make a lane change without realizing that the fast car is now trapped with nowhere to go and not enough time to stop. Did the slower car "cause" the accident? Maybe in one sense, yes, but rear-end a car when you're doing 70 in a 45-mile-per-hour zone and see how fast you need a lawyer.

Exemplification is one of the most commonly used rhetorical options in practical contexts, as the following examples illustrate:

- A manager trying to change a workplace policy and using an example of how this policy tends to be counterproductive
- A cost analyst trying to explain how a quarterly budget will not (or did not) work by using a practical example of a flaw built into the budget
- A fisheries biologist arguing that state recreational fishing quotas must be changed, citing the example of overfishing in a particular area

### Process Analysis

Process analysis has two purposes. One is to explain to the reader how to do something: perform a task, repair machinery, and so on. The second purpose is to explain how an activity happened in the past or happens routinely. (For more on process analysis, see Chapter 8.)

The first of the following two examples uses the "how to" approach to lead the reader through the "process" of falling asleep:

> The first step takes place in the two or three hours before bedtime. This period is not a good time to eat the evening meal, unless you want to run the risk of being awakened by indigestion. Similarly, anything containing alcohol or caffeine can disrupt your ability to fall asleep. Old novels tell of characters drinking a glass of heated milk before bed. It sounds awful, but it works for many people. A warm bath just before bed may also help. The main objectives are to avoid anything that will disrupt sleep and to take measures conducive to sleep.

The next example shows how otherwise promising sales presentations can fail:

> The other extreme has its own problems. In my division we call these presentations "two young guys in red flannel shirts." When the techies show up, they are prepared to wow you. And they do. Their fingers fly across their ergonomic keyboards; technical wizardry rises up like a powerful genie in the room. However, the real problem with this type of presentation happens, oddly enough, at the same juncture as in the previous type. Ask one of these phenoms an application question, and watch what happens. Some of them can't communicate at all; some can't even look you in the eye. All in all, the solitude that draws many very smart but very shy people into computer/software design does not lend itself to interaction with the lay public.

The process that the writer is analyzing has happened in the past; presumably, it will happen in the future as well. Note that this paragraph comes from a definition essay that uses process analysis as an internal strategy.

Analyzing and explaining processes is one of the most useful strategies that writers employ. Consider some of the various contexts in which you might find yourself using this option in the future:

- Explaining to readers how to use your company's radically new software
- Explaining to your company vice president how your proposed budget will be used in the next quarter
- Explaining to a residential client how you can remodel her house

### Causal Analysis

Paragraphs developed using causal analysis normally concentrate on either cause or effect. (For more on causal analysis, see Chapter 9.) In this first example, Naomi Wolf considers possible causes for a perceived change in attitude:

> Thus, feminism stopped being seen as guaranteeing every woman's choice—whatever that may be—and fell captive to social attitudes held only by a minority that often could not even reach agreement among its own members. To be sure, this development might have been inescapable, a result of the abortion wars that demanded an us-and-them worldview. But, the ideological overloading closed the word

"feminism" off to enormous numbers of people: women who are not sure about, or who actively oppose, abortion; women who are terrified of being tarred with the brush of homophobia; women who strongly resist identifying themselves as victims; women who are uneasy with what they see as man bashing and blaming; conservative women; and men themselves.

—from Naomi Wolf, *Fire with Fire*

The second example concentrates on effects:

To the British, the Eskimos were like children—untutored savages who could only benefit from the white man's ways. This paternalism was quite unjustified. In the decades that followed, the real children in the Arctic would be the white explorers. Without the Eskimos to care for them, hunt for them, and guide them through that chill, inhospitable realm, scores more would have died of starvation, scurvy, exhaustion, or exposure. Without the Eskimos, the journeys to seek out the Pole and the Passage would not have been possible. Yet their contribution has been noted only obliquely. It was the British Navy's loss that it learned so little from the natives. Had it paid attention, the tragedies that followed might have been averted.

—from Pierre Berton, *The Arctic Grail*

If, Berton argues, the British naval explorers had tried to learn from the Inuit rather than seeing them as hopeless savages, the exploration of the Arctic would have been easier and not quite so deadly.

Causal analysis is an enormously versatile option, both in academic work and in the workplace. Here are a few of the contexts in which real-world writers employ this approach:

- A fire marshal explaining the origins of a house fire
- A contractor explaining cost overruns to a client
- An oncologist warning that a cancer treatment plan could have some atypical side effects

### Definition

Writers use definition to clear up possible confusion about a troublesome term or to bring new meaning to a commonplace word or idea. (For more on definition, see Chapter 10.) Note how the following paragraph defines the idea of "living on the economy budget":

Members of families existing on the economy budget never go out to eat, for it is not included in the food budget; they never go out to a movie, concert, or ball game or indeed to any public or private establishment that charges admission, for there is no entertainment budget; they have no cable television, for the same reason; they never purchase alcohol or cigarettes; never take a vacation or holiday that involves any motel or hotel or, again, any meals out; never hire a baby-sitter or have any other paid child care; never give an allowance or other spending

money to the children; never purchase any lessons or home-learning tools for the children; never buy books or records for the adults or children, or any toys, except in the small amounts available for birthday or Christmas presents ($50 per person over the year); never pay for a haircut; never buy a magazine; have no money for the feeding or veterinary care of any pets; and never spend any money for preschool for the children, or educational trips for them away from home, or any summer camp or other activity with a fee.
  —from John E. Schwarz and Thomas J. Volgy, *The Forgotten Americans*

Notice the internal strategy that Schwarz and Volgy use. They define the economy budget by using exemplification; we learn the misery faced by people trapped in this economic bracket by example after example of what the poor can't afford to do. Almost involuntarily, the reader compares these examples to his or her situation.

The definition option is frequently used in today's business world as managers and executives try to redefine their company's approaches in order to keep up in an increasingly competitive global market. Here are workplace issues that need to be redefined periodically:

- Promotion and retention policies
- Short-term design, production, and/or financial goals
- The company's obligations to its shareholders as well as its obligations to its employees—for example, its benefits package

## Classification

Writers classify when they take large subjects and divide them into smaller subjects. (For more on classification, see Chapter 11.) Classification is a way of making a subject clear by discussing its parts or categories, as in the following example:

In this country, we waste an enormous amount of time and energy disapproving of one another in three categories where only personal taste matters: hair, sports, and music. We need not review the family trauma, high dudgeon, tsk-tsking, and lawsuits caused over the years by hair and how people wear it. Consider the equally futile expenditure of energy in condemning other people's sports. And in music, good Lord, the zeal put into denouncing rock, sneering at opera, finding classical a bore, jazz passé, bluegrass fit only for snuff-dippers—why, it's stupefying. It's incomprehensible.
  —from Molly Ivins, *"Honky Tonking"*

For writers on the job, classification works the same way as it does in the classroom: it is a way of making sense of large collections of information. Consider some ways that people in the working world use classification as they organize data and make decisions:

- An emergency room supervisor drawing up guidelines on which patients will be treated first—the triage process

- A cost-containment specialist categorizing a company's workers as full-time, part-time, and contract employees
- A day-care manager summarizing her branch's expenses by type for the monthly report to the home office auditors

## Comparison/Contrast

When you compare and contrast two subjects, you have two options for structuring your paragraph or essay. If you use the subject-by-subject approach, you discuss one of the subjects first, then the other. In an essay, you can use various paragraph strategies, including most of the ones in this section. If you use the point-by-point approach, however, you compare and contrast the two subjects in relation to one point of comparison per sentence or group of sentences. (For more on comparison/contrast, see Chapter 12.) The point-by-point approach requires a careful use of transitions, as in the following example:

> In terms of gas mileage, my current vehicle is vastly superior to its predecessor. My old car averaged 22 miles per gallon. In contrast, my new vehicle averages 36 m.p.g. The clunker that I suffered with for so long needed a tune-up every year; however, my new car is guaranteed not to need a tune-up for at least 100,000 miles. Finally, I'm saving a dime each time I buy a gallon of gas, for my old car needed mid-grade gas whereas my new one burns regular.

In the workplace, comparison and contrast is a very effective planning tool. Consider the following examples, in which the people featured are asked to make choices and then back them up in a report:

- An information technology specialist considering two very different networking software packages
- A flooring contractor explaining to a client the pros and cons of two types of tile
- A human resources manager choosing between two health insurance plans that cost the same but have radically different approaches to benefits

## Argument

You can use any type of paragraph when developing an argument, but most paragraphs used in an argument make and support assertions. (For more on argument, see Chapter 13.) In the following example, the writer is arguing against a proposal to offer free tuition to community college students in her state:

> I would feel sorry for college instructors who suddenly had to teach this newly defined group of students. A college professor must be seen as an expert, and suddenly he or she must teach students with no incentive to learn whatsoever. Surely this situation would be demoralizing. Community college faculty would become like those notorious American high school teachers I've heard about so much: tired, depressed functionaries with no control and no hope.

In an argument essay, you are, obviously, trying to prove your point. However, any subject worth arguing has very good arguments on each side. The **yield** is a type of paragraph that acknowledges the other side's assertions. Yield paragraphs do not appear in all argument essays, but they are useful devices. The following yield is the second paragraph of the same argument about tuition:

> To one style of thinking, it is hard to oppose this idea. There are a great many people who find one difficulty standing between them and a college degree: money. These folks will become the very smart mechanic, the brilliant secretary, the underused office manager. Telling these people "no" just seems wrong.

In this paragraph, the writer acknowledges that her position may seem harsh and that those who oppose her may well have sound reasons for doing so. The writer is—temporarily—yielding to the other side before resuming her argument.

Argument permeates our lives: we continually find ourselves having to mount our own stands and react to the claims of others. The following are examples of common situations in which argument is the logical rhetorical option:

- A manager justifying to an employee why he should receive no raise in salary
- The employee writing a response to the manager asking that she reconsider his case and providing evidence in his favor
- A health insurance claims reviewer denying payment for a new procedure and explaining why the decision is valid
- A medical office manager responding to the insurance denial and providing justification for the use of the new procedure

**CATALYST 2.0**

**MORE OPTIONS ONLINE**
For more help with body paragraphs, go to www.mhhe.com/ writingtoday.

## EXERCISE 3.1

Each chapter in Part 2 (chapters 5–14) ends with a photograph chosen to illustrate the rhetorical option that the chapter discusses. For example, the narration chapter (Chapter 6) has a photograph reflecting a story, the comparison/contrast chapter (Chapter 12) has a photograph showing a sharp contrast between two images, and so on. Turn to Part 2, and select a photograph that interests you. Note the title of the chapter, and write a paragraph in response to the photograph, using the rhetorical option covered in the chapter to develop your idea.

## Concluding Paragraphs

A short essay normally ends with only one concluding paragraph. Along with the introduction, the conclusion of an essay often gives students trouble.

Many students make the error of bringing up new topics in the conclusion, frequently topics that beg to be explored, but not at the end of an essay. If you find yourself in this situation, reexamine the structure of your introduction and your body paragraphs. Should the new topic or topics be developed within your essay, or should they not be mentioned at all?

● *Consider Your Options*

Exercise 3.1 asks you
to examine a visual
representation (a pho-
tograph), consider an
abstraction (a rhetori-
cal option), and then
respond in words (by
writing a paragraph).
Try this: listen to your
favorite music for a
day, and list the rhetor-
ical options that you
hear used by your
favorite artists.

The worst approach to take in a conclusion is to contradict the ideas and positions already developed in the body paragraphs. You might shake your head and wonder who would do such a thing, but we see this problem often enough in students' essays to mention that it is a common pitfall.

The conclusion is the last part of your essay; it should logically derive from the paragraphs that precede it. Therefore, avoid using "In conclusion" or similar phrasing. Your reader can see that this is the end of your essay, so there is no need to announce it. Also avoid stilted sentences such as "As this essay has shown. . . ." Such language can lower the reader's evaluation of an otherwise effective essay.

Short essays rarely need a summary in their conclusion. Readers are frequently put off by encountering a recap of what they have just read and can still easily remember. Instead, use your conclusion to comment about your essay and its implications. Here are some proven approaches to writing effective conclusions.

### Reinforcing Your Thesis

Don't *repeat* your thesis; *reinforce* it. In "A Very Secret Santa," Verlinda includes her thesis statement within this sentence:

> Yet inside Walter Wallace was, if not a heart of gold, then the next best thing: he was the most charitable man I've ever met.

If in her conclusion Verlinda had repeated her thesis—"he [Walter] was the most charitable man I've ever met"—she would have missed an opportunity to make a strong final impression. However, note her very effective conclusion, especially its last sentence, which *reinforces* her thesis:

> In general, I feel that when someone does something "nice" for another, his or her motives are not altogether altruistic—being nice makes the giver feel good about himself or herself. In the case of Walter Wallace, however, the motive seems to have been more involuntary. Does this make Walter any less admirable? I don't think so; I wish the world were full of men like him.

### Commenting on Your Essay's Implications

If in your essay you have analyzed a situation, for example, now is the time to comment on the implications of your analysis. The following paragraph concludes an essay that examines the problem of boredom in modern life (see page 54 for the first two paragraphs of this essay). The writer believes that the modern world's noisy and intrusive entertainment and advertising culture is one of the main causes of boredom.

> In the future, two things are likely to happen. One is that the entertainment/advertising phalanx will turn to even more violence, noise, and intrusion. These techniques have worked for a long time, and they are not likely to disappear. Correspondingly, the ability to appreciate anything that requires a "quiet faculty"—such as a garden, an art museum, or an algebra textbook—will certainly dwindle even more. Our culture is about to become the slave of its own entertainment industry.

### Using a Call to Action

An essay that analyzes a problem can make a recommendation on how to solve the problem or at least improve the situation. The following paragraph concludes an essay defining the ideal sales presentation (excerpted on page 59). The essay points out what is wrong with most corporate sales presentations, and the concluding paragraph offers a remedy for this ongoing problem:

> I have a feeling that most vendors would prosper if they were able to sit in on presentations that actually convinced my company to pull the trigger. The androids-in-suits crowd would be horrified by how "unprofessional" a successful presentation is; the red-flannel boys would be alarmed at the apparent lack of nuclear widgets. However, in the middle is not mediocrity, but success.

### Showing the Aftermath

Many essays are either straight narratives or use a narrative framework to accomplish another purpose. In such essays, the conclusion can explain what happens *after* the narrative. The following example concludes a narrative of unexpected heroism in a basketball game (excerpted on page 57). The story itself ends in the last body paragraph, and the conclusion provides the aftermath, allowing the writer to comment on his life since basketball:

> My height is useful in different ways now. While going to college, I work part time as a stocker for Target, and I can reach shelves unattainable by my colleagues. The rest of the time, I study. I don't even own a basketball, but my brief moment of glory will never fade.

### Referring to an Earlier Anecdote or Example

Page 58 of this chapter contains a paragraph from an exemplification essay in which the writer discusses dangerous driving. In that paragraph, the writer introduces the example of a car moving at 70 mph in a 45-mph speed zone. The writer uses this hypothetical example in each of his body paragraphs, then returns to it in his conclusion:

> The driver cruising at 70 mph in a 45-mph zone is one of the worst of all traffic problems. Mr. Careless is driving too fast to react to slower traffic. The drivers of the slower cars, in turn, may not realize that a maniac is in their midst. And, if the distractions of cell phones, CD players, radios, and refreshments are present—for any or all of the drivers—then a dynamic recipe for trouble emerges.

### Using an Authoritative Quotation

Taking advantage of someone else's words can produce a powerful conclusion. The following is the concluding paragraph of an essay warning of the dangers of credit-card debt for college students:

> All students want to have fun while going to school; it's part of the tradition. But do they want to be paying for that fun many years from

**CATALYST 2.0**

**MORE OPTIONS ONLINE**
For more help with concluding paragraphs, go to
www.mhhe.com/
writingtoday.

now? When I talked to Teresa Espinoza, a Student Life counselor, she provided a grisly anecdote: "The worst case this office has seen was a student who—beyond the normal package of student loans—owed $27,000 in credit debt at the end of her junior year. When this student is in her forties or fifties, she may still be paying off this debt."

# WRITING EFFECTIVE TOPIC SENTENCES

Just as the thesis statement represents the controlling idea of an essay, the **topic sentence** indicates the specific subject of a paragraph. Readers expect a clear topic sentence and a unified paragraph on one idea. Moving from one main idea to another within a paragraph, or digressing from the main idea and then returning to it, results in a lack of unity.

The topic sentence may be handled in a variety of ways, normally depending on its placement in the paragraph. The topic sentence may also be implied—not stated but evident from the development of the paragraph—or it may be carried over from the preceding paragraph.

## Topic Sentence at the Paragraph's Beginning

Starting a paragraph with a topic sentence is the most common approach, as in the following example (the topic sentence is highlighted):

> **It was a world of difference marked by possessions.** Between Saturday night movies and winter vacations; weekly pay envelopes and checking accounts; Easter outfits bought on the layaway plan and designer clothes ordered a season ahead; social security checks and stock dividends; kids who slept on sofa beds and children with nannies; in short, between an envious life and an enviable one. Because these symbols of class changed visibly from top to bottom, they seemed unnatural, perhaps unjust, and we resented them. Because male-female roles changed very little from their elegant dinner parties to our kitchen tables, they seemed natural, and very just indeed.
> —from Gloria Steinem, *Moving Beyond Words*

Steinem illustrates the general statement in her topic sentence with specific evidence. Her concluding sentences comment on the situation that she describes.

Steinem's paragraph is part of an analytical discussion of a complex subject, and her topic sentence is appropriate for her subject matter. In more informal writing, however, a topic sentence might try to engage, interest, or even humor the reader. The following paragraph presents a great deal of information and develops it quite well, but the topic sentence is as flat as roadkill:

> **There are many problems with local road construction.** The expansion of the Midtown Expressway toll plaza seems to take place only between the hours of 7 and 9 a.m. and 4 and 6 p.m. It's as if the Department of Transportation is trying to show us their sincerity. An obvious solution would be to move this work to nighttime hours, when

traffic on the Midtown is about one-tenth of rush-hour volume. Another example is the widening of the emergency lanes on the six miles of the interstate east of downtown. This project has already consumed two years and doesn't seem close to being finished. One wonders how much work is actually being done.

Notice how much better a livelier topic sentence would work with the same paragraph:

> Is anyone in our area actually "in charge" of road construction?

In this case, asking a pointed question is a much more effective lead-in than the boring "There are many . . ." approach. Writing topic sentences intended to "hook" the reader is largely a matter of judgment and degree; starting every paragraph with a question would seem labored and artificial. However, keep in mind that the purpose of an essay is not just to pass along information; a well-written essay engages the reader.

## Ending with the Topic Sentence

The standard development pattern—with the topic sentence first, followed by supporting details—can be reversed. Some paragraphs begin with evidence and details, then conclude with the topic sentence, which gathers the preceding sentences into a general idea:

> But then there was Spanish. *Español:* my family's language. *Español:* the language that seemed to me a private language. I'd hear strangers on the radio and in the Mexican Catholic church across town speaking in Spanish, but I couldn't really believe that Spanish was a public language, like English. Spanish speakers, rather, seemed related to me, for I sensed that we shared—through our language—the experience of feeling apart from *los gringos.* It was thus a ghetto Spanish that I heard and I spoke. Like those whose lives are bound by a barrio, I was reminded by Spanish of my separateness from *los otros, los gringos* in power. **But more intensely than for most barrio children—because I did not live in a barrio—Spanish seemed to me the language of home. (Most days it was only at home that I'd hear it.) It became the language of joyful return.**
> —from Richard Rodriguez, "Los Otros, Mis Hermanos"

In his essay, Rodriguez uses the comparison/contrast option as his overall strategy, but he uses narrative as this paragraph's internal strategy. This approach works well in paragraphs that recount events and then build up to a defining conclusion. Note that Rodriguez's topic sentence is actually three sentences, the last three of the paragraph.

Placing the topic sentence at the end of a paragraph is a strategy that works only in certain situations. Writers who use this device too often have probably planned poorly. In other words, they wrote the paragraph, figured out what they meant, and then added a topic sentence at the end. Note the following example:

> The presenters have spent a great deal of time—and money—in ensuring that they look just right. The women dress like Miranda in *Sex and the City*; the men all watch *Boston Legal*. Somewhere in the histories of these people are rich orthodontists, as their teeth could blind you in direct sunlight. Their delivery is practiced and polished. These people are, to be frank, very easy to look at. So what's the problem? It's obvious: most of these people could push Chryslers or furniture as well as they can move whatever technical stuff they're trying to sell my company. Over the past fifteen years, computer/software/support items have been the focus of many of these presentations, and lately that focus has narrowed, with the Internet and its possibilities taking over. But ask one of these well-tailored androids a question that's not in the "script," and the façade weakens. Then a noticeable anger rises from me and my colleagues. **Most high-powered presentations favor style over substance.**

The logical position for the topic sentence in this paragraph is at the beginning, not the end, where it seems like an afterthought. Consider how much better the paragraph would read, and how much easier it would be to understand, if its topic sentence appeared at the beginning.

## Topic Sentence Within the Paragraph

The strategy of placing the topic sentence within the paragraph can be very useful, especially when you need to give your reader background information. A few (or several) sentences introduce the main idea, which is then presented; the rest of the paragraph develops and supports the main idea, as in the following example:

> There've been a lot of famous corpses in Chicago over the years, but John Wilkes Booth probably wasn't one of them. You do bring up an interesting topic, though. **The circumstances surrounding the death of John Wilkes Booth are hazy—hazy enough, in fact, to have kept a rumor in circulation for some years after his death (or "death," if you prefer) that J. W. was alive and kicking.** According to the history books, Booth died on the night of April 26, 1865. Heading south from Washington after the assassination, he reached the rolling Rappahannock River in Virginia on the twelfth night of his flight, and took refuge, along with one of his co-conspirators, in a tobacco barn belonging to the farm of one Richard Garrett. Federal troops in the area were tipped off, and the barn was surrounded and set on fire at about three in the morning. The troops had been instructed to take Booth alive, but he was found inside the burning building with a fatal bullet wound, an apparent suicide. A sergeant named Boston Corbett later took credit for the shooting, claiming that "Providence directed me" to disobey the order, but the point was never settled. Booth lived for some hours after the shooting, muttering the words "useless, useless," according to a popular account. The badly burned body was taken to Washington, where it was identified by some

of Booth's friends, but the corpse had been damaged severely enough to make a positive identification impossible. The body, whoever it was, was secretly buried in the floor of a Washington warehouse to keep it safe from molestation. Four years later, the corpse was exhumed and taken to the Booth family plot in Baltimore, where as far as anybody knows or cares, it has remained ever since.

—from Cecil Adams, *The Straight Dope*

The purpose of Adams's very popular newspaper column is to entertain as well as inform; thus, he prefaces his serious topic sentence ("The circumstances surrounding the death . . .") with sentences that establish his context and provide an effective lead-in. A more straightforward approach would have been informative but much less conversational in tone and, hence, less entertaining.

## Topic Sentence Used for Two Paragraphs

Occasionally, a writer begins a paragraph with a topic sentence and then develops the idea over two paragraphs (and sometimes more). Remember, a paragraph must develop a single idea, but this guideline does not mean that every idea must be developed in only one paragraph. Careful writers will sometimes break up a long paragraph into shorter paragraphs that are more easily digested, as in the following example:

As a group, today's parents have been portrayed as selfish and uncaring: Yuppie parents abandon the children to the au pair; working parents hang a key around their kids' necks and a list of emergency numbers on the refrigerator. Even in the healthiest families, parents fail to put their children first.

The indictment of parents is pervasive. In a survey by the Carnegie Foundation, 90 percent of a national sample of public school teachers say a lack of parental support is a problem in their classrooms. Librarians gathered at a national convention to draft a new policy to deal with the problem of parents who send unattended children to the library after school. Day-care workers complain to Ann Landers that all too often parents hand over children with empty stomachs and full diapers. Everywhere, parents are flunking the most basic tests.

—from Barbara Dafoe Whitehead, "Where Have All the Parents Gone?"

## The Implied Topic Sentence

When a writer implies the main idea rather than stating it, he or she is gambling that the development and support within the paragraph will make the main idea obvious, as in the following example:

I am over 21 years of age. I am a citizen of the United States. I have not been convicted of a felony. And I have not been treated or confined for drug addiction, drunkenness, or mental illness. According to the National Firearms Act of 1934, I thus qualify to purchase a fully automatic machine gun capable of firing hundreds of bullets with a single squeeze of the trigger. A few months ago, I decided to try.

—from Mathew Maranz, "Guns 'R' Us"

What is the topic of this paragraph? It could be stated this way: "Guns are too readily available in the United States." Would the paragraph be better if it had included this sentence? No—Maranz's point is self-evident.

However, think about the danger that lurks in the word *implied*. As a writer, you can attempt to imply your point, but your attempt will be fruitless if your reader does not grasp your implication. In other words, you are assuming that your reader will *infer* your meaning, a risky proposition. Be careful.

### EXERCISE 3.2

Each of the following paragraphs is missing its topic sentence. Read the paragraph carefully; then add the topic sentence where it will be most effective.

1. I wake up too late, and have to rush to get ready. Because I've been rushing, I forget a key piece of my schoolwork. And the later I start in the morning, the worse the traffic is during rush hour. I get to school late and enter my first class ten minutes after it has begun, receiving a puzzled glare from the instructor, who probably believes that I'll be late for my own funeral. And finally, to make my day complete, I learn much later in the afternoon that he increased our reading assignment and announced a quiz for the next class—information I would have received earlier if my day wasn't so off-kilter.

2. According to a story in yesterday's student newspaper, this school has spent $11 million on its football program over the last four years. During this time, the team's record has been a combined 12 wins, 32 losses. Seven football players have been arrested for violent crimes, and fifteen more have been arrested for theft, drug possession, or alcohol-related offenses. The university also plans to spend $15 million to renovate its football stadium.

## ACHIEVING UNITY

A paragraph needs to develop one idea. When a paragraph has done this successfully, it is said to be unified. Lack of **unity** is a problem that hinders many student writers, but paragraphs with unity problems are frequently the result of poor planning and no sense of purpose.

Chapter 2 discusses the need for planning and offers prewriting techniques that writers can use to help them determine where they are going before they begin the first draft of a paragraph or an essay.

The following paragraph is a good example of what happens when someone starts writing on a subject without prewriting and without determining a specific purpose:

America is a melting pot, and Florida is a state, like New York or Massachusetts, that has an incredibly diverse population. Immigrants have come to Florida for more than four centuries. Florida became a state in 1837. The first immigrants in Florida were the Spanish in the 1500s. Then came French and British settlers. Today, many immigrants from Cuba, Puerto Rico, and the non-Hispanic parts of the Caribbean live in Florida. These people are largely from Jamaica, Haiti, and the Bahamas. Early in the century, many Greeks settled on the Gulf Coast north of Clearwater in the Tarpon Springs area. Tarpon Springs is neat. They have a Sponge Museum and other sponge-related attractions. Many black people were brought to Florida as slaves, and many more came to Florida after the Civil War. Also, the Minorcans helped settle Florida in the St. Augustine-New Smyrna area in the 1800s. Only the Native Americans of South Florida are nonimmigrants.

This paragraph wanders like a toy boat in a gale. What is the writer's purpose? If it is to point out that different areas of Florida retain an ethnic flavor due to immigration patterns, it fails. If it is to list the major waves of immigration to Florida over time, it fails as well. There is no sense of chronology here.

Let's assume that the purpose of this paragraph is the second one: to list—generally—the historical immigration patterns in Florida. Using a narrative (chronological) strategy for development, the writer can revise the paragraph so that it is unified:

The United States has often been described as a melting pot, and one of its largest states, Florida, is a very good example of the immigrant tradition. Florida has received immigrants for over four centuries. The first were the Spanish, who arrived on the Atlantic coast in the 1500s, followed in later centuries by the French and the British. An interesting (and ultimately tragic) contingent was the Minorcans, who were brought to the St. Augustine-New Smyrna area as laborers. Black slaves became involuntary Florida residents up to the end of the Civil War. In the twentieth century, various groups have settled in specific areas of the state: Greeks who were attracted by the sponges off the Tarpon Springs coastline, Cubans and Puerto Ricans who settled in Miami and other population centers. The most recent wave of immigrants has come from Jamaica, Haiti, and the Bahamas. The only Floridians who aren't immigrants are the Native Americans of South Florida, and relatively few of this band remain, concentrated in the area around the Everglades.

Another problem with unity occurs when a writer has a clear purpose for a paragraph but includes irrelevant statements within it, leading the reader off the track of the paragraph's central idea. Called *digressions,* these wanderings can distract and confuse the reader. In the following example, the irrelevant sentences are highlighted:

If current trends continue, stores will soon start offering Christmas merchandise on June 1. For years, the Christmas shopping season commenced on the day after Thanksgiving. Everyone remembers that frantic Friday. (Once, I saw a four-way fistfight over a mall parking spot.) However, retailers have now succeeded in pushing this date forward to mid-October. There is no law against this practice. The general freedom given to business in this country allows Wal-Mart, say, to sell Christmas decorations in March if company officials feel like it. **This kind of freedom is what has allowed the United States to become so wealthy. The marketing genius of American retailers is the envy of the rest of the world.** But starting the Christmas shopping season earlier every year is becoming increasingly bizarre. Also, this practice is turning an occasion that is already a problem for many people into a true ordeal.

### EXERCISE 3.3

The following paragraphs lack unity. Read each and underline the sentences that lead the text in the wrong direction. Then revise the paragraph to correct the problem.

1.  The dog is the most useful creature humanity has ever known. Farmers and ranchers, in particular, have made great use of dogs. Dogs can be used to herd sheep and to help in the herding of horses. Horses themselves are quite useful agrarian animals. So is the mule, which is the offspring of a male donkey and a female horse, and the hinny, which is the offspring of a male horse and a female donkey. Oxen have also been used on farms and ranches. Dogs in rural areas can be used to guard property against trespassers and to help control vermin. Cats can also be used to control vermin, but not to repel intruders.

2.  My roommate had his semester fall apart on him this weekend, and while I feel sorry for him, he has only himself to blame. Mike is taking three classes and working thirty hours a week. On Friday afternoon, he got his latest calculus test back and found that he made a 51. Now he probably can't pass the course. Calculus is one of the hardest courses for many students at this school. Of course, it's not as boring as statistics, but that's its only saving grace. I tried to commiserate with Mike; however, he was down and stayed there. He went out to a local club that night and didn't get back until 4:00 a.m. A good band was playing at the Emerald, which is one of my favorite night spots. They have great specials and attract the best crowds in town. Mike stayed much too long and then came home and slept until 2:30 p.m. When he awoke, he found a message on the answering machine from his boss, letting Mike know that he had been fired for missing work. On both Saturday night and Sunday night, Mike also hit the club scene. On Monday, he managed to sleep both through his biology exam and past the deadline for his research paper in Comp 2. I'm going to have a talk with him about getting some help over at the counseling center.

## ACHIEVING COHERENCE

When someone is trying to talk and is babbling or cannot form words, the person is said to be incoherent. In terms of paragraph development, however, **coherence** has a more technical meaning. A paragraph is coherent when the writer has succeeded in guiding the reader through the text. Three common techniques that will help you achieve coherence in your paragraphs are

(1) using effective transitions, (2) choosing nouns and pronouns carefully, and (3) writing with parallel structures.

## Using Effective Transitions to Improve Coherence

**Transitions** are text markers—words and phrases that guide the reader through the text. When a paragraph does not include transitions, the reader faces a string of unconnected sentences and is forced to impose order on and make connections among the various thoughts without the writer's help.

| TRANSITIONAL EXPRESSIONS | |
|---|---|
| Relationship | Expression |
| Addition | also, in addition, too, moreover, and, besides, furthermore, equally important, then, finally |
| Example | for example, for instance, thus, as an illustration, namely, specifically |
| Contrast | but, yet, however, on the other hand, while, nevertheless, nonetheless, conversely, in contrast, still, at the same time |
| Comparison | similarly, likewise, in the same way |
| Concession | of course, to be sure, certainly, granted |
| Time | first, second, third, next, then, finally, afterwards, before, soon, later, meanwhile, subsequently, immediately, eventually, currently |
| Location | in the front, in the foreground, in the back, in the background, at the side, adjacent, nearby, next to, in the distance, here, there, to the left, to the right, inside, outside |
| Result | therefore, thus, as a result, so, accordingly |
| Summary | hence, in short, in brief, in summary, in conclusion, finally |

Effective transitions are one of the true marks of good writing—and this technique is one of the most painless to learn. Note the following paragraph, which uses no transitions at all:

> On our date last Saturday, my boyfriend ran over a nail. His left front tire went flat. The car jack had never been used before. It was stiff. Eduardo tried to loosen the tire lugs. They were almost frozen. He found a piece of pipe. He used it to gain leverage on the tire iron. The car was parked in some mud. Eduardo got the flat tire off and slipped and fell into the mud. He was filthy. Eduardo got the spare tire in place. We continued on our "date."

This paragraph is written in a telegraphic style: Sentence. Stop. Sentence. Stop. Now see how adding transitional words and phrases improves the paragraph's coherence:

> On our date last Saturday, my boyfriend ran over a nail, **so** his left front tire went flat. The car jack had never been used before; **as a result,** it was stiff. **First,** Eduardo tried to loosen the tire lugs, **but** they were almost frozen. **Then** he found a piece of pipe, and he used it to gain leverage on the tire iron. **However,** the car was parked in some mud. **Once** Eduardo got the flat tire off, he slipped and fell into the mud. **Thus,** he was filthy **by the time** he got the spare tire in place **and** we could continue on our "date."

Most of the transitions used in this paragraph show the passage of time (*first, then, once*) and cause/effect (*so, as a result, thus*). The transitions in the following paragraph help the writer build a sense of opposition, or contrast:

> The key to the industrial revolution was discovering that non-human forms of energy substituted for human forms could increase the wealth of a nation beyond anyone's wildest dreams. **But** there was a catch. To realize this great wealth, non-human energy needed huge complexes called factories with hundreds, even thousands of workers collected into one factory. **Moreover,** several factories in one central place made the generation of energy more efficient. **Almost overnight,** the Western world was transformed from a rural and agricultural country to an urban and industrial state. Our technological advance seems to no longer fit our social structure: In a sense, the Japanese can better cope with modern industrialism. **While** Americans still busily protect our rather extreme form of individualism, the Japanese hold their individualism in check and emphasize cooperation.
>
> —from William Ouchi, "Japanese and American Workers: Two Casts of Mind"

CATALYST 2.0

**MORE OPTIONS ONLINE**
For more help with
paragraph coherence,
go to
www.mhhe.com/
writingtoday.

This paragraph is part of Ouchi's argument that Japanese workers and American workers approach their jobs very differently. Hence, Ouchi uses transitions of opposition, such as *but* and *while,* as well as other transitions, such as *moreover,* which help him introduce additional details.

## EXERCISE 3.4

The following paragraphs have very few transitions and, as a result, very little coherence. Revise each paragraph, adding transitional words and phrases to improve the paragraph's coherence.

1. Today, war is fought differently than it was in the past. Traditional combat depended on information gained from scouts and spies. These brave souls placed their lives in danger by infiltrating enemy lines or attacking exposed areas such as beaches or hills. Modern combat uses satellites and computers to get the job done. In the past, soldiers fought hand to hand and face to face. Soldiers today are frequently miles apart and never see their opponents up close. They are able to kill much more efficiently due to the technology at their command.

2. Colleges sometimes spend money like water, as one need leads to another. I work as a student assistant for the Student Activities (SA) office,

which recently launched a new and revamped intramural program. SA hired a new coordinator. He needed someone to answer the phone and handle written communication. He hired a secretary. The coordinator found that he could not trust the secretary to make decisions while he was away. He then hired a woman to be his assistant. She is an organizational type who likes delegating authority. She hired two student assistants. First we had one person hired to perform a function. Now we have five, all in the space of a month.

## Achieving Coherence Through Careful Choice of Nouns and Pronouns

Pronouns enable us to avoid the needless repetition of nouns, thereby making reading easier and faster. At the same time, the words that pronouns are replacing—their **antecedents**—must be clear, or the reader will wonder what the writer is referring to. Developing a sense of how to use pronouns and when *not* to use a pronoun—instead, repeating the noun for clarity and emphasis—will help you make your paragraphs and essays more coherent.

Note the skillful use of pronouns in the following two paragraphs by Axel Madsen:

> Gabrielle was twenty-seven when **she** fell in love with Arthur Capel. To **her**, Boy Capel was someone solid, someone who assumed **she** had a mind and asked what **she** thought. To **him, she** was a singular beauty. Slim, straight, and with an aristocratic head on a long, graceful neck, **she** looked like a Gainsborough duchess in profile. Yet full face, with **her** mocking raven eyes, generous mouth, charming dimple and knowing presence, **she** was an alluring street urchin.
>
> During the week in the Pyrenees **he** had come to appreciate **her** acid charm, **her** spontaneity and sharp tongue. **She** was energetic, frank, and witty, yet just beneath **her** deceptively accessible and limpid demeanor there was something severe. **She** loved what was beautiful and detested what was merely pretty. **Her** taste was nervy and **she** divined the phony, the contrived, the spurious in people. That **she** was Etienne's mistress somehow added to **her** stature in Boy's eyes. Etienne's persistent reminders that **he** would be going to Argentina for an extended visit practically invited Boy to attempt **her** conquest.
>
> —from Axel Madsen, *Chanel: A Woman of Her Own*

Here the pronouns *she, her, he,* and *him* are used twenty-one times, but there is never a question about which person each pronoun refers to. Notice in the last two sentences that Madsen is able to continue to use *she* and *her* (referring to Gabrielle) while using mostly nouns to refer to the two men, Arthur ("Boy") and Etienne.

In the preceding example, the careful use of pronouns contributes to clarity and ease of reading. Sometimes, however, to achieve greater emphasis, writers deliberately repeat nouns or use synonyms for greater emphasis, as in the following example:

Social change may be slow to occur, but as we have seen, the democratic process is the best way to effect equitable progress. The democratic process lets people have their say. The democratic process then lets elected leaders judge the desires of the populace and make informed decisions. Finally, the democratic process allows judicial, principled review of new laws to ensure that our nation's basic ideas are not violated.

### Using Parallelism to Improve Coherence

**Parallelism** is the use of the same constructions for similar ideas. The following sentence has a problem with parallelism:

John enjoyed reading, dancing, and to swim.

The writer's pattern is gerund ("reading"), gerund ("dancing"), and then, illogically, infinitive ("to swim"). Obviously, the writer should have continued the pattern established by the two gerunds:

John enjoyed reading, dancing, and swimming.

Problems with parallelism can also occur within paragraphs. Note in the following paragraph how careless wording causes a lack of parallelism and a corresponding lack of coherence:

**To change** a practice that has long been followed can be difficult. **Modifying** the practice may be seen as the first step. Smokers find that **to vary** the intervals between cigarettes may help disturb the pattern of counting on a smoke at certain times. **To modify** one element of a habit can be the first step in **losing** the habit altogether.

The boldface terms should be made parallel for greater coherence, as in the revision below:

**Changing** a practice that has long been followed can be difficult. **Modifying** the practice may be seen as the first step. Smokers find that **varying** the intervals between cigarettes may help disturb the pattern of counting on a smoke at certain times. **Modifying** one element of a habit can be the first step in **losing** the habit altogether.

See chapters 4 and 25 for more on the subject of parallelism.

# ACHIEVING SPECIFICITY THROUGH THE USE OF CONCRETE DETAILS

Effective paragraph development is always a matter of degree and a matter of context. Some paragraphs deal with abstract or general subjects and do not—and should not—depend on specific, concrete details, as in the following example:

The American premise is an existential one, and our moral code is political, its object being to allow for the widest horizons of sight and the broadest range of expression. We protect the other person's liberty in the interest of protecting our own, and our virtues conform to the terms and conditions of an arduous and speculative journey. If we look into even so coarse a mirror as the one held up to us by the situation comedies on prime-time television, we see that we value the companionable virtues— helpfulness, forgiveness, kindliness, and, above all, tolerance.

—from Lewis H. Lapham, "Who and What Is American?"

*Consider Your Options*

Think about the last paragraph that you have written—for this or another class, at work, or in a message to a friend. Could it have been improved by adding more concrete and specific details? What details could you have chosen to add?

The closest that Lapham gets to using concrete details is his reference to television. Yet there's nothing wrong with this paragraph (and a great deal that is right). Many paragraphs in academic writing take this approach.

However, in essays that deal with more specific and more practical issues, using concrete details will help develop your paragraphs and inform your reader. We frequently groan (sometimes inwardly, sometimes not) when we read paragraphs like this one:

Breakfast is the most important meal of the day. Getting nutritious food into your system in the morning starts your metabolism working and provides you with energy. People who don't eat breakfast sometimes encounter ill effects later in the morning.

We don't learn much from this paragraph. How about some specific breakfast-food choices? Are some better than others? Should we ingest all the sugar-laden products that we can find? What if we want to eat a couple of barbecue sandwiches? And what, exactly, happens to people who don't eat breakfast? Do they feel a sudden lack of energy, experience a mild headache, or start lurching about like the zombies in *Night of the Living Dead*? This paragraph cries out for specific examples. Note the following revision:

Breakfast is the most important meal of the day. When people wake up, they need energy for the morning, and energy comes from food. What kind of food, though? The remains of last night's pizza or barbecue? Sugar-loaded Breakfast Bombs? Technically, these are sources of energy, but not very good ones. Better choices are bran cereal, fruit, or even green vegetables. The last suggestion may sound strange, but a simple salad is a very nutritious breakfast, and a good breakfast can help avoid problems later in the morning. People who don't eat breakfast—or who eat very little at breakfast—can suffer a variety of late-morning problems, such as lack of energy, headaches, and fluctuating glucose levels. Taking the time to eat a good breakfast is a simple way to make the morning better and the day easier.

## EXERCISE 3.5

Read the following paragraphs. Determine if each one is sufficiently specific in terms of its subject matter and purpose. If it is not, add specific details of your choosing.

1. Most people don't exercise enough. Exercise gets the heart and lungs working. It also helps burn calories and leads to weight loss. People who exercise feel better and look better. A lack of exercise can lead to significant health problems in later life.

2. Many observers note that college does a poor job of training students for the world of work. Although such training is only a part of what colleges do, these complaints are valid. However, such a discrepancy is inevitable. For one thing, the business world changes faster than the academic world can adapt. Business is based on the need for profit, and decisions on changing policies can be made in an afternoon. Colleges, on the other hand, are based on tradition and bureaucracy. Change occurs more slowly here. Another problem is that "training" in college comes from professors, and many professors do not alter their methods over time. In other words, if they see that their approaches are reasonably successful, most instructors won't alter them just to "keep up" with the needs of the private-sector workplace.

3. This university has a very good reputation, but it may have the ugliest campus in North America. The buildings are very old, for one thing—not distinguished old but crumbling old. They are dirty and poorly maintained as well. The campus is very bare, with almost no greenery. A busy commercial section of town is literally next door, and this strip is decaying, not improving. All in all, our campus is not much of an advertisement for this university.

## EXERCISE 3.6

Write a fully developed paragraph on one of the following topics. Remember to use specific, concrete examples and details.

1. **Description.** Choose an object that you are planning to buy or want to buy in the future.

2. **Narration.** What was the most amazing thing you heard someone say this week? Go beyond one or two sentences. For example, explain the circumstances or context in which it was said. Narrate the events that led up to and came after this comment. Identify the speaker and the listeners.

3. **Exemplification.** State a general "rule of thumb"; then give an example of what happens if someone violates this rule.

4. **Process analysis.** Show the reader how to get up and get ready in the morning without wasting time. Or write about another task that you complete regularly.

5. **Causal analysis.** What is one cause of student failure? What is one effect experienced by spending too much time surfing the Internet? Choose one of these questions.

6. **Definition.** What is the ideal roommate? What is the ideal neighbor? What is the ideal boss? Choose one of these questions. Rely on definition, but also use examples as necessary.

7. **Comparison and contrast.** Contrast your two closest friends in terms of one personality trait.

8. **Argument.** Argue against one policy of your college or university.

## Responding to Visuals

Companies that are at the top of their industries tend to use their advertising to remind us of that fact. After all, they've achieved the right to do so. Porsche is one of these companies.

Examine the accompanying ad, and answer the questions.

- How many of the nine rhetorical options can you find used here? (See pages 57–63 in this chapter.)

- To what purpose are they used?

- What is your personal response to this ad? Does it work for you, or not? Explain your reaction.

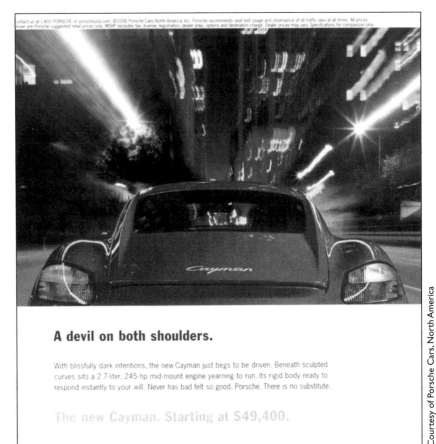

Courtesy of Porsche Cars, North America

ontact us at 1-800-PORSCHE or porscheusa.com. ©2006 Porsche Cars North America, Inc. Porsche recommends seat belt usage and observance of all traffic laws at all times. All prices hown are Porsche suggested retail prices only. MSRP excludes tax, license, registration, dealer prep, options and destination charge. Dealer prices may vary. Specifications for comparison only.

**A devil on both shoulders.**

With blissfully dark intentions, the new Cayman just begs to be driven. Beneath sculpted curves sits a 2.7-liter, 245-hp mid-mount engine yearning to run. Its rigid body ready to respond instantly to your will. Never has bad felt so good. Porsche. There is no substitute.

The new Cayman. Starting at $49,400.

## Using the Internet

Go to these Web sites to find more tips, techniques, and insights on developing paragraphs:

### Guide to Grammar and Writing

This Web site, maintained by Capital Community College of Hartford, Connecticut, provides a discussion of several topics relating to paragraph unity, coherence, development, and variety: **http://grammar.ccc.commnet.edu/grammar**.

### The University of Victoria Hypertext Writer's Guide

The University of Victoria's English Department Web site includes helpful information on the rhetorical functions of paragraphs, the topic sentence, unity and coherence, paragraph development, and paragraph patterns: **http://web.uvic.ca/wguide**.

**CATALYST 2.0**

**MORE OPTIONS ONLINE**
You can access the Web sites listed in "Using the Internet" by going to www.mhhe.com/ writingtoday.

### CHAPTER 4

# RESHAPING YOUR ESSAY

## Revising, Editing, and Proofreading

The Renaissance dramatist Ben Jonson once wrote about his contemporary, William Shakespeare, that he was believed to have "never blotted out a line." The implication is that Shakespeare produced flawless first drafts, never needing to revise or make corrections. This statement is surely a product of Elizabethan hype; no one believes that Shakespeare wrote his prodigious body of work as a series of uncorrected first drafts.

ALL WRITERS REVISE. **Revision** is the process of modifying what you have written so that it is more effective and economical. You can forgo revising only when time pressures keep you from it, such as when you are taking an essay examination that asks for more than you can deliver in the allotted time.

In the first half of this chapter, we concentrate on comprehensive issues that are sometimes called, collectively, "global" revision. Global issues include unity, coherence, language level, tone, and the effectiveness of an essay's introduction, body, and conclusion. Being able to write dynamic sentences is a valuable ability; unfortunately, it is possible to write a paragraph or essay full of strong sentences that don't relate to one another and don't work together to develop the paragraph's or essay's controlling idea.

The second half of this chapter looks at issues that are more specific yet no less important: editing and proofreading. This section concentrates on developing clear, succinct sentences that say exactly what you want them to say. It shows you how to produce varied sentence patterns and to avoid creating major sentence errors. It moves on to the subject of words themselves, discussing the many pitfalls that writers face when trying to communicate in English and showing you ways around these problem areas.

Therefore, this chapter moves from the general to the specific. However, we begin with a discussion of a highly effective and widely used revision technique: peer review and response.

*Consider Your Options*

When you write, how much revising do you normally do? (Be honest.) Has anyone ever pointed out that your writing process seems incomplete? In our experience, lack of revision is the main cause of weak writing at the college level.

## PEER RESPONSE AND REVIEW

A good way to approach revision is to ask for the opinions of your peers. Consulting another person or persons allows you to get past the "blinders" that all writers have, to one degree or another, regarding their own work. "Everyone needs an editor" is a statement that sounds like a simpleminded aphorism, but it is not. It is true. Why? One reason has to do with human nature and the need for self-esteem (It's mine! I wrote what I meant! Leave it alone!), but the full picture is not as obvious. Even professionals who are deeply involved with the mysteries of language—rewrite specialists and copy editors—report that they have trouble editing their own work.

Therefore, the reactions of your student colleagues can be an essential part of your revising process. As in any other potentially worthwhile activity, however, pitfalls lurk. The following are some guidelines to help you avoid wasting your peer response time or, even worse, incorporating changes into your writing that will actually damage it:

1. **Treat peer review seriously.** Meeting with your peers is not a time for getting together with friends or finding someone to date. If your peer review time degenerates into socializing, you will have lost a valuable opportunity.

2. **Take part.** Some students are shy, and some come from cultures in which group interaction is much more formal than the atmosphere typically found in a peer review session. If you are uncomfortable with the peer review process, remember that its rewards outweigh its problems.

3. **Understand how groups operate.** Some people like to take charge (in current pop terminology, they are "alphas"); others ("betas") prefer to cooperate and get along. However, the desire to be in charge doesn't correspond to the ability to revise English prose. An alpha member may have the worst skills or judgment of the group; he or she may also be the one who wants to talk, not work.

4. **Be receptive to suggestions.** For the same reason that it is hard for writers to read their own work with a cold eye, most of us resist the help of others. Group review was not invented for the purpose of challenging your ego; therefore, listen to what your classmates tell you without reacting defensively. If, for example, you are working with a partner who marks twenty-four places that need improvement, do not take offense. Perhaps only twelve of the responses are actually valid; if so, your partner has done you a huge favor.

5. **Use a checklist.** To make sure that you have covered all the important revision issues, use a checklist of standard questions (see below).

> *Consider Your Options*
>
> A sign of true maturity is the ability to listen to constructive criticism, not get upset, and then profit from the advice. Can you recall a situation in your life when you used constructive criticism as it was intended?

## *Peer Review Checklist*

Answer the following questions as you review your partner's draft:

1. Does the introduction provide sufficient and appropriate background and context?

2. Does the introduction include a clear thesis statement?

3. After you read the rest of the essay, reread the thesis statement. Is it supported by the rest of the essay? If not, should it be revised, or should one or more body paragraphs be revised?

4. Is the topic sentence of each body paragraph effective? If not, should it be revised, or should the rest of the paragraph be revised?

5. Are the topic sentences in the body paragraphs supported by specific and concrete evidence?

6. Is the conclusion an effective commentary on the essay, or does it merely repeat the thesis and summarize the essay or have other problems?

7. Overall, does the essay suffer from problems in any of the following areas?

   - Unity (in terms of the essay as a whole and each paragraph)
   - Coherence (in terms of the essay as a whole and each paragraph)
   - Language level (see pages 88–90)
   - Tone (see page 93)

6. **Refer matters of grammar and punctuation to the authorities.** Suppose that you are a beta type, and your essay is being reviewed by the group's alpha person. "Aha!" he says. "I think this is a comma splice. In fact, I'm *sure* it is." Two other group members then read the sentence, and their responses are not helpful: "I'm not sure." "Beats me." Here is the sentence:

Some scientists believe that viruses are immortal, whereas other researchers are finding ways to combat these destructive organisms.

If you follow the alpha person's guidelines, here is the result:

Some scientists believe that viruses are immortal; whereas, other researchers are finding ways to combat these destructive organisms.

You've just changed a perfectly good complex sentence into a sentence with an error—a semicolon should not be used to join an independent and a dependent clause. And your "helpful reviewer" will not share in the harm he caused. On questions about grammar, punctuation, and mechanics, consult your instructor or Part 4 of this text.

Peer review sessions are not intended to be error-hunting sessions. Larger issues, such as organization and level of detail, should be dealt with here; finding specific grammatical or mechanical errors is a matter of editing and proofreading—*your* editing and proofreading.

## Responding to Suggestions for Revision

When another person—a peer, a tutor, your instructor—has reviewed your draft and suggested changes, you are faced with a series of decisions. If someone has gone over a draft for you, you will see specific corrections that you will want to make without delay, but you will also note suggestions, queries, and overview comments, all of which you will need to consider carefully before choosing which revisions to make.

· · · · · · · ·
CATALYST 2.0

**MORE OPTIONS ONLINE**
For more help with
peer review,
go to
www.mhhe.com/
writingtoday.

## One Writer's Decisions

After Verlinda wrote the first draft of "A Very Secret Santa," she exchanged drafts with her partner, Daniel, and each reviewed the other's work. Here is Daniel's response to Verlinda's draft, followed by Verlinda's handwritten revision plan. Can you suggest any further changes?

*Peer-Reviewed Draft*

### A Very Secret Santa

All my years growing up; Betty Wallace was my very best friend.

I spent a lot of time at her house, she spent a lot of time at my

house. Our parents were good friends. Each couple trusted the other

*seems wordy*

*seems wordy*

implecitly. I grew to see Walter and Leona Wallace as uncle and aunt figures.

*than what?*

Walter was more interesting, but not at first glance. An accountent, he seem to want to fit in. Walter dressed conservatively, which matched his features and size: a black man of middle height, a little over weight, rimless glasses and the only "daring" feature a very neatly trimmed mustache. His personality also seemed boring. He

*wrong word*

was quite, a bit shy, and not really sociable or pleasant. Given his choice, he would sit alone in his big lounge chair and smoke a pipe

*strengthen thesis*

while watching T.V. Yet Walter Wallace, he was the most charitable man I've ever met.

I remember an example of Walter's secret side. It was before

*wordy*

Christmas, years ago, Betty and I were ten years old and going shopping with Mr. and Mrs Wallace at the mall. After Walter finaly found a parking space we noticed a comotion a few cars over. A young woman and her seven-year-old were trying to quiet down the three-year-old. He had been pulled from the last store visited without getting what he wanted. The mother looked entirely flustered and she

*Make two sentences*

was obviously quite poor, the little boy was screaming like he had been scalded. We walked toward the mall, listening to this squabble unfold behind us, suddenly Walter disappeared. Mrs. Wallace told us to keep walking, that Walter would catch up. When he did he said nothing.

*fix dialogue*

I waited until Betty and I were alone to ask for an explanation. "He went back to give that woman some money", Betty explained, "He's done this a thousand times".   *why tiny paragraph?*

At the Wallaces' home there was always six to ten dogs and cats. Strays knew where to go. Over the objections of Leona, Walter would take them in, carry them to the vet, pay for shots, nutering, and medicine, and keep them if he couldn't convince some one else to take them off his hands. As a child I remember loving the fact that the Wallace home was full of animals, but I don't think Leona Wallace shared my enjoyment. She didn't like dogs, and would freeze in midsentence if a cat jumped in her lap. Then launching the cat back towards the floor.          *abrupt*

Christmastime is wonderful for kids, and it is one of my fondest memories'. My family and the Wallaces attended Trinity United Methodist, a mostly white church with a middle class population. The arrival of Santa Claus was a great event. Walter Wallace as Santa was a complete transformation from Walter Wallace as bespectacled, quiet taxadvisor. His voice and laughter booms          *shift?* through the church as he talks to his small "clients". Walter took his act on the road, at the area hospitals and the children's hospise.

Did Walter Wallace have the proverbeal heart of gold? Or was he motivated by guilt—a successful man who is a success story and can't help looking back to a time when he was poor? Neither one. Walter          *confusing* helped young and old, black and white, human and nonhuman; only because he couldn't keep himself from doing so. Betty told me that her father was miserable, if he percieved that he had not done enough. She told me that Walter's activities caused signifigant friction in his marriage. But he would not be stopped.

I feel that when people do something "nice" for another that their motives are not altogether altruistic being nice makes the giver feel good about him or herself. In the case of Walter Wallace however the motive seems to have been more involuntary. Does this make Walter less admirable? I don't think so, I wish the world was full of men like him.

*V: This is a good start. Walter sounds like a really good guy. Here are some problem areas you might went to look at, though:*

1. *It's like you're writing to yourself. Why would your reader be interested in Walter?*

2. *I'm not sure what you're trying to accomplish here. Think about your thesis.*

3. In places, this doesn't hang together—more transitions?

4. I noticed a lot of specific stuff that we're not really supposed to mark. You might want to drop by the Writing Center. Good Luck!

   1. *Daniel's right—it's like I'm talking to myself. This doesn't flow.*

   2. *Transitions will help my paragraphs. It's like they start at one point and then jump from sentence to sentence without much connection.*

   3. *Read this aloud when revising.*

   4. *<u>Proofread</u>—yes, the Writing Center could help.*

## Using a Computer to Revise

If you start your assignment on the computer—including your preliminary thoughts and your prewriting strategies—you will be able to exploit your computer's memory by building upon each previous step. Even if you realize that your first draft will need substantial revision, it's there for you to revise. The following guidelines will help:

1. **Take advantage of the computer's ability to duplicate your draft.** In Chapter 2 a student sets up files for prewriting and drafting the third essay of the semester. All draft file names start with "E3." The student keys in a first draft, named E3A, then copies the file twice under new names: E3B and E3C. E3B is the file that she will revise. As she revises E3B, she marks any text that seems questionable, adds parenthetical comments, and suggests new wording, all by using boldface type. Boldface is easy to see on the computer screen, and words and sentences in bold type can be easily changed or deleted in the final draft. After revising file E3B, the student has two choices: (1) merge E3B into E3C or (2), if the software permits, view E3C and E3B simultaneously. Recall that E3C is a duplicate of E3A. The student can now revise the first draft by using the revision notations in E3B. If anything goes wrong, the student still has a copy of the original first draft.

   Use this cautious approach. Two major problems can occur when you work with only one file: (1) if you decide to go back to text used in a previous version, that text no longer exists and must be reconstructed, and (2) you may lose the single file due to some unthinkable misadventure.

   *Note:* Many word processors allow you to make revisions in a different color font so that you can easily compare one draft with another.

2. **Use your printer frequently.** Print out your work at important moments, such as when you are finished working for the day or have completed a revision stage.

3. **Learn the cut-and-paste (block) functions.** Word-processing software allows you to duplicate, move, and save text. You can change the order of

your body paragraphs with a few mouse clicks, or you can go into the file containing your first draft or prewriting and "salvage" text that you have left behind.

4. **Listen to your text.** If your computer is equipped with Simpletext or a similar program and has speakers, you can "hear" your essay. Talking programs are very useful, especially for auditory learners.

# REVISING YOUR ESSAYS

Quite often, students are surprised by comments made by their instructors in the margins of their graded essays. "But I didn't mean it that way" is a frequent student response.

Remember that your instructor can't read your mind. Your intentions are, essentially, private. Your instructor's judgment of your work is based on the pieces of paper that you submit. We all know about good intentions.

What happens between the time that you start planning an essay and the time that your instructor finishes reading it is a complicated process with many sometimes mysterious variables. For example, you can't control your instructor's reaction, nor is there any single "correct" response to a writing assignment. However, most of these variables *can* be controlled, and the revision process is the point at which you are in the best position to do so.

We'll begin by looking at general areas of concern, then tackle more specific problems. Remember that your ability to address these issues successfully can make the difference between an *A* essay and a *C* essay.

## Checking for Unity

Does your essay address the ideas you have asserted in your thesis statement, or does it wander from idea to idea, like a moth flying near stadium lights? Remember that **unity** is closely connected to purpose. (See Chapter 3, page 70.) If you clearly understand your purpose for writing an essay, then unity is easier to achieve. For example, if your purpose is to convince the reader that real-estate developers are corrupting your local zoning commission, then a paragraph about the history of "old downtown" will probably be out of place.

Sometimes, however, students have an overly narrow view of unity. They are afraid to let *anything* appear in their essays that is not strictly related to the thesis. These students sometimes produce "tunnel vision" essays that read like product manuals. However, skillful writers know that they have the option of introducing brief comparisons, adding the occasional funny or ironic comment, and conveying a sense, generally, of the world around them. Their writing has a thematic texture that goes beyond their thesis. Effective writing is always a balancing act, with the writer constantly thinking thoughts such as the following:

> I love this paragraph, but have I gone too far this time? The rest of my essay is rather sober, but this part of the subject is something that I've always found ludicrous. Still. . . .

For an example of a student writer's work that reflects this kind of balance, see Sam Leininger's essay contrasting two types of moviegoers (Chapter 12, pages 403–405).

Achieving unity requires a series of judgment calls about what to keep and what to drop, decisions that you will have to make during the revision process. If you err, err on the side of conservativism. In other words, is the potential reward worth the risk that you're considering?

## Improving Coherence

As you will recall from Chapter 3, a document that is **coherent** will (1) follow the direction implied by its thesis statement and (2) use effective transitions to help make connections between paragraphs. When you revise, you need to ask yourself if you have made all the relationships clear for your readers. Will they be able to read your essay straight through without having to reread some of the sections?

Coherence is closely related to the issue of audience. As a writer, you should be trying to write an essay that accommodates the needs of an adult reader. This is not a matter of keeping your text simple (using common words, simple sentences, and easy transitions). It is more an issue of being able to perceive a possible interpretation problem and taking steps to avoid confusion.

Chapter 3 provides strategies for achieving coherence at the paragraph level, including the use of transitional expressions, pronouns, repeated nouns and synonyms, and parallel structures. (See pages 72–76.) All four of these strategies are useful at the essay level as well. In addition, transitional sentences such as the following can help you clearly link a paragraph to the one that precedes or follows it:

> Although Buffalo's location on Lake Erie has been a blessing, the heavy industry that was attracted by its access to the cities on the Great Lakes and the abundant energy provided by Niagara Falls has also brought a curse: pollution.

The sentence refers back to the preceding paragraph about the advantages of Buffalo's location and, at the same time, prepares readers for the topic of the next paragraph.

## Using the Appropriate Language Level

There are many ways to categorize language levels, but for our purposes let us concentrate on three types: informal, standard, and formal.

Informal English is conversational. In many ways, it reflects the diction of spoken English, of good friends talking to one another without worrying about being overheard. Because informal English is casual in tone and tends to include slang, it is usually not appropriate for college-level writing, although it may be suitable for a personal narrative. Developing and using a personal voice are important, but at the same time you must consider your audience; in the case of slang, which changes very quickly, your audience may not even know what your words mean.

Here is an example of a paragraph written in informal English:

> The downtown club scene must be real trouble for newcomers. There're more than twenty clubs and seventy bands coming and going, so who knows where to look for the good stuff. One thing is key: the choice bands don't hook up with the "nice" clubs. A rule of thumb: the cleaner the club and the higher the cover, the worse the act and the general scene. The "nice" places will be filled with burb types, along with the crews moving in and out. Downtown is like what Austin and Athens used to be: if you want the hot sound, find the grungy-looking crib.

**Consider Your Options**

Which language level do you use most frequently? Can you recall an instance in which using an inappropriate language level caused you trouble?

Standard English avoids the casual tone and slang of informal English but also avoids the complex vocabulary and syntax of formal English. This paragraph is a good example of standard English:

> A few yards up the hill, I found a protected platform beneath a thick barrier of trees. The forest canopy deflected the wind, filtered the sunlight, and dispersed the rain into a fine mist. The green mosses and yellow-green lichens on the forest floor were spongy and comfortable. A roar in the canopy overhead reminded me that the storm still raged, but that was another world, far removed from my burrow within the rain forest. I sat in the mist with my back against a rock, watched the water drip off my parka, and relaxed. Then I pitched my tent and crowded inside to brew a hot cup of tea.
>
> —from Jon Turk, *Cold Oceans*

Formal English is the language of scholarly writing and applied technology. It avoids the personal voice and uses complex sentence structure and diction to achieve a tone of thoroughly objective discussion. Here is an example:

> The habitual reference to the emotions and processes of the poet's mind for the source of poetry altered drastically the established solutions to that basic problem of aesthetics, the discrepancy between the subject matter in poetry and the objects found in experience. According to the central tradition hitherto, poetry departs from fact principally because it reflects a nature which has been reassembled to make a composite beauty, or filtered to reveal a central form or the common denominator of a type, or in some fashion culled and ornamented for the greater delight of the reader. To the romantic critic, on the other hand, though poetry may be ideal, what marks it off from fact is, primarily, that it incorporates objects of a sense which have already been acted on and transformed by the feelings of the poet.
>
> —from M. H. Abrams, *The Mirror and the Lamp: Romantic Theory and the Critical Tradition*

You probably won't be expected to write at precisely the same language level in all of your essays. What is appropriate for one purpose may well be unsuitable for another. For example, the personal narrative may employ informal language, whereas the analytical options—process, cause and effect, and classification—tend to require a language level closer to standard English or even formal English. For most of your college-level writing, your safest choice is standard English. For some writing assignments, however, you may need to move toward formal English.

Consider your purpose as you start revising a first draft. Is your language level appropriate for this purpose? If the language level seems generally adequate, then think about this possible problem: Are there some places where you've used language that clashes with the rest of your text? Have you used a slang expression in, say, the fourth paragraph? If so, then this gaffe may lodge in the reader's memory. We occasionally read otherwise sound essays that contain a minor or mid-level obscenity, perhaps thrown in for effect. Such a usage is almost always inappropriate in academic writing, and this misjudgment truly stands out.

### EXERCISE 4.1

The following passage is written in informal English. Working alone, revise the paragraphs so that they are more suitable for college-level work.

My favorite computer/music/video store gives me a load of problems at the same time. It's in the low-rent part of town, but that's the least of my worries. Great merchandise, scuzzy store, weird salesguys are the normal bill of fare.

I went there last Saturday to look at some new speakers. Walking past a pack of wireheads arguing about the latest downloader, I tripped over a gizmo that even I, good with computers, couldn't put a name to. In the stereo section I ran into the guy who would help my quest. He had obviously been hiding when the Dork Patrol made its latest sweep. But he knew a lot about sound systems. He found me the speakers I wanted. He dug up a rebate coupon from somewhere. He gave me enough info so that I wouldn't fry myself when I got home. And the price was right. So, what's to moan about?

### EXERCISE 4.2

The following passage uses elevated language and syntax to describe a subject that would be better handled with standard English. Working with a partner or in a small group, revise it. Use a dictionary if needed.

Television serial comedies have reached their nadir. This reference is, of course, to the programs that display young people using the workplace for both gainful employment and riotous romance. The result is an unfortunate admixture of unproductive work hours and chaotic personal lives.

Hitherto, workplace propinquity, an issue of some inevitability, was less of a staple on network broadcasts. To be sure, the work environment was seen as a source of humor, but not as a breeding ground. In current offerings, young people seem to attend work only to wear the latest accoutrements and spend their tenure trying to gain the amorous attention of other similarly attired and like-intentioned foragers. The results are ludicrous, pathetic, and forced.

## Making Your Language More Concrete and Specific

Concrete language usually communicates your ideas and details more effectively than abstract language. Concrete language appeals to the senses: sight, hearing, taste, smell, and touch. Notice the strength of impact, interest, and precision that the sentences on the right have when compared to those on the left:

| Abstract | Concrete |
|---|---|
| He was envious of the success of others. | He mocked others who were successful. |
| My grandmother was affectionate. | My grandmother often kissed and hugged us. |
| We were uncomfortable in the overcrowded waiting room. | Our faces and hands became sweaty, and we had trouble breathing in the overcrowded waiting room. |
| The old man's fingers were arthritic. | The fingers of the old man's right hand were swollen, and they curled into a useless claw. |

Remember, concrete language gives your readers a verbal portrait of what you are communicating and allows them to experience it in their imaginations. Abstract language simply tells readers something. In some contexts, however, abstract language is appropriate, as in the following example, excerpted from Lewis H. Lapham's "Who and What Is American?"

> We [Americans] protect the other person's liberty in the interest of protecting our own, and our virtues conform to the terms and conditions of an arduous and speculative journey.

Nevertheless, when you want to transmit your experience of a person, object, place, or problem, abstract language often leaves your readers with only a vague sense of what you mean. Even when student writing is unified, coherent, and pointed, it can be weakened by discussions that take place in the realm of the abstract—no concrete details support the student's assertions.

The following paragraph is a good example of writing that lacks specificity:

> During fall and spring registration, a place that students avoid and dread is the preliminary table. If their advising forms are complete,

students can avoid this step. However, students who are forced to deal with the preliminary table will face general rudeness, incompetence, and delay.

This paragraph is not badly written, but it could be so much stronger if specific, concrete detail were included, as in the following revision:

> A careful student never goes to registration at Parker College without having his or her documents in order. Much like a hero trying to cross a European border in a World War II movie, it is worth one's health and future to have these documents in order. "Your papers, please?" is what I remember the monocled inspector demanding in those old films. At Parker's registration, students breathe a sigh of relief if they pass this stage. If not, they are directed to the dreaded preliminary table. Here members of the Records Department shuffle paper, lose forms, and stamp the wrong documents. My friend Heather once waited five minutes for the "registration specialist" to find her name in an alphabetized printout. "It was pathetic," Heather reported. "I can read upside-down, like most people, and I saw the man go past my name at least six times. But you don't want to anger these people." Another acquaintance, Jeff, waited for over a half hour. The person who was "helping" him got up and took his documents to a supervisor's office. Along the way, this nimrod got distracted and laid the documents down. Most of the delay, Jeff figured, was spent in finding the missing forms. The conclusion to be drawn? Avoid the preliminary desk if at all possible, for there be monsters.

As you revise your essay, look for places where specific, concrete details would make your ideas clearer for your audience.

## Achieving Specificity

Notice that the items on the right are much more effective and clear than those on the left.

| General | More Specific | Very Specific |
|---|---|---|
| book | novel | *The Scarlet Letter* |
| artwork | oil painting | Rembrandt's self-portrait |
| residence | house | three-bedroom ranch |
| exercise | aerobic exercise | jogging |
| motor vehicle | sports utility vehicle | Ford Explorer |
| restaurant | fast-food restaurant | McDonald's |
| evergreen | pine | Norwegian spruce |
| municipality | city | Los Angeles |
| boat | sailboat | schooner |

### EXERCISE 4.3

Working alone, read the following paragraph, which lacks concrete, specific details that would make the writer's meaning clearer. Prepare a list of suggestions for the writer to indicate where specific examples and support will help.

> Shopping for home-decorating products is a lot of fun, but there are also pitfalls. The same products can vary in price by 100%. The worst offenders are, of course, mall stores. An item costing $40 at the mall may well be available for $20–$25 at the discount department stores or the "warehouse" home-decorating outfits. Deep sales at the mall don't really equalize matters either. A 40%-off sale sounds great, but the $40 item now costs $24, and the off-price outlet only needs a 10% sale to stay lower. A final problem is that many people seem to use the mall as a place to handle things, touching them almost compulsively. By the time the 40%-off sale takes place, the desired item has felt many hands, and this is not a picture that I find appealing.

## Finding the Right Tone

Your **tone** is your essay's attitude toward your subject. Should your essay's tone be angry, calm, impassioned, or joyful? Usually, your rhetorical option, your purpose, and your subject matter will help determine the appropriate tone. A humorous tone may well be appropriate for a narrative essay about misinterpreted directions, but a similarly humorous tone would certainly not work in an essay about the lives of terminally ill children.

Another issue is consistency of tone. Does your essay start off with an edge of anger but then end with a completely different tone? If so, why? Examine your purpose again; then try to tell where and why the tone of your essay changed.

## Checking Your Introductory Paragraphs and Thesis

Remember that your introduction should (1) establish a context for your essay and (2) include a thesis statement that both informs your reader of the essay's direction and expresses the essay's controlling idea. Read your draft's introduction to make sure that it provides the proper context. Students frequently err by doing too little or too much here, either writing a huge explanation for their essay that threatens to dwarf the essay itself or a tiny introduction: "Last summer I moved to a new apartment with no help. I'll never forget that day." (Chapter 3, pages 53–56, provides a list of ways to introduce an essay.)

Next, check your thesis statement against the body of your draft. Read your thesis, then each topic sentence. Does your thesis accurately reflect your essay's content, or did your essay take a new direction during the writing process? If the latter is true, do you need to revise your thesis statement so that it reflects this change in approach? Or, as we discuss in the next section, do you need to revise body paragraphs to bring them back into line with your controlling idea and the purpose implied in your thesis?

## Checking Your Topic Sentences and Body Paragraphs

Your thesis statement promises the reader that your essay will follow a specific approach. When you read your first draft, do the essay's body paragraphs deliver on this promise? Or do they begin to deliver and then change course or seem to weaken?

If there is a conflict or weakness, many students are tempted to go back to the introduction and modify the thesis. After all, it's easier to rewrite the thesis than to rewrite a whole paragraph or two. However, revising the thesis isn't always the best approach. If the body of your essay has lost its direction or doesn't seem to fulfill the promise of your thesis, then patching the thesis statement won't fix the problem. You will need to revise the body so that it corresponds to your purpose.

### Revising for Effective Topic Sentences

If you find a unity problem in the body of your essay, pay close attention to the topic sentences of your body paragraphs. Frequently, a key to your problem can be found here. Does each topic sentence support your thesis, or does one or more of them wander off in a different direction? If so, ask yourself if you can revise them to fix the problem or if you need to delete and replace the paragraph.

Even if the topic sentences support the thesis, you also need to make sure that they are strong topic sentences that work with the rest of the paragraph. Just as a thesis statement controls an essay, a topic sentence controls a paragraph. Sometimes, a topic sentence is too general, providing a weak focus. Other times, a topic sentence can be misleading, promising one type of development while the paragraph actually develops in new, unexplained directions. And when the topic sentence appears at the end of the paragraph as a summary of the paragraph's ideas, the summary may not adequately reflect the paragraph that it is concluding.

### EXERCISE 4.4

Each of the following paragraphs has a faulty topic sentence. Working alone, replace the topic sentence with a more effective one.

1.  TV weather forecasters make inaccurate judgments about the weather. These "specialists" are upbeat in any situation except for the truly catastrophic. A case in point: last July, our area went the entire month without rain. Both the days and nights were extremely hot. But each morning and evening, the local forecasters would chirp on about the beautiful day we were about to have, when a more mature judgment would have been to concentrate on the need for rain. However, Mr. or Ms. Tallhair is just giving us what surveys tell TV consultants that we really want: happy weather.

Commercial television is a business, and I suppose that in one sense we shouldn't blame these "forecasters" for fulfilling our stated needs.

2.  A sixteen-year-old boy wanders through Landon Department Store. He finally comes to the music department and spends almost an hour looking through the compact discs. Eventually, he goes to a cash register and pays $12 for a CD, takes his purchase, and leaves the store. But although he has paid for one CD, he has shoplifted three more, hidden in his back-pack. Shoplifting is a problem that must be stopped.

## Revising for Stronger Body Paragraphs

Just as you need to check your essay as a whole for unity and coherence, you should check each of your body paragraphs to make sure that your ideas all relate to the topic sentence and that a reader can follow your ideas without having to double back. Delete any sentences that do not support your topic sentence. Add transitional expressions and use parallelism to help readers follow your ideas. (For help with improving a paragraph's coherence, including a list of transitional expressions, see pages 72–76 in chapter 3.) Finally, as you read each paragraph, look for opportunities to add the specific, concrete details that will make your essay clearer and more forceful.

### EXERCISE 4.5

Working alone, read the following paragraph, and underline sentences that have strayed from the point.

> Students who disrupt college classes should be removed from those classes. My major will be economics, and I'm taking the intro economics courses as well as finishing up my general-ed courses. Three of these courses are in Ryan Hall. In every one of my classes this semester there is at least one clown who detracts from the lecture or discussion by calling attention to himself. In fact, the same clown is in two of my classes—Renaissance humanities and macroeconomics. These two aren't the best anyway. The humanities instructor is a complete bore who reads from the textbook. The economics professor mumbles while he is facing the board and trying to clarify his shaky graphs. The clown sits and talks to his friends and laughs at anything unexpected coming from either instructor. He seems to have learned how to approach a college lecture by watching too many episodes of *Mystery Science Theater 3000*. I dream that someday a large campus security officer will loom up behind him and take him away. He'll never be seen again, of course, and this fact will help dissuade future clowns from making the same mistake.

### EXERCISE 4.6

Working with a partner or in a small group, read the following paragraphs, and make any changes that will improve coherence. (For suggestions on how to improve a paragraph's coherence, see pages 72–76 in Chapter 3.)

1. Many people these days seem desperate to produce children. These people can spend a fortune on "pre-pregnancy" treatments: fertility testing, genetic testing, artificial fertilization. If successful, these people then produce a child. The costs of raising and to educate a child are immense. The costs can average a half million dollars per child. The costs are prohibitive. Personal pressure, family pressure, and pressure from society all work together to ensure that people continue to want babies.

2. Our entertainment options today are vastly different from the opportunities for entertainment before World War II. In the 1930s, the standard picture was of families sitting in the living room listening to the huge radios or record players of the time. Or perhaps the family would go to a live concert, or perhaps a play was being performed. Modern families have radio, television is available, computer games and the Internet are popular. Modern families don't have to go to a performance to be entertained. Modern families can have the entertainment come to them. Pay-per-view movies can be ordered, and premium sporting events can be ordered. Modern families have a wealth of entertainment options.

## Checking Your Conclusion

Finally, ask these questions about your conclusion:

1. Does this paragraph appear brief when compared to my other paragraphs?

2. Is the conclusion a simple summary of my essay?

3. Have I brought up any new topics here that will divert my reader from the main idea of the essay that he or she has just read?

4. Have I included a self-conscious reference to my essay ("In this essay I have shown . . .")?

If your answer to any of these questions is yes, then you need to revise your conclusion. (For ways to conclude an essay, see Chapter 3, pages 63–66.) Students sometimes forget a very basic fact: normally, the conclusion is the last part of the essay that an instructor reads before determining a grade. An otherwise strong essay with a weak or confusing conclusion has made its mistake in the wrong place. It's as if you met a new person, made a satisfactory first impression, had a positive conversation, and then muttered an obscure thought while parting.

### EXERCISE 4.7

At the end of Chapter 2, you were asked to prepare, prewrite, and draft a response to one of the topics on pages 49–50. (If you haven't completed this assignment yet, do so now.) Find and revise this draft, using the techniques discussed in this section. Then exchange drafts with a partner and review (1) the first draft and (2) your partner's suggested changes to his or her essay. Use the checklist questions on page 82 to guide your review. What else can you suggest that will improve your partner's revision?

## Writing an Effective Title

At this point, the structure of your essay is in place, so it's time to give your essay a title. The following guidelines explain your options:

CATALYST 2.0

**MORE OPTIONS ONLINE**
For more information about revision checklists, go to
www.mhhe.com/writingtoday.

1. Avoid using a vague or an overly general title:

   My Adventure                    Aunt Rita's Greenhouse

   Such titles sound juvenile and tell your reader very little.

2. Avoid a strained and overly specific title:

   The Problem Caused by Feral Cats and What the Current Proposal (AR-1789) Before the Sparks County Commission Can Do to Solve It

3. Use a title suitable to your purpose. Narratives and descriptions frequently have fairly short titles primarily designed to entice the reader:

   The Mystery of Spring Water            Jason's Revenge

   Remember the title of Verlinda's essay: "A Very Secret Santa." It is both accurate, meaning that it reflects the essay as a whole, and interesting.

   In the case of more analytical essays, however, titles need to be more informative. Consider using a colon to separate the main part of a title from its descriptive second part. "How to Wax a Car" is a factual (and probably accurate) but boring title. How about "Waxing a Car: Three Easy Steps"? "The Modern Root Canal" is off-putting, to say the least. How about "The Modern Root Canal: Less Pain, Less Time"? This title would interest readers, not repel them.

4. Do not add extra formatting to your title (extra quotation marks, bold type, italic type, underlining, or all-capital letters). Center it, and capitalize its important words. (For more on capitalization, consult chapter 31.)

   To the Losers Go the Rest

## Completing Your Essay on a Computer

If you are using a computer to write your essay, at this point you should have your latest draft on a backup disk and also on the hard drive, if possible. You should also have a paper copy of the draft with handwritten revision comments on it. Now you are ready to finish your essay by revising your existing file. The following guidelines will help:

1. Check your existing electronic draft for any areas that are highlighted or marked in boldface. Also check for any annotations or comments that you may have inserted.

2. Make your revisions from paper to screen. Once you are satisfied that you have finished this step, save and print out the corrected version. Now check this printout against the paper source; it's easy to miss corrections when revising on computer.

3. After you have made your last correction, print out a paper copy and read it again. This is the proofreading stage, in which you try to find the last few errors.

4. Run the spell-checker. If your computer has a grammar-checking program, you might use this as well. You should not *rely* on either one, however. Such software programs aren't perfect. For example, a spell-checker can't distinguish among *their, there,* and *they're.* A grammar checker might highlight sentences that have no errors but seem too long, according to the software's programming. Remember that the quality of the essay is your responsibility.

5. Read your essay aloud. (If your computer has the appropriate software, let your computer read your essay back to you.) *Listen* for problems that you might not see when reading silently. At this stage, you can catch awkward phrasings and unintentional rhymes.

6. When preparing your essay for its final printing, check your assignment one last time. Is there any requirement that you missed or forgot? Does the instructor include information about how he or she wants your typed essay to be formatted? Now is the time to confirm that your response meets the physical demands of the assignment.

7. Use a standard typeface of easily readable size, and double-space your printout. One of the great advantages of the computer is that it allows you to determine font, point size, and line spacing, so is it any wonder that composition instructors get angry when they receive a paper in ten-point type, single-spaced? Use a nondisplay font—the older, conservative fonts such as Times Roman, Courier, Garamond, Goudy, and Palatino will work well. Use 12-point type unless your instructor specifies differently. Don't use a cursive font, all-capital letters, or any other formatting that will distract your reader. Use one-inch margins, and don't crowd your page.

8. After you have printed out the final draft of your essay, save your work once again to two different places, in case disaster strikes. Also, consider keeping an "electronic portfolio": your entire semester's work on a backup disk or drive. You never know when you might need a file from the disk, and it is often useful to be able to look back over your semester's work and see how far you've progressed.

# EDITING AND PROOFREADING YOUR ESSAYS

All experienced writers edit and proofread their work, and learning to do so will only improve your college-level writing. Your writing instructor, along with your other instructors, is an expert reader. Such readers are impatient with sloppy, wasteful writing: twelve words used when six would suffice; "weasel words," which are terms used in an attempt to avoid speaking plainly; and euphemisms, terms constructed to avoid the painful facts of human existence and/or the responsibilities of the person controlling the situation.

In addition, any reader hates being made to squint. "Squinting" is an expression normally used to describe poorly placed modifiers, but the idea can be applied more generally. You make your reader squint when he or she has to read a sentence or larger passage more than once. Yes, it is possible that your reader has simply misread your passage (it happens to the best of us), and it is possible that your reader has decided to go back and reread your text because it is wonderful. In general, however, writing that needs to be read more than once is simply unclear, ambiguous, or without a controlling focus.

Finally, learning to edit and proofread will help you in the competitive environment of higher education. You are a smart person pitted against other smart people. Your instructors will inevitably compare your work with that of your classmates. Be assured that the best writers in all of your classes will be taking the time to refine their work by editing and proofreading.

This part of the chapter concentrates on revising sentences and words. We discuss here the problems that afflict most English prose, along with ways to fix these problems. If you need additional help with the topics covered in these sections, consult Part 4 of this text.

**CATALYST 2.0**

**MORE OPTIONS ONLINE**
For more help with the topics in this chapter, go to
www.mhhe.com/ writingtoday.

# COMBINING SENTENCES

> The Internet is a new world. It is an exciting world. This world contains many possibilities. One possibility is research. Another possibility is shopping. Another possibility is investing. Students can research topics from home. They don't have to go to a library. Shoppers can buy products. They don't have to go to a store. Investors can buy mutual funds directly. They don't have to call a broker. The Internet is a major convenience.

As the passage suggests, you can write English prose in single-clause sentences, with each sentence containing a subject and verb and expressing a single idea. These are called **simple sentences,** the most basic type. However, this approach has two major limitations:

1. The resulting text sounds immature, as if written by a child.
2. The text is inefficient—too many words and too much space are wasted when you use a sentence for each thought.

Sentence combining allows writers to create mature, economical text by merging connected ideas and showing their relationships to one another. In this section, we'll look at two methods of combining sentences:

1. Merging and submerging
2. Coordinating and subordinating

## Merging and Submerging Related Ideas

### Merging
The most basic way to combine sentences is to merge parallel ideas:

ORIGINAL    **The Civic Center is old. It is run-down. It is hazardous.**

|  |  |
|---|---|
| REVISED | **The Civic Center is old, run-down, and hazardous.** |
| ORIGINAL | **The Parker Hotel was built in 1911. It was once a resort hotel. Time passed by. The hotel is now a collection of apartments. These apartments are used by senior citizens.** |
| REVISED | **The Parker Hotel, built in 1911 and once regarded as a resort, now provides apartments for senior citizens.** |

### Submerging

There are five basic ways to join sentences by submerging:

1. **Turn one of the sentences into a relative clause.** A relative clause has a subject and verb and starts with *who, whom, whose, that,* or *which.* Relative clauses modify nouns.

|  |  |
|---|---|
| ORIGINAL | **There is the car. I saw it near the elementary school yesterday.** |
| REVISED | **There is the car that I saw near the elementary school yesterday.** |
| ORIGINAL | **Atlanta is the capital of Georgia. It is located in the northern half of the state.** |
| REVISED | **Atlanta, which is the capital of Georgia, is located in the northern half of the state.** |

Notice the distinction between *that* and *which. That* is used to begin **essential clauses,** which are clauses that define. ("There's the car." "Which car?" "The car that I saw near the elementary school yesterday.") Do not use commas to set off essential clauses. On the other hand, **nonessential clauses** offer extra, explanatory information, not defining information. Atlanta is a well-known city and doesn't need to be defined; that it is the capital of Georgia is extra information. Use *which,* along with a comma or commas, for nonessential clauses.

Here is an easy way to remember the essential/nonessential distinction. Note the following phrases:

my sister Mary

my sister, Mary

The writer of the first phrase has more than one sister. The name *Mary* answers the question "Which sister?" The writer of the second phrase has only one sister. The comma precedes the name, which is extra, explanatory information.

You will sometimes see *which* used in place of *that* at the beginning of an essential clause:

ACCEPTABLE    **There is the car which I saw near the elementary school yesterday.**

However, the reverse won't work. In a nonessential relative clause, a comma + *that* can't be substituted for a comma + *which:*

INCORRECT    **Atlanta, that is the capital of Georgia, is located in the northern half of the state.**

*That* and *which* are used to refer to everything except people and named animals. *Who* is used for these two groups. When you are forming an essential relative clause beginning with *who,* do not use a comma or commas; for a nonessential clause, use a comma or commas:

NONESSENTIAL   **I'm going back home to help my father, who is**
MODIFIER   **moving to an apartment.**

Each human can have only one father.

ESSENTIAL    **Ed is my cousin who once served in the legislature.**
MODIFIER

Each person can have many cousins. The relative clause *who once served in the legislature* answers the question "Which cousin?"

2. **Change one sentence into an appositive. An appositive** is a word or phrase used to modify an adjacent noun. As with relative clauses, you must use a comma or commas to set off an appositive if it provides extra information:

Atlanta, the capital of Georgia, is located in the northern half of the state.

In this sentence, the appositive functions in much the same way as does the relative clause in the example on page 100, but *which is* has been deleted, turning the clause into a phrase.

Appositives can also function as essential modifiers:

My sister Mary is here for the weekend.

No commas are used here because the writer has more than one sister; *Mary* answers the question "Which sister?"

3. **Change one sentence into a participial phrase. Participles** are adjectives formed from verbs; they end in *-ed, -d, -t, -en,* or *-ing.* Note the following sentences:

Butter is derived from milk. Butter is high in fat content.

We can combine these two short sentences by changing the first sentence into a phrase beginning with the participle *derived:*

Butter, derived from milk, is high in fat content.

4. **Turn one sentence into a prepositional phrase.** A prepositional phrase begins with a preposition such as *for, at, to, in, by,* or *on.*

ORIGINAL    The hitter wished for good luck. He tapped the plate three times with the end of the bat.

REVISED    For good luck, the hitter tapped the plate three times with the end of the bat.

*For good luck* is a prepositional phrase beginning with the preposition *for*.

5. **Change one sentence into an absolute phrase.** An **absolute phrase** modifies the entire sentence.

ORIGINAL    The car's front tires were flat. The car limped along the shoulder of the road.

REVISED    Its front tires flat, the car limped along the shoulder of the road.

## EXERCISE 4.8

Working alone, combine the following sentence pairs by using any method discussed in this section.

1. The search engine was slow today. The Web search took seven minutes.
2. That's Angela. She is my cousin's wife.
3. Tomatoes were once thought to be poisonous. They are now enjoyed by millions of people.
4. The movie *Manhunter* is based on Thomas Harris's novel *Red Dragon.* The movie is the "prequel" to *Silence of the Lambs.*
5. Sunshine came through the open window. The sunshine kept me awake.
6. There's the skeleton of the snake. The snake was run over last month.
7. The death of Ralph Miley came as a shock. He was mayor for twelve years.
8. Jason's new company didn't have outside financial support. The new company was doomed.

## EXERCISE 4.9

Working with a partner or in a small group, revise the following paragraphs, which are strings of related sentences. Combine the sentences by merging or submerging related ideas.

1. Hepatitis C is a very serious disease. It affects the liver. Many people have it. However, they may not know that they have it. Some victims may not get medical treatment. If so, these people could become very ill and die. Scientists are working on a cure. So far, they have been unsuccessful.
2. The storm caused a great deal of damage. The damage was mainly in the eastern part of the city. Trees were knocked down. Power lines were also knocked down. The rain lasted for three hours. It was torrential. However, the wind did most of the damage. It approached tornado strength. Luckily,

the storm hit at 3:00 a.m. Very few people were out in the open or driving in their cars.

## Coordinating and Subordinating Related Ideas

**Coordination** and **subordination** are additional sentence-combining techniques designed to connect sentences of roughly equal weight. When you combine sentences by using coordination and subordination, you can indicate both obvious and subtle connections, control your level of formality, and produce sentences appropriate for your purpose.

**Conjunctions,** words used to join words, phrases, and sentences, come in four varieties. Of the four types, two are related: **coordinating conjunctions** and **conjunctive adverbs/transitional expressions.** (See the chart on pages 104 and 105.) These two types are used to join **independent clauses,** word groups that can stand alone as sentences, in order to form **compound sentences,** sentences made up of more than one independent clause. For example,

ORIGINAL    Alice enjoyed spending time in online chat rooms. Lisa had never even been on the Internet.

REVISED    Alice enjoyed spending time in online chat rooms, **but** Lisa had never even been on the Internet.

Here the two sentences are joined with the coordinating conjunction *but,* preceded by a comma, to form a compound sentence. Notice how a similar effect can be achieved by using a conjunctive adverb:

Alice enjoyed spending time in online chat rooms; **however,** Lisa had never even been on the Internet.

When you use *however* or any other conjunctive adverb/transitional expression to join two sentences, place a semicolon before it and a comma after it. Note that this sentence has a more formal tone than the compound sentence formed by using *but.*

Notice how another type of sentence connector, the **subordinating conjunction,** can be used to join two sentences:

ORIGINAL    Lisa had an unreasonable fear of the Internet. She had read stories about cybercrime.

REVISED    Lisa had an unreasonable fear of the Internet **because** she had read stories about cybercrime.

OR    **Because** Lisa had read stories about cybercrime, she had an unreasonable fear of the Internet.

The revised sentence is not a compound sentence; it is called a **complex sentence** because it has one independent clause and one dependent clause. What happened to the other independent clause? The addition of the subordinating conjunction *because* made it dependent. As the name suggests, this type of word is used to *subordinate* an independent clause—to make it lower in rank, so to speak. It has become a **dependent clause,** one that cannot stand alone as a sentence.

The following chart lists coordinating conjunctions, conjunctive adverbs/transitional expressions, and subordinating conjunctions.

| SENTENCE CONNECTORS | | |
| --- | --- | --- |
| **Coordinating Conjunctions** | **Conjunctive Adverbs/ Transitional Expressions** | **Subordinating Conjunctions** |
| and | accordingly | after |
| but | additionally | although |
| for | also | as |
| nor | as an illustration | because |
| or | at the same time | before |
| so | besides | even if |
| yet | certainly | even though |
| | consequently | if |
| | conversely | in order that |
| | finally | once |
| | for example | provided that |
| | for instance | rather than |
| | furthermore | since |
| | hence | so that |
| | however | so (that) |
| | in addition | than |
| | in brief | that |
| | in conclusion | though |
| | in contrast | unless |
| | in short | until |
| | in summary | when |
| | in the same way | whenever |
| | indeed | where |
| | instead | whereas |
| | likewise | wherever |
| | meanwhile | whether |
| | moreover | while |
| | namely | |
| | nevertheless | |

| **SENTENCE CONNECTORS** *(continued)* | | |
| --- | --- | --- |
| Coordinating Conjunctions | Conjunctive Adverbs/ Transitional Expressions | Subordinating Conjunctions |
| | next | |
| | nonetheless | |
| | of course | |
| | on the other hand | |
| | otherwise | |
| | similarly | |
| | specifically | |
| | still | |
| | subsequently | |
| | then | |
| | therefore | |
| | thus | |
| | to be sure | |
| | (Note that other adverbs can also function as con-junctives: *clearly, slowly, eagerly,* and so on.) | |

Correlative conjunctions, the fourth type, are discussed on pages 109–110.

## Using Coordinating Conjunctions

The words in the first column on page 104 are the seven coordinating con-junctions. Small words of either two or three letters, they are very old mem-bers of the English language. When you use them as sentence connectors, be aware of these key issues:

1. Don't place a comma in front of every *and* or *but* that you write. Besides being used with a comma to form compound sentences, these seven words can also be used as simple conjunctions, joining two nouns, verbs, or phrases. In both of the following sentences, the conjunction is not used as a sentence connector but as a simple conjunction—hence, no preceding comma is needed:

Miguel **and** Angelica are here.

We traveled to Tampa **but** not to Clearwater.

For a complete discussion of comma usage, consult chapter 29.

2. By using a coordinating conjunction with a comma to form a compound sentence, you can avoid the major errors known as the **comma splice** and the **fused sentence**. The following sentence is an example of a comma splice:

COMMA SPLICE  Julia reminded Eddie to set his alarm clock, he still overslept.

In a compound sentence, a comma can separate the two independent clauses only if a coordinating conjunction follows the comma:

CORRECT **Julia reminded Eddie to set his alarm clock, yet he still overslept.**

The fused sentence is the comma splice made worse. Here, even the comma is missing:

FUSED SENTENCE **Julia reminded Eddie to set his alarm clock he still overslept.**

CORRECT **Julia reminded Eddie to set his alarm clock, yet he still overslept.**

3. The coordinating conjunctions are useful little words, but as a category they have some limitations. Although there are seven coordinating conjunctions, two of them—*but* and *yet*—are synonyms and are virtually interchangeable. Also, two more of the coordinating conjunctions—*or* and *for*—are not used very often to connect independent clauses. Note this sentence:

We will drive to St. Louis, or we will fly to Kansas City.

This construction, although a clear example of a compound pattern, is probably not the way that most writers would express this idea. Normally, a reader would expect a more concise pattern:

We will either drive to St. Louis or fly to Kansas City.

If you were to use only coordinating conjunctions to connect sentences, you would show that you have mastered a punctuation strategy, avoid comma splices and fused sentences, and communicate in a common, centuries-old sentence pattern. However, you would also severely restrict your ability to communicate precisely. Look at the much longer list of words and phrases in the second column of the sentence connector chart on pages 104 and 105. These connectors, discussed in the following section, cover a far wider range of meanings than do the seven coordinating conjunctions.

## Using Conjunctive Adverbs/Transitional Expressions

The conjunctive adverbs and the words and phrases collectively known as **transitional expressions** are the other group of sentence connectors that you can use to form compound sentences.

These words and phrases are extremely useful, provided that you choose carefully and keep the following issues in mind:

1. The semicolon-before, comma-after pattern holds for all these connectors except one, the last in the following group of sentences:

Trouble awaits applicants who put off filing; **however,** the deadline is still two weeks away. Anyone who needs help with the paperwork can call on a number of resources; **for instance,** there is a company office not two blocks from here. Most people call this office first; **then** they can get all the assistance they need.

Note that in these examples, *then* is the only connector not followed by a comma. All the other words and phrases in the second column of the chart on pages 104 and 105 follow the semicolon-connector-comma pattern.

2. Unlike coordinating conjunctions, conjunctive adverbs/transitional expressions can appear in different positions within a clause:

Maria was ready; **however,** Eduardo was not.

Maria was ready; Eduardo, **however,** was not.

Maria was ready; Eduardo was not, **however.**

The semicolon is the boundary point between the two independent clauses, but the conjunctive adverb *however* can be placed at the beginning, in the middle, or at the end of the second independent clause.

Is there a preferred position? You should normally place the connector at the beginning. When the connector appears in the beginning position, the reader sees how the two independent clauses are related before reading the second clause. In the third example, the reader doesn't get to the negative transition until the very end: "Eduardo was not, however." The word *however* doesn't appear when the reader really needs it (at the beginning).

3. The semicolon can stand alone without a connector. Think of the semicolon as an internal period: it brings the sentence to a stop but, unlike the period, allows the writer to continue with the sentence instead of starting a new one:

Maria was ready; Eduardo was not.

This sentence communicates well enough. It seems a bit abrupt, yet not drastically so. But notice how much the sentence improves with the addition of a conjunctive adverb:

Maria was ready; **however,** Eduardo was not.

Here the writer has given his or her audience more direction.

4. Many conjunctive adverbs can also function as regular adverbs. An **adverb** is a word that modifies a verb, an adjective, or another adverb.

We are asked to vote for every referendum the mayor proposes, **however** misguided it might be.

In this sentence, *however* is a simple adverb modifying the adjective *misguided.* It is not a conjunction and should not be preceded by a semicolon.

5. If you are careless when punctuating compound sentences that use conjunctive adverbs or transitional expressions, you can end up with comma splices or fused sentences (see pages 105–106):

COMMA SPLICE    D. W. Griffith was a great film pioneer, in addition, he was one of the founders of United Artists.

CORRECT    D. W. Griffith was a great film pioneer; in addition, he was one of the founders of United Artists.

FUSED
SENTENCE
**Most people remember Mary Pickford as a silent-film star nevertheless she was also a founder of United Artists.**

CORRECT
**Most people remember Mary Pickford as a silent-film star; nevertheless, she was also a founder of United Artists.**

## Using Subordinating Conjunctions

Subordinating conjunctions connect sentences differently than do coordinating conjunctions or conjunctive adverbs/transitional expressions. When you join two sentences by adding a subordinating conjunction, one of the two sentences loses its status as an independent clause. Note the following two sentences:

I wasn't sure how to use the new software. I gave it a try.

We can use the word *although* to subordinate the first clause:

**Although** I wasn't sure how to use the new software, I gave it a try.

We can also subordinate the second clause:

I wasn't sure how to use the new software, **although** I gave it a try.

When the second clause starts with a subordinating conjunction, it doesn't need to be preceded by a comma unless it represents a contrasting thought. However, even in this case the use of the comma is optional.

As with coordinating conjunctions and conjunctive adverbs/transitional expressions, subordinating conjunctions have special features that you should keep in mind:

1.  Most of the time, a writer will use a complex sentence (independent clause followed by dependent clause, or the reverse order) to show that the independent clause contains information that is more important than the information contained in the dependent clause, as in this construction:

    Although she stumbled at the start, Angela won the race easily.

    The outcome of the race is more important than Angela's stumbling.
    However, writers sometimes use complex sentences simply to provide variety. The two sentences are equal in weight, and the writer subordinates one to the other only to vary the sentence pattern for his or her reader, who might otherwise become tired of sentences joined by *and, but,* and *however.*

    The Wallace family loved Christmas, whereas the Jacksons saw it as merely a grim duty.

    Which fact is more important, that the Wallaces are Christmas lovers or the Jacksons are Christmas haters? Neither is. The writer is using the subordinating conjunction *whereas* to provide stylistic variety.

2.  A dependent clause standing alone is not a complete sentence; it is a **sentence fragment,** a group of words that is treated like a sentence but is missing a subject and/or a verb or that does not represent a complete thought. A fragment is as severe an error as a comma splice or a fused sentence.

    In the following example, the first sentence is correct; the second is a fragment:

    FRAGMENT       **I couldn't get to work on time. Because my car wouldn't start.**

    Revision is easy in this case; simply form a complex construction by combining the sentence and the fragment:

    CORRECT        **I couldn't get to work on time because my car wouldn't start.**

    The next example is more troubling:

    FRAGMENT       **Although, I could have asked my neighbor for a ride.**

    In this case, the writer obviously believes that *although* is a conjunctive adverb, not a subordinating conjunction. Fixing this fragment is easy; simply replace *although* with the appropriate conjunctive adverb:

    CORRECT        **Nevertheless, I could have asked my neighbor for a ride.**

    For more help with recognizing and correcting sentence fragments, consult chapter 25.

3.  Two of the subordinating conjunctions—*since* and *while*—are troublesome because each has two different meanings. *Since* can mean either "during the time after" or "because":

    AMBIGUOUS      **Since my refund check arrived, I have felt better.**

    Has the writer felt better in the days after the check arrived, or because the check arrived? Does it make any difference? Of course it does, especially if the reader has to sit and think about the meaning.

    *While* can mean "during the time that" or "whereas":

    AMBIGUOUS      **Jane enjoyed swimming while Kathryn played the piano.**

    The writer probably intended *while* to mean "whereas" in this case. Otherwise, the scene it brings to mind is a bit bizarre, though possible. If the writer did mean "whereas," why not just use that word and avoid the possible confusion?

## Using Correlative Conjunctions

**Correlative conjunctions,** a fourth type of conjunction, are not used to join sentences, so they do not appear in the sentence connectors chart. These are paired conjunctions that emphasize relationships *within* sentences:

**Both** walnuts **and** cashews are delicious.

**Either** Juan **or** Elena will be here soon.

**Neither** Bill **nor** Edna voted in the last election.

You should **not only** study for your physics test **but also** attend the group study session.

Remember to use a "whole" pair of correlative conjunctions. For example, *not only* must be followed by *but also,* not *but* alone.

## EXERCISE 4.10

Each sentence in the following paragraph consists of a single independent clause. Working with a partner or in a small group, use coordination and subordination to combine sentences and make the paragraph read more smoothly. If necessary, add the appropriate sentence connector to show logical relations between ideas. Make sure that you punctuate your newly combined sentences correctly.

> Someone needs to establish a janitorial service for the Internet—not to clean up the raunchy parts but to get rid of the abandoned, ancient Web sites. The Internet has been in popular use for a relatively short time. However, there are an alarming number of outmoded, useless sites. New Web sites tend to have all the bells and whistles. Old Web sites have a reek of early technology. New Web sites tend to rely on graphics. Old Web sites are dependent on text. Old Web sites also tend to contain information current in the year they were last updated—say, 1996. This information is no longer needed. Perhaps someday an agency will be allowed to do a search-and-destroy mission on these ancient outposts.

## EXERCISE 4.11

Many of the following sentences are incorrectly punctuated, causing comma splices and fused sentences. Working alone, correct any faulty punctuation.

1.  I frequently hear people complain about the high salaries paid to professional athletes. They make too much money, no one should get that much for playing a game. This is the way that the argument normally goes. People complain all the time about athletes, however you rarely hear them complain about movie actors. I believe the reason is twofold. One is that most of us have played sports at some time in our lives therefore we have a familiarity with what athletes are doing. The second is the opposite, most of us have never tried to act, so we give actors more credit than they might deserve.

2.  I'm at war with a bluejay that lives in a tree near my apartment's parking lot. I like the looks of jays in general and this one's looks in particular, nevertheless, we're locked in battle. The jay is guarding a nest, so anyone who walks by is a threat. The bird will fly fifty feet to swoop down at me. This is not to say I disapprove of the bird's protective instinct, I just won-

der why jays are the only ones that act this way. You walk past a nesting robin nothing happens. Jays, however, treat humans as enemies.

## EXERCISE 4.12

The following paragraph contains fragments caused by treating dependent clauses as sentences. Working alone, find the fragments and fix them in one of two ways: (1) by revising the fragment so that it becomes part of an adjacent sentence or (2) by changing the subordinating conjunction into a conjunctive adverb. Make sure that you punctuate your revised sentences correctly.

> The era of the box-office idol seems a thing of the past. People used to go to movies based on who was starring. Because these stars had drawing power that in some cases lasted for decades. Today, no star seems to be able to carry a film singlehandedly. Tom Cruise, Julia Roberts, Brad Pitt, and Tom Hanks are all contemporary superstars. Although, each of these actors has seen failure at the box office. Perhaps the director is today's new superstar. People will turn out in droves to see anything directed by Steven Spielberg or Peter Jackson. Maybe because these directors always aim for blockbuster success.

## Using Hybrid Sentence Patterns

Sentences joined by coordination and subordination form recognizable patterns with formal names, some of which we have already encountered:

**. . . . . . . .**

**CATALYST 2.0**

**MORE OPTIONS ONLINE**
For more help with sentence combining, go to www.mhhe.com/ writingtoday.

**COMPOUND SENTENCES**

My computer is three years old, but it still suits my needs.

My computer is three years old; however, it still suits my needs.

**COMPLEX SENTENCES**

Although my computer is three years old, it still suits my needs.

My computer still suits my needs although it is three years old.

When a sentence contains both compound and complex elements, it is called a **compound-complex sentence:**

**COMPOUND-COMPLEX SENTENCES**

Although my computer is three years old, it still suits my needs, so I probably won't buy a new one for a few more years.

Although my computer is three years old, it still suits my needs; therefore, I probably won't buy a new one for a few more years.

My computer still suits my needs although it is three years old, so I probably won't buy a new one for a few more years.

My computer still suits my needs although it is three years old; therefore, I probably won't buy a new one for a few more years.

I probably won't buy a new computer for a few more years; my current computer still suits my needs although it is three years old.

> I probably won't buy a new computer for a few more years;
> although my current computer is three years old, it still suits
> my needs.

You can generate a limitless number of new sentences by changing the subject, changing the verb, changing the connector, and so on. You can also generate sentences that contain many clauses—collections of independent clauses and dependent clauses that represent increasingly complex thoughts. However, be careful: long sentences are not necessarily wrong, but think of your reader. Do you want to subject your audience to eighty-five-word sentences? Of course not. The patterns that we have explored will allow you to generate sentences of any length, long or short. It is up to you to use these options wisely.

## Using Periodic and Climactic Sentence Structure to Create Emphasis

Creating emphasis may require you to structure sentences so that your most important words and phrases are highlighted. Two methods of highlighting are the periodic sentence and the climactic sentence.

The majority of declarative sentences are **cumulative;** they begin with the main idea and then add any modifiers or details needed. For emphasis (and variety), try using a **periodic** sentence from time to time; in such a sentence, the main idea comes *last,* preceded by its modifiers. Note the difference in emphasis between the following two sentences:

CUMULATIVE    **The governor is in sad shape, beset by a hostile press, charges of corruption, and dissension within her own party.**

PERIODIC    **Beset by a hostile press, charges of corruption, and dissension within her own party, the governor is in sad shape.**

A **climactic** sentence arranges its ideas in order of importance, ending with the most important idea:

CLIMACTIC    **During that week, Jason sold his car, found someone to date, and graduated from college after six years of trying.**

## EXERCISE 4.13

Examine each set of word groups below, and construct a sentence displaying the best possible emphasis.

**1.** My friend Jason. 1997. Graduated. Got engaged. Moved to Oregon.
**2.** Dark clouds. High winds. Heavy rains. Ruined picnic.
**3.** Bad relief pitching. Slow base runners. Strange managerial decisions. Won 11–3.

4. Flat tire. Crashed hard drive. Monthly sales award. Nice bonus. Strange day at the office.

5. Torn ear. Blind eye. Arthritic hip. Horrible excuse for a dog.

# CHOOSING WORDS CAREFULLY

You may find that your first draft contains phrases and sentences that are overly complicated or that do not say what you intended them to say. You may also find passages that are not emphatic; weak phrasing has caused your writing to lose its punch. And you may also discover passages that are simply awkward. This section discusses these problems and ways to correct them.

## Striving for Parallelism

When you give equal emphasis to two or more ideas, actions, things, or feelings, try to use **parallel** structures. In other words, group nouns with nouns, verbs with verbs, prepositional phrases with prepositional phrases, and so on:

| | |
|---|---|
| NOT PARALLEL | **In Japan, heavy rains are frequent, and the country also experiences volcanic eruptions as well as typhoons.** |
| MADE PARALLEL BY USING NOUNS | **In Japan, heavy rains, typhoons, and volcanic eruptions are frequent.** |
| NOT PARALLEL | **Mia has two ambitions: graduating from college and to get a job.** |
| MADE PARALLEL BY USING INFINITIVES | **Mia has two ambitions: to graduate from college and to get a job.** |

Parallelism can also help make comparisons and contrasts clear and emphatic:

| | |
|---|---|
| UNCLEAR | **The candidate was greeted with cheers, and he did not hear the hisses and boos he had expected.** |
| MADE PARALLEL BY USING PREPOSITIONS | **The candidate was greeted with cheers, not with the hisses and boos he had expected.** |

Some pairs of words help make a sentence parallel if used correctly. These are the correlative conjunctions: *both/and, either/or, neither/nor,* and *not only/but also* (see also pages 109–110 in this chapter). When you use these correlatives, make sure the elements they are joining are parallel:

| | |
|---|---|
| NOT PARALLEL | **In January, the weather is either cool and rainy or we get frigid temperatures and lots of snow.** |
| PARALLEL | **In January, the weather is either cool and rainy or cold and snowy.** |

Note that not everything in English can be made parallel. As the examples below illustrate, sometimes you might have to restructure the sentence:

| | |
|---|---|
| **INCORRECT** | **Raul is poised, witty, and gives great presentations.** |
| **CORRECT** | **Raul is poised and witty; therefore, he gives great presentations.** |

## Including All Necessary Words

Faulty parallelism and poor communication are frequently caused by the omission of key words:

| | |
|---|---|
| **WORD OMITTED** | **The striking workers were angry and grumbling in low tones.** |
| **REVISED** | **The striking workers were angry and were grumbling in low tones.** |
| **WORD OMITTED** | **The professor gave high grades to Laura, Bill, and to Anne.** |
| **REVISED** | **The professor gave high grades to Laura, to Bill, and to Anne.** |

Although words can often be omitted from a pair or series without sacrificing clarity, make sure that the word you are leaving out is expendable. If not, you may create an error like the one below:

| | |
|---|---|
| **WORD OMITTED** | **Is it similar or different from our old model?** |
| **REVISED** | **Is it similar to or different from our old model?** |

In this situation, each verb requires its own preposition: *to* and *from,* respectively. Preposition usage is highly idiomatic; refer to chapter 23 or a dictionary if you are unsure about which preposition to use in a given context.

A similar problem is sometimes caused by the omission of the subordinator *that.* Most of the time, writers can leave out this word:

Shannon believed [that] she would win the race.

In this instance, omitting *that* causes no problem for the reader. But how about this example?

| | |
|---|---|
| **AWKWARD** | **Mark felt the car was overpriced.** |

The reader understands what is meant, but *Mark felt the car* can be misread. Don't omit *that* if doing so causes your reader to pause or to stumble.

| | |
|---|---|
| **CLEAR** | **Mark felt that the car was overpriced.** |

You should also avoid constructions such as this one:

FAULTY          **Keith understood the process would be lengthy and that he was looking at three months of hard work.**

Here, the writer has used *that* to *explicitly* subordinate the second idea but, by omitting *that,* has only *implicitly* subordinated the first idea. It is clearer and more logical to treat both ideas in the same way by subordinating them explicitly.

CLEAR           **Keith understood that the process would be lengthy and that he was looking at three months of hard work.**

The following sentence omits a needed word in a comparison:

INCORRECT       **Ms. Tompkins sings better than any member of her church choir.**

Ms. Tompkins is a member of the choir, so the comparison indicates that she sings better than herself. Note the revision:

CORRECT         **Ms. Tompkins sings better than any other member of her church choir.**

Because of missing words, some comparisons are ambiguous:

AMBIGUOUS       **Anna likes Pablo more than Esteban.**

The meaning is unclear. Here are two revisions:

CLEAR           **Anna likes Pablo more than she likes Esteban.**

CLEAR           **Anna likes Pablo more than Esteban does.**

## Avoiding Awkward Repetition

Key words and concepts can be repeated for emphasis:

Mr. Desmond is a **fine** employee and a **fine** human being.

Oral presentations enable an instructor **to gauge a student's** thinking, **to gauge a student's** preparation, and **to gauge a student's** confidence.

However, needless repetition should be avoided:

AWKWARD         **A teacher who teaches middle school students usually learns a great deal about teaching.**

REVISED         **A middle school teacher usually learns a great deal about teaching.**

## Avoiding Faulty Comparisons

When you compare things, they have to be logically comparable:

INCORRECT       **More Euromongo Supremes are on the highways than any other car company.**

In effect, this sentence tries to compare a car to a car company. Note the revision:

CORRECT **More Euromongo Supremes are on the highways than any other car.**

## EXERCISE 4.14

Check for faulty parallelism, omitted words, awkward repetition, or faulty comparisons in the following sentences, and revise them.

1. Do you want to walk or go swimming?
2. The fighter fought four fighters in the next weight class up.
3. Lisa can spell better than any six-year-old I've ever known.
4. The painting was more complicated than any other modern artist.
5. Mario likes to swim, to dance, and he likes playing soccer.

## Using Only Words That Matter

You do not necessarily need to write each thought in as few words as possible. Writing in this manner produces text that is flat and over-controlled; it sounds as if it has been produced by a machine. But don't waste words. Don't use six words when two will suffice. Otherwise, your reader will become impatient with your text, much as a listener grows edgy when a speaker takes five minutes to tell a thirty-second story. Don't think that you must always avoid using

| AVOID WORDINESS | |
| --- | --- |
| Wordy Phrase | Simpler Equivalent |
| during the time that | while |
| due to the fact that | because |
| in excess of | more than |
| in all probability | probably |
| in many instances | often |
| in a similar manner | similarly |
| in the event that | if |
| whether or not | whether |
| on the part of | by |
| a large number of | many |
| a large amount of | much |
| a small number of | few |
| a small amount of | little |
| it is clear that | clearly |
| it is obvious that | obviously |
| speaking with the truth | speaking truthfully |

| AVOID WORDINESS *(continued)* | |
|---|---|
| Wordy Phrase | Simpler Equivalent |
| walking with care | walking carefully |
| shouting with excitement | shouting excitedly |
| not a few | many |

a phrase from the left-hand column; at times, one of these phrases may be useful and appropriate. However, if you *consistently* use these terms in place of their simpler equivalents, your writing will seem bloated.

You should also avoid using **fillers,** well-known but essentially empty expressions used when a more basic expression—or none at all—would suffice:

all in all

needless to say

first and foremost

Note the following paragraph and its revision:

WORDY    **It can be clearly seen that our division's profits may or may not increase next year, with this issue based on the question of whether or not a large number of our current clients adopt the offer on the part of our main competition to sign package deals. Needless to say, in the event that our competitor succeeds, our business's profits, in all probability, will falter.**

REVISED    **Clearly, our division's profits next year depend on whether many of our current clients adopt our rival's package-deal offer. If our competitor succeeds, our business's profits will falter.**

Unrevised first drafts are frequently as wordy as the original paragraph above. One of the purposes of revision is to clear away some of the deadwood from the original forest of prose.

## EXERCISE 4.15

Working alone, revise the following sentences so that they are more concise.

1.  When all is said and done, I believe that the art gallery's new show is a hit.

2.  If and when the new stadium is completed, I doubt that it will meet the financial estimates of the planning committee.

3.  The attempt on the part of the art gallery's management to restrict audience numbers in excess of seventy-five will be seen to be futile.

4.  In all probability, the planning committee's estimates will be exceeded by 50 percent or more.

5.  Shouting with happiness, Robert approached Anne, who shivered with nervousness.

6.  Not a few of the art gallery patrons complained about the number of restrictions; however, the vast majority of those who got in were made happy by the experience.

7.  Needless to say, the company's profit margin is my main concern.

8.  A small number of the new stadium's supporters are speaking with care about the rash optimism that prevailed during the time that the initial budget planning took place.

### EXERCISE 4.16

Working with a partner or in a small group, revise the following paragraphs to eliminate wordiness.

1.  The deep rivers of the Midwest and Great Plains have always fascinated not a small number of visitors. During the time that Mark Twain wrote about attempts on the part of steamship companies to master the Mississippi, it is obvious that the romance of the great rivers existed in a prior time and that Twain was building on a myth that was not new. Due to the fact that obstacles placed in the river by nature and obstacles placed in the river by accident forced riverboat pilots to navigate in a cautious manner, an inevitable theme rose up of the fact of humanity at war with its natural environment.

2.  "Dahlia, if you'll join me in matrimony, I think you'll find in all probability that in many measures I will surprise you as a husband. I am not ungifted in the arts of love, despite any preconceptions on that issue you might have formed, and in a similar way you will grow to love my home bequeathed to me by my ancestors. Ignore those attempts on the part of your friends to persuade you; it is obvious that they do not know the interests that are best for you."

## Avoiding Redundancy

**Redundancy**—the use of two or more words together that mean the same thing—is another common word-choice problem. The following are common redundancies:

| Redundant Phrase | Simpler Equivalent |
| --- | --- |
| small in size | small |
| brown in color | brown |
| and therefore | therefore |

| Redundant Phrase | Simpler Equivalent |
| --- | --- |
| so therefore | so *or* therefore |
| and so | so |
| and yet | yet |
| but yet | but *or* yet |
| outside of | outside |
| future plans | plans |
| advance reservations | reservations |
| prior planning | planning |
| visible to the naked eye | visible |
| square in shape | square |
| quite precise | precise |
| vanish from view | vanish |
| recur again | recur |
| advance ahead | advance |
| can possibly | can |
| very unique | unique |
| plan ahead | plan |
| retreat backward | retreat |
| completely clear | clear |
| totally obvious | obvious |
| in this day and age | now |
| over and over | continually *or* regularly |
| each and every | each *or* every |
| deliberately plan | plan |
| review again | review |
| past experience | experience |
| prior experience | experience |
| personal friend | friend |
| review again | review |
| final result | result |
| end result | result |
| final total | total |
| my own personal | my |
| my own | my |

A writer who uses any of the terms from the left-hand column in a final draft
is not paying enough attention to what he or she is actually communicating.

## EXERCISE 4.17
Working alone, revise the following sentences to eliminate redundant constructions.

1. Prior experience tells us that the end result of this initiative will be failure.
2. I think that Jared deliberately planned to ruin my party.
3. Your motives are totally obvious, Laura.
4. After failing to break the enemy lines, the patrol returned back to head-quarters.
5. The mall was closed, and so we had to postpone our Christmas shopping.
6. Eddie left the car, but yet he forgot to give me his key.
7. The mysterious guest vanished from view when approached by Dr. Herzel.
8. It's a small device, gray in color and oval in shape—it's absolutely unique.
9. My own personal opinion is that modern physics has become too special-ized for anyone except people with doctorates in the subject.
10. Unless you have the surgery, Mr. Walker, these symptoms will recur again.

## Avoiding Euphemisms

**Euphemisms** are words and phrases used to mask the painful realities of life. We sometimes use euphemisms to avoid making a troubling situation worse ("Uncle Mike passed on last night") or to avoid saying what we actually mean ("Jenkins, we're going to have to let you go"). In some situations, a euphemism can be appropriate—for example, "going to the bathroom." However, if you want to write directly and clearly, using euphemisms is a bad habit.

### EXERCISE 4.18

Working alone, read the following sentences. Decide if the highlighted term is a euphemism. If so, replace it with a more direct or appropriate expression.

1. Wanda's in trouble with the boss; it looks like she **fudged** on her travel account.
2. Our former accountant **expired** this morning.
3. During our journey, we frequently had to stop so that my young son could go **tinkle.**
4. The police arrested seventeen people after last night's **civil unrest** in which cars were smashed and businesses were looted.
5. The new tolls on the Midtown Expressway will **enhance revenues** for the city.
6. Henry never gives to any charities; he's very **parsimonious.**
7. Seventy-four employees were **downsized** in the company's latest cost-cutting efforts.
8. Aunt Linda's **frugality** kept her family going after the death of Uncle Carter.

## Using Figurative Language Appropriately

**Figurative language** does not represent a subject directly or literally; instead, it compares the subject in some way to something else. The result creates a relationship that helps explain, define, or add information about the subject.

> Harrison's wrongful-termination lawsuit is **the wheel upon which our company may be broken.**

The lawsuit is not literally a wheel; it's a legal filing. But claiming that the lawsuit is "the wheel upon which our company may be broken" evokes images of a torturer's wheel, a medieval device used to strain and kill its victim.

Note how the author of the following passage uses figurative language to help him make his point:

> The whiskey-jack showed up again around here a couple of years ago. I encountered one down in the cedar swamp in the pasture, where I had gone to look for a fox's den. The bird, instead of showing alarm at my intrusion, followed me about, jumping silently from branch to branch in the thick woods, seemingly eager to learn what I was up to. I found it spooky yet agreeable to be tailed by a bird, and a disreputable one at that. **The Canada jay looks as though he had slept in his clothes.**
> —from E. B. White, "Home-Coming"

In this passage, White uses a **simile.** This figure of speech is a direct comparison, claiming that something is *like* something else ("looks *as though*"). White's use of the simile gives the paragraph a vivid conclusion.

Here is another approach:

> Prices continued to move firmly upward on the Wall Street stock exchanges, and Alan Greenspan, that great and good chairman of the Federal Reserve Bank named *de facto* captain of the American ship of state since President Clinton had fallen overboard with Monica Lewinsky, saw nothing on the calm horizon but blue sky and white sailboats.
> —from Lewis H. Lapham, "Sucking at Straws"

Lapham is using a **metaphor.** Like a simile, a metaphor tries to amplify meaning by linking one idea to another, but a metaphor does so directly, without using *like* or similar words that signal comparison. With a metaphor, the writer says that the item being described *is* (figuratively) the other. Lapham compares the U.S. government to a "ship" crossing rough waters, then suggests that Alan Greenspan has become "captain" in place of the embattled President Clinton.

Note the following two examples:

SIMILE      **After Mike's grueling day at the office, Laura's welcoming smile was like a rainbow of sanctuary.**

METAPHOR    **After Mike's grueling day at the office, Laura's welcoming smile was a rainbow of sanctuary.**

As you can see in the two examples above, the metaphor is more forceful than the simile. However, the metaphor is also somewhat harder to use properly.

A problem area in figurative language involves **mixed metaphors**, which occur when multiple comparisons are used in a single text passage:

> The bottom line is that Geena would be in the lap of luxury if she had nipped that drinking problem in the bud. When push came to shove, the world was her oyster last year; now, she'll be lucky if her company doesn't kick the bucket before the cows come home.

This isn't direct communication; it's a form of code. Seven different themes are used here, and the reader is being bounced from figurative phrase to figurative phrase—to no purpose. Moreover, each figurative phrase is a cliché, discussed in the next section of this chapter.

A third type of figurative language is **personification**, in which human characteristics are given to nonhuman entities:

> The night's wind whispered a mystery story.

Obviously, as this sentence indicates, writers who use personification must keep control of their imagination. A sentence that personifies the night wind is striking, but if the wind whispers through an entire paragraph, readers will soon tire of the idea.

## Avoiding Clichés

Using vivid figures of speech will improve your writing; using **clichés** will hurt it. How can you tell the difference? If an expression is very common, a phrase that you've known most of your life, an "old standard," it's probably a cliché:

> My sister is blind as a bat without her glasses.

Besides the needless cruelty of *blind as a bat,* this worn-out phrase is not going to make your reader admire your language skills. However, note how the writer of the following passage makes good use of a cliché:

> Peter McMichaels was hired at the same time as four other people. His work has been no better or worse than theirs. He has no outstanding characteristics other than his willingness to complain when he doesn't get his way. Yet Peter got a raise this month whereas the other four people didn't. It's clearly an instance of the "squeaky wheel" syndrome.

The writer has taken a very old cliché ("The squeaky wheel gets the grease") and used it to good effect. The reader can be expected to know the cliché. However, remember that only rarely can you put a cliché to good use; you should avoid clichés as much as possible.

### EXERCISE 4.19

Working alone, read the following sentences. If a sentence can be made more lively, revise it. Be creative. If a sentence contains a cliché or a mixed metaphor, revise the sentence to eliminate the problem. Some sentences are acceptable.

1. Mrs. Parker hit the nail on the head when she suggested that we pull out all the stops and call everyone in the neighborhood.

2. My brother-in-law isn't the swiftest arrow in the quiver, but he's a good family man.

3. Find him—leave no stone unturned!

4. Myra went up the corporate ladder quickly until her career ran aground after her company was taken over.

5. The recent campaign to "beautify" Parkersville is like putting makeup on a hog.

6. The salmon swam very hard against the current.

7. After her oral presentation bit the dust, Laurel considered dropping her business communications class.

8. This cake batter is as light as a feather.

9. Luis's petition got a shot in the arm when the committee steamrolled the only objection.

10. In a nutshell, here's the straight dope.

## Learning to Use Denotation and Connotation

**Denotation** refers to the actual meaning or meanings of a word. Students sometimes misunderstand the denotative meaning of a word and misuse it. When this happens, the reader may understand what the writer intends but will still note the error. In the worst cases, however, the reader has no idea what the writer is attempting to communicate. A college-level dictionary is your best guide when you want to be sure that you are using a word with the correct denotation. As well, a usage glossary such as the one at the end of this text will help you make accurate decisions.

### EXERCISE 4.20

Working with a partner or in a small group, read the following sentences. Do the highlighted terms mean what the writer seems to intend? If not, replace the term with a correct one or revise the sentence so that the term is correct. Use a college-level dictionary and/or this text's usage glossary for help.

1. The disabled singer received **fulsome** praise from her proud fans.

2. The judge was clearly **biased** in his opinion.

3. A crime was **omitted** last night in Parkersville.

4. I had to have my car's **breaks** replaced again; this kind of **maintenance** drives me crazy.

5. My government teacher has given me five *A*'s in a row—I can't stand all this **opprobrium**.

6. Go to the **Personal** Department if you want to get your health insurance forms.

7. When you spoke harshly to me, were you **inferring** that I was to blame for our financial situation?

8. Michael's father was a **conscious** objector during the Vietnam War era.

Whereas **denotation** is what words *mean* (their dictionary definition), **connotation** is what words *suggest*. Note the difference between these two sentences:

Mr. Newsome owned and managed old apartment complexes in the central city.

Mr. Newsome was a slum lord.

The first sentence is an objective statement; it does not imply anything about Newsome and his buildings. However, the second sentence is highly *suggestive. Slum lord* brings up a raft of associations, none of them positive. These associations are called the connotation of a term.

### Two Connotation Pitfalls

1. Sometimes, writers who fail to recognize the connotations of words can create sentences with unintended and inappropriate humor:

The directions for this laxative are very irregular.

The writer has made an inadvertent pun—wouldn't *unusual* work better than *irregular*? Humor is frequently a plus, but missteps such as this one will cause people to laugh *at* you, not *with* you.

2. Frequently, inadvertent **sexism** is another result of problems with connotation. If a friend mentions that she plans to run for the Student Assembly, the following response may not have the desired effect:

Brenda, I'm so happy that you're going to try to become an assemblyman.

For Brenda to do so will involve both (a) winning the election and (b) having a sex-change operation. We doubt that she is considering the second option. Many traditional terms and titles of standard English were formed when, largely, men ran things and women kept house. This situation hasn't been true for a very long time.

Concern about sexism in language is frequently described as "political correctness," as if avoiding sexism (and racism and ageism, for that matter) were something that people *had* to do under the watchful eye of some shadowy monitoring group. No—careful writers avoid sexist language because they don't want to offend others or to alienate their readers.

Therefore, Brenda probably doesn't want to become an "assemblyman." But she likely wants to be a *member* of the Student Assembly or, perhaps, a *representative*. If a writer shows no sensitivity about this issue, the reader will think that the writer doesn't know any better or, worse, doesn't care. Remember, you should always write for your audience, not for yourself.

The built-in sexism of American English can be countered, but you don't have to sacrifice your style to do so. For example, you can't change every word ending in *-man* to a word ending in *-person* without producing awkwardness.

Use common sense. For instance, "guard" seems more logical than "watch person," and "postal carrier" seems more natural than "mail person."

### EXERCISE 4.21

Working with a partner or in a small group, read the following sentences and choose the *best* word or phrase from the choices in parentheses.

1. Her job as a (waiter, waitress, waitperson, server) kept Gwen afloat during her senior year.

2. The accused man looked (nervous, shifty) as the bailiff ordered all to rise.

3. Irena del Valles is the (congressman, congresswoman, representative) for our district.

4. I felt (strange, funny) as I waited for the comedian to start his act.

5. If they don't fix that pothole in front of my house, I'm going to call the city (ombudsman, ombudsperson, mediator).

6. Moria went to school to learn how to become a computer (repairman, repairwoman, technician).

7. We elected Lydia Kelly as (chairman, chairwoman, chair) of the Goals 2010 committee.

8. Your grandfather seems rather (crotchety, irritable) today.

9. Her hands visibly (shaking, fluttering), Ms. Walters asked the (policeman, police officer) to come inside.

10. That pile of dead spiders is (creepy, disturbing).

## Using Idiomatic English

Like all languages, English has its own **idioms**—customarily accepted phrasings and ways of ordering words. To an international student who is learning English, a sentence such as "The butler called me a cab" must seem very strange indeed. (A native speaker of English would find similar oddities in the international student's first language.)

However, even experienced writers of English sometimes run into trouble with idioms. (Should you use *different from* or *different than*? The former, usually.) People who read a great deal have an advantage in this area because they see edited language that, by virtue of sheer repetition, helps them learn the correct forms. But for everyone else, the problem remains, and some phrasings can't be constructed logically: you must either know the correct form or look it up. You can get help choosing the correct word or phrase by using a good ESL dictionary, such as *The Newbury House Dictionary of American English,* or the usage notes in a college-level dictionary.

### EXERCISE 4.22

In the following passage, the highlighted words and phrases are unidiomatic. Working with a partner or in a small group, revise this passage to eliminate the errors. Use a college-level dictionary or an ESL dictionary for assistance.

I went to get my mail **at my mailbox** last Sunday, and **from the mail** I got a shock. It seems that my health insurance claims were not approved **through school's insurance policy.** I had to make a special trip to school, **during that** I planned my argument.

The health insurance office is **found at** the Student Services Building, **besides** the financial aid office. I **asked** with the representative for almost an hour, and she apologized about the problem. She **told me also** what she planned **on doing** to correct the error. I concurred **about** her idea; it seemed to be a good way **of to take care with** the problem.

A friend of **my** later told **to me** to **be accustomed** with this mixup; it happens **all the while.** She also told me that the university **health blanketing** is **much preferable than providers on the outside** because of its **lowered** cost. So I **took a word with the wise** and will be prepared **for scrutinizing** all **documents of university health insurance sent at me.**

## Using Active, Specific Language

Students in college-level writing classes sometimes make the process of composing more complicated than it is. In their attempt to sound "formal," they forget one of the first guidelines for communicating clearly: *good writing is good speaking correctly transcribed to paper.* Students sometimes write sentences that they would not dream of saying, such as "Formulated in the early morning hours, the proposal was designed to facilitate interaction among the two sides in the labor dispute." First off, is it necessary to "formulate" a proposal? Second, who did this deed? Third, what in the world does *facilitate* really mean, anyway? Here is a plainer version of this sentence: "Early in the morning, the committee finished the proposal that would bring both sides to the bargaining table." In other words, write what you mean. Don't cloak your meaning in ornate language.

In this section, we look at three related problems that can make your writing seem static instead of active: relying on complicated noun structures when direct verbs would be better, relying too much on the passive voice, and relying on abstract words when concrete words would be more emphatic.

1.  **Prefer verbs over nouns.** Examine the following sentence:

    There was an immediate burst of applause from the crowd when the popular governor started her speech.

    It communicates well enough, but it lacks a certain punch. Note the revision:

    The crowd applauded immediately when the popular governor started speaking.

    The revised sentence depends on verbs (*applauded, started speaking*), not nouns, to show what happened, and it gets directly to the point. In the next two examples, the original sentences have a similar problem:

    ORIGINAL     **The baking of cakes is a source of much pleasure for my retired uncle.**

REVISED    **My retired uncle really enjoys baking cakes.**

ORIGINAL    **It was in the supervision of trainees that Manuel Gomez found his niche.**

REVISED    **Manuel Gomez excelled at supervising trainees.**

As we mentioned earlier, the goal is not to write each sentence with the fewest possible words, but to remember that each sentence tells the story of an actor and an action. Concentrate on showing this relationship with active verbs and clear, direct expression.

2.  **Prefer the active voice.** In sentences in the active voice, subjects act; in sentences in the passive voice, subjects are acted upon. Overusing the passive voice causes weak, flabby writing. Examine these two sentences:

PASSIVE    **The bonus money was given to us by Ms. Thompson.**

ACTIVE    **Ms. Thompson gave us the bonus money.**

The sentence using the passive voice fades away like the dying note of a song, whereas the sentence in the active voice gives the reader the information directly. Keep in mind these simple guidelines: use the passive voice only (1) when you can't—or really don't want to—reveal who did the action or (2) when you want to emphasize the receiver of the action.

Consider the following situation. Police officers checking the back door of a restaurant find a male corpse. It has four visible bullet wounds. No other human beings are in the area. How will the local newspaper "lead" with this story? Probably this way:

A man was murdered last night. . . .

The active voice won't work here because the writer doesn't know the identity of the actor.

Also, you may want to choose the passive voice when you know the responsible party but don't want to mention the name—perhaps the guilty party is your boss, for example.

TACTFUL    **Mistakes were found in the billing of the Andrews project.**

The alternative might be dangerous:

BLUNT    **Mr. Waddell committed errors when billing the Andrews project.**

Finally, sometimes you will want to emphasize the receiver, not the actor:

The murder weapon was found behind a shed.

The person who found the weapon is not important; the actual discovery is.

3.  **Use concrete terms.** Don't overuse abstract words when specific, concrete words would work much better. (See pages 91–92.) Most readers find that "weasel words" such as *facilitate, facilitation, enable, enabler, utilize,* and *utilization* make their skin crawl. Again, college-level writing does not require the construction of such jewels as "I perceived the letter carrier at the door." You wouldn't say such a thing, so why put it on paper?

 In "Politics and the English Language," the British novelist and essayist George Orwell claims that sloppy, inefficient writing is the result of sloppy, inefficient thinking. Moreover, Orwell points out that one breeds the other in a vicious cycle. However, the opposite is also true. Think clearly, and write your thoughts clearly; then you are ready for an even better attempt the next time out.

## EXERCISE 4.23

Working alone, look for problem areas in the following sentences and revise as needed. Use a college-level dictionary for reference.

1.  Hi, I'm here to facilitate this meeting.
2.  According to our statistics, utilization of coffee by our secretaries has undergone an increase of 20 percent.
3.  The bad news was communicated by Inspector Laurence.
4.  Don't bug me, Eddie; I'm cogitating!
5.  The termination process of an employee found to be ineffective has been estimated by our personnel department to cost over $5,000.
6.  I'm trying to conceptualize the scene that you're describing.
7.  The ball was hit by the bat and began the process of arcing through the air in the general proximity of the shortstop.
8.  My apprehension of your meaning is faulty.

## EXERCISE 4.24: SUMMARY

The following paragraphs contain all the problems that we have discussed in the "Choosing Words Carefully" section of this chapter. Working with a partner or a small group, revise these paragraphs so that they are clear, concise, and active. Use a college-level dictionary for reference.

1.  The endless parade of children in their trick-or-treat regalia I find fascinating, but yet I feel a sensation of pleasure when I perceive that the last child is here no more. The last piece of firm confectionary made largely of sucrose has been given out, and the final, last gamine has been dispatched. I sink back and down into my soft recliner, and I cogitate back to my days of youthfulness. During the time that my days of trick-or-treating were active, a hard doughnut or roll was our most frequent gift. Costumes were

hand sewn by our mothers using needle and thread, and no child ever faced the eventuality of a cookie infiltrated with medicine, or some other unspeakable, monstrous act. Ah, each and every time I think of it, times change, but never for the better.

2. Ms. Lawrence, in your role as foreman of the safety crew, your conduct has been found to be above average. We wish that there were some financial perquisite that you could receive, but our shaky contingencies forbid that eventuality. So, therefore, we ask you to toe the line and act like a trouper, for your day in the sun will come.

3. Don't think that I'm not receptive to your generous and charitable offer, Jeffrey. My mind has entered a state of chaos, much like a horde of flies fighting over an abandoned pudding. I have perused your suggestion with care, Jeffrey, and its potentialities and possibilities are not unpleasant to my style of thought. Perhaps at some time of a future date I will be able to give you my final and ultimate response.

### EXERCISE 4.25: SUMMARY

The following paragraph is from the first draft of "A Very Secret Santa." Working with a partner or in a small group, fix any error that you find. Then compare your corrected version of the paragraph with the final version on pages 19–20.

> I remember the first time I saw an example of Walter's secret side. It was before Christmas, years ago, Betty and I were ten years old and going shopping with Mr. and Mrs Wallace at the mall. After Walter finaly found a parking space we noticed a comotion a few cars over. A young woman and her seven-year-old were trying to quiet down the three-year-old. He had been pulled from the last store visited without getting what he wanted. The mother looked entirely flustered and she was obviously quite poor, the little boy was screaming like he had been scalded. We walked toward the mall, listening to this squabble unfold behind us, suddenly Walter disappeared. Mrs. Wallace told us to keep walking, that Walter would catch up. When he did he said nothing.

### *Responding to Visuals*

Cartoonists often use visual metaphors to make their point. Here, the cartoonist uses the image of a fallen tree and its shriveled roots (which presumably caused the tree to fall) to identify some of the reasons behind the educational decline. Examine the accompanying cartoon, and answer the following questions:

- What is your personal response to this cartoon? Explain your reaction.

- Why is the image of a fallen tree a powerful metaphor for the decline in schools?

- How would you revise this cartoon? Are there other "root" problems with America's schools you might add to the image? Which ones?

Dropout Roots

By permission of Gary Varvel and Creators Syndicate, Inc.

garyvarvel.com

### Using the Internet

Go to these Web sites to find more tips on, techniques for, and insights on revising words and sentences:

### The University of Victoria Hypertext Writer's Guide

The section titled "Writing Your Essay: Getting It Down" offers suggestions on writing and revising first drafts and creating effective introductions and conclusions. Other advice covers writing well-developed, coherent body paragraphs that relate to the essay's thesis: **http://www.web.uvic.ca/wguide**.

### LEO Write Place Catalogue

Maintained by St. Cloud State University, this site provides advice on organization and coherence in paragraphs and essays. Transitions and thesis statements receive special coverage. You can also find information on writing essay introductions and conclusions: **http://leo.stcloudstate.edu/catalogue.html**.

### The American Heritage Book of English Usage

This commercial online reference tool contains sections on style, word choice, and matters regarding gender in writing: **http://www.bartleby.com/64**.

### The Elements of Style

This is an online edition of the classic work of American usage, written by William Strunk, Jr., for his students at Cornell University. It was later revised by E. B. White, who had been one of those students: http://www.bartleby.com/141

### Guide to Grammar and Style

Created by Professor Jack Lynch of Rutgers University, this Web site contains a search engine that allows you to access information on English usage. The list of additional readings on grammar and usage is also useful: http://andromeda.rutgers.edu/~jlynch/Writing

### Guide to Grammar and Writing

Among the most useful pages on this site are "Notorious Confusables," which lists words "we get mixed up," and "Plague Words and Phrases," which "we should avoid": http://grammar.ccc.commnet.com/grammar.

### LEO Write Place Catalogue

Maintained by St. Cloud State University, this site contains abundant resources on sentence structure and style, including advice on how to combine sentences for variety and clarity, techniques to avoid and correct wordiness, and coverage of matters pertaining to word choice: http://leo.stcloudstate.edu/catalogue.html.

### University of Richmond Writer's Web

The Web site of the University of Richmond's Writing Center, the Writer's Web contains advice on editing for clarity and style, with emphasis on avoiding sexist language, distinguishing between commonly confused words, and avoiding clichés: http://writing2.richmond.edu/writing/wweb.html.

**Y**our college and the working world that looms before you contain a number of **discourse communities.** Each field of study or employment has its own preferred approaches to communication, its own specialized language and shorthand. These you will learn as you choose your major and immerse yourself in a field of study and application.

However, you need some general tools and skills before you begin to specialize in a chosen field. The chapters in Part 2 discuss strategies that underlie the writing you will be expected to produce. Each chapter concentrates on one strategy. We call these strategies **rhetorical options.** They are ways to approach a writing situation.

Students sometimes find the process of learning one new approach after another to be stressful. Having become comfortable with one strategy, they don't see the point of learning a new one. They believe that in the working world, they won't need all of these specific approaches. It's true that your boss will never assign you a project report and say "Write a process analysis." By the same token, your boss will know what he or she wants—a process analysis—and will expect you to be able to write the appropriate document without having to tell you how to proceed. Similarly, if your boss sends you a set of data and asks you to analyze it, he or she is probably not going to tell you which algebraic technique to employ—sampling, graphing, guessing, or consulting a psychic. But your algebra instructor made you process similar data in a specific way—the most reliable and economical way—so that you could avoid guesswork. In short, the techniques that you learn in college "skill classes" will extrapolate to the world of work.

We do not see composition as a captive part of the humanities. Instead, we see writing as a responsibility that every adult has—both on the job and off. To that end, we offer the following ten chapters with the "real" world in mind. Each chapter begins with a vignette from the business world. A new employee is faced with a boss (Bob) who is sometimes lazy and sometimes sadistic—and who always seems to need a new report written. The new hire is forced to scramble, to conceive, to come up with the best way to respond to Bob's need for documents. As a manager, Bob is not atypical of a supervisor in the corporate world, and his requests (demands) will show you how the skills discussed in each chapter can be extrapolated into "real" situations (as if the sweat and hope and worry that you'll put into English composition aren't "real").

Nine of the ten chapters in Part 2 are each devoted to a specific rhetorical option. The final chapter in this part, "The Blended Essay," takes a combined approach, covering situations that do not fit well under the umbrella of one particular strategy or another. In these situations, the writer needs to employ multiple strategies, and we discuss how to choose the best strategies for such an essay and produce a well-organized, successful piece of writing.

When working through these chapters, remember that *options* is an important word in the title of this text. Our aim is always to avoid a formulaic, cookie-cutter approach to writing an essay. When we include a model essay, it is just that—a model, not a blueprint. As we mention elsewhere, if five students earn an *A* on the same writing assignment and you had the opportunity to read all five essays, you would be surprised at how *different* the essays are. If you had access to each student's writing process—prewriting, first draft, revisions, and final draft—you would also see that each student took a very different road to get to the same good outcome. Learn the strategies in the following ten chapters, and make them your own. •

PART

2

STRUCTURES

Dilbert © Scott Adams/Dist. by Universal Feature Syndicate, Inc.

# Writing in Context

You've had a busy afternoon. After applying to Osprey Online Technologies last month, you had your interviews today.

You had a good experience. The preliminary interviews went well, and the next meeting—with Bob, the man who would be your supervisor—went quite well indeed.

Returning home, you make a phone call, as promised, to a friend who wants a report on your big day. When you start telling her about what happened, she interrupts: "No, tell me what the company is *like*. The *place*. The *people*."

Note that the friend doesn't want to hear a story but wants, instead, a "picture" of the experience.

# HOW DOES DESCRIPTION WORK?

As a general strategy, **describing** is used in many forms of writing. Readers use their imagination as they read, and descriptive details help make the subject matter real for them. Visual forms of expression—photography, painting, and film, to name a few—have the advantage of fully engaging one of our senses— sight—but they are still limited. For example, film can appeal to both our eyes and our ears, but three more senses remain: touch, taste, and smell. Good descriptive writing can stimulate the reader's imagination to form sensory responses from all five senses. Frequently, the reader has no choice: many people cannot read an article about the taste of citrus fruits, for example, without having a physical response to the imagined taste. And a passage about a specific food left out of the refrigerator too long will produce a shudder from readers as they imagine the resulting smell.

Description is a powerful strategy, one that allows the writer to exercise a great deal of control over the reader's perceptions. Compare these two sentences:

The boy stood outside the shack.

The small, ragged boy, who looked as though he hadn't bathed for a few days, stood outside the lopsided, unpainted shack.

The first sentence provides a dim picture, a stick-figure outline of the scene. The second sentence indicates dysfunction and despair. Poverty is the obvious problem, but the alert reader will infer that the boy has another, more sinister problem as well: in our culture, poor hygiene is seen as a symptom of abuse, neglect, and/or depression.

Description is also a strategy we use in our daily interactions. No doubt, you frequently describe different kinds of subjects to your friends and family. One category consists of objects and items:

- The outfit you spotted at the mall and are now thinking of buying
- The new sports car from Mongo Euromotors that fills you with consumer lust
- The weird bone that the dog brought into the yard
- The Picasso on loan to the local art museum
- The meal of a lifetime—a five-course extravaganza at your city's finest restaurant

You can also describe places—either natural or constructed:

- The amazing tide swing in the Bay of Fundy
- A large, ornate house that sits in the middle of a group of smaller houses with much more modest designs
- The new sports stadium
- A quiet street lined with camphor trees
- A desert scene at night
- Your dorm during finals week

Taking a slightly different tack, you can describe people: the very old, the very young, those who are striking, those who are extremely unattractive, those who are in any way distinctive.

Obviously, you can use description as a specific strategy within an essay written with a different overall strategy. An essay contrasting the performance styles of two popular singers might describe each singer's physical appearance to help the reader get a fuller picture. An essay narrating a senseless crime in a quiet neighborhood would probably describe the neighborhood prior to telling the shocking story. Used as a strategy—as an option—description brings texture to any type of writing.

However, in some essays your main strategy is to describe something, perhaps simply to entertain your audience or to make a serious point about your subject. Here, you attempt to convey the *essence* of the subject by using sensory details to appeal to your reader's imagination. As much as possible, you should try to evoke all five senses:

- Sight: "The mountain rose, green and verdant, above the white, sandy beach below."
- Hearing: "The quail burst out of the thicket with an explosion of pounding wings."
- Touch: "Weathered by almost a century, the old man's arm felt as if it were covered with elephant skin."
- Taste: "My slice of apple pie tasted the way I expected it to until I noticed a hint of raspberries."
- Smell: "The part of the cave where the bear had nested had a sharp, earthy, almost rank scent."

Not every context will allow you to provide details that appeal to all five senses. However, remember that your purpose is to capture for your audience the essence of the subject you are describing, using as much detail as your writing context allows you.

The descriptive essay comes in two basic forms: objective and subjective. **Objective description** is used in the sciences, in business, and in technology; writers using this approach attempt to describe their subject without including their personal responses. A medical examiner's report on what caused the death of a person found in an alley is an example of objective description. So is the report of a business planner who has been sent to look at a tract of land and determine its suitability for development as a shopping center. When a certain type of machinery is needed for production, a company's engineers will describe the machine *before* it is built, laying out the required physical and dynamic specifications. Note that personal bias is out of place in this context. Instead, the emphasis is on impartiality—on providing a disinterested description.

**Subjective description**, on the other hand, allows the writer to show a personal connection to his or her subject. For example, if you wrote an essay describing your aunt's dog, Rusty—a lovable rogue with a talent for madcap adventures and digging up disgusting objects—you would be writing from your limited experience of this dog. If your aunt had taken on this assignment, however, her response would probably be much different. She's the one who has to deal with this creature day in and day out, and what seems "lovable" to an occasional visitor may well require teeth-gritting forbearance from the caretaker.

Such a difference in response to a subject is normal and to be expected. After all, a subjective description requires a *personal* bias. A subjective description is also different from an objective description in this way: the writer is usually exploring his or her emotions. In this context, "feelings" aren't really physical responses. However, our emotional reaction to a subject helps determine the physical details we choose to describe it. Think of the example of the small boy standing outside the shack (page 136). The first, unadorned description is neutral. The second description implies that the writer feels pity for the young boy and his obviously troubled life. In general, we describe positively those things or people that we personally like; we describe sympathetically those things or people that we pity. The opposite is also true.

Some contexts require both subjective and objective description. In the first reading selection of this chapter, Thomas McGuane's "Roanie" (pages 139–142), the author describes a horse that is both a working animal (requiring objective description) and a personal pet (requiring subjective description). McGuane's context dictated his approach.

Whether you are using an objective or a subjective approach (or a combination of both), you need to work from a **dominant impression**, a focus that controls the structure and details of your descriptive essay. In an objective description, your intellectual evaluation of the qualities of your subject matter will shape your dominant impression; in a subjective description, your feelings toward the person or thing you are describing will govern your approach.

*Consider Your Options*

List various environmental stimuli with which you come into contact every day. Then, referring to one or more of the five senses, describe the way each stimulus in the list affects you.

# READING THE DESCRIPTIVE ESSAY WITH A WRITER'S EYE

The following three essays are largely subjective descriptions. In the first one, Thomas McGuane describes the best horse he ever owned, an animal of quirky genius. In the second, Maxine Hong Kingston gives us her impressions of an old photograph of her mother and father. Finally, the actress Hildegard Knef describes her father and what his death did to her as a young girl. As you read each essay, try to judge the writer's connection with his or her audience. For what audience is each essay written?

Following the essays, the second half of this chapter features strategies for writing the descriptive essay with a reader's eye (pages 152–161). If you decide to write on one of the topics that follow the three essays below, make sure that you have read the strategies section before you begin. Also note that additional writing topics are listed at the end of the chapter (page 166).

# Roanie

## THOMAS MCGUANE

*Thomas McGuane is the author of ten novels, including* Ninety-Two in the Shade, *which was nominated for the 1973 National Book Award;* Panama *(1978);* Nothing But Blue Skies *(1999); and* The Cadence of Grass *(2002). He has also written screenplays, including those for* The Missouri Breaks *(1976) and* Tom Horn *(1980). Increasingly, however, McGuane is becoming well-known for his skills as an essayist, especially after the publication of his 2000 collection* The Longest Silence: A Life in Fishing, *which showcased his sharp wit and elegant style. McGuane lives in Sweet Grass County, Montana.*

*In this essay, from McGuane's collection* Some Horses *(1999), the author describes a rather remarkable horse, one that seems to transcend his species. "Cutting horses" have traditionally been used to separate a chosen cow from a herd. Typically, the cow does not want to leave the herd's safety and will do everything in its power to elude the horse. The cutting horse must be smarter, faster, and more agile than the cow. In the twentieth century, cutting evolved into a sport, with regular competitions and even a hall of fame. "Roanie" describes this world.*

There is a notion that you get only one great  1
horse in a lifetime, a persistent notion that I hope isn't true; because, if that is the case, I've already had mine, in fact still have him though he is an arthritic old man twenty-six years old. His name is Lucky Bottom 79 and he was already a terrific horse when I acquired him over twenty years ago, though for some reason, he wasn't doing much and had a reputation for being a bronc that had probably kept someone else from buying him. He is called Roanie for his red roan coat, a coat that turns almost purple in the summer, and he is not a very pretty horse. In fact, he won an informal contest one year in Hamilton for being the ugliest horse in Montana. He has a slight Roman nose, actually called the "Burt bump" for a trait inherited from his grandsire Burt. As to the length of his head, it's been remarked that he can drink from a fifty-gallon drum and still keep an eye on you. His sire was a good horse called Lucky Star Mac, an Oklahoma Star–bred

horse; and his mother was a racehorse named Miss Glimpse. Roanie is one of those hotheaded horses about which people say, "The only safe place is on his back." He can kick in any direction, has actually stripped the buttons off the front of a man's shirt, and the extreme suspicion that is continuously in his eye doesn't come from nowhere. Roanie was not the sort of horse Buster prefers but he once said to me, "Boy, when he was on, that roan horse was unbelievable!"

Lucky Bottom 79 was trained by a part-  2
Cherokee cowboy named Ed Bottom, who is, any way you look at it, an outstanding horseman who had made an everlasting mark training calf-roping and cutting horses for nearly half a century. Like Buster Welch, Ed is a member of the Cutting Horse Hall of Fame. Yesterday, I tried to catch swaybacked old Roanie in a twenty-foot loafing shed. He went by me like mercury, low, quick, and throwing me such an elegant head fake I'm lucky I didn't fall down.

Ed Bottom lives in Asher, Oklahoma, next  3
door to the Barrow farm, former home of Clyde Barrow. One of Ed's childhood heroes was a family friend, Pretty Boy Floyd, and Ed remembers Pretty Boy coming home from robberies, hiding his shot-up Hudson in a sheep shed, giving all the kids silver dollars, and pitching horseshoes with the grown-ups.

I traveled to Oklahoma to try Roanie and I  4
remember two things distinctly. When I went out to the corral to saddle and work a cow on him, Mrs. Bottom said, "Don't fall off."

Responding to this nicely, I said, "I won't."  5
Mrs. Bottom said, "You won't?"  6
I had some time to think about this as we got  7
Roanie ready. Roanie hadn't seen me before and I have never been around a horse that exuded such

all-consuming distrust of strangers. However, once I was on his back and loping in a circle all was well, with the exception of one small thing: the horse kept his head turned so that he could look back and watch me the whole while.

I cut the first cow on him. The cow stopped, looked, prepared for sudden motion, and Roanie began to sink. I guess you would call it a crouch. But it was level all around and I simply sensed the ground coming up: this horse had a working altitude of about a man's waist and I soon found that he had real speed and the ability to turn right through himself like a dishrag. And he understood cattle. He could mesmerize them or stop them with sheer speed, all at hot-rod roadster height. And as I would learn over the years, either his sense of play or his sense of rightness in the world made him purely at home only when he was working cattle. At such a time, you couldn't spur him or misride him to the wrong spot with the strength of Superman. He knew with certainty where he wanted to be and the door to the suggestion box was nailed shut. Over the years, several outstanding cutting-horse riders have competed on him without success. Evidently, he disliked all their opinions and convictions. I was too ignorant and perhaps intimidated by him to let him do anything but what he wanted to do. That proved to be the right approach. For a few years, I made more money on his back than I did at my actual job. It was a great feeling to know you were probably going to win a cutting before you even unloaded the horse from the trailer.

I bought Roanie on the condition he pass a veterinary exam. We took him to the local vet and after Roanie kicked the X-ray plates all over the building and took a couple of shots at the X-ray machine itself, we decided to forgo the exam and accept instead Ed's statement, "You can't hurt him with an axe handle." The demoralized veterinarian was reduced to inquiring rhetorically, "Why do you people always want to X-ray everything?" Ed gave me two bits made by another Cherokee,

John Israel, identical except for the length of the shanks and beautifully fashioned from salvaged old hay rakes. "Tune him in the long shanks and show him in the short ones." That was the end of the operating instructions. We headed home.

It was early spring on the ranch, snowy and muddy. A friend of mine stopped by to see Roanie and the muck sucked his overshoe off in the corral. He looked at the slush filling the boot as he stood in his stocking foot. "There it is," he said, "ag world." I led Roanie around, then put him in a box stall to protect him from the change of Montana weather and settled in to start building a relationship with him.

Roanie had not always done well in box stalls. At the national futurity for three-year-olds, he had a record-setting run that brought the audience to its feet. Afterward, Ed put him in one of the assigned box stalls. Someone had placed a blanket in the stall that Roanie had never seen before. By the time Roanie spotted it, his friend Ed was back in the bleachers and Roanie felt he had little choice but to kick the door, its latch and hinges, off the box stall and race out in equine hysteria to scatter spectators. Ed was summoned on the loudspeaker and things were soon put right. If there was a big problem, it was lost on Ed, who is the last word in cool-headed. His comment on Roanie's escapade: "I guess he didn't want to be in there."

I didn't know that story at the time I got Roanie home. All I know is that when I went into the box stall with him, he flattened himself against the wall in terror and when I moved, he began to whirl. . . . Sharing a tiny room with an eleven-hundred-and-fifty pound whirling panicked animal is a situation that impresses one with its gravity. I had to do something. The check hadn't cleared yet and I could hardly confine our relationship to watching him through the window. This was not a public aquarium.

The next day, I moved a small school desk into Roanie's stall. Then I went in and sat down and did my work. For the first hour, Roanie seemed to be trying to smear himself into the plank walls. He trembled from head to toe. At the end of the hour, I was still writing and he was getting tired of his exertions. He was standing with his weight equally distributed on all four feet. When I got up to pet him, he flattened himself once more. I found myself, pen in hand, seated at my desk, hunched over a legal pad, making such plaintive cries as, "Roanie, I gotta take a leak!" In three days, he was tired of my writing life, trying to figure out how to get around the desk to the hay. We'd made a start.

We began riding out on the ranch. This he 14 adored: new country. It was always a special pleasure to simply use him as a saddle horse because he was the sort of horse that always seemed to pull you through the country, head stretched forward, ears pricked, drinking up the new space. There is nothing quite like looking over wild land from horseback.

I don't know how Roanie would have done in 15 battle though I think once he'd gotten the idea of what the job was, he would have excelled. His panic attacks, however, would have been dangerous to friend and foe alike. Early in my ownership of him, his feet, accustomed to red Oklahoma dirt, got sore on the rocks where I live. Finally, he went quite lame. It turned out to be merely a stone bruise but a shadow on his X-rays suggested a fractured coffin bone. I sent him immediately to Colorado State University's outstanding equine veterinary center in Fort Collins and called the excellent lameness specialist there. I explained to this specialist that Roanie could be quite unpredictable; to avoid having people getting hurt, I urged caution.

"Mr. McGuane, we are well accustomed to 16 handling horses of all kinds. Owners often give us these sorts of warnings and, while we think it is considerate, we don't worry about it too much." The doctor, a cultivated Australian, took me for a nervous sort.

Within a few days, he called me. His voice was 17 elevated in both pitch and intensity. "Your horse is going to get this university sued back to the stone age! I have had to rescue several of my graduate students from him and I have hung a skull and crossbones on his stall!" They had tranquilized my horse from the sort of range usually considered appropriate for the rhinoceros and managed to examine him enough to conclude that his hoof injury wasn't serious. When his health papers came back with him, a notation read, "Lucky Bottom 79's rectal temperature not taken as he continually endangered human life."

"I'd like a photograph of someone riding this 18 horse," were the doctor's last words to me.

"The only safe place is on his back," I said but 19 I think it fell on deaf ears.

In any case, he was soon sound once again 20 and in glistening physical condition. We worked cattle at home and he was quick and smooth. I decided to take him to a cutting-horse contest in Blackfoot, Idaho, on the weekend. I knew I had a special horse.

The cutting was held in a city park right in the 21 middle of town. It seemed kind of odd not to have a lot of open country around us but the cattle had been, in the words of Chuck Tyson, a great old cow man, "surrounded by cleverness" and things were rather orderly. Roanie had not been to a cutting in a good while and, as I was to learn, he knew the difference between a cow in a contest and a cow anywhere else. As soon as I unloaded him and he heard the bawling cattle and saw the spectators, his blood began to boil. I tried to gallop him down but he just got crazier. I decided to walk him and keep him calm. He gaped around at everything, froze, and shied from paper cups, cigarette wrappers, the light off windshields; children who'd never seen a horse flare its nostrils, snort, and run backward from a gum wrapper gathered around and made my composure worse with their astonished questions. "Hey mister, what's the matter with your horse?" Or, "He's loco, ain't he?" I consoled myself by knowing that as soon as I rode him into the herd, everything would settle down and the eternal cowhorse logic would take over. Boldly, I entered both the open and the non-professional classes.

I had an excellent draw in the open. I hired my herd holders and turn-back man and rode confidently toward the herd. I thought Roanie's walk was uncustomarily jerky but gave it little thought as we turned through the cattle and began to drive out. A pretty baldface heifer slipped up onto the point of the herd and I eased forward, cut her, and put my rein hand down on Roanie's neck. Roanie stood bolt upright, the perfect position, I thought, for him to jump out of his skin. He looked bug-eyed at the cow until she moved and then he reared up on his hind legs, pawing the air like Roy Rogers' Trigger on LSD, and with several huge kangaroo leaps shot past the turn-back horses, blowing snot in two directions, and bolted into the Blackfoot city park, scattering strollers and people of all ages. When I got him stopped, I turned to look back at the cutting-horse contest. All I could see was a wall of blank faces. The judge gave me a zero because he was unaware of a lower number.

I decided that the only way around this was through it and so I did not scratch from the next class; and I was only mildly unnerved by the voices I heard as I rode toward the cattle: "He's not going in there *again,* is he?" In the crowd were some unmitigated gawkers of the kind that swarm to accident scenes. I cut two cows in the course of my run and Roanie laid down a performance that was absolutely faultless. We won the cutting by a serious margin. It seemed to be that we had gotten through something together because I became abruptly more sensitive to the world as he saw it. I used to think that when I led him out of his box stall at a cutting I could tell by the look in his eye if he was going to win it that day. If he seemed to gaze upon the world with easy vigilance, I knew that we would be deep in the money. If the look of incomplete understanding was there, if he fixated on a bucket or a snakelike curve of garden hose, I knew we would have to find some way to cool out before we began, often by a ride around the neighborhood or, if we were at a local Montana cutting, a visit to one of his horse friends at another trailer. In any case, from then on the pressure was on me to cut my cows correctly and to ride him well; in doing such a tremendous job of holding up his end, he gave me much room for error. I tried not to abuse it.

I felt so competitive when I was riding this horse that I went to every last little cutting in the region and got a wonderful education in the geography of the Northern Rockies, so many little towns in which the fairgrounds were the only public gathering place. It's been more than a decade since I rode him in a contest but people still inquire about him everywhere I go. "How's the old roan horse?" they ask, shaking their heads in awe. It's so nice to tell them he's fine, and free, in a big grassy place. Not that I don't sometimes wish it were long ago and I were throwing a saddle up on his powerful withers with the feeling that I could hardly wait for my draw.

*Vocabulary*

The following terms are identified by paragraph number. Make sure that you understand each term's meaning in its context. If you're not sure that you understand a term, look it up in a college-level dictionary.

| | | |
|---|---|---|
| notion (1) | mesmerize (8) | gravity (12) |
| bronc (1) | rhetorically (9) | plaintive (13) |

swaybacked (2)  equine (11)  unmitigated (23)

exuded (7)  escapade (11)  vigilance (23)

## Style and Strategy

1.  Which of the five senses does McGuane evoke in this essay?

2.  What is your dominant impression of McGuane's horse?

3.  Find examples of McGuane's use of the following strategies: narration (see Chapter 6), process analysis (Chapter 8), causal analysis (Chapter 9), definition (Chapter 10), and comparison/contrast (Chapter 12). What does each strategy contribute to the essay as a whole?

## Questions for Critical Thinking and Discussion

1.  Many people who work in farming and ranching do so because they grew up on a farm or a ranch. However, Thomas McGuane *chose* to become a rancher. Thus, what is the significance of the comment of McGuane's friend whose boot is sucked away by the mud: "There it is . . . ag world" (paragraph 10)?

2.  Some observers believe that using animals such as horses and dogs on ranches and farms is acceptable but that using animals in sports such as racing or rodeos is not. What is the difference between the two types of activities? In your opinion, is the competition that McGuane describes a "fair use" of a horse like Roanie? Why or why not?

3.  Someone who answers "yes" to the preceding question might point out that without competitions such as racing and shows, a horse such as Roanie would never have been bred at all—in other words, Roanie owes his very existence to cutting competitions. Is this a valid argument? Why or why not?

## Suggestions for Writing

1.  In 500 to 750 words, discuss the "personality" of a dog, cat, or other pet that has been part of your family. Does the animal exhibit interesting, odd, or distinctive behavior? Does he or she have special skills (for example, a cat who can open closet doors)? Does he or she respond in a unique way to certain kinds of stimuli, such as loud noises or bright lights? What kinds of human behavior cause the animal to react in distinctive ways?

2.  In 500 to 750 words, describe someone you know who, like Roanie, is brilliant at a particular skill or activity but seems to require "special handling" in other areas of life.

## Speaking Assignment

Prepare a presentation in which you argue that cruelty to domestic animals should receive the same punishment under the law as comparable offenses to humans. If this assignment doesn't interest you, prepare a presentation on one of the following:

- Killing animals for food is (or is not) cruel and unnecessary.
- Zoos should be closed.
- Zoos perform valuable services for both people and animals.
- Harvesting fur to make coats and other garments should be prohibited.
- Using animals in medical research should (or should not) be discontinued.

For more help with oral presentations, see Chapter 18.

# Photographs of My Parents

## MAXINE HONG KINGSTON

*Born in Stockton, California, Maxine Hong Kingston grew up in the United States listening to her immigrant parents and relatives talk of their homeland in China. Two of Kingston's books,* The Woman Warrior: Memoirs of a Girlhood Among Ghosts *(1975) and* China Men *(1980), reflect both her own and her parents' and ancestors' diverse experiences.*

*"Photographs of My Parents" shows the world of meaning that a picture can convey—especially if the photo is from another time and place.*

Once in a long while, four times so far for me, my mother brings out the metal tube that holds her medical diploma. On the tube are gold circles crossed with seven red lines each—"joy" ideographs in abstract. There are also little flowers that look like gears for a gold machine. According to the scraps of labels with Chinese and American addresses, stamps, and postmarks, the family airmailed the can from Hong Kong in 1950. It got crushed in the middle, and whoever tried to peel the labels off stopped because the red and gold paint came off too, leaving silver scratches that rust. Somebody tried to pry the end off before discovering that the tube pulls apart. When I open it, the smell of China flies out, a thousand-year-old bat flying heavy-headed out of the Chinese caverns where bats are as white as dust, a smell that comes from long ago, far back in the brain. Crates from Canton, Hong Kong, Singapore, and Taiwan have that smell too, only stronger because they are more recently come from the Chinese.

Inside the can are three scrolls, one inside another. The largest says that in the twenty-third year of the National Republic, the To Keung School of Midwifery, where she has had two years of instruction and Hospital Practice, awards its Diploma to my mother, who has shown through oral and written examination her Proficiency in Midwifery, Pediatrics, Gynecology, "Medecine," "Surgary," Therapeutics, Ophthalmology, Bacteriology, Dermatology, Nursing and Bandage. This document has eight stamps on it: one, the school's English and Chinese names embossed together in a circle; one, as the Chinese enumerate, a stork and a big baby in lavender ink; one, the school's Chinese seal; one, an orangish paper stamp pasted in the border design; one, the red seal of Dr. Wu Pak-liang, M.D., Lyon, Berlin, president and "Ex-assistant étranger à la clinique chirugicale et d'accouchement de l'université de Lyon"; one, the red seal of Dean Woo Yin-kam, M.D.; one, my mother's seal, her chop mark larger than the president's and the dean's; and one, the number 1279 on the back. Dean Woo's signature is followed by "(Hackett)." I read in a history book that Hackett Medical College for Women at Canton was founded in the nineteenth century by European women doctors.

The school seal has been pressed over a photograph of my mother at the age of thirty-seven. The diploma gives her age as twenty-seven. She looks younger than I do, her eyebrows are thicker, her lips fuller. Her naturally curly hair is parted on the left, one wavy wisp tendrilling off to the right. She wears a scholar's white gown, and she is not thinking about her appearance. She stares straight ahead as if she could see me and past me to her grandchildren and grandchildren's grandchildren. She has spacy eyes, as all people recently from Asia have. Her eyes do not focus on the camera. My mother is not smiling; Chinese do not smile for photographs. Their faces command relatives in foreign lands—"Send money"—and posterity forever—"Put food in front of this picture." My mother does not understand Chinese-American snapshots. "What are you laughing at?" she asks.

The second scroll is a long narrow photograph of the graduating class with the school officials seated in front. I picked out my mother immediately. Her face is exactly her own, though forty years younger. She is so familiar, I can only tell whether or not she is pretty or happy or smart by comparing her to the other women. For this formal group picture she straightened her hair with oil to make a chinlength bob like the others'. On the other women, strangers, I can recognize a curled lip, a sidelong glance, pinched shoulders. My mother is not soft; the girl with the small nose and dimpled underlip is soft. My mother is not humorous, not like the girl at the end who lifts her mocking chin to pose like Girl Graduate. My mother does not have smiling eyes; the old woman teacher (Dean Woo?) in front crinkles happily, and the one faculty member in the western suit smiles westernly. Most of the graduates are girls whose faces have not yet formed; my mother's face will not change anymore, except to age. She is intelligent, alert, pretty. I can't tell if she's happy.

The graduates seem to have been looking elsewhere when they pinned the rose, zinnia, or chrysanthemum on their precise black dresses. One thin girl wears hers in the middle of her chest. A few have a flower over a left or right nipple. My mother put hers, a chrysanthemum, below her left breast. Chinese dresses at that time were dartless, cut as if women did not have breasts; these young doctors, unaccustomed to decorations, may have seen their chests as black expanses with no reference points for flowers. Perhaps they couldn't shorten that far gaze that lasts only a few years after a Chinese emigrates. In this picture too my mother's eyes are big with what they held— reaches of oceans beyond China, land beyond oceans. Most emigrants learn the barbarians' directness—how to gather themselves and stare rudely into talking faces as if trying to catch lies. In America my mother has eyes as strong as boulders, never once skittering off a face, but she has not learned to place decorations and phonograph needles, nor has she stopped seeing land on the other side of the oceans. Now her eyes include the relatives in China, as they once included my father smiling and smiling in his many western outfits, a different one for each photograph that he sent from America.

He and his friends took pictures of one another in bathing suits at Coney Island beach, the salt wind from the Atlantic blowing their hair. He's the one in the middle with his arms about the necks of his buddies. They pose in the cockpit of a biplane, on a motorcycle, and on a lawn beside the "Keep Off the Grass" sign. They are always laughing. My father, white shirt sleeves rolled up, smiles in front of a wall of clean laundry. In the spring he wears a new straw hat, cocked at a Fred Astaire angle. He steps out, dancing down the stairs, one foot forward, one back, a hand in his pocket. He wrote to her about the American custom of stomping on straw hats come fall. "If you want to save your hat for next year," he said, "you have to put it away early, or else when you're riding the subway or walking along Fifth Avenue, any stranger can snatch it off your head and put his foot through it. That's the way they celebrate the change of seasons here." In the winter he wears a gray felt hat with his gray overcoat. He is sitting on a rock in Central Park. In one snapshot he is not smiling; someone took it when he was studying, blurred in the glare of the desk lamp.

There are no snapshots of my mother. In two small portraits, however, there is a black thumbprint on her forehead, as if someone had inked in bangs, as if someone had marked her.

"Mother, did bangs come into fashion after you had the picture taken?" One time she said yes. Another time when I asked, "Why do you have fingerprints on your forehead?" she said, "Your First Uncle did that." I disliked the unsureness in her voice.

The last scroll has columns of Chinese words. The only English is "Department of Health, Canton," imprinted on my mother's face, the same photograph as on the diploma. I keep looking to see whether she was afraid. Year after year my father did not come home or send for her. Their two children had been dead for ten years. If he did not return soon, there would be no more children. ("They were three and two years old, a boy and a girl. They could talk already.") My father did send money regularly, though, and she had nobody to spend it on but herself. She bought good clothes and shoes. Then she decided to use the money for becoming a doctor. She did not leave for Canton immediately after the children died. In China there was time to complete feelings. As my father had done, my mother left the village by ship. There was a sea bird painted on the ship to protect it against shipwreck and winds. She was in luck. The following ship was boarded by river pirates, who kidnapped every passenger, even old ladies. "Sixty dollars for an old lady" was what the bandits used to say. "I sailed alone," she says, "to the capital of the entire province." She took a brown leather suitcase and a seabag stuffed with two quilts.

*Vocabulary*

The following terms are identified by paragraph number. Make sure that you understand each term's meaning in its context. If you're not sure that you understand a term, look it up in a college-level dictionary.

| | | |
|---|---|---|
| ideographs (1) | posterity (3) | emigrants (5) |
| abstract (1) | expanses (5) | province (9) |
| enumerate (2) | emigrates (5) | |

*Style and Strategy*

1. Kingston first describes the photographs of her mother, then the ones of her father. In your opinion, why did she choose this order?

2. Reread Kingston's description of her mother's photographs. How much of her discussion is based on pure observation, and how much is her interpretation of what she observes?

3. The last paragraph tells of the death of the couple's first two children. Were you surprised by this development? Why do you think Kingston saved this information for the end of her essay?

## Questions for Critical Thinking and Discussion

1. In our digital era, photographs can be scanned, altered, and output again. In addition, many good-looking people don't photograph well, whereas many ordinary-looking people are quite photogenic. In terms of "capturing a moment," how reliable is photography?

2. Many people in the United States spend dozens of hours each year chronicling their family or documenting their travels. Why is photography so popular?

## Suggestions for Writing

1. Kingston discusses many of the challenges that her mother had to overcome as a young woman. In an essay of 500 to 750 words, discuss the obstacles or problems that a relative of yours—perhaps a parent or grandparent—had to face when he or she was about your age. How did your subject overcome these obstacles or face these problems? Does the way in which he or she responded reveal something about his or her character? If possible, interview your subject or someone who has known your subject. If appropriate, complete library or Internet research to learn more about the kinds of health, financial, social, or other problems that your subject might have faced.

2. Look through a photograph album or a series of photographs of a particular person in your family, perhaps someone you have never met or someone who died before you were born. What does each of these tell you about his or her character and lifestyle? Write down your impressions. Then, if possible, interview another family member who knew your subject. Put all of this information into a 500- to 750-word essay that describes this person. If needed, complete library or Internet research to learn more about the times or places in which this individual lived.

## Speaking Assignment

Prepare a presentation in which you use old photographs of a close relative to explain the challenges and opportunities that he or she faced during the time(s) in his or her life that the photographs were taken. (See Chapter 18 for more help with oral presentations.)

# *From* The Gift Horse

## HILDEGARD KNEF

**Translated by David Anthony Palastanga**

*Born in Germany, Hildegard Knef (1925–2002) survived her father's early death, the Nazi regime, and cancer to become an international film star. Late in her career she published two highly regarded memoirs,* The Gift Horse *(1970) and* The Verdict

*(1975). These fascinating accounts of Knef's life clearly transcend the typical movie star "autobiography."*

*In this selection (Chapter 4 of* The Gift Horse*), Knef paints a portrait of herself as a very conflicted and thoroughly unpromising young girl.*

I, Hildegard Frieda Albertina, had given my mother, Frieda Auguste, very little joy. There were the constant, endless, countless, family-disrupting illnesses, streams of drops and medicines. "Hilde is always ill," they said. There was my fear when she was out, my fear when she was there, fear that she might go out again. There was the waiting around hallway doors, fear of darkness, fear of being alone, of forgetfulness. There were swollen eyes and sties, wobbly polio legs, a broken collarbone that wouldn't mend, rheumatism that kept me and her awake all night. One nose, broken; one jaw, operated on; one foot, cut open with a razor blade because Mother was at the movies and still not home at eleven. There was anemia and there were blood tests, ghostly pale face, shadows under the eyes, and there was jolly sympathy from the neighbors. And if the flood of horror was once stemmed for a short while and I was allowed to visit her, perhaps, one afternoon at Siemens in the big room where she typed, where forty typewriters all chattered simultaneously, where she typed until the chain of chocolate, tobacco, shoemaker shops began—then I promptly fell down. Fell on the stairs, got bumps on my forehead and other places, brought disgrace, snot, and pain where proud presentation had been wished for, expected.

"It really is a trial with that child," she would sometimes say, when all hope forsook her. And the grand ball, the only one—I spoiled that for her too. Ruined it. It was at the Imperial Ballroom in Lichterfelde. Mother and Stepfather's first ball together—Mother in long gown, Stepfather in navy blue, scrubbed and eager, already in the taxi. And the torchlight procession for the children. Chinese lanterns in the twilight, orchestra plays something by Lincke, parents clap, beam, are proud, puffed up. I stand there, look at torches, the procession does a sudden turn, I lose sight of Mother—panic. A man comes, lifts me onto the stage, light, fanfare.

"We have found a stray child. Now what's your name?" Chuckles and sniggers from below.

"What's your name?" Louder, sharper. Don't know. Panic. "Now, now," he says beside me, above me, "it's not as bad as all that."

Mother pulls me down. "Dear God," she says, "dear God, can't you take care of yourself for two minutes?"

The children poke each other in the ribs, laugh. The adults exchange glances, smile. Stepfather drinks a quick beer, too quick, starts coughing, goes his asthma color, lilac at its most lilac. We go. No one says a word. Go home on the train, in long festive black.

And I wasn't pretty either, God knows, nobody but Grandfather thought I was pretty. The saleswoman in the bookshop next door once said: "You get more like your Aunt Hulda every day," and although I loved Aunt Hulda dearly, I didn't want to look like her. And Mother said to Stepfather, one night as it was getting dark: "A pity Hilde isn't prettier." And Stepfather, cranky, wanting to sleep, murmured: "Yes, but she looks quite interesting."

That was a blow. A worse one fell the day Lieselotte wanted to go to the movies with her friend. She took me along because her mother had said, "You're not to go alone." Her friend brought his friend, pimply, damp hands, rubbing his cheeks and rolling his eyes, sighing: "This shaving drives me crazy." When the film was over, the three of them said: "Auf Wiederseh'n." Left me standing at the cinema in the black-out, said Wiederseh'n and went.

And Mother was beautiful, very beautiful. She had the longest, loveliest legs in Schöneberg, the greenest eyes, was healthy, slender, tough, powerful, fearless. A little disappointed perhaps, disappointed because she had such a lovely clear high voice, but had not, after all, become a singer. There wasn't enough money for the training, and to go around begging for a scholarship—no, one was too proud for that, if it came to that, one would rather not fulfill one's most cherished dreams. She had been brought up on Prussian discipline and when she was twenty-three my grandmother asked her whether she still had a right to wear that white summer dress. She didn't. She had met my father. It was love at first sight and I believe my mother still loved him when she died thirty-five years after him.

His name was Hans Theodor, he was big, wild, 9 restless, red-haired, he charged through life and professions like an express train through stations, won races swimming against the current in the Rhine, football trophies, amateur boxing contests.

He was desperate.    10

I would like to have known him.    11

At seventeen he was awarded the Iron Cross 12 second class, at seventeen and a half the Iron Cross first class. He had volunteered, was at the Somme, at Verdun, and was once in a brothel. And when the war was over, the revolutionaries tore off his ribbons and epaulettes at the railway station in Berlin. What remained was the illness. "Cured," the doctor said a year later, "got away with it this time."

He had trouble adjusting himself to a Ger- 13 many reeking of cabbages and turnips, sought war, sought a fight—until he found his Frieda Auguste. They got married. Packed, unpacked, moved, moved again; it was a marriage on the move. He had success and a chauffeur-driven car, lost both, landed in Ulm. Then came the biggest, once-in-a-lifetime, puts-everything-else-in-the-shade chance: Turkey, own factory, independence. I put an end to that. I made my entrance in December. My father ran through the apartment shouting: "Is her blood all right, Doctor, is her blood in order too?" It was. (father morphine)

A month later Mother found the syringe. In 14 the hall was a high cupboard, in the high cupboard a carton, in the carton the syringe. What's the syringe for? she asked.

The illness I had once has come back. I'm hav- 15 ing treatment, giving myself the injections, they say it will go away again.

It didn't. He got fever, he got angina. 16 Whether the one had anything to do with the other the doctors didn't know. He was taken to the hospital. Mother too—she had appendicitis. He lay on the second floor, she on the first. Ten days later he screamed for his Auguste, the priest came. Taking him gently by the hand, he spoke: My son, he said, we all have to die one day, it is God's will. We have to find the way to *Him, He* is good, *He* is great. *He,* in his mercy, will take care of you, let us pray.

Hans Theodor stood up, took the comforting 17 priest by the throat and throttled him until he turned purple, screamed and screamed: I am twenty-eight I have a wife and a child of six months it's not true it isn't *His* will can't be *His* will you're lying. . . . Then he fell over the unconscious priest and died.

My mother was informed four hours later; 18 they had simply forgotten about her.

She took the urn and a hammock, strung me 19 up between two luggage racks, and traveled back to Berlin and her parents. There was no money left, she had to work in offices again, as she had done before she was married. Grandmother and I went regularly to the Schöneberg cemetery and she said, "If we water the grave well enough, perhaps Father will grow again, we must be patient and wait until spring," but in spring the cemetery and the grave looked the same as ever, Father had not grown again and I was disappointed and cried all the way home.

When in thirty-three the Nazis took over 20 Berlin with parades and uproar and children waving little flags and squealing Heil Hitler, my mother said: "A blessing that he's not alive, a blessing that he's not alive." He had been a Social Democrat, and despite his many professions, had even spoken in the Reichstag* once; but she wasn't thinking of this so much as his inability to avoid a row, to take anything lying down; stupidity and fanaticism threw him into a rage, besides which he'd never been averse to a good fight.

---

*Reichstag: German legislature.

My stepfather went about things in a more prudent manner. He had a shop together with a Herr Gold, and when the Nazis advised him to join the party and get rid of Herr Gold, he asked simply and quietly how much it might cost not to become a party member as he had asthma and would not be able to take part in the sporting activities of the community. They said uncertainly that they would leave this up to him, so he pulled out his wallet and cordially placed a one-mark piece on the table. He was looking for a new shop the next day.

He didn't like hanging out the flag either and was currently being warned by the Blockleiter. Finally he bought one, about the size of a child's handkerchief, and was warned again. The Blockleiter said severely that the flag must be relative in size to the shop window. So Stepfather bought one relative in size to the shop window, but it hung down onto the pavement and people got tangled up in it; with a really good gust of wind it would envelope whole families. The Blockleiter came again and demanded something shorter, so Stepfather rolled it up around the pole so that the black swastika in the white circle disappeared and we now had a flag of exactly the requisite dimensions, but red—which at that time was not at all fashionable. Several inquisitive people, who probably thought that they'd misunderstood the latest news bulletins, gathered in front of the shop and asked excitedly what the new flag meant. The purple-faced Blockleiter steamed up and put an end to the disorder with a threatening: "If one more incident comes to my notice . . ." and then left Stepfather's haven of quiet mirth without reporting him.

I always carried with me a small photo of my father; he looked sad and angry with his deep-set, somewhat slanting eyes, his square chin and soft mouth. I always looked at him when I had troubles, or when I was especially happy about something. My stepfather was jealous of my quiet photo love affair, Mother pacified him with: "But she's only a child." As I got bigger, she often looked at me in astonishment and said: "You laugh just like your father—he always bellowed like that too and laughed till the tears rolled down his face." I tried to tame my wild laughter, but sometimes I forgot and then Mother looked startled, grew pale, went out.

## Vocabulary

The following terms are identified by paragraph number. Make sure that you understand each term's meaning in its context. If you're not sure that you understand a term, look it up in a college-level dictionary.

| | | |
|---|---|---|
| polio (1) | reeking (13) | cordially (21) |
| rheumatism (1) | syringe (14) | envelope (22) |
| anemia (1) | throttle (17) | requisite (22) |
| forsake (2) | urn (19) | inquisitive (22) |
| procession (2) | fanaticism (20) | mirth (22) |
| fanfare (2) | averse (20) | bellow (23) |
| epaulettes (12) | prudent (21) | |

## Style and Strategy

1. Descriptive essays need to evoke the senses. How well does Knef accomplish this? To which senses does she appeal the most? Does she neglect to evoke any of the five senses?

2. Find the two most *emphatic* sentences in this essay. How does Knef use these as part of her description?

3. Knef uses the internal strategy of comparison/contrast (see Chapter 12) several times during this essay. Find these instances, and analyze why Knef uses this strategy.

4. What is the tone of this essay? How does Knef achieve this tone, and how does she use it to make her point?

## Questions for Critical Thinking and Discussion

1. In your childhood, did you have to adjust to the presence of a new stepparent? If so, how were you affected?

2. As a person ages, does the loss of a close relative ever get any easier to bear?

3. Are you the same person you were as a child? If not, how have you changed, and what caused you to change?

## Suggestions for Writing

1. Write a 500- to 750-word essay in which you describe yourself at a time in your life when you felt supremely awkward and out of place.

2. In a 500- to 750-word essay, describe your most notable or interesting relative.

3. Knef writes that her father "charged through life . . . like an express train. . . ." Do you know someone who lives his or her life in a similar way? If so, relate events from his or her life that might prove your point. On the other hand, you might want to write about someone like Knef's stepfather, who "went about things in a more prudent manner." In either case, write an essay of between 500 and 750 words, and fill it with the kinds of details that will support your assessment of your subject.

4. Write an essay in which you describe someone whose personality was profoundly affected by a momentous occurrence. The event might have been quite personal, such as losing a parent when this individual was only a child. Then again, his or her character might have been influenced by a more universal phenomenon such as a war or an economic depression. If need be, do library or Internet research to learn more about the kinds of psychological effects your subject might have suffered or about the difficult years that he or she had to live through.

## Speaking Assignment

Prepare a presentation that informs your audience of a problem you faced as a child. Explain what caused the problem, its serious effects, and, if appropriate, how it was resolved. Also consider discussing the lasting effects it had on your life. (For more help with oral presentations, see Chapter 18.)

# WRITING THE DESCRIPTIVE ESSAY WITH A READER'S EYE

When you write, you are striving to produce a document that successfully meets your goals (your purpose) while satisfying your reader's needs. Think like a reader as you write. For example, if a passage seems unclear to you or lacks sufficient details, your reader will undoubtedly also sense this flaw. Externalize your effort by trying to foresee how what you write will be perceived by your audience. The following advice will help you think like your reader as you consider your assignment and then prewrite, draft, revise, and edit your descriptive essay.

## Issues to Keep in Mind

Some students find that a descriptive essay is relatively easy to write; others struggle with this type of essay. Here are four issues for you to consider as you work on your essay:

1. Audience and language level
2. The tendency to write a narrative essay instead of a description
3. The question of objective approach versus subjective approach
4. Choosing an effective structure for description

### Audience and Language Level

Depending on the topic that you choose and the focus of your assignment, you will need to think hard about your essay's effect on the person or persons who will read it. For example, if you are writing a straightforward, objective description of an orange for your writing class (it sounds like an easy task, but it's not—try it), considering your audience should be fairly easy. You are trying to find clear, specific language to draw a "word picture" of this common fruit. You can probably think of words that both you and your reader will understand; the challenge will be to find a way to engage your reader's imagination.

But suppose that you have been assigned to write about your most treasured possession. In your case, it would be your retooled 1971 Plymouth Roadrunner with hemispheric carburetion and all the "improvements" that you have been able to add to it. The danger here is that you might lapse into technological shorthand and **jargon**—the specialized language that is acceptable if your audience is composed of fellow Roadrunner fans but that is strange and even unintelligible to people who don't share that interest. Failure to define or clarify terms that readers are not likely to know—in general, failure to consider your reader—may well result in a negative reception for your essay. Unfortunately, some writers see writing in the language of a specialized field as a form of showing off. However, most readers hate a show-off.

For a general audience, then, you should avoid jargon. But even when you are writing for a general audience, you may find it necessary to use technical language; just make sure that you define an unfamiliar term the first time you use it, as in the following example:

> The ancient skeleton had ossified (hardened until brittle).

Thereafter, you are free to use *ossified* whenever it is appropriate.

Often, descriptions are too bland rather than too technical. When describing a common object or scene, a writer may fail to realize that his or her description adds little to the reader's understanding, as in this example:

> The beach had white sand leading down to the water.

The reader's response to such a sentence is likely to be something like "Noted." This description is what most readers will picture when they see the word *beach*. However, you can find ways around this problem. Note the following revision:

> The beach was like a postcard, with gleaming white sand leading to azure water that broke in a gentle surf.

Descriptive writing is a natural context for **figurative language**, especially **similes** such as the one in the sentence above (see pages 121–122 in Chapter 4 for more on figurative language). Frequently, writers will describe something by comparing it to another, more familiar object:

> This variety of orange has a brownish tint, the same color as a regulation basketball.
>
> The tiny house on the slope of the mountain looked like a person hanging on to the edge of a cliff.
>
> The indigo snake's skin feels like an expensive glove.
>
> The old firefighter had a voice like a foghorn: loud, insistent, and monotonous.

However, remember to avoid **clichés**, which are overused figures of speech (for example, "old as the hills"). As noted in Chapter 4, if you use an expression fairly frequently, it's probably not going to be fresh for your readers.

### Description and Narration

Many descriptive essays concentrate on sensory details and emotional responses. Maxine Hong Kingston's "Photographs of My Parents" (pages 144–146) is a good example of this type. However, in many descriptive essays, description is embedded in a narrative structure. **Narrative** (see Chapter 6) is a powerful tool for communicating our ideas about people and places: our first impulse is always to tell a story—to recount events—when we are asked to explain ourselves or something outside ourselves. And many descriptive essays use brief narratives, or *anecdotes,* to good effect. In this chapter, Thomas McGuane's "Roanie" (pages 139–142) includes a good deal of narration. However, note that the anecdotes McGuane loosely groups together are not the dominant feature in the essay; instead, he concentrates on sensory descriptions that help readers see what makes his horse unique, and these sensory details are what readers will most likely remember.

When you are writing a descriptive essay, you can use anecdotes to help make your subject come to life for your readers, and you can even use a narrative structure to arrange your details. However, make sure that if the assignment calls for a description, you are not just writing a narrative with some description added here and there.

### Objective Description Versus Subjective Description

Although we have discussed *objective* and *subjective* description as two separate concepts, rarely, if ever, can an essay be described as purely objective or purely subjective. Instead, essays tend to lean in one direction or the other, being *primarily* objective or *primarily* subjective.

You should determine whether your essay will be primarily objective or subjective either before or during the prewriting stage. Often, this decision is made for you—your instructor might specifically request an objective approach or a subjective approach as part of the assignment. In general, though, the subject matter and your purpose for writing will help determine your response. If you are asked to describe your favorite vacation location in order to entertain your readers, then a subjective response is obviously appropriate. On the other hand, if you are asked to describe a car, a basketball, or a hand tool in order to inform your readers, then an objective response is clearly indicated.

However, problems can occur when the writer suddenly shifts gears. A writer should not suddenly switch from impartial, unbiased description to an overtly personal or subjective approach; similarly, a subjective description that suddenly becomes dry and objective will seem strange. In either case, the essay will have lost its **unity.**

### Structuring Your Description

How you present your description to your reader will affect its impact. If your description jumps from detail to detail without a logical or coherent plan, the essay will be disjointed and the reader will be confused and unsure of the dominant impression you are trying to convey. Note how the following paragraph proceeds without plan or logic:

> The old woman sat across the table from me. Her eyes were dark and very small, almost beady, and they nervously flitted from left to right. Her clothing was old, a faded windbreaker worn over a man's shirt. Her hair was almost white and flew out of control away from her head. The skin on the woman's hands was very thin, with freck-

les and liver spots covering her knuckles. The wrinkles in her brow and cheeks showed the effects of too much worry, a life spent in anxiety over what would happen next.

This passage is in many ways competent, with a number of well-chosen, specific details, but it suffers because of its poor structure. The writer moves haphazardly through the woman's eyes, clothes, hair, hands, and face without establishing a logical pattern. Unless there is a good—and apparent—reason for taking such a scattered approach, the writer is asking the reader to make connections that would not have been necessary if the writer had done a better job of organizing and planning. The revised paragraph paints a clearer picture because it is logically structured. The writer first describes the woman's clothes and hands, then focuses on her face:

The old woman sat across the table from me. Her clothing was old, a faded windbreaker worn over a man's shirt. The skin on the woman's hands was very thin, with freckles and liver spots covering her knuckles. Her hair was almost white and flew out of control away from her head. Her eyes were dark and very small, almost beady, and they nervously flitted from left to right. The wrinkles in her brow and cheeks showed the effects of too much worry, a life spent in anxiety over what would happen next.

The following two patterns are commonly used options for descriptive essays. Both patterns are *logical* and *natural* ways of arranging descriptive details:

1. **Outside (fringes) to inside (nucleus).** This approach works well if the most important feature that you are describing is at the center of an area:

The large room was mainly empty, with only a few papers next to several computer terminals and artists' tables. As I moved closer to the center of the room, however, evidence of hard work began to appear: stacks of yellowing pages, drawings, artists' tools. Then I came upon a blizzard of activity: two graphic artists, one at a computer and the other at her inclined table, talked feverishly as cigarette smoke swirled around them and coffee fumes filled the air. The hubbub was intense; these two nervous people faced a ten o'clock deadline, and time was running out.

Note that you can reverse this pattern for ironic effect:

> The two nervous graphic artists faced a ten o'clock deadline, and time was running out. One sat at a computer, the other at her inclined table. Both were talking feverishly as cigarette smoke and coffee fumes filled the air. But the two occupied only the center of a large room, and as I walked away, I noticed the vestiges of past projects at several computer terminals and artists' tables. The rest of the room was empty.

2. **Left to right, right to left, top to bottom, bottom to top.** In this approach, the writer cues the reader to the pattern by using **transitions of location** (see also page 73 in Chapter 3). These words and terms "show" your reader where one item is located relative to another, as in the following example:

> The used-car lot had ten rows of about fifteen cars apiece. The row **nearest** to the highway had bright, shiny models with high prices. Obviously, these were the most desirable cars with the highest potential for profit. In the **next row back,** the cars were a bit less desirable. But when you walked four or five rows deeper into the lot, the segregation became even more pronounced: cars with weird, rough paint jobs, dents, and hopeful window signs (Air works great!). The **farthest** row from the highway held the dregs, cars whose bright and shiny days were long past. These cars were **distanced** from most customers and would attract only those driving similar eyesores.

Remember to build your description with your audience in mind. You are trying to *help* your reader, who should be able to perceive the organization you are using and comfortably follow your progress through the arrangement of your details and your use of transitions.

## Choosing a Topic

Your instructor may assign you a specific topic for your description: an item or object, a place or building on campus, a person you know well, and so on. Alternatively, your instructor may allow you to choose a specific topic from some general categories or from the suggestions for writing that follow the readings in this chapter. If you are allowed to choose your own topic, you have two factors to consider: the "size" of your topic and its level of difficulty.

1. If you choose a topic that is too broad, you will find yourself trying to describe something too large to fit into a standard essay. If you tried to describe your college's campus in 600 to 700 words, for example, your essay would need to be very general in order to cover all of the campus's features. Remember that good description captures *specific* sensory details. You might be able to provide specific details for one of the campus's buildings in an essay of this size, but then you would have even less room to describe the rest of the campus.

   On the other hand, if you choose a very limited topic, you may not have enough subject matter to work with. Suppose you decide to describe an ornate hairbrush that has been handed down through your family for two centuries. You may find yourself working very hard to "fill" your essay. This topic is also so personal that it may not result in an essay that interests your audience. Although highly personal topics can be the source of excellent essays, when you describe something that is both very limited and extremely personal, you run the risk of developing a "private" essay that does not engage its intended audience. Lacking a personal connection to the hairbrush, the reader might very well think, "So what?"

2. You also need to consider your topic's degree of difficulty. Although you don't necessarily need to choose the most difficult topic from a list of possibilities—this is not mountain climbing, after all—you should keep in mind the need for a certain "perceived level of difficulty" in your writing. Have you ever watched high divers in competition, perhaps in the Olympics? Each dive is first judged by its level of difficulty. Potentially, a diver can earn a higher score by attempting a more difficult combination. Instructors often use similar—though usually unstated—criteria when judging essays. If you choose the easiest possible subject to describe—a treasured object with which you are completely familiar—it is likely that your essay will be somewhat limited. Push yourself a bit—try to go beyond the easy or the expected. Your instructor will notice your effort, and you will grow as a writer by taking on more difficult tasks.

## Prewriting

Chapter 2 presents a variety of prewriting strategies to choose from. Many writers find that the less formal strategies work best when they are generating ideas for a descriptive essay. For example, clustering and brainstorming are very useful for generating sensory details. (See pages 30–35 for help with these two strategies.) Remember, when you are prewriting, more is better. Having more details than you can possibly use is preferable to straining for details as you write your initial draft. Write down everything you can think of about your subject.

As you prewrite, you can also start to make some important decisions about your essay. First, if you are not sure whether a subjective approach or an objective approach is appropriate, the details you generate while you are prewriting may help you decide. Second, as you come up with ideas and details, you will probably get a sense of the dominant impression that you wish to convey to the reader and begin to develop your working thesis. Third, once you have your raw materials down on paper or on a computer screen, you should be able to plan your method of organization.

## Organizing

Once you have generated a sufficient number of ideas and developed your working thesis, the best way for you to organize this raw material is to arrange it into an outline. (Chapter 2 covers informal, sentence, and formal outlines.) As you develop an outline of your draft, make sure that you consider the most effective order for your body paragraphs.

## Drafting

To illustrate an approach to writing the descriptive essay, we have included an essay ("Frozen Moment") written in response to the photograph shown on page 159. Note that the student's response is subjective; the people in the picture are strangers to her, and sometimes she relies on both her impressions and logical conjecture.

### The Introduction

The introductory paragraph or paragraphs provide the context and background that the reader needs in order to make sense of the essay. Student writers often tend to treat the introduction as a formality, writing only a few sentences. However, a good descriptive essay needs a strong introduction that will draw readers in. Remember the guideline from Chapter 2: the fact that the introduction comes first does not mean that you have to write it first. Rather than agonizing over the first paragraph, you can come back to this section of your essay after you've completed the body.

Note how the first paragraph of our sample essay sets up the rest of the writer's response to the photograph:

Frozen Moment

Although it was taken over 50 years ago, Kathryn Abbe's photograph *Lisa Fonssagrives-Penn and Her Son, Tom* seems surprisingly modern. Here we see an older, aristocratic mother with her "trophy" son. In many ways this photo seems staged, but I have to believe it is not. **These are clearly people who are born to dominate, and the woman's haughtiness must be seen as sincere, not staged.**

● *Consider Your Options*

Often, it's a good idea to avoid starting your description in your introduction. Instead, use the introduction for context and background.

The writer's thesis appears at the end of the paragraph. The woman in the picture clearly believes that she is important, and this dominant impression will shape the rest of the student writer's response essay.

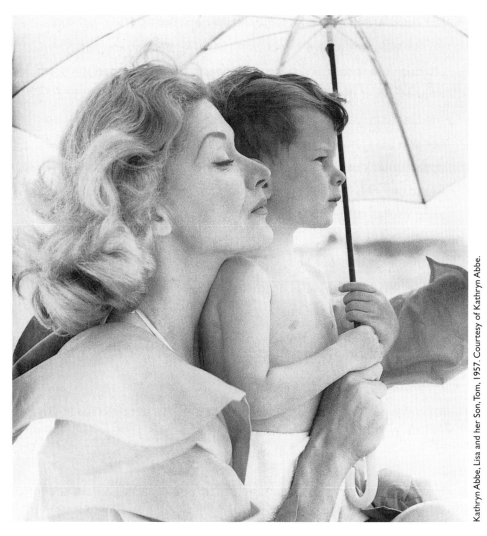

Kathryn Abbe, Lisa and her Son, Tom, 1957. Courtesy of Kathryn Abbe.

## The Body

In a descriptive essay, the **body**—or **development**—paragraphs should support the dominant impression with significant sensory details. In this case, the writer is limited to visual clues; in many contexts, however, all of the senses will be evoked.

For her response essay on the photograph, the student writer decided to describe the woman first, then the son. Note in the next two paragraphs how the topic sentences indicate this pattern without stating it overtly:

> The woman in the picture is clearly from the upper class. First,
>
> there is her name, Lisa Fonssagrives-Penn. At that time, ordinary
>
> people didn't have hyphenated names; in fact, it seems like the
>
> name of a character in a literary farce. Second, her clothes indicate

her class. Although she is clearly in a recreational setting, her sundress has almost a cowl effect as it rises over her bathing suit. Third, although the setting is apparently a beach, the mother and son seem to be alone. If the woman is at the beach, then she is probably using the umbrella/parasol to avoid the direct sunlight, which could harm her skin tone. Also, a beach setting would explain the woman's apparent lack of makeup, which makes her look older than she would probably like. She is about 40 but looks a bit older here: a regal woman holding her prize, her son.

The boy's face lacks the extreme definition that characterizes his mother's face, but he is still clearly an aristocrat in the making. The button nose sets off a handsome profile, much more formal than you would normally see in a boy who is only two to three years old. Even at that young age, he does not turn to Mother but looks *with* her: to sea, to his limitless future. The world *should* be his, if this photograph tells us anything at all.

Carefully constructed topic sentences such as the ones in these paragraphs give both you and your reader a focus for each body paragraph and keep the essay on track.

### The Conclusion

Students frequently dread writing the conclusion even more than the introduction. For one thing, they are often tired at this point, having expended a great deal of mental energy on developing the draft. Second, many students don't see the necessity for a conclusion and resist putting too much effort into it. However, keep in mind that your conclusion allows you to bring the points you have made throughout your essay together and emphasize them. It's your chance to leave your reader with a strong final impression. The conclusion is *not* a place to (a) summarize your essay or (b) bring up new ideas that lead off in startling directions. However, note that the conclusion may include *evaluative* statements, as the sample descriptive essay does:

Lisa Fonssagrives-Penn and her son present an image of pride, almost arrogance. The future (as well as the present) belongs to people such as these two, but seeing these shining specimens also reminds viewers of the aging process and the inevitability of decay. The woman will grow old and die, and her son will go through the

• *Consider Your Options*

Consider description as a way to conclude any type of writing. For example, describing the mangled wreck of a car might be an effective way to end an essay arguing for stiffer penalties for drunk driving.

same heartbreaks and tragedies that happen to all of us. Yet for one frozen moment, these bluebloods dominate the camera's eye.

## EXERCISE 5.1

Write a sentence outline of "Frozen Moment." (For help with sentence outlines, see Chapter 2, pages 41–42.) What does the outline reveal about the essay's organization? Would a different organization work better? Why?

### Revising Your Draft

After you have completed a draft of your descriptive essay, your next step is to revise it, using your own analysis and comments from classmates or friends. During peer review, answer the questions below about the draft you are reviewing, whether it is yours or another student's.

After reviewing for content, you need to go over your peer reviewers' responses to your essay and then revise for unity, coherence, language level, and tone (see Chapter 4). When you have revised your draft and are basically satisfied with it, read your draft for grammatical and mechanical errors. Concentrate on finding and correcting major sentence errors (fragment, comma splice, fused sentence), errors in pronoun agreement and subject-verb agreement, and spelling.

Once you have made your corrections, *read your essay one more time* to catch any errors made during revision and find errors missed during your earlier reviews.

**CATALYST 2.0**

**MORE OPTIONS ONLINE**
For more help with the step-by-step development of the descriptive essay, go to **www.mhhe.com/ writingtoday.**

**CATALYST 2.0**

**MORE OPTIONS ONLINE**
For more help with revision, go to **www.mhhe.com/ writingtoday.**

## Questions for Reviewing a Descriptive Essay

1. Does this essay have an introduction that engages the reader and sufficiently explains the situation? How could it be improved?

2. What is the thesis statement? In what ways, if any, could it be strengthened?

3. Does the description create a complete picture of the subject? Has the writer fulfilled his or her purpose for writing the essay?

4. Is the pattern of organization effective? Would another pattern work better?

5. Are the topic sentences clear and properly located? Where is a more effective topic sentence needed?

6. Are the body paragraphs fully developed? Where are additional details, or more specific details, needed?

7. Does the writer use transitions to guide the reader? Where are transitional words or sentences needed?

8. Does the essay have an effective conclusion? How could it be improved?

## Student Essay

The following essay is Jennifer Janisz's response to an assignment that asked for a descriptive essay. The final draft is presented first. Then Jennifer's first draft is presented, with her comments about this draft and what she needed to do in the revision stage.

In the essay, Jennifer describes her sensations during what must be a major life event for anyone who has experienced it: the removal of her wisdom teeth.

### Jennifer's Final Draft

#### Help! Anyone!

The moment I walk through the mirrored door and into the      1
peach reception room, a sense of trepidation washes over me as a
mixture of plastic and mint invades my nostrils. Slowly, I approach
the Hispanic woman at the circular, cream desk. "Can I help you?"
she asks with a smile, flashing her perfect white teeth. I give her my
name and drag myself over to one of the chairs covered in scratchy
cloth, which makes it impossible to get comfortable and perhaps
pretend, for just a moment, that I am anywhere else but here. Gazing around the room, desperate for anything to get my mind off
of the pain I know I'm about to endure, I find only children's books
and little toy blocks. My eyes fixate on the pyramid design on the
wallpaper.

Before I can count to 200 blocks of pyramid, my name is called.      2
The tingling in my legs becomes more paralyzing with every step I
take closer to the back room. Passing through the heavy apricot-
colored door, I swear I hear shrieks from the poor victims of the dental hygienist. Other dental hygienists are crowded around a sink putting on fresh latex gloves. My jaw starts throbbing at the very sight
of the torture devices neatly lined up on the table next to them. The
receptionist ushers me past tearful children, strapped down to chairs
and enduring the same fate I will soon have the pleasure of enduring. She leads me into a brightly lit, private room. I have no choice
but to sit down in the cold, gray, vinyl chair.

Silently, I wait in agony for the torment to begin. My premonitions get stronger, and my heart starts racing faster and faster, yet nothing happens. I sit in complete silence, except for the second hand on the black-and-white wall clock that my eyes are fixated on. I desperately want this experience to just be over so I can go home and block it all out of my memory. Maybe I should make a run for it while I still can. Too late, the door opens, and in walks the dentist in his blue paper face mask and cap. He slips on his funny-looking glasses and sits down with a sigh.

Much against my will, the dentist is now in control of my mouth. My thoughts are screaming at me to clamp my mouth shut and do as much damage to his hand with my teeth as I possibly can. My mouth doesn't listen to the screams and continues to do whatever the dentist requests. I can feel my blood pounding through my entire body as I open my eyes just in time to see the dentist reach for a pair of blindingly shiny, silver clamps. "All right, now keep your head steady and your mouth open wide. You shouldn't feel that much pain." I would love to believe him. Still, even though I taste the piña-colada-flavored numbing gel and my lip feels like it's touching the ground, I know better. In complete agony I lie in the chair, unable to shut my eyes, move, or even utter a sound. Yet I'm very able to feel and hear him searing through my gums and into my jaw. The clamps enclose my tooth, and I can literally hear each crack as he tries as gingerly as possible to extract it from my jaw. Blood gushes from my mouth as tears cascade down my cheeks. I have no idea how much longer I will be able to survive this suffering as I feel my tooth dangling from just one side of my jaw. I hear one final snap, and relief washes over me as the pain slowly subsides.

"Great job! Only three more left to go!" exclaims the dentist. I shudder at the thought of even one more second in this chair. I take a deep breath and just thank God that I only have one set of wisdom teeth.

## Help! Anyone!

My goal was to make the reader feel what it was like to be in the dentist chair and understand why I hate that place so much.

The moment I walk through the mirrored door and into the peach receptionist room, a sense of trepidation washes over me, plastic and mint invade my nostrils. Slowly, I approach the Spanish looking receptionist. "Can I help you?" she asks with a smile, flashing her perfect white teeth. I give her my name and sit down in one of the chairs in the room covered in scratchy cloth, which makes it impossible for me to get comfortable and perhaps, just for a moment, that I'm anywhere else. Gazing around the room, desperate for something to get my mind off of the pain I know I'm about to endure, I find only children's books and toys. My eyes fixate on the pyramid design on the wallpaper. Before I could reach 200 blocks of pyramids my name is called. The tingling in my legs gets stronger with every step I take towards the back room. Passing through the heavy apricot colored door, I swear I hear the screams of dental hygienist victims. A group of dental hygienists are crowded around a sink putting on fresh latex gloves. My jaw starts throbbing at the very sight of the torture devices neatly lined up on the table next to them. The receptionist ushers me into a private room and into a gray colored vinyl chair. Silently I wait for the torture to begin. Although my premonitions get stronger and my heart races faster and faster, nothing happens. The only thing moving is the second hand on the black and white wall clock that my eyes are fixated on. I just want to go hone and forget about it. Maybe I should make a run for it while I still can. Too late, the door slides open and in walks the dentist with his blue paper face mask and cap and funny looking glasses. Very unwillingly, the dentist is in control of my mouth. My brain's telling me to clamp shut, but my mouth does exactly what the dentist requests. I can feel my blood pounding through my entire body as I open my eyes just in time to see the dentist reach for a pair of blindingly shiny, silver clamps.

I added more description of the walk to the examining room and the room itself so that the reader could actually picture the events.

I also tried to make my essay a little bit longer, but I chose the details I added carefully so that the reader would think about my overall impression.

"Alright, now keep your head steady and your mouth open wide. You shouldn't feel much pain." I would love to believe him. And even though I taste the pina colada flavored numbing gel and my lip feels about ten times too big, I know better. In complete agony I lay in the chair, unable to shut my eyes, move or even scream. Yet very able to feel and hear him searing through my gums and into my jaw. The clamps enclose on the tooth and I can literally hear each cracking of my tooth as he tries as gingerly as possible to extract the tooth from my jaw. Blood gushes from my mouth as tears cascade down my cheeks. "Great job! Only three more to go!" the dentist exclaims. I shudder at the thought of even one more second in this chair. I just thank God that you only get wisdom teeth once.

*I wrote my first draft in one fast block. When I revised, I had to go back and establish my paragraphs. Since I was using a narrative structure, I started a new paragraph each time something happened.*

## EXERCISE 5.2: REVISING

The following is the first draft of a student's descriptive essay. Working in pairs or in small groups, review this essay. Using the Questions for Reviewing a Descriptive Essay on page 161, decide what revisions you would suggest. If you have any questions that the student needs to consider, write them in the margin or on a separate piece of paper. If your instructor directs you to, rewrite one or more paragraphs to make them stronger and to eliminate any grammatical or mechanical errors.

### "Dorm Room From Hell"

I live in a dorm room with too other dudes, they are also students here. The place is always a mess, pizza boxes and beer cans everwhere. Tim is the worst offender but James at least trys to keep things neet. I'm sort of in the middle.

The livingroom has a couple of chairs, a couch and a T.V. The rug hasn't been cleaned in awhile and it needs it. Weve spilled stuff everywhere. One Saturday we were all going to pitch in to cleanup, but James got called into work and Tim was sleeping off one. Somehow nothing got done.

We each have a bedroom, Tim's is the worse as you might imagine. There's stuff everywhere, including old food. He hasn't made his bed in months and he rarely change the sheets. His girl friend says, it looks like hes a tornado victim.

James' room is the neatest, he at least trys to keep it neat. But, he works so much that he doesn't have a lot of time. My room is sometimes neat only do to the fact that I try to keep my possesions at a minemum. Otherwise I'm almost as bad of a slob as Tim.

Whenever we move out of this apartment well have a lot of cleaning to do. Unless, of course, the land lord wants to donate it as a museum of male messiness.

## Additional Writing Topics

1. Some people look different because of birth, disease, or accident, but many people have a distinctive appearance because of personal choice. Choose a person you know who has a very personal style, and describe him or her.

2. What is the most distinctive public building or private house that you have seen lately? Describe the exterior of this structure.

3. Have you been in a very interesting room in a public building or in someone's house? Describe it.

4. Where do you go to get comfortable and be alone? Describe this place.

5. **Writing on the job.** Think of the place where you work or where you used to work. Choose a distinctive physical feature of this workplace, and write an essay describing it for a potential employee.

## Description and Visual Representations

Today, tourism is such a major and accepted industry that it is easy to forget about its basic business plan. In short, people come to an area and spend money—sometimes large amounts of money—in the local economy. This spending produces jobs in the area, and in many cases tourists pay taxes that the locals don't.

However, the trick is to get the tourists to come. Some venues—Niagara Falls, for example—are so established that the local tourism authorities don't have to advertise very much: the crowds will come anyway. But what if the venue is not a "standard," accepted destination? Then advertising becomes crucial.

In 1981 the Jamaica Tourist Board hired the U.S. agency Young & Rubicam to create a series of magazine advertisements designed to describe Jamaica in a new way. Many potential tourists knew that Jamaica was a subtropical island nation in the Caribbean, but many had fears about their safety, especially during the early years of the drug wars. The collection of ads developed by Young & Rubicam, one of which is shown on page 167, was designed to offer a new description of Jamaica.

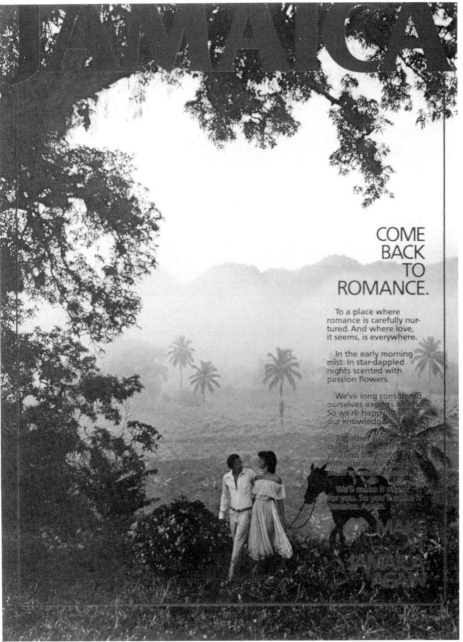

JAMAICA

COME
BACK
TO
ROMANCE.

To a place where
romance is carefully nur-
tured. And where love,
it seems, is everywhere.

In the early morning
mist. In star-dappled
nights scented with
passion flowers.

We've long considered
ourselves experts in love.
So we're happy to share
our knowledge.

Together with your
travel agent we'll help
you find the most
romantic places.

We'll make it easy
for you. So you'll want to

MAKE
IT
JAMAICA
AGAIN

Courtesy of Jamaica Tourist Bureau.

Also in the 1980s, the North Carolina Department of Tourism undertook
a similar campaign with the McKinney & Silver agency. The problem that the
state board faced was that most travelers of the time didn't think of North
Carolina as a vacation destination—certainly not in the sense of Florida,

California, Hawaii, or New York. McKinney & Silver's award-winning series of ads, one of which is shown here, successfully introduced potential tourists to what North Carolina has to offer.

1. Write a response to these ads. What are your thoughts and impressions? As you write, refer to Questions for Reviewing a Visual Representation.

2. Both of these ads were commissioned by governmental tourism boards. Research the role of such agencies. When have their efforts been especially innovative and successful, and when have they been abject failures? Try to find examples of the actual advertisements produced. Then either write an essay containing your findings and documenting your sources (see also Chapter 21) or develop an oral presentation based on your research and conclusions (see also Chapter 18).

## Questions for Reviewing a Visual Representation

- Is the representation forceful, passive, or something in between?

- What is the purpose of the representation—in other words, what is it trying to do to you, the reader/viewer?

- If the representation uses words, do they reinforce the visual image or in some way contradict it?

- What is the presumed audience for the representation—men, women, children, the elderly? Or does it have a broader appeal?

- If the representation is an advertisement, is it trying to sell a product or to get you to adopt a way of thinking?

- If the representation is an advertisement, does it try to persuade you in a fair manner, or do you feel manipulated?

## Responding to an Image

During the Great Depression, Walker Evans worked for the Farm Security Administration, a branch of the federal government that tried to aid the nation's farmers. Evans traveled widely, photographing the inhabitants of rural areas. While roaming through Alabama in 1936, Evans did an extensive study of the Floyd Burroughs family. One of his photographs is reproduced below.

From the collections of the Library of Congress.

1. Write an informal response to the photograph. What do you notice? How does the image make you feel? How does the photograph make use of the description option?

2. In 1936 many of the safeguards that we now take for granted—Social Security, Medicare, and Medicaid, for instance—did not exist. The Great Depression was also marked by an extensive drought, so U.S. farmers struggled with poor agricultural conditions as well as a poor economy. Some farm families lost their land; others actually starved. Using a combination of library and online research, explore the life of the small farmer or sharecropper of the 1930s. Write a documented essay describing what daily life was like for a representative family. (For more information on documented essays, see Chapter 21.)

## Using the Internet

Search the Internet for insights and information to use in descriptive papers.

1. Visit at least two Web sites containing information on a city, state, country, or region of the world that you have always wanted to see.

Take notes on points of interest. Gather information about one or more of the following: historical attractions, important buildings, museums and galleries, folk festivals, native food and dress, and social and religious observances. However, don't forget to gather information about the natural environment of the place as well. Turn these notes into a full-length descriptive essay designed to entice outsiders to visit this locale.

2. Search for information on the places where your parents or grandparents were born, grew up, or lived most of their lives. Draw this material from at least two different Web sites. Then write a descriptive essay that explains the kind of place in which your parents or grandparents once lived. Be as specific as you can about special aspects of the natural and social environment of this town or city. Also describe the kind of people who inhabit it, if possible. If you have visited this place, draw on your own experience as well as the information you gather from the Web.

3. In her essay about the extraction of her wisdom teeth, Jennifer Janisz does more than describe a place or explain a dental procedure. She also describes her state of mind, and she even verges on technical description when she talks about those "shiny silver clamps." Using her essay as inspiration, search the Internet to learn about a new instrument or machine that represents a significant advance in medicine, dentistry, or another health-related field. You might want to search for information about a device used to treat an illness that you or someone you know is suffering from. Describe what this instrument looks like, and explain what it can do.

### CHAPTER 6

# NARRATION

# Writing in Context

RIGHT, RIGHT. THIS IS THE STORY OF THE HYDRAULIC PUMP (Fig. 1), THE WHEEL SHAFT FLANGE (Fig. 2), AND THE EVIL PATENT INFRINGEMENT.

I WANT A *GOOD* STORY.

You have been "called back" for a second interview at Osprey. On Wednesday afternoon you show up determined to nail down this job.

First, you have another interview with Bob, the man who would be your boss. Bob is all teeth, smiles, and suit, but you notice that he is smart enough to protect himself by carefully avoiding a commitment at this point.

Next, you are sent back to Human Resources. There is yet another psychological profile test for you to complete, administered by one of the quiet, synthetically pleasant people who hover around the area. (At this point you wouldn't be surprised if one of them produced a rubber mallet and asked to check your reflexes.) After the profile, one of the HR people sits down with you, hands over a clipboard and some writing paper, and asks this question: "Can you tell us about the single most important event in your college years, the one that led you here today?"

And how shall you begin?

Indeed, we all know how to tell stories, but finding the most effective one and telling it to maximum benefit is a complex process.

# HOW DOES NARRATION WORK?

The **narrative** is the oldest structured form of human communication. The ability to process the standard elements of a narrative seems to be genetically hardwired into the human system. Parents teach language to very young children by telling them stories. Moreover, people spend the rest of their lives telling stories: informing the traffic officer about what happened in the accident, explaining to the boss what happened in the client conference, letting the spouse know about the huge argument at work, explaining to children the events that happened when they were too young to remember. When you are old, you will probably tell young people about how strange the decades before and after the turn of the century were.

Except when people are asleep and slaves to their subconscious, the events of their world unfold in a continuous narrative. In some sense, every life is a narrative, a chronology of events both small and large.

Most of life's events are, indeed, small. Think what your typical morning would look like if captured on film. You wake up, shower, prepare, dress. You leave for school. Your first class is algebra, where you are either attentive or bored, depending on your general level of interest, the specific subject matter, and the lecturer's skill. Your next class is economics, where you go through the same scenario. At 10:00 you have an hour break, during which you grab some food and study for a while. At 11:00 you have English. At noon your morning is over.

The resulting "film" of your average morning is unlikely to win any best-documentary awards. More likely, it would bore viewers to tears. This narrative is *unstructured,* like most of our experiences in real life. In fact, there is a significant subcategory of narrative writing that is deliberately unstructured. Read a police officer's incident report or the court transcript of eyewitness testimony, and you'll find narratives in which the "story" is lost in a mass of seemingly extraneous details and impressions. However, the person relating the narrative is just following directions. The *whole* story is needed; others will figure out what is important. The minutes of meetings produce a similar effect: all motions and discussions are listed in order, the important along with the trivial, and the reader is left to interpret the results. However, most written narratives are *structured*—that is, they convey a sense of their significance and a point or "moral." Moviemakers edit out the dull parts; similarly, writers of short stories, novels, and plays concentrate on the significant events of the plot and minimize others.

The success of a personal narrative essay depends on this search for significance. The narrative essay tells a story, to be sure, but the true value of the narrative comes from what the writer and reader learn from it. Thus, what may well be suitable in a short story—for example, an amusing series of events—may not work so well as the subject of a personal narrative essay. Read the following short essay, and then consider its "point":

> In 1958 I was three years old. My father had just been transferred seven hundred miles from our home to a power-plant construction project in a very remote part of the lower Midwest. The place and the area must have been hellish for my parents—especially my mother—but I didn't care.

At three years of age, I found the world an endlessly fascinating place no matter where I was.

During the day I played outside in the yard, or watched life through the window. One afternoon in the late summer of 1958, I saw a strange episode unfold. Our next-door neighbor, Joe Marshall, was Dad's age, and the next neighbor down was a retired coal miner, Albert McGinnis. For some reason, Mr. Marshall was home from work that day, working in his yard, and for a probably more complicated reason, Mr. McGinnis snapped and took out after Mr. Marshall with a shovel.

The old man chased Joe Marshall down the middle of the street, and suddenly Joe stopped and started to chase Mr. McGinnis. After this went on for a few hundred feet, the old man apparently realized that he was the one with the deadly weapon, and the race suddenly reversed itself again.

Finally, Joe Marshall took the shovel away from Albert McGinnis, and eventually the sheriff came. Mr. McGinnis was taken away, and Mr. Marshall recovered his equilibrium.

That night at supper, my parents discussed the incident. My mother asked me if I'd seen this bizarre event. When I answered yes, she was amazed: "Why didn't you say anything?"

"Because it was like a cartoon," I answered. I didn't have to say anything else. My parents looked at each other, and the conversation ended.

Even at the age of three, I was sure that no one was going to be hurt during the Marshall-McGinnis debacle. For it was just like a cartoon, and I'm sure that I, somehow, some way, would have known otherwise if actual violence had been about to occur.

Do you see the problem with this essay? The writer recounts an odd event, one that could be very funny in a movie or a novel, but what is the point? Cartoons are bad? Encounters that initially seem violent can end up being comical? No, there isn't really a resulting message issuing from this essay. The raw materials are certainly present, but they really don't lead anywhere.

However, the structured personal essay—the formal type that you'll be writing in response to classroom assignments—*does* need to make a point. The writer has experienced something in his or her past that proved significant; perhaps it changed the way that he or she understands the world. The preceding essay about the young boy, though interesting, has no real point, but a less interesting narrative—say, one about the day you learned the result of touching a hot stove top—would be about an event that changed the way you experience the world: a narrative whose significance is lasting. Note that we're not advising dreary, moralistic approaches to the essay. "How I Learned Not to Drive Drunk" and "My Horrible Experience with Credit-Card Debt" may well be the titles of interesting essays, but you don't need to take this approach. People learn from good experiences as well as from bad ones.

Another way you will employ structured narrative is to develop paragraphs for essays based on other rhetorical options. For example, a process analysis essay (see Chapter 8) is frequently ordered chronologically, as the writer explains to the reader how to complete a series of steps. As well, you will find yourself using smaller narratives (brief recountings of events known as

• *Consider Your Options*

When was the last time you chose to use a narrative? What was your purpose? How did this purpose help you shape your account?

anecdotes) to help develop paragraphs in almost every type of essay that you write. Narrative pervades our world.

The effective personal narrative has a story to tell and a point to make; it also uses an economical structure and has a clear sense of its audience. Later in this chapter we talk about how to handle time in an essay and how to use transitions to guide the reader. Note how the writers of the following professional essays make their points, structure their stories, and engage their readers.

## READING THE NARRATIVE ESSAY WITH A WRITER'S EYE

In the three works that follow, Lynda Barry writes about a childhood spent in such dysfunctional circumstances that school became a haven for her, Sandra Cisneros shows how going against her father's very traditional expectations paid off for her, and Annie Dillard recounts an experience from her youth in Pittsburgh. As you read each essay, concentrate on the writer's **thesis**—the point that the writer is trying to make and the focus that drives each of these narratives.

The second half of this chapter features strategies for writing the personal narrative with a reader's eye (pages 186–196). If you decide to write on one of the topics that follow the three essays, make sure that you have read the strategies section before you begin. Additional writing topics are listed at the end of the chapter (page 201).

# The Sanctuary of School

## LYNDA BARRY

*Lynda Barry is best known for her syndicated cartoons, but she has also written an important novel about adolescence, The Good Times Are Killing Me (1988). She has a profound understanding of the issues facing children and teenagers.*

*"The Sanctuary of School" first appeared in the New York Times in 1992. In it, Barry portrays her childhood response to her family situation, made dysfunctional by strife and alcohol.*

I was 7 years old the first time I snuck out of the house in the dark. It was winter and my parents had been fighting all night. They were short on money and long on relatives who kept "temporarily" moving into our house because they had nowhere else to go.

My brother and I were used to giving up our bedroom. We slept on the couch, something we actually liked because it put us that much closer to the light of our lives, our television.

At night when everyone was asleep, we lay on our pillows watching it with the sound off. We watched Steve Allen's mouth moving. We watched Johnny Carson's mouth moving. We watched movies filled with gangsters shooting machine guns into packed rooms, dying soldiers hurling a last grenade and beautiful women crying at windows. Then the sign-off finally came and we tried to sleep.

The morning I snuck out, I woke up filled with a panic about needing to get to school. The sun wasn't quite up yet but my anxiety was so fierce that I just got dressed, walked quietly across the kitchen and let myself out the back door. 4

It was quiet outside. Stars were still out. Nothing moved and no one was in the street. It was as if someone had turned the sound off on the world. 5

I walked the alley, breaking thin ice over the puddles with my shoes. I didn't know why I was walking to school in the dark. I didn't think about it. All I knew was a feeling of panic, like the panic that strikes kids when they realize they are lost. 6

That feeling eased the moment I turned the corner and saw the dark outline of my school at the top of the hill. My school was made up of about 15 nondescript portable classrooms set down on a fenced concrete lot in a rundown Seattle neighborhood, but it had the most beautiful view of the Cascade Mountains. You could see them from anywhere on the playfield and you could see them from the windows of my classroom—Room 2. 7

I walked over to the monkey bars and hooked my arms around the cold metal. I stood for a long time just looking across Rainier Valley. The sky was beginning to whiten and I could hear a few birds. 8

In a perfect world my absence at home would not have gone unnoticed. I would have had two parents in a panic to locate me, instead of two parents in a panic to locate an answer to the hard question of survival during a deep financial and emotional crisis. 9

But in an overcrowded and unhappy home, it's incredibly easy for any child to slip away. The high levels of frustration, depression and anger in my house made my brother and me invisible. We were children with the sound turned off. And for us, as for the steadily increasing number of neglected children in this country, the only place where we could count on being noticed was at school. 10

"Hey there, young lady. Did you forget to go home last night?" It was Mr. Gunderson, our jani- 11 tor, whom we all loved. He was nice and he was funny and he was old with white hair, thick glasses and an unbelievable number of keys. I could hear them jingling as he walked across the playfield. I felt incredibly happy to see him.

He let me push his wheeled garbage can between the different portables as he unlocked each room. He let me turn on the lights and raise the window shades and I saw my school slowly come to life. I saw Mrs. Holman, our school secretary, walk into the office without her orange lipstick on yet. She waved. 12

I saw the fifth-grade teacher, Mr. Cunningham, walking under the breezeway eating a hard roll. He waved. 13

And I saw my teacher, Mrs. Claire LeSane, walking toward us in a red coat and calling my name in a very happy and surprised way, and suddenly my throat got tight and my eyes stung and I ran toward her crying. It was something that surprised us both. 14

It's only thinking about it now, 28 years later, that I realize I was crying from relief. I was with my teacher, and in a while I was going to sit at my desk, with my crayons and pencils and books and classmates all around me, and for the next six hours I was going to enjoy a thoroughly secure, warm and stable world. It was a world I absolutely relied on. Without it, I don't know where I would have gone that morning. 15

Mrs. LeSane asked me what was wrong and when I said "Nothing," she seemingly left it at that. But she asked me if I would carry her purse for her, an honor above all honors, and she asked if I wanted to come into Room 2 early and paint. 16

She believed in the natural healing power of painting and drawing for troubled children. In the back of her room there was always a drawing table and an easel with plenty of supplies, and sometimes during the day she would come up to you for what seemed like no good reason and quietly ask if you wanted to go to the back table and "make some pictures for Mrs. LeSane." We all had 17 a chance at it—to sit apart from the class for a while to paint, draw, and silently work out impossible problems on 11 X 17 sheets of newsprint.

Drawing came to mean everything to me. At the back table in Room 2, I learned to build myself a life preserver that I could carry into my home. 18

We all know that a good education system saves lives, but the people of this country are still told that cutting the budget for public schools is necessary, that poor salaries for teachers are all we can manage and that art, music and all creative activities must be the first to go when times are lean. 19

Before- and after-school programs are cut and we are told that public schools are not made for baby-sitting children. If parents are neglectful temporarily or permanently, for whatever reason, it's certainly sad, but their unlucky children must fend for themselves. Or slip through the cracks. Or wander in a dark night alone. 20

We are told in a thousand ways that not only are public schools not important, but that the children who attend them, the children who need 21

them most, are not important either. We leave them to learn from the blind eye of a television, or to the mercy of "a thousand points of light" that can be as far away as stars.

I was lucky. I had Mrs. LeSane. I had Mr. Gunderson. I had an abundance of art supplies. And I had a particular brand of neglect in my home that allowed me to slip away and get to them. But what about the rest of the kids who weren't as lucky? What happened to them? 22

By the time the bell rang that morning I had finished my drawing and Mrs. LeSane pinned it up on the special bulletin board she reserved for drawings from the back table. It was the same picture I always drew—a sun in the corner of a blue sky over a nice house with flowers all around it. 23

Mrs. LeSane asked us to please stand, face the flag, place our right hands over our hearts and say the Pledge of Allegiance. Children across the country do it faithfully. I wonder now when the country will face its children and say a pledge right back. 24

## Vocabulary

The following terms are identified by paragraph number. Make sure that you understand each term's meaning in its context. If you're not sure that you understand a term, look it up in a college-level dictionary.

| | |
|---|---|
| sign-off (3) | easel (17) |
| nondescript (7) | abundance (22) |

## Style and Strategy

1. What was the only part of Barry's home that she enjoyed? How does she illustrate this aspect of her home life?

2. Where does the narrative end? What follows the end of the narrative?

3. Barry tells us that her second-grade teacher was named Claire LeSane, an obviously fictional name. Why did Barry choose this pseudonym for her teacher?

4. In paragraph 22, note the two questions that Barry asks. These are called *rhetorical* questions because Barry does not intend to answer them. Why, then, does she ask them? What do they contribute to her narrative?

## Questions for Critical Thinking and Discussion

1. Do you know a family whose situation is similar to the situation that Barry describes? If so, how do the children cope? What options do they have?

2. Comment on this statement: "You have to buy a license to catch fish, but you can produce all the children that you want while the government turns a blind eye." Given the high value most people in the United States attach to individual liberty and freedom of choice, what, if anything, can the government do about situations such as the one Barry faced as a child?

## Suggestions for Writing

1. When you were a child, where did you go to "hide"? Write a 500-word essay about a time when you felt the need to escape to that place.

2. In 500 to 750 words, write about a family crisis and how you reacted to it.

3. Barry states that "high levels of frustration, depression and anger in my house made my brother and me invisible." Write an essay of 500 to 750 words in response to this statement. Explain what she means. Then narrate an event or discuss a time during which you felt "invisible." What caused this? What were its effects on you physically, emotionally, or in other ways? How did you overcome feeling "invisible"?

4. Have you ever known a teacher or other school employee like "Claire LeSane"? If so, write a 500- to 750-word essay that explains ways in which this person affected or even changed you. Narrate at least one incident— more if you can—to explain how and to what extent this person helped, inspired, or encouraged you.

## Speaking Assignment

Prepare a presentation about the most difficult problem you faced in elementary school or high school. Explain whether you addressed the problem and, if so, how you addressed it. Conclude by explaining what you learned from the experience. If this assignment doesn't interest you, talk about your most embarrassing experience and what you learned from it. (For more help with oral presentations, see Chapter 18.)

# Only Daughter

## SANDRA CISNEROS

*Sandra Cisneros was born in Chicago to a Mexican father and a Mexican-American mother. She attended the prestigious Master of Fine Arts program at the University of Iowa before producing her* well-regarded collections of short stories and poetry—The House on Mango Street *(short fiction, 1983),* My Wicked Wicked Ways *(poetry, 1987),* Woman Hollering Creek *(short fiction, 1991), and Loose Women (poetry, 1994). She has also written a children's book,* Hairs-Pelitos *(1994). In 1995, Cisneros was awarded a MacArthur fellowship.*

*In "Only Daughter," first published in 1990 in* Glamour, *Cisneros writes about the push/pull of traditional culture (her father's) and modern culture (North America's).*

Once, several years ago, when I was just starting out my writing career, I was asked to write my own contributor's note for an anthology I was part of. I wrote: "I am the only daughter in a family of six sons. *That* explains everything." 1

Well, I've thought about that ever since, and yes, it explains a lot to me, but for the reader's sake I should have written: "I am the only daughter in a *Mexican* family of six sons." Or even: "I am the only daughter of a Mexican father and a Mexican-American mother." Or: "I am the only daughter of a working-class family of nine." All of these had everything to do with who I am today. 2

I was/am the only daughter and only a daughter. Being an only daughter in a family of six sons forced me by circumstance to spend a lot of time by myself because my brothers felt it beneath them to play with a girl in public. But that aloneness, that loneliness, was good for a would-be writer—it allowed me time to think and think, to imagine, to read and prepare myself. 3

Being only a daughter for my father meant my destiny would lead me to become someone's wife. That's what he believed. But when I was in the fifth grade and shared my plans for college with him, I was sure he understood. I remember my father saying, "*Que bueno, ni'ja,* that's good." That meant a lot to me, especially since my brothers thought the idea hilarious. What I didn't realize was that my father thought college was good for girls—good for finding a husband. After four years in college and two more in graduate school, and still no husband, my father shakes his head even now and says I wasted all that education. 4

In retrospect, I'm lucky my father believed daughters were meant for husbands. It meant it didn't matter if I majored in something silly like English. After all, I'd find a nice professional eventually, right? This allowed me the liberty to putter about embroidering my little poems and stories without my father interrupting with so much as a "What's that you're writing?" 5

But the truth is, I wanted him to interrupt. I wanted my father to understand what it was I was scribbling, to introduce me as "My only daughter, the writer." Not as "This is my only daughter. She teaches." *Es maestra*—teacher. Not even *profesora*. 6

In a sense, everything I have ever written has been for him, to win his approval even though I know my father can't read English words, even though my father's only reading includes the brown-ink *Esto* sports magazines from Mexico City and the bloody *¡Alarma!* magazines that feature yet another sighting of *La Virgen de Guadalupe* on a tortilla or a wife's revenge on her philandering husband by bashing his skull in with a *molcajete* (a kitchen mortar made of volcanic rock). Or the *fotonovelas,* the little picture paperbacks with tragedy and trauma erupting from the characters' mouths in bubbles. 7

My father represents, then, the public majority. A public who is uninterested in reading, and yet one whom I am writing about and for, and privately trying to woo. 8

When we were growing up in Chicago, we moved a lot because of my father. He suffered bouts of nostalgia. Then we'd have to let go of our flat, store the furniture with mother's relatives, load the station wagon with baggage and bologna sandwiches, and head south. To Mexico City. 9

We came back, of course. To yet another Chicago flat, another Chicago neighborhood, another Catholic school. Each time, my father would seek out the parish priest in order to get a tuition break, and complain or boast: "I have seven sons." 10

He meant *siete hijos,* seven children, but he translated it as "sons." I have seven sons. To anyone who would listen. The Sears Roebuck employee who sold us the washing machine. The short-order cook where my father ate his ham-and-eggs breakfasts. "I have seven sons." As if he deserved a medal from the state. 11

My papa. He didn't mean anything by that 12 mistranslation, I'm sure. But somehow I could feel myself being erased. I'd tug my father's sleeve and whisper: "Not seven sons. Six! And *one daughter.*"

When my oldest brother graduated from med- 13 ical school, he fulfilled my father's dream that we study hard and use this—our heads, instead of this—our hands. Even now my father's hands are thick and yellow, stubbed by a history of hammer and nails and twine and coils and springs. "Use this," my father said, tapping his head, "and not this," showing us those hands. He always looked tired when he said it.

Wasn't college an investment? And hadn't I 14 spent all those years in college? And if I didn't marry, what was it all for? Why would anyone go to college and then choose to be poor? Especially someone who had always been poor.

Last year, after ten years of writing profession- 15 ally, the financial rewards started to trickle in. My second National Endowment for the Arts Fellowship. A guest professorship at the University of California, Berkeley. My book, which sold to a major New York publishing house.

At Christmas, I flew home to Chicago. The 16 house was throbbing, same as always; hot tamales and sweet tamales hissing in my mother's pressure cooker, and everybody—my mother, six brothers, wives, babies, aunts, cousins—talking too loud and at the same time, like in a Fellini film, because that's just how we are.

I went upstairs to my father's room. One of my 17 stories had just been translated into Spanish and published in an anthology of Chicano writing, and

I wanted to show it to him. Ever since he recovered from a stroke two years ago, my father likes to spend his leisure hours horizontally. And that's how I found him, watching a Pedro Infante* movie on Galavisión* and eating rice pudding.

There was a glass filmed with milk on the bed- 18 side table. There were several vials of pills and balled Kleenex. And on the floor, one black sock and a plastic urinal that I didn't want to look at but looked at anyway. Pedro Infante was about to burst into song, and my father was laughing.

I'm not sure if it was because my story was 19 translated into Spanish, or because it was published in Mexico, or perhaps because the story dealt with Tepeyac, the *colonia* my father was raised in and the house he grew up in, but at any rate, my father punched the mute button on his remote control and read my story.

I sat on the bed next to my father and waited. 20 He read it very slowly. As if he were reading each line over and over. He laughed at all the right places and read lines he liked out loud. He pointed and asked questions: "Is this So-and-so?" "Yes," I said. He kept reading.

When he was finally finished, after what 21 seemed like hours, my father looked up and asked: "Where can we get more copies of this for the relatives?"

Of all the wonderful things that happened to 22 me last year, that was the most wonderful.

*Pedro Infante (1917–1957):* a Mexican film star and singer.

*Galavisión:* a major Hispanic cable television network in the United States.

## Vocabulary

The following terms are identified by paragraph number. Make sure that you understand each term's meaning in its context. If you're not sure that you understand a term, look it up in a college-level dictionary.

retrospect (5)  philandering (7)  Chicano (17)

embroidering (5)  nostalgia (9)

## Style and Strategy

1.  Cisneros spends the first four paragraphs of her essay commenting on the significance of her being the only sister of six brothers. Why does she open the essay in this way? How successful is this strategy?

2.  What is this essay's thesis? Is it stated overtly, or is it implied?

3.  "The turning point of this narrative is paragraph 12." Do you agree with this statement? Why or why not?

## Questions for Critical Thinking and Discussion

1.  The idea that young women should be given the same opportunities as young men is widely accepted in modern North American culture. However, Cisneros's father believed that young women should be both protected and provided for. Do you know someone who holds a similar opinion? What might be some of the consequences of this idea?

2.  What do your parents expect of you over the next ten years? Are you willing to try to satisfy those expectations? What are your own expectations? If any of your expectations differ from those of your parents, how have you handled this conflict?

## Suggestions for Writing

1.  Write a 500- to 750-word essay about an occasion on which you had every reason to succeed at a task but somehow failed.

2.  Write a narrative essay of 500–750 words in which you explain the frustration you experienced while trying to impress an older person whom you held in high esteem—a coach, a teacher, an employer, a member of the clergy, or a parent, for example. In addition to explaining what you did, explain the other person's reactions, and tell your reader something about his or her personality and/or motives. Finally, if you succeeded in your attempts to impress this person, explain how you did so.

3.  Sandra Cisneros's father had certain well-defined expectations for his daughter. However, these were not the same as those she had for herself. In an essay of 500–750 words, narrate an incident—or series of incidents—in which your expectations for yourself clashed with those that your parent or parents had for you. In the process, try to reveal something about your character and the character of your parent(s).

## Speaking Assignment

Cisneros provides several definitions of herself at the beginning of her essay. Develop an oral presentation in which you explain the most important influence your family has had on your development as the person you are today. (For more help with oral presentations, see Chapter 18.)

# The Chase

## ANNIE DILLARD

*Annie Dillard, best known for her Pulitzer Prize-winning* Pilgrim at Tinker Creek *(1975), is the author of eight other books, including a novel,* The Living *(1992); a collection of essays,* Teaching a Stone to Talk: Expeditions and Encounters *(1982); and her memories of growing up,* An American Childhood *(1987).*

*In "The Chase," excerpted from* An American Childhood, *Dillard looks back at her early days in Pittsburgh and recounts a moment in which she gained a better understanding of the nature of adults. Have you ever had a similar experience?*

Some boys taught me to play football. This was fine sport. You thought up a new strategy for every play and whispered it to the others. You went out for a pass, fooling everyone. Best, you got to throw yourself mightily at someone's running legs. Either you brought him down or you hit the ground flat out on your chin, with your arms empty before you. It was all or nothing. If you hesitated in fear, you would miss and get hurt; you would take a hard fall while the kid got away, or you would get kicked in the face while the kid got away. But if you flung yourself wholeheartedly at the back of his knees—if you gathered and joined body and soul and pointed them diving fearlessly—then you likely wouldn't get hurt, and you'd stop the ball. Your fate, and your team's score, depended on your concentration and courage. Nothing girls did could compare with it.

Boys welcomed me at baseball, too, for I had, through enthusiastic practice, what was weirdly known as a boy's arm. In winter, in the snow, there was neither baseball or football, so the boys and I threw snowballs at passing cars. I got in trouble throwing snowballs, and have seldom been happier since.

On one weekday morning after Christmas, six inches of new snow had just fallen. We were standing up to our boot tops in snow on a front yard on trafficked Reynolds Street, waiting for cars. The cars traveled Reynolds Street slowly and evenly; they were targets all but wrapped in red ribbons, cream puffs. We couldn't miss.

I was seven; the boys were eight, nine, and ten. The oldest two Fahey boys were there—Mikey and Peter—polite blond boys who lived near me on Lloyd Street, and who already had four brothers and sisters. My parents approved Mikey and Peter Fahey. Chickie McBride was there, a tough kid, and Billy Paul and Mackie Kean too, from across Reynolds, where the boys grew up dark and furious, grew up skinny, knowing, and skilled. We had all drifted from our houses that morning looking for action, and had found it here on Reynolds Street.

It was cloudy but cold. The cars' tires laid behind them on the snowy street a complex trail of beige chunks like crenellated castle walls. I had stepped on some early; they squeaked. We could have wished for more traffic. When a car came, we all popped it one. In the intervals between cars we reverted to the natural solitude of children.

I started making an iceball—a perfect iceball, from perfectly white snow, perfectly spherical, and squeezed perfectly translucent so no snow remained all the way through. (The Fahey boys and I considered it unfair actually to throw an iceball at somebody, but it had been known to happen.)

I had just embarked on the iceball project when we heard tire chains come clanking from afar. A black Buick was moving toward us down the street. We all spread out, banged together some regular snowballs, took aim, and, when the Buick drew nigh, fired.

A soft snowball hit the driver's windshield right before the driver's face. It made a smashed star with a hump in the middle.

Often, of course, we hit our target, but this time, the only time in all of life, the car pulled over and stopped. Its wide black door opened; a man got out of it, running. He didn't even close the car door.

He ran after us, and we ran away from him, 10 up the snowy Reynolds sidewalk. At the corner, I looked back; incredibly, he was still after us. He was in city clothes: a suit and tie, street shoes. Any normal adult would have quit, having sprung us into flight and made his point. This man was gaining on us. He was a thin man, all action. All of a sudden, we were running for our lives.

Wordless, we split up. We were on our turf; 11 we could lose ourselves in the neighborhood backyards, everyone for himself. I paused and considered. Everyone had vanished except Mikey Fahey, who was just rounding the corner of a yellow brick house. Poor Mikey, I trailed him. The driver of the Buick sensibly picked the two of us to follow. The man apparently had all day.

He chased Mikey and me around the yellow 12 house and up a backyard path we knew by heart: under a low tree, up a bank, through a hedge, down some snowy steps, and across the grocery store's delivery driveway. We smashed through a gap in another hedge, entered a scruffy backyard and ran around its back porch and tight between houses to Edgerton Avenue; we ran across Edgerton to an alley and up our own sliding woodpile to the Halls' front yard; he kept coming. We ran up Lloyd Street and wound through mazy backyards toward the steep hilltop at Willard and Lang.

He chased us silently, block after block. He 13 chased us silently over picket fences, through thorny hedges, between houses, around garbage cans, and across streets. Every time I glanced back, choking for breath, I expected he would have quit. He must have been as breathless as we were. His jacket strained over his body. It was an immense discovery, pounding into my hot head with every sliding, joyous step, that this ordinary adult evidently knew what I thought only children who trained at football knew: that you have to fling yourself at what you're doing, you have to point yourself, forget yourself, aim, dive.

Mikey and I had nowhere to go, in our own 14 neighborhood or out of it, but away from this man who was chasing us. He impelled us forward; we compelled him to follow our route. The air was cold; every breath tore my throat. We kept running, block after block; we kept improvising, backyard after backyard, running a frantic course and choosing it simultaneously, failing always to find small places or hard places to slow him down, and discovering always, exhilarated, dismayed, that only bare speed could save us—for he would never give up, this man—and we were losing speed.

He chased us through the backyard labyrinths 15 of ten blocks before he caught us by our jackets. He caught us and we all stopped.

We three stood staggering, half blinded, 16 coughing, in an obscure hilltop backyard: a man in his twenties, a boy, a girl. He had released our jackets, our pursuer, our captor, our hero: he knew we weren't going anywhere. We all played by the rules. Mikey and I unzipped our jackets. I pulled off my sopping mittens. Our tracks multiplied in the backyard's new snow. We had been breaking new snow all morning. We didn't look at each other. I was cherishing my excitement. The man's lower pants legs were wet; his cuffs were full of snow, and there was a prow of snow beneath them on his shoes and socks. Some trees bordered the little flat backyard, some messy winter trees. There was no one around: a clearing in a grove, and we the only players.

It was a long time before he could speak. I 17 had some difficulty at first, recalling why we were there. My lips felt swollen; I couldn't see out of the sides of my eyes; I kept coughing.

"You stupid kids," he began perfunctorily. 18

We listened perfunctorily indeed, if we lis- 19 tened at all, for the chewing out was redundant, a mere formality, and beside the point. The point was that he had chased us passionately without giving up, and so he had caught us. Now he came down to earth. I wanted the glory to last forever.

But how could the glory have lasted forever? [20] We could have run through every backyard in North America until we got to Panama. But when he trapped us at the lip of the Panama Canal, what precisely could he have done to prolong the drama of the chase and cap its glory? I brooded about this for the next few years. He could only have fried Mikey Fahey and me in boiling oil, say, or dismembered us piecemeal, or staked us to anthills. None of which I really wanted, and none of which any adult was likely to do, even in the spirit of fun. He could only chew us out there in the Panamanian jungle, after months or years of exalting pursuit. He could only begin, "You stupid kids," and continue in his ordinary Pittsburgh accent with his normal righteous anger and the usual common sense.

If in that snowy backyard the driver of the [21] black Buick had cut off our heads, Mikey's and mine, I would have died happy, for nothing has required so much of me since as being chased all over Pittsburgh in the middle of winter—running terrified, exhausted—by this sainted, skinny, furious redheaded man who wished to have a word with us. I don't know how he found his way back to his car.

## Vocabulary

The following terms are identified by paragraph number. Make sure that you understand each term's meaning in its context. If you're not sure that you understand a term, look it up in a college-level dictionary.

| | | |
|---|---|---|
| trafficked (3) | scruffy (12) | perfunctorily (18) |
| cream puff (3) | mazy (12) | redundant (19) |
| crenellated (5) | improvising (14) | dismembered (20) |
| translucent (6) | exhilarated (14) | piecemeal (20) |
| turf (11) | labyrinth (15) | exalting (20) |

## Style and Strategy

1. Dillard uses a brief thesis statement (see paragraph 2). Could she have expanded it, or is it more effective the way it is? Explain.

2. Why does Dillard open her essay with some comments about playing football? How is this section relevant to the rest of her essay? How does Dillard establish this relevance for readers?

3. How does Dillard use description (see Chapter 5) in this essay?

4. In paragraph 13, Dillard comes to an important realization about adults. Restate this realization in your own words.

## Questions for Critical Thinking and Discussion

1. In what way or ways can the unidentified "furious redheaded man" be said to function as a role model for Dillard and her friends?

2. Although this narrative about Dillard and her childhood friends has a satisfactory outcome, consider this question: What could have gone very wrong during such an encounter?

### Suggestions for Writing

1. When you were a child, did you ever have an initially negative encounter with an adult that ended up having a positive outcome? Write a 500- to 750-word essay about such an encounter.

2. Sober, industrious adults will sometimes display an otherwise hidden joy for life. In 500 to 750 words, write a narrative about an event in which an adult of your acquaintance showed such an unexpected side.

3. Like Dillard, have you ever been in a situation that was both exciting and dangerous? Did you, like Dillard, "cherish" the excitement? Would you want to relive this experience or have another one that is similar? In an essay of at least 500 words, narrate your story by using the kind of vivid and exciting language we see in "The Chase."

4. In some ways, Dillard's essay resembles the kind of story you might read about in the sports pages of a newspaper. Think back to an athletic event in which you competed. In an essay of at least 500 words, tell your story by trying to recreate the excitement you felt as you prepared for and participated in this competition.

### Speaking Assignment

Pretend that you are the parent of a seven-year-old child who has just taken part in an escapade like the one narrated in "The Chase." What might you say to this child? (For more help with oral presentations, see Chapter 18.)

# WRITING THE PERSONAL NARRATIVE WITH A READER'S EYE

The audience for a personal narrative wants to read an interesting, well-structured story that has a point to make. The advice that follows will help you think like your reader as you consider your assignment and then prewrite, draft, revise, and edit your narrative essay.

## Issues to Keep in Mind

The personal narrative deals with events that transpire over a period of time; time itself, along with how it is presented, is the most central issue in structuring this type of writing. Here are four aspects of presenting time for you to consider as you plan, write, and revise your personal narrative:

1. Strategies that expand, compress, and manipulate time
2. Transitions
3. Paragraphing and topic sentences
4. Dialogue

## *Using Time Economically*

The writer of a personal narrative needs to make choices similar to those made by a film editor. Think about how movies work. The events of two days, or two weeks, or two years are condensed into a product that takes about two hours to view. The boring parts are left out. So it is with the personal narrative essay. Events taking hours or days can be covered in a relatively small number of paragraphs if the writer carefully selects what is central to the narrative and ignores what is not.

Similarly, the film editor can *expand* time. Say that the hero, played by Ben Affleck, is fighting his penultimate battle against the villain, played by Gary Oldman. They are on a balcony three stories above the street. By a singularly underhanded maneuver, Oldman is able to tumble Affleck off the balcony. In real life, the ensuing fall would take about five seconds. However, the smart film editor will make it last twenty seconds to exploit the audience's horror over the possibility of Ben's going splat. Slow motion, various camera angles, long shots, and close-ups will be used to show the falling Ben, and "reaction shots"—the smirk of the evil villain, the terror of Ben's sweetheart, the upturned faces of the pedestrians below—will prolong and accentuate the moment.

When you write a personal narrative, the duration of the event about which you're writing becomes a raw resource; you can use it, alter it, and control it. Of course, you could write a "straight" narrative that sticks closely to **chronological** time, but very few narrative topics work well this way. Think about it: you can read the body paragraphs of a 700-word essay in under five minutes. Do you want to write your essay about a five-minute life experience? Perhaps, but searching for such a topic would truly restrict your opportunities.

More likely, you will want to depend on the use of **psychological** time—time as we remember it, time as it is important in a narrative structure. This approach can sometimes result in the expansion of time, as you describe your reaction to a small but extremely important event. Normally, however, you will need to condense a longer event into a narrative that is more compact and therefore more compelling. Notice how the writer of the following narrative passage, not wanting to leave anything out, tells us a bit more than we need to know:

> Highway 35 is a big bunch of curves, and Jason seemed to take this as a challenge. On we rode, going much too fast in his car with its brakes that Jason knew to be bad. After about two miles the idiot finally learned the reality of his situation when the car ran straight through a curve and landed us in a shallow ditch. No one was hurt, thank God, but we were certainly stuck.
>
> Laura used her cell phone to call a wrecker, and we waited. I had been having a nagging problem with the little toe on my right foot, so I took my shoe off and rubbed the toe, but it still hurt. Then I remembered that I had a test on the following Friday in U.S.

government, and I made a mental note to set aside some time on Thursday evening to study, which meant going home right after work and not going out with Laura.

When help arrived, it wasn't a wrecker; it was a county deputy. She asked what had happened, and Jason, the idiot, said, "My brakes failed." (Not "I swerved to avoid a cat" or "I overcorrected coming into the curve.") The cop wrote Jason a ticket for going too fast for conditions and also one for not maintaining a safe vehicle. If he had had a brain, he probably could have avoided both tickets and the inevitable lecture.

Do you see the problem with this passage? The first paragraph is fine, as is the third. But the second paragraph has only one useful sentence: "Laura used her cell phone. . . ." Whatever narrative tension has been built up by the first paragraph is dissipated in the rest of the second paragraph, as the reader lets us know about the problems with her foot (thanks!) and her need to study (yawn). Then the third paragraph picks us up again, but the damage has already been done.

What would have worked better here is a **flashforward**, going from one significant narrative event to the next while omitting the waiting period. (Waiting is almost always boring, unless a quarrel breaks out.) Note how the writer could have used this device to unify her narrative:

Highway 35 is a big bunch of curves, and Jason seemed to take this as a challenge. On we rode, going much too fast in his car with its brakes that Jason knew to be bad. After about two miles the idiot finally learned the reality of his situation when the car ran straight through a curve and landed us in a shallow ditch. No one was hurt, thank God, but we were certainly stuck.

Laura used her cell phone to call a wrecker, and we waited. **And waited. And waited. Surely, I thought, we're not that far from town. But it took forever.**

**Finally,** when help arrived, it wasn't a wrecker; it was a county deputy. . . .

The highlighted words act as a "bridge" between the two important events.

A similar technique is a **flashback,** which takes the reader to a significant moment in a time preceding the immediate event:

It was three minutes until ten, and Randall still hadn't arrived. I was cursing myself for allowing the least active group member to "finally do something" at the end, and he was carrying the folder that contained our project. A glance at Luis and Brenda indicated that they were also beating themselves up.

Years ago, when I was in middle school, a similar disaster occurred. I remember my mother's verdict: "Don't trust important stuff to trivial people. They'll screw you up every time, and then they'll ask 'What's the big deal?'"

Today I thought about my mother, who had spent her working life managing teenagers at a restaurant, and I realized how right she was. I—and my team—faced an *F* on a crucial assignment because of our heedless trust in Randall.

You'll probably use the flashforward technique more often than the flashback; the latter strategy is more specialized and stylistic, whereas the former strategy fulfills a routine, practical need in narratives.

### Transitions

Too often, students' narratives suffer from the "and then" syndrome, as in the following paragraph:

Then Bobby decided to end the foolishness, and he grabbed the dead raccoon by the tail and heaved it off the roof. Then Bobby and Jane climbed down and got ready to leave. Mr. Johnson, Jane's dad, was there and he was mad. The raccoon corpse had narrowly missed him on the way down, and he was standing beside it. Then Bobby took off running, and Mr. Johnson took off after him.

And so on. Then so on some more. Narratives that depend on *and then* have the rushed quality of stories reported by children: a sort of needlessly breathless effect. Remember from Chapter 3 that there are many transitions you can use to indicate shifts in chronological time:

first, second, third, next, then, finally, afterwards, before, soon, later, meanwhile, subsequently, immediately, eventually, currently

Such time transitions help you create a *smooth* narrative; they also help you control the way that your reader processes your text. Note how even a straightforward use of transitions (shown highlighted) shapes the following paragraph:

Our **first** problem occurred because Amy and I were physically separated and couldn't communicate. I was in Chicago, and she was in Milwaukee. I assumed that buying the Christmas tree was my responsibility, and I **immediately** started scouring the church, school, and commercial lots. **Meanwhile,** Amy's search exemplified our second confusion: she thought we needed an artificial tree for our Christmas celebrations. **Subsequently,** she arrived at our apartment with a six-foot spruce in a box, thinking she had done her part. Imagine her surprise when I **finally** arrived, dragging a seven-foot fir up the steps.

Time transitions can also allow you to delay climactic moments or to surprise your reader when he or she least expects it.

### Paragraphing and Topic Sentences

A problem related to the "and then" syndrome is the formless narrative. In this kind of faulty narrative, the body paragraphs tell a continuous story, but in one big sweep. The paragraphs begin and end for no discernible reason, as if the writer had decided "that one's long enough" and then embarked on a new one.

Remember that paragraphs are controlled by ideas, not word count. A narrative can be organized into a logical structure in the same way that any piece of writing can be organized. When prewriting, look for logical breaks in the action, such as these:

1. Sudden complications—in other words, the direction of the narrative is quickly changed by a new and surprising event.
2. Cause and effect—one event logically leads to another.
3. Dead time—as mentioned, the waiting time between key events is frequently a good point to flashforward to the next event.

Don't let your narrative just unfold; instead, plan your series of paragraphs carefully. Then make sure that the topic sentences of your body paragraphs clearly indicate the narrative's structure. Readers don't need topic sentences that read like directions from the owner's manual for a hair dryer; however, readers do look for structure in a narrative, and it is your job as the writer to provide it. Using time transitions will help you in this effort.

### Dialogue

Effective narratives often include conversations between people in the story by placing these exchanges in quotation marks. This is called **dialogue.** If you summarize or report what was said in a conversation, the reader processes this information quickly. However, using dialogue slows down the pace of a narrative—sometimes a good idea—and is also more specific and "real." Dialogue can also be used to communicate a person's conversations with himself or herself. In other words, it can be a good way to reveal what an individual is thinking.

Dialogue can serve many purposes in a narrative. It can be used to introduce important information that the reader needs to learn to understand the significance of the events being related. In some cases, a character's words will recall events that occurred well before the story began. In others, a character's words will help advance the plot by telling the reader what is happening. In still others, they will convey information about the time and place in which the story is set. However, the most important functions of dialogue are to reveal important information about the people who inhabit the story—their motives, values, and personalities—and to develop the narrative's theme or implied thesis. Look back to "Only Daughter," by Sandra Cisneros. Here, the author uses her father's words to explain his hopes and fears for her future, to describe their relationship, and, most important, to convey the strength and nobility of the man's character.

Note that authors take pains to make sure that speakers are always identified and that each statement or question is directly attributable to someone. As well, remember that when you use dialogue from two or more speakers, each speaker gets a new paragraph, as in this example:

> "Are you going to the party?" Andrea asked.
> "Nope. Got too much to do," I mumbled.

(For more on the mechanics of including dialogue, see Chapter 30.)

CATALYST 2.0

**MORE OPTIONS ONLINE**
For more help with problem areas in the narrative essay, go to www.mhhe.com/writingtoday.

## Choosing a Topic

Many of the problems students have with narrative essays are caused by the topics they choose. The following guidelines will help you choose a subject that can be handled in an academic assignment:

1. Write about one event or sequence of events, not your life's story. If the assignment asks for 700 words, you will have trouble recounting your sophomore year in high school, or the summer that followed, or perhaps even a week during that summer. Choose a *limited* subject, one that you can exploit within the limits of the assignment.

2. Avoid personally painful issues. No one gets through life unscathed, and many people suffer horrible, unspeakable wrongs along the way. If you have been the victim of a dreadful circumstance, this experience might not be a good subject for your narrative. Writing an essay about a personal tragedy may require you to deal with your emotions as much as the demands of the assignment. Remember that your goals are to write an accomplished essay, improve your composition skills, and receive a desirable grade. Choose a topic that will allow you to concentrate on the writing process, not on your emotions.

3. Consider your audience. Sometimes, a personal experience may seem so intense and special to a writer that he or she may forget that it is old news

to an adult audience. For example, instructors really don't like to read a personal narrative about the loss of the writer's virginity—not necessarily for prudish reasons, but because this life event happens to most people in much the same way. In other words, an event that seems unique to the writer is simply part of the general human experience.

4. Be sure that you can make a thematic point. As we illustrated in the passage on pages 174–175, some narratives recount interesting but essentially pointless events: random violence, sudden bad luck, and so on. Instead, look for events that taught you something, or changed your career goals, or put you in a new city or in a new school when you were quite happy with the old city or school.

5. Consider choosing a humorous topic. Humor has an honorable place in the long history of the personal narrative. There's no reason that you should look for a serious, sober topic if you tend to see the funny side of most situations. Besides, if you are able to bring a smile to your instructor's face during the sometimes grim process of grading a stack of papers, you may well have accomplished something.

6. Consider writing about someone close to you. The personal essay doesn't always have to be about the narrator. Many students would rather write about someone other than themselves, and the experiences of a family member or close friend may prove to be a promising topic. You were there; you saw what your sister or your boyfriend went through; you commiserated or joined in the celebration; you learned something about life because of your connection to the story's central figure. Some excellent essays have been written using this approach; however, check with your instructor before you proceed.

## Prewriting

Use one of the "data-gathering" strategies—freewriting, listing, or clustering—outlined in Chapter 2 to generate the raw material of your composition. After having done so, determine the most important events of the story. Concentrate on these, and decide how you will deal with the less important events. Also, review your prewriting to see if your resulting essay will make a point. If so, you should be able to come up with your working thesis at this time.

## Organizing

Use one of the outlining methods discussed in Chapter 2 to help you find a coherent structure for your story. Remember, you want to avoid writing a formless narrative with indeterminate paragraphs. You might consider writing the topic sentences for body paragraphs before you begin drafting. You may end up revising these sentences, but they will help you to establish an initial structure for your narrative.

## Drafting

To illustrate one writer's approach to writing the narrative essay, we have included the essay "Chaos at the Veterinary Clinic."

### The Introduction

Too often, students dive into their narrative without establishing its context. Remember that your reader knows very little about you. If, for example, you are writing about being uprooted from your home in Portland, Oregon, and moving to a new home in Portland, Maine, because of your mother's job transfer, you first need to tell readers something about your life prior to the move. What was Oregon like? Were you happy? How many siblings did you have, if any? Was the move a complete surprise, or was it an issue that your family had discussed at length? Notice how the writer of the following essay uses two introductory paragraphs to establish her story:

Avoid starting your narrative in your introduction. Use the introduction for context and background. The reader needs this information to make sense of the story that follows. (See Chapter 3 for more on introductions.)

*Consider Your Options*

### Chaos at the Veterinary Clinic

My five-year-old cat, Raymond, is a magnificent creature. He is coal-black and very large, weighing eighteen pounds with no apparent fat. But it's his personality that makes Raymond special. He has very little fear, rather a bold curiosity with which he meets the world. He's a very loving cat as well and a good judge of my moods. His only drawback is his habit of jumping on my lap when I'm preoccupied, landing with a force strong enough to almost knock the wind out of me.

Raymond's health needs are dealt with at the Oakland Veterinary Clinic, owned and run by the very skillful (and very cute) Dr. Scott McNabb. Dr. McNabb has treated Raymond since he was a kitten, and I've made many trips there, carrying increasingly large cat carriers. However, last Tuesday the cat carrier was under a bunch of boxes in the utility room, so, on a whim, I carried Raymond to the car and let him ride in the passenger seat. As I expected, he was fine during the six-block ride to the clinic, standing up and watching the world go by outside the window. **However, the fun really began at the clinic.**

Note that the last sentence of the introduction is the writer's thesis statement. Should she have been more explicit about the events that were about to unfold? No—to do so would have spoiled the story for her readers.

*The Body*

The main section of the narrative is where the actual event or sequence of events is recounted. Note how the writer maintains control of the reader's perception of time while adding sensory detail to help amplify her story's effect:

> The waiting room looked peaceful enough. Three people were there with dogs in carriers, and two people had cats. Besides Raymond, the only "loose" animal was a small kitten playing on the lap of its owner. After surveying the room and sniffing the weird, ever-present medicinal smell, Raymond settled down on my lap and seemed perfectly happy.
>
> Suddenly, the door to the kennel burst open and a stream of dogs rushed into the waiting area. The dogs in their carriers immediately started barking, as did the intruders, who rushed up to their caged colleagues and checked them out. From the cat carriers came a frenzied clicking sound, as if someone had poured ice water on a nest of rattlesnakes. The kitten disappeared. Raymond stood up on my lap, digging in with his back claws (thank heaven his front ones had been removed), swelling up like a cobra. To say he resembled a black cat in a Halloween decoration would be both a cliché and an understatement; those cats aren't nearly as big as Raymond was at that point.
>
> Next, a loud rumbling bark reverberated from the kennel; a huge Rottweiler appeared, followed by Dr. McNabb. I've never really cared for Rottweilers, especially this one, which headed straight for me and Raymond. My great tom had met his match. He became very small (as small as an eighteen-pound cat can become), sinking down in my lap as if he were in a World War I bunker, staring at the approaching foe.
>
> During the crisis, Dr. McNabb retained his cool, acting as if this were business as usual. He grabbed the Rottweiler by the collar and had the presence of mind to reach over and scratch Raymond's ears.

Behind Dr. McNabb, his assistants rounded up the remaining dogs, which seemed to take an hour but actually took about five minutes.

Finally, all the dogs were led, dragged, or carried back to the kennel. The waiting room was eerily silent. The dogs had stopped barking, but the cats still apparently believed that Armageddon was in process. Raymond didn't move; his only reaction was to let down his hackles.

### The Conclusion

The concluding section of your essay recounts the aftermath, the wrapping up of loose ends. What were the immediate effects of your experience? What did you learn? Note how the writer of our model essay used two paragraphs to wrap up the story of her chaotic experience at the clinic:

When it was finally time for Raymond's shots, he submitted meekly. I waited until Dr. McNabb had finished before I asked the obvious question: "What happened?" He answered sheepishly, "My son's day care is closed today because of renovations. I brought him in to work with me, and he decided it would be fun to set the kennel dogs free."

Raymond has another appointment with Dr. McNabb in six weeks. I can only expect that we won't see a repeat of last Tuesday's events, but if we do, Raymond will be watching from inside his carrier. His days as a free-range clinic cat are over.

### EXERCISE 6.1

Write a sentence outline of "Chaos at the Veterinary Clinic." (For help with sentence outlines, see Chapter 2, pages 41–42.) What does the outline reveal about the essay's organization?

## Revising Your Draft

After you have completed a draft of your narrative essay, your next step is to revise it, using your own analysis and comments from classmates or friends. During peer review, answer the Questions for Reviewing a Narrative Essay (page 196) in regard to the draft you are reviewing, whether it is yours or another student's.

After reviewing for content, you need to go over your peer reviewers' responses to your essay and then revise for unity, coherence, language level, and tone (see Chapter 4). When you have revised your draft and are basically satisfied with it, read your draft for mechanical and grammatical errors. Concentrate on finding and correcting major sentence errors (fragment, comma splice, fused sentence), errors in pronoun agreement and subject-verb agreement, inappropriate shifts in verb tense, and spelling.

Now that you have made your corrections, *read your essay one more time* to catch any errors made during revision and find errors missed during your earlier reviews.

## Student Essay

The following essay is Claire Reid's response to a narrative assignment. Claire's mother had gone to considerable trouble so that her daughter could "come out in society." However, Claire had other ideas. This essay won first place in the personal essay contest held at her college. The final draft is presented first, followed by Claire's first draft, with her comments about this draft and what she needed to do in the revision stage.

### Claire's Final Draft

After the Fray

From the earliest time I can remember, my mother was always

instructing me on how to be a lady. She would dress me every morn-

1

- - - - - - - - - - - - - - - - - - - - - - - - - - - - - - - - - - - - - - - - -

## Questions for Reviewing a Narrative Essay

1   Does the introduction give the reader enough context? Does it capture the reader's interest? How could the introduction be strengthened?

2   What is the thesis statement? Has the writer placed it in the best position within the essay? How could it be improved? If there is no thesis statement, is the main point of the narrative clear from the way the writer presents the key events?

3   Does the narrative relate a significant event or series of events? How has the writer fulfilled his or her purpose for writing the essay?

4   Is the organization effective? Where would a flashforward help the writer get from one key event to the next? Where would a flashback be useful?

5   Do the topic sentences indicate the structure of the narrative?

6   Are the body paragraphs fully developed? Where are additional sensory details needed? Where could dialogue be added to make the narrative more lively and immediate?

7   Does the writer use time transitions to guide the reader? Where are transitional words or sentences needed?

8   Does the essay have an effective conclusion? How could it be improved?

ing in a freshly pressed dress, pin my hair back perfectly with tiny bows, and polish my patent leather shoes until they gleamed. "Sugar, spice, and everything nice, that's what little girls are made of," she'd say as she handed me my Barbie lunchbox and kissed me goodbye. I would come home at the end of the day, pink taffeta dress saturated in mud, hair matted into little knots around my bows, and pantyhose run clear to my thigh. "Claire," my mother would exclaim as she stripped me down and ripped through my hair, "someday I'm gonna make a lady out of you, even if it kills me!" I never doubted her when she took that tone of voice, and something told me, even then, that it was going to take a fight.

My time finally came when I was thirteen years old. One morning    2
I woke up to find an invitation to the Winter Park Women's Club Ball placed neatly on my breakfast plate. I ate that meal like it was my last supper. As my mother busied herself with invitations, reservations, and other plans to carry out my doom, I followed behind her, making it quite clear that I would rather die a miserable death than submit to this form of torture. I was convinced that she hated me and relished my suffering.

The following week was a whirlwind of dancing and etiquette    3
classes, fitting sessions, and rehearsals for the gala event. Out of pure spite toward my mother, I fought the whole way. I made every retailer on Park Avenue suffer as I flung dresses out of the stalls, raked the nerves of even the most composed etiquette teachers, and dragged my mother, exasperated and humiliated, through it all. After a week of all-out temper tantrums (on both of our parts), the day had finally come to take my place among society's finest bunch of clueless individuals. I spent the morning raging through the house, performing the grand finale I had worked up all week. She spent the morning locked in her room crying to my father, thinking I was disconnected and extreme, and blaming herself for all of my shortcomings. Finally, my father, put out by this whole chain of events,

demanded I put on my dress and comply with my mother's wishes for the rest of the evening. He then rounded up the family and herded us to the car.

The event went by in a whirlwind, and I hardly even noticed the elders who stopped to compliment me on my hair or tell me what an absolute princess I had become. I soon felt the room closing in on me and sought refuge behind the clubhouse on the fairway. As I stepped outside, I thought I could hear the faint sniffles of someone crying. Turning to my right and walking down the green, I stumbled upon my mother, sitting on the grass in her rumpled peach dress, crying like a baby. In her left hand was a wad of tissues, and in her right, much to my dismay, was a cigarette. "You know I don't usually smoke," she blurted out.

"I know," I replied, and plopped down next to her on the soft, fragrant grass. I'm not so sure how it happened, but in those few minutes behind that clubhouse full of little debutantes and their estranged parents, I caught the first glimpse of my mother. I saw her not as the one who cleans your cuts and tucks you in at night, but as a real person . . . and right then and there began our everlasting quest to understand each other.

Even now, my mother still swears she'll make a lady out of me or die trying. But after that day, she became a little less pushy and a little more trusting. She tells me she's gonna let the cards fall where they may, but she hopes the wind will push them in the right direction. And I, well, I'm learning that having an overbearing mother isn't so bad after all, and sometimes, just sometimes, it helps to take your mother's advice. The older I get, the more frequently I tell her, half joking but more seriously than she knows, that someday she just may make a lady out of me. "I've never doubted you when you use that tone of voice," she replies, "but I have a feeling it's gonna be a fight."

*Claire's First Draft*

### After the Fray

From the time I can Remember, my mother was always instructing me on how to be a lady. "Sugar, spice, and everything nice, that's what little girls are made of", she'd say as she hand me my Barbie lunchbox and kissed me goodbye. I would come home at the end of the day, pink taffetta dress saturated in mud, hair matted into little knots around my bows, and pantyhose run clear to my thigh. "Claire", my mother would exclaim as she stripped me down and ripped through my hair, "someday I'm gonna make a lady out of you, even if it kills me"! I never doubted her when she took that tone of voice, and something told me, even then, that it was going to take a fight.

My time finally came when I was thirteen years old. One morning I woke up to find an invitation to the Winter Park woman's club Ball placed neatly on my breakfast plate. I ate that meal like it was my last supper. I was convined that she hated me and relished in my suffering.

The following week was a whirlwind of dancing and etiquette classes, fitting sessions, and rehersals for the gala event.Out of pure spite toward my mother, I fought the whole way. I made every retailer on Park avenue suffer as I flung dresses out of the stalls, raked the nerves of even the most composed etiquitte teachers, and dragged my mother, exasperated and humiliated, through it all. after a week of all out temper tantrums (on both of our parts), the day had finally come to take my place among society's finest bunch of clueless individuals. I spent the morning raging through the house, performing the grand finale I had worked up all week. She spend the morning locked in her room crying to my father, thinking I was disconnected and extreme, and blaming herself for all of my shortcomings. Finally my father, put out by this whole chain of events,

1   I added details about how my mother would dress me to give the reader a better sense of our conflict.

2   I added some details here to show our conflict more clearly.

3

I'm not the best speller in the world, or the best typist. I made five proofreading passes through this to get rid of all the errors, but I didn't do the proofreading all at the same sitting.

demanded I don on my dress and comply for the rest of the evening. He then rounded up the family, and herded us to the car.

The event went by in a whirlwind, and I hardly even noticed the elders who stopped to complement me on my hair, or ell me what an absolute princess I had become. I soon felt the room closing in on me and sought refuge behind the clubhouse on the fairway. As I stepped outside, I thought I could hear the faint sniffles of someone crying. Turning to my right and walking down the green, I stumbled upon my mother, sitting on the grass in her rumpled peach dress, crying like a baby. In her left hand was a wad of tissues, and in her right, much to my dismay, was a cigarette. I'm not so sure how it happened, but in those few minutes behind that clubhouse full of little debutantes and their estranged parents, I caught the first glimpse of my mother. I saw her as not the one who cleans you cuts and tucks you in at night, but the real person . . . and right then and there began the everlasting quest to understand eachothther.

4

*I added some dialogue here to make the scene stronger.*

Even to this day, my mother still swears she'll make a lady out of me, or die trying. but after that day, she became a little less pushy and a little more trusting. She tells me she's gonna let the cards fall where they may, but she hopes the wind will push them in the right direction. And I, well, I'm learning that having an overbearing mother isn't so bad after all, and sometimes, just sometimes, it helps to take your mothers advice.

5

*My classmate thought I needed more here so I added a final quote.*

## EXERCISE 6.2: REVISING

The following is the first draft of a student's narrative essay. Working in pairs or in small groups, review this essay. Using the Questions for Reviewing a Narrative Essay on page 196, decide what revisions you would suggest. If you have any questions the student needs to consider, write them in the margin or on a separate sheet of paper. If your instructor directs you to, rewrite one or more paragraphs to make them stronger and to eliminate any grammatical or mechanical errors.

"stupid is it's own reward"

When I was seven I did the dumbest thing imaginable, I got my tongue stuck to a pumphandle.

I new not to do this. Like every one. But my brother Mike talk me in to it.

It was very cold that day, it was atleast 20 degrees. We got up and got dress in a hury, it was so cold. Mike and me went out side and we noticed what snow had left was frozen into ice.

Then we saw the old pump the one not hookedup any more. Then Mike dared me to put my tongue on the handle. I told him he was loony if he thought Id do that. Then he 'called me chicken'. And I couldnt let that go.

I was 8 years old, Mike was ten. He was my big brother - still is, but I new he was likely to play crule tricks on me. 'Just touch it with your tongue', he said, 'be quick and you wont get hurt'.

I did as he said my tongue froze instantly to the handle. Mike ran away laughing and I was trapped with terror and pain.

I forgiven Mike after awhile. Although, I still dont trust him.

## Additional Writing Topics

1. What is the most significant event that happened to you before you were five years old?

2. We all end up spending a great deal of our time in school. Write about an event that occurred in your K–12 years.

3. During high school, what was your single most "formative" experience? That is, was there an event that led you here today?

4. **Writing on the job.** What's the most interesting experience that you have had while working? Did it change your view of the job market? Write a narrative for someone who is about to enter the work force.

## Narration and Visual Representation

The daily newspaper has long been a standard part of our lives. However, over time the newspaper industry has been threatened by the rise of new technologies, beginning with radio, then television, and finally the Internet and related media. Newspapers have had to work harder to stay profitable. One method adopted by *USA Today,* which has been copied by many other print companies, is to create a more striking page: shorter articles, attention-grabbing story titles and photo captions, and other graphic devices designed to keep the attention of a public with an increasingly visual orientation.

Parodies were inevitable. The most successful is undoubtedly *The Onion,* a newspaper that was started in 1988 by two students at the University of Wisconsin and has since grown far beyond the confines of Madison. Today, *The*

*Onion* is available nationally, online, and in annual collections and specialty collections, such as *Our Dumb Century*.

*The Onion* portrays a breathless, sometimes brainless approach to the news, ruthlessly skewering "happy journalism" and its excesses. The page reproduced here was originally published in the 20 December 2001–16 January 2002 issue and then collected in *The Onion Ad Nauseam* (2003), edited by Robert Siegel.

**CATERERS** from previous page

"The last time, Five-Time Fatty loaded up his plate, I could see Matt making all these faces at me from across the room," said Salerno, who staffed the buffet table's ziti station for much of the party. "But Five-Time

> **"I've seen not one but two different people wearing pastel sweaters knotted around their necks,"** said Blaine, 20, during a cigarette break outside. **"I think we accidentally stepped into a time machine set for Dipwadville, 1984."**

was trying to chat me up, so I couldn't laugh. I knew Matt was praying that I'd bust up right in front of the guy."

While most partygoer-mocking is traditionally done during a party itself, Feather & Fennel staffers have been known to mock particularly memorable guests weeks or even months after an event.

"One guy at a bar mitzvah got so shitfaced, he passed out in a plate of kugel," Blaine said. "Ever since, whenever we see somebody who looks like he's about to pass out, we say, 'Uh-oh, better hide the kugel.' Man, that guy was seriously plowed."

Experts say mockery of the well-to-do by the serving class is a millennia-old tradition.

> While most partygoer-mocking is traditionally done during a party itself, Feather & Fennel staffers have been known to mock particularly memorable guests weeks or even months after an event.

"Whenever people are forced to serve others, resentment and derision are inevitable," said Dr. Henry Janssen, a University of Georgia anthropologist. "This tradition dates back to Ancient Greece, where servants at grand Athenian feasts would sneak into the kitchen to put on short plays lampooning the foibles of their wealthy, gluttonous guests. As long as there are people who stuff their faces

*Above: The Dawes grimly watch* It's A Wonderful Life.

# Emotionally Distant Family Spends Holidays Watching Touching Family Dramas Together

RUTLAND, VT—In what has become an annual holiday tradition, the dysfunctional Dawes family came together Sunday to sit in front of the TV and watch touching, feel-good family dramas in stony silence.

"We see each other so rarely," said Nicole Dawes, 44, whose three children were all home from college. "It's so nice to all sit down together and have a peaceful time. And [son] Kevin didn't bring up that awful new girlfriend of his once the entire time."

Following a special holiday dinner of turkey, artichokes, and spiced yams, Nicole and sullen daughter Gabrielle, an 18-year-old freshman at the University of Vermont, were put in charge of selecting the movies to watch. The two shared a wordless 10-minute car trip to their local Blockbuster video store, where Gabrielle ruled out most of her mother's choices as "stupid" or "lame." Tired of saying no and eager to leave the store, Gabrielle finally assented to the holiday classic *It's A Wonderful Life* and the 1994 remake of *Miracle On 34th Street*.

"I can't believe we got *Miracle On 34th Street* again," Gabrielle said. "Still, it's better than some of the other stuff my mom was pulling off the shelves. I mean, *The Santa Clause*? How gay is that? I hate Tim Allen."

Added Gabrielle, "I wish we hadn't gotten *It's A Wonderful Life*. It's so

every December?"

Upon Nicole and Gabrielle's return, *It's A Wonderful Life* was promptly inserted into the living-room VCR. Familiar with the annual routine, the

> **"I can't believe we got** *Miracle On 34th Street* **again,"** Gabrielle said. **"Still, it's better than some of the other stuff my mom was pulling off the shelves. I mean,** *The Santa Clause***? How gay is that? I hate Tim Allen."**

family members huddled around the TV without exchanging a word, just as they have since the holiday tradition began in 1991.

As the movie played, Kevin, 22, a senior at Southern Vermont College, paid little attention, wrapped up in thoughts of his impending graduation. The few times he did focus on the film, it was to negatively compare his own family to the Baileys.

"That movie always makes me think

said. "He'd probably blame us and drag us all down with him. Good thing he isn't trusted with much money at his job."

Following the conclusion of *It's A Wonderful Life*, an awkward 80-second silence occurred as the videotape rewound. The silence was briefly broken by daughter Gina, 20, who remarked that the evening's dinner had been "really good." Peter, her father, grunted in agreement.

As *Miracle On 34th Street* played, Peter sat in rapt attention, pushing aside anxieties about work, aging, and his chilly relationship with his children.

"The original was one of my all-time favorites," Peter said. "I was trying to spot the differences between the two. I was just glad to have something to focus on besides trying to make conversation with the kids. I have no idea what they're up to these days. Jesus, they're all grown up, able to vote and all. I wonder if they hate me."

Some 40 minutes into the movie, having consumed three snifters of brandy, Peter fell asleep.

When the second movie finished, the three children claimed exhaustion and trundled off to their childhood bedrooms, feigning excitement for the following day's Christmas-tree shopping excursion.

"It's good to see all the kids together again. It reminds me of when they'd

1. Write a response to this newspaper page and the full article contained within it ("Emotionally Distant Family Spends Holidays Watching Touching Family Dramas Together"). What are your thoughts and impressions? As you write, refer to Questions for Reviewing a Visual Representation.

2. As mentioned, *The Onion* was founded by two college students. Research another major company or organization that began when its founder was still in college. (Microsoft is the most famous example, but look for others.) Then either write an essay about the company history, remembering to document your sources (see also Chapter 21), or develop an oral presentation on the same subject (see also Chapter 18).

## Questions for Reviewing a Visual Representation

- Is the representation forceful, passive, or something in between?

- What is the purpose of the representation—in other words, what is it trying to do to you, the reader/viewer?

- If the representation uses words, do they reinforce the visual image or in some way contradict it?

- What is the presumed audience for the representation—men, women, children, the elderly? Or does it have a broader appeal?

- If the representation is an advertisement, is it trying to sell a product or to get you to adopt a way of thinking?

- If the representation is an advertisement, does it try to persuade you in a fair manner, or do you feel manipulated?

## Responding to an Image

In Roman Polanski's *Chinatown* (1974-R), Jack Nicholson plays Jake Gittes, a Los Angeles private detective who, in the late 1930s, is investigating a very complex case involving the death of the city's water commissioner. His widow, Evelyn Mulray, played by Faye Dunaway, hires Jake to help her.

In this scene, Jake and Evelyn are clearly growing fond of each other. However, each has a dark secret. When Evelyn won't tell Jake what she knows, she plunges the pair into grave danger.

© Paramount/The Kobal Collection.

1. Some narrative essays are able to use a very effective device: withholding key information from the reader until the crucial moment. Write a personal narrative that uses this technique. Caution: make sure that your reader doesn't feel cheated; in other words, don't withhold information unfairly.

2. Watch *Chinatown* to find out what Jake eventually learns. Why is the secret so closely guarded? Does the 1930s setting affect the keeping of the secret? Would the issue be treated differently today? Write an essay in which you explore these ideas.

## Using the Internet

Search the Internet for insights and information to use in narrative essays.

1. Search the Internet to find information about the use or prohibition of the death penalty in your state, in a neighboring state, or in another country. Use this information to write a short history of capital punishment in your state. Focus on a few questions:

   - When was capital punishment first used?
   - How often has it been used and for what crimes?
   - Is capital punishment still used? Has it ever been banned by law?
   - What method(s) of execution have been used?
   - Have any death row inmates been exonerated?

   Rely on more than one Internet source to find information.

2. Go online to find sites that contain and/or discuss myths, tales, or legends used by any culture of your choice to teach people about death, illness, poverty, suffering, infidelity, sin, or some other aspect of the darker side of human existence. Write about this topic by first summarizing a tale or myth. Then explain how this story might help you explain the existence of a particular evil or harsh reality to a child. As an alternate assignment, summarize two different myths or tales on the same subject; then compare and/or contrast their messages (see Chapter 12) and how the stories present them.

DILBERT © Scott Adams/Dist. by United Feature Syndicate, Inc.

### CHAPTER 7

# EXEMPLIFICATION

# Writing in Context

www.dilbert.com

SO I EMBARKED ON A THREE-YEAR MISSION TO MAKE THE BANK ADMIT ITS MISTAKE!

WOULD HE FIT IN?

UNFORTU- NATELY, YES.

Bob has called a meeting to discuss subcontracting part of a new software project. Osprey Online Technologies has used various vendors for this kind of help in the past, with varying results. The boss wants to talk about which company is best suited for the current project.

The meeting is attended by Bob, Stephanie (his assistant), two software developers, and Jason, who, along with you, will supervise the subcontractors.

Shortly after the meeting begins, Jason raises his hand. "I just want to say that whichever outfit we choose, I hope it's not IBDmc. We've had a lot of trouble with them in the past two years. They're sloppy. I figure —"

Bob interrupts. "Give me some specifics."

"What?" Jason seems surprised, as if Bob had happened to question whether the sun will rise and set.

"Refresh my memory. Give me some *examples* of problems that we've had. In writing, please."

Bob is making a reasonable request here: ground the complaint in actual fact. Jason's distrust of the vendor may be justified, but where's the evidence?

# HOW DOES EXEMPLIFICATION WORK?

When writers back up their assertions with a specific example or examples, they are using **exemplification**. Exemplification has two distinct uses. One is as an internal strategy, a way of providing concrete details to back up assertions and claims of every type. Most essays that you write will use these concrete details. You will find that you need to provide examples to develop paragraphs and essays written for many different purposes. Readers appreciate a well-written passage that presents an interesting or provocative general statement ("Rubbernecking is as dangerous as drunk driving"), but they will like that passage much more if it backs up the general statement with concrete evidence and details. Notice the difference between the following two paragraphs:

> Sometimes a false picture emerges of the U.S. generals in World War II. The exploits of a few romantic individuals, each of whom saw himself as the leader of a historical crusade, tend to overshadow the reality of how the American end of the war was run. Our command was actually in the hands of generals who were effectively bureaucrats—competent managers who didn't let their personalities get in the way of the larger effort.

> Sometimes a false picture emerges of the U.S. generals in World War II. A few generals had a somewhat romantic view of their roles. George S. Patton in the European theater and Douglas MacArthur in the Pacific each saw himself as the leader of a historical crusade. But such individuals overshadow the reality of how the American end of the war was run. Our command was actually in the hands of generals who were effectively bureaucrats—competent managers such as Dwight Eisenhower, Omar Bradley, and Mark Clark. These men didn't let their personalities get in the way of the larger effort. They in turn reported to the ultimate manager, George Marshall, who "ran the war" just as a company president "runs the firm."

The first paragraph seems acceptable until you read the second one. Your writing instructor knows the value of specific examples and will likely prompt you to include them if you have neglected to do so. No other strategy connects abstract thought to human reality as effectively as a well-chosen example.

The second use of exemplification is as an overall pattern for an essay. A writer of an exemplification essay wants to illustrate a situation or make a point; the writer explains and supports the thesis with examples drawn from his or her experience or research into a topic. Some essays will analyze one extended example for this purpose. But how does exemplification differ from the other rhetorical options that are used to explain something to readers?

In Chapter 8 and Chapter 9 you will be introduced to two forms of **analysis**: process analysis in Chapter 8 and causal analysis in Chapter 9. Process analysis shows *how* something happens or has happened. Causal analysis shows *why* something happened or what might happen as the result of some action. The exemplification essay has a similar but more general goal—to explain a situation or problem. Exemplification is actually a form of analysis, a way of looking into a problem or situation and explaining it.

Consider the following scenario: your campus has been ravaged by tornadoes, but so far the administration has managed to avoid canceling a large number of classes. Here is how the three types of analysis could be used to address this situation:

- **Causal analysis.** You could write an essay that answers this question: What were the *effects* of the tornadoes? In your essay, you would probably discuss the destruction of all or parts of buildings on campus, the classes that had to be moved from their normally scheduled rooms to temporary areas, and whatever class cancellations were inevitable.

- **Process analysis.** You could write an essay that considers *how* the administration is coping with the problems caused by the storms. In your essay, you would probably focus on the steps that the administration has taken: ordering emergency repair estimates, moving classes, rescheduling labs, and so on.

- **Exemplification.** For this kind of essay, you would probably answer this question: *What is* the current situation on campus after the recent tornadoes? In your essay, you would concentrate on *illustrating* the problems faced by students, staff, and faculty by providing specific examples of each one. For instance, you might mention the decrease in the number of student parking spots resulting from the fact that a large oak fell onto the main student lot.

You will use exemplification in many writing situations throughout your college career. For example, Chapter 19 of this text covers the essay examination, a form of testing that you can expect to face in many of your courses. In an American history class, for instance, you might see this item on an essay test: "Discuss the situation faced by the Confederate army after its defeat at Gettysburg." This question is designed to let you display your knowledge in an essay format. Let's say that you decide to concentrate on these three areas in your essay: momentum, morale, and manpower. Besides the nifty alliteration produced by those *m*'s, you believe that these were the three most important issues for the Confederates after Gettysburg. However, your history instructor doesn't want to read an essay filled with generalizations. ("Both sides fought hard." "Many lives were lost." "It was a great victory for the North.") Instead, he or she wants to see general statements backed up by **evidence**: examples that consist of facts, quotations, and statistics. When you support your general statements with this kind of evidence, you demonstrate that you have studied and assimilated the material; your resulting essay shows that you understand the evidence in context.

The exemplification option is useful not only in response to essay examination questions but in many other writing situations as well. For example, suppose that a student journalist were given this assignment: "Describe the current controversy over the misuse of Student Government funds." Despite the presence of the word *describe,* the prompt is really asking the writer to explain, to *elucidate,* using examples.

Exemplification is enormously versatile. Writers often use it to explain their world, as we see in the readings that follow.

**Consider Your Options** •

How might you use exemplification strategies on the job? What circumstances would call for you to explain a workplace situation by using specific examples?

# READING THE EXEMPLIFICATION ESSAY WITH A WRITER'S EYE

In the three works that follow, Brent Staples writes about dealing with the general public's fear of unknown black men, Lars Eighner writes about what it is like to dine from a Dumpster, and Harry F. Waters illustrates the false picture of American society that television provides. As you read these essays, concentrate on the authors' *purpose*. What are they trying to prove? Writers of exemplification essays are usually presenting their generalizations and examples for a reason; readers always appreciate concrete examples, which makes this option ideal for getting a writer's message across.

Following the essays, the second half of this chapter features strategies for writing the exemplification essay with a reader's eye (pages 226–231). If you decide to write on one of the topics that follow the three essays below, make sure that you have read the strategies section before you begin. Also note that additional writing topics are listed at the end of the chapter (page 237).

# Just Walk on By

## BRENT STAPLES

*Brent Staples received a doctorate in psychology from the University of Chicago and taught psychology before becoming a writer and an editor. He worked for the* Chicago Sun-Times *and then the* New York Times, *where he serves on the editorial board and is an editorial writer. His 1994 memoir,* Parallel Time: Growing Up in Black and White, *won the Anisfield Wolff Book Award.*

*"Just Walk on By" originally appeared in* Ms. *in 1986 and then in a revised version, "Black Men and Public Space," in* Harper's *(1987). In this widely anthologized essay, Staples gives readers vivid examples of one middle-class black man's experience in a country dominated by whites.*

My first victim was a woman—white, well dressed, probably in her early twenties. I came upon her late one evening on a deserted street in Hyde Park, a relatively affluent neighborhood in an otherwise mean, impoverished section of Chicago. As I swung onto the avenue behind her, there seemed to be a discreet, uninflammatory distance between us. Not so. She cast back a worried glance. To her, the youngish black man— a broad six feet two inches with a beard and billowing hair, both hands shoved into the pockets of a bulky military jacket—seemed menacingly close. After a few more quick glimpses, she picked up her pace and was soon running in earnest. Within seconds she disappeared into a cross street.

That was more than a decade ago. I was 22 years old, a graduate student newly arrived at the University of Chicago. It was in the echo of that terrified woman's footfalls that I first began to know the unwieldy inheritance I'd come into—the ability to alter public space in ugly ways. It was clear that she thought herself the quarry of a mugger, a rapist, or worse. Suffering a bout of insomnia, however, I was stalking sleep, not defenseless wayfarers. As a softy who is scarcely able to take a knife to a raw chicken—let alone hold it to a person's throat—I was surprised, embarrassed, and dismayed all at once. Her flight made me feel like an accomplice in tyranny. It also made it clear that I was indistinguishable from the muggers who occasionally seeped into the area from the surrounding ghetto. That first encounter, and those that followed, signified that a vast, unnerving gulf lay between nighttime pedestrians—particularly women—and me. And I soon gathered that being perceived as dangerous is a hazard in itself. I only needed to turn a corner into a dicey situation, or crowd some frightened, armed person in a foyer somewhere, or make an errant move after being pulled over by a policeman. Where fear and weapons meet—and they often do in urban America—there is always the possibility of death.

In that first year, my first away from my hometown, I was to become thoroughly familiar with the language of fear. At dark, shadowy intersections in Chicago, I could cross in front of a car stopped at a traffic light and elicit the thunk, thunk, thunk, thunk of the driver—black, white, male, or female—hammering down the door locks. On less traveled streets after dark, I grew accustomed to but never comfortable with people who crossed to the other side of the street rather than pass me. Then there were the standard unpleasantries with police, doormen, bouncers, cab drivers, and others whose business it is to screen out troublesome individuals before there is any nastiness.

I moved to New York nearly two years ago and I have remained an avid night walker. In central Manhattan, the near-constant crowd cover minimizes tense one-on-one street encounters. Elsewhere—visiting friends in SoHo, where sidewalks are narrow and tightly spaced buildings shut out the sky—things can get very taut indeed.

Black men have a firm place in New York mugging literature. Norman Podhoretz in his famed (or infamous) 1963 essay, "My Negro Problem—And Ours," recalls growing up in terror of black males; they "were tougher than we were, more ruthless," he writes—and as an adult on the Upper West Side of Manhattan, he continues, he cannot constrain his nervousness when he meets black men on certain streets. Similarly, a decade later, the essayist and novelist Edward Hoagland extols a New York where once "Negro bitterness bore down mainly on other Negroes." Where some see mere panhandlers, Hoagland sees "a mugger who is clearly screwing up his nerve to do more than just ask for money." But Hoagland has "the New Yorker's quickhunch posture for broken-field maneuvering," and the bad guy swerves away.

I often witness that "hunch posture," from women after dark on the warrenlike streets of Brooklyn where I live. They seem to set their faces on neutral and, with their purse straps strung across their chests bandolier style, they forge ahead as though bracing themselves against being tackled. I understand, of course, that the danger they perceive is not a hallucination. Women are particularly vulnerable to street violence, and young black males are drastically overrepresented among the perpetrators of that violence. Yet these truths are no solace against the kind of alienation that comes of being ever suspect, against being set apart, a fearsome entity with whom pedestrians avoid making eye contact.

It is not altogether clear to me how I reached the ripe old age of 22 without being conscious of the lethality nighttime pedestrians attributed to me. Perhaps it was because in Chester, Pennsylvania, the small, angry industrial town where I came of age in the 1960s, I was scarcely noticeable against a backdrop of gang warfare, street knifings, and murders. I grew up one of the good boys, had perhaps a half-dozen fist fights. In retrospect, my shyness of combat has clear sources.

Many things go into the making of a young thug. One of those things is the consummation of the male romance with the power to intimidate. An infant discovers that random flailings send the baby bottle flying out of the crib and crashing to the floor. Delighted, the joyful babe repeats those motions again and again, seeking to duplicate the feat. Just so, I recall the points at which some of my boyhood friends were finally seduced by the perception of themselves as tough guys. When a mark cowered and surrendered his money without resistance, myth and reality merged—and paid off. It is, after all, only manly to embrace the power to frighten and intimidate. We, as men, are not supposed to give an inch of our lane on the highway; we are to seize the fighter's edge in work and in play and even in love; we are to be valiant in the face of hostile forces.

Unfortunately, poor and powerless young men seem to take all this nonsense literally. As a boy, I saw countless tough guys locked away; I have since buried several, too. They were babies, really—a teenage cousin, a brother of 22, a childhood friend in his mid-twenties—all gone down in episodes of bravado played out in the streets. I came to doubt the virtues of intimidation early on. I chose, perhaps even unconsciously, to remain a shadow—timid, but a survivor.

The fearsomeness mistakenly attributed to me in public places often has a perilous flavor. The most frightening of these confusions occurred in the late 1970s and early 1980s when I worked as a journalist in Chicago. One day, rushing into the office of a magazine I was writing for with a deadline story in hand, I was mistaken for a burglar. The office manager called security and, with an ad hoc posse, pursued me through the labyrinthine halls, nearly to my editor's door. I had no way of proving who I was. I could only move briskly toward the company of someone who knew me.

Another time I was on assignment for a local paper and killing time before an interview. I entered a jewelry store on the city's affluent Near North Side. The proprietor excused herself and returned with an enormous red Doberman pinscher straining at the end of a leash. She stood, the dog extended toward me, silent to my questions, her eyes bulging nearly out of her head. I took a cursory look around, nodded, and bade her good night. Relatively speaking, however, I never fared

as badly as another black male journalist. He went to nearby Waukegan, Illinois, a couple of summers ago to work on a story about a murderer who was born there. Mistaking the reporter for the killer, police hauled him from his car at gunpoint and but for his press credentials would probably have tried to book him. Such episodes are not uncommon. Black men trade tales like this all the time.

In "My Negro Problem—And Ours," Podhoretz writes that the hatred he feels for blacks makes itself known to him through a variety of avenues—one being his discomfort with that "special brand of paranoid touchiness" to which he says blacks are prone. No doubt he is speaking here of black men. In time, I learned to smother the rage I felt at so often being taken for a criminal. Not to do so would surely have led to madness—via that special "paranoid touchiness" that so annoyed Podhoretz at the time he wrote the essay.

I began to take precautions to make myself less threatening. I move about with care, particularly late in the evening. I give a wide berth to nervous people on subway platforms during the wee hours, particularly when I have exchanged business clothes for jeans. If I happen to be entering a building behind some people who appear skittish, I may walk by, letting them clear the lobby before I return, so as not to seem to be following them. I have been calm and extremely congenial on those rare occasions when I've been pulled over by the police.

And on late-evening constitutionals along streets less traveled by, I employ what has proved to be an excellent tension-reducing measure: I whistle melodies from Beethoven and Vivaldi and the more popular classical composers. Even steely New Yorkers hunching toward nighttime destinations seem to relax, and occasionally they even join in the tune. Virtually everybody seems to sense that a mugger wouldn't be warbling bright, sunny selections from Vivaldi's *Four Seasons*. It is my equivalent of the cowbell that hikers wear when they know they are in bear country.

## Vocabulary

The following terms are identified by paragraph number. Make sure that you understand each term's meaning in its context. If you're not sure that you understand a term, look it up in a college-level dictionary.

| | | |
|---|---|---|
| affluent (1) | errant (2) | consummation (8) |
| discreet (1) | elicit (3) | bravado (9) |
| billowing (1) | extol (5) | labyrinthine (10) |
| unwieldy (2) | bandolier (6) | affluent (11) |
| quarry (2) | perpetrator (6) | proprietor (11) |
| insomnia (2) | solace (6) | cursory (11) |
| wayfarer (2) | alienation (6) | bade (11) |
| tyranny (2) | entity (6) | berth (13) |
| dicey (2) | lethality (7) | skittish (13) |
| foyer (2) | retrospect (7) | congenial (13) |

## Style and Strategy

1. In the opening sentence, why does Staples refer to his "first victim"? How does Staples's opening paragraph capture readers' attention?

2. What is the contrast between the "real" Staples and how he is perceived by others? How does Staples make that contrast clear?

3. Most of Staples's examples are from his own experience. What other examples does he provide? What do they add to the essay?

4. Staples has every right to be angry about what he has gone through. Is the tone of this essay angry? Explain.

## Questions for Critical Thinking and Discussion

1. This essay is about the harmful effects of stereotyping—white Americans frequently fear young black men, so Staples is feared. How often, and in what contexts, do you see negative stereotyping in your daily life?

2. Consider the following situation. You walk into a busy office where four young workers are frantically running around and getting into loud arguments with one another. In the midst of these four is an older woman working calmly and serenely, never showing the tension and apprehensiveness that afflict her colleagues. Who are you going to go to for assistance? If you said "the older woman," is this an example of positive stereotyping? How?

3. We all depend a great deal on first impressions—how a person looks and behaves, and how those features fit in with our past experiences. How often are your first impressions wrong? In other words, explain a situation in which you got to know a person and found him or her to be quite unlike your presumption.

*Suggestions for Writing*

1. Staples discusses an identity problem caused by the way in which he is perceived by others. Obviously, he has been a victim of stereotyping. But there are many reasons for which people might misperceive others. Using examples taken from your own experiences, write a 500- to 750-word essay that explains some of the ways in which people have misperceived you or someone you know well. In the process, explain the cause of this misperception.

2. Staples mentions several ways in which he tried to reassure people he came across during his late-night walks that they had nothing to fear from him. In other words, he attempted to change their perception of him. Have you ever been misjudged or seen as something you were not? Write an essay of 500 to 750 words in which you develop examples of the kinds of things you did (or do) to correct misperceptions that others had (or have) about you.

3. Many of the examples that Staples uses recall dangerous situations. Staples's problem was directly related to his sex, age, and race, but many of us frequently face danger because of who we are, where we live, the roads we travel, or the kinds of jobs we hold. Some of us even place ourselves in danger through the kinds of activities we choose to engage in. Write an essay in which you use examples to show that you or someone you know faces danger on a relatively frequent basis.

*Speaking Assignment*

Have you ever been unfairly stereotyped and not known how to respond? Do you know someone else who has been in this situation? If so, prepare a presentation that begins by briefly summarizing the experience. Then spend the rest of the time explaining how you or your subject might respond if this ever happens again. In other words, give yourself or the other person some advice to prepare for a recurrence. (For more help with oral presentations, see Chapter 18.)

# On Dumpster Diving

## LARS EIGHNER

*When Lars Eighner wrote "On Dumpster Diving," he was homeless after having been fired from his job in Austin, Texas. With Lizbeth, his Labrador retriever, Eighner spent three years on the streets.*

*"On Dumpster Diving" is a revised version of an essay origi-nally published in 1991 in* Threepenny Review *and included in the book* Travels with Lizbeth: Three Years on the Road and on the *Streets (1993). In it, Eighner uses a series of examples to comment on how what we throw away defines the way we live.*

Long before I began Dumpster diving I was impressed with Dumpsters, enough so that I wrote the Merriam-Webster research service to    1 discover what I could about the word *Dumpster.* I learned from them that it is a proprietary word belonging to the Dempster Dumpster company. Since then I have dutifully capitalized the word, although it was lowercased in almost all the citations Merriam-Webster photocopied for me. Dempster's word is too apt. I have never heard these things called anything but Dumpsters. I do not know anyone who knows the generic name for these objects. From time to time I have heard a wino or hobo give some corrupted credit to the original and call them Dipsy Dumpsters.

I began Dumpster diving about a year before I became homeless. 2

I prefer the word *scavenging* and use the word *scrounging* when I mean to be obscure. I have heard people, evidently meaning to be polite, use the word *foraging,* but I prefer to reserve that word for gathering nuts and berries and such, which I do also according to the season and the opportunity. *Dumpster diving* seems to me to be a little too cute and, in my case, inaccurate because I lack the athletic ability to lower myself into the Dumpsters as the true divers do, much to their increased profit. 3

I like the frankness of the word *scavenging,* which I can hardly think of without picturing a big black snail on an aquarium wall. I live from the refuse of others. I am a scavenger. I think it a sound and honorable niche, although if I could I would naturally prefer to live the comfortable consumer life, perhaps—and only perhaps—as a slightly less wasteful consumer, owing to what I have learned as a scavenger. 4

While Lizbeth and I were still living in the shack on Avenue B as my savings ran out, I put almost all my sporadic income into rent. The necessities of daily life I began to extract from Dumpsters. Yes, we ate from them. Except for jeans, all my clothes came from Dumpsters. Boom boxes, candles, bedding, toilet paper, a virgin male love doll, medicine, books, a typewriter, dishes, furnishings, and change, sometimes amounting to 5

many dollars—I acquired many things from the Dumpsters.

I have learned much as a scavenger. I mean to put some of what I have learned down here, beginning with the practical art of Dumpster diving and proceeding to the abstract. 6

What is safe to eat? 7

After all, the finding of objects is becoming something of an urban art. Even respectable employed people will sometimes find something tempting sticking out of a Dumpster or standing beside one. Quite a number of people, not all of them of the bohemian type, are willing to brag that they found this or that piece in the trash. But eating from Dumpsters is what separates the dilettanti from the professionals. Eating safely from the Dumpsters involves three principles: using the senses and common sense to evaluate the condition of the found materials, knowing the Dumpsters of a given area and checking them regularly, and seeking always to answer the question "Why was this discarded?" 8

Perhaps everyone who has kitchen and a regular supply of groceries has, at one time or another, made a sandwich and eaten half of it before discovering mold on the bread or got a mouthful of milk before realizing the milk had turned. Nothing of the sort is likely to happen to a Dumpster diver because he is constantly reminded that most food is discarded for a reason. Yet a lot of perfectly good food can be found in Dumpsters. 9

Canned goods, for example, turn up fairly often in the Dumpsters I frequent. All except the most phobic people would be willing to eat from a can, even if it came from a Dumpster. Canned goods are among the safest of foods to be found in Dumpsters but are not utterly foolproof. 10

Although very rare with modern canning methods, botulism is a possibility. Most other forms of food poisoning seldom do lasting harm to a healthy person, but botulism is almost certainly fatal and often the first symptom is death. 11

Except for carbonated beverages, all canned goods should contain a slight vacuum and suck air when first punctured. Bulging, rusty, and dented cans and cans that spew when punctured should be avoided, especially when the contents are not very acidic or syrupy.

Heat can break down the botulin, but this requires much more cooking than most people do to canned goods. To the extent that botulism occurs at all, of course, it can occur in cans on pantry shelves as well as in cans from Dumpsters. Need I say that home-canned goods are simply too risky to be recommended.

From time to time one of my companions, aware of the source of my provisions, will ask, "Do you think these crackers are really safe to eat?" For some reason it is most often the crackers they ask about.

This question has always made me angry. Of course I would not offer my companion anything I had doubts about. But more than that, I wonder why he cannot evaluate the condition of the crackers for himself. I have no special knowledge and I have been wrong before. Since he knows where the food comes from, it seems to me he ought to assume some of the responsibility for deciding what he will put in his mouth. For myself I have few qualms about dry foods such as crackers, cookies, cereal, chips, and pasta if they are free of visible contaminates and still dry and crisp. Most often such things are found in the original packaging, which is not so much a positive sign as it is the absence of a negative one.

Raw fruits and vegetables with intact skins seem perfectly safe to me, excluding of course the obviously rotten. Many are discarded for minor imperfections that can be pared away. Leafy vegetables, grapes, cauliflower, broccoli, and similar things may be contaminated by liquids and may be impractical to wash.

Candy, especially hard candy, is usually safe if it has not drawn ants. Chocolate is often discarded only because it has become discolored as the cocoa butter de-emulsified. Candying, after all, is one method of food preservation because pathogens do not like very sugary substances.

All of these foods might be found in any Dumpster and can be evaluated with some confidence largely on the basis of appearance. Beyond these are foods that cannot be correctly evaluated without additional information.

I began scavenging by pulling pizzas out of the Dumpster behind a pizza delivery shop. In general, prepared food requires caution, but in this case I knew when the shop closed and went to the Dumpster as soon as the last of the help left.

Such shops often get prank orders; both the orders and the products made to fill them are called *bogus*. Because help seldom stays long at these places, pizzas are often made with the wrong topping, refused on delivery for being cold, or baked incorrectly. The products to be discarded are boxed up because inventory is kept by counting boxes: A boxed pizza can be written off; an unboxed pizza does not exist.

I never placed a bogus order to increase the supply of pizzas and I believe no one else was scavenging in this Dumpster. But the people in the shop became suspicious and began to retain their garbage in the shop overnight. While it lasted I had a steady supply of fresh, sometimes warm pizza. Because I knew the Dumpster I knew the source of the pizza, and because I visited the Dumpster regularly I knew what was fresh and what was yesterday's.

The area I frequent is inhabited by many affluent college students. I am not here by chance; the Dumpsters in this area are very rich. Students throw out many good things, including food. In particular they tend to throw everything out when they move at the end of a semester, before and after breaks, and around midterm, when many of them despair of college. So I find it advantageous to keep an eye on the academic calendar.

Students throw food away around breaks because they do not know whether it has spoiled or will spoil before they return. A typical discard is a half jar of peanut butter. In fact, nonorganic peanut butter does not require refrigeration and is unlikely to spoil in any reasonable time. The student does not know that, and since it is Daddy's money, the student decides not to take a chance. Opened containers require caution and some attention to the question "Why was this discarded?" But in the case of discards from student apartments, the answer may be that the item was thrown out through carelessness, ignorance, or wastefulness. This can sometimes be deduced when the item is found with many others, including some that are obviously perfectly good.

Some students, and others, approach defrosting a freezer by chucking out the whole lot. Not only do the circumstances of such a find tell the story, but also the mass of frozen goods stays cold for a long time and items may be found still frozen or freshly thawed. 23

Yogurt, cheese, and sour cream are items that are often thrown out while they are still good. Occasionally I find a cheese with a spot of mold, which of course I just pare off, and because it is obvious why such a cheese was discarded, I treat it with less suspicion than an apparently perfect cheese found in similar circumstances. Yogurt is often discarded, still sealed, only because the expiration date on the carton had passed. This is one of my favorite finds because yogurt will keep for several days, even in warm weather. 24

Students throw out canned goods and staples at the end of semesters and when they give up college at midterm. Drugs, pornography, spirits, and the like are often discarded when parents are expected—Dad's Day, for example. And spirits also turn up after big party weekends, presumably discarded by the newly reformed. Wine and spirits, of course, keep perfectly well even once opened, but the same cannot be said of beer. 25

My test for carbonated soft drinks is whether they still fizz vigorously. Many juices or other beverages are too acidic or too syrupy to cause much 26 concern, provided they are not visibly contaminated. I have discovered nasty molds in vegetable juices, even when the product was found under its original seal; I recommend that such products be decanted slowly into a clear glass. Liquids always require some care. One hot day I found a large jug of Pat O'Brien's Hurricane mix. The jug had been opened but was still ice cold. I drank three large glasses before it became apparent to me that someone had added rum to the mix, and not a little rum. I never tasted the rum, and by the time I began to feel the effects I had already ingested a very large quantity of the beverage. Some divers would have considered this a boon, but being suddenly intoxicated in a public place in the early afternoon is not my idea of a good time.

I have heard of people maliciously contaminating discarded food and even handouts, but mostly I have heard of this from people with vivid imaginations who have had no experience with the Dumpsters themselves. Just before the pizza shop stopped discarding its garbage at night, jalapeños began showing up on most of the thrown-out pizzas. If indeed this was meant to discourage me, it was a wasted effort because I am a native Texan. 27

For myself, I avoid game, poultry, pork, and egg-based foods, whether I find them raw or cooked. I seldom have the means to cook what I find, but when I do I avail myself of plentiful supplies of beef, which is often in very good condition. I suppose fish becomes disagreeable before it becomes dangerous. Lizbeth is happy to have any such thing that is past its prime and, in fact, does not recognize fish as food until it is quite strong. 28

Home leftovers, as opposed to surpluses from restaurants, are very often bad. Evidently, especially among students, there is a common type of personality that carefully wraps up even the smallest leftover and shoves it into the back of the refrigerator for six months or so before discarding it. Characteristic of this type are the reused jars 29 and margarine tubs to which the remains are committed. I avoid ethnic foods I am unfamiliar with. If I do not know what it is supposed to look like when it is good, I cannot be certain I will be able to tell if it is bad.

No matter how careful I am I still get dysen- 30 tery at least once a month, oftener in warm weather. I do not want to paint too romantic a picture. Dumpster diving has serious drawbacks as a way of life.

## Vocabulary

The following terms are identified by paragraph number. Make sure that you understand each term's meaning in its context. If you're not sure that you understand a term, look it up in a college-level dictionary.

| | | |
|---|---|---|
| proprietary (1) | refuse (4) | pathogens (16) |
| dutifully (1) | niche (4) | advantageous (21) |
| citations (1) | sporadic (5) | deduced (22) |
| apt (1) | bohemian (8) | expiration (24) |
| generic (1) | dilettanti (8) | staples (25) |
| corrupted (1) | phobic (10) | spirits (25) |
| frankness (4) | qualms (14) | dysentery (30) |

## Style and Strategy

1.  Many Americans see homelessness as a vast national tragedy. (In such a prosperous country, how could so many people be adrift?) Does Eighner's tone reflect this attitude, or does it indicate that he is taking a different approach? Explain.

2.  At times, this essay almost seems as if it were written by a sociologist studying Americans' discards in order to analyze consumer habits. (Such studies have been conducted.) But who is Eighner's audience? How will this audience react to Eighner's examples?

3.  Explain how Eighner incorporates the following three strategies as part of his exemplification essay: process analysis (see Chapter 8), causal analysis (Chapter 9), and comparison and contrast (Chapter 12).

## Questions for Critical Thinking and Discussion

1.  Are there people in your city or town who are *involuntarily* homeless? Do you know what caused them to lose their homes?

2.  Why would someone *choose* to be homeless?

3.  Are you an efficient consumer, or would a "scavenger" welcome the chance to sort through your garbage? Explain.

**4.** Would you take something from a garbage can or a Dumpster if the item appealed to you? Explain.

## Suggestions for Writing

**1.** Write a 500-word essay about an activity that most people dislike and avoid (for example, cleaning an apartment or doing laundry) but that you perversely enjoy. Give examples that show why you enjoy this activity.

**2.** Write a 500-word essay about an activity that most people enjoy but that you dread. Give examples that show why you dislike this normally "positive" experience.

**3.** Eighner shows us that people can survive on very little money and can, in fact, eat for free. As a college student, you have probably had to stretch a dollar in order to make ends meet. Write a 500- to 750-word exemplification essay that discusses ways in which college students on a limited budget can make the most of their money. For your intended audience, pretend that you are writing to a group of freshmen who have just started classes at your college.

**4.** Do Americans waste food and other precious resources? Provide several examples of the kinds of wasteful behavior that people engage in regularly. If possible, extend your discussion by offering recommendations that might help your readers conserve.

## Speaking Assignment

In some ways, Eighner's essay is a guide to survival. Prepare a presentation in which you explain various ways to survive a particular situation that you or your classmates are apt to face. For example, explain a few ways to survive a bad blind date, a trip to the dentist, or the end of a romantic relationship. (For more help with oral presentations, see Chapter 18.)

# Life According to TV

## HARRY F. WATERS

*Television plays a major role in the United States, even for people who don't watch it very often. Television's influence is vast and incalculable. However, is television an accurate reflection of life in the United States? Harry F. Waters, a staff writer for* Newsweek *(where this essay appeared on December 6, 1982), doesn't think so. Drawing on the work of media scholar George Gerbner, Waters's essay shows, by example after example, that television is a faulty mirror of American society.*

The late Paddy Chayefsky, who created Howard Beale,* would have loved George Gerbner. In *Network*, Chayefsky marshaled a scathing fictional

---

*****Howard Beale:** a character in the film *Network*, a satire of the television industry's pursuit of ratings. Played by Peter Finch, Beale is remembered for screaming "I'm mad as hell, and I'm not going to take this anymore!"

assault on the values and methods of the people who control the world's most potent communications instrument. In real life, Gerbner, perhaps the nation's foremost authority on the social impact of television, is quietly using the disciplines of behavioral research to construct an equally devastating indictment of the medium's images and messages. More than any spokesman for a pressure group, Gerbner has become the man that television watches. From his cramped, book-lined office at the University of Pennsylvania springs a steady flow of studies that are raising executive blood pressures at the networks' sleek Manhattan command posts.

George Gerbner's work is uniquely important 2 because it transports the scientific examination of television far beyond familiar children-and-violence arguments. Rather than simply studying the link between violence on the tube and crime in the streets, Gerbner is exploring wider and deeper terrain. He has turned his lens on TV's hidden victims—women, the elderly, blacks, blue-collar workers and other groups—to document the ways in which video-entertainment portrayals subliminally condition how we perceive ourselves and how we view those around us. Gerbner's subjects are not merely the impressionable young; they include all the rest of us. And it is his ominous conclusion that heavy watchers of the prime-time mirror are receiving a grossly distorted picture of the real world that they tend to accept more readily than reality itself.

The 63-year-old Gerbner, who is dean of 3 Penn's Annenberg School of Communications, employs a methodology that meshes scholarly observation with mundane legwork. Over the past 15 years, he and a tireless trio of assistants (Larry Gross, Nancy Signorelli and Michael Morgan) videotaped and exhaustively analyzed 1,600 prime-time programs involving more than 15,000 characters. They then drew up multiple-choice questionnaires that offered correct answers about

the world at large along with answers that reflected what Gerbner perceived to be the misrepresentations and biases of the world according to TV. Finally, these questions were posed to large samples of citizens from all socioeconomic strata. In every survey, the Annenberg team discovered that heavy viewers of television (those watching more than four hours a day), who account for more than 30 percent of the population, almost invariably chose the TV-influenced answers, while light viewers (less than two hours a day) selected the answers corresponding more closely to actual life. Some of the dimensions of television's reality warp:

### Sex

Male prime-time characters outnumber females by 4 3 to 1 and, with a few star-turn exceptions, women are portrayed as weak, passive satellites to powerful, effective men. TV's male population also plays a vast variety of roles, while females generally get typecast as either lovers or mothers. Less than 20 percent of TV's married women with children work outside the home—as compared with more than 50 percent in real life. The tube's distorted depictions of women, concludes Gerbner, reinforce stereotypical attitudes and increase sexism. In one Annenberg survey, heavy viewers were far more likely than light ones to agree with the proposition: "Women should take care of running their homes and leave running the country to men."

### Age

People over 65, too, are grossly underrepresented 5 on television. Correspondingly, heavy-viewing Annenberg respondents believe that the elderly are a vanishing breed, that they make up a smaller proportion of the population today than they did 20 years ago. In fact, they form the nation's most rapidly expanding age group. Heavy viewers also believe that old people are less healthy today than they were two decades ago, when quite the opposite is true. As with women, the portrayals of old people transmit negative impressions. In general, they are cast as silly, stubborn, sexually inactive and eccentric. "They're often shown as feeble grandparents bearing cookies," says Gerbner. "You never see the power that real old people often have. The best and possibly only time to learn about growing old with decency and grace is in youth. And young people are the most susceptible to TV's messages."

### Race

The problem with the medium's treatment of blacks is more one of image than of visibility. Though a tiny percentage of black characters come across as "unrealistically romanticized," reports Gerbner, the overwhelming majority of them are employed in subservient, supporting roles—such as the white hero's comic sidekick. "When a black child looks at prime time," he says, "most of the people he sees doing interesting and important things are white." That imbalance, he goes on, tends to teach young blacks to accept minority status as naturally inevitable and even deserved. To access the impact of such portrayals on the general audience, the Annenberg survey forms included questions like "Should white people have the right to keep blacks out of their neighborhoods?" and "Should there be laws against marriages between blacks and whites?" The more that viewers watched, the more they answered "yes" to each question.

### Work

Heavy viewers greatly overestimated the proportion of Americans employed as physicians, lawyers, athletes and entertainers, all of whom inhabit prime-time in hordes. A mere 6 to 10 percent of television characters hold blue-collar or service jobs vs. about 60 percent in the real work force. Gerbner sees two dangers in TV's skewed division of labor. On the one hand, the tube so overrepresents and glamorizes the elite occupations that it sets up unrealistic expectations

among those who must deal with them in actuality. At the same time, TV largely neglects portraying the occupations that most youngsters will have to enter. "You almost never see the farmer, the factory worker or the small businessman," he notes. "Thus not only do lawyers and other professionals find they cannot measure up to the image TV projects of them, but children's occupational aspirations are channeled in unrealistic directions." The Gerbner team feels this emphasis on high-powered jobs poses problems for adolescent girls, who are also presented with views of women as homebodies. The conflicting views, Gerbner says, add to the frustration over choices they have to make as adults.

### Health

Although video characters exist almost entirely on junk food and quaff alcohol 15 times more often than water, they manage to remain slim, healthy and beautiful. Frequent TV watchers, the Annenberg investigators found, eat more, drink more, exercise less and possess an almost mystical faith in the curative powers of medical science. Concludes Gerbner: "Television may well be the single most pervasive source of health information. And its over-idealized images of medical people, coupled with its complacency about unhealthy life-styles, leaves both patients and doctors vulnerable to disappointment, frustration and even litigation."

### Crime

On the small screen, crime rages about 10 times more often than in real life. But while other researchers concentrate on the propensity of TV mayhem to incite aggression, the Annenberg team has studied the hidden side of its imprint: fear of victimization. On television, 55 percent of prime-time characters are involved in violent confrontations once a week; in reality, the figure is less than 1 percent. In all demographic groups in every class of neighborhood, heavy viewers overestimated the statistical chance of violence in their own lives and harbored an exaggerated mistrust of strangers—creating what Gerbner calls "mean-world syndrome." Forty-six percent of heavy viewers who live in cities rated their fear of crime "very serious" as opposed to 26 percent of light viewers. Such paranoia is especially acute among TV entertainment's most common victims: women, the elderly, nonwhites, foreigners and lower-class citizens.

Video violence, proposes Gerbner, is primarily 10 responsible for imparting lessons in social power: it demonstrates who can do what to whom and get away with it. "Television is saying that those at the bottom of the power scale cannot get away with the same things that a white, middle-class American male can," he says. "It potentially conditions people to think of themselves as victims."

At a quick glance, Gerbner's findings seem to 11 contain a cause-and-effect, chicken-or-the-egg question. Does television make heavy viewers view the world the way they do or do heavy viewers come from the poorer, less experienced segment of the populace that regards the world that way to begin with? In other words, does the tube create or simply confirm the unenlightened attitudes of its most loyal audiences? Gerbner, however, was savvy enough to construct a methodology largely immune to such criticism. His samples of heavy viewers cut across all ages, incomes, education levels and ethnic backgrounds—and every category displayed the same tube-induced misconceptions of the world outside.

Needless to say, the networks accept all this 12 as enthusiastically as they would a list of news-coverage complaints from the Ayatollah Khomeini.* Even so, their responses tend to be tinged with a singular respect for Gerbner's personal and professional credentials. The man is no ivory-tower recluse. During World War II, the Budapest-born Gerbner parachuted into the mountains of Yugoslavia to join the partisans fighting the Germans. After the war, he hunted down and personally arrested scores of high Nazi officials. Nor is Gerbner some videophobic vigilante. A Ph.D. in communications, he readily acknowledges TV's beneficial effects, noting that it has abolished parochialism, reduced isolation and loneliness and provided the poorest members of society with cheap, plug-in exposure to experiences they otherwise would not have. Funding for his research is supported by such prestigious bodies as the National Institute of Mental Health, the Surgeon General's office, and the American Medical Association, and he is called to testify before congressional committees nearly as often as David Stockman.*

## Mass Entertainment

When challenging Gerbner, network officials focus 13 less on his findings and methods than on what they regard as his own misconceptions of their industry's function. "He's looking at television from the perspective of a social scientist rather than considering what is mass entertainment," says Alfred Schneider, vice president of standards and practices at ABC. "We strive to balance TV's social effects with what will capture an audience's interests. If you showed strong men being victimized as much as women or the elderly, what would comprise the dramatic conflict? If you did a show truly representative of society's total reality, and nobody watched because it wasn't interesting, what have you achieved?"

CBS senior vice president Gene Mater also 14 believes that Gerbner is implicitly asking for the theoretically impossible. "TV is unique in its problems," says Mater. "Everyone wants a piece of the action. Everyone feels that their racial or ethnic group is underrepresented or should be portrayed as they would like the world to perceive them. No popular entertainment form, including this one, can or should be an accurate reflection of society."

---

*Ayatollah Khomeni:* a religious leader who came to power after the 1979 Iranian revolution.

*David Stockman:* a prominent and controversial official during Ronald Reagan's presidency.

On that point, at least, Gerbner is first to 15 agree; he hardly expects television entertainment to serve as a mirror image of absolute truth. But what fascinates him about this communications medium is its marked difference from all others. In other media, customers carefully choose what they want to hear or read: a movie, a magazine, a best seller. In television, notes Gerbner, viewers rarely tune in for a particular program. Instead, most just habitually turn on the set—and watch by the clock rather than for a specific show. "Television viewing fulfills the criteria of a ritual," he says. "It is the only medium that can bring to people things they otherwise would not select." With such unique power, believes Gerbner, comes unique responsibility: "No other medium reaches into every home or has a comparable, cradle-to-grave influence over what a society learns about itself."

## Match

In Gerbner's view, virtually all of TV's distortions of 16 reality can be attributed to its obsession with demographics. The viewers that prime-time sponsors most want to reach are white, middle-class, female and between 18 and 49—in short, the audience that purchases most of the consumer products advertised on the tube. Accordingly, notes Gerbner, the demographic portrait of TV's fictional characters largely matches that of its prime commercial targets and largely ignores everyone else. "Television," he concludes, "reproduces a world for its own best customers."

Among TV's more candid executives, that the- 17 ory draws considerable support. Yet by pointing a finger at the power of demographics, Gerbner appears to contradict one of his major findings. If female viewers are so dear to the hearts of sponsors, why are female characters cast in such unflattering light? "In a basically male-oriented power structure," replies Gerbner, "you can't alienate the male viewer. But you can get away with offending women because most women are pretty well brainwashed to accept it." The Annenberg dean

has an equally tidy explanation for another curious fact. Since the corporate world provides network television with all of its financial support, one would expect businessmen on TV to be portrayed primarily as good guys. Quite the contrary. As any fan of "Dallas," "Dynasty," or "Falcon Crest" well knows, the image of the company man is usually that of a mendacious, dirty-dealing rapscallion. Why would TV snap at the hand that feeds it? "Credibility is the way to ratings," proposes Gerbner. "This country has a populist tradition of bias against anything big, including big business. So to retain credibility, TV entertainment shows businessmen in relatively derogatory ways."

In the medium's Hollywood-based creative 18 community, the gospel of Gerbner finds some passionate adherents. Rarely have TV's best and brightest talents viewed their industry with so much frustration and anger. The most sweeping indictment emanates from David Rintels, a two-time Emmy-winning writer and former president of the Writers Guild of America, West. "Gerbner is absolutely correct and it is the people who run the networks who are to blame," says Rintels. "The networks get bombarded with thoughtful, reality-oriented scripts. They simply won't do them. They slam the door on them. They believe that the only way to get ratings is to feed viewers what conforms to their biases or what has limited resemblance to reality. From 8 to 11 o'clock each night, television is one long lie."

Innovative thinkers such as Norman Lear, 19 whose work has been practically driven off the tube, don't fault the networks so much as the climate in which they operate. Says Lear: "All of this country's institutions have become totally fixated on short-term bottom-line thinking. Everyone grabs for what might succeed today and the hell with tomorrow. Television just catches more of the heat because it's more visible." Perhaps the most perceptive assessment of Gerbner's conclusions is offered by one who has worked both sides of the industry street. Deanne Barkley, a former NBC vice president who now helps run an independent production house, reports that the negative depictions of women on TV have made it "nerve-racking" to function as a woman within TV. "No one takes responsibility for the social impact of their shows," says Barkley. "But then how do you decide where it all begins? Do the networks give viewers what they want? Or are the networks conditioning them to think that way?"

Gerbner himself has no simple answer to that 20 conundrum. Neither a McLuhanesque* shaman nor a Naderesque crusader, he hesitates to suggest solutions until pressed. Then out pops a pair of provocative notions. Commercial television will never democratize its treatments of daily life, he believes, until it finds a way to broaden its financial base. Coincidentally, Federal Communications Commission chairman Mark Fowler seems to have arrived at much the same conclusion. In exchange for lifting such government restrictions on TV as the fairness doctrine and the equal-time rule, Fowler would impose a modest levy on station owners called a spectrum-use fee. Funds from the fees would be set aside to finance programs aimed at specialized tastes rather than the mass appetite. Gerbner enthusiastically endorses that proposal: "Let the ratings system dominate most of prime time but not every hour of every day. Let some programs carry advisories that warn: 'This is not for all of you. This is for nonwhites, or for religious people or for the aged and the handicapped. Turn it off unless you'd like to eavesdrop.' That would be a very refreshing thing."

---

*McLuhanesque:* derived from the name Marshall McLuhan (1911–1980), a pioneer in media studies and the source of the observation "The medium is the message."

### Role

In addition, Gerbner would like to see viewers 21 given an active role in steering the overall direction of television instead of being obliged to passively accept whatever the networks offer. In Britain, he points out, political candidates debate the problems of TV as routinely as the issue of crime. In this country, proposes Gerbner, "every political campaign should put television on the public agenda. Candidates talk about schools, they talk about jobs, they talk about social welfare. They're going to have to start discussing this all-pervasive force."

There are no outright villains in this docu- 22 drama. Even Gerbner recognizes that network potentates don't set out to proselytize a point of view; they are simply businessmen selling a mass-market product. At the same time, their 90 million nightly customers deserve to know the side effects of the ingredients. By the time the typical American child reaches the age of reason, calculates Gerbner, he or she will have absorbed more than 30,000 electronic "stories." These stories, he suggests, have replaced the socializing role of the preindustrial church: they create a "cultural mythology" that establishes the norms of approved behavior and belief. And all Gerbner's research indicates that this new mythological world, with its warped picture of a sizable portion of society, may soon become the one most of us think we live in.

Who else is telling us that? Howard Beale and 23 his eloquent alarms have faded into off network reruns. At the very least, it is comforting to know that a real-life Beale is very much with us . . . and *really* watching.

*Vocabulary*

The following terms are identified by paragraph number. Make sure that you understand each term's meaning in its context. If you're not sure that you understand a term, look it up in a college-level dictionary.

| | | |
|---|---|---|
| late (1) | curative (8) | derogatory (17) |
| scathing (1) | acute (9) | adherents (18) |
| cramped (1) | savvy (11) | conundrum (20) |
| subliminally (2) | recluse (12) | shaman (20) |
| strata (3) | parochialism (12) | levy (20) |
| satellites (4) | mendacious (17) | proselytize (22) |
| quaff (8) | rapscallion (17) | |

## Style and Strategy

1.  What is the thesis of this essay? Where is it?

2.  Waters's *primary* purpose is to provide examples of ways that television, overall, presents a distorted picture of life in the United States. What is his *secondary* purpose? (Hint: look for his references to causes and effects.)

3.  Find and list examples of Waters's use of (1) causal analysis (see Chapter 9) and (2) classification (Chapter 11) as internal strategies.

4.  Does Waters come to a definitive conclusion? Summarize the last three paragraphs of this essay.

## Questions for Critical Thinking and Discussion

1.  This essay is more than twenty-five years old. How has television changed since this essay was published in 1982? Is television now a more accurate reflection of society, or has it become even less accurate?

2.  In paragraphs 13 and 14, Waters includes rebuttals from two network executives, who point out that (a) people don't want to see social realism on television and (b) television cannot please everyone. Discuss these ideas. Would you watch a prime-time drama about families living on the social and economic margin?

## Suggestions for Writing

1.  Today, companies and institutions seem devoted to "mission statements" and "values statements." Write a 500- to 750-word essay about a company or institution whose "projected" image is at odds with the reality of the company or institution itself. Use specific examples.

2.  Select a local company or institution whose services are undervalued or unappreciated—a food bank, for instance. Write a 500- to 750-word essay explaining the value that this company or institution provides.

3.  "Life According to TV" mentions a number of contemporary television's failings. But should we tar every program and network with the same brush? Isn't there anything good to be said about today's television? If you were to nominate several television shows—of whatever genre—as representatives of what you think television should be, which programs would you choose? Write about these shows in a 500- to 750-word essay that explains what you think is worthwhile about each.

**4.** Do you agree with the conclusions presented in this essay? For example, are African Americans underrepresented and misrepresented on television? Do "male prime-time characters outnumber females by 3 to 1"? Focusing on one or two categories used in "Life According to TV," write a 500- to 750-word essay that discusses examples from your own viewing that might challenge the conclusions presented by Waters.

### Speaking Assignment

We sometimes become interested in and even fascinated by literary, movie, or television characters because we identify with them. Make a short presentation in which you provide examples to show that you and a favorite literary or screen character are alike in two or three ways. For example, compare personality traits, values, temperaments, or the kinds of problems both of you have to face every day. (For more help with oral presentations, see Chapter 18.)

# WRITING THE EXEMPLIFICATION ESSAY WITH A READER'S EYE

**CATALYST 2.0**

**MORE OPTIONS ONLINE**
If you would like to read additional exemplification essays, go to www.mhhe.com/ writingtoday.

Essays that depend on abstractions and generalities usually fail to connect with the audience and fulfill their purpose. Use effective, believable examples to support your general statements and reach out to your readers. The advice that follows will help you think like your reader as you consider your assignment and then prewrite, draft, revise, and edit your exemplification essay.

## Issues to Keep in Mind

The usual purpose of an exemplification essay is to inform your reader about a topic or persuade your reader by providing clear, concrete examples. Consequently, as you begin to think about your essay, you'll need to decide on the kinds of examples you'll need and where to find them. Thinking about the following issues will help you to choose the best examples for your purpose:

1. Using examples from personal experience and from sources
2. Finding relevant and representative examples

### Sources of Examples

For a great many essays, you can find plenty of examples from your personal experience, often more than you can use. However, if you have been assigned a topic that does not ask you to depend on your personal experience, you may need to spend some time at the library or online to find supporting information for your thesis. In fact, some assignments will stipulate that you do some basic research. Such assignments aren't necessarily asking you to produce a full-fledged research paper, just to go beyond your own experience. Whether you are required to use sources or not, if you use researched information in an essay, remember that you will be expected to cite the source. Moreover, there is a substantial difference between widely available information, known as **common knowledge**, that you encountered for the first time during your research and highly specific, specialized information that needs to be documented, including facts that are not readily available, opinions, and someone else's words. For example, if your instructor read the following sentence in one of your essays, he or she would probably not even slow down:

> Wyoming is one of the western states that regularly experiences heavy snowfalls.

All the people who live in Wyoming, and many people who live elsewhere, know that it snows a great deal in that state. However, the following sentence would probably draw a comment:

> Wyoming's population was only 340,000 in 1970, and the state remains sparsely settled today.

"What's your source?" "Where did you find this?" "You must give credit to the source that provided this information." These are the types of comments you could expect to find in the margin next to a sentence like this one. Your instructor would be trying to alert you to the dangers of playing fast and loose with researched material.

In the academic world, you are allowed to borrow from someone else's work, whether it be published or unpublished, but only if you acknowledge having done so. Not citing the sources of any facts (other than common knowledge), opinions, or quotations that you use is **plagiarism**, a term that you should hope to encounter only in the abstract. You don't want to be accused of lifting someone else's work. When in doubt, as always, ask your instructor. (Chapter 21 gives more details about the various transgressions that can be interpreted as plagiarism and provides guidelines for documenting your sources.)

When writing an essay that draws on their personal experience, some students are tempted to "construct" examples. Whatever your opinion on the morality of such a practice, we advise against it. Our opinion is rooted in practicality: a constructed example tends to stick out a bit, like a third eye in the center of someone's forehead. Most of us aren't very good writers of fiction, and most of us aren't very convincing liars; constructing examples requires talent in both areas. A paragraph like this one reeks of artificiality:

> The endless period of rain we have lived through is interesting, but everyone wishes it was gone. For example, my friend Emily has had a cold for two weeks. The walkways are slippery as well. For example, my friend Jennifer slipped on the sidewalk and sprained her ankle.

The paragraph is generally routine and lifeless; moreover, its two examples seem more like chalk outlines than real human beings. Working hard to come up with genuine examples will always help your essay; constructing examples will almost always introduce a false note.

### *Relevant and Representative Examples*

For each example that you find, you need to ask yourself the following questions: Does the example actually help illustrate my point, or is it irrelevant? Even worse, does it *contradict* my point? Once again, careful planning and prewriting will allow you to weed out defective examples, perhaps preventing you from writing a paragraph like this one on the topic of laws against drunk driving:

> Our state's new .08 blood alcohol content limit for drunk driving is a problem. For example, my roommate, Eddie, blew a .10 and was convicted of driving while intoxicated (DWI). He lost his license for six months, he has to complete 100 hours of community service, he had to pay his lawyer $1500.00, and he will be facing sky-high insurance rates when he gets his license back.

Although admirable in its use of specific details, this paragraph does not illustrate the writer's idea that the new law is a problem; instead, it proves that Eddie behaved foolishly. A DWI law is not passed in secrecy. The issue of drunk driving always generates publicity and controversy, and Eddie either didn't pay attention or decided to ignore the new reality. Moreover, the writer has let his sympathy for his roommate override his common sense.

Here is another question to ask yourself about each example that you consider: Is it truly representative? For example, a student who is developing an essay claiming that "volunteerism" has become a major part of student life at her college may want to use as an example a truly committed volunteer, a young man who has been profiled in the student newspaper for his involvement in six different charity drives and fund-raisers. But this person is not *representative* of the student body; instead, he is the *model* of the student volunteer. To find more effective examples, the student would need to do research on the total number of fund-raisers and charity drives on campus and the level of student involvement with these activities. With more broad-based examples, the writer can more convincingly support her assertion that volunteering has indeed become a fact of student life.

## Choosing a Topic

To write an effective exemplification essay, you need to find a general statement about your topic that you can illustrate with clear, relevant, and representative examples. The following guidelines will help you choose a promising topic for your essay:

1. Choose a topic that you're comfortable with. Why choose a topic such as "the great value of books" if you don't like to read but prefer to watch seven hours of television every day? Wouldn't you be better off with "television: an underrated resource"?

● ● ● ● ● ● ●
CATALYST 2.0

**MORE OPTIONS ONLINE**
For more help with problem areas in the exemplification essay, go to www.mhhe.com/ writingtoday.

**2.** Look for a topic that you can successfully illustrate. Exemplification works best when connected to the particulars of everyday life. Think of the subject matter of the three readings in the previous section: walking the streets at night, sorting through garbage, watching television. The three authors drew upon observable reality. You would have trouble developing an exemplification essay on a large, abstract, and complicated subject such as the inequities in U.S. immigration laws because such a topic requires a great deal of abstract discussion.

**3.** Consider your audience and the interaction that readers will bring to your text. Many essay assignments will include a specific audience and purpose, and you can use this context to guide you as you work. The more you consider your audience, the better your chances of success. As you select your topic, though, don't try to "score points" with your audience by attempting to determine the culturally appropriate response—the response you think they expect. If given a choice between reading a well-written essay on the value of books or a well-written essay on the undervaluation of television, we'd go straight for the latter. It's got more potential; the challenge is greater.

## Prewriting

Once you have chosen your topic, use one of the informal prewriting strategies to generate ideas and examples: listing, freewriting, or clustering. (See Chapter 2 for more on these strategies.) Remember that you are always better off generating more examples than you will actually use. If examples from your personal experience will not be enough to support the topic, consider going to the library or on the Internet to look for additional support. If you plan to research your topic, however, check with your instructor first.

At this point, see if you can develop a working or preliminary thesis. If you can do so, and if you begin to visualize the direction that your essay will take, you are now ready to organize your prewriting.

## Organizing

Once you have generated a sufficient number of examples and developed your working thesis, the best way for you to organize this raw material is to arrange it into an outline. (Chapter 2 covers informal, sentence, and formal outline structures.) The typical structure of an exemplification essay is straightforward and logical: a thesis supported by topic sentences supported by specific examples. As well, make sure that you consider the most effective order for your body paragraphs and examples. Ending with your most compelling example is frequently a good approach.

## Drafting

To illustrate one approach to writing an exemplification essay, we have included the essay "Tattoos: Thinking in the Present Tense."

## The Introduction

The introductory paragraphs of an exemplification essay should literally introduce your reader to your main idea and the world that it inhabits. If readers do not have sufficient context, it can hinder their ability to appreciate an exemplification essay. Someone has forgotten to turn on some of the lights, as it were, and the reader is forced to stumble around in the dark, trying to get a fix on what the writer is up to. Note how the following introductory paragraph grounds the reader in the writer's reality:

### Tattoos: Thinking in the Present Tense

Recently, I heard a caller to a conservative talk-radio show complain about the appearance of young people: their weird hair, their body piercings, their tattoos. I told myself that young people always look strange to older people, and the caller sounded old. But of her three points, only one is truly worth exploring. **Tattoos are effectively permanent, and a person who has decided to get a tattoo is saying a lot about his or her view of life, especially in the location and type of tattoo.** Is it visible, or is it hidden? What is its subject matter?

Note the position of the thesis statement, toward the end of the paragraph, but with two questions following it for elaboration.

## The Body

Here the writer proceeds to develop the ideas presented in her introduction with topic sentences and examples:

People who have easily visible tattoos are making the strongest statement. A tattoo on the hand/wrist, leg/calf, or face or neck will almost always be there for anyone to examine. The striking shoulder and neck tattoo worn by George Clooney's character in *From Dusk Till Dawn* and Harvey Keitel's facial cat stripes in *The Piano* were the first traits that viewers noticed. However, many young people get "in-your-face" tattoos without realizing that within a short time they may be going on an interview for that big first career job and looking into the eyes of an interviewer who is transfixed by the impossible-to-hide choice made in a somewhat more exuberant moment.

People who have hidden tattoos are playing it safe, in one sense. The tattoo won't prevent them from landing a good job. But the hidden tattoo can play a more devious role. My friend Siobhan uses hers as a flirtation device. When she's at a club and meets a guy she likes, she always lets him know that she has a tattoo. When the stooge asks "Where?" Siobhan always says "I'm not telling." It's obvious where that strategy is designed to lead.

The subject matter of the tattoo is also important. The favorite tattoos of the past—"Mom" and "Born to Lose"—seem to have been replaced by images only—a rose, a floral design, a snake. Images can be taken to extremes, however. I recently saw a man at a convenience store who was shirtless, and around his chest and back was a mural, a cyclorama, of the man's sexual fantasies. It was utterly ghastly. This man should not be allowed go into public without a shirt, or at least an NC-17 rating.

### The Conclusion

Your conclusion needs to reinforce your thesis—the idea that your body paragraphs and examples have developed. You might even go further and offer a judgment based on the evidence you have presented. Note here how the writer comes to two judgments about the decision to get a tattoo, both of which are logically derived from her essay's body paragraphs:

> Tattoos seem like a lot of fun, but they are indeed permanent. Attempts to surgically remove tattoos always leave a scar. Perhaps my father, who is from Texas, sums it up best: "Sure, tattoos should be legal. But the minimum age ought to be 65. By then, people'd be mature enough not to screw up their future."

## EXERCISE 7.1

Write a sentence outline of "Tattoos: Thinking in the Present Tense." (For help with sentence outlines, see Chapter 2, pages 41–42.) What does the outline reveal about the essay's organization? Could you suggest a different organization for this essay? Why?

*Consider Your Options*

In the conclusion of a short essay you don't need to summarize, nor do you need to repeat your thesis. But keep your thesis in mind as you choose your approach. One common approach for this type of essay is to comment on the situation or problem that you have just explained. (See Chapter 3 for more approaches.)

**CATALYST 2.0**

**MORE OPTIONS ONLINE**
For more help with the step-by-step development of the exemplification essay, go to **www.mhhe.com/writingtoday**.

## Revising Your Draft

After you have completed a draft of your exemplification essay, your next step is to revise it, using your own analysis and comments from classmates or friends. During peer review, answer the Questions for Reviewing an Exemplification Essay about the draft you are reviewing, whether it is yours or another student's.

After reviewing for content, you need to go over your peer reviewers' responses to your essay and then revise for unity, coherence, language level, and tone (see Chapter 4). When you have revised your draft and are basically satisfied with it, read your draft for mechanical and grammatical errors. Concentrate on finding and correcting major sentence errors (fragment, comma splice, fused sentence), errors in pronoun agreement and subject-verb agreement, and spelling.

Now that you have made your corrections, *read your essay one more time* to catch any errors made during revision and find errors missed during your earlier reviews.

## Student Essay

The following essay is Jennifer Janisz's response to an exemplification assignment. The final draft is presented first. Then Jennifer's first draft is presented, with her comments about this draft and what she needed to do in the revision stage.

## Questions for Reviewing an Exemplification Essay

1. Does the introduction give the reader enough context? Does it capture the reader's interest? How could the introduction be strengthened?

2. What is the thesis statement? Has the writer placed it in the best position within the essay? How could it be improved?

3. Has the writer offered enough examples to support the thesis? If not, should the writer add more? Has the writer fulfilled his or her purpose for writing the essay?

4. Do the content and the structure work together, or is there a better way of organizing the examples? If so, how should they be organized?

5. Does the draft sound mechanical, as if each paragraph has been "set up" so that an example can illustrate it? Or are the examples integral and natural elements of their respective paragraphs? Where are transitional words or sentences needed?

6. Do any of the examples seem irrelevant, contradictory, artificial, or just strange? If so, point them out.

7. Are the body paragraphs fully developed? Where are additional details, or more specific details, needed?

8. Does the essay have an effective conclusion? How could it be improved?

*Jennifer's Final Draft*

## Three Families

It's Christmas day, and the entire family is at my house. Eating dinner, I overhear several conversations and start to realize just how different the branches of my family are. I have three sets of aunts and uncles: my mom's sister, Gwen, and her husband, Ben; my dad's brother, John, and his wife, Kelly; and my dad's sister, Nicole, and her husband, Tom. Each set of relatives has at least one child yet very distinct ideas about how to raise and treat him or her. Gwen's family is laid back and cooperative. John's family is under his strict watch and command at all times. Nicole's family is free to do whatever they desire without repercussions. Though all three of these families have personal theories on the process of raising children, it's clear that no single approach is the perfect solution for everyone.

Gwen's family is the easygoing type. She and Ben don't worry too much about anything. Basically, they can have this attitude because the family members all trust one another. Gwen and Ben have two children, Billy and Christie. These two are responsible and levelheaded and do not need to be constantly watched by their parents. Billy and Christie are not perfect children. Like every child who is growing up, they make mistakes. Because of the respect these family members have for one another, however, it is easy for them to trust each other. When something does go wrong, the problem is handled rationally. A perfect example of this approach happened when Billy was sixteen. He went to a party that provided alcohol, and he ended up getting drunk. Most kids his age would have kept this secret from their parents. Billy, though, told his parents exactly what happened. Instead of grounding him, Gwen and Ben felt that he had learned his lesson from the experience and trusted him not to do it again.

John's family is not that trusting. The respect in this house is          3
built out of fear. John and Kelly have one daughter, Mariah, who is
far from meeting their high expectations. When Mariah does something wrong, even something petty, she can be sure that the punishment will be severe. John and Kelly don't want to take chances in
raising their daughter. They want to make sure that she knows what
is expected of her and feel that she should respect their wishes, simply because they are her parents. Unfortunately, Mariah craves
attention of any kind, so she doesn't strive to be what her parents
demand, which only angers them that much more. Neither John nor
Kelly smokes, so when Mariah brought home a pack of cigarettes she
got from her friend, her parents were furious. John caught her with
the pack and made her smoke every last cigarette in front of him.
Indeed, John and Kelly can be sure that she won't smoke again for a
long time. But even though John and Kelly's rules are effective, the
motives behind their rules aren't based on trust.

Nicole's family, on the other hand, is entirely different from          4
both of the other two families. Although Gwen's and John's families
are dissimilar, both are based on respect. By contrast, Nicole and
Tom, who have two sons, Martin and Charlie, get no respect from
either one. Martin and Charlie come and go as they please and don't
bother to tell their parents where they're going and when they
might be home. If Nicole and Tom were to punish one of them, he
would simply ignore his parents and continue to enjoy his freedom.
Once when Martin was seventeen, he "borrowed" Tom's car. After a
week he finally returned but only to ask for money from his parents
(which they gave without question). Nicole and Tom are not worried
about whether they are raising their children right. They believe
that the most important role they play is to make sure that their
children are happy. This method doesn't seem to work with many
families because people usually don't have an unlimited supply of
patience and understanding. However, it works for Nicole and Tom.

As I look around the table, it is easy to see just how different these families are. Their actions and reactions all seem unusual to me, but each family has its own vision of how children should be raised and treated, and I can't say if any particular method is the best one. A one-size-fits-all plan clearly wouldn't work in my family.

5

*Jennifer's First Draft*

### Three Families

It's Christmas day, and the whole family is at my house. Listening to three different conversations at the dinner table I start to realize just how diffrent the branches of my family are. I have three sets of aunts and uncles: my mom's sister, Gwen, and her husband Ben, my dad's brother, John, and his wife Kelly, and my dad's sister, Nicole, and her husband Tom. Each set has at least one child, yet very distinct ways of raising them. Gwen's family is laid back and co-operative, John's family is under his strict watch at all times, Nicole's family is free to do whatever they desire. All of these families are different.

1 The rough draft was the "bones" of what I eventually wanted to write. I wanted to get the basic structure and events on paper.

John's family is not very trusting. The respect in that house is built on fear. John and Kelly have one daughter, Mariah. John and Kelly are extremely strict with Mariah; who is far from their high expectations. When Mariah does something wrong, she can be sure that the punishment will be severe. Unfortunately, Mariah craves attention of any kind so she doesn't strive to be who her parents want. True, John and Kelly's rules are effective, but that couldn't be too happy of a living environment.

2 I changed the order of these two paragraphs because I thought that it would be more effective to move from the less strict family to the more strict one.

By contrast, Gwen's family is the easy going type. Her and Ben never worry about too much about anything. Basically, they can do this because there is a trust that bonds their family together. Gwen and Ben have two children, Billy and Christie. They are responsible and level headed and do not need to be constantly watched by their parents. Billy and Christie are not perfect children, like every child who is grow- ing up, they make mistakes too, but because of the strong respect

3 In the final draft I added detail like the story about Billy and the party. I realized that a reader of the first draft would be seeing just names and opinions. I needed more.

these family members have for one another, it is easy for them to trust each other, and when something does go wrong, it is handled rationally.

Nicole's family is entirely diffrent from both of the others. Gwen's    4
and John's families, though unalike, were both based on respect. Nicole and Tom, who have two sons, Martin and Charlie, get no respect from either. Martin and Charlie come and go as they please. When Martin was seventeen, he "borrowed" Tom's car. He finally returned only to withdraw more money from his parents. This method doesn't really appear to get results, but all Nicole and Tom are worried about is their childrens happiness.

As I look around the table, it is easy to see just how diffrent these    5
families are. There actions and reactions are all unusual, but the results each separate family desire is unusual also. So even though no particular method is the best one, the chosen method for each individual family is the best for them.

### EXERCISE 7.2: REVISING

The following is the first draft of a student's exemplification essay. Working in pairs or in small groups, review this essay. Using the Questions for Reviewing an Exemplification Essay on page 232, decide what revisions you would suggest. If you have any questions the student needs to consider, write them in the margin or on a separate sheet of paper. If your instructor directs you to, rewrite one or more paragraphs to make them stronger and to eliminate any grammatical or mechanical errors.

*"T.V. ads"*

T.V. ads tell us a lot about ourselves, as Americans. They tell us we are thrifty, love luxury and want to be sexey.

We love luxury, for example, there is the car ads on TV; also, the cruiseline ads. Car dealers advertise cars costing up to $60,000 dollars; the price of a small house. These cars are like living space, in fact, they're nicer than some people's living space. Many people lust at these.

We are thrifty, we love to save a buck. TV ads frequently scald the viewer for spending to much for a products. Whereas savers are seen as smart.

We wont to be sexey. Back to the car ads again. They don't show ugly people or fat people or deformed people. Rich sleke people drive rich sleke cars. The women are prizes. Buy one and your sex life will improve.

Obviously the ideal American is thrifty, luxury loving and sexy.

## Additional Writing Topics

1.  Proverbs frequently become clichés, but they always have some truth built into them. Write an essay explaining one of the following proverbs, using examples to illustrate the proverb's core meaning:
    a.  A rolling stone gathers no moss.
    b.  Make hay while the sun shines.
    c.  Clothes make the person.
    d.  Let a smile be your umbrella.
    e.  A bird in the hand is worth two in the bush.
    f.  Don't put all your eggs in one basket.
    g.  It's always darkest before the dawn.
    h.  You can't judge a book by its cover.
    i.  Every cloud has a silver lining.
    j.  Still waters run deep.
    k.  Don't look a gift horse in the mouth.
    l.  You can't make a silk purse out of a sow's ear.
    m.  If wishes were horses, beggars would ride.
    n.  It was the straw that broke the camel's back.
    o.  In for a penny, in for a pound.

2.  **Writing on the job.** Think of the place where you work or where you used to work. Choose one workplace policy, procedure, or practice that you believe to be either highly effective or highly ineffective. Write a memo for your boss essay analyzing this policy by using examples to support your assertions. (See Chapter 17 for help with writing a memo.)

## Exemplification and Visual Representations

Many of us carry small objects for good luck, such as a rabbit's foot, a coin, or an object with religious significance. Other people carry objects that remind them of strong relationships with people in their lives—loved ones and the departed.

For soldiers in wartime, such items become priceless memories of home and everything else they have left behind. *Time* magazine photographer Yuri Kozyrev traveled in Iraq with the soldiers of Kilo Company, Third Battalion, Eighth Marine Regiment. On November 11, 2006, he published "Talismans" on the *Time* Web site (http://www.time.com/time/photoessays/2006/talismans _multimedia_new). His photographs are arranged as a photo essay, a form that uses photographs connected by theme, usually with captions, and, in this case, with voice-over narration. The photos and captions shown here are excerpted from Kozyrev's work.

© Yuri Kozyrev

Sergeant Winston Daley, 25, wears a bandanna with Psalms 91 printed on it.

© Yuri Kozyrev

Corporal Michael Compton, 22, carries a pair of his wife's underwear.

© Yuri Kozyrev

Captain Andrew DelGandio, the company commander, carries a picture of his mother and a prayer card, as well as the funeral card of First Lieutenant Ronnie Winchester, killed in action in Iraq.

© Yuri Kozyrev

Lance Corporal Jairo Muycando, 20, carries a Bible, dog tags, the Virgin of Guadelupe, the Virgin Mary, Jesus and two rosaries.

© Yuri Kozyrev

Lance Corporal Richard J. Caseltine carries a dog tag that belonged to his grandfather who served in the Korean War. Caseltine writes, "It is a good-luck charm which worked. I was shot in the head on April 8, 2006. Yet I am alive. To me God was with me and so was my grandfather who taught me everything I know about being a man."

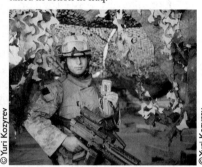

© Yuri Kozyrev

Lance Corporal Anton Volkov carries a card of St. Michael, the patron saint of soldiers and warriors.

1. Write a response to this collection of photographs. What are your thoughts and impressions? As you write, refer to Questions for Reviewing a Visual Representation.

2. The United States has not had a military draft for more than thirty years. Who joins today's Army, Navy, Air Force, Marines, and Coast Guard? Use both library and Internet research to find out about the backgrounds of U.S. enlisted men and women. Look for large categories and significant trends. Is today's military different from the one of the 1950s, for example? Write an essay containing your findings and documenting your sources (see also Chapter 21), or develop an oral presentation based on your research and conclusions (see also Chapter 18).

### Questions for Reviewing a Visual Representation

- Is the representation forceful, passive, or something in between?
- What is the purpose of the representation—in other words, what is it trying to do to you, the reader/viewer?

- If the representation uses words, do they reinforce the visual image or in some way contradict it?
- What is the presumed audience for the representation—men, women, children, the elderly? Or does it have a broader appeal?
- If the representation is an advertisement, is it trying to sell a product or to get you to adopt a way of thinking?
- If the representation is an advertisement, does it try to persuade you in a fair manner, or do you feel manipulated?

## Responding to an Image

This lineup scene takes place early on in Bryan Singer's *The Usual Suspects* (1995-R). (In a police lineup, a crime victim or witness examines "usual suspects" and other individuals to try to identify a perpetrator.)

© Corbis/Sygma

1. Write an informal response to this film still. What is your reaction to this collection of men?

2. As the film goes forward, we eventually learn that one of the men is the notorious master criminal Keyser Soze. Can you guess which one? Watch the film, and then write an essay explaining how you were tricked, as was the customs inspector (played by Chazz Palminteri).

## Using the Internet

Search the Internet for insights and information to use when developing essays with examples.

1. Write an exemplification essay on the popularity of online shopping. Locate the Web sites of as many "e-tailers" as you can, and use these examples to demonstrate the variety of goods and services on the Web and the extent to which e-business is expanding. Refer in detail to as many specific Web sites as you can.

2. We often hear that government wastes our tax money. Using the Internet, find outlandish examples of government waste on the local, state (provincial), or national level. Use these examples in an essay that alerts your reader to the extent of the problem.

   As an alternate assignment, search the Web for examples of useful human services that a government—local, state (provincial), or national—provides its citizens. Using these examples, write an essay that you or someone you know might find helpful as a guide to government assistance, information, or funding.

"O.K. now. You got it straight what you're supposed to do?"

### CHAPTER 8

# PROCESS ANALYSIS

# Writing in Context

You are at your desk one afternoon finishing an intermediate report on the Medlock project when you sense the presence of another. It is, of course, Bob, and he is wearing his shifty expression, the one that says he is about to give you work that he should be doing himself but finds too difficult.

"This new software documentation is brutal. Read through this and see if you can make me sort of a summary of steps to follow."

You sigh. Stephanie the Capable, Bob's assistant, is out of the office today, or she would have been stuck with this task. You also want to finish your report on the Medlock project by quitting time. You wonder darkly why you are working for a man who can't read.

When you go through the documentation, however, you agree with Bob about the central problem: this stuff is atrocious. You read the instructions again, and this time you find yourself making notes. These notes become a clear set of steps for you to hand to Bob so that he can begin to use his new software update.

The documentation that has stymied Bob is a poorly written example of process analysis, a rhetorical option that is used throughout the business world and in many other writing situations as well.

# HOW DOES PROCESS ANALYSIS WORK?

When people want to learn how to do something, or how something works or is done, most try to find an expert who can break the process down into a clear set of steps (and not make the listener or reader feel stupid in the bargain). In other words, they look for a process analysis. Writing that uses process analysis is seemingly everywhere. For example, most bookstores feature a large number of titles in the self-help section. Here, people can buy books that are designed to improve their sex life, self-esteem, negotiating skills, and hairstyle, just to name a few areas for self-improvement. Other sections of the bookstore contain books and magazines that claim to help the reader improve his or her golf swing, learn to use the latest tax-accounting program, attract a desirable mate, and transform a mundane picnic into a gala affair.

The instructions that come with most of the products that you buy are an even more specific form of process analysis. Product instructions are examples of technical writing, and here the ever-important need for the writer to know his or her audience is especially critical. Everyone has had to deal with defective product instructions. If the product is imported, the confusion may have been caused by a writer who was struggling with English. More often, however, the writer simply forgot to think about the reader's needs. The following instructions for formatting a computer diskette for a different use may or may not have actually accompanied a product, but they illustrate the risks—and possible disturbing consequences—of ignoring the audience:

**Step 1.** Erase all existing files from the disk.

**Step 2.** Make sure that you have saved any important
files before proceeding with Step 1.

These two types of process analysis—self-help and product directions—have an **instructional** purpose. However, most academic writing that uses process analysis is more likely to be **informative.** In other words, a writer tells you how something happened—for example, how the Confederacy, although it was the underdog, kept the American Civil War going on for so long. Or how the "Miracle Mets," a baseball franchise that had been in existence for only seven years at the time, won the 1969 World Series. Or how Mother Teresa's humble street mission eventually brought its founder international acclaim and the Nobel Peace Prize. Sometimes writers use process analysis to explain why a problem or situation is so hard to change or remedy—for example, why it is so hard to keep stalkers away from their victims; why teenagers continue to take up cigarette smoking, despite the overwhelming evidence of the harmful effects of this habit and the billions of dollars spent on cautionary advertising campaigns each year; why the heroin market remains such a profitable enterprise; why it is becoming more and more difficult for college students to complete a traditional four-year degree in four years.

Process writing that attempts to inform or comment has a broader focus than instructional writing. Often, the writer has a larger purpose for presenting information in this way: to argue against an injustice, for example, or to show why a particular government policy that looks good on paper is imbecilic in practice. Usually, the writer will make this aim clear in a thesis statement that makes a point about the process being described. The essays in the following section are examples of process analysis, but in each one the writer has a compelling point to make about the process that he or she is describing.

In addition, think about the value of using process analysis in other types of essays. An analysis of the cause of a problem (see Chapter 9) might also need to explore *how* the problem developed as well as *why* the problem developed. An essay arguing that a policy is ineffective and/or unfair (see Chapter 13) will need to explain *how the policy works.* Process analysis is a "core option," one that appears in a variety of contexts and with a variety of purposes.

## READING THE PROCESS ANALYSIS ESSAY WITH A WRITER'S EYE

In the following essays, Jerry Jesness shows how the high schools in which he has taught have corrupted the academic process. Malcolm X writes about the time in the 1940s when he was still Malcolm Little, not Malcolm X, and had his hair straightened—a seemingly innocuous process that leads the author to comment on a much more insidious practice. Finally, Umberto Eco explains how the advent of fax machines and cell phones has led to unexpected—and mostly negative—situations. As you read these essays, be aware of the authors' purpose: each author is using the process option as a useful strategy to reveal a higher meaning.

Following the essays, the second half of this chapter features strategies for writing the process analysis essay with a reader's eye (pages 256–262). If you decide to write on one of the topics that follow the three essays, make sure that you have read the strategies section before you begin. Also note that additional writing topics are listed at the end of the chapter (pages 267–268).

# Why Johnny Can't Fail

## JERRY JESNESS

*Jerry Jesness teaches special education in Los Fresnos, Texas. He has published more than forty articles, columns, and commentaries on the subject of education. This essay first appeared in* Reason *magazine in August 1999. (*Reason *is a publication devoted to "free minds and free markets," seeking to make "a principled case for liberty and individual choice in all areas of human activity.") Do you recognize any of the occurrences that Jesness describes?*

I confess. I am a grade-inflating teacher guilty of "social promotion." I have given passing grades to students who failed all of their tests, to students who refused to read their assignments, to students who were absent as often as not, to students who were not even functionally literate. I have turned a blind eye to cheating and outright plagiarism, and have given As and Bs to students whose performances were at best mediocre. Like others of my ilk, I have sent students to higher grades, to higher education, and to the workplace unprepared for the demands that would be made of them.

I am, in short, a servant of the force that thwarts nearly every effort to reform American education. I am a servant of the floating standard.

I was introduced to the floating standard in 1979, while teaching for the Bureau of Indian Affairs on a reservation in western South Dakota. My predecessor, considered a capable if imprudent instructor by his former students and peers, had been forced to resign after failing nearly half of his students. In his absence, the failing grades were changed and his students were promoted to the next grade.

Even though I knew my predecessor's fate, I gave some failing grades the first term. After a few warnings, however, I fell into line. There was no point in doing otherwise. The students already knew that failing grades would mysteriously self-correct over the summer. I opted for self-preservation.

A few years later I moved to Texas's lower Rio Grande Valley. Since I now was more experienced, I was confident that I would be able to grade fairly. Besides, my future principal spoke movingly at my interview about the need to push our students to their limits. In the first grading period, I boldly flunked a number of students, including the daughter of an administrator of a local elementary school and a star fullback who was also the nephew of a school-board member.

Shortly thereafter I was called in to meet with my principal and the aggrieved parents. Such was my naïveté that I actually bothered to bring evidence. I showed the administrator her daughter's plagiarized book report and the book from which it had been copied, and I showed the fullback's father homework bearing his son's name but written in another person's handwriting. The parents offered weak apologies but maintained that I had not treated their children fairly.

My principal suddenly discovered a number of problems with my teaching. For the next few weeks he was in my class almost daily. Every spitball, every chattering student, every bit of graffiti, was noted. When there were discipline problems, my superiors sided with the offending students. Teaching became impossible.

So again I learned to turn a blind eye to cheating and plagiarism, and to give students, especially athletes, extra credit for everything from reading orally in class to remembering to bring their pencils. Along the way, I gained the cooperation of my students and the respect and support of my superiors.

But not until my fifth year of teaching did I finally accept that my only choices were to embrace the floating standard or to abandon public education. That year my assignment was to teach English as a second language and lower-level language arts. My principal was particularly adamant about having all the students pass.

In language arts, no test was to be graded below 50, even one that was turned in blank. Daily assignments were to be graded according to the number of questions answered, even if all of the answers were wrong. If eight of ten questions were answered, the grade was to be 80, regardless of the quality of the answers. Those who still were failing at the end of the grading period were to be offered the opportunity to do reports or projects for extra credit. My neighbor, another lower-group teacher who was held up to me as a mentor, boasted that he left the week's spelling words on the blackboard during spelling tests and recommended that I do the same. I pulled in my horns too late to save myself that year. The principal recommended that my contract not be renewed.

That job and its $17,000 annual salary were hardly worth fighting for, so I left quietly. After a year as a salesperson and graduate student, however, I began to miss the classroom and decided to give teaching one more try. I returned to the district where I had flunked the star fullback. My superiors correctly assumed that I had learned my lesson and welcomed the return of the prodigal teacher. Just as Orwell's Winston Smith was finally able to achieve victory over himself and love Big Brother, I was ready to embrace the floating standard.

In the ensuing seven years, only two of my 12 students failed. My evaluations were "above expectations" twice and "clearly outstanding" five times. By my fifth year I had climbed to the top of the Texas teachers' career ladder and earned an annual bonus of $3,300.

The funny thing is that I really did become a 13 better teacher after my reincarnation, if only because my students and superiors were now cooperative. My classes were better behaved once I stopped trying to force students to learn more than they cared to. I no longer met with hostility when I sent students to the principal's office. I tried to be as honest as possible with my charges. All of my students and any parents who bothered to visit my classroom or return my phone calls understood that grades above 80 honestly reflected performance, while those in the 70 range were fluffed up with extra credit. I explained to the parents of my immigrant students that here in America passing grades may be given for attendance and minimal effort and do not necessarily reflect mastery of the course material. Students who needed to be pushed lost out, but that was the price of harmony.

It does not matter what changes we make in 14 curricula. The floating standard guarantees the reign of mediocrity. If standards are set high but students lack the skills or motivation to meet them, the standards will inevitably change. If a number of students in a given class take part-time jobs, homework will be reduced. If drugs sweep through a school, lower expectations will compensate for weakened ability. Americans want quality education, but when lower grades and higher failure rates reach their own children's classes, they rebel and schools relent. Americans hate public education because standards are low but love their local schools because their children perform so well there.

Schools have their own reasons to play along. 15 Flexible standards mean fewer complaints. When parents are happy, there are fewer lawsuits; when students are happy, there are fewer discipline problems. What's more, schools that fail students assume the expense and unpopular obligation of retaining them.

In the short term, floating standards make 16 everybody a winner. Students build self-esteem, parents gain peace of mind, and schools save money. By giving high grades and class credit to anyone willing to occupy space in a classroom, schools create the illusion that their students are learning. Only after leaving school and facing work or college do the students discover that they are ignorant and ill prepared.

Imagine that you are required to teach *Hamlet* 17 to a group of students who are either unwilling or unable to read such a work. If you demand that your charges read and understand the play, most will fail and you will be blamed. If you drop *Hamlet* and convert the class into a remedial reading course, you will be out of compliance with the curriculum. If you complain that your students are not up to the mandated task, you will be labeled insensitive and uncaring.

Fear not: The floating standard will save you. 18 If the students will not or cannot read the play, read it to them. If they will not sit still long enough to hear the whole play, consider an abridged or comic-book version, or let them watch the movie. If they cannot pass a multiple-choice test, try a true-or-false or a fill-in-the-blank test that mirrors the previous day's study sheet. If they still have not passed, allow them to do an art project. They could make a model of the Globe Theatre with Popsicle sticks or draw a picture of a Danish prince, or Prince Charles, or even the Artist

Formerly Known As Prince. Those not artistically inclined could make copies of Shakespearean sonnets with macaroni letters on construction paper. If all else fails, try group projects. That way you can give passing grades to all the students, even if only one in five produces anything.

19  Keep dropping the standard, and sooner or later everyone will meet it. If anyone asks, you taught *Hamlet* in a nonconventional way, one that took into account your students' individual differences and needs.

20  For three decades, dismayed Americans have watched their children's test scores slip relative to those of children in other industrialized nations. Our leaders have responded with hollow excuses. Too many American children live in poverty, they say. But so do many Koreans. Many American children are raised in single-parent homes. But so are many Swedes. The United States is an ethnically diverse country. But so is Singapore. The biggest lie is that we are the only nation in the world that seeks to educate children of all socioeconomic classes. That has not been true for decades. The reality is simpler than that. Those other nations have fixed standards.

21  American schools offer fixed standards for their best and worst students, but not for the largest group, those in the middle. Advanced Placement tests are the same throughout the country. The International Baccalaureate program offers uniform curricula and standards to top-notch students in the United States and in English-language schools throughout the world. Ever-increasing numbers of states have mandated that their students pass a basic skills test before graduating. In Texas, the Texas Assessment of Academic Skills

(TAAS) is the standard. In order to prevent schools from ignoring any class of students, Texas wisely chose to track test scores by racial and economic group. The state has demanded basic skills for all students, and the schools are delivering.

22  For those who seek to learn more than basics, however, the result has been negative. Like other state-mandated minimum skills tests, the TAAS is helping to solve one problem while creating another: basic skills are now so strongly stressed that real academics suffer. It should be obvious that a student who has read and analyzed the works of Charles Dickens or Mark Twain would be better able to determine the sequence of events or identify the main idea of a paragraph than would a student who spent his academic year reading sample test passages, yet teachers who once taught from novels now assign reams of single-page reading passages followed by multiple-choice questions.

23  Perhaps there is another way. Those who take Advanced Placement or International Baccalaureate tests submit to a voluntary outside standard. There is no reason that we cannot extend this option to other students as well. Textbook publishers, educators, and others could produce competing tests, to be given at the end of certain courses. Schools could submit the works of literature read and historical eras studied to private testing companies and receive tests based on that material. These tests would free teachers from the pressure to adjust the content of their courses and would assure students and their parents that the standard for each course is fixed, not floating. If *Hamlet* is tested, then *Hamlet,* not Popsicle-stick or macaroni art, will be taught.

*Vocabulary*

The following terms are identified by paragraph number. Make sure that you understand each term's meaning in its context. If you're not sure that you understand a term, look it up in a college-level dictionary.

social promotion (1)     adamant (9)          remedial (17)

functionally literate (1) prodigal (11)        compliance (17)

plagiarism (1)           ensuing (12)         mandated (17)

thwart (2)               reincarnation (13)   sonnets (18)

imprudent (3)            harmony (13)         diverse (20)

aggrieved (6)            curricula (14)       reams (22)

naïveté (6)

## Style and Strategy

1.  What is this essay's intended audience?

2.  What is the author's thesis, and where is it located? Find the specific examples that Jesness uses to back up his thesis.

3.  What is the problem that the author analyzes, and what process must teachers follow in order to deal with the problem?

4.  How would you evaluate the author's tone?

5.  At the end of the essay, the author proposes a solution. Given the tone of his essay, do you think that he expects the solution to be adopted? Explain.

6.  Jesness uses process analysis and exemplification. What other rhetorical options does he use in this essay? Point to specific paragraphs.

## Questions for Critical Thinking and Discussion

1.  Consider the following statement: "The American system of education in grades K through 12 is a complete fraud—they might as well call it the national day-care initiative." Do you agree or disagree? Explain.

2.  Some states have adopted a version of the voucher system, in which parents have the option of placing their children in private schools and receiving some form of tuition reimbursement from tax revenues. What is your opinion of this policy?

3.  What is the main problem—or group of problems—that you remember from your K–12 years? Can you suggest a way to solve this problem?

## Suggestions for Writing

1.  Have you ever participated in an organization that didn't follow its own rules or practices, leaving you feeling somehow defrauded? Write a 500-word essay about this experience.

2.  Write a 500- to 750-word process analysis essay that shows how an activity turned sour—for example, a party, a trip, or a sporting event that started promisingly but went bad.

3.  Pretend that you have been asked to write a 500- to 750-word essay titled "Preparing for College," which is to be distributed to first-year high school students. What advice might you offer them about using the next four years to prepare themselves for the kind of work they will find in college?

Include both dos and don'ts. Of course, you can rely on your own experience as a source of information, but you can find more on this subject in the library or on the Internet.

4.  Jesness admits to being "a servant of the floating standard." Bad habits are sometimes easy to fall into. For example, have you ever been tempted to skimp on academic assignments, or have you ever completed a job at home or at work in a perfunctory manner—without giving it your all? Have you ever sacrificed your integrity just to avoid conflict with others? Did this kind of behavior become habitual? If so, write an essay of between 500 and 750 words in which you trace the process by which you too became the "servant" of a bad habit or inappropriate behavior.

### Speaking Assignment

Create a presentation aimed at a teacher or at teachers you had in high school. What advice would you give them about motivating students better, about getting students to reach for higher goals, and, in general, about avoiding becoming servants of the "floating standard"? Caution: Do not reveal the teachers' real names. (For more help with oral presentations, see Chapter 18.)

# My First Conk

## MALCOLM X

*The civil rights movement of the 1950s and 1960s had two great leaders: Martin Luther King, Jr., and Malcolm X (1925–1965). King believed in civil disobedience—peaceful resistance to unfair and unconstitutional laws (see his essay in Chapter 11, pages 348–349). However, Malcolm X believed that African Americans had been acquiescent for too long; he favored a more militant response. A native of Omaha, Nebraska, Malcolm Little converted to Islam while serving a prison sentence and later became a leading member of the Black Muslim movement. In his middle age, he returned to orthodox Islam and channeled his political energy into his black separatist movement, the Organization for Afro-American Unity. Malcolm X was assassinated in 1965.*

*"My First Conk," excerpted from* The Autobiography of Malcolm X *(1965), is about two processes, one physical and one social. Notice how easily the author moves from one to the other.*

Shorty soon decided that my hair was finally long enough to be conked. He had promised to school me in how to beat the barber shops'   1

three- and four-dollar price by making up congolene, and then conking ourselves.

I took the little list of ingredients he had printed out for me, and went to a grocery store, where I got a can of Red Devil lye, two eggs, and two medium-sized white potatoes. Then at a drugstore near the poolroom, I asked for a large jar of vaseline, a large bar of soap, a large-toothed comb and a fine-toothed comb, one of those rubber hoses with a metal spray-head, a rubber apron, and a pair of gloves.   2

"Going to lay on that first conk?" The drugstore man asked me. I proudly told him, grinning, "Right!"   3

Shorty paid six dollars a week for a room in his cousin's shabby apartment. His cousin wasn't at home. "It's like the pad's mine, he spends so   4 much time with his woman," Shorty said. "Now, you watch me—"

He peeled the potatoes and thin-sliced them into a quart-sized Mason fruit jar, then started stirring them with a wooden spoon as he gradually poured in a little over half the can of lye. "Never use a metal spoon; the lye will turn it black," he told me. [5]

A jelly-like, starchy-looking glop resulted from the lye and potatoes, and Shorty broke in the two eggs, stirring real fast—his own conk and dark face bent down close. The congolene turned pale-yellowish. "Feel the jar," Shorty said. I cupped my hand against the outside, and snatched it away. "Damn right, it's hot, that's the lye," he said. "So you know it's going to burn when I comb it in—it burns bad. But the longer you can stand it, the straighter the hair." [6]

He made me sit down, and he tied the string of the new rubber apron tightly around my neck, and combed up my bush of hair. Then, from the big vaseline jar, he took a handful and massaged it hard all through my hair and into the scalp. He also thickly vaselined my neck, ears and forehead. "When I get to washing out your head, be sure to tell me anywhere you feel any little stinging," Shorty warned me, washing his hands, then pulling on the rubber gloves, and tying on his own rubber apron. "You always got to remember that any congolene left in burns a sore into your head." [7]

The congolene just felt warm when Shorty started combing it in. But then my head caught fire. [8]

I gritted my teeth and tried to pull the sides of the kitchen table together. The comb felt as if it was raking my skin off. [9]

My eyes watered, my nose was running. I couldn't stand it any longer; I bolted to the washbasin. I was cursing Shorty with every name I could think of when he got the spray going and started soap lathering my head. [10]

He lathered and spray-rinsed, lathered and spray-rinsed, maybe ten or twelve times, each [11] time gradually closing the hot-water faucet, until the rinse was cold, and that helped some.

"You feel any stinging spots?" [12]

"No," I managed to say. My knees were trembling. [13]

"Sit back down, then. I think we got it all out okay." [14]

The flame came back as Shorty, with a thick towel, started drying my head, rubbing hard. *"Easy, man, easy!"* I kept shouting. [15]

"The first time's always worst. You get used to it better before long. You took it real good, homeboy. You got a good conk." [16]

When Shorty let me stand up and see in the mirror, my hair hung down in limp, damp strings. My scalp still flamed, but not as badly; I could bear it. He draped the towel around my shoulders, over my rubber apron, and began again vaselining my hair. [17]

I could feel him combing, straight back, first the big comb, then the fine-tooth one. [18]

Then, he was using a razor, very delicately, on the back of my neck. Then, finally, shaping the sideburns. [19]

My first view in the mirror blotted out the hurting. I'd seen some pretty conks, but when it's the first time, on your *own* head, the transformation, after the lifetime of kinks, is staggering. [20]

The mirror reflected Shorty behind me. We both were grinning and sweating. And on top of my head was this thick, smooth sheen of shining red hair—real red—as straight as any white man's. [21]

How ridiculous I was! Stupid enough to stand there simply lost in admiration of my hair now looking "white," reflected in the mirror in Shorty's room. I vowed that I'd never again be without a conk, and I never was for many years. [22]

This was my first really big step toward self-degradation: when I endured all of that pain, literally burning my flesh to have it look like a white man's hair. I had joined that multitude of Negro men and women in America who are brainwashed [23] into believing that the black people are "inferior"—and white people "superior"—that they will even violate and mutilate their God-created bodies to try to look "pretty" by white standards.

Look around today, in every small town and big city, from two-bit catfish and soda-pop joints into the "integrated" lobby of the Waldorf-Astoria, and you'll see conks on black men. And you'll see black women wearing these green and pink and purple and red and platinum-blonde wigs. They're all more ridiculous than a slapstick comedy. It makes you wonder if the Negro has completely lost his sense of identity, lost touch with himself. 24

You'll see the conk worn by many, many so-called "upper class" Negroes, and, as much as I hate to say it about them, on all too many Negro entertainers. One of the reasons that I've especially admired some of them, like Lionel Hampton and Sidney Poitier, among others, is that they have kept their natural hair and fought to the top. I admire any Negro man who has never had himself conked, or who has had the sense to get rid of it—as I finally did. 25

I don't know which kind of self-defacing conk is the greater shame—the one you'll see on the heads of the black so-called "middle class" and "upper class," who ought to know better, or the 26

one you'll see on the heads of the poorest, most downtrodden, ignorant black men. I mean the legal-minimum-wage ghetto-dwelling kind of Negro, as I was when I got my first one. It's generally among these poor fools that you'll see a black kerchief over the man's head, like Aunt Jemima; he's trying to make his conk last longer, between trips to the barbershop. Only for special occasions is this kerchief-protected conk exposed—to show off how "sharp" and "hip" its owner is. The ironic thing is that I have never heard any woman, white or black, express any admiration for a conk. Of course, any white woman with a black man isn't thinking about his hair. But I don't see how on earth a black woman with any race pride could walk down the street with any black man wearing a conk—the emblem of his shame that he is black.

To my own shame, when I say all of this, I'm talking first of all about myself—because you can't show me any Negro who ever conked more faithfully than I did. I'm speaking from personal experience when I say of any black man who conks today, or any white-wigged black woman, that if they gave the brains in their heads just half as much attention as they do their hair, they would be a thousand times better off. 27

## Vocabulary

The following terms are identified by paragraph number. Make sure that you understand each term's meaning in its context. If you're not sure that you understand a term, look it up in a college-level dictionary.

| | | |
|---|---|---|
| conk (1) | lye (2) | slapstick (24) |
| congolene (1) | self-degradation (23) | |

## Style and Strategy

1.  In which paragraph does the thesis appear? Why does Malcolm X reveal his purpose at that point of the essay?

2. Locate the following internal strategies: comparison/contrast (see Chapter 12), causal analysis (Chapter 9), argument (Chapter 13), exemplification (Chapter 7), and definition (Chapter 10). What does each rhetorical option contribute to the essay?

3. In this process analysis, Malcolm X is actually analyzing two processes. What are they?

## Questions for Critical Thinking and Discussion

1. When Malcolm X got his hair conked, he was clearly bowing to peer pressure—the desire to look like his contemporaries so that they would accept him. How much peer pressure do you experience or notice your friends experiencing?

2. Can peer pressure ever be a positive phenomenon?

3. Malcolm X is writing about a situation that reflects the social structure that was prevalent in the middle of the twentieth century, when African Americans were encouraged to imitate the look and standards of the dominant European American majority. In what ways has this situation changed, and even reversed? In what ways is it the same?

## Suggestions for Writing

1. Malcolm X talks about a practice that he once engaged in, then rejected. Have you ever had a habit or engaged in a kind of behavior that you now regret? Write a 500-word essay in which you explain the process by which you broke the habit or changed your behavior.

2. Many people seek to change their appearance by coloring their hair, using tinted contact lenses, sitting under tanning lamps, getting tattoos, or even having surgery. Have you ever tried to change your appearance in such a significant way? If not, do you know anyone else who has? In an essay of 500 to 750 words, explain the step-by-step procedure by which this process occurred. As you do so, make sure to tell your readers whether you now approve of the process.

3. Write a 500- to 750-word essay about one of these processes: (a) conforming to a trend in order to be perceived as stylish or hip; (b) ignoring current trends in clothing and personal appearance and seeking to create a personal style and image.

## Speaking Assignment

Prepare a presentation that argues for or against a practice used by young people to change or enhance their appearance. For example, you might discuss tattooing, body piercing, dieting, or even shaving one's head. (For more help with oral presentations, see Chapter 18.)

# How Not to Use the Fax Machine and the Cellular Phone

## UMBERTO ECO

*Umberto Eco is professor of semiotics at the University of Bologna, in Italy. (Semiotics is the linguistic study of signs, symbols, and meanings.) Eco is best known for his novels, such as Foucault's Pendulum (1989), The Name of the Rose (1994), The Island of the Day Before (1995), and Baudolino (2002). Eco has also written numerous scholarly works and collections of essays.*

*The following essay, from* How to Travel with a Salmon *(1995), examines two processes: how people use technology and how technology can dominate people's lives.*

The fax machine is truly a great invention. For anyone still unfamiliar with it, the fax works like this: you insert a letter, you dial the number of the addressee, and in the space of a few minutes the letter has reached its destination. And the machine isn't just for letters: it can send drawings, plans, photographs, pages of complicated figures impossible to dictate over the telephone. If the letter is going to Australia, the cost of transmission is no more than that of an intercontinental call of the same duration. If the letter is being sent from Milan to Saronno, it costs no more than a directly dialed call. And bear in mind that a call from Milan to Paris, in the evening hours, costs about a thousand lire.* In a country like ours, where the postal system, by definition, doesn't work, the fax machine solves all your problems. Another thing many people don't know is that you can buy a fax for your bedroom, or a portable version for travel, at a reasonable price. Somewhere between a million five and two million lire.** A considerable amount for a toy, but a bargain if your work requires you to correspond with many people in many different cities.

Unfortunately, there is one inexorable law of technology, and it is this: when revolutionary inventions become widely accessible, they cease to be accessible. Technology is inherently democratic, because it promises the same services to all; but it works only if the rich are alone in using it. When the poor also adopt technology, it stops working. A train used to take two hours to go from A to B; then the motor car arrived, which could cover the same distance in one hour. For this reason cars were very expensive. But as soon as the masses could afford to buy them, the roads became jammed, and the trains started to move faster. Consider how absurd it is for the authorities constantly to urge people to use public transport, in the age of the automobile; but with public transport, by consenting not to belong to the elite, you get where you're going before members of the elite do.

In the case of the automobile, before the point of total collapse was reached, many decades went by. The fax machine, more democratic (in fact, it costs much less than a car), achieved collapse in less than a year. At this point it is faster to send something through the mail. Actually, the fax encourages such postal communications. In the old days, if you lived in Medicine Hat, and you had a son in Brisbane, you wrote him once a week and you telephoned him once a month. Now, with the fax, you can send him, in no time, the snapshot of his newborn niece. The temptation is irresistible. Furthermore, the world is inhabited by people, in an ever-increasing number, who want to tell you something that is of no interest to you: how to choose a smarter investment, how to pur-

---

*Up until 2002, the *lira* was the basic unit of currency in Italy. In 1995, a thousand lire was equivalent to approximately sixty-three cents.

**A million five lire** was approximately $945 in 1995; **two million lire** was approximately $1,260.

chase a given object, how to make them happy by sending them a check, how to fulfill yourself completely by taking part in a conference that will improve your professional status. All of these people, the moment they discover you have a fax, and unfortunately there are now fax directories, will trample one another underfoot in their haste to send you, at modest expense, unrequested messages.

As a result, you will approach your fax machine every morning and find it swamped with messages that have accumulated during the night. Naturally, you throw them away without having read them. But suppose someone close to you wants to inform you that you have inherited ten million dollars from an uncle in America, but on condition that you visit a notary before eight o'clock: if the well-meaning friend finds the line busy, you don't receive the information in time. If someone *has* to get in touch with you, then, he has to do so by mail. The fax is becoming the medium of trivial messages, just as the automobile has become the means of slow travel, for those who have time to waste and want to spend long hours in gridlocked traffic, listening to Mozart and Dire Straits.*

Finally, the fax introduces a new element into the dynamics of nuisance. Until today, the bore, if he wanted to irritate you, paid (for the phone call, the postage stamp, the taxi to bring him to your doorbell). But now you contribute to the expense, because you're the one who buys the fax paper.

How can you react? I have already had letterhead printed with the warning "Unsolicited faxes are automatically destroyed," but I don't think that's enough. If you want my advice, I'd suggest keeping your fax disconnected. If someone has to send you something, he has to call you first and ask you to connect the machine. Of course, this can overload the telephone line. It would be best for the person who has to send a fax to write you

first. Then you can answer, "Send your message via fax Monday at 5.05.27 P.M., Greenwich mean time, when I will connect the machine for precisely four minutes and thirty-six seconds."

It is easy to take cheap shots at the owners of cellular phones. But before doing so, you should determine to which of the five following categories they belong.

First come the handicapped. Even if their handicap is not visible, they are obliged to keep in constant contact with their doctor or the 24-hour medical service. All praise, then, to the technology that has placed this beneficent instrument at their service. Second come those who, for serious professional reasons, are required to be on call in case of emergency (fire chiefs, general practitioners, organ-transplant specialists always awaiting a fresh corpse, or President Bush,* because if he is ever unavailable, the world falls into the hands of Quayle). For them the portable phone is a harsh fact of life, endured, but hardly enjoyed. Third, adulterers. Finally, for the first time in their lives, they are able to receive messages from their secret lover without the risk that family members, secretaries, or malicious colleagues will intercept the call. It suffices that the number be known only to him and her (or to him and him, or to her and her: I can't think of any other possible combinations). All three categories listed above are entitled to our respect. Indeed, for the first two we are willing to be disturbed even while dining in a restaurant, or during a funeral; and adulterers are very discreet, as a rule.

Two other categories remain. These, in contrast, spell trouble (for us and for themselves as well). The first comprises those persons who are unable to go anywhere unless they have the possibility of chattering about frivolous matters with the friends and relations they have just left. It is hard to make them understand why they shouldn't do it.

———————————

*Dire Straits:** a band popular in the mid-to-late 1980s.

*President George H. W. Bush:** 41st President of the United States and father of President George W. Bush. Dan Quayle was his vice president.

And finally, if they cannot resist the compulsion to interact, if they cannot enjoy their moments of solitude and become interested in what they themselves are doing at that moment, if they cannot avoid displaying their vacuity and, indeed, make it their trademark, their emblem, well, the problem must be left to the psychologist. They irk us, but we must understand their terrible inner emptiness, be grateful we are not as they are, and forgive them—without, however, gloating over our own superior natures, and thus yielding to the sins of spiritual pride and lack of charity. Recognize them as your suffering neighbor, and turn the other ear.

In the last category (which includes, on the 10 bottom rung of the social ladder, the purchasers of fake portable phones) are those people who wish to show in public that they are greatly in demand, especially for complex business discussions. Their conversations, which we are obliged to overhear in airports, restaurants, or trains, always involve monetary transactions, missing shipments of metal sections, an unpaid bill for a crate of neckties, and other things that, the speaker believes, are very Rockefellerian.*

Now, helping to perpetuate the system of 11 class distinctions is an atrocious mechanism ensuring that, thanks to some atavistic proletarian defect, the nouveau riche, even when he earns enormous sums, won't know how to use a fish knife or will hang a plush monkey in the rear window of his Ferrari or put a San Gennaro** on the dashboard of his private jet, or (when speaking his native Italian) use English words like "management." Therefore he will not be invited by the Duchesse de Guermantes (and he will rack his brain trying to figure out why not; after all, he has a yacht so long it could almost serve as a bridge across the English Channel).

What these people don't realize is that Rocke- 12 feller doesn't need a portable telephone; he has a spacious room full of secretaries so efficient that at the very worst, if his grandfather is dying, the chauffeur comes and whispers something in his ear. The man with power is the man who is not required to answer every call; on the contrary, he is always—as the saying goes—in a meeting. Even at the lowest managerial level, the two symbols of success are a key to the executive washroom and a secretary who asks, "Would you care to leave a message?"

So anyone who flaunts a portable phone as a 13 symbol of power is, on the contrary, announcing to all and sundry his desperate, subaltern position, in which he is obliged to snap to attention, even when making love, if the CEO happens to telephone; he has to pursue creditors day and night to keep his head above water; and he is persecuted by the bank, even at his daughter's First Holy Communion, because of an overdraft. The fact that he uses, ostentatiously, his cellular phone is proof that he doesn't know these things, and it is the confirmation of his social banishment, beyond appeal.

---

*Rockefellerian:* an adjective derived from "Rockefeller," the surname of a wealthy American family.

**San Gennaro:** a statue of the patron saint of the Italian city of Naples.

*Vocabulary*

The following terms are identified by paragraph number. Make sure that you understand each term's meaning in its context. If you're not sure that you understand a term, look it up in a college-level dictionary.

| | | |
|---|---|---|
| dictate (1) | adulterer (8) | monetary (10) |
| duration (1) | malicious (8) | perpetuate (11) |

| lire (1) | suffices (8) | atrocious (11) |
| inexorable (2) | comprises (9) | atavistic (11) |
| inherently (2) | frivolous (9) | proletarian (11) |
| elite (2) | compulsion (9) | nouveau riche (11) |
| notary (4) | solitude (9) | chauffeur (12) |
| dynamics (5) | vacuity (9) | flaunts (13) |
| unsolicited (6) | trademark (9) | sundry (13) |
| beneficent (8) | irk (9) | subaltern (13) |
| practitioners (8) | gloating (9) | ostentatiously (13) |

## Style and Strategy

1. In which paragraph is Eco's thesis? Restate it in your own words.

2. Eco analyzes a process, the development of problems with fax machines and with cellular phones, but they aren't the same problems. In your own words, explain the problems that Eco identifies with each type of technology.

3. In paragraphs 2–3, Eco explains a *paradox* (contradiction) that developed when fax machines went on the market. What is this paradox, and what historical *analogy* (extended comparison) does Eco use to illustrate it?

4. In paragraph 4, Eco explains the effects of the proliferation of fax machines. Is this paragraph meant to be taken literally? Explain.

5. Eco uses classification in paragraphs 7–13. What is his purpose for doing so?

6. This essay does not have a formal conclusion. Would it have been improved by the addition of a final, concluding paragraph? Explain.

## Questions for Critical Thinking and Discussion

1. Comment on the following statement: "The recent developments in consumer technology have had the unfortunate result of making U.S. culture noisier and ruder. Cell phones, pagers, boom boxes, and modern sound systems for cars have turned rudeness into an art form."

2. Comment on the following statement: "Cell phones don't play the same role they did in the past. For many people, the vast number of minutes they have to use each month prompts them to use the phone as much as possible. Some people can't seem to walk a hundred yards without making a 'Whassup?' phone call."

## Suggestions for Writing

1. Write a 500- to 750-word essay on the following topic: "how not to use e-mail." Note that this essay could employ either the instructional approach or the informational approach.

2. Has a specific kind of technology—cell phones or personal digital assistants (PDAs), for example—ever taken up more of your life than you expected it to? Write a 500- to 750-word essay that analyzes how this process developed.

**3.** Write a 500- to 750-word essay on the following topic: how to use a cell phone responsibly.

*Speaking Assignment*

Give a presentation that explains how the lives of Americans (or any other people) have changed in your lifetime because of technology. Limit yourself to the effects of three or four major inventions or developments. (For more help with oral presentations, see Chapter 18.)

# WRITING THE PROCESS ANALYSIS ESSAY WITH A READER'S EYE

**CATALYST 2.0**

**MORE OPTIONS ONLINE**
If you would like to read additional process analysis essays, go to www.mhhe.com/ writingtoday.

When you are writing a process essay, your ability to understand your reader's needs is crucial. Look at it this way: you are telling your reader how to do something or how a process occurs. Since you probably know more about the subject than your reader does, you shouldn't assume that your reader will understand the process if you write down the steps just as they occur to you. Beware of writing an essay that seems very effective—to you—but that baffles an intelligent reader who needs a clearer, more detailed explanation of the process you are analyzing. The advice that follows will help you think like your reader as you consider your assignment and then prewrite, draft, revise, and edit your process analysis essay.

## Issues to Keep in Mind

When writing a process analysis, you may choose a topic that leads you to write an instructional ("how-to") essay, or you may prefer the informational approach, in which you show how a significant process works. In either case, take some time to think about the following three issues:

**1.** Audience analysis

**2.** Language level

**3.** Voice

*Audience Analysis*

If you needed to explain how to use a new type of optical scanner, you wouldn't write the same instructions for every possible audience. A novice computer user would need a simple, painstakingly clear set of steps, whereas someone with extensive computer experience could probably understand a less detailed set of instructions. Therefore, before you begin to write any kind of process analysis, you need to consider how much you can expect your audience to know about the process that you are analyzing. The answer to this question will determine both how you plan your essay and how much explanatory information you will need to include.

In addition, once you have completed a draft, you can use peer review to help you discover places where readers will have problems following the process. Choose a reviewer who is part of your target audience, and ask him or her this question at the start: "Does my essay make *sense* to you?"

### Language Level

As you think about how much your audience is likely to know, you also need to think about the kind of language to use in your essay. If you are writing about a mechanical or technical process, you need to be careful about including **jargon**, specialized language that only members of a particular group are likely to understand. For example, the following sentence appeared in an essay for a general audience on how baseball managers choose relief pitchers: "Ryan Howard went yard with the bases juiced." Perhaps one out of three U.S. readers would understand the meaning of this mysterious line—that Ryan Howard (the batter) hit a grand slam (a home run with runners on all three bases). Unless you know that all of the members of your audience will understand it, it's usually best to avoid using jargon in a process analysis.

Although you can usually avoid jargon, sometimes you will need to explain general technical terms in order to make readers understand the process you are describing. In an essay on working out, for instance, the writer could use a parenthetical definition to clarify a term that some readers might not know: "Performing regular sets of this exercise will strengthen the deltoids (shoulder muscles)." As in this example, you should usually define terms simply and economically; an essay filled with complex definitions will frustrate readers. Moreover, any topic that requires you to define a large number of terms may be too specialized for your purposes.

### Voice

Students are usually told to avoid using *you* in their essays. Normally, when students write *you,* they mean a generalized, vague "someone." However, in an instructional process analysis, the writer is addressing a specific *you:* the reader. Using *you* is appropriate in this situation. On the other hand, an informational process essay does not tell the reader how to perform a process, so the use of *you* should usually be avoided in such writing.

## Choosing a Topic

CATALYST 2.0

**MORE OPTIONS ONLINE**
For more help with problem areas in the process analysis essay, go to www.mhhe.com/writingtoday.

As always, think of your reader. Most writing instructors have already read a great many weak, boring papers on such topics as "How to Pack a Suitcase" and "How to Change a Flat Tire on an Imported Car." At the very least, you want your essay to be informative *and* entertaining. The following guidelines will help you choose a promising topic for your process analysis:

1. Find a topic that is neither too narrow nor too broad. A narrow, mundane topic will probably lead to a narrow, mundane essay, like the sleep-inducing essays on packing suitcases and changing tires mentioned above. On the other hand, some topics are clearly too broad for the confines of the short essay. "How the Federal Reserve Came to Be More Important Than the Supreme Court" is an interesting subject, but you could spend the rest of your life researching it and writing about it. Find a topic that can be

successfully undertaken within the limits of your assignment—for example, the process that the justices of the U.S. Supreme Court use to decide whether to hear a case.

2. Find a topic that interests you. Students sometimes worry that their interests and those of their instructor may be very far apart; hence, they may discard certain topics because they fear the topic will not be "pleasing" to the instructor. Remember that composition teachers tend to be a fairly open-minded group of people. They like good writing, regardless of the subject, and they are continually surprised by students' ability to develop interesting papers on unexpected themes. Consider the following topic: "How Country Music Videos Have Succeeded as Television Programming." One of the authors of this text believes that country music is enjoyable, historically important, and culturally significant; the other hates country music, doesn't listen to it, and wishes that it would go away. Yet we'd both like to read a student's paper on this subject.

3. Consider whether you want to choose a topic that will require research. Although you may know a great deal about a particular subject, research might help broaden your scope. However, before proceeding with a topic that requires research, check with your instructor about whether he or she will allow you to include secondary material in your essay. And if you do include information from other sources, make sure that you document this information properly (see also Chapter 21).

## Prewriting

The process essay sets forth a series of steps. To develop these steps, you need to generate plenty of material before you decide how to organize your essay. Freewriting works well for generating the steps or stages in a process, as does clustering or brainstorming (see Chapter 2, pages 30–35). As you choose your topic and start your prewriting, you will be able to determine whether your essay will be instructional or informational, and this decision will help later as you begin to draft your introduction. If your essay will use the instructional approach, you should think about how learning the process will help your reader. If your essay is informational, you should consider the overall point that you are trying to make. Also at this time, you should be able to develop a preliminary thesis statement.

## Organizing

Once you have generated a list of the steps or stages in the process and developed your working thesis, the best way for you to organize this raw material is to arrange it into an outline. (Chapter 2 covers informal, sentence, and formal outline structures. See pages 40–43.) A sentence outline works well for process analysis, giving you (and perhaps your peer reviewer) a look at how the essay will present the process for readers. Make sure that you are comfortable with your essay's proposed outline before you begin drafting and that your outline doesn't reveal gaps in the process. Outlines are easy to revise, but essays can be much more of a problem.

## Drafting

To illustrate one approach to writing a process analysis essay, we have included the essay "Shaping a Better Beast."

### The Introduction

The introduction to a process analysis must establish background and context— what your reader needs to know before working through your process analysis. Many students, concentrating on the process that will form the body of the essay, write very short introductions, forgetting what the reader needs to know:

- In an informational essay, the context and the larger significance of the process being analyzed
- In an instructional essay, the context and the importance of learning how to master the process (and in the case of a highly practical essay, such as how to sand and finish a wooden cabinet, the tools and other materials that will be required)

Remember that you can write your introduction after you write the body of your essay. Many writers find it hard to introduce text that has not yet been written, so consider postponing the introduction until after you have written the draft of your body paragraphs.

The introductory paragraph for our sample essay effectively establishes the importance of the process, setting up the rest of the essay:

### Shaping the Better Beast

Today, cats are the most popular pets in American homes. But before cats grow up, they start as kittens, creatures that are very different from mature felines in many ways. Most people love kittens; they are a delight to be around. As the saying goes, though, "The problem with kittens is that they grow up and become CATS." Many adult cats are mean, distant, neurotic, or just plain weird. However, the personality of a mature cat is not "hard-wired" genetically. The development of a cat's temperament is a function of environment and handling. **By working closely with a kitten from the moment you bring it home, you can have a good chance of developing a kind, loving companion.**

Note the thesis statement at the end of this paragraph. In many types of writing that you will be assigned, your instructor may require a specific thesis statement that lists all the issues you plan to cover. Such a thesis can help readers follow the structure of your essay, but in a process essay this "list" approach

> *Consider Your Options* •
>
> A process analysis might be written in different ways to fulfill a variety of purposes. Make sure to understand your purpose and to state it clearly in your introduction. (For more on introductions, see Chapter 3.)

can make the essay seem more mechanical than it needs to. Moreover, in some cases listing all the steps in the process is unwieldy; your thesis would have to consist of either multiple sentences or one long, crowded sentence that would be hard to make parallel. Therefore, a general thesis statement is usually the best option for a process essay.

## The Body

The writer now provides the steps—both specific and general—that the reader should follow:

First, make sure that you bring your kitten home to a nonthreatening environment. A dwelling filled with noisy roommates, parties, and loud music is not a good place to raise a kitten. Cats are afraid of loud noises and prefer quiet. Similarly, if you own a dog or other cats, these other animals will make it more difficult for your kitten to adjust and develop. You should also be aware that your kitten needs quiet places: things to hide under, such as table coverings and drapes. A kitten is much more likely to feel at home in a place that matches its instinctive needs.

Second, spend as much time as possible playing with your kitten. Human children who are routinely ignored can grow up to be cold, distant adults. The same is true with cats. Kittens are dynamos: they want to play, sometimes at a maniacal level. Indulge this need: play with your kitten as much as you can if you want it to bond with you for life. For better or for worse, your kitten sees you as a surrogate mother, so spend as much time as you can with your "child."

Finally, listen to your kitten and be aware of its signals. Each cat is different. Try to figure out your kitten's personality very early on. For example, if you are playing with your kitten and it suddenly seems angry or aggressive, let it cool off. As you interact with your kitten, you can also let it know that some of its signals are unacceptable. Biting, excessive use of claws, and interminable crying in the presence of a closed door are behaviors that you can adjust at this point. However, although you can mold your kitten's behavior to a degree, keep in mind that cats aren't robots. A friend of mine thinks

she has raised the perfect cat, and her cat is usually docile and
pleasant, but if he has access to her bedroom at night, she will
invariably wake up at three or four in the morning with a sixteen-
pound Bengal Tiger perched on top of her head. She has tried to
change his behavior, but it continues. Oddly enough, her cat didn't
start this behavior until he was four years old.

Note the writer's use of topic sentences:

- First, make sure that you bring your kitten home to a nonthreatening environment.
- Second, spend as much time as possible playing with your kitten.
- Finally, listen to your kitten and be aware of its signals.

These sentences guide the reader effectively through the process. In Chapter 3, "Developing Strong Paragraphs," we point out that writers can sometimes use implied topic sentences or topic sentences that end, rather than begin, a paragraph. However, avoid these approaches in an instructional process essay. Instead, begin each body paragraph with a clear topic sentence.

Second, notice how the writer has used transitions to link ideas. Time-order transitions (for example, *first, next, then, finally*) are frequently useful in process analysis, as this essay proves, but causal transitions such as *therefore* and *consequently* can also work well. See Chapter 3, page 73, for the chart on transitions, and use them liberally in any process analysis essay you write. Especially if your essay tells readers how to do something, it may sound a bit more formulaic and mechanical than other essays you write. If readers find it clear and easy to follow, though, they will be grateful and your essay will be a success.

Third, notice how the writer employs other rhetorical options as she develops her body paragraphs. Description, narration, exemplification, causal analysis, definition, and comparison/contrast all help to make these paragraphs more effective.

### The Conclusion

The dreaded "summary" approach to concluding your process essay ("In this essay I have explained three steps for making the shoe-shining process a snap. These are . . .") is rarely a good choice. Although you should avoid bringing up new subjects in your conclusion, you should certainly feel free to comment on the significance of your subject or offer an effective anecdote:

A few weeks ago, my friend Amy asked me to come by and see
her cat, a Russian Blue named Nita. I knew that Amy already had a
dog and another cat, and I knew as well that Russian Blues are sometimes neurotic, so I was curious to see what this one might be like.

*Consider Your Options*

Instead of summarizing your essay in the conclusion of a process analysis, ask yourself what needs to be stressed to your reader at this point. (For more on conclusions, see Chapter 3.)

During my ninety minutes at Amy's, I got just three brief glimpses of her "pet." Whenever Nita emerged from her hiding place, either the Labrador or the orange tom ran after her and chased her away. When I tried to pick Nita up, she raked my arm because of her fear of contact. Amy said, "I haven't been home much since I adopted Nita. I've been letting her get to know the others on her own." Because of Amy's "process" of raising her kitten, she doesn't have a pet; she has a hostage.

The conclusion to the process essay is your opportunity to finish what is sometimes a fairly mechanical essay with your own signature flourish. Take advantage of this opportunity.

### EXERCISE 8.1

Write a sentence outline of "Shaping the Better Beast." (For help with sentence outlines, see Chapter 2, pages 41–42.) What does the outline reveal about this essay's organization? How would a different organization work for this essay?

### Revising Your Draft

After you have completed a draft of your process analysis essay, your next step is to revise it, using your own analysis and comments from classmates or friends. During peer review, answer the Questions for Reviewing a Process

## Questions for Reviewing a Process Analysis Essay

1   Does the introduction sufficiently explain the background and context for the process?

2   Does the essay include a thesis statement that informs the reader about the analysis to follow, either stating why it is important to learn or making a point about it? Is the writer's purpose clear?

3   Do the steps and the commentary make sense? Do you feel that you understand the process that is being described? Point out any places where you were confused.

4   Point out any step or comment that doesn't ring true.

5   Are topic sentences both clear and properly located? Where are the steps unclear for readers, and where does a step need more explanation?

6   Does the writer use enough transitions to guide the reader through the process? Where are transitional words and sentences needed?

7   Does the essay have an effective conclusion? How could it be improved?

Analysis Essay (on page 262) whether you are reviewing your own draft or the work of another student.

After reviewing for content, you need to go over your peer reviewers' responses to your essay and then revise for unity, coherence, language level, and tone (see Chapter 4). When you have revised your draft and are basically satisfied with it, read your draft for mechanical and grammatical errors. Concentrate on finding and correcting major sentence errors (fragment, comma splice, fused sentence), errors in pronoun agreement and subject-verb agreement, and spelling.

Now that you have made your corrections, *read your essay one more time* to catch any errors made during revision and find errors missed during your earlier reviews.

**CATALYST 2.0**

**MORE OPTIONS ONLINE**
For more help with revision, go to www.mhhe.com/ writingtoday.

## Student Essay

In the following essay, Manny Meregildo writes about the problem of trying to hold down a job while attending college. The final draft is presented first. Then Manny's first draft is presented, with his comments about this draft and what he needed to do in the revision stage.

### Manny's Final Draft

#### Get the Right Job

Unfortunately, most of us do not live in an ideal world where Mom and Dad pay for all of our school and living expenses. If most college students plan to have any type of social life or buy their first car, they will have to find a job. Eventually, serious college students find out that attending college is extremely difficult, and having to get a job to pay for some of the expenses is not a pleasant experience. Even though most employers value a higher education, the business world and the college environment sometimes collide, creating extreme conflicts.

Attending college is a job in itself. You are expected to be on time for class and attend every lecture—which in some cases means attending a class three times a week. You are also expected to study several hours a day and complete any assignment that has been given, which can take several hours as well. That leaves very little time for an employer to work with; however, when managers are creating the schedules for the following week, they are not concerned about the number of hours that you need for studying or whether the schedule they are creating conflicts with your current course schedule. Fortunately, there is a way out of this situation: find a job with flexible hours and a work environment that is not tyrannical.

Flexibility is an extremely important attribute for both school and work. Usually, college instructors will hand out a syllabus listing what will be done during that semester, and this schedule is normally followed. However, there are always unexpected circumstances when the class runs late, you need to stay after class to speak with the professor, or the date of an exam is pushed back. These unexpected events can cause problems when you have to work on the same day. Unfortunately, some students have to deal with an employer like mine, who will refuse to give anyone the day off, even if it means failing the class. Is having to deal with this dilemma worth the risk of losing three months of your life?

For every class hour, students should spend a minimum of three hours studying—well, at least that is the recommended time given by instructors. Your main goal is to achieve an *A* in the class; therefore, to accomplish this task, you need to study as much as possible. Unfortunately, having a job takes away precious studying time—doing the math shows why. Some employers allow their employees to bring their schoolbooks to work so that they can study while on the job. However, if your boss is strict like mine, and he or she doesn't care if business is slow or not, the boss will not allow any materials that are not work-related on the floor. Nevertheless, what your boss and other bosses do not know won't hurt them. You can usually find a way to study where you work.

The best option is to avoid working altogether while attending college, unless you can find a supervisor who believes that education comes first and will fight for you, or who needs the extra studying time too and is willing to overlook some of the company's policies. However, not all of us are fortunate enough to enjoy such pleasures; instead, we battle with time to get everything done.

*Manny's First Draft*

### Getting the Right Job

Unfortunately, we all do not live in an ideal world where mom and dad pay for all of our school or living expenses. If we as students plan to have any type of life, we will have to find a job. Eventually, serious college students find out that attending college is extremely difficult, and having to get a job to pay for some of the expenses is not a pleasant experience. Even though most employers value a higher education, the business world and the college environment sometimes collide, creating a catastrophic event.

Attending college is a job in itself. We as college students are expected to attend every lecture - which in some cases are about three times a week. We are also expected to study several hours a day, which can take several hours as well. That leaves very little time for an employer to work with; however, when managers are creating the work schedules for the following week, they are not concerned about whether the schedule they are creating conflicts with our current course schedule, creating a problem for the student. Fortunately, there is an easy way out of this situation: finding the right job, one that is flexible and not tyrannical.

College instructors usually will hand out a listing of what would be done during that semester. Thus, there are those unexpected circumstances where the class runs late, if the students needs to stay after class to speak with the professor, or if the date of an exam is pushed back. This could be a problem, because the student might have to work that day. Unfortunately, some students have to deal with an employer like mine who will refuse to give any one the day off. Is having to deal with this dilemma worth the risk of losing three months of your life?

For every class hour there should be a minimum of three hours of studying. A student's main goal is to achieve an A in the class;

1   When I wrote my first draft, I wasn't really sure which way to go with it, so it didn't seem very focused when I read it over. Sometimes it's informational, sometimes instructive. I realized that I was better off giving advice here, even though that complicated the revision.

2   I wasn't sure whether to use "you" or talk about college students—this went along with my problems in focusing the essay.

3   A classmate pointed out that this paragraph needed a point, so I added a topic sentence.

4

My first drafts frequently have verb problems and clunky language; this one is a good example.

therefore, to accomplish this task, lots of studying is required. Unfortunately, having a job takes away from our studying time, and if we were to do the math we will see why. Some employers would allow their employees to bring their schoolbooks to work so that they could study while on the job. Thus, if the student has a strict boss like I do who does not care if business is slow or not, the boss will not allow any materials that are not work related on the floor.

If possible, avoid working while attending college at all cost, unless you can find a supervisor who will fight for you and believes that education comes first or he or she needs the extra studying time too and is willing to overlook some of the company's policies. However, we are all not that fortunate to enjoy such pleasures; instead, we battle with time to get the job done.

5

### EXERCISE 8.2: REVISING

The following is the first draft of a student's process analysis essay. Working in pairs or in small groups, review this essay. Using the Questions for Reviewing a Process Analysis Essay on page 262, decide what revisions you would suggest. If you have any questions the student needs to consider, write them in the margin or on a separate sheet of paper. If your instructor directs you to, rewrite one or more paragraphs to make them stronger and to eliminate any grammatical or mechanical errors.

### "Losing Weight"

Everyone seems to be trying to lose weight. A good idea, since most Americains are overweight to some degree or the other. Irregardless of how much weight people want - or need - to loose, there are three simple steps that will help bring the gross weight down and help to acheive a healthy life style; eliminating fat from the diet, regualar intake and an exercise program.

1

A large cheese burger from a fastfood restarant may contain as many as 125 grams of fat. This is enough fat for a week! on the other hand, chicken - with the skin removed - has far less fat. And so does fish. But you cant fry either chicken or fish and hope to loose weight

2

do to the fat in the fring oils. Never the less, avoiding fastfoods is one way to cut down fat. A diet that consists of skinless chicken and fish are the way to go, therefore, think of these as your key to thiness.

3

When I start my tuesdays they are very different than my Mondays which are very different from my wednesdays and so on, etc. My schedual changes everyday. So does my meal times. Eating on a regualar schedual helps one acheive selfdiscipline, and you can then look forward to a self controled diet. If you cant eat on a regualar schedual than try to plan what you eat before its time to eat it. It might be that it is dificult for you to plan a meal before you eat it, never the less, make the attempt.

4

Exercise has any number of health related benefits and it is the best way to burn extra calories and it is also the way to tone the bodies mussels. Hard exercise is best it strenthens the muscles and improves the heart's activities. Any one of any age, from infants to geezers will have their life improved by hard exersise.

5

So, as you can see, in the previous essay I have given three easy steps to improve your health: exercise, avoid fat and eat regualar. Try it, it just might make a differance!

## Additional Writing Topics

1. *Deflated expectations.* You had great hopes for that first date with a new someone, but after ten minutes you realize that you are in what government types call a "damage control situation." What steps can you take to survive the evening and return to the safety of your home?

2. *The collection agent awaits.* The credit cards have been fun, but the bills are piling up. What can you do to stabilize your financial situation?

3. *Grand Central Station.* You live in a home with three (or four, or whatever) roommates. How can this situation be managed so that chaos is not the normal condition?

4. *Time control.* You love to shop, but time is not as free for you as it used to be. How can you efficiently maximize your enjoyment of shopping in a limited amount of time?

5. *Practical stuff.* Teach your readers how to
   a. Customize a Web browser.
   b. Change the oil in a fifty-year-old car.

    c.  Improve their poker-playing skills.

    d.  Get rid of a slice (or a hook) in golf.

    e.  Accessorize clothing.

    f.  Use a thumb drive.

    g.  Meet new friends.

    h.  Break up with a sweetheart.

    i.  Improve their public image.

    j.  Become a better public speaker.

    k.  Set up an aquarium.

    l.  Keep a ferret, an iguana, or other exotic animal as a pet.

    m. Make a good first impression.

    n.  Make a horrible first impression.

    o.  Pass a particularly difficult course.

    p.  Fail a particularly easy course.

**6.  Writing on the job.** Write an essay in which you explain to the reader either (a) how to succeed in a job interview or (b) how to fail miserably in a job interview.

### Process Analysis and Visual Representations

Workers in the United States are ranked among the most productive in the world. Is it because of the strong work ethic that is a national tradition? Partly, but there is another reason as well. The following is a brief lesson in macroeconomics.

Companies always want to increase revenues and profits, but in strongly competitive markets they have few options. A company could raise its prices, but if its competitors did not follow suit, it would lose market share, thus lowering revenues. A company could try to minimize its costs for raw materials, but chances are it's already done that. And, below a certain level, a company's products would be seen by buyers as substandard. They would look to the company's competitors as an alternative. A third option is to cut labor costs. One approach here is to keep wages down. A second is to ask workers to work much harder for the wages they receive.

Since World War II, the manufacturing sector of the U.S. economy has dwindled; the nation has increasingly become more service and information oriented. The factory jobs that were the mainstay of the economy went overseas. "Good" jobs became hard to find, and women grew up planning to enter the workplace, for most married couples could not survive on just one income. Many jobs that were previously paid by the hour were reclassified by companies as salaried positions to avoid federal overtime laws.

Companies tried to inculcate positive attitudes by stressing teamwork and sacrifice. A whole industry sprang up to service this initiative. Doubtless you have seen countless motivational posters, books, and other media throughout your life.

However, U.S. workers have begun to burn out, and a new "counter-motivational" movement has emerged. If you've ever watched NBC's *The Office* (or the British original of the same name), you've seen people who want to keep their jobs but don't want to work themselves to death to do so. The poster you see here was produced by Despair, Inc., a company that produces "Demotivators": posters, calendars, coffee cups, and so on that are parodies of the motivational industry's products. The company's motto is "No matter how lackluster you are, you have the potential to be so much less."

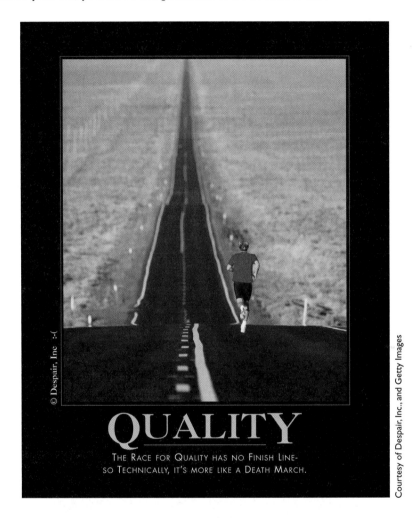

© Despair, Inc :-(

Courtesy of Despair, Inc., and Getty Images

1.  Write a response to this poster. What are your thoughts and impressions? As you write, refer to Questions for Reviewing a Visual Representation.

2.  Research the topic of stress and the workplace. Use both library and Internet resources. You will probably want to concentrate on specific subtopics—for example, the stress faced by working mothers or by people with more than one job. Then either write an essay containing your findings and documenting your sources (see also Chapter 21) or develop an oral presentation based on your research and conclusions (see also Chapter 18).

## Questions for Reviewing a Visual Representation

- Is the representation forceful, passive, or something in between?
- What is the purpose of the representation—in other words, what is it trying to do to you, the reader/viewer?
- If the representation uses words, do they reinforce the visual image or in some way contradict it?
- What is the presumed audience for the representation—men, women, children, the elderly? Or does it have a broader appeal?
- If the representation is an advertisement, is it trying to sell a product or to get you to adopt a way of thinking?
- If the representation is an advertisement, does it try to persuade you in a fair manner, or do you feel manipulated?

## Responding to an Image

Shari Springer Berman and Robert Pulcini's *American Splendor* (2003-R) tells the real-life story of Harvey Pekar (played by Paul Giamatti), who, although he cannot draw, has become one of North America's most famous and respected comic-book authors.

© Good Machine/HBO/The Kobal Collection/Clifford, John.

1. First, write an informal response to the depiction of Pekar shown in the film still.

2. Watch the film. How does Pekar develop his career, despite his limitations? Write an essay analyzing this process.

## Using the Internet

Search the Internet for insights and information to use when explaining a process.

1. Use the Internet to find information on an art, task, or process that is now rare or no longer practiced. Examples include mummifying the body of an ancient Egyptian; making wine without the use of a press; churning butter; building an Egyptian or Mayan pyramid; cremating a Viking chieftain; building a cliff dwelling, long house, or other Native American home; painting a fresco; hunting with falcons; printing a book or newspaper in colonial America; throwing a masquerade ball; hauling freight along the Erie Canal; sailing a merchant schooner; practicing medicine with leeches; and fueling and driving a coal-fired steam locomotive. Use this information to write an essay that instructs the reader in the steps required to perform this art, task, or process.

2. Explain a natural process such as photosynthesis, the circulation of the blood in a human body, the formation of rain clouds, the eruption of a volcano, the creation of oil or coal deposits, the migration of birds, or the metamorphosis of a butterfly. Once again, use the Internet to find sources of information.

3. Go online to learn how to build a Web page and to put it on the Internet. Explain this process in an essay addressed to a novice Web user.

Meet Jack

He studied hard at College

Jack earned a Degree

It cost him 4 years and
Tens of Thousands of Dollars

Jack partied hard at College

He put it all on MySpace.com

Potential Employers found it

It cost him 4 years and
Tens of Thousands of Dollars

By permission of Gary Varvel and Creators Syndicate, Inc.

### CHAPTER 9

# CAUSAL ANALYSIS

# Writing in Context

One of Osprey's major revenue sources is the sale of networking software; unfortunately, because of the way that the software has been developed over time, some clients have older versions, with updates provided only by high-level client-specific "patches" to the ongoing software program.

Bob has called a meeting to unveil his new marketing plan. Bob's plan is both simple and audacious: offer all current business users an up-to-date version of the program, which would cost the clients a hefty sum, then guarantee future updates at a reduced price. This is a one-time-only offer; clients must decide within thirty days.

The idea sounds good to you, but Bert Alvarez, one of the company's vice presidents, has doubts. "Perhaps a feasibility study would be in order," he says.

"Exactly," Bob agrees. He turns in your direction. "How are our current clients likely to react? Will they run to our competitors? Speaking of them, will they try to undercut us? You've got till Friday to give us an answer."

The document that Bob has requested, a *feasibility study*, examines the possible *effects* of a change in policy. A very common type of business writing, it calls for an option that is used widely in the academic and business worlds.

# HOW DOES CAUSAL ANALYSIS WORK?

Feasibility studies such as the one Bob has asked for require use of the **causal analysis** option, in which a writer explores the causes and/or effects of an event, a policy, or a situation. Note that this feasibility study will need to be *hypothetical*. The writer is being asked to predict the future by considering the firm's current circumstances and researching the past behavior of its clients.

In other circumstances, the writer might be asked to write a report exploring the effects of a past event. For example, perhaps a policy change was made in the past, and the vice president wants to determine its effects. Did everything go according to plan, or were there any surprises?

This kind of causal analysis can be used for a great many subjects in numerous academic disciplines as well as in business and in daily life, as the following brief list of possible topics for an essay exploring effects makes clear:

- In 1990, Iraq invaded Kuwait and goaded the United States into the military response that came to be known as Desert Storm. What happened to Iraq after losing this war?

- A year ago, a twenty-two-year-old woman decided to divorce her chronically unemployed husband, return to college, and try to establish a better life for herself and her two very young children. Did she succeed? What were the effects of this momentous choice?

- Ten years ago, a student informed his parents that he was changing his major from finance to humanities and planned to attend graduate school after receiving his bachelor's degree. Ten years later, how have things worked out for him?

- A maple tree has been encroaching on the sight lines of motorists as they approach a stop sign. The county commission has been told repeatedly that the tree must be cut back, but it has never taken action. What are the effects of this nondecision?

- A state decides to limit welfare benefits to two years, after which the recipients must fend for themselves. Five years after the new law was enacted, the state commissions a study to find out what has happened to the people who were affected by the law. Did they thrive, or did they starve?

When a writer explores the effects of past events, he or she concentrates on factual situations that can be studied and understood. In the case of a state cutting back on welfare availability, though, it is likely that both approaches would be used. Before the law was approved, the state government would have looked into what *would probably* happen as a result of the new welfare law (the feasibility approach); five years later, the state orders a study to examine what *actually* happened.

The third basic version of causal analysis looks at *why* events happened or why a situation has arisen, such as in the following instances:

- Police intervene in an argument between two patrons outside a downtown club. Five minutes later, a riot is in progress.

- A weird odor fills the air near the water treatment plant on the Generic River.
- In the past three years, the student dropout rate has tripled at Area Consolidated Comprehensive High School.
- Your cat insists on sitting directly in front of the television during *Ugly Betty.*
- It has become almost impossible to find a parking spot on your college's campus.

A writer investigating these situations needs to concentrate on *causes.* What is the explanation for these curious events? What factors have changed? Are there any causes that are not immediately evident but seem obvious after some thought and investigation?

Writers who use causal analysis tend to concentrate on either causes or effects (whether historical or hypothetical); however, it is impossible to discuss causes without discussing effects, and vice versa. The distinction is more a matter of emphasis, of looking at a situation and finding the best way to analyze it. For example, would you emphasize causes or effects when writing about the following situations?

- Your university has announced that any student who misses more than three classes, or "contact hours," in a semester will be dropped from that class.
- Over the past month, your lover has become listless, moody, and irritable.
- In 1863, Robert E. Lee ignored the advice of his generals and continued on with his plans during the battle of Gettysburg.

In each of these situations, the best strategy seems fairly obvious. The first scenario makes one wonder what the effects of the change in attendance policy will be. Will students have to put in extra semesters to make up for uncompleted classes? Will students need to change their habits? If you were writing about this situation, you would probably look at the hypothetical: What effects could be *expected*? On the other hand, the second scenario would prompt you to look for *causes.* What's going on with your loved one? Why is he or she changing? The third scenario would most likely lead you to investigate what actually happened after Lee made his ill-fated decision: the Confederacy lost its vital momentum, and the Civil War turned in favor of the Union.

Causal analysis essays tend to follow these basic patterns:

- **Multiple causes of one effect.** In this pattern, a writer concentrates on the cause of a situation by explaining how an outcome is the product of a combination of causes—for example, a failed birthday party caused by a number of factors that went awry.
- **One major cause with several effects.** Here, one event or factor has various ramifications, and the essay concentrates on effects—for example, a writer might relate how the death of his or her father just after the writer's graduation from high school affected (a) the emotional

well-being of all the surviving family members, (b) the financial/occupational status of the writer's mother, and (c) the college prospects of both the writer and his or her brothers and sisters.

- **Hypothetical effects of a proposed change.** This approach speculates: "What would happen if . . . ?" The writer produces a hypothetical scenario that attempts to logically forecast the results of a policy change or structural change, such as "What would happen if the United States severely restricted immigration quotas?" The essay would explore the positive and negative outcomes that could be expected from such a change in policy.

- **Causal chains.** This term may best be explained as "one thing leads to another." In a basic example, the writer might explain about one recent morning when she overslept, causing her to run late in getting her daughter ready for school, resulting in her daughter's missing the school bus, requiring the writer to call a taxi and accompany her daughter to school and then return home, making her late for her own city bus to college, causing her to miss half of her economics class on final exam day, fail the exam, and have to take economics again.

In the examples above, the purpose for writing determines whether the emphasis is on cause or effect.

Occasionally, an essay will weigh causes and effects equally. How might you respond to the following scenario? Your paternal grandparents have been married for forty-eight years. They suddenly announce that they are splitting up. What is the best way to write about this situation? One approach would be to look at the causes of this surprising decision. Were your grandparents secretly unhappy with each other? Did one of them, at around age seventy, fall in love with someone else? (Don't laugh; it happens.) Has one of them changed so much over the last several years that the marriage is no longer viable?

The other approach would be to examine the potential effects of this decision. Will one (or both) of your grandparents be emotionally devastated? Financially devastated? How about the effects on their children, including, of course, your father? How about the effects on their grandchildren, including you?

Actually, your grandparents' divorce could be discussed from either angle. The situation also presents an opportunity to write an essay in which you concentrate equally on causes and effects, with causes discussed first and effects discussed later. However, most topics lead the writer in one direction or the other.

As these examples demonstrate, causal analysis, along with two other forms of analysis—exemplification (Chapter 7) and process analysis (Chapter 8)—are powerful tools that enable us to look at the world around us and make sense of it. For this reason, these strategies are commonly used by instructors in other courses when they ask you to explain the content you have learned in their classes. And your future writing, on the job or in the laboratory, will doubtless require you to employ these standard options.

In many essays that use a different overall strategy, you will need to consider either causes or effects in order to support your thesis and fulfill your purpose. For example, if you are explaining how to do something on the job (a process analysis essay), you may need to warn readers about the effects of neglecting to follow a particular step. If you are classifying a group of events for a history course, you might decide to categorize them according to their causes or their effects.

In other essays, however, causal analysis will be your main strategy. A note of caution: students occasionally get so fixated on the idea of causal analysis that they never stray from their initial idea, producing essays showing how one event leads to another, which leads to another, and so on, like some kind of demented parlor game. However, the purpose of causal analysis is much broader. Here, as in the other two analytical options—exemplification and process analysis—the writer has the opportunity to discuss the world as he or she sees it. The causal option forms the backbone of such an essay. A writer might explore the causes and/or effects of a situation, event, or policy in order to explain to readers how it came about or how it will affect them. Alternatively, the writer might analyze causes and/or effects in order to persuade the reader to do something about them—for example, to agree to an increase in student fees so that the college can build more parking lots.

Being able to show the linkages that make up our world is a powerful skill, as demonstrated in the essays that follow.

> *Consider Your Options*
>
> How might you use causal analysis on the job? What circumstances would call for you to analyze a situation by using this strategy?

## READING THE CAUSAL ANALYSIS ESSAY WITH A WRITER'S EYE

In the works that follow, the social commentator Barbara Ehrenreich examines a modern attitude toward being busy, Gore Vidal examines the causes and results of the "war on drugs," and Richard Rhodes attacks the idea that entertainment violence leads to real violence. These essays all demonstrate the importance of **prewriting.** As you read them, you will notice that a great deal of thought went into constructing the causal connections that these writers present.

The second half of this chapter features strategies for writing the causal analysis essay (pages 287–297). If you decide to write on one of the topics that follow the three essays below, make sure that you have read the strategies section before you begin. Note that additional writing topics are listed at the end of the chapter (pages 304–305).

# The Cult of Busyness

## BARBARA EHRENREICH

*Barbara Ehrenreich is a keen observer of the world. Writing on a wide variety of social topics, she has published scores of magazine articles and a number of books of social criticism, including the fol-* *lowing: Fear of Falling: The Inner Life of the Middle Class (1989), The Worst Years of Our Lives: Irreverent Notes on a Decade of Greed (1990), The Snarling Citizen (1995), Blood Rites: The*

Origins and History of the Passions of War *(1997), and* Nickel and Dimed: On (Not) Getting By in America *(2001). In the following essay, she illustrates a problem by approaching it with common sense and a clear eye.*

Not too long ago a former friend and soon-to-be acquaintance called me up to tell me how busy she was. A major report, upon which her professional future depended, was due in three days; her secretary was on strike; her housekeeper had fallen into the hands of the Immigration Department; she had two hours to prepare a dinner party for eight; and she was late for her time-management class. Stress was taking its toll, she told me: her children resented the fact that she sometimes got their names mixed up, and she had taken to abusing white wine.

All this put me at a distinct disadvantage, since the only thing I was doing at the time was holding the phone with one hand and attempting to touch the opposite toe with the other hand, a pastime that I had perfected during previous telephone monologues. Not that I'm not busy too: as I listened to her, I was on the alert for the moment the dryer would shut itself off and I would have to rush to fold the clothes before they settled into a mass of incorrigible wrinkles. But if I mentioned this little deadline of mine, she might think I wasn't busy enough to need a housekeeper, so I kept on patiently saying "Hmm" until she got to her parting line: "Look, this isn't a good time for me to talk, I've got to go now."

I don't know when the cult of conspicuous busyness began, but it has swept up almost all the upwardly mobile, professional women I know. Already, it is getting hard to recall the days when, for example "Let's have lunch" meant something other than "I've got more important things to do than talk to you right now." There was even a time when people used to get together without the excuse of needing something to eat—when, in fact, it was considered rude to talk with your mouth full. In the old days, hardly anybody had an appointment book, and when people wanted to know what the day held in store for them, they consulted a horoscope.

It's not only women, of course; for both sexes, busyness has become an important insignia of upper-middle-class status. Nobody, these days, admits to having a hobby, although two or more careers—say, neurosurgery and an art dealership—is not uncommon, and I am sure we will soon be hearing more about the tribulations of the four-paycheck couple. Even those who can manage only one occupation at a time would be embarrassed to be caught doing only one *thing* at a time. Those young men who jog with their headsets on are not, as you might innocently guess, rocking out, but are absorbing the principles of international finance law or a lecture on one-minute management. Even eating, I read recently, is giving way to "grazing"—the conscious ingestion of unidentified foods while drafting a legal brief, cajoling a client on the phone, and, in ambitious cases, doing calf-toning exercises under the desk.

But for women, there's more at stake than conforming to another upscale standard. If you want to attract men, for example, it no longer helps to be a bimbo with time on your hands. Upscale young men seem to go for the kind of woman who plays with a full deck of credit cards, who won't cry when she's knocked to the ground while trying to board the six o'clock Eastern shuttle, and whose schedule doesn't allow for a sexual encounter lasting more than twelve minutes. Then there is the economic reality: any woman who doesn't want to wind up a case study in the feminization of poverty has to be successful at something more demanding than fingernail maintenance or come-hither looks. Hence all the bustle, my busy friends would explain—they want to succeed.

But if success is the goal, it seems clear to me that the fast track is headed the wrong way. Think of the people who are genuinely successful—path-breaking scientists, best-selling novelists, and designers of major new software. They are not, on the whole, the kind of people who keep glancing shiftily at their watches or making small lists entitled "To Do." On the contrary, many of these people appear to be in a daze, like the distinguished professor I once had who, in the middle of a lecture on electron spin, became so fascinated by the dispersion properties of chalk dust that he could not go on. These truly successful people are childlike, easily distractable, fey sorts, whose usual demeanor resembles that of a recently fed hobo on a warm summer evening.

The secret of the truly successful, I believe, is 7 that they learned very early in life how *not* to be busy. They saw through that adage, repeated to me so often in childhood, that anything worth doing is worth doing well. The truth is, many things are worth doing only in the most slovenly, halfhearted fashion possible, and many other things are not worth doing at all. Balancing a checkbook, for example. For some reason, in our culture, this dreary exercise is regarded as the supreme test of personal maturity, business acumen, and the ability to cope with math anxiety. Yet it is a form of busyness which is exceeded in futility only by going to the additional trouble of computerizing one's checking account—and that, in turn, is only slightly less silly than taking the time to discuss, with anyone, what brand of personal computer one owns, or is thinking of buying, or has heard of others using.

If the truly successful manage never to be 8 busy, it is also true that many of the busiest people will never be successful. I known this firsthand from my experience, many years ago, as a waitress. Any executive who thinks the ultimate in busyness consists of having two important phone calls on hold and a major deadline in twenty minutes, should try facing six tablefuls of clients simultaneously demanding that you give them their checks, fresh coffee, a baby seat, and a warm, spontaneous smile. Even when she's not busy, a waitress has to look busy—refilling the salt shakers and polishing all the chrome in sight—but the only reward is the minimum wage and any change that gets left on the tables. Much the same is true of other high-stress jobs, like working as a telephone operator, or doing data entry on one of the new machines that monitors your speed as you work: "success" means surviving the shift.

Although busyness does not lead to success, 9 I am willing to believe that success—especially when visited on the unprepared—can cause busyness. Anyone who has invented a better mousetrap, or the contemporary equivalent, can expect to be harassed by strangers demanding that you read their unpublished manuscripts or undergo the humiliation of public speaking, usually on remote Midwestern campuses. But if it is true that success leads to more busyness and less time for worthwhile activities—like talking (and listening) to friends, reading novels, or putting in some volunteer time for a good cause—then who needs it? It would be sad to have come so far—or at least to have run so hard—only to lose each other.

## Vocabulary

The following terms are identified by paragraph number. Make sure that you understand each term's meaning in its context. If you're not sure that you understand a term, look it up in a college-level dictionary.

| | | |
|---|---|---|
| pastime (2) | tribulations (4) | distractable (6) |
| monologue (2) | ingestion (4) | fey (6) |

| | | |
|---|---|---|
| incorrigible (2) | upscale (5) | demeanor (6) |
| conspicuous (3) | feminization (5) | adage (7) |
| upwardly mobile (3) | shiftily (6) | slovenly (7) |
| insignia (4) | dispersion (6) | acumen (7) |
| neurosurgery (4) | | |

## Style and Strategy

1. Describe the way Ehrenreich opens her essay. Is her introduction effective? Why or why not?

2. What is the author's thesis? Where has she placed it?

3. Ehrenreich presents the contemporary "cult of busyness" as a *paradox*, a statement that seems contradictory but that is nevertheless true. Explain this paradox.

4. Find two instances where the author uses definition (see Chapter 10). How does her use of definition support her causal analysis?

5. Do you accept Ehrenreich's conclusion? Why or why not?

## Questions for Critical Thinking and Discussion

1. "Success in United States culture is becoming more and more dependent on personal image. It doesn't matter whether you're any good at what you do as long as you *say* you're good at what you do and look and dress the part." Do you agree or disagree with this statement?

2. Over the past twenty years, the media have devoted considerable attention to Americans who are too busy to pause for breath. Yet it is likely that these career-fixated, time-obsessed people are still a distinct minority. The majority still follow the example of Homer Simpson: come home at 5:30, eat supper, and watch television. What have you observed about people and their attitudes toward work? Have you noticed any differences between the way women approach this issue of work versus leisure time and the way men do?

## Suggestions for Writing

1. Write a 500- to 750-word essay in which you analyze a well-intentioned approach to solving a problem or completing a project that got bogged down. Consider what caused the problem. Were there defects in the planning stage and/or misplaced priorities?

2. Write a 500- to 750-word essay about a person who has a positive reputation that is unearned. How did this person come to be seen as smart, able, kind, or "cool"?

3. Ehrenreich writes that many of us live busy lives because we wish to succeed but that busyness does not lead to success. Are there consistent factors that lead people to become successful in their careers? Pick a profession or career type, perhaps one that you may be thinking about

entering after graduation. Then write a 500- to 750-word essay that explains the various factors—other than hard work—that contribute to success in that field. If you need to learn more about the demands of this career, try using the library or the Internet for research.

4. Write a 500- to 750-word essay that explains why a particular "cult" or obsession develops. You can focus on a religious or semi-religious cult, but there are many other possible choices. If necessary, support your thesis with library or Internet research in addition to your own knowledge and insights.

### Speaking Assignment

Ehrenreich characterizes busyness as a "cult." Create a short presentation in which you characterize any common, contemporary behavior, activity, or belief as a "cult" or an obsession. For example, think about people who can't go a day without visiting the mall, going to the gym, or reading their horoscope. (For more help with oral presentations, see Chapter 18.)

# Drugs

## GORE VIDAL

*Novelist, playwright, screenwriter, actor, and political commentator, Gore Vidal has alternately edified and infuriated his audience for more than sixty years. As an unabashed political independent, Vidal has found himself arguing unorthodox and/or unpopular positions for decades. He published his first novel, Williwaw (1946), at the age of nineteen, and has written more than thirty books, including Burr (1973), 1876 (1976), Duluth (1983), Lincoln (1984), Empire (1987), and The Golden Age (2000).*

*"Drugs," first published in 1970 in the New York Times, examines both the causes and the effects of the ongoing American war on illegal narcotics.*

It is possible to stop most drug addiction in the United States within a very short time. Simply make all drugs available and sell them at cost. Label each drug with a precise description of what effect—good and bad—the drug will have on the taker. This will require heroic honesty. Don't say that marijuana is addictive or dangerous when it is neither, as millions of people know—unlike "speed," which kills most unpleasantly, or heroin, which is addictive and difficult to kick.

For the record, I have tried—once—almost every drug and liked none, disproving the popular Fu Manchu theory that a single whiff of opium will enslave the mind. Nevertheless many drugs are bad for certain people to take and they should be told why in a sensible way.

Along with exhortation and warning, it might be good for our citizens to recall (or learn for the first time) that the United States was the creation of men who believed that each man has the right to do what he wants with his own life as long as he does not interfere with his neighbor's pursuit of happiness (that his neighbor's idea of happiness is persecuting others does confuse matters a bit).

This is a startling notion to the current generation of Americans. They reflect a system of public education which has made the Bill of Rights, literally, unacceptable to a majority of high school graduates (see the annual Purdue reports) who now form the "silent majority"—a phrase which that underestimated wit Richard Nixon took from Homer who used it to describe the dead.

Now one can hear the warning rumble begin: if everyone is allowed to take drugs everyone will and the GNP will decrease, the Commies will stop us from making everyone free, and we shall end up a race of Zombies, passively murmuring "groovie" to one another. Alarming thought. Yet it seems most unlikely that any reasonably sane person will become a drug addict if he knows in advance what addiction is going to be like.

Is everyone reasonably sane? No. Some people will always become drug addicts just as some people will always become alcoholics, and it is just too bad. Every man, however, has the power (and should have the legal right) to kill himself if he chooses. But since most men don't, they won't be mainliners either. Nevertheless, forbidding people things they like or think they might enjoy only makes them want those things all the more. This psychological insight is, for some mysterious reason, perennially denied our governors.

It is a lucky thing for the American moralist that our country has always existed in a kind of time-vacuum: we have no public memory of anything that happened before last Tuesday. No one in Washington today recalls what happened during the years alcohol was forbidden to the people by a Congress that thought it had a divine mission to stamp out Demon Rum—launching, in the process, the greatest crime wave in the country's history, causing thousands of deaths from bad alcohol, and cre-

ating a general (and persisting) contempt among the citizenry for the laws of the United States.

The same thing is happening today. But the government has learned nothing from past attempts at prohibition, not to mention repression.

Last year when the supply of Mexican marijuana was slightly curtailed by the Feds, the pushers got the kids hooked on heroin and deaths increased dramatically, particularly in New York. Whose fault? Evil men like the Mafiosi? Permissive Dr. Spock? Wild-eyed Dr. Leary? No.

The Government of the United States was responsible for those deaths. The bureaucratic machine has a vested interest in playing cops and robbers. Both the Bureau of Narcotics and the Mafia want strong laws against the sale and use of drugs because if drugs are sold at cost there would be no money in it for anyone.

If there was no money in it for the Mafia, there would be no friendly playground pushers, and addicts would not commit crimes to pay for the next fix. Finally, if there was no money in it, the Bureau of Narcotics would wither away, something they are not about to do without a struggle.

Will anything sensible be done? Of course not. The American people are as devoted to the idea of sin and its punishment as they are to making money—and fighting drugs is nearly as big a business as pushing them. Since the combination of sin and money is irresistible (particularly to the professional politician), the situation will only grow worse.

## Vocabulary

The following terms are identified by paragraph number. Make sure that you understand each term's meaning in its context. If you're not sure that you understand a term, look it up in a college-level dictionary.

| | | |
|---|---|---|
| exhortation (3) | prohibition (8) | vested interest (10) |
| mainliners (6) | curtailed (9) | wither (11) |
| perennially (6) | bureaucratic machine (10) | |

## Style and Strategy

1. What is Vidal's proposal? Does he qualify or weaken it in any way? Where does he present it, and what is the effect of its placement in the essay?

2. List the causes that Vidal cites for the ongoing American war on illegal substances.

3. List the effects of the war on illegal substances, as Vidal sees them.

4. How would you describe Vidal's tone?

5. A *rhetorical question* is one asked by a writer who really doesn't want an answer but wants to raise the issue mentioned in the question. Where in this essay does Vidal use rhetorical questions? In what way does he use them? What is their effect?

## Questions for Critical Thinking and Discussion

1. What would the United States be like if all currently illegal drugs could be sold legitimately? Would our society find a way to accommodate the open use of these drugs, or would chaos reign?

2. Do you think that people who do not take illegal drugs would try them if they were legal?

3. Most adult Americans believe that marijuana is less harmful than alcohol, but alcohol is legal (and culturally accepted) whereas possession of marijuana will lead straight to arrest. Moreover, some commentators believe that this apparent paradox reflects the power struggle among the American social classes—in other words, the rich make the rules and the rich prefer alcohol, so drinking is encouraged whereas smoking pot is a criminal offense. Do you agree or disagree?

4. "If all drugs were legalized, the inner-city ghetto and barrio would disappear." What is the reasoning behind this comment?

5. Reread paragraph 12. What assumptions does Vidal make here about the American public and its government? Do you agree? Why or why not?

## Suggestions for Writing

1. Write a 500- to 750-word essay about a social program or policy that doesn't seem worth the trouble—in other words, the effects of this program fail to justify the program's costs.

2. When Vidal writes about the rise of organized crime during the 1920s, he is referring to the Law of Unintended Consequences. In other words, the federal government made the sale of alcoholic beverages illegal; then, to everyone's horror, organized, vicious criminals appeared to satisfy the national demand for alcohol. Write a 500- to 750-word essay about a situation in which a change in a policy or procedure brought about an unintended consequence—whether positive or negative.

3. Write a 500- to 750-word essay in which you argue for a change in or the reversal of a college policy that you believe is counterproductive or unfair.

Try to predict the effects of this change or reversal, using as much detail as possible in order to support your thesis and convince your readers.

*Speaking Assignment*

In response to this essay, give a presentation arguing that a particular drug or other illegal substance should not be legalized. On the other hand, you might argue that a particular substance that is now legal should be made illegal. In either case, emphasize the ill effects of using this substance. (For more help with oral presentations, see Chapter 18.)

# Hollow Claims About Fantasy Violence

## RICHARD RHODES

*Richard Rhodes is best known for his* The Making of the Atomic Bomb *(1987), which was awarded the Pulitzer Prize for Nonfiction, the National Book Award, and a National Book Critics Circle Award. He is also the author of eighteen other books, including* Nuclear Renewal: Common Sense About Energy *(1993),* Dark Sun: The Making of the Hydrogen Bomb *(1995),* Why They Kill: The Discoveries of a Maverick Criminologist *(1999), and* Masters of Death: The SS-Einsatzgruppen and the Invention of the Holocaust *(2002).*

*"Hollow Claims About Fantasy Violence," which first appeared in the* New York Times *on September 17, 2000, challenges beliefs held by many laypersons as well as many social scientists. Does violent entertainment cause violent behavior? Rhodes doesn't think so.*

1 The moral entrepreneurs are at it again, pounding the entertainment industry for advertising its Grand Guignolesque* confections to children. If exposure to this mock violence contributes to the development of violent behavior, then our political leadership is justified in its indignation at what the Federal Trade Commission has reported about the marketing of violent fare to children. Senators John McCain and Joseph Lieberman have been especially quick to fasten on the FTC report as they make an issue of violent offerings to children.

---
*__*Grand Guignolesque:__ referring to a Parisian theater that specialized in productions that were designed to shock and horrify audiences.*

2 But is there really a link between entertainment and violent behavior?

3 The American Medical Association, the American Psychological Association, the American Academy of Pediatrics, and the National Institute of Mental Health all say yes. They base their claims on social science research that has been sharply criticized and disputed within the social science profession, especially outside the United States. In fact, no direct, causal link between exposure to mock violence in the media and subsequent violent behavior has ever been demonstrated, and the few claims of modest correlation have been contradicted by other findings, sometimes in the same studies.

4 History alone should call such a link into question. Private violence has been declining in the West since the media-barren late Middle Ages, when homicide rates are estimated to have been 10 times what they are in Western nations today. Historians attribute the decline to improving social controls over violence—police forces and common access to courts of law—and to a shift away from brutal physical punishment in child-rearing (a practice that still appears as a common factor in the background of violent criminals today).

The American Medical Association has based its endorsement of the media violence theory in major part on the studies of Brandon Centerwall, a psychiatrist in Seattle. Dr. Centerwall compared the murder rates for whites in three countries from 1945 to 1974 with numbers for television set ownership. Until 1975, television broadcasting was banned in South Africa, and "white homicide rates remained stable" there, Dr. Centerwall found, while corresponding rates in Canada and the United States doubled after television was introduced.

A spectacular finding, but it is meaningless. As Franklin E. Zimring and Gordon Hawkins of the University of California at Berkeley subsequently pointed out, homicide rates in France, Germany, Italy, and Japan either failed to change with increasing television ownership in the same period or actually declined, and American homicide rates have more recently been sharply declining despite a proliferation of popular media outlets—not only movies and television but also video games and the Internet.

Other social science that supposedly undergirds the theory, too, is marginal and problematic. Laboratory studies that expose children to selected incidents of televised mock violence and then assess changes in the children's behavior have sometimes found more "aggressive" behavior after the exposure—usually verbal, occasionally physical.

But sometimes the control group, shown incidents judged not to be violent, behaves more aggressively afterward than the test group; sometimes comedy produces the more aggressive behavior; and sometimes there's no change. The only obvious conclusion is that sitting and watching television stimulates subsequent physical activity. Any kid could tell you that.

As for those who claim that entertainment promotes violent behavior by desensitizing people to violence, the British scholar Martin Barker offers this critique: "Their claim is that the materials they judge to be harmful can only influence us by trying to make us be the same as them. So horrible things will make us horrible—not horrified. Terrifying things will make us terrifying—not terrified. To see something aggressive makes us feel aggressive—not aggressed against. This idea is so odd, it is hard to know where to begin in challenging it."

Even more influential on national policy has been a 22-year study by two University of Michigan psychologists, Leonard D. Eron and L. Rowell Huesmann, of boys exposed to so-called violent media. The Telecommunications Act of 1996, which mandated the television V-chip, allowing parents to screen out unwanted programming, invoked these findings, asserting, "Studies have shown that children exposed to violent video programming at a young age have a higher tendency for violent and aggressive behavior later in life than children not so exposed."

Well, not exactly. Following 875 children in upstate New York from third grade through high school, the psychologists found a correlation between a preference for violent television at age 8 and aggressiveness at age 18. The correlation—0.31—would mean television accounted for about 10 percent of the influences that led to this behavior. But the correlation only turned up in one of three measures of aggression: the assessment of students by their peers. It didn't show up in students' reports about themselves or in psychological testing. And for girls, there was no correlation at all.

Despite the lack of evidence, politicians can't resist blaming the media for violence. They can stake out the moral high ground confident that the First Amendment will protect them from having to actually write legislation that would be likely to alienate the entertainment industry. Some use the issue as a smokescreen to avoid having to confront gun control.

But violence isn't learned from mock violence. 13 There is good evidence—causal evidence, not correlational—that it's learned in personal violent encounters, beginning with the brutalization of children by their parents or their peers.

The money spent on all the social science 14 research I've described was diverted from the National Institute of Mental Health budget by reducing support for the construction of community mental health centers. To this day there is no standardized reporting system for emergency-room findings of physical child abuse. Violence is on the decline in America, but if we want to reduce it even further, protecting children from real violence in their real lives—not the pale shadow of mock violence—is the place to begin.

## Vocabulary

The following terms are identified by paragraph number. Make sure that you understand each term's meaning in its context. If you're not sure that you understand a term, look it up in a college-level dictionary.

| | | |
|---|---|---|
| entrepreneur (1) | barren (4) | desensitizing (9) |
| Grand Guignol (1) | attribute (4) | critique (9) |
| confections (1) | endorsement (5) | mandated (10) |
| mock (1) | proliferation (6) | invoked (10) |
| indignation (1) | undergird (7) | smokescreen (12) |
| fare (1) | marginal (7) | diverted (14) |

## Style and Strategy

1. In paragraph 1, Rhodes refers to the "moral entrepreneurs." What does he mean by this term?
2. Rhodes uses an implicit thesis statement. State his thesis in your own words.
3. What does Rhodes see as the real cause of juvenile violence?
4. In analyzing a very complicated and controversial subject, Rhodes refers to a number of studies and authorities, sometimes specifically and sometimes more generally. In your opinion, does he present a convincing analysis? Explain.

## Questions for Critical Thinking and Discussion

1. "Rhodes may be right about violent entertainment not causing violent behavior. However, the barrage of media violence faced by Americans of all ages is coarsening us as a people. We *are* becoming desensitized to violence, if to the extent only that reports of it on the news don't affect us the way they might have in the past." Do you agree?
2. Do you believe in censorship? If not, do you believe that under certain circumstances you could change your mind? Explain.

*Suggestions for Writing*

Rhodes's essay is about *false* (or *spurious*) *causality*—the tendency of people to believe they understand the cause of a phenomenon even without sufficient proof. Write a 500- to 750-word essay in which you examine one of the following phenomena and explain why its commonly accepted cause is not its real cause:

1. Why the U.S. high school dropout rate is very high
2. Why many U.S. teenage girls become pregnant before marriage
3. Why many U.S. college students gain weight during their freshman year
4. Why the voting rate among U.S. college students is very low

*Speaking Assignment*

Do the media influence our lives? If the answer is no, then why are billions spent on television, print, and other types of advertising? Prepare a presentation that explains one way that a particular medium—television, pop music, or the Internet, for example—influences people your age. (For more help with oral presentations, see Chapter 18.)

· · · · · · · ·
**CATALYST 2.0**

**MORE OPTIONS ONLINE**
If you would like to read additional causal analysis essays, go to
**www.mhhe.com/ writingtoday.**

# WRITING THE CAUSAL ANALYSIS ESSAY WITH A READER'S EYE

Causal analysis essays must have a logical, believable development; otherwise, they will not connect with their audience and will fail to accomplish their purpose. The advice that follows will help you think like your reader as you consider your assignment and then prewrite, draft, revise, and edit your causal analysis essay.

## Issues to Keep in Mind

The usual purpose of a causal analysis essay is to explain a situation to the reader. Consequently, as you begin to plan your essay, you will need to consider the best way to present causes and/or effects. Thinking about the following two issues will help you as you prepare:

1. Considering the nature and importance of each cause or effect
2. Choosing internal development strategies

*Weighing Causes or Effects*

Three critical issues in developing a causal analysis essay are the following:

1. **Determining major causes and/or effects and then concentrating on them.** Many events, policies, or situations have more than one cause and result in more than one effect. Because of this complexity, writers often have to sort out primary causes or effects from minor ones or even from false ones. One pitfall that you need to watch out for in particular is

building an essay on a bad foundation—a cause or effect that turns out to be minor—while the essay ignores the much more important—and obvious—primary cause or effect.

To avoid this potential problem, you need to spend the time necessary to consider—and weigh—all of the causes or effects. As you prewrite, don't just seize the first causes or effects that come to mind. Evaluate the results of your prewriting to determine the *most* important causes or effects; then concentrate on these as you develop your essay. For example, suppose you write about the *nearest* cause—the one that happened closest in time to the situation you are considering—as if it were the sole reason for the situation. But reality is complicated; the *nearest* cause may not be the *primary* cause. Notice how the writer of the following passage avoids this error by moving from an immediate, superficial reason for a new law to a less obvious but more substantial one:

> The city council has stated that the guidelines it recently passed to curtail downtown activity are meant "to bring stability to the central business district in the nighttime hours." Thus, more police officers will now patrol the sidewalks and check for violations of the open-container law, apprehend the inebriated, and enforce the parking regulations, which now extend around the clock.
>
> Yes, downtown activity will be "controlled" all right—to the point of extinction. And this is the council's true motive. The city council—and, presumably, their most vocal constituents—are made uncomfortable by the strange-looking young people who congregate downtown after hours to hear the latest bands in the most current club. Surely they must be sent away.
>
> This metropolis was a much smaller city only a few decades ago, and it is still run as if the year were 1959. The city council members are always mourning the death of "family values," and clearly the young people with the brilliant hair, the tattoos, and the pierced noses and lips don't have a place in the family values picture. But here's where the city council has missed the point: without those clubs, downtown is as dead as a post. The kids spend money, they cause very little real trouble, and they make this city a greater draw than it would be otherwise. Perhaps the city council members should actually go downtown and watch. In fact, they could go along with me; I'm a cop, and I've spent the last year patrolling the downtown district. Perhaps the "family values" crowd could then get past their horror over weird hair and look at the vibrant downtown scene for what it is: a cultural and financial bonanza.

On the other hand, sometimes the primary cause is important but doesn't warrant much discussion. Suppose, for example, that your area has been ravaged by wildfires that have been able to spread because of an ongoing drought. The primary cause of this situation is a shift in the El Niño weather patterns. Although this shift needs to be mentioned in any discussion of the causes of the fires, there is very little that can be done about it—scientists can't, at this point, reprogram El Niño. Hence, even though the drought is a secondary cause, writers will probably concentrate on its nature, predictions about its duration, and ways to counter its effects in order to prevent additional fires.

You will also need to keep the big picture in mind when you write about effects. For instance, suppose that your school has decided to increase fees by fifty dollars per student per year in order to augment its construction fund. An essay in which you complain about the narrow, short-term effect of this increase on students (meaning the writer of the essay, who is speaking personally) would probably appear to be self-indulgent because the writer is not considering the long-term effects of the increase. Wouldn't it be nice to have an extra parking lot or two so that students could park more quickly and get to their classes sooner, thus ending the usual morning madness? Even if the parking lots will not be completed until after the writer graduates, he or she will gain credibility by considering long-term benefits rather than debating the issue solely in terms of how it affects students right now. Composition instructors tend to view causal analysis essays written with a narrow, self-interested focus as products of immaturity; the responsible writer will look instead to the larger picture.

Thus, it is essential to weigh all possible causes or effects when you are preparing to write a causal analysis essay. Peer review can help you do this at every stage. Consider showing a classmate your completed prewriting, in which you've listed all of the causes or effects and indicated the ones you consider most important. Your classmate's comments may alert you to potential problems in your thinking. Also, keep in mind that a causal essay is easy to "repair" early in the process, but if it is not built on a solid base, it is a nightmare to revise.

2.  **Mistaking correlation for causation.** Events often occur simultaneously and are even associated with each other in people's minds, but that does not necessarily mean that one event has caused the other, only that they are correlated. For instance, dark, puffy cumulus clouds normally accompany rain, but do they *cause* rain? No. Rain is the product of a much more complicated **causal chain**—defined above as a scenario in which "one thing leads to another"—and cumulus clouds are but one link in that chain. As another example, you may have noticed a bitter, cold wind blowing on each of the last five mornings. At the same time, each morning you have noticed that your neighbor's dog, which lives outdoors, has been steadily barking. Did the wind cause the dog's behavior? Maybe—further investigation is required. Did the dog's barking cause the wind to blow? We hope not (tabloid headline: "Demon Dog Controls Local Climate"). As with the issue of choosing the *most* important causes or effects, you must think critically about how causation occurs: this rhetorical option requires an active brain.

3.  **Recognizing the Law of Unintended Consequences.** Sometimes an organization will change one of its policies or rules with a confident sense

that the organization will benefit from the effects of this new approach. However, such confidence can fall victim to the Law of Unintended Consequences. This maxim, loosely related to the general series of laws associated with Mr. Murphy, states that we cannot know what the future will bring—that if we change the dynamics of a situation, then we cannot predict the outcome with certainty. As an example, Gore Vidal points out in "Drugs" (pages 281–282) that the American people and their legislators greatly misjudged the situation in 1919 when the legislation outlawing alcoholic beverages, known as the Volstead Act, was enacted and Prohibition became the law of the land. Americans didn't stop drinking; they just started buying their alcohol from illegal providers. Hence, organized crime was born on a national level and, of course, remains with us today.

You need to be aware of unintended consequences in two varieties of causal analysis essays. The first is an essay in which you explain how a change in policy caused an important and unanticipated effect—much as Vidal does in "Drugs." The second is an essay in which you are exploring a "what-if" scenario. As you prewrite your essay, you need to be aware that the policy change that you are considering could have unexpected consequences of its own—ones that you might miss but that your reader may see as obvious.

### *Choosing Internal Strategies*

Good causal analysis essays avoid a narrow, formulaic approach to their subjects. You will most likely need to use several internal strategies to develop your essay fully and to fulfill your purpose. For example, consider how the three readings in the first half of the chapter were developed:

- In "The Cult of Busyness," Barbara Ehrenreich uses narrative (see Chapter 6) and process analysis (Chapter 8) as she asks the question "Why are people suddenly so busy?"

- In "Drugs," Gore Vidal uses comparison and contrast (comparing the war on drugs to the previous war on alcohol—see Chapter 12) and argument (presenting these campaigns as illogical and impractical—see Chapter 13) to illustrate the unanticipated effects of the anti-drug campaign.

- In "Hollow Claims About Fantasy Violence," Richard Rhodes uses argument (see Chapter 13) to criticize the claims of those who see a link between media violence and real violence.

The internal strategies that you will need to use to develop your causal analysis will depend on your context—your subject, your focus (emphasizing cause or effect), your audience, and your purpose.

In the "Drafting" section (pages 292–297), we will show how two student essays were developed, one concentrating on causes and the other on effects. When you read these examples, notice the number and range of internal strategies used.

CATALYST 2.0

**MORE OPTIONS ONLINE**
For more help with problem areas in the causal analysis essay, go to
www.mhhe.com/
writingtoday.

## Choosing a Topic

When you are writing a causal analysis essay, bear in mind that you will need to choose a topic that you can deal with adequately within the scope of the assignment. If you have been assigned a topic, you will still need to narrow it down to a manageable size. You should also decide whether to concentrate on causes or effects or both and consider whether you will need to do some research in order to gain a fuller understanding of your topic.

1. Choose a topic that you can deal with. Would any of the following be good topics for a causal analysis essay?
   - The reasons behind the Civil War
   - Why salmon migrate upstream
   - The fallout from the Great Depression

   Perhaps these topics would work, if you don't mind writing an essay the length of an encyclopedia. If that prospect doesn't appeal to you, could you investigate causes and effects by limiting one of these topics into a more specific, manageable form? Certainly, but note how even a very limited version of each of the above ideas might be hard to handle in a 750-word essay:
   - The South went to war against the North because it followed the hotheads of a relatively unimportant state, South Carolina, rather than the more reasoned attitudes of a key state, Virginia.
   - What is important about the spawning migration of salmon is not that they swim upstream, swim downstream, or perhaps hitchhike; it's that they are genetically programmed to return home to breed.
   - One effect of the Great Depression is our current crop of retirees, the richest group of older people in our nation's history, who still eat at early-bird specials and order water with meals.

   Handling any of these revised topics in under a thousand words would be difficult. The more you limit your topic, the better you can control the resulting essay. One way to test the "size" of your topic is to measure the amount of prewriting that you produce. If your prewriting seems to go on forever, you probably need to scale down the size of your topic—and the reverse is also true. If you find it difficult to generate ideas in the prewriting stage, you need to broaden your topic.

2. Decide whether to concentrate on causes or effects or both. As we discuss in the introduction to this chapter (see pages 274–277), this decision is usually a fairly straightforward one—your subject matter and writing context tend to make the decision for you.

3. Consider the possible need to research the topic and, if so, the kind of research you will need to conduct. Whether your instructor has assigned a specific topic or set of topics from which to choose or you are choosing your own topic, you will need to decide if the topic is within your "comfort zone" of knowledge or is one that you need to research in the library or on the Internet. For a personal topic, you can usually rely on your own knowledge. For most other topics, however, you may need to conduct

research either for specific information or for general background knowledge in order to write authoritatively. Chapters 20 and 21 offer advice on locating and documenting library and Internet sources.

## Prewriting

As mentioned, causal analysis essays are easy to fix in the early stages but hard to revise if the fundamental analysis is wrong. The following approach will help you to generate ideas. First, use an informal, idea-gathering strategy such as brainstorming, clustering, or freewriting to develop possible causes or effects (see Chapter 2, pages 30–35). Review your results carefully. At this point, you may want to stop, come back later, and prewrite some more. If you have determined that you need to research your topic, this is the time to do so. As we discuss in "Issues to Keep in Mind" (pages 287–290), your analysis of your prewriting is crucial: your essay must concentrate on major causes or effects, must avoid confusing cause and correlation, and must not miss any obvious (and important) causes or effects that an able reader would expect to see. Make sure that you have done thorough prewriting before you go on to the organizing stage. Consider having a peer reviewer go over your prewriting as well and give you his or her thoughts on your analysis.

## Organizing

After your prewriting, you should have a good idea of how to "shape" your essay. You may be writing about multiple effects stemming from a single cause or about a major effect caused by multiple factors. If your prewriting indicates a causal chain (one factor causing another, which causes another, and so on), keep in mind that your essay will most likely employ a narrative framework. Now is the time to build a thorough sentence outline. (For help with sentence outlines, see Chapter 2, pages 41–42.) When you review your completed outline, you will have a good sense of where your essay will go, and you may also find some weaknesses, which are much easier to correct at this stage than later in the writing process. As in the prewriting stage, consider having a peer reviewer go over your outline at this point; a second pair of eyes—and accompanying brain—are always helpful.

## Drafting

Because causal analysis includes two differing strategies, we have included two causal analysis essays: "Listening Intently," which explores the causes of an ironic world view, and "Never a Dull Moment," which looks at the unintended effects of a change in educational policy.

### The Introduction

In the introduction to your causal analysis essay, you need to provide your reader sufficient context: your reader needs the background of your subject. Sometimes, this situation requires two or more introductory paragraphs, but in most essays of under 1,000 words, a single, well-developed paragraph will suffice.

> **• Consider Your Options**
>
> As is true of other types of writing, introductions to causal analysis essays can take a variety of forms. Consider description or definition as strategies to build an effective introduction. Other strategies are to contradict a popular opinion or belief, to define a controversial issue, to state a problem, or to ask a question that the rest of the essay will answer.

Both of the introductory paragraphs that follow were written after the writer had completed the body of the essay. Since causal analysis can be a fairly complex option, developing the essay first and then creating its introduction is frequently a good idea. With this approach, you avoid the danger that your body paragraphs will drift away from what your introduction has promised.

## Essay A: Cause Focus

### Listening Intently

During the late 1990s, the media were obsessed with "Generation X": the slackers, the irony-transfixed whiners who seemed to have no productive place in society. In a time when wealth was readily available to those who were bright and ambitious, the Gen X crowd seemed to prefer black clothes, black coffee, and black humor. Why? Centrally, irony (and its related negativisms, cynicism and nihilism) is learned, not innate. **Three American institutions have a lot to answer for in fostering this negativity: our politicians, our schools, and our parents.**

The writer sets up his analysis by contrasting the go-go acquisitiveness of the late twentieth century with the values of the quizzical, passive generation that was just coming into adulthood at that time. The thesis statement, which appears at the end of the paragraph, is specific, pointing to three causes of the phenomenon.

## Essay B: Effects Focus

### Never a Dull Moment

Because of the recent budget surplus in our state, the legislature has decided to use some of the extra money to establish merit scholarships. Basically, any student who maintains a 3.0+ GPA through high school and then keeps above this threshold in college gets a sizable scholarship. This program has made the difference for a lot of students who either couldn't have afforded to attend a state university or any other kind of college or would have gone heavily into debt. However, a perhaps unexpected problem has resulted. To maintain the scholarship, students must earn a 3.0 or better cumulative GPA. **As an outcome, our student body is grade conscious**

**to an extent that is terrifying. Learning seems to be way back on this bus; the magical GPA now rules everything.**

In this introduction, the writer refers to the Law of Unintended Consequences as she sets up the rest of her essay. Note that, unlike the previous introduction, the thesis statement does not offer a preview of what will follow; however, the reader's interest is sufficiently aroused.

### The Body

Each writer has set up a context in which he or she can explore causes or effects, thus avoiding the "cookie-cutter" phenomenon, wherein causes and effects are discussed as if they followed a formula. Note how the two sets of body paragraphs develop in very different ways:

**Essay A: Cause Focus**

Americans' contempt for politicians and the political process is nothing new, but our negative attitudes have sharpened ever since the Watergate scandal in the 1970s. Part of the cause lies with the media themselves. In the past, the media's attitude toward public figures was more respectful. For example, White House correspondents knew that President Kennedy had extramarital affairs, but there was never any question of publishing this information. Today, of course, the media see the private lives of politicians as a gold mine of opportunity. Furthermore, the media breed cynicism by openly questioning politicians' motives. The way elected figures now tend to exploit the media also exacerbates this problem. Many thought the media had hit a new low when then governor Bill Clinton played his saxophone on *Arsenio Hall*; however, that performance was topped several years later by former senator Bob Dole's shilling for Viagra. (At this point the concept of "new low" becomes frightening.) Growing up during this era, I—and the vast majority of my contemporaries—did not see politicians as public servants; we saw them as money-grubbing hypocrites. Can you imagine one of us hanging a printed portrait of the president on our living room wall?

The cynicism bred by politics is more than matched, however, by the pessimism four years in high school can cause. When I watch *The Simpsons,* I view this program as sociology as much as entertainment, especially in its depiction of the school Bart and Lisa attend. After talking to my peers, I find that my experiences in public education were typical, which is a frightening thought. My high school classes were presided over by two types of teachers: those who passed the time and those who used their cleverness to pass the time. For the first group, a successful day at the job site meant that no student became mutilated, pregnant, unconscious, or dead while in their charge. This is the Daycare Model. The second group was actually worse. These teachers depended on clever, gimmick assignments to "stimulate" students, to somehow prod them into a "passion for learning." Thus, in the space of one week during my sophomore year I was asked to write my own obituary (Journalism), to write a letter to my long-dead great-grandparents to let them know what 1995 was like (English), and to "design my ideal mammal" (Biology). When I got to college, I learned that my language classes would have done me a favor if they had taught me how to analyze text, and that if I had learned something about the human musculoskeletal system I would be better prepared for university-level biology. But such activities wouldn't have been "stimulating," just a lot of hard work, and they wouldn't have been "fun" either—for the teachers as well as for their intellectually dispossessed students.

Our parents are another source of cynicism. In the past, parents were portrayed as remote, prepossessing figures who sacrificed a good deal for the welfare of their brood. I don't see these traits in my parents or in most of the parents I know. They seem to be merely older versions of adolescents. They still have a mania to get and spend (does this never end?), and they work hard in order to buy more toys and satisfy the credit card companies. If this is maturity, I don't see much to look forward to.

See if you can find the following internal strategies used in the body paragraphs above: classification (see Chapter 11), exemplification (Chapter 7), and process analysis (Chapter 8).

### Essay B: Effects Focus

The first visible result of the pressures to maintain grade point average is rampant cheating. Before, most students who cheated probably did so out of a desire for convenience: too lazy to study, they got the answers the easy way. Now, however, students have a very real need to practice this dishonesty: they need to stay in school. According to a recent article in the *Signal,* the number of cases of academic dishonesty referred to the Review Council has tripled from the same time period over two years ago. A girl down my hall was caught with her boyfriend breaking into a chemistry instructor's office. Not only did they get expelled from school, but they are facing criminal charges as well.

Professors with a reputation for difficult classes are being avoided at all costs. Softer touches, formerly just popular, are now being mobbed. An interesting incident happened during the drop/add period for this term. A certain tenured humanities professor reacted to a dispute with his department head by giving all *A's* to all four sections that he taught in the fall semester. Once news of his generosity got around, students were lined up around the block trying to get into this man's spring classes, on the hope that his campaign would continue.

Faculty members who teach classes where the grading is perceived by students as "subjective" must really hate the new scholarship program. At the end of each semester since the program's inception, they have been pestered by students trying to wheedle a better grade. Some real sob stories are offered. I sat outside my speech instructor's office one afternoon in December as someone from my dorm went through a psychodrama. At first I thought she really might have been responding to some bizarre academic assignment, but then I realized she was merely having a fit. When she emerged her face was flushed, she had tears streaming down her cheeks, and she muttered imprecations as she sped down through the hall. I asked Mr. Gonzalez if I should come back later, but he said that I should stick around, unless I had something similar in mind.

See if you can find the following internal strategies used in the body paragraphs above: exemplification (see Chapter 7), comparison/contrast (Chapter 12), narration (Chapter 6), and description (Chapter 5).

### The Conclusion

As in most essays, you should avoid a summary conclusion, which is often dull and adds little to the essay. Instead, try to come to an *evaluative* conclusion, which comments on the implications of the essay's analysis. The evaluative conclusion is a more effective and informative approach. Note the angles the two writers use to end their essays on Generation X and the problematic education policy.

*Consider Your Options*

Good ways to end a causal analysis are to offer your reader advice, look to the future, or explain the applicability of the analysis to your reader's life. (For more on conclusions, see Chapter 3.)

### Essay A: Cause Focus

Children learn by imitation. What the members of so-called Generation X have learned is that truth is rare and that greed, mendacity, and ineptitude are the controlling features of their world. So why should they be enthusiastic, and why isn't irony an appropriate lens through which to view this mess?

### Essay B: Effects Focus

The legislators undoubtedly had good intentions when they passed the scholarship bill, but they have opened a particularly active can of worms with the new merit scholarship initiative. Letting deserving students go to college is a good idea, but not if a secondary effect is to cheapen education and alter the whole process.

CATALYST 2.0

**MORE OPTIONS ONLINE**
For more help with the step-by-step development of the causal analysis essay, go to www.mhhe.com/ writingtoday.

### EXERCISE 9.1

Write a sentence outline of "Listening Intently" or "Never a Dull Moment." (For help with sentence outlines, see Chapter 2, pages 41–42.) What does the outline reveal about each essay's organization? How would a different organization work?

## Revising Your Draft

After you have completed a draft of your causal analysis essay, your next step is to revise it, using your own analysis and comments from classmates or friends. Use the peer review stage to make sure that your essay's structure and content are sound. During peer review, answer the questions below about the draft you are reviewing, whether it is yours or another student's.

After reviewing for content, you need to go over your peer reviewers' responses to your essay and then revise for unity, coherence, language level, and tone (see Chapter 4). When you have revised your draft and are basically satisfied with it, read your draft for mechanical and grammatical errors. Concentrate on finding and correcting major sentence errors (fragment, comma splice, fused sentence), errors in pronoun agreement and subject-verb agreement, and spelling.

Now that you have made your corrections, *read your essay one more time* to catch any errors made during revision and find errors missed during your earlier reviews.

**CATALYST 2.0**

**MORE OPTIONS ONLINE**
For more help with
revision, go to
www.mhhe.com/
writingtoday.

## Student Essay

The following essay is Noelani Jones's response to a causal analysis assignment. Noelani, a native of Hawaii, writes about the effects caused by that state's isolation from the U.S. mainland. The final draft is presented first. Then Noelani's first draft is presented, with her comments about this draft and what she needed to do in the revision stage.

## Questions for Reviewing a Causal Analysis Essay

1. Is the writer's purpose for the essay clear? Does the essay include an introduction that gives readers important background information?

2. Is there a clear thesis statement that indicates whether the writer is concentrating on causes, effects, or both? If not, how could the thesis be improved?

3. Point out any explanation of a cause or an effect that doesn't ring true. Point out any place where the writer has mistaken correlation for causation.

4. Has the writer used an effective organization for the causes and/or effects? What other organization would be more effective?

5. Has the writer used the right strategy to explain each cause or effect? Where does a cause or an effect need additional clarification or development?

6. Are topic sentences both clear and properly located?

7. Does the writer use transitions to guide the reader? Where are transitions needed?

8. Does the essay have an effective conclusion? How could it be improved?

*Noelani's Final Draft*

Worlds Apart

When people make general statements about the United States
as a whole country, I notice that their comments often exclude
Hawaii and Alaska. This often bothered me, growing up in Hawaii,
but now that I also live in the continental United States I can understand how easy it is to exclude Alaska and Hawaii when thinking of
the "United" States. Hawaii's detachment from the rest of the states
truly makes it special and gives Hawaii its unique identity, but this
isolation comes with several pitfalls for the people of Hawaii as well.

The remoteness and unique tropical beauty of this small chain of
islands are what make it so attractive to the world. Hawaii benefits
greatly from tourism, its leading industry. Hundreds of thousands of
beach-loving tourists make their way to the shores of Hawaii each
year. You can always find a game show or sweepstakes offering a
free vacation to Hawaii as a prize because a trip to Hawaii is something that just about anyone in the general population would want to
have. The film industry in Hawaii is also booming. Hundreds of television shows and movies have been and are now still being filmed in
Hawaii because viewers love to see its rare beauty. Hawaii's reputation as a remote tropical paradise is the bread and butter of its people because most of the jobs in Hawaii depend upon the tourism
industry.

Hawaii's seclusion from the rest of the United States leads to a
much higher cost of living, however. Just about everything under the
sun, other than the local agricultural produce, must be shipped to the
islands by barge or by plane over the wide, blue ocean, which makes
practically everything more expensive. A good example of this is oil.
Because oil needs to be shipped in by boat, the average price for gas
these days is one and a half times as much as it is in Florida. In addition to that, prices are also hiked because the major consumers are

the wealthy tourists who can afford to pay a little more while they're on vacation. All the same, limited space, the high demand for real estate, and the additional difficulty of importing building materials lead to a much higher cost of housing than in most other states.

The Hawaiian people are just as unique as the character of their land. Hawaii is often called the "melting pot of the Pacific." Hawaii is just as close to, or even closer to, Asia than it is to America, and just as the continental United States has received many immigrants from European and Latin American countries, Hawaii over the years has seen a great influx of Asians and Polynesians. The Asian influence on Hawaii today is strong and predominant in all aspects of our culture. I myself am not native Hawaiian by race; I am a mixture of Chinese, Japanese, Irish, and Welsh blood. The Asian influence is very evident in the personality of our people, our gift-giving customs, the style of food we eat, even the language we use. "Pidgin English," our colloquial language, is a random mixture of broken English, Hawaiian, Japanese, Filipino, and Chinese, and it is one of the many differences that separate us from the "haoles" (Caucasians) on the mainland. "We no can understand what da haoles say, 'cuz dey talk da kine proper English," I might say.

Isolation from the rest of the United States has created a strong subculture that quite surpasses the small variations between the different regions of the continental United States. This great difference between cultures makes it fairly difficult for people who grow up in Hawaii to move to other states. Most often, students who stay in Hawaii for college end up staying in Hawaii their whole lives. But Hawaii is losing its highest-quality students to the renowned universities on the mainland, which in turn means that the islands also lose the best of their work force. The students with the most potential are most often the ones who do leave Hawaii for college. They often remain on the mainland, adapting to the mainland's culture, its low cost of living, and its large job market, none of which can be found in Hawaii. The saddest aspect of the situation is that the students have to travel so far from home to access such opportunities.

Whenever I call home to Hawaii, my brother and sister always remark in a remorseful way how I've lost my Hawaiian accent. They tease me that I've become like the haoles. The stark contrast between the two cultures and its effect on me is evident even over the phone. I am one of these students who have left Hawaii for the vast opportunities of the mainland. Hawaii will always be my homeland, but it's not likely that I will ever choose to go back to live there. To me, Hawaii would just be a great place to visit for a vacation.

6

*Noelani's First Draft*

### Worlds Apart

When people make general statements about the United States as a whole country, I notice they often leave out Hawaii, and Alaska. This often bothered me growing up in Hawaii, but now that I also live on the continental United States I can understand how easy it is to forget that the union extends past the boarders of California, Oregon and Washington. Hawaii's isolation from the rest of the "united" states makes it special and gives Hawaii its unique identity but isolation has it's pitfalls for the islanders of Hawaii as well.

1

The remoteness and unique tropical beauty of this small, chain of islands is what makes it so attractive to the world. Tourism is by far Hawaii's leading industry. Hundreds of thousands of beach-loving tourist make their way to the shores of Hawaii a year. A free trip to Hawaii is always a popular game show prize, because it's everyone's dream to vacation there. The film industry in Hawaii is booming. Thousands of television shows, and movies have shown the world the

2

I shortened and refined the end of the second paragraph because it did not support the topic sentence, and it included altogether too much information.

beauty of Hawaii. And new upcoming shows have recently been contracted to be filmed there, because viewers love to see the rare beauty of Hawaii. Many wealthy people own beautiful houses in Hawaii because it's a great place to "get away from it all" if you can afford it. Hawaii is known worldwide as a remote tropical paradise, and the people profit from this reputation with an economy supported heavily by tourism.

But isolation and remoteness from the rest of the United States leads to a higher cost of living. Just about everything, except for the local agricultural produce, must be shipped in by barge or by plain, which makes practically everything, we buy more expensive. A good example of this is oil. Because oil needs to be shipped in by boat, the average price for gas these days is one and a half times as much as it is in Florida. In addition to that, prices are also hiked because the major consumers are the wealthy tourists who can afford to pay a little more while they're on their two week vacation. Limited space, and the high demand for real estate in Hawaii leads to an extremely higher cost of housing in Hawaii, than in most other states of America.

Being isolated from the rest of the United States makes it difficult for people from the state of Hawaii to know, understand, or distinguish the different cultural regions that make up the conitental U.S. A man from New York could most likely distinguish a Texan from a Californian by their dress, and accent, because he's had friends that came from those parts, he's had business dealings with companies in those states, and he often visits his cousins who live in LA, and his sister who is studying in Austin, TX. But Americans who grow up in Hawaii often refer to people from all other states simply as "Mainlanders" or "haole's", which means "white foreigners". They have a hard time, because they are not exposed as much to the different types of cultures in the U.S. The distance limits our interaction with the rest of the US, thus making it harder for us to learn

3

4

I took out most of the "we's" and "our's" in the essay because I didn't use them throughout the paper consistently, and it seemed misleading for me to write as if I were still a part of Hawaii, when the main focus was to show that I am now separate from Hawaii.

I repeated the words "isolation" and "isolated" too many times, so I replaced them with other similar words.

I totally deleted the fourth paragraph because it was too trivial and discussed a very small idea in a roundabout, wordy way. The main idea I wanted to emphasize was also a part of the fifth paragraph, so I just eliminated the whole fourth paragraph.

about different types of mainlanders or be able to distinguish them apart

Hawaii's people are unique. Hawaii is often called the "melting pot of the Pacific." Hawaii is just as close, or even closer to Asia than it is to America, and just as (while) the continental US received many immigrants from European and Latin American countries, Hawaii, over the years has seen a great influx of Asians, and Polynesians. The Asian influence on Hawaii today is strong and predominant in all aspects of our culture and greatly contrasts the similar regional cultures of the continental US. It is evident in the personality of our people, our gift giving customs, the style of food we eat, even the language we use. "Pidgin English", our colloquial language, is a random mixture of broken English, Hawaiian, Japanese, Filipino, and Chinese, and is one of the many differences that separate us from the "haole's" (Caucasians) on the mainland. "We no can understand what da haole's say, 'cuz dey talk da kine proper English," I might say. Isolation from the rest of the United States has created a strong and quite (far away) subculture that quite surpasses the small variations between the different regions of the continental US. This great difference between cultures makes it fairly difficult for people who grow up in Hawaii to move to other states. Most often, students who stay in Hawaii for college end up staying in Hawaii their whole lives. But Hawaii is loosing its highest quality students to the renowned universities on the mainland, which in turn means that it also loses the best of our potential work force. The students that do leave often end up staying on the mainland, because they've adapted to the mainland culture, the low cost of living, and the large job market that they can not find in Hawaii.

I am one of these students who have left Hawaii for college, and I may never return to live there again. Whenever I call home, my brother and sister always remark in a remorseful way that I've lost my pidgin accent. They tease me and tell me I've become a haole.

5

6

I changed the first sentence of the fifth paragraph because it was choppy/messy. I added the fifth sentence to the fifth paragraph to back up the sentence before it and to give interesting insight into my life and viewpoint, that of an average person from Hawaii. I also broke up this paragraph because it seemed too long.

Hawaii will always be my homeland, but now it seems like just a great place to visit and take vacations in. I don't think I could every call it home again.

### EXERCISE 9.2: REVISING

The following is the first draft of a student's causal analysis essay. Working in pairs or in small groups, review this essay. Using the Questions for Reviewing a Causal Analysis Essay on page 298, decide what revisions you would suggest. If you have any questions that the student needs to consider, write these in the margin or on a separate sheet of paper. If your instructor directs you to, rewrite one or more paragraphs to make them stronger and to eliminate any grammatical or mechanical errors.

### "A Bad Move Gentleman"

Our college has a new policy, it's a horrible policy: any student that misses more than 3 'contact hours' will be dropped from their class. The effects are going to hurt badly individual students: they will be punished unfairly.

First in a three-day a week class over 16 weeks has 45 class meetings, therefore, at least 42 classes must be attended orelse the student is dropped. Thats too much. What if you get sick. What if your car wont start. And besides everyone gets a day off every once in a while, dont they?

Students with too absenses could find themselves living in fear because they know their on the edge.

Moreover students, we, pay the tuition that runs this school, who is the school to cancel us after we've paid are money? The whole thing sucks if you ask me. We putup with alot with this school anyway; bad parking, old classrooms. What are they thinking?

In conclusion, as I have clearly pointed out, the new rules is too hard on students and unfair toboot. Think it over, gentleman.

### Additional Writing Topics

1. Are you a different person than you were four years ago? If so, why?

2. Describe a problem that exists at your college, and discuss (a) its cause, (b) its effects, or (c) both.

3. Most college students are eighteen or older, so they are normally eligible to vote. However, college students are notoriously underrepresented among voters in local, state, and federal elections. Why?

4. Over the past fifteen years, most states have raised their drinking ages to twenty-one (in other states, twenty-one was already the legal drinking age). In your experience, what have been the effects of this change?

5. How would your life change, in all probability, if you found yourself in one of the following situations?
   - A close relative dies, leaving you with custody of her two-year-old son.
   - Your physician tells you that you must avoid all caffeine.
   - Because of a change in your financial situation, you find that you must work twenty more hours per week at your current job or at a new one.
   - You find, to your amazement, that you have the winning ticket in the state Lotto drawing. You will receive, after taxes, $247,395 for each of the next twenty years.

6. **Writing on the job.** In any line of work, workers can count on foul-ups with at least one procedure. At your current job or at a former job, what was the major procedural difficulty? Write a memo for your supervisor that analyzes this problem and discusses its causes and possible solutions. (For help with writing memos, see Chapter 17.)

## Causal Analysis and Visual Representations

Many consumer items are popular because of the prestige associated with owning them. Having a product made by Rolex, Tiffany, or Porsche, just to name a few examples, constitutes "double value." These companies make fine products, and their consumers enjoy not only this value but also the envy of their peers.

However, the design and manufacture of some products, such as luxury handbags and shoes, can be closely imitated. Such a practice is legal. But if the imitator also includes the original manufacturer's logo or emblem, then the trouble begins.

The *Harper's Bazaar* magazine page reproduced here is not trying to get the reader to buy anything; instead, it's attempting to get the reader *not* to buy certain categories of products. It asserts a causal relationship: "Profits from counterfeit sales fund organized crime including drug cartels, child labor and even terrorist organizations." This is a strong statement, one that is designed to arouse the conscience of the reader.

1. Write a response to this ad. What are your thoughts and impressions? As you write, refer to Questions for Reviewing a Visual Representation.

2. The central claim of this ad is that "Profits from counterfeit sales fund organized crime including drug cartels, child labor and even terrorist organizations." Do some research to see if this claim is true. Then either write an essay explaining what you discovered (remember to document your sources—see also Chapter 21) or develop an oral presentation based on your research and conclusions (see also Chapter 18).

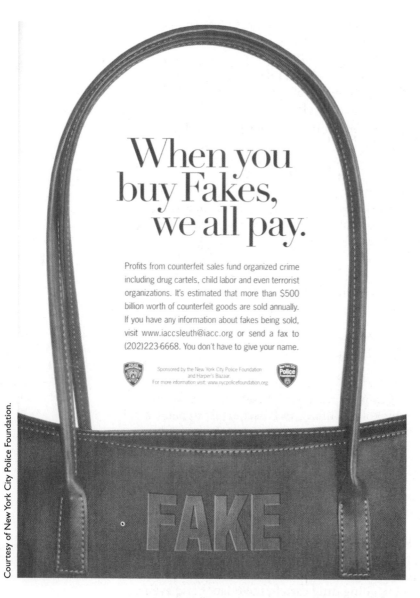

## When you buy Fakes, we all pay.

Profits from counterfeit sales fund organized crime including drug cartels, child labor and even terrorist organizations. It's estimated that more than $500 billion worth of counterfeit goods are sold annually. If you have any information about fakes being sold, visit www.iaccsleuth@iacc.org or send a fax to (202)223-6668. You don't have to give your name.

Sponsored by the New York City Police Foundation
and Harper's Bazaar.
For more information visit: www.nycpolicefoundation.org

FAKE

### Questions for Reviewing a Visual Representation

- Is the representation forceful, passive, or something in between?
- What is the purpose of the representation—in other words, what is it trying to do to you, the reader/viewer?
- If the representation uses words, do they reinforce the visual image or in some way contradict it?
- What is the presumed audience for the representation—men, women, children, the elderly? Or does it have a broader appeal?
- If the representation is an advertisement, is it trying to sell a product or to get you to adopt a way of thinking?
- If the representation is an advertisement, does it try to persuade you in a fair manner, or do you feel manipulated?

### Responding to an Image

In 1955, in Montgomery, Alabama, Rosa Parks, an African American, refused to surrender her bus seat to a white passenger. Parks was arrested, and in response to the incident, black citizens of Montgomery boycotted the city bus system. Dan Weiner took this photograph soon after the boycott began.

**1.** Write an informal response to the photograph. What do you notice? How does the image make you feel? How does the photograph make use of the causal analysis option?

Dan Weiner. *Boycotted Bus, Montgomery.* 1956. Courtesy of Sandra Weiner.

2. The 1950s and 1960s were the heyday of the U.S. civil rights movement. In response to racial discrimination, leaders such as Martin Luther King, Jr., planned nonviolent actions to show the resolve of the African American citizenry. Using a combination of library and online research, explore an event that prompted a coordinated, nonviolent response from King or from another black leader. Write a documented essay exploring the causes and the effects of the event. (For more information on documented essays, see Chapter 21.)

*Using the Internet*

Search the Internet for insights and information to use when explaining causes and effects.

1. Find several Web sites that use a layperson's language to explain the causes, symptoms, and probable outcomes of physical or mental illnesses. After some preliminary "surfing," focus on a particular disease and gather information about your subject from at least three different Web sites. Use this information in an essay that explains the causes, symptoms, and probable outcomes of this illness. If the disease can be treated, explain how this treatment works and discuss the extent to which it is effective in arresting the disease's progress, alleviating its symptoms, or curing the patient entirely.

2. Gore Vidal and Richard Rhodes analyze subjects that generate endless debate. Another divisive subject is the military draft. Go online to research the history of selective service. Write an essay on what happened after the draft was abandoned in the 1970s in favor of an all-volunteer military.

Shock Jocks

### CHAPTER 10

# DEFINITION

# Writing in Context

You've been at Osprey Online for over a month now. At lunch, you are talking to a colleague, Jason, about Bob and his shortcomings as a manager. Jason has worked for Bob for two years, and he has a long list of complaints.

"Bob's manipulative, lazy, and—frankly—rude. Sometimes he's talking to a client and forgets that he's not dealing with one of us. Then you see something click in his face, and suddenly he becomes nice again. He doesn't have an ounce of sincerity. He's successful because of the hard work of people like you and me, not that this fact has ever occurred to him, and not that he'd ever admit it."

Jason's description matches some of the traits you've noticed during your brief working relationship with Bob; however, you decide to play devil's advocate.

"Jason, all bosses cause problems for the people who work for them, even the best ones. What's your definition of the ideal manager, anyway?"

Jason might find that the answer to this question requires some serious thought.

# HOW DOES DEFINITION WORK?

A writer trying to explain the qualities of an ideal manager might be in for a few surprises. The ideal manager wouldn't let his or her workers goof off all day, call in "sick" whenever they felt like it, or come and go as they pleased. With such lax supervision, the enterprise would soon go bankrupt, and all concerned would lose their jobs. No, the writer would likely discover—and reveal to the reader— that the ideal boss would insist on professional behavior and productivity.

When you use **definition**, you explain the meaning of a term or concept in order to shed new light on it. Your purpose is to show your readers a new way of looking at a concept, perhaps with the goal of changing their attitudes. You can use definition as an internal strategy, in which you define a term or concept in order to clarify some larger issue or discussion. You can also use definition as the basis of an entire essay.

Often, students will use a dictionary definition in the course of an essay, sometimes making the definition part of their introduction. However, most of the time a formal definition does not tell the reader anything new and sometimes even insults the reader's intelligence. Quoting the formal definition of a word from a standard college dictionary won't help your essay unless you are able to use the word's meaning in a fresh, surprising way. For example, in the following paragraph from an essay about the stock market boom of the 1990s, a secondary meaning of the word *rush* proves to be illuminating:

> According to my dictionary, one of the definitions of *rush* is "the movement of people to a new site in search of financial reward," as in a gold rush. Just as the hopeful thronged to California in the middle of the nineteenth century and to Alaska at the end of the century, during the 1990s investors "rushed" to the brave new digital world of Internet stocks. The movement wasn't so much a boom as it was an exploratory adventure. Like the gold-obsessed pilgrims of the nineteenth century, many of the investors had no idea where to look for treasure and what to do when they found promising options. Thus, fortunes were made and lost in weeks or days, as some new companies paid off dramatically and others turned out to be empty mines.

In order to shed light on a subject, a writer can also examine the historical roots of the word being defined, as Nancy Gibbs does in the following excerpt from "When Is It Rape?"

> The present debate over degrees of rape is nothing new: All through history, rapes have been divided between those that mattered and those that did not. For the first few thousand years, the only rape that was punished was the defiling of a virgin, and that was viewed as a property crime. A girl's virtue was a marketable asset, and so a rapist was often ordered to pay the victim's father the equivalent of her price on the marriage market. In early Babylonian and Hebrew societies, a married woman who was raped suffered the same fate as an adulteress—death by stoning or drowning. Under William the Conqueror, the penalty for raping a virgin was castration and loss of both eyes—unless the violated

woman agreed to marry her attacker, as she was often pressured to do. "Stealing an heiress" became a perfectly conventional means of taking—literally—a wife.

Here Gibbs uses the history of the concept of *rape* to help explain current attitudes toward sexual violence.

Sometimes, a writer may need to use a highly personal definition of a word, called a **stipulated definition**. In other words, the writer asks the reader to agree to his or her "spin" on a term's meaning, as in the following example:

> When I think of "welfare," I don't think about small sums of money going to mothers trying to raise children on their own. Instead, I think about state legislatures and the U.S. Congress finding new ways to give businesses money to keep them afloat. I think of the artificial price structures that are maintained for tobacco and sugar so that American businesses can compete in the global marketplace. I think about companies that never actually pay fines for their illegalities; they simply pass the costs on to their customers, who foot the bill. That's what "welfare" means to me.

In an **extended definition**, the writer devotes an entire essay to exploring the meaning of a term or concept—once again, to show the reader a new way of looking at the topic or to change the reader's opinion. Writers can choose from a limitless number of possible topics and employ a wide variety of internal strategies. For example, over the course of an essay you could define selfishness, honesty, the optimum fitness plan, the perfect dinner date, or the typical fraternity member. To explain the **defining features** of your term or concept, the aspects of it that set it apart, you could use one or more of the rhetorical options discussed in Part 2 of this book.

Definition essays normally have an **objective** focus or a **subjective** focus. An objective definition seeks to inform the reader and usually does not contain the preferences or opinions of the writer. A subjective definition represents the writer's personal definition of a term or concept. However, note that rarely is a definition completely objective or completely subjective; the focus is more on one than on the other.

*Consider Your Options*

Make a list of topics relating to your role as a student that might be discussed by using an extended definition.

# READING THE DEFINITION ESSAY WITH A WRITER'S EYE

In the three essays that follow, the writers present extended definitions on a range of topics. Judy Brady offers an exhaustive (and daunting) definition of society's expectations of wives, William Raspberry points out that social definition can be self-perpetuating, and Annie Dillard provides a subjective definition of adolescence. As you read these selections, note the effects that the authors are able to achieve from the starting point of definition. As a rhetorical option, definition may seem basic; however, it is anything but that. A good definition can change a reader's most strongly held assumptions.

Following the essays, the second half of this chapter provides strategies for writing the definition essay with a reader's eye (pages 320–329). If you decide to write on one of the topics that follow the three essays below, make sure that you have read the strategies section before you begin. Also note that additional writing topics are listed at the end of the chapter (page 336).

# Why I Want a Wife

## JUDY BRADY

*Written by essayist and political activist Judy Brady, "Why I Want a Wife" is one of the most famous and enduring essays of our times. First published in the Spring 1972 issue of* Ms.*, it has become both a rallying cry for women seeking equality and a penetrating look into the sociology of the American family.*

I belong to that classification of people known as wives. I am A Wife. And, not altogether incidentally, I am a mother. 1

Not too long ago a male friend of mine appeared on the scene fresh from a recent divorce. He had one child, who is, of course, with his ex-wife. He is looking for another wife. As I thought about him while I was ironing one evening, it suddenly occurred to me that I, too, would like to have a wife. Why do I want a wife? 2

I would like to go back to school so that I can become economically independent, support myself, and, if need be, support those dependent upon me. I want a wife who will work and send me to school. And while I am going to school I want a wife to take care of my children. I want a wife to keep track of the children's doctor and dentist appointments. And to keep track of mine, too. I want a wife to make sure my children eat properly and are kept clean. I want a wife who will wash the children's clothes and keep them mended. I want a wife who is a good nurturant attendant to my children, who arranges for their schooling, makes sure that they have an adequate social life with their peers, takes them to the park, the zoo, etc. I want a wife who takes care of the children when they are sick, a wife who arranges to be around 3

when the children need special care, because, of course, I cannot miss classes at school. My wife must arrange to lose time at work and not lose the job. It may mean a small cut in my wife's income from time to time, but I guess I can tolerate that. Needless to say, my wife will arrange and pay for the care of the children while my wife is working.

I want a wife who will take care of *my* physical needs. I want a wife who will keep my house clean. A wife who will pick up after me. I want a wife who will keep my clothes clean, ironed, mended, replaced when need be, and who will see to it that my personal things are kept in their proper place so that I can find what I need the minute I need it. I want a wife who cooks the meals, a wife who is a *good* cook. I want a wife who will plan the menus, do the necessary grocery shopping, prepare the meals, serve them pleasantly, and then do the cleaning up while I do my studying. I want a wife who will care for me when I am sick and sympathize with my pain and loss of time from school. I want a wife to go along when our family takes a vacation so that someone can continue to care for me and my children when I need a rest and change of scene. 4

I want a wife who will not bother me with rambling complaints about a wife's duties. But I want a wife who will listen to me when I feel the need to explain a rather difficult point I have come across in my course of studies. And I want a wife who will type my papers for me when I have written them. 5

I want a wife who will take care of the details of my social life. When my wife and I are invited out by friends, I want a wife who will take care of the babysitting arrangements. When I meet people at school that I like and want to entertain, I want a wife who will have the house clean, will prepare a special meal, serve it to me and my friends, and not interrupt when I talk about the things that interest me and my friends. I want a wife who will have arranged that the children are fed and ready for bed before my guests arrive so that the children do not bother us. I want a wife who takes care of the needs of my guests so that they feel comfortable, who makes sure that they have an ashtray, that they are passed the hors d'oeuvres, that they are offered a second helping of the food, that their wine glasses are replenished when necessary, that their coffee is served to them as they like it. And I want a wife who knows that sometimes I need a night out by myself.

I want a wife who is sensitive to my sexual needs, a wife who makes love passionately and eagerly when I feel like it, a wife who makes sure that I am satisfied. And, of course, I want a wife who will not demand sexual attention when I am not in the mood for it. I want a wife who assumes the complete responsibility for birth control, because I do not want more children. I want a wife who will remain sexually faithful to me so that I do not have to clutter up my intellectual life with jealousies. And I want a wife who understands that *my* sexual needs may entail more than strict adherence to monogamy. I must, after all, be able to relate to people as fully as possible.

If, by chance, I find another person more suitable as a wife than the wife I already have, I want the liberty to replace my present wife with another one. Naturally, I will expect a fresh, new life; my wife will take the children and be solely responsible for them so that I am left free.

When I am through with school and have a job, I want my wife to quit working and remain at home so that my wife can more fully and completely take care of a wife's duties.

My God, who *wouldn't* want a wife?

## Vocabulary

The following terms are identified by paragraph number. Make sure that you understand each term's meaning in its context. If you're not sure that you understand a term, look it up in a college-level dictionary.

| | | |
|---|---|---|
| nurturant (3) | hors d'oeuvres (6) | adherence (7) |
| attendant (3) | replenish (6) | monogamy (7) |

## Style and Strategy

1. Write down the major defining features of wives that Brady includes, and note their arrangement. How does Brady organize her definition?

2. Writers use *irony* when they say the exact opposite of what they mean in order to create humor or emphasize a point. *Sarcasm,* a form of irony, has a biting or critical tone. Locate the places where Brady uses irony and/or sarcasm.

3. Both the first paragraph and the last paragraph are very brief, but they are also very effective. Explain why.

## Questions for Critical Thinking and Discussion

1.  Why is it appropriate that Brady thought of this subject "while I was ironing one evening" (paragraph 2)?

2.  Brady is writing about the typical wife's domestic duties in the early 1970s. Three decades later, how much has changed for the "typical wife"? How much has changed for the "typical husband"?

3.  James Thurber, another chronicler of relationships and strife, titled one of his books *The War Between Men and Women.* What, do you think, causes resentment between men and women?

## Suggestions for Writing

1.  Write an ironic essay of at least 500 words in which you answer Brady by explaining why you want a husband. If you want, pattern your response on Brady's. Then again, you might want to try a new approach.

2.  Write a 500- to 750-word essay that uses definition to explain why "I want/don't want to get married."

3.  Woody Allen's film *Sleeper* (1973) envisions a world in which people are served by robotic butlers. Write an essay of 500 to 750 words in which you pretend that you have entered such a world. Explain what you would want such a butler to do for you. Next, explain what you would do with all of the free time that resulted from having this butler. Finally, explain what your answers tell you about yourself. As you have probably guessed, this is an assignment in self-definition.

## Speaking Assignment

Complete the following statement: "I want a _____!" Then prepare an oral presentation that uses irony to define the term you have chosen. (For more help with oral presentations, see Chapter 18.)

# The Handicap of Definition

## WILLIAM RASPBERRY

*A native of Mississippi, William Raspberry is one of the most respected journalists in the United States, with a commanding insight into the problems of American society and politics. In 1991, Raspberry published* Looking Backward at Us, *a collection of his nationally syndicated columns for the* Washington Post, *where the following essay was first published in 1982.*

*In "The Handicap of Definition," Raspberry explains the problems caused by accepting a narrow definition of oneself and one's culture. He then shows how these limitations can be overcome.*

I know all about bad schools, mean politicians, economic deprivation and racism. Still, it occurs to me that one of the heaviest burdens black Americans—and black children in particular—have to bear is the handicap of definition: the question of what it means to be black.       1

Let me explain quickly what I mean. If a basketball fan says that the Boston Celtics' Larry Bird       2 plays "black," the fan intends it—and Bird probably accepts it—as a compliment. Tell pop singer Tom Jones* he moves "black" and he might grin in appreciation. Say to Teena Marie or the Average White Band** that they sound "black" and they'll thank you.

But name one pursuit, aside from athletics, entertainment or sexual performance, in which a white practitioner will feel complimented to be told he does it "black." Tell a white broadcaster he talks "black" and he'll sign up for diction lessons. Tell a white reporter he writes "black" and he'll take a writing course. Tell a white lawyer he reasons "black" and he might sue you for slander.

What we have here is a tragically limited definition of blackness, and it isn't only white people who buy it.

Think of all the ways black children can put one another down with charges of "whiteness." For many of these children, hard study and hard work are "white." Trying to please a teacher might be criticized as acting "white." Speaking correct English is "white." Scrimping today in the interest of tomorrow's goals is "white." Educational toys and games are "white."

An incredible array of habits and attitudes that are conducive to success in business, in academia, in the nonentertainment professions are likely to be thought of as somehow "white." Even economic success, unless it involves such "black" undertakings as numbers banking, is defined as "white."

And the results are devastating. I wouldn't deny that blacks often are better entertainers and athletes. My point is the harm that comes from too narrow a definition of what is black.

One reason black youngsters tend to do better at basketball, for instance, is that they assume they can learn to do it well, and so they practice constantly to prove themselves right.

Wouldn't it be wonderful if we could infect black children with the notion that excellence in

math is "black" rather than white, or possibly Chinese? Wouldn't it be of enormous value if we could create the myth that morality, strong families, determination, courage and love of learning are traits brought by slaves from Mother Africa and therefore quintessentially black?

There is no doubt in my mind that most black youngsters could develop their mathematical reasoning, their elocution and their attitudes the way they develop their jump shots and their dance steps: by the combination of sustained, enthusiastic practice and the unquestioned belief that they can do it.

In one sense, what I am talking about is the importance of developing positive ethnic traditions. Maybe Jews have an innate talent for communication; maybe the Chinese are born with a gift for mathematical reasoning; maybe blacks are naturally blessed with athletic grace. I doubt it. What is at work, I suspect, is assumption, inculcated early in their lives, that this a thing our people do well.

Unfortunately, many of the things about which blacks make this assumption are things that do not contribute to their career success—except for that handful of the truly gifted who can make it as entertainers and athletes. And many of the things we concede to whites are the things that are essential to economic security.

So it is with a number of assumptions black youngsters make about what it is to be a "man": physical aggressiveness, sexual prowess, the refusal to submit to authority. The prisons are full of people who, by this perverted definition, are unmistakably men.

But the real problem is not so much that the things defined as "black" are negative. The problem is that the definition is much too narrow.

Somehow, we have to make our children understand that they are intelligent, competent

---

*Tom Jones: a pop singer who had a number of hit songs in the late 1960s and early 1970s.

**Teena Marie; the Average White Band:** Teena Marie is a singer and songwriter whose most popular hits were released in the eighties; Average White Band is a popular soul group from the seventies.

people, capable of doing whatever they put their minds to and making it in the American mainstream, not just in a black subculture.

What we seem to be doing, instead, is raising up yet another generation of young blacks who will be failures—by definition. 16

## Vocabulary

The following terms are identified by paragraph number. Make sure that you understand each term's meaning in its context. If you're not sure that you understand a term, look it up in a college-level dictionary.

| | | |
|---|---|---|
| deprivation (1) | conducive (6) | innate (11) |
| diction (3) | numbers banking (6) | inculcated (11 |
| reasons (3) | quintessential (9) | prowess (13) |
| slander (3) | elocution (10) | subculture (15) |
| scrimping (5) | | |

## Style and Strategy

1. This essay was originally published as a newspaper column. Newspaper columnists have a limited amount of space in which to make their point. Note that Raspberry delivers his thesis early—in the second sentence. How might Raspberry have begun this essay if he had written it for a different audience and purpose?

2. Raspberry first attacks a number of definitions or assumptions about African Americans, then provides a better definition for the future. What does he claim to be the fatal flaw of the existing assumptions?

3. Paragraphs 15 and 16 serve as Raspberry's conclusion. Raspberry is following journalistic convention by using short paragraphs throughout his essay; however, these two paragraphs could be easily be merged into one. Can you think of another reason why using two paragraphs is effective here?

## Questions for Critical Thinking and Discussion

1. Chapter 7 contains an essay by Brent Staples titled "Just Walk on By" (pages 210–212). In it, Staples describes a series of typical experiences he had as a young black male walking alone at night. He found that if people saw him approaching on the sidewalk, they would nervously cross the street to avoid him because he fit their definition of "danger." How much of this perhaps unconscious definition do you experience in your life? Do you act on it? Have you ever been the victim of it?

2. Many observers believe that young people can be trapped in their parents' or families' expectations—in other words, the previous generation's "definition" of a young person's future. Is this syndrome a factor in your life?

## Suggestions for Writing

1. Write a 500- to 750-word essay about a teacher or supervisor who had an inaccurate perception of you. Explain how you overcame (or were unable to overcome) this definition.

2. Write a 500- to 750-word essay on the following topic: "I may appear to be a(n) _____, but I'm actually a(n) _____."

3. Raspberry argues against a "tragically limited definition of blackness." Write a 500- to 750-word essay in which you examine the image of another group in society that suffers from being defined in too limited a fashion. Like Raspberry, address the misleading and inaccurate public images that this definition comprises. In other words, explain how outsiders see these people. Are these images accurate? Also discuss the ways in which members of the group see themselves. Is their perception healthy, or does it need to be changed?

4. Raspberry says that some of the assumptions that "black youngsters make about what it is to be a 'man'" often lead to dire consequences. What assumptions does our society make about what it means to be a man, a woman, a father, a mother, a student, a businessperson, a soldier, or a member of the clergy (or any other term you wish to consider)? Write an essay of 500 to 750 words in which you discuss a number of these assumptions; then explain whether you agree with them. If you don't agree, explain why.

## Speaking Assignment

In paragraph 11, Raspberry mentions "the importance of developing positive ethnic traditions." Use definition to discuss a positive tradition, practice, or value that you have inherited from your family, ethnic group, or other source. (For more help with oral presentations, see Chapter 18.)

# So This Was Adolescence

## ANNIE DILLARD

Annie Dillard, best known for her Pulitzer Prize–winning Pilgrim at Tinker Creek (1975), is the author of eight other books, including a novel, The Living (1992); a collection of essays, Teaching a Stone to Talk: Expeditions and Encounters (1982); and her memories of growing up, An American Childhood (1987).

In "So This Was Adolescence," excerpted from An American Childhood, Dillard looks back at her adolescence. As you read this selection, think about your own adolescence. Do you recognize any of the situations, problems, and emotions that Dillard recounts?

When I was fifteen, I felt it coming; now I was sixteen, and it hit.

My feet had imperceptibly been set on a new path, a fast path into a long tunnel like those many turnpike tunnels near Pittsburgh, turnpike tunnels whose entrances bear on brass plaques a roll call of those men who died blasting them. I wandered witlessly forward and found myself going down, and saw the light dimming; I adjusted to the slant and dimness, traveled further down, adjusted to greater dimness, and so on. There wasn't a whole lot I could do about it, or about anything. I was going to hell on a handcart, that was all, and I knew it and everyone around me knew it, and there it was.

I was growing and thinning, as if pulled. I was getting angry, as if pushed. I morally disapproved most things in North America, and blamed my innocent parents for them. My feelings deepened and lingered. The swift moods of early childhood—each formed by and suited to its occasion—vanished. Now feelings lasted so long they left stains. They arose from nowhere, like winds or waves, and battered at me or engulfed me.

When I was angry, I felt myself coiled and longing to kill someone or bomb something big. Trying to appease myself, during one winter I whipped my bed every afternoon with my uniform belt. I despised the spectacle I made in my own eyes—whipping the bed with a belt, like a creature demented!—and I often began halfheartedly, but I did it daily after school as a desperate discipline, trying to rid myself and the innocent world of my wildness. It was like trying to beat back the ocean.

Sometimes in class I couldn't stop laughing; things were too funny to be borne. It began then, my surprise that no one else saw what was so funny.

I read some few books with such reverence I didn't close them at the finish, but only moved the pile of pages back to the start, without breathing, and began again. I read one such book, an enormous novel, six times that way—closing the binding between sessions, but not between readings.

On the piano in the basement I played the maniacal "Poet and Peasant Overture" so loudly, for so many hours, night after night, I damaged the piano's keys and strings. When I wasn't playing this crashing overture, I played boogie-woogie, or something else, anything else, in octaves—otherwise, it wasn't loud enough. My fingers were so strong I could do push-ups with them. I played one piece with my fists. I banged on a steel-stringed guitar till I bled, and once on a particularly piercing rock-and-roll downbeat I broke straight through one of Father's snare drums.

I loved my boyfriend so tenderly, I thought I must transmogrify into vapor. It would take spectroscopic analysis to locate my molecules in thin air. No possible way of holding him was close enough. Nothing could cure this bad case of gentleness except, perhaps, violence: maybe if he swung me by the legs and split my skull on a tree? Would that ease this insane wish to kiss too much his eyelids' outer corners and his temples, as if I could love up his brain?

I envied people in books who swooned. For two years I felt myself continuously swooning and continuously unable to swoon; the blood drained from my face and eyes and flooded my heart; my hands emptied, my knees unstrung, I bit at the air for something worth breathing—but I failed to fall, and I couldn't find the way to black out. I had to live on the lip of a waterfall, exhausted.

When I was bored I was first hungry, then nauseated, then furious and weak. "Calm yourself," people had been saying to me all my life. Since early childhood I had tried one thing and then another to calm myself, on those few occasions when I truly wanted to. Eating helped; singing helped. Now sometimes I truly wanted to calm myself. I couldn't lower my shoulders; they seemed to wrap around my ears. I couldn't lower my voice although I could see the people around me flinch. I waved my arm in class till the very teachers wanted to kill me.

I was what they called a live wire. I was shooting out sparks that were digging a pit around me, and I was sinking into that pit. Laughing with Ellin at school recess, or driving around after school with Judy in her jeep, exultant, or dancing with my boyfriend to Louis Armstrong across a polished dining-room floor, I got so excited I looked around wildly for aid; I didn't know where I should go or what I should do with myself. People in books split wood.

When rage or boredom reappeared, each 12 seemed never to have left. Each so filled me with so many years' intolerable accumulation it jammed the space behind my eyes, so I couldn't see. There was no room left even on my surface to live. My rib cage was so taut I couldn't breathe. Every cubic centimeter of atmosphere above my shoulders and head was heaped with last straws. Black hatred clogged my very blood. I couldn't peep, I couldn't wiggle or blink; my blood was too mad to flow.

For as long as I could remember, I had been 13 transparent to myself, unselfconscious, learning, doing, most of every day. Now I was in my own way; I myself was a dark object I could not ignore. I couldn't remember how to forget myself. I didn't want to think about myself, to reckon myself in, to deal with myself every livelong minute on top of everything else—but swerve as I might, I couldn't avoid it. I was a boulder blocking my own path. I was a dog barking between my own ears, a barking dog who wouldn't hush.

So this was adolescence. Is this how the peo- 14 ple around me had died on their feet—inevitably, helplessly? Perhaps their own selves eclipsed the sun for so many years the world shriveled around them, and when at last their inescapable orbits had passed through these dark egoistic years it was too late, they had adjusted.

Must I then lose the world forever, that I had 15 so loved? Was it all, the whole bright and various planet, where I had been so ardent about finding myself alive, only a passion peculiar to children, that I would outgrow even against my will?

## Vocabulary

The following terms are identified by paragraph number. Make sure that you understand each term's meaning in its context. If you're not sure that you understand a term, look it up in a college-level dictionary.

| | | |
|---|---|---|
| roll call (2) | overture (7) | exultant (11) |
| witlessly (2) | transmogrify (8) | ardent (15) |
| appease (4) | spectroscopic (8) | peculiar (15) |
| demented (4) | swoon (9) | |
| borne (5) | live wire (11) | |

## Style and Strategy

1. Where is Dillard's thesis statement? Why did she present the thesis in this position?

2. Besides definition, what other rhetorical options does Dillard employ in this essay? Cite specific passages and paragraphs.

3. In the first paragraph, Dillard writes that "When I was fifteen, I felt it coming. . . ." As you read this essay, when did you realize what "it" is?

4. In your opinion, does Dillard expect the questions in the final paragraph to be answered? Explain.

### Questions for Critical Thinking and Discussion

1. "Anyone who survives to age twenty-one can probably expect to live to be eighty." Comment on this statement. What does it imply about the vicissitudes of adolescence?

2. What advice would you give to teenagers undergoing adolescence?

### Suggestions for Writing

1. Choose a period in your life, and define it in an essay of 500 to 750 words.

2. Was your adolescence different from the stormy times that Dillard describes? If so, write a 500- to 750-word essay defining adolescence in terms of your experience.

3. Dillard isolates a few characteristics of her adolescence: she was opinionated, intense, and egotistic. What common characteristics would you discuss if you were asked to define people in your age group? Write an essay of 500 to 750 words in which you do just that. Use information from your own observations, from what you have heard people from other age groups say about your generation, and from the image of your generation that is portrayed in the media.

4. In defining herself as an adolescent, Dillard calls herself a "live wire." Choose another label that you might use when defining a personality type. Like Dillard, you might pick an informal term such as a "nerd," "geek," "jock," "shopaholic," or "prom queen." Then again, you might use a term from psychology such as introvert, extrovert, neurotic, type-A personality, or obsessive-compulsive. Write a 500- to 750-word essay that defines this personality type. Rely on your own knowledge to gather relevant detail, but also research your topic in the library or on the Internet, if appropriate.

### Speaking Assignment

Few of us can look back on our adolescence and not ask why or how our parents, teachers, or other adults put up with us. In a presentation, define your most obnoxious quality as an adolescent, making sure to explain how obnoxious it was. If you're really brave, however, define a current quality that you or others find obnoxious in you. (For more help with oral presentations, see Chapter 18.)

**CATALYST 2.0**

**MORE OPTIONS ONLINE**
If you would like to read additional definition essays, go to www.mhhe.com/ writingtoday.

# WRITING THE DEFINITION ESSAY WITH A READER'S EYE

As you write a definition essay, you will need to be constantly aware of your reader's knowledge of, and interest in, your topic as well as your purpose for writing. The term or concept that you choose to define will largely determine whether you take an objective or subjective (personal) approach to your material. (For more on objective and subjective definition, see pages 322–325.) If you will be writing a subjective definition, you need to be especially sure that you think like a member of your audience from the prewriting stage through your final draft. The advice that follows will help you think like a reader as you consider your assignment and then prewrite, draft, revise, and edit your extended definition essay.

## Issues to Keep in Mind

If you consider the following four issues as you plan and write your extended definition essay, you will have a better chance of making your definition clear for your readers:

1. Using brief definitions
2. Using negative definitions
3. The differences between objective definition and subjective definition
4. Strategies for developing a definition essay

### Using Brief Definitions

Providing a brief definition is a good internal strategy that you can use when developing extended definition essays as well as essays that employ other rhetorical options. Often you will need to indicate to your reader the meaning of a term or concept that you are using. Sometimes a more common synonym for the term in question is sufficient, such as in the following example:

> Environmental changes can sometimes be detected by examining a tortoise's carapace (shell).

In other instances, you will need to provide a longer, more detailed definition of a term. Note how this process works:

>         *name*                    *category*                              *distinguishing features*
> A "backpack" is a computer hard drive that is portable and is used to copy the contents of one regular hard drive, such as that found in a PC, to another hard drive.

The definition first names or labels the term or item, then shows what type or category it is found within, and then shows how the term or item differs from other terms or items within that category. Thus, a "backpack" is not used as part of a standard computer but is used to copy one computer's contents to another computer.

Writers sometimes make careless errors when writing simple definitions:

1. **Defining too broadly.** "A car is a four-wheeled, internal-combustion vehicle used to carry people and objects from place to place" does not distinguish a car from a truck.
2. **Defining too narrowly.** "The tomato is a common vegetable that is rendered to produce ketchup" ignores the fact that tomatoes are used in many other areas of food production.

3. **Using a circular definition.** "A word processor is a machine used to process words" tries to define *word processor* by using *process;* for a reader unfamiliar with such a machine, *processor* is probably the term that needs to be defined.

4. **Omitting the category or type.** "In substance-abuse counseling, an intervention is when family members or friends confront the person at risk and try to persuade him or her to enter treatment" neglects to define the category. *Is when* does not give the reader a clear sense of what an intervention actually is: a face-to-face, surprise confrontation. Using *is when* is also faulty grammar.

## Using Negative Definitions

Sometimes, defining something by what it *is not* is more effective than merely defining what it *is,* as in the following paragraph:

> The city's new police chief has announced that her emphasis will be on crime prevention—in other words, "proactive" policing, stopping crime before it happens rather than tracking down criminals after the fact. Crime prevention would seem to indicate a more healthy relationship between citizens and law enforcement: community policing, better access to the police to report concerns, and so on. But what has actually transpired is a vast network of speed traps. Although an intended crime is sometimes thwarted by the results of a traffic stop, putting every available officer behind a radar gun (1) ignores neighborhood concerns and (2) raises the old suspicions that the police are just there to raise revenues through the traffic court system. What we are seeing is not crime prevention but a policy that makes local driving an immense pain for residents and makes outsiders glad to leave our city limits behind them.

The writer provides an "ideal" definition of what crime prevention should entail, but the paragraph concentrates on a faulty approach to crime prevention—in the writer's view, what "proactive" police work should *not* be.

## Objective Definition and Subjective Definition

The goal of an objective definition is usually to inform the reader about a term or concept. Objective definitions usually avoid personal opinions or biases. However, a subjective definition tries to show the reader a new way of considering a term or concept or even to make a radical change in the reader's opinion of that term or concept. Which approach is the better one for you to take? That depends upon your purpose for writing.

***Objective Definition*** Suppose that for your next assignment your instructor handed you a topic sheet with the following photograph of a typical dog:

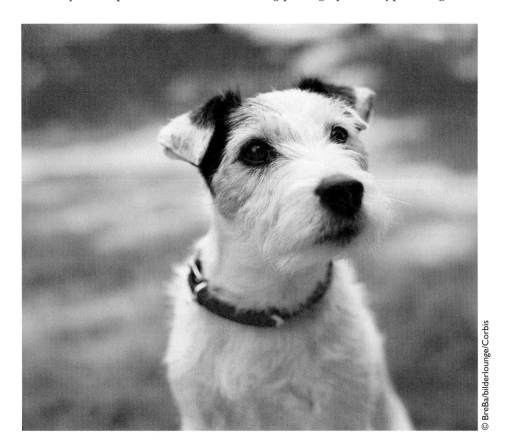

© BreBa/bilderlounge/Corbis

You are asked to define this creature. In this assignment, your instructor is asking for an **objective definition**, one in which the observation "I like dogs" is probably irrelevant. What your instructor wants, instead, is an essay in which you demonstrate your ability to plan, organize, write, and revise a definition of this familiar type of domesticated animal. Such an assignment might seem like a dry exercise, but it's actually quite useful and a lot harder than it looks.

The main problem with objective definition is to decide what to leave in and what is too specific or irrelevant. Do you need to point out that a dog is a carbon-based life form? Probably not. Do you need to point out that a dog is a mammal? Maybe, if you need to separate dogs from lizards and ticks. Should you say that dogs are descended from wolves and still resemble them in many ways? Yes. The following is a paragraph from an essay responding to this assignment:

Dogs are descendants of wolves, those rapidly disappearing predators that once prowled most of the world. Early peoples domesticated wolves, probably by the simple device of offering them food and warm shelter. However, the modern dog is still closely related to the wolf: both are fur-bearing mammals with prominent ears, eyes, and nose. Selective breeding over the centuries has produced dog breeds that range from barely 10 pounds to almost 200 pounds; however, look closely at any dog and you'll see signs of its wild ancestor: the face, the general body shape, the teeth. And although dogs are millennia removed from wolves, they can still revert to feral, predatory behavior.

This paragraph covers a lot of factual ground without lapsing into tedium, proving that seemingly mundane topics can be turned into interesting reading.

**Subjective Definition**    When you write a **subjective definition**, your purpose is different from that of the objective approach. You are trying to influence readers so that they understand a concept from your point of view. When you define *your* ideal (or least-favorite) vacation, evening, car, or article of clothing, the purpose of this essay is different from that of the objective definition.

In the preceding section, we illustrated how one student used a paragraph to define what a dog is. The result was objective and was clearly intended to inform the reader. A different slant on the topic—what is your *ideal* dog?—produces a different result. Now the reader is trying both to inform the reader and to convince him or her that the writer's choice is worthy of consideration. Here is a paragraph from a student's essay on the second topic:

I first discovered hounds when I was a child spending summer vacations on my uncle's farm. Uncle Ed raised hounds for bird hunting, but by that point in his life he was more interested in the dogs than in chasing quail. I liked his German shorthairs very well. These are mid-sized dogs, usually with a steady temperament and very little viciousness. They like people and join in various activities but are not "needy," a trait I dislike. Dynamo, who is now six years old and whom I raised from puppyhood, is the great-grandson of one of Uncle Ed's hunters. He likes riding in the car but doesn't get cranky if he has to stay home. He likes attention but doesn't demand it. I can leave him at home for a weekend without his going crazy and trashing the place. For me, the German shorthair is the ideal dog to own.

Using subjective definition, the writer is clearly "lobbying" for his favorite breed of dog, trying to convince the reader of the rightness of his preference.

However, note that because your personal view of the topic controls the structure and content of the essay, there is a danger that you will end up writing a "private" essay, one that loses its connection to the reader as you burrow deeper and deeper into your own world. A related danger is that the "private" essay doesn't *define;* it usually just *describes.* For example, when asked to define the ideal living quarters, one student writer decided to use her own apartment as an example and proceeded to describe her (admittedly) well-furnished and desirable abode. Here is one of the body paragraphs:

> The living room is all modular glass and steel, with black leather furniture chosen to match the modular effect. I avoided bright colors here: the wall decorations are all black-and-white prints or photographs. The appliances are also minimized, with the clock wafer-thin against the wall and the television recessed. The carpet is equally muted: a very dark gray.

Why is this décor scheme important to the writer? What does it have to do with the ideal living quarters? The writer has not really defined anything but has instead described her unstated preference with objective, surface details. Note how the following revision makes the description serve the definition:

> Many people over-decorate their living rooms and use too much color, as if they were putting together an outfit for a party instead of providing a suitable environment. The best furniture and decorations are unobtrusive and uncluttered. My living room is all modular glass and steel, with black leather furniture chosen to match the modular effect. The wall decorations are all black-and-white prints or photographs. The appliances are also minimized, with the clock wafer-thin against the wall and the television recessed. The carpet is equally muted: a very dark gray. My living room doesn't occupy me; I occupy it.

### Strategies for Developing a Definition

Note how you can use the other rhetorical options to help you develop an extended definition:

1. **Description** (Chapter 5). Defining a physical object virtually requires you to describe it.
2. **Narration** (Chapter 6). Use an anecdote to give your reader a better sense of the term or concept being defined.
3. **Exemplification** (Chapter 7). If you are defining a type of machine, for example, you could list and analyze different name-brand examples of that machine.

4. **Process analysis** (Chapter 8). You could show how the thing you are defining happens or works.

5. **Causal analysis** (Chapter 9). You could show some of the effects of the term or concept when it is used in practice; alternatively, you could explain why a term or concept has come to mean something quite different from its earlier meaning.

6. **Classification** (Chapter 11). A key step in defining a term or concept is showing what type of thing it is, so you could discuss the term or concept in relation to other terms or concepts in the same category.

7. **Comparison/contrast** (Chapter 12). A negative definition explains what a term or concept is *not;* the contrast strategy is obviously useful here.

8. **Argument** (Chapter 13). A subjective definition frequently tries to convince the reader that the writer's point of view is valid and worthy of consideration.

**CATALYST 2.0**

**MORE OPTIONS ONLINE**
For more help with problem areas in the definition essay, go to www.mhhe.com/ writingtoday.

## Choosing a Topic

Your first step in writing an effective extended definition is to choose a term or concept that you are interested in and can successfully define for your audience. The following guidelines will help you choose a promising topic for your essay:

1. Think about your purpose for writing about this topic. Do you want to write an objective definition that informs your readers about a topic, or do you want to write a subjective definition that amuses readers or convinces them to share your viewpoint? What is the point that you are trying to make?

2. Whether you will be writing an objective definition or a subjective definition, concentrate on finding a topic that you can make interesting for your reader. If you are writing a subjective definition, beware of topics that might lead you to write a "private" essay that your readers will be unable to relate to. Remember, it's not a question of what your preferences are on a given topic; it's a matter of *why.*

3. Avoid a topic that is too large or too vague. Trying to define "love" or "honor" in 500 to 750 words is a recipe for disaster.

4. Consider what your reader is already likely to know about a subject. For example, an objective definition of a supermarket would probably bore most readers; however, a subjective definition of the same term might be quite effective.

## Prewriting

To write an extended definition, you need to try to capture the defining features of the term or concept as you plan and prewrite. One student writer tackled the topic "What is the perfect job supervisor?" As he began to think about his topic, he realized that this mythical person had to possess certain general attributes: the ability to be fair, the ability to punish, and the ability to praise.

Using clustering, the writer started with this group of three general attributes, then added specific attributes for each of the three general ones. Note that freewriting or brainstorming would also have been a good choice at this stage (see Chapter 2 for more on prewriting strategies).

At this point, see if you can develop a working or preliminary thesis. Does your thesis match your purpose? If so, and if you begin to visualize the direction that your essay will take, you are now ready to organize your prewriting.

## Organizing

The writer of the essay on the perfect supervisor produced a sentence outline before beginning his essay. This step helped him see that his essay's structure was logical and balanced. (For more information on outlines, see Chapter 2.)

## Drafting

To illustrate some approaches to writing an extended definition, we have included the essay "The Brave and the Humane."

### The Introduction

In an extended definition, the introduction needs to present the term or concept to be defined and capture the reader's interest, often by relating the topic to his or her own experience. Introductions often move from general to specific, which is the approach that the student writer has chosen for his essay defining the ideal boss:

The Brave and the Humane

Most people have a number of problems with their job. Even those who like what they do find that most mornings they would rather sleep in or go the beach. However, if work were all fun and games, the company wouldn't need to pay employees for their efforts.

The main demon most people dread at work is the boss. This person probably occupies more space in the average adult American's psyche than Mom, Dad, spouse, or children, largely because of his or her ability to wound us, harm our self-esteem, and even make us feel like moral failures. But what kind of supervisor would be ideal? Many people might long for a weak or absent boss, but most businesses wouldn't keep such a supervisor for long. **Instead, the mythical "perfect boss" needs to have three qualities: the ability to be fair, the ability to punish, and the ability to reward.**

Note the position of the thesis, at the end of the second paragraph, where it follows two paragraphs that have a writing pattern of general to specific.

## The Body

The writer has set up a clear pattern of organization for his essay in his thesis. However, clearly spelling out the essay structure in this way can set up either a mechanical, perfunctory essay or a lively, interesting one. Read on to discover how the student writer carried out his plan:

Everyone wants a piece of the boss. The strategies that employees use to manipulate their supervisors are endless. If Charley has discovered that the boss likes golf, he'll make sure to drop in and schmooze about his iron shot to the eleventh green at Invisible Lakes last Sunday and, maybe, drop off a few half-price greens fee coupons. If Karen knows that the boss has a soft spot for family issues—specifically, kids—she'll keep the boss updated on little Amy's ongoing, time-consuming, and expensive battle with ear infections. Yet when it comes time to decide on rewards for performance (raises, days off, promotions, overtime pay, and so on), the good boss is going to put all personal considerations aside.

The punishment of wrongdoers is another sticky subject. Some supervisors turn into sadistic prison guards at that point, clearly enjoying this part of their job, drawing the process out, twisting the knife. Others have the opposite problem: they can't even look the offender in the eye or form complete sentences. However, the ideal manager gets to the point, clearly stating the problem and the consequences in as short a time as possible. There is no reason for the employee to come away with fears or bad feelings. It's a matter of stating the facts, explaining the situation, and coming to an agreement. Life goes on.

Finally, why can't some bosses ever find a way to praise their subordinates? Some supervisors are like pinch-faced Puritan judges from the seventeenth century. They act as if they're giving up part of their soul if they say "Job well done." Although a good boss can't hand out financial rewards like Halloween candy, he or she must know how a well-judged compliment can motivate employees.

Note how the writer uses comparison/contrast and exemplification as internal strategies to develop the body paragraphs.

### The Conclusion

The conclusion of an extended definition needs to reinforce the main point about the term or concept or move beyond it. For example, the student writer could have summarized his extended definition in his conclusion, but a summary would not have added anything to his essay. Instead, notice how he is able to show the logical point to be drawn from his essay:

Even when they have an ideal boss, people will still have problems at work. Most workplaces do not offer much emotional gratification. But the good supervisor will know what people need and what they can tolerate. And most people, if they believe they are being treated <u>fairly,</u> in all senses of the word, will be willing to come back tomorrow and put in an honest day's effort.

### EXERCISE 10.1

Write an outline of "The Brave and the Humane." (For help with outlines, see Chapter 2, pages 41–42.) What does the outline reveal about the essay's organization? Would a different organization work better? Explain.

## Revising Your Draft

After you have completed a draft of your extended definition, your next step is to revise it, using your own analysis and comments from classmates or friends. During peer review, answer the questions on page 330 about the draft you are reviewing, whether it is yours or another student's.

After your review for content, you need to go over your and your peer reviewers' responses to your essay and then revise for unity, coherence, language level, and tone (see Chapter 4). When you have revised your draft and are satisfied with it, read your draft for mechanical and grammatical errors. Find and correct major sentence errors (fragments, comma splices, fused sentences), errors in pronoun agreement and subject-verb agreement, and spelling.

Now that you have made your corrections, *read your essay one more time* to catch any errors you may have made during revision and find errors missed during your earlier reviews.

*Consider Your Options*

The conclusion of a definition essay gives you the opportunity to comment on what you have written. Don't summarize here. Use this section to reinforce the significance of what you have written in the body of your essay. (To read more about strategies for concluding an essay, see Chapter 3.)

CATALYST 2.0

**MORE OPTIONS ONLINE**
For more help with step-by-step development of the definition essay, go to www.mhhe.com/ writingtoday.

## Student Essay

The following essay is Curtis Ray Mosley's response to a definition assignment. The final draft is presented first. Then Curtis's first draft is presented, with his comments about this draft and what he needed to do in the revision stage.

Even the final version of this essay, which won first place in a student writing contest, is strong stuff. Curtis Mosley is working with potentially controversial subject matter here. As you read, ask yourself how you might respond to Mosley's essay if you were to give him comments as a peer reviewer. What are its strengths and weaknesses as a definition of the concept of a "moment of truth"?

*Curtis's Final Draft*

My "Moment of Truth"

A moment of truth is, more accurately, a moment of decision. Faced with an adequate amount of information, the person in a given situation still faces a difficult choice. If good judgment and common sense prevail, then he or she chooses the correct alterna-

1

## Questions for Reviewing an Extended Definition

1  Does the essay's opening introduce the topic and capture the reader's interest? How could the introduction be strengthened?

2  What is the thesis statement, and has the writer placed it in the best position within the essay? In what ways, if any, could it be strengthened?

3  Is the term or concept that is being defined clear? What is the writer's purpose for defining this term or concept? Has the writer fulfilled this purpose?

4  If the definition is subjective, does the essay speak to an audience, or does it seem written for the writer only?

5  Does the extended definition seem complete? Point out any important defining feature of the term or concept that the writer has left out.

6  Is the organization effective? Should the defining features be given in a different order? If so, what order would be better?

7  Do the topic sentences introduce each defining feature? Is each feature fully developed? Where could the writer use a different rhetorical option to explain a feature more effectively?

8  Does the writer use transitions to guide the reader? Where are transitional words or sentences needed?

9  Does the essay have an effective conclusion? How could it be improved?

tive. If not, then he or she walks away feeling like a dope, as I did recently.

One afternoon a week or so ago, I was sitting on the lowered tailgate of my friend Bubba's pickup, feeling out of place. The central artery of The Pines Trailer Park in the small town of Bithlo was clogged with wild, screaming children just released from school. I was worried about the impression we gave them, drinking Budweiser at three in the afternoon. The antlike scurrying of the children was disrupted only by the dustdevil swarms of future athletes that marked the frequent basketball goals placed by the road.

As I ceremoniously crushed an empty can in my hand, something down the road caught my eye. Walking toward us, parting the throng of children as Moses parted the Red Sea, was the distinctive shape of an attractive young woman. Although she was still twenty-odd mobile homes away, I could not keep my eyes off her. She paused in the road and was joined by another girl, this one a little overweight. They both were adorned in tube tops and cut-off blue jean shorts. The overweight one was bulging over the top, while the thin one hung out the bottom. Neither wore shoes. They commanded an audience of young boys as they held hands and whispered in each other's ear. Standing in the middle of the road, they were totally oblivious to a car trying to fight its way through.

"Where do you think they're going?" I asked Bubba.

"Oh, you don't want to mess with them. Trust me."

I wondered what he meant. The two girls were slowly coming into focus, and I came to realize their beauty was best admired from afar. Each face was heavily coated in makeup. The thin one had blue mascara streaking back from her eyes like Endora on *Bewitched*; the fat one had red cheeks like Krusty the Clown. Turning suddenly, the two went up to a trailer window, talked for a minute, and went inside.

"Bubba, what's the danger here?"

"Well, you see, those two are making their early rounds. They're 8
checking out the scene. They want to find out who has some money,
beer, or cigarettes, along with anything else a man will give them.
That way, later tonight they know where to party."

"How do they make a living? Do they have any children?" 9

"Of course they have children. They just don't have any hus- 10
bands. They're virtual experts in matters concerning food stamps,
WIC (Women and Infant Care), and the legal entitlements of child
support. Shoot, that skinny one is so good she collects from two guys
for the same kid."

It all seemed a little professional to me. Could they be prosti- 11
tutes? How could they finagle every night without a conflict arising
between would-be suitors? Bubba's explanation was enlightening.
"Take it from me. Those two are slicker than greased owl poop. The
good-looking one teases you out of the goods, while the fat one gives
her a reason to go home early. It's the old good cop, bad cop with a
Bithlonian twist."

This would seem to be enough information to convince a reason- 12
able man that he should seek romance elsewhere, but after all of
Bubba's warnings, I was still thinking I would like to meet that thin
one. I did not have long to wait. Reaching for another Bud, I caught
a whiff of fake designer perfume and looked up to find myself face
to face with danger.

"Those Budweisers sure look tasty, and you look pretty tasty 13
yourself, working man," she purred seductively.

Bubba instinctively grabbed the now tepid twelve pack, pulling it 14
close as if it were a woman's purse on a crowded subway. The thin
one positioned her foot on the tailgate between Bubba and me, presenting an erotic barrier that was hard to ignore. The other one was
flirting with the now eunuch-like Bubba, to no avail.

At this point, of course, I still could have found a way out of the    15
situation. However, my better judgment and overall common sense
were growing weaker by the moment. As Miss Piggy asked to turn up
the radio in my car (Bubba had blown his speakers), I crumbled
under the pressure. Prying the beer from Bubba's hand, I gave them
each one. Only two remained.

"Hey, maybe I can give you a call sometime?" I sheepishly asked    16
Skinny.

"Sure. Got a red?" she replied, grabbing my pack of Marlboros.    17
Without waiting for an answer, she shook out the last of the Mohicans and quickly lit up. She instantly ripped the five Marlboro miles
off the side of the pack and stuffed them into her tube top. "I'm
sav'n for that Snake River wet-dry duffel bag. It's only three thousand miles. Got a pen?" She squirmed noticeably while writing her
initials and number on my now worthless pack of smokes. "I don't
want your old lady coming down here to kick my butt," she quipped
in regard to the initials.

Feeling like Mr. Macho, I surrendered my last beer, bid everyone    18
farewell, and headed for Orlando. After giving up only three beers,
five miles, and one Marlboro red, I had procured a phone number
and was ready for romance. I was on the East-West Expressway
before I noticed my wallet was not in its regular place in the con-
sole. Everything became crystal clear, as I remembered the chunky
one's request to turn up my radio because her favorite song was on.
Furious, I retrieved my cell phone and called the newly acquired
number.

Listening to the operator's recorded message, "The number you    19
have dialed has been temporarily disconnected," I recalled Bubba's
early warning: "You don't want to mess with them. Trust me."

*Curtis's First Draft*

### Trailer Park Girls

My peer review partner mentioned that my essay didn't have much of a plot. She suggested that I needed to introduce some sort of story line that entertains readers. I added more description and narration to the final version, including figurative language ("as Moses parted the Red Sea") and humor.

As I read this draft, I began to worry about using the behavior of two people to define an entire group of women. My peer reviewer echoed my concern. I decided that the real issue was my own careless judgment during the encounter and that an analysis of that "moment of decision" was a better topic for a definition essay.

Adding the paragraph placing the overweight girl in the car was all that I needed to set up the surprise ending, when I have my "moment of truth."

Sitting on the lowered tailgate of Bubba's pickup, I felt out of place. The Pines Trailer Park in the small town of Bithlo was clogged with wild, screaming children. I was worried about the impression we gave them, drinking Budweiser at three in the afternoon.

Something down the road caught my eye. Walking toward us was an attractive young woman. She was soon joined by another girl, this one a little overweight. They both were wearing cut-off blue jean shorts. They commanded an audience of young boys as they held hands and whispered in each other's ear.

The two girls were slowly coming into focus, and I came to realize their beauty was best admired from afar. Each face was heavily coated in makeup. Turning suddenly, the two went up to a trailer window, talked for a minute, and went inside.

As we drank, Bubba warned me about trailer park girls. "Trailer park girls all have children. They just don't have any husbands. They are all experts in matters concerning food stamps, WIC (Women and Infant Care), and the legal entitlements of child support."

"Take it from me. Those two are slicker than greased owl poop. The good-looking one teases you out of the goods, while the fat one gives her a reason to go home early."

Even after Bubba's warning, I was still thinking I would like to meet that thin one. I did not have long to wait. Reaching for another Bud, I caught a whiff of fake designer perfume and looked up to find myself face to face with a genuine Bithlo trailer park girl!

Bubba instinctively grabbed the now tepid twelve pack, pulling it close as if it were a woman's purse on a crowded subway. The thin one positioned her foot on the tailgate between Bubba and me, presenting an erotic barrier that was hard to ignore. The other one was flirting with the now eunuch-like Bubba, to no avail. Crumbling under the pressure, I pried the beer from Bubba's hand, and gave them each one. Only two remained.

"Hey, maybe I can give you a call sometime?" I sheepishly asked Skinny.

8

"Sure. Got a red?" she replied, grabbing my pack of Marlboros. Without waiting for an answer, she shook out the last of the Mohicans and quickly lit up. "Got a pen?" She asked, squirming noticeably while writing her initials and number on my now worthless pack of smokes. "I don't want your old lady coming down here to kick my butt," she quipped in regard to the initials. Against Bubba's advice, I was about to become acquainted with a trailer park girl.

9 In my final draft I "poured some gravy on the potatoes" by adding more dialogue in the characters' authentic dialect. Finally, I changed the title to reflect my new focus.

## EXERCISE 10.2: REVISING

The following is the first draft of a student's definition essay. Working in pairs or in small groups, review this essay. Using the Questions for Reviewing an Extended Definition on page 330, decide what revisions you would suggest. If you have any questions the student needs to consider, write them in the margin or on a separate sheet of paper. If your instructor directs you to, rewrite one or more paragraphs to make them stronger and to eliminate any grammatical or mechanical errors.

### "TEEN-AGED DISCRIMINATION"

'Discrimination' is a hot topic today. Minority groups are sick of it, women are sick of it, foriegners are sick of it. But another group faces discrimination everyday, these are teen-agers.

In highschool teenagers are treated like crap, we were used to it. After school, on the weekends, in the summers, are kids treated any better? No!!!

Teen-age discrimination takes many forms. One is stores. When young people go to the mall they' can expect to be followed around by store security. This isnt an opinion its a fact. Teens are seen to be either criminals, or criminals about to happen. We want to spend money but we can take it for granite that stores think were their to steel.

An other discrimination is police. Last summer I was going fifty in a 35-zone, and got pulled over. Not only did the cop right me a ticket, he gave me a 'young lady' lecture as well. My self of steam suffered that day, I felt like, you know a second class citizen.

Teenagers are a target group; no doubt about it. This type of discrimination hurts everytime it hits; although, noone wants to talk about it.

## Additional Writing Topics

1.   Write an extended definition of one of the following terms:
     a.   Road rage
     b.   Passive-aggressive drivers
     c.   Cyber loafing
     d.   A blown semester
     e.   The ideal academic advisor

2.   **Writing on the job.** At work, you may have heard someone refer to taking a "mental health" day off. What does this term mean? Write an extended definition as a memo for your company's human resources department in which you incorporate both your sense of this term and the interpretations of your co-workers. (See Chapter 17 for help with writing a memo.)

## Definition and Visual Representations

When you think of the insurance industry, what are your first impressions? Do you see this as an exciting, fast-paced field? Or are your perceptions somewhat different?

Advertising is a subtle art for insurance companies. Insurance is a serious, multi-billion-dollar business in the United States, but advertising, after all, aims to attract attention. The magazine ad for Travelers reproduced here goes out on a limb. Both the subject of synchronized swimming and mention of the boy band 'N Sync are likely to evoke a reaction from most readers. But notice how the tone quickly shifts from the ironic to the serious as it explores the definition of *in-synch*.

1.   Write a response to this ad. What are your thoughts and impressions? As you write, refer to Questions for Reviewing a Visual Representation.

2.   How does the concept of being "in-synch" apply to your life today? How is the role of a college student different from the same role twenty years ago? Research this idea. Then either write an essay explaining your findings and documenting your sources (see also Chapter 21) or develop an oral presentation based on your research and conclusions (see also Chapter 18).

Courtesy of Travelers Insurance

Exactly what is "in-synch"?

And does it always involve sequined swim caps?

· · · · · · · · · · · · · · · · · · · · · · · · · · · · · · · · · · · · · · · · · · · · · · · · · · · · · · · · · ·

No, it's not an underwater dance troupe. Or a boy band. In-synch is simply a more evolved approach to insurance. An approach that acknowledges that the world is always changing — so why shouldn't your insurance? At Travelers, our goal is simple—never to stop working to understand the intricacies of your world, so we can make sure your insurance always keeps up. Ask your independent agent about all the benefits of being in-synch. Just don't ask about the swim caps.

 **TRAVELERS**
*Insurance. In-synch.*

travelers.com

## Questions for Reviewing a Visual Representation

- Is the presence forceful, passive, or something in between?

- What is the purpose of the representation—in other words, what is it trying to do to you, the reader/viewer?

- If the representation uses words, do they reinforce the visual image or in some way contradict it?

- What is the presumed audience for the representation—men, women, children, the elderly? Or does it have a broader appeal?

- If the representation is an advertisement, is it trying to sell a product or to get you to adopt a way of thinking?

- If the representation is an advertisement, does it try to persuade you in a fair manner, or do you feel manipulated?

### Responding to an Image

In James Cameron's *Aliens* (1986-R, second film in the Aliens quartet), Sigourney Weaver plays Lieutenant Ellen Ripley, who in this futuristic thriller must battle a horrific alien who is trying to protect her young. This film still shows Sigourney Weaver and the director James Cameron.

© Bob Penn/Sygma/Corbis

1. First, write an informal response to the film image. What do you notice about Ripley?

2. Many observers believe that Weaver's Ripley singlehandedly invented the role of woman as action hero. Watch the film, and write an essay exploring this definition.

### Using the Internet

Search the Internet for insights and information to use when writing extended definitions.

1. Many definition topics ask the writer to define an "ideal" or "perfect" example of some subject or thing, such as a day. What might be a perfect day for an avid golfer, tennis player, gourmet, hiker, camper, bowler, beer drinker, basketball player, video-game enthusiast, shopper, or Internet addict? Find three or four Web sites dedicated to a sport or activity you enjoy. Combine information from these sites with your own ideas in an essay that defines what you imagine to be a "perfect day" spent in this sport or activity.

2. Until the twentieth century—before the era of universal education and instant telecommunications—there were many regional and local dialects of American English. In fact, most major languages have numerous dialects. Even today, the Chinese dialects of Mandarin and Cantonese differ markedly, and the French spoken in Quebec is quite different from the French spoken in Paris. Even English continues to have many varieties. Consider the differences between the language as it is spoken in the United States and as it is spoken in England, Scotland, Australia, or South Africa. Search the Internet for information about the various forms or dialects of any spoken language of your choice. Then focus on a specific dialect of that language and do some more online research. Use this material in a definition essay that explains the major characteristics of that dialect to someone who has little knowledge of it.

   As an alternative assignment, use the Internet to discover information about a particular sect or branch of a world religion. For example, you might search for materials on Hasidic Jews, Coptic Christians, or Shiite Muslims. Again, use the information you find in a definition essay.

### CHAPTER 11

# CLASSIFICATION

# Writing in Context

You have been asked to start attending the regular Monday morning meeting at Osprey Online. You are sitting with your colleagues at a conference table headed by Bob. "It's quarterly sales report time," he says, tapping a very large folder packed full of paperwork. Bob grins, then slides the mountainous package down the table toward you. "It's your turn. Welcome to the team."

Back in your office, you start to wonder about Bob. He seems to have a certain sadistic quality. But your more important question is right in front of you. Your classes in business school taught you a lot about sales and profit breakdowns, but not how to write about them.

At first, you try to figure this task out on your own but don't make much progress. Then Bob's assistant, Stephanie, suggests using last quarter's report as a guide. You quickly realize that the solution is right in front of you. Virtually all of your division's revenues come from three sources: new software, software upgrades, and outsourced consulting. You take the folder's contents apart and then separate the paperwork into three stacks. The rest of your work day is substantially free of stress, as you organize last quarter's business by category.

* * * * * * * * * * *  *Classification* is a way of organizing material in order to make better sense of it. In the example above, what first seemed chaotic made sense once classification came into the picture.

# HOW DOES CLASSIFICATION WORK?

**Classification** is a powerful option that allows a writer to make sense of a large subject by dividing it into smaller categories, each one consisting of similar items. In fact, this strategy is sometimes called **division** because the first step requires the writer to divide the larger subject into smaller units. The writer then classifies specific entities according to which smaller category they fit into.

Regardless of the terminology used to describe this strategy, classification is widely employed. In the sciences, for example, classification is a standard strategy. The Swedish biologist Carolus Linnaeus established the taxonomy that we use to classify plants and animals. When we refer to a creature as belonging to a certain family, genus, or species, we are using Linnaeus's system. Similarly, if you find yourself in a chemistry class, you'll probably see the periodic table of elements hanging on the wall nearby, courtesy of Dmitri Mendeleev and Henry Moseley. On this chart, the elements are arranged from top to bottom and left to right, according to their electron structure. The elements of each category behave similarly in chemical combinations.

Classification is not confined to the sciences, however. This method appears in every discipline and in every type of writing. In his classic account of driving the back roads of America, *Blue Highways,* William Least Heat Moon describes the Hopi method of classifying human development:

> The Hopi believes mankind has evolved through four worlds: the first a shadowy realm of contentment; the second a place so comfortable the people forgot where they had come from and began worshipping material goods. The third world was a pleasant land too, but the people, bewildered by their past and fearful for their future, thought only of their own earthly plans. At last, the Spider Grandmother, who oversees the emergences, told them: "You have forgotten what you should have remembered, and now you have to leave this place. Things will be harder." In the fourth and present world, life is difficult for mankind, and he struggles to remember his source because materialism and selfishness block a greater vision. The newly born infant comes into the fourth world with the door of his mind open (evident in the cranial soft spot), but as he ages, the door closes and he must work at remaining receptive to the great forces. A human being's grandest task is to keep from breaking with things outside himself.

Even topics that we try *not* to think about may lend themselves to classification. In 1992 former Vice President Al Gore, Jr., wrote this paragraph as part of *Earth in the Balance,* his plea to clean up the environment:

> Perhaps the most visible evidence of the waste crisis is the problem of how to dispose of our mountains of municipal solid waste, which is being generated at the rate of more than five pounds a day for every citizen of this country, or approximately one ton per person per year. But two other kinds of waste pose equally difficult challenges. The first is

the physically dangerous and politically volatile material known as hazardous waste, which accompanied the chemical revolution of the 1930s and which the United States now produces in roughly the same quantities as municipal solid waste. (This is a conservative estimate, one that would double if we counted all the hazardous waste that is currently exempted from regulation for a variety of administrative and political reasons.) Second, one ton of industrial solid waste is created each week for every man, woman, and child—and this does not even count the gaseous waste steadily being vented into the atmosphere. (For example, each person in the United States also produces an average of twenty tons of $CO_2$ each year.) Incredibly, taking into account all three of these conservatively defined categories of waste, every person in the United States produces *more than twice his or her weight in waste every day.*

You can classify by theme, by type, by appearance, by behavior. The way you choose to classify your subject is your **basis of classification.** In his narrative about his middle-school years, student writer Kevin Hunkovic shows the "pecking order" that existed at the ironically named Liberty Middle School (see Chapter 14 for the entire essay):

In 1988 Liberty Middle School had a student body of about 1,700 students, give or take a few hundred. I was overwhelmed by the multitudes of diverse people around me. My classes were huge. There were 40-65 students per class. These numbers dwarfed me as I became a very small part of a whole. Soon after I started the sixth grade, I began to notice a system underlying the way students and faculty interacted with each other. I later realized that it was a social class system. The highest members were the intellectuals, or nerds as they were called. They enjoyed special privileges that others did not have, such as getting to leave class and study alone in the library or move through the hallways without a pass. Then there was the middle class, those who weren't the best or the worst students. This group usually contained the athletes, cheerleaders, and the somewhat popular students. It constituted the majority of the student body. Next, there were the troublemakers, or the Future Criminals of America, as I called them. Those students tended to receive bad grades and get into trouble when they weren't causing it. Above all of this was the school faculty. Until I entered middle school, I thought the faculty were just the people who distributed the information to the students. At Liberty Middle School, however, the faculty took on all the functions of a small government: executives to run it, legislators to make the rules, and judges to punish wrongdoers with detentions. Finally, I noticed a class of outsiders, who for one reason or another did not fit into any category. They weren't mean enough to be in the lower class, or popular enough to converse with the middle class, or good enough at studying to be in the upper class. These students went unnoticed for the most part and were overlooked by teachers in an overcrowded classroom. The fourth class of people slipped through the cracks of the system, so to speak. In other words, they became victims of the institution.

Hunkovic uses classification as an internal strategy here, one that organizes the people of the school into recognizable groups.

In an informative classification essay about a factual subject, such as a report classifying moths or word-processing software, your purpose is to provide your reader with as clear a picture of the subject as possible. In the personal essay, however, your purpose is often both to enlighten and entertain. Therefore, the basis for your classification will be essential to the success of your essay. For example, if asked to classify your blood relatives, you could organize your essay according to genetic proximity—your siblings are closest to you, your parents are next, your extended relatives are further removed, and so on. But an essay on this topic will probably bore its readers. Why not find a more inventive way to classify your relatives? Consider the following categories:

1. Relatives whom I'd want in my life even if we weren't related

2. Relatives who are in my life only because of blood ties

3. Relatives who are not in my life because they are dysfunctional

• *Consider Your Options*

Choose your categories carefully when classifying people. A degree of sensitivity is needed here. Be sure to avoid categories that have been used to stereotype or hurt people.

This second approach has a much better chance of captivating an audience than the first one. It has more potential: everyone has both beloved and obnoxious relatives. The essay could be either grim or funny, according to the writer's personal circumstances.

As you read the essays that follow, note that the classification strategy always requires three or more categories. If you have a subject that can be broken into only two categories, then you're probably better off using the comparison/contrast strategy (see Chapter 12), which allows you to concentrate on the similarities and differences between the two groups. When you use classification, you examine each group separately.

## READING THE CLASSIFICATION ESSAY WITH A WRITER'S EYE

In the three selections that follow, Fran Lebowitz sorts out the types of music that assault her, unbidden; Martin Luther King, Jr., evaluates three methods of responding to social oppression; and Paul Fussell takes a systematic look at social class in the United States. In the wrong hands, classification can be a dry and boring option; however, note how skillfully these writers make this rhetorical strategy come alive.

The second half of this chapter features strategies for writing the classification essay with a reader's eye (pages 357–363). If you decide to write on one of the topics that follow the three essays, make sure that you have read the strategies section before you begin. Note that additional writing topics are listed at the end of the chapter (page 369).

# The Sound of Music: Enough Already

## FRAN LEBOWITZ

*Fran Lebowitz is known for her satiric commentary on urban living. Her love-hate relationship with city life is the usual topic of her essays, which have been collected in* Metropolitan Life *(1978),* Social Studies *(1981), and* The Fran Lebowitz Reader *(1994). She is also a writer of fiction, a popular lecturer on the college circuit, and an occasional guest on late-night TV talk shows.*

*In "The Sound of Music," from* Metropolitan Life, *Lebowitz uses classification to comment upon our noisy, intrusive world. This essay is thirty years old, but as you read, consider whether Lebowitz's conclusions are still valid today.*

First off, I want to say that as far as I am concerned, in instances where I have not personally and deliberately sought it out, the only difference between music and Muzak is the spelling. Pablo Casals* practicing across the hall with the door open—being trapped in an elevator, the ceiling of which is broadcasting "Parsley, Sage, Rosemary, and Thyme"—it's all the same to me. Harsh words? Perhaps. But then again these are not gentle times we live in. And they are being made no more gentle by this incessant melody that was once real life. 1

There was a time when music knew its place. No longer. Possibly this is not music's fault. It may be that music fell in with a bad crowd and lost its sense of common decency. I am willing to consider this. I am willing even to try and help. I would like to do my bit to set music straight in order that it might shape up and leave the mainstream of society. The first thing that music must understand is that there are two kinds of music—good music and bad music. Good music is music that I want to hear. Bad music is music that I don't want to hear. 2

*Pablo Casals (1876–1973): famous twentieth-century cellist, composer, and conductor.

So that music might more clearly see the error of its ways I offer the following. If you are music and you recognize yourself on this list, you are bad music. 3

### 1. Music in Other People's Clock Radios
There are times when I find myself spending the night in the home of another. Frequently the other is in a more reasonable line of work than I and must arise at a specific hour. Ofttimes the other, unbeknownst to me, manipulates an appliance in such a way that I am awakened by Stevie Wonder. On such occasions I announce that if I wished to be awakened by Stevie Wonder I would sleep with Stevie Wonder. I do not, however, wish to be awakened by Stevie Wonder and that is why God invented alarm clocks. Sometimes the other realizes that I am right. Sometimes the other does not. And that is why God invented *many* others. 4

### 2. Music Residing in the Hold Buttons of Other People's Business Telephones
I do not under any circumstances enjoy hold buttons. But I am a woman of reason. I can accept reality. I can face the facts. What I cannot face is the music. Just as there are two kinds of music—good and bad—so there are two kinds of hold buttons—good and bad. Good hold buttons are hold buttons that hold one silently. Bad hold buttons are hold buttons that hold one musically. When I hold I want to hold silently. That is the way it was meant to be, for that is what God was talking about when he said, "Forever hold your peace." He would have added, "and quiet," but he thought you were smarter. 5

### 3. Music in the Streets

The past few years have seen a steady increase in the number of people playing music in the streets. The past few years have also seen a steady increase in the number of malignant diseases. Are these two facts related? One wonders. But even if they are not—and, as I have pointed out, one cannot be sure—music in the streets has definitely taken its toll. For it is at the very least disorienting. When one is walking down Fifth Avenue, one does not expect to hear a string quartet playing a Strauss waltz. What one expects to hear while walking down Fifth Avenue is traffic. When one does indeed hear a string quartet playing a Strauss waltz while one is walking down Fifth Avenue, one is apt to become confused and imagine that one is not walking down Fifth Avenue at all but rather that one has somehow wound up in Old Vienna. Should one imagine that one is in Old Vienna one is likely to become quite upset when one realizes that in Old Vienna there is no sale at Charles Jourdan.* And that is why when I walk down Fifth Avenue I want to hear traffic.

### 4. Music in the Movies

I'm not talking about musicals. Musicals are movies that warn you by saying, "Lots of music here. Take it or leave it." I'm talking about regular

---

*Charles Jourdan:* an international chain of stores selling high-end shoes, with two locations in New York City.

movies that extend no such courtesy but allow unsuspecting people to come to see them and then assault them with a barrage of unasked-for tunes. There are two major offenders in this category: black movies and movies set in the fifties. Both types of movies are afflicted with the same misconception. They don't know that movies are supposed to be movies. They think that movies are supposed to be records with pictures. They have failed to understand that if God had wanted records to have pictures, he would not have invented television.

### 5. Music in Public Places Such as Restaurants, Supermarkets, Hotel Lobbies, Airports, Etc.

When I am in any of the above-mentioned places I am not there to hear music. I am there for whatever reason is appropriate to the respective place. I am no more interested in hearing "Mack the Knife" while waiting for the Shuttle to Boston than someone sitting ringside at the Sands Hotel is interested in being forced to choose between sixteen varieties of cottage cheese. If God had meant for everything to happen at once, he would not have invented desk calendars.

### Epilogue

Some people talk to themselves. Some people sing to themselves. Is one group better than the other? Did not God create all people equal? Yes, God created all people equal. Only to some he gave the ability to make up their own words.

---

### Vocabulary

The following terms are identified by paragraph number. Make sure that you understand each term's meaning in its context. If you're not sure that you understand a term, look it up in a college-level dictionary.

| | | |
|---|---|---|
| incessant (1) | malignant (6) | barrage (7) |
| unbeknownst (4) | disorienting (6) | |

## Style and Strategy

1. What are Lebowitz's purpose and thesis?

2. What is Lebowitz's tone? How might she have changed her tone if she had had a different purpose?

3. In the first three paragraphs, Lebowitz *personifies* music—in other words, she treats it as a living thing, with motives and responsibilities. Why do you think she uses personification in this way?

4. Lebowitz uses six subheads—five to indicate her classification scheme and one for her conclusion. Subheads are features normally found in technical documents, not personal essays. Why do you think Lebowitz uses this device?

5. What purpose do the author's frequent references to God serve?

## Questions for Critical Thinking and Discussion

1. We do indeed live in a noisy and obtrusive world. Unwanted music, intrusive advertising, and rude people often combine to assault our peace of mind. What can a person do to insulate himself or herself against this collective intruder? What are the consequences of this self-insulation?

2. Should personal privacy be protected by law? Possible areas to consider are noise pollution; the availability of personal information, including income, debt, and shopping habits; and unsolicited calls, e-mails, or visits to the home.

## Suggestions for Writing

1. Lebowitz classifies "bad" music. Write a 500- to 750-word essay in which you classify "good" music.

2. In a 500- to 750-word essay, classify any artistic or entertainment form unrelated to music. For example, you might classify the kinds of movies popular in contemporary cinema. You might classify various works now being produced by science fiction writers. You might even discuss a recent television genre.

3. What type of music do you listen to? Write an essay of 500 to 750 words in which you discuss the various subgroups of a particular type of music. For example, if you enjoy rock music, you might include soft rock, classic rock, punk rock, and New Wave. Your purpose is to show that the genre you have picked is quite varied. Therefore, as your thesis, you might write the following: "Although many think of classical as the kind of music heard in symphony halls, this form is actually quite varied."

## Speaking Assignment

What kinds of things cross the boundary into your private space on a regular basis? In a short presentation, classify the sounds, the activities, the people, or any other type of unwanted intrusion that violates your privacy or serves to distract you. (For more help with oral presentations, see Chapter 18.)

# Three Types of Resistance to Oppression

## MARTIN LUTHER KING, JR.

*The American civil rights movement has had many leaders from the 1950s through today, but Martin Luther King, Jr. (1929–1968), was its leader at the most crucial times, from the Alabama sit-ins and boycotts of the 1950s through the national movement of the 1960s. In 1968, King was murdered by white assassin James Earl Ray in Memphis.*

*King believed in civil disobedience—nonviolent protest against legal inequities. However, many people in the civil rights movement believed that a more forceful response was needed to "shake things up." In the following essay, first published as part of his book* Stride Toward Freedom *(1958), note the delicate balancing act that King is able to achieve in renouncing violence but also decrying acquiescence.*

Oppressed people deal with their oppression in three characteristic ways. One way is acquiescence: the oppressed resign themselves to their doom. They tacitly adjust themselves to oppression, and thereby become conditioned to it. In every movement toward freedom some of the oppressed prefer to remain oppressed. Almost 2,800 years ago Moses set out to lead the children of Israel from the slavery of Egypt to the freedom of the promised land. He soon discovered that slaves do not always welcome their deliverers. They become accustomed to being slaves. They would rather bear those ills they have, as Shakespeare pointed out, than flee to others that they know not of. They prefer the "fleshpots of Egypt" to the ordeals of emancipation. 1

There is such a thing as the freedom of exhaustion. Some people are so worn down by the yoke of oppression that they give up. A few years ago in the slum areas of Atlanta, a Negro guitarist used to sing almost daily: "Been down so long that down don't bother me." This is the type of negative freedom and resignation that often engulfs the life of the oppressed. 2

But this is not the way out. To accept passively an unjust system is to cooperate with that system; thereby the oppressed become as evil as the oppressor. Noncooperation with evil is as much a moral obligation as is cooperation with good. The oppressed must never allow the conscience of the oppressor to slumber. Religion reminds every man that he is his brother's keeper. To accept injustice or segregation passively is to say to the oppressor that his actions are morally right. It is a way of allowing his conscience to fall asleep. At this moment the oppressed fails to be his brother's keeper. So acquiescence—while often the easier way—is not the moral way. It is the way of the coward. The Negro cannot win the respect of his oppressor by acquiescing; he merely increases the oppressor's arrogance and contempt. Acquiescence is interpreted as proof of the Negro's inferiority. The Negro cannot win the respect of the white people of the South or the peoples of the world if he is willing to sell the future of his children for his personal and immediate comfort and safety. 3

A second way that oppressed people sometimes deal with oppression is to resort to physical violence and corroding hatred. Violence often brings about momentary results. Nations have frequently won their independence in battle. But in spite of temporary victories, violence never brings permanent peace. It solves no social problem; it merely creates new and more complicated ones. 4

Violence as a way of achieving racial justice is both impractical and immoral. It is impractical because it is a descending spiral ending in destruction for all. The old law of an eye for an eye leaves everybody blind. It is immoral because it seeks to humiliate the opponent rather than win his understanding; it seeks to annihilate rather than to con- 5 vert. Violence is immoral because it thrives on hatred rather than love. It destroys community and makes brotherhood impossible. It leaves society in monologue rather than dialogue. Violence ends by defeating itself. It creates bitterness in the survivors and brutality in the destroyers. A voice echoes through time saying to every potential Peter, "Put up your sword." History is cluttered with the wreckage of nations that failed to follow this command.

If the American Negro and other victims of oppression succumb to the temptation of using violence in the struggle for freedom, future generations will be the recipients of a desolate night of bitterness, and our chief legacy to them will be an endless reign of meaningless chaos. Violence is not the way. 6

The third way open to oppressed people in their quest for freedom is the way of nonviolent resistance. Like the synthesis in Hegelian philosophy, the principle of nonviolent resistance seeks to reconcile the truths of two opposites—acquiescence and violence—while avoiding the extremes and immoralities of both. The nonviolent resister agrees with the person who acquiesces that one should not be physically aggressive toward his opponent; but he balances the equation by agreeing with the person of violence that evil must be resisted. He avoids the nonresistance of the former and the violent resistance of the latter. With nonviolent resistance, no individual or group need 7

submit to any wrong, nor need anyone resort to violence in order to right a wrong.

It seems to me that this is the method that must guide the actions of the Negro in the present crisis in race relations. Through nonviolent resistance the Negro will be able to rise to the noble height of opposing the unjust system while loving the perpetrators of the system. The Negro must work passionately and unrelentingly for full stature as a citizen, but he must not use inferior methods to gain it. He must never come to terms with falsehood, malice, hate, or destruction. 8

Nonviolent resistance makes it possible for the Negro to remain in the South and struggle for his rights. The Negro's problem will not be solved by running away. He cannot listen to the glib suggestion of those who would urge him to migrate en masse to other sections of the country. By grasping his great opportunity in the South he can make a lasting contribution to the moral strength of the nation and set a sublime example of courage for generations yet unborn. 9

By nonviolent resistance, the Negro can also enlist all men of good will in his struggle for equality. The problem is not a purely racial one, with Negroes set against whites. In the end, it is not a struggle between people at all, but a tension between justice and injustice. Nonviolent resistance is not aimed against oppressors but against oppression. Under its banner, consciences, not racial groups, are enlisted. 10

*Vocabulary*

The following terms are identified by paragraph number. Make sure that you understand each term's meaning in its context. If you're not sure that you understand a term, look it up in a college-level dictionary.

| | | |
|---|---|---|
| acquiescence (1) | yoke (2) | synthesis (7) |
| tacitly (1) | corroding (4) | glib (9) |
| fleshpot (1) | momentary (4) | sublime (9) |
| emancipation (1) | annihilate (5) | |

### Style and Strategy

1.  King was a Baptist minister and a great public speaker. Note that he uses one of the elements of a spoken sermon: repetition. What is the effect of this rhetorical device?

2.  Each type of resistance is discussed in a group of three paragraphs. What does each paragraph in each group accomplish? See paragraphs 1–3, 4–6, and 7–9.

3.  Read King's conclusion once more (paragraph 10). Is his contrasting device ("it's not this; it's that") effective? Is King summarizing here, or is he evaluating the points made in his essay?

### Questions for Critical Thinking and Discussion

1.  King preached patience; Malcolm X (see his essay on pages 248–250) preached direct action. Is violence ever acceptable as a device to effect social change?

2.  In your daily life, do racial issues play a large role? Is the way that you see the world affected in any way by discrimination because of race, color, religion, or ethnic origin? If so, how have you responded?

3.  Comment on the following statement: "The greatest social development in the United States in the last forty years has been the rise of the black middle class." Do you agree? Why or why not?

### Suggestions for Writing

1.  In a 500- to 750-word essay, classify the ways that you could respond to a police officer if you were pulled over in a traffic stop.

2.  King advocates nonviolent resistance as the best way to secure human rights. Think about a government polity or practice (local, state, or national) that you want to see rescinded or abolished. In an essay of 500 to 750 words, explain the kinds of nonviolent methods that you and those who agree with you might use to accomplish your goal.

3.  Think back to an altercation you were involved in that resulted in violence—whether verbal or physical—or that simply ended in a way that you now regret. Write a 500- to 750-word essay in which you explain what happened. In addition, discuss several ways in which the problem might have been resolved more amicably.

### Speaking Assignment

Develop an oral presentation in which you discuss major events in Dr. King's life to demonstrate his effect on the advancement of human rights. You may have to complete some Internet or library research for this assignment. (For more help with oral presentations, see Chapter 18.)

# Notes on Class

## PAUL FUSSELL

*Paul Fussell, the Donald T. Regan Professor Emeritus of English at the University of Pennsylvania and noted scholar of eighteenth-century British literature, is well known for his accomplishments in a variety of areas. As an officer in World War II, he was twice wounded and won the Bronze Star and the Purple Heart. He has published thirteen books: on literature, especially poetry; on his wartime experiences; on travel; and on social class. His study of World War I and its surrounding literature,* The Great War and Modern Memory *(1976), won the National Book Award.*

*Fussell has also studied modern behavior and social expectations. His essays and books on class structure, vulgarity, and modern expressions of personal taste are pungent, biting examinations of the way we live. "Notes on Class," adapted from* The Boy Scout Handbook and Other Observations *(1982), examines a "dirty little secret": our obsession with social class status.*

If the dirty little secret used to be sex, now it is the facts about social class. No subject today is more likely to offend. Over thirty years ago Dr. Kinsey generated considerable alarm by disclosing that despite appearances one-quarter of the male population had enjoyed at least one homosexual orgasm. A similar alarm can be occasioned today by asserting that despite the much-discussed mechanism of "social mobility" and the constant redistribution of income in this country, it is virtually impossible to break out of the social class in which one has been nurtured. Bad news for the ambitious as well as the bogus, but there it is.

Defining class is difficult, as sociologists and anthropologists have learned. The more data we feed into the machines, the less likely it is that significant formulations will emerge. What follows here is based not on interviews, questionnaires, or any kind of quantitative technique but on perhaps a more trustworthy method—perception. Theory may inform us that there are three classes in America, high, middle, and low. Perception will tell us that there are at least nine, which I would designate and arrange like this:

> Top Out-of-Sight
> Upper
> Upper Middle
>
> ────────────────
>
> Middle
> High-Proletarian
> Mid-Proletarian
> Low-Proletarian
>
> ────────────────
>
> Destitute
> Bottom Out-of-Sight

In addition, there is a floating class with no permanent location in this hierarchy. We can call it Class X. It consists of well-to-do hippies, "artists," "writers" (who write nothing), floating bohemians, politicians out of office, disgraced athletic coaches, residers abroad, rock stars, "celebrities," and the shrewder sort of spies.

The quasi-official division of the population into three economic classes called high-, middle-, and low-income groups rather misses the point, because as a class indicator the amount of money is not as important as the source. Important distinctions at both the top and bottom of the class scale arise less from degree of affluence than from the people or institutions to whom one is beholden for support. For example, the main thing distinguishing the top three classes from each other is the amount of money inherited in relation to the amount currently earned. The Top Out-of-Sight Class (Rockefellers, du Ponts, Mellons, Fords,

Whitneys) lives on inherited capital entirely. Its money is like the hats of the Boston ladies who, asked where they got them, answer, "Oh, we *have* our hats." No one whose money, no matter how ample, comes from his own work, like film stars, can be a member of the Top Out-of-Sights, even if the size of his income and the extravagance of his expenditure permit him temporary social access to it.

Since we expect extremes to meet, we are not surprised to find the very lowest class, Bottom Out-of-Sight, similar to the highest in one crucial respect: it is given its money and kept sort of afloat not by its own efforts but by the welfare machinery or the prison system. Members of the Top Out-of-Sight Class sometimes earn some money, as directors or board members of philanthropic or even profitable enterprises, but the amount earned is laughable in relation to the amount already possessed. Membership in the Top Out-of-Sight Class depends on the ability to flourish without working at all, and it is this that suggests a curious brotherhood between those at the top and the bottom of the scale.

It is this also that distinguishes the Upper Class from its betters. It lives on both inherited money and a salary from attractive, if usually slight, work, without which, even if it could survive and even flourish, it would feel bored and a little ashamed. The next class down, the Upper Middle, may possess virtually as much as the two above it. The difference is that it has earned most of it, in law, medicine, oil, real-estate, or even the more honorific forms of trade. The Upper Middles are afflicted with a bourgeois sense of shame, a conviction that to live on the earnings of others, even forebears, is not entirely nice.

The Out-of-Sight Classes at top and bottom have something else in common: they are literally all but invisible (hence their name). The façades of Top Out-of-Sight houses are never seen from the street, and such residences (like Rockefeller's upstate New York premises) are often hidden away deep in the hills, safe from envy and its ultimate attendants, confiscatory taxation and finally expropriation. The Bottom Out-of-Sight Class is equally invisible. When not hidden away in institutions or claustrated in monasteries, lamaseries, or communes, it is hiding from creditors, deceived bail-bondsmen, and merchants intent on repossessing cars and furniture. (This class is visible briefly in one place, in the spring on the streets of New York City, but after this ritual yearly show of itself it disappears again.) When you pass a house with a would-be impressive façade addressing the street, you know it is occupied by a mere member of the Upper or Upper Middle Class. The White House is an example. Its residents, even on those occasions when they are Kennedys, can never be classified as Top Out-of-Sight but only Upper Class. The house is simply too conspicuous, and temporary residence there usually constitutes a come-down for most of its occupants. It is a hopelessly Upper- or Upper-Middle-Class place.

Another feature of both Top and Bottom Out-of-Sight Classes is their anxiety to keep their names out of the papers, and this too suggests that socially the President is always rather vulgar. All the classes in between Top and Bottom Out-of-Sight slaver for personal publicity (monograms on shirts, inscribing one's name on lawn-mowers and power tools, etc.), and it is this lust to be known almost as much as income that distinguishes them from their Top and Bottom neighbors. The High- and Mid-Prole Classes can be recognized immediately by their pride in advertising their physical presence, a way of saying, "Look! We pay our bills and have a known place in the community, and you can find us there any time." Thus hypertrophied house-numbers on the front, or house numbers written "Two Hundred Five" ("Two Hundred and Five" is worse) instead of 205, or flamboyant house or family names blazoned on façades, like "The Willows" or "The Polnickis."

(If you go behind the façade into the house itself, you will find a fairly trustworthy class indicator in the kind of wood visible there. The top three classes invariably go in for hardwoods for doors and panelling; the Middle and High-Prole Classes, pine, either plain or "knotty." The knotty-pine "den" is an absolute stigma of the Middle Class, one never to be overcome or disguised by temporarily affected higher usages. Below knotty pine there is plywood.)

9    Façade study is a badly neglected anthropological field. As we work down from the (largely white-painted) bank-like façades of the Upper and Upper Middle Classes, we encounter such Middle and Prole conventions as these, which I rank in order of social status:

*Middle*    1. A potted tree on either side of the front door, and the more pointy and symmetrical the better.

2. A large rectangular picture-window in a split-level "ranch" house, displaying a table-lamp between two side curtains. The cellophane on the lampshade must be visibly inviolate.

3. Two chairs, usually metal with pipe arms, disposed on the front porch as a "conversation group," in stubborn defiance of the traffic thundering past.

*High-Prole*  4. Religious shrines in the garden, which if small and understated, are slightly higher class than

*Mid-Prole*  5. Plaster gnomes and flamingos, and blue or lavender shiny spheres supported by fluted cast-concrete pedestals.

*Low-Prole*  6. Defunct truck tires painted white and enclosing flower beds. (Auto tires are a grade higher.)

7. Flower-bed designs worked in dead light bulbs or the butts of disused beer bottles.

The Destitute have no façades to decorate, and of course the Bottom Out-of-Sights, being invisible, have none either, although both these classes can occasionally help others decorate theirs—painting tires white on an hourly basis, for example, or even watering and fertilizing the potted trees of the Middle Class. Class X also does not decorate its façades, hoping to stay loose and unidentifiable, ready to re-locate and shape-change the moment it sees that its cover has been penetrated.

10    In this list of façade conventions an important principle emerges. Organic materials have higher status than metal or plastic. We should take warning from Sophie Portnoy's aluminum venetian blinds, which are also lower than wood because the slats are curved, as if "improved," instead of classically flat. The same principle applies, as *The Preppy Handbook** has shown so effectively, to clothing fabrics, which must be cotton or wool, never Dacron or anything of that prole kind. In the same way, yachts with wood hulls, because they must be repaired or replaced (at high cost) more often, are classier than yachts with fiberglass hulls, no matter how shrewdly merchandised. Plastic hulls are cheaper and more practical, which is precisely why they lack class.

11    As we move down the scale, income of course decreases, but income is less important to class than other seldom-invoked measurements: for example, the degree to which one's work is supervised by an omnipresent immediate superior. The more free from supervision, the higher the class, which is why a dentist ranks higher than a mechanic working under a foreman in a large auto shop, even if he makes considerably more money than the dentist. The two trades may be thought equally dirty: it is the dentist's freedom from supervision that helps confer class upon him. Likewise, a high-school teacher obliged to file weekly "lesson plans" with a principal or "curriculum

---

**The Official Preppy Handbook:* a book by Lisa Birnbach, published in 1980, that satirically explains the typical "preppy," or upper-class, lifestyle.

co-ordinator" thereby occupies a class position lower than a tenured professor, who reports to no one, even though the high-school teacher may be richer, smarter, and nicer. (Supervisors and Inspectors are titles that go with public schools, post offices, and police departments: the student of class will need to know no more.) It is largely because they must report that even the highest members of the naval and military services lack social status: they all have designated supervisors—even the Chairman of the Joint Chiefs of Staff has to report to the President.

Class is thus defined less by bare income than 12 by constraints and insecurities. It is defined also by habits and attitudes. Take television watching. The Top Out-of-Sight Class doesn't watch at all. It owns the companies and pays others to monitor the thing. It is also entirely devoid of intellectual or even emotional curiosity: it *has* its ideas the way it has its money. The Upper Class does look at television but it prefers Camp offerings, like the films of Jean Harlow or Jon Hall. The Upper Middle Class regards TV as vulgar except for the highminded emissions of National Educational Television, which it watches avidly, especially when, like the Shakespeare series, they are the most incompetently directed and boring. Upper Middles make a point of forbidding children to watch more than an hour a day and worry a lot about violence in society and sugar in cereal. The Middle Class watches, preferring the more "beautiful" kinds of non-body-contact sports like tennis or gymnastics or figure-skating (the music is a redeeming feature here). With High-, Mid-, and Low-Proles we find heavy viewing of the soaps in the daytime and rugged body-contact sports (football, hockey, boxing) in the evening. The lower one is located in the Prole classes the more likely one is to watch "Bowling for Dollars" and "Wonder Woman" and "The Hulk" and when choosing a game show to prefer "Joker's Wild" to "The Family Feud," whose jokes are sometimes incomprehensible. Destitutes and Bottom Out-of-Sights have in common a problem involving choice. Destitutes usually "own" about three color sets, and the problem is which three programs to run at once. Bottom Out-of-Sights exercise no choice at all, the decisions being made for them by correctional or institutional personnel.

The time when the evening meal is consumed 13 defines class better than, say, the presence or absence on the table of ketchup bottles and ashtrays shaped like little toilets enjoining the diners to "Put Your Butts Here." Destitutes and Bottom Out-of-Sights eat dinner at 5:30, for the Prole staff on which they depend must clean up and be out roller-skating or bowling early in the evening. Thus Proles eat at 6:00 or 6:30. The Middles eat at 7:00, the Upper Middles at 7:30 or, if very ambitious, at 8:00. The Uppers and Top Out-of-Sights dine at 8:30 or 9:00 or even later, after nightly protracted "cocktail" sessions lasting usually around two hours. Sometimes they forget to eat at all.

Similarly, the physical appearance of the vari- 14 ous classes defines them fairly accurately. Among the top four classes thin is good, and the bottom two classes appear to ape this usage, although down there thin is seldom a matter of choice. It is the three Prole classes that tend to fat, partly as a result of their use of convenience foods and plenty of beer. These are the classes too where anxiety about slipping down a rung causes nervous overeating, resulting in fat that can be rationalized as advertising the security of steady wages and the ability to "eat out" often. Even "Going Out for Breakfast" is not unthinkable for Proles, if we are to believe that they respond to the McDonald's TV ads as they're supposed to. A recent magazine ad for a diet book aimed at Proles stigmatizes a number of erroneous assumptions about body weight, proclaiming with some inelegance that "They're all a crock." Among such vulgar errors is the proposition that "All Social Classes Are Equally Overweight." This the ad rejects by noting quite accurately:

Your weight is an advertisement of your social standing. A century ago, corpulence was a sign of success. But no more. Today it is the badge of the lower-middle-class, where obesity is *four times* more prevalent than it is among the upper-middle and middle classes.

It is not just four times more prevalent. It is at least four times more visible, as any observer can testify who has witnessed Prole women perambulating shopping malls in their bright, very tight jersey trousers. Not just obesity but the flaunting of obesity is the Prole sign, as if the object were to give maximum aesthetic offense to the higher classes and thus achieve a form of revenge.

Another physical feature with powerful class 15 meaning is the wearing of plaster casts on legs and ankles by members of the top three classes. These casts, a sort of white badge of honor, betoken stylish mishaps with frivolous but costly toys like horses, skis, snowmobiles, and mopeds. They signify a high level of conspicuous waste in a social world where questions of unpayable medical bills or missed working days do not apply. But in the matter of clothes, the Top Out-of-Sight is different from both Upper and Upper Middle Classes. It prefers to appear in new clothes, whereas the class just below it prefers old clothes. Likewise, all three Prole classes make much of new garments, with the highest possible polyester content. The question does not arise in the same form with Destitutes and Bottom Out-of-Sights. They wear used clothes, the thrift shop and prison supply room serving as their Bonwit's and Korvette's.

This American class system is very hard for for- 16 eigners to master, partly because most foreigners imagine that since America was founded by the British it must retain something of British institutions. But our class system is more subtle than the British, more a matter of gradations than of blunt divisions, like the binary distinction between a gentleman and a cad. This seems to lack plausibility here. One seldom encounters in the United States the sort of absolute prohibitions which (half-comically, to be sure) one is asked to believe define the gentleman in England. Like these:

> A gentleman never wears brown shoes in
>    the city, or
> A gentleman never wears a green suit, or
> A gentleman never has soup at lunch, or
> A gentleman never uses a comb, or
> A gentleman never smells of anything but
>    tar, or
> "No gentleman can fail to admire Bellini"
> —W. H. Auden.

In America it seems to matter much less the way you present yourself—green, brown, neat, sloppy, scented—than what your backing is—that is, where your money comes from. What the upper orders display here is no special uniform but the kind of psychological security they derive from knowing that others recognize their freedom from petty anxieties and trivial prohibitions.

## Vocabulary

The following terms are identified by paragraph number. Make sure that you understand each term's meaning in its context. If you're not sure that you understand a term, look it up in a college-level dictionary.

| | | |
|---|---|---|
| formulations (2) | confiscatory (6) | protracted (13) |
| proletarian (2) | expropriation (6) | inelegance (14) |
| hierarchy (2) | lamaseries (6) | corpulence (14) |

| quasi-official (3) | façade (6) | prevalent (14) |
| affluence (3) | slaver (7) | perambulating (14) |
| beholden (3) | hypertrophied (7) | aesthetic (14) |
| philanthropic (4) | blazoned (7) | gradations (16) |
| honorific (5) | stigma (8) | cad (16) |
| bourgeois (5) | inviolate (9) | plausibility (16) |
| forebears (5) | highminded (12) | prohibitions (16) |

## Style and Strategy

1. What is Fussell's purpose in writing this essay? Would you guess that Fussell likes his fellow humans, or not?

2. What is the tone of this essay, and how does Fussell's word choice contribute to it?

3. Fussell points out that the traditional three-way categorization of American social class is flawed; he then proceeds to identify nine social classes along with a "floating" class. Which two groups does he compare? How does this comparison add to the essay?

4. Fussell analyzes his nine (plus one) groups in terms of a number of defining attributes. What are these attributes?

5. How has Fussell organized his presentation of the categories? What other organization might he have used?

## Questions for Critical Thinking and Discussion

1. *Snobbery* can be defined as the disparagement of those who are perceived to have a lower status in society. When and where have you experienced snobbery? How did you deal with it?

2. Comment on this statement: "In the past, American society was striated by race. Today, race is less of an issue, and class has become the deciding factor. The average middle-class white family, given the choice of living next door to a poor white family or a middle-class black family, will choose the black family. They share more values." Do you agree? Why or why not?

3. How would you define *poor people*? In your experience, are the poor generally seen as unfortunate victims of circumstance or as unworthy? How do society's assumptions affect the lives and prospects of the poor?

## Suggestions for Writing

1. Many people live lives that could place them into more than one of Fussell's categories. In other words, one could be a self-employed dentist (high status) who eats supper every evening at 5:00 (low status), watches almost no television (high status) but is forty pounds overweight (low status). Write a 500- to 750-word essay in which you explain how your life—or that of someone you know—compares to Fussell's classification.

2. Consider your extended family. Write a 500- to 750-word essay in which you categorize the members of your family according to social class.

3. Write an essay of at least 500 words in which you paraphrase Fussell's explanation of the class system. However, define each class in your own way, and use your own appropriate examples to explain it.

4. In paragraph 1, Fussell argues that "it is virtually impossible to break out of the social class in which one has been nurtured." Do you agree? If not, write a 500- to 750-word essay that discusses three or four examples of people who have broken out of the social class in which they were raised. Choose examples from people you know personally or from those you have read about. Spend the bulk of your time on people who have risen in the social ranks. However, also consider writing about someone who fell from a higher into a lower class. If appropriate, use library or Internet research in this paper.

### Speaking Assignment

In an oral presentation, take issue with Fussell's definition of one of the social classes discussed in this essay. Reference the text closely. (For more help with oral presentations, see Chapter 18.)

**CATALYST 2.0**

**MORE OPTIONS ONLINE**
If you would like to read additional classification essays, go to www.mhhe.com/writingtoday.

# WRITING THE CLASSIFICATION ESSAY WITH A READER'S EYE

At first glance, classification may seem like a dry, almost boring rhetorical option. However, we have found over the years that some of our favorite essays are classifications. The choices that you make in planning and drafting your essay will largely determine your reader's response, so exploit your opportunity.

## Issues to Keep in Mind

In this section, we explore three important topics that you need to think about as you write and revise a classification essay:

1. The method you use to identify a category within a paragraph or section
2. Your purpose for writing a classification essay
3. Your language level

### Methods of Explaining Categories

Let's assume that you are classifying teaching styles and are drawing on your own experience to develop the categories. In effect, you are classifying the instructors and teachers whom you've experienced over the years. You find that they fall into three basic groups: the lecturer, the mixer, and the time server. Note that you need to define each type as you introduce it, as in the following paragraph:

The lecturer does just what the label indicates: lectures, usually from notes. The best of this type is a highly efficient purveyor of information. Teaching a class that won't quite fit into a semester, he or she will cover ground swiftly and effectively. However, this person is a rarity. Most instructors who use the lecture method will cause the class members to be torn between the need to take notes and a desperate desire to fall asleep. An example is my current history instructor (who shall remain nameless). I've always found history to be an exciting, lively subject, full of surprises, but Dr. Lecture seems intent on squeezing the life out of it for me and whoever else in my class seems interested in the subject.

This paragraph first defines the type—*lecturer* can have multiple meanings, and the speaker clearly wants to differentiate between effective and ineffective lecturers—then develops the classification by including an example, his history professor. Would more than one example have worked? Of course it would have, within the boundaries of what a paragraph can hold. Note how the writer uses a different internal strategy, narration, to develop the next paragraph:

The opposite of the lecturer is the mixer, the sort of person who can work a room at a party. This person probably also has a side job selling Tupperware or Mary Kay. Involvement means everything to this dynamo. The class members are virtually forced to participate because of the barrage of questions and mandatory discussion groups. My psychology professor is an example of this type. Although, on the whole, she is a very effective instructor, she finds psychology to be the most important field of study conceived in human history, and she is amazed when she encounters a student who doesn't share that belief. (She must live in a perpetual state of amazement.) This attitude *does* help involve the student and make class time fly by; however, some days it's just a bit much. Last Monday, for example, one of my "colleagues" fell asleep during class. From the looks of him, he had been out a bit late the night before. Dr. Dynamo tried speaking to him to rouse him from his slumbers; when that failed, she walked over and prodded him, as if he were a

drunk who had fallen asleep on her front porch. He woke up
(briefly), stared at her, and said, "Give it a rest, will ya?" Dr.
Dynamo was crushed. I sympathized with her on one level, but some
days most students in the class find her a bit hard to take.

First, note the skillful transition used to open the paragraph: "The opposite
of. . . ." Then the writer uses a definition strategy similar to the one that he
employed in his previous body paragraph: he provides a few key details that
describe the type of teacher. But after the middle of the paragraph, he switches
to a narrative strategy, using an anecdote to illustrate what can annoy students
about "Dr. Dynamo's" teaching style. In his final body paragraph, the writer
uses yet another development strategy:

Time must pass by slowly for those who have grown sick of teaching. You can spot these people a mile away. They have a slightly
glazed look to them, a little distracted, as if they were mildly
drugged, which is a distinct possibility. I'm not talking about professors a few years away from retirement; I'm talking about those who
are clearly sick of what they're doing. If you get close enough to
them to look at their lecture notes, these pages will be yellow around
the edges. My feeling is that these individuals are to be pitied, not
scorned. They are not like Ms. Krebabble of *The Simpsons*, a contemptible and contemptuous functionary who couldn't care less
about her profession. No, these folks have burned out on their career
and are careening toward something else. I feel sorry for them.

In the second half of this paragraph, the writer uses contrast to explain what
these people are *not*. This isn't a strategy that works in all situations, but it is
effective in certain contexts.

As you can see from these examples, you can use definition, description,
narration, exemplification, and/or comparison/contrast to explain your categories. You could also use causal or process analysis, depending on your topic
and your purpose for writing.

### Informative Classification Versus Personal Classification

The example paragraphs we have been discussing are based on one writer's
personal experience. Another student who chooses the same topic will likely
come up with different categories in which to group his or her instructors.
These paragraphs also show that the writer knows how to "externalize" his
experiences by explaining his categories so that his audience can understand—and be entertained by—his point of view about instructors. However,

some assignments will ask you to take a more objective approach to your subjects. In these situations, your purpose will be to inform.

Note that these two types of classification essays aren't complete opposites. The personal essay also informs, and the informative essay gains nothing by being dry and boring. But the audience for an informative classification essay has different expectations—the readers assume that the writer knows more about the subject than they do. During the prewriting stage, then, the writer needs to spend more time thinking about the needs of his or her readers:

1. How much can the reader be expected to know about this subject?

2. Will I need to define certain terms? If so, what is the best way to do so?

For example, in the excerpts from an essay that appears on pages 362–363, the writer is discussing a subject—types of turtles—that most readers will know very little about. Note how each paragraph includes information that the reader needs in order to understand the essay.

### *Language Level*

Self-conscious, artificially formal language is never appropriate; however, many students are tempted to use such language when they write a classification essay, as in the following example:

> To classify breakfast foods is a matter of finding adequate categories.
>
> Logical division indicates that nutrition value, time of preparation, and
>
> tastiness must be considered. Therefore, in this paper I will classify break-
>
> fast foods in the following three categories: foods that are nutritious,
>
> foods that take little time to prepare, and foods that taste good.

We don't want to read the rest of this essay. The language alone is enough to repel us. Also, note that the categories are hazy and that they overlap (a breakfast food could be nutritious, easy to prepare, and tasty at the same time). Use concrete language and active verbs to describe your categories. Also, make sure that your categories are clearly distinct from one another.

## Choosing a Topic

When writing a classification essay, you first need to decide whether you will be writing an essay that is primarily informative or primarily personal:

1. If you choose to write an *informative classification,* you are probably thinking of a topic with which you are already familiar. Your purpose will be to explain this topic to your reader so that he or she will gain a better understanding of the subject. However, consider the following two issues:
   - Although you know the subject matter quite well, you should still consider doing some online and library research to look for new ideas and information. For more information on research and on writing documented essays, see chapters 20 and 21.

**CATALYST 2.0**

**MORE OPTIONS ONLINE**
For more help with problem areas in the classification essay, go to
www.mhhe.com/
writingtoday.

- Consider your audience and your purpose as you think about a topic for an informational classification. We have read many classification essays that were technically proficient but on subjects that didn't need to be explored by using classification—such as "types of socks." The students who wrote these papers obviously thought that they had fulfilled the assignment, but the writer never established a reason for the reader to be interested in these very tedious essays.

2. If you choose to write a primarily *personal classification,* remember that in this context, *personal* doesn't mean "private." Think of your audience. Is the subject that you are choosing going to be one that you can develop to the point that your reader will be thoroughly engaged, or is this an essay that will best be appreciated by the person who has written it?

## Prewriting

Once you have chosen your topic, use one of the informal prewriting strategies to generate ideas: listing, freewriting, brainstorming, or clustering. (See Chapter 2 for more on these strategies.) Consider using two steps. First, you could brainstorm the categories that you will use. Then you could use a prewriting strategy for each category to develop definitions, differences between categories, and examples.

At this point, see if you can develop a working or preliminary thesis. If you can do so, you are now ready to organize your prewriting.

## Organizing

After you have generated your categories and a sufficient number of examples and developed your working thesis, the best way for you to organize this raw material is to arrange it into an outline. (Chapter 2 covers informal, sentence, and formal outline structures.) As you work on your outline, think about how a body paragraph in a classification essay typically works:

1. General (names the category)

   to

2. More specific (defines and/or explains the category)

   to

3. Even more specific (gives examples of items within the category along with specific information about some of the items)

As well, make sure that you consider the most effective order for your body paragraphs. The normal order is **emphatic,** with the most interesting or complexly developed body paragraph coming last, just before the conclusion.

## Drafting

To illustrate one approach to writing a classification essay, we have included the essay "The Last Dinosaurs."

## The Introduction

When writing a classification essay, some students write an introduction that is little more than an expanded thesis statement. Remember that an essay's introduction must first establish the essay's *context;* this way, the reader understands the general subject matter and the reasons that the writer has decided to explore it—in this case, by dividing it into separate yet approachable categories. You also need to spark your reader's interest.

Remember also that you don't have to write your introduction first. The writer of our essay in progress wrote this introduction after producing the body of his essay:

Choose an approach that allows you to convey the context and background in a lively way. (See Chapter 3 for ways to introduce an essay.) You need to introduce your topic sufficiently; otherwise, your reader will not understand why you are using classification.

*• Consider Your Options*

### The Last Dinosaurs

When people think of turtles, they probably visualize a generic version of this large family of reptiles. Turtles are part of our collective consciousness: children are fascinated by them, and most adults seem to retain a fondness for these creatures. However, there are three very different types of turtles, and the distinctions among them are both illuminating and interesting. **Turtles, terrapins, and tortoises are the three main groups that make up the order <u>Testudinata</u>.**

The writer has used a straightforward thesis statement that indicates the three categories and the order in which he will explain them in the body of the essay.

## The Body

The writer has mentioned three types—or categories—of turtles in the introduction. Now he proceeds to develop a paragraph on each category. Notice the development pattern. The first part of each paragraph names the type. Then the writer explains how the type is distinctive from other turtles. Finally, the writer gives specific details to help develop the idea of the paragraph. The pattern used is general, to less general, to specific:

The word <u>turtle</u> is used generically, but the term really applies only to the so-called soft-shell turtles. Most people have never seen one and would be surprised at their appearance. These aquatic reptiles have, as their name suggests, a soft carapace (shell) without the bony plates that form the "armor" common to the other two types. The neck is elongated, and the head is noticeably pointed at the snout. They look quite fierce—because they are. Soft-shells are territorial creatures that will not hesitate to bite an intruder. Swimmers should beware of these aggressive reptiles.

The second group, terrapins, is also found in water. Once again, many people have never seen these or have perhaps seen them only in zoos. These turtles have the bony plates that most of us visualize, and the carapace is very hard. The head is broad, with a rather pugnacious-looking snout. Some terrapins, such as the group made up of snapping turtles, are very aggressive and dangerous. By the time it is fully grown, an alligator snapper may have a head the size of a football; biting off a swimmer's or an angler's finger is no problem for this beast.

The third group, tortoises, is found on dry land, normally in wooded areas. These are what most people think of when the word turtle is mentioned. Tortoises range from a few inches in length to several feet, in the case of the mammoth Galapagos tortoise. Usually, tortoises are not aggressive, and they make fairly good pets. However, a wild tortoise will bite if threatened, inflicting a painful wound on the unwary.

### The Conclusion

Having shown the differences among the three groups, the writer now returns to the features that all turtles have in common:

Turtles are said to be the oldest living dinosaurs, and it is clear that they are winners when it comes to natural selection and evolution. The hard shell protects some turtles, and aggressive fighting abilities protect others. All three types continue to occupy a valuable niche in the world's ecosystem.

> **Consider Your Options**
>
> Don't summarize here; comment instead. The conclusion allows you to reinforce the importance of what you have just written. (For more on strategies for concluding an essay, see Chapter 3.)

> **CATALYST 2.0**
>
> **MORE OPTIONS ONLINE**
> For more help with the step-by-step development of the classification essay, go to www.mhhe.com/writingtoday.

### EXERCISE 11.1

Write an outline of "The Last Dinosaurs." (For help with outlines, see Chapter 2, pages 40–43.) What method has the writer used for organizing the categories? What other method could he have used?

## Revising Your Draft

After you have completed a draft of your classification essay, your next step is to revise it, using your own analysis and comments from classmates or friends.

During peer review, answer the questions on this page about the draft you are reviewing, whether it is yours or another student's.

After reviewing for content, go over your peer reviewers' responses to your essay and then revise for unity, coherence, language level, and tone (see Chapter 4). When you have revised your draft and are basically satisfied with it, read your draft for mechanical and grammatical errors. Concentrate on finding and correcting major sentence errors (fragments, comma splices, fused sentences), errors in pronoun agreement and subject-verb agreement, and spelling.

Now that you have made your corrections, *read your essay one more time* to catch any errors made during revision and find errors missed during your earlier reviews.

### Student Essay

The following essay is Sam Leininger's response to a classification assignment. The final draft is presented first. Then Sam's first draft is presented, with his comments about this draft and what he needed to do in the revision stage.

## Questions for Reviewing a Classification Essay

1 Does the introduction explain the basis for classifying the topic as well as interest the reader? How could it be improved?

2 What is the thesis statement? Has the writer placed it in the best position within the essay? In what ways, if any, could it be improved?

3 Has the writer fulfilled his or her purpose for writing the essay? Is the writer's tone appropriate for this purpose?

4 Does the way that the writer has classified the topic make sense? Point out any obvious categories that have been omitted. Are the categories differentiated, or could two of them be combined?

5 Is the organization effective? Should the categories be presented in a different order?

6 How do the topic sentences introduce each new category, or how do they introduce a new aspect of a previous category? In other words, point out any topic sentences that do not have a clear role in introducing or further defining a category.

7 Is each category fully developed? Where does the writer need to add more detail to make the distinctions between categories clearer?

8 Does the writer use transitions to guide the reader from one category to the next? Where are transitional words or sentences needed?

9 Does the essay have an effective conclusion? How could it be improved?

*Sam's Final Draft*

Fraud Alert

A new brand of retail store has developed over the past several
years. The superstore overwhelms smaller, independent competitors
with its larger inventory, lower prices, and multiple locations. The
chain bookstore is a unique kind of superstore: part store, part library,
part café, it's a place where the emphasis has shifted from selling
books to getting people to visit, apparently. The staff is extremely
nonconfrontational. Most of the time, they won't even acknowledge a
customer's existence. It is the policy of these stores not to pressure
customers, and they usually provide ample tables and sofas. This laid-
back atmosphere has created a new breed of bookstore patron. In
fact, there are specific types of customers at these bookstores, and
they can be easily distinguished by their purpose for being there.

The status-challenged group likes to maintain a high degree of
visibility by simply spending an enormous amount of time in these
stores. These folks are under the impression that merely setting foot
inside a bookstore raises their cultural status. So they grab a few
magazines, or perhaps the *History of* Playboy *Magazine Covers,* find
a comfortable, visible seat, and begin to pore over their selection
with a mock intensity that rivals any politician's. The easiest way to
spot these people is to note the frequency with which they look up
from their books: almost every time someone walks by, they will
stop reading and look up, just in case it's someone they know. One
time, I made eye contact with one of them, and I could swear he
was silently begging me not to expose him for the fake that he is.

The hipsters are also easily recognizable. The patrons of all
those coffee houses that have sprung up in the last few years have
migrated to the bookstores. You can usually find them in the café
section, double latte in hand, or staring lovingly at the shelves in the
poetry section. Some of them may even work at the store. Most of

the hipsters have some sort of backpack or bag, and most wear Birkenstocks, yet every single one of them has a notepad in which they manically scribble poetry, but only when people are watching. If the café tables are in plain view, this is usually where they set up camp. Some of the wealthier hipsters substitute a notebook computer for actual paper, but there's a greater chance that they are playing solitaire than writing poetry.

The worst phenomenon of these stores is the "in-and-outers." These are the people who rush into the store, grab whatever book has been chosen for the best-seller display at the store's entrance, and rush out. Rarely ever seen as more than a blur, these patrons can be observed closely only when the cashier line is backed up. They may blend into the line, but if you notice someone tapping his or her feet and rattling car keys, you may just have spotted the elusive "in-and-outer."

These new kinds of shoppers are almost enough to keep me out of the bookstore. I am embarrassed to be seen at the same store as a hipster, although I must admit that it's fun to watch them scamper when you mention that you just saw an employee stocking some new editions of Jack Kerouac's* books. However, the worst group is the "in-and-outers." Not only do they promote the monopoly that these few big bookstores are developing by grabbing the latest romance, spy, or horror novel that has absolutely no literary value, but they also diminish the country's intellectual level faster than professional wrestling. Soon, even these big bookstores with all their excess capital will start to narrow down their selections, because 100 extra copies of the new Tom Clancy book will sell while that collection of essays on Marxism will probably stay on the shelf for months. So the next time you see one of these bookstore types, take action. Hand a

---

*Jack Kerouac (1922–1969): an icon of the 1950s counterculture, also known as the "Beat Generation," a phrase he coined. His novel *On the Road*, published in 1957, has been highly influential.

hipster a Thomas Pynchon* novel, offer one of the magazine readers a book by Bertrand Russell,** and see if you can steer an in-and-outer to *Jane Eyre* instead of the latest offering from Danielle Steele. You'd be doing your duty for your country.

*Sam's First Draft*

## Fraud Alert

A new brand of retail store has developed over the past five years. The superstore uses its massive volume to overwhelm any smaller, independent competitors with a larger inventory, lower prices, and multiple locations. The bookstore has become a unique entity; part store, part library, part cafe, the emphasis has shifted from selling books to getting people to visit, apparently. The atmosphere creates a new breed of bookstore patrons. In fact, there are many different types of customers at these bookstores.

The Hipsters are easily recognizable. Remember all those coffee houses? Their patrons have transplanted to the bookstores. You can usually find them in the cafe section, double latte in hand, or staring lovingly at the poetry section. Every single one of them has a notepad that they scribble manic poetry into, but only when people are watching. Some of the richer Hipsters substitute a notebook computer for actual paper, but there's a greater chance that the solitaire program is being run than the word processor.

Another group often spends an enormous amount of time in these stores. These folks are under the impression that merely stepping foot inside a bookstore raises their cultural status. So they grab something from the shelf, find a comfortable seat, and begin to pour over their selection with mock intensity. The easiest way to spot

1  I made my thesis stronger by adding the basis of my classification.

2  When I read my draft, I noticed first off that the order of the body paragraphs seemed wrong. I realized that the best approach was to put my categories into the "order of increasing annoyance value," so I switched the first two body paragraphs.

3  I wanted to add more detail, to fill in the picture. For example, I added a fuller description of the status-challenged group.

---

*Thomas Pynchon** (b. 1937): a respected contemporary novelist. His greatest work, *Gravity's Rainbow* (1973), won the National Book Award in 1974.

**Bertrand Russell** (1872–1970): an influential twentieth-century philosopher, who is also remembered for his social and political activism. He was a leader of both the anti-war and the ban-the-bomb movements in Europe. He won the Nobel Prize in Literature in 1950.

these people is the frequency with which they look up from their books: almost every time someone walks by, they will stop reading and look up, just in case it's someone they know.

I needed to tighten the language in the body paragraphs: my first drafts are always more wordy than they need to be.

Although the lingering groups are annoying, the worst phenomenon of these stores is the "in-and-outers." These are the people who rush into the store, grab whatever book has been chosen for the best seller display at the store's entrance, and rush out. The best chance to see these patrons is when the cashier line is backed up. They may blend in, but check for people rattling their car keys, and you may just have spotted the elusive "in-and-outer." 4

These new classes of shoppers are almost enough to keep me out of the bookstore; I am embarrassed to be seen at the same store as a Hipster, although I must admit that it's fun to watch them scamper when you mention that you just saw an employee stocking some new Jack Kerouac books. However, the worst are the "in-and-outers." Not only do they promote the monopoly that these few big bookstores are developing, by grabbing the latest romance, spy, or horror novel that has absolutely no literary value, they are sending the country's intellectual level down faster than professional wrestling. So the next time you see a hipster, hand him or her a Thomas Pynchion novel; smack one of the magazine readers in the face with a Bertrand Russell book, and set up a snare for the "in-and-outer," take them in the back, and just beat them senseless until they've agreed that Danielle Steele is not literature. 5

I changed the ending to make it less shocking and add a final comment.

## EXERCISE 11.2: REVISING

The following is the first draft of a student's classification essay. Working in pairs or in small groups, review this essay. Using the Questions for Reviewing a Classification Essay on page 364, decide what revisions you would suggest. If you have any questions the student needs to consider, write them in the margin or on a separate sheet of paper. If your instructor directs you to, rewrite one or more paragraphs to make them stronger and to eliminate any grammatical or mechanical errors.

*"Bars"*

Bars and taverns are popular spots to relax. Although, there are several different types of bars. In this essay I will classify bars and show that they fall in to 3 main categories, and the reader will have a better understanding of this subject.

The first classification are neighborhood bars, these are also known as taverns. They specialize in providing constant service to working men and retired men. It takes awhile to become welcome here.

Second type are grilles. These are usually franchises, part of the place is a resturent, the rest is a central bar. These places are sometimes trendy.

The third type are my favorite. These are clubs, they are designed for younger costomers. Their is usually a dj, drinks specials an loud music for dancing. Theyre great places to meet women. Some local favorites are: Magma, Club 2009 and the Snake Pit. These places guaranty a classy enviroment by: (1) having a covercharge (2) haveing a strict dresscode (3) security guards. They are hot places to spend an evenning.

I hope the reader now understands better the subject of bars. Know what you want, then find the right place for your needs.

## Additional Writing Topics

1.  Write an essay in which you divide one of the following subjects into its categories:
    a. Infomercials
    b. First dates
    c. Newscasters
    d. Auto repair companies
    e. College support personnel

2.  **Writing on the job.** Think about where you work now or a place where you worked in the past, and write a memo to your manager classifying your customers or clients. Your purpose is to increase sales. (For help with writing a memo, see Chapter 17.)

## Classification and Visual Representations

One of America's leading vacation destinations is Las Vegas, Nevada. People have been traveling there for many decades, attracted to the legal gambling, the all-night party atmosphere, a relaxed attitude toward sexual activity, and, at least in the early years, the convenience of the Nevada divorce and marriage laws.

You've probably read or seen the recent Las Vegas tourist campaign that builds upon the idea that "what happens here stays here." In other words, tourists are invited to come to Vegas, lose their normal inhibitions, and then return to their normal lives with no questions asked and no harm done (but, of course, with substantial cash having been spent while in Nevada).

However, the print ad reproduced on the next page shows a different approach. The Las Vegas of today is much different from the Las Vegas of even fifteen years ago. Many of the tourist amenities are clearly aimed at families rather than gamblers or party monsters. Las Vegas is transforming into a more "family-friendly" environment. Examine the four categories of "Las Vegas alibis."

1. Write a response to this ad. What are your thoughts and impressions? As you write, refer to Questions for Reviewing a Visual Representation.

2. In the past fifty years, Las Vegas has changed a great deal. Do some research to see what types of changes have occurred. Then either write an essay classifying these changes (remember to document your sources—see also Chapter 21) or develop an oral presentation based on your classification scheme (see also Chapter 18).

## Questions for Reviewing a Visual Representation

- Is the representation forceful, passive, or something in between?

- What is the purpose of the representation—in other words, what is it trying to do to you, the reader/viewer?

- If the representation uses words, do they reinforce the visual image or in some way contradict it?

- What is the presumed audience for the representation—men, women, children, the elderly? Or does it have a broader appeal?

- If the representation is an advertisement, is it trying to sell a product or to get you to adopt a way of thinking?

- If the representation is an advertisement, does it try to persuade you in a fair manner, or do you feel manipulated?

## Responding to an Image

By the end of the nineteenth century, the violent conflicts between Native Americans and settlers in the United States were effectively over. Many Native Americans became the legal equivalent of wards of the U.S. government, forced to

# 4 Las Vegas Alibis

## "What did you do in Vegas?"
Here are some easy answers to use in mixed company.

### The Entertainment Alibi

"I gawked from the front row at every headliner I could find."

### The Fine Dining Alibi

"I broke my diet in a very big way."

### The Shopping Alibi

"I'll tell you what I did. I blew a whole month's budget, on clothes."

### The Golf Alibi

"I couldn't stop swinging."

For more alibis, go to VisitLasVegas.com

Courtesy of Las Vegas Convention & Visitors Authority

live on reservations and submit to the new culture and its demands. An unknown photographer took this picture, titled "Seven Little Children in Four Stages of Civilization," around 1900.

Unknown photographer, Before entering school, Sioux, *Seven Little Indian Children in Four Stages of Civilization*, ca. 1900. The Photography Collection, Harvard University.

1. Write an informal response to the photograph. What do you notice? How does the image make you feel? How does the photograph make use of the classification option?

2. At the time of the photograph, Native Americans were not classified as full citizens. Using a combination of library and online research, explore the status of Native Americans at the start of the twentieth century. (A good way to narrow your topic is to concentrate on one Native American tribe or on one tribe in a single geographical area.) Write a documented essay showing how Native Americans were classified, viewed, and treated. (For more information on documented essays, see Chapter 21.)

## Using the Internet

Search the Internet for insights and information to use when writing classification essays.

1. Find Web sites devoted to a subject relating to your college major or to an academic discipline that interests you. Focus on a limited subject. For example, instead of researching "biology," try "microbiology," "human physiology," "entomology," or "parasitology"—the more specific the better. Try to limit your search to sites devoted exclusively to your subject, and visit as many sites as you can. Then classify these sites into at least three logical categories. Finally, write an essay explaining the principle you used to classify each Web site. For example, one category might

three logical categories. Finally, write an essay explaining the principle you used to classify each Web site. For example, one category might consist of sites maintained by professional organizations. Another might include sites established by colleges or universities. A third might consist of Web sites dedicated to professional, online journals.

Describe each site thoroughly, and explain the similarities that the sites within each category share. You will need to use the techniques of description and comparison/contrast as well as those associated with classification. (See chapters 5 and 12 for help with these patterns.)

2. Search the Internet to find the Web sites of online news providers—news services, newspapers, and/or magazines. In a classification essay, discuss at least ten to twelve different sites by organizing them into three or four categories. To classify the sites, consider layout, extent and nature of news coverage, quality of news coverage, editorial leanings, prominence of advertising, or any other relevant governing principles.

©2007 CREATORS SYNDICATE INC.
WWW.GORRELLART.COM
GORRELL

MARCH MADNESS

PRODUCTIVITY

MISMATCH

By permission of Bob Gorrell and Creators Syndicate, Inc.

# COMPARISON AND CONTRAST

### CHAPTER 12

# Writing in Context

Bob appears at your cubicle yet again.

"What do you know about optical scanners?" he asks.

"I know what they do. And I know that some of them are geared more toward text processing and some of them are graphics oriented."

"Good," Bob replied. "Here, take this." He hands you two folders. "We need to decide which one of these to buy. Talk to Stephanie if you want the background. I'll need an analysis by Friday."

You start looking through the folders Bob has left with you. They contain mainly sales brochures and listings of technical specifications. You know you'll need to grill Stephanie, and probably other people, before you feel confident about starting the report.

Then it will be a matter of writing an evaluation, a side-by-side examination of the distinctions between the two scanners. Even at this point you can see the "shape" of your report.

You can see its shape because this task so clearly calls for an option known as comparison and contrast, in which two things are compared, often with the aim of producing an evaluation, perhaps an evaluation that will enable readers to arrive at some decision.

# HOW DOES COMPARISON/ CONTRAST WORK?

We frequently engage in the act of comparing. When shopping for food, clothing, cars, or almost any other product, we tend to face multiple choices, not to mention a barrage of marketing intended to sway our decision. Usually, we are able to narrow the field down to a few likely suspects, and then the serious comparison begins.

The same process tends to occur when we choose a service:

- The college or university we'll attend
- The tax preparer who will mediate our relationship with the Internal Revenue Service
- The dentist to whom we'll pay substantial sums of money to inflict pain upon us and disrupt our daily lives

In the case of the dentist, for instance, we might make our choice based on a comparison like this one:

> Dr. Burns is a great dentist, but he's got the patient-relation skills of a repo man. And you have to schedule months in advance. On the other hand, Dr. Chen is young and has not yet shown that she is a "great" dentist, but she's funny, I like her, and she keeps evening hours.

As with comparison and contrast in daily life, writers—whether working on the job, in school, or in other contexts—often use comparison and contrast in order to evaluate. That is, they use it to try to reach a judgment based on a serious and objective look at relevant features of the entities that they are comparing.

However, writers may also use the comparison/contrast strategy in order to inform readers—that is, to illustrate, to describe, or simply to reveal the similarities and differences that exist between two subjects. For example, a writer might describe her two uncles, who are twins. Her purpose might be to show how different the two men are—an approach that would be particularly effective because it would tend to work against the reader's expectations (when most of us think of twins, we automatically think in terms of similarity, not difference). Clearly, the writer's goal is not to "evaluate" her uncles— it's not as if she's trying to convince the reader to buy her uncles or marry them. Rather, she is painting a picture—explaining, perhaps entertaining, showing the reader how twins can be very different. In a similar vein, if your political science professor asks you to compare the U.S. electoral system to the Australian electoral system on an essay exam, he or she hasn't asked for an evaluation of the two systems, but rather for a discussion of the points on which they are similar and different. In short, comparison and contrast can be used for two general purposes: an evaluative purpose and a more general descriptive and informative purpose.

Just as there are two general purposes for using the strategy, there are also two organizational approaches. The **subject-by-subject** method fully examines the first of two subjects being compared and then fully examines the second. A broad outline for such an essay might look like this:

Piano A
- Tone
- Design
- Keyboard

Piano B
- Tone
- Design
- Keyboard

The **point-by-point** method examines both subjects in terms of the first point of the comparison, then examines both in terms of the second point, and so on. A very broad outline for such an essay might look like this:

Tone
- Piano A
- Piano B

Design
- Piano A
- Piano B

Keyboard
- Piano A
- Piano B

In the vignette that opens this chapter, Bob wants information. Specifically, he wants an analysis of key performance and technical issues that will determine which of two scanners will best serve the company's needs. This analysis will probably be easiest for him to read if the writer compares and contrasts the two scanners on one point at a time. Therefore, the writer will probably use the point-by-point method, perhaps selecting these three areas:

- Purpose—to what extent is each scanner designed for text scanning (with less emphasis on graphics scanning) or graphics scanning (with less emphasis on text scanning)?
- Software compatibility—which scanner is better suited for painless hookup to the company's network?
- Processing speed—which scanner gets more work done in a given period of time?

Bob probably doesn't want to be told whether the scanner is beige or gray or to be given interesting information about the development of each product. That information is likely irrelevant to him. He wants to know which product to buy. The areas included in the comparison and contrast are the ones that will help him make this decision. As in this example, in many cases when your purpose is evaluative, you will find a point-by-point organization particularly useful.

However, if your purpose is to inform and describe—to provide readers with a picture of the two subjects—the subject-by-subject method may well be the better choice. This is especially true for comparison/contrast essays that use narration as an internal strategy—for example, comparing and contrasting a wonderful vacation and a horrible one. By analyzing first one event and then the next, you give your readers clear accounts of both events. On the other hand, if you were to use a point-by-point approach here, you'd wind up fragmenting those accounts, in a sense reducing the dynamics of the experiences to mere categories of information (hotels stayed at, meals eaten, places seen, and so on). Your reader deserves better treatment. After all, you are trying to fulfill your purpose of providing a clear picture of the two subjects.

In most comparison/contrast essays, the emphasis will be on contrast. Obviously, if your purpose is evaluative, you want to find and focus on differences. Even if your purpose isn't evaluative, it is usually more instructive and interesting to readers to show how two entities are different than to show how they are similar (however, see page 396 for examples of situations in which comparison is the best option). For example, consider this idea: for decades, American automakers tended to produce a car model and then package it under different "nameplates." A midsize Chevy was virtually identical to a midsize Pontiac, and the same was true of Ford and Mercury, and Plymouth and Dodge. Presumably, a buyer might buy a Mercury that was virtually the same as the (normally) lower-priced Ford because the Mercury line had more prestige. Would you want to write an essay comparing these two very similar cars? It's hard to see how you could write a fully developed, interesting paper when trying to compare two items that are so similar. However, keep in mind that comparison/contrast essays that emphasize contrast may also use comparison, just as those that emphasize comparison will surely include some contrasts.

Technically, the comparison/contrast option is not limited to two subjects. A writer could compare three subjects (or four, or ten, or twenty, for that matter). But a three-way comparison asks a great deal of your reader, and any number beyond three would probably be too hard for your reader to comprehend in an essay. The three-way approach tends to appear only in technical/business contexts that use a point-by-point approach. In the opening vignette, for example, Bob could have requested an analysis of three scanners rather than of two. However, for general purposes, most essays concentrate on two subjects only. If a situation seems to call for a three-way analysis, you may find that using a classification or definition approach is a better option.

Note also that you can use comparison/contrast to help you develop essays that concentrate on other rhetorical options. For a good example, see Umberto Eco's "How Not to Use the Fax Machine and the Cellular Phone" in Chapter 8 ("Process Analysis"). While showing how consumer technology can come to dominate the consumer, Eco makes a firm distinction between people who need cell phones and those who do not.

The comparison/contrast essay can be difficult to write yet a joy to read, as the following essays indicate.

• *Consider Your Options*

How might you use comparison/contrast strategies at work? How could this approach help you evaluate situations as they arise?

# READING THE COMPARISON/CONTRAST ESSAY WITH A WRITER'S EYE

In the works that follow, Bharati Mukherjee examines two very different ways for immigrants to approach life in a new country; David Sedaris contrasts his fun-loving family with his serious, analytical father; and Barbara Mellix contrasts "home English" with "public English." As you read these essays, note the method of organization used by each author. As well, note how the author uses the comparison/contrast option to achieve his or her purpose.

The second half of this chapter features strategies for writing the comparison/contrast essay (pages 391–402). If you decide to write on one of the topics that follow the three essays below, make sure that you have read the strategies section before you begin. Also note that additional writing topics are listed at the end of the chapter (pages 407–408).

# Two Ways to Belong in America

## BHARATI MUKHERJEE

*Bharati Mukherjee was born in India, where she received a bachelor's degree and master's degree before immigrating to the United States in 1961. She attended the University of Iowa, where she earned a master's in fine arts and a doctorate in English and comparative literature. A renowned writer of fiction, Mukherjee has published the novels* The Tiger's Daughter *(1972),* Wife *(1975),* Jasmine *(1989),* The Holder of the World *(1993),* Leave It to Me *(1997), and* Desirable Daughters *(2002). Her short-story collection* The Middleman and Other Stories *(1988) won the National Book Critics Circle Award.*

*Immigration and identity are frequent themes in Mukherjee's works. The following essay was written for the* New York Times *in 1996 to comment upon controversial proposals and legislation regarding the rights of immigrants.*

This is a tale of two sisters from Calcutta, Mira and Bharati, who have lived in the United States for some 35 years, but who find themselves on different sides in the current debate over the status of immigrants. I am an American citizen and she is not. I am moved that thousands of long- 1

term residents are finally taking the oath of citizenship. She is not.

Mira arrived in Detroit in 1960 to study child psychology and pre-school education. I followed her a year later to study creative writing at the University of Iowa. When we left India, we were almost identical in appearance and attitude. We dressed alike, in saris; we expressed identical views on politics, social issues, love, and marriage in the same Calcutta convent-school accent. We would endure our two years in America, secure our degrees, then return to India to marry the grooms of our father's choosing. 2

Instead, Mira married an Indian student in 1962 who was getting his business administration degree at Wayne State University. They soon acquired the labor certifications necessary for the green card of hassle-free residence and employment. 3

Mira still lives in Detroit, works in the Southfield, Mich., school system, and has become 4 nationally recognized for her contributions in the fields of pre-school education and parent-teacher relationships. After 36 years as a legal immigrant in this country, she clings passionately to her Indian citizenship and hopes to go home to India when she retires.

In Iowa City in 1963, I married a fellow stu- 5 dent, an American of Canadian parentage. Because of the accident of his North Dakota birth, I bypassed labor-certification requirements and the race-related "quota" system that favored the applicant's country of origin over his or her merit. I was prepared for (and even welcomed) the emotional strain that came with marrying outside my ethnic community. In 33 years of marriage, we have lived in every part of North America. By choosing a husband who was not my father's selection, I was opting for fluidity, self-invention, blue jeans and T-shirts, and renouncing 3,000 years (at least) of caste-observant, "pure culture" marriage in the Mukherjee family. My books have often been read as unapologetic (and in some quarters overenthusiastic) texts for cultural and psychological "mongrelization." It's a word I celebrate.

Mira and I have stayed sisterly close by phone. 6 In our regular Sunday morning conversations, we are unguardedly affectionate. I am her only blood relative on this continent. We expect to see each other through the looming crises of aging and ill health without being asked. Long before Vice President Gore's "Citizenship U.S.A." drive, we'd had our polite arguments over the ethics of retaining an overseas citizenship while expecting the permanent protection and economic benefits that come with living and working in America.

Like well-raised sisters, we never said what 7 was really on our minds, but we probably pitied one another. She, for the lack of structure in my life, the erasure of Indianness, the absence of an unvarying daily core. I, for the narrowness of her perspective, her uninvolvement with the mythic depths or the superficial pop culture of this society. But, now, with the scapegoatings of "aliens" (documented or illegal) on the increase, and the targeting of long-term legal immigrants like Mira for new scrutiny and new self-consciousness, she and I find ourselves unable to maintain the same polite discretion. We were always unacknowledged adversaries, and we are now, more than ever, sisters.

"I feel used," Mira raged on the phone the 8 other night. "I feel manipulated and discarded. This is such an unfair way to treat a person who was invited to stay and work here because of her talent. My employer went to the I.N.S. and petitioned for the labor certification. For over 30 years, I've invested my creativity and professional skills into the improvement of *this* country's pre-school system. I've obeyed all the rules, I've paid my taxes, I love my work, I love my students, I love the friends I've made. How dare America now change its rules in midstream? If America wants to make new rules curtailing benefits of legal immigrants, they should apply only to immigrants who arrive after those rules are already in place."

To my ears, it sounded like the description of 9 a long-enduring, comfortable yet loveless marriage, without risk or recklessness. Have we the right to demand, and to expect, that we be loved? (That, to me, is the subtext of the arguments by immigration advocates.) My sister is an expatriate, professionally generous and creative, socially courteous and gracious, and that's as far as her Americanization can go. She is here to maintain an identity, not to transform it.

I asked her if she would follow the example of 10 others who have decided to become citizens because of the anti-immigration bills in Congress. And here, she surprised me. "If America wants to play the manipulative game, I'll play it, too," she snapped. "I'll become a U.S. citizen for now, then change back to India when I'm ready to go home. I feel some kind of irrational attachment to India that I don't to America. Until all this hysteria against legal immigrants, I was totally happy. Having my green card meant I could visit any place in the world I wanted to and then come back to a job that's satisfying and that I do very well."

In one family, from two sisters alike as peas in a pod, there could not be a wider divergence of immigrant experience. America spoke to me—I married it—I embraced the demotion from expatriate aristocrat to immigrant nobody, surrendering those thousands of years of "pure culture," the saris, the delightfully accented English. She retained them all. Which of us is the freak?

Mira's voice, I realize, is the voice not just of the immigrant South Asian community but of an immigrant community of the millions who have stayed rooted in one job, one city, one house, one ancestral culture, one cuisine, for the entirety of their productive years. She speaks for greater numbers than I possibly can. Only the fluency of her English and the anger, rather than fear, born of confidence in her education, differentiate her from the seamstresses, the domestics, the technicians, the shop owners, the millions of hard-working but effectively silenced documented immigrants as well as their less fortunate "illegal" brothers and sisters.

Nearly 20 years ago, when I was living in my husband's ancestral homeland of Canada, I was always well-employed but never allowed to feel part of the local Quebec or larger Canadian society. Then, through a Green Paper that invited a national referendum on the unwanted side effects of "nontraditional" immigration, the Government officially turned against its immigrant communities, particularly those from South Asia.

I felt then the same sense of betrayal that Mira feels now. I will never forget the pain of that sudden turning, and the casual racist outbursts the Green Paper elicited. That sense of betrayal had its desired effect and drove me, and thousands like me, from the country.

Mira and I differ, however, in the ways in which we hope to interact with the country that we have chosen to live in. She is happier to live in America as expatriate Indian than as an immigrant American. I need to feel like a part of the community I have adopted (as I tried to feel in Canada as well). I need to put roots down, to vote and make the difference that I can. The price that the immigrant willingly pays, and that the exile avoids, is the trauma of self-transformation.

## Vocabulary

The following terms are identified by paragraph number. Make sure that you understand each term's meaning in its context. If you're not sure that you understand a term, look it up in a college-level dictionary.

| | | |
|---|---|---|
| oath (1) | scapegoating (7) | aristocrat (11) |
| sari (2) | adversaries (7) | cuisine (12) |
| quota (5) | subtext (9) | ancestral (13) |
| fluidity (5) | expatriate (9) | referendum (13) |
| renouncing (5) | divergence (11) | betrayal (14) |
| mythic (7) | demotion (11) | trauma (15) |

### Style and Strategy

1. Mukherjee's thesis is suggested in her first few paragraphs but isn't explicitly stated until later. Where is it explicitly stated?

2. Mukherjee uses a point-by-point organization. Write a sentence outline of this essay to help reveal her organization.

3. Is the writer objective in this essay, or is she favoring her choice over her sister's? Explain.

4. Why does the author include (in paragraphs 13 and 14) her experiences in Canada?

### Questions for Critical Thinking and Discussion

1. Does someone living in the United States on a temporary permit have responsibilities to the United States? If so, what are those responsibilities?

2. Some people immigrate to the United States solely for financial purposes. Like the author's sister, they have no interest in becoming an "American." At the same time, many U.S. corporations "emigrate" to countries with lower labor costs and less stringent regulations. Are these two phenomena comparable? Why or why not?

### Suggestions for Writing

1. In a 500-word essay, compare and contrast these two approaches to the college experience: (a) the student who explores the life of the campus, joins clubs, and takes widely varied electives; (b) the student who shows up for classes and leaves the campus immediately afterward.

2. In a 500- to 750-word essay, compare and contrast the following types of romantic relationships: intense and monogamous versus casual and "no strings attached."

3. How does your hometown differ from what it was a century ago? Write a 500- to 750-word essay in which you use library or Internet research as well as what you have learned just from living in that town. Limit your paper to three or four important points of contrast. If appropriate, also talk about what has *not* changed in your town.

4. Write a 500- to 750-word essay in which you contrast two cities or towns that you have lived in or two places that you have visited on vacation. If you choose the latter, make sure that your subjects fit into the same class. In other words, don't contrast a vacation on a Caribbean island with a sightseeing trip through Europe.

### Speaking Assignment

Give an oral presentation in which you explain what Mukherjee means in her last sentence: "The price that the immigrant willingly pays, and that the exile avoids, is the trauma of self-transformation." Make frequent and careful reference to the text. (For more help with oral presentations, see Chapter 18.)

# Family Engineering

## DAVID SEDARIS

*David Sedaris is a humorist who, along with his sister Amy Sedaris, makes up a comedy team known as the Talent Family. David Sedaris's books include* Barrel Fever: Stories and Essays *(1994),* Holidays on Ice *(1997),* Naked *(1997),* Me Talk Pretty One Day *(2001), and* Dress Your Family in Corduroy and Denim *(2004).*

*In "Family Engineering," first published in the August 24–31, 1999, edition of* The New Yorker, *Sedaris pits his mysteriously serious father against the rest of his normal, fun-loving family.*

My father always struck me as the sort of man who, under the right circumstances, might have invented the microwave oven or the transistor radio. You wouldn't seek him out for advice on a personal problem, but he'd be the first one you'd call when the dishwasher broke or someone flushed a hairpiece down your toilet. As children, we placed a great deal of faith in his ability, but learned to steer clear while he was working. The experience of watching was ruined, time and time again, by an interminable explanation of how things were put together. Faced with an exciting question, science tended to provide the dullest possible answer. Ions might charge the air, but they fell flat when it came to charging the imagination—my imagination, anyway. To this day, I prefer to believe that inside every television there lives a community of versatile, thumb-size actors, trained to portray everything from a thoughtful newscaster to the wife of a millionaire stranded on a desert island. Fickle gnomes control the weather, and an air-conditioner is powered by a team of squirrels, their cheeks packed with ice cubes.

Once, while rifling through the toolshed, I came across a poster advertising an I.B.M. computer the size of a refrigerator. Sitting at the control board was my dad the engineer, years younger, examining a printout no larger than a grocery receipt. When I asked about it, he explained that he had worked with a team devising a memory chip capable of storing up to fif-

teen pages' worth of information. Out came the notepad and pencil, and I was trapped for hours as he answered every question except the one I had asked. "Were you allowed to wear makeup and run through a variety of different poses, or did they get the picture on the first take?"

To me, the greatest mystery of science continues to be that a man could father six children who shared absolutely none of his interests. We certainly expressed enthusiasm for our mother's hobbies, from smoking and napping to the writings of Sidney Sheldon.* (Ask my mother how the radio worked and her answer was simple: "Turn it on and pull out the goddam antenna.") I once visited my father's office, and walked away comforted to find that at least there he had a few people he could talk to. We'd gone, my sister Amy and I, to settle a bet. She thought that my father's secretary had a sharp, protruding chin and long blond hair, while I imagined that the woman might more closely resemble a tortoise—chinless, with a beaky nose and a loose, sagging neck. The correct answer was somewhere in between. I was right about the nose and the neck, but Amy won on the chin and the hair color. The bet had been the sole reason for our visit, and the resulting insufferable tour of Buildings A through D taught us never again to express an interest in our father's workplace.

My own scientific curiosity eventually blossomed, but I knew enough to keep my freakish experiments to myself. When my father discovered my colony of frozen slugs in the basement freezer, I chose not to explain my complex theories of suspended animation. Why was I filling the

---

*Sidney Sheldon (1917–2007): a Hollywood producer, a director, and the author of popular novels such as *Rage of Angels.*

hamster's water bottle with vodka? "Oh, no reason." If my experiment failed, and the drunken hamster passed out, I'd just put her in the deep freeze, alongside the slugs. She'd rest on ice for a few months and, once thawed and fully revived, would remember nothing of her previous life as an alcoholic. I also took to repairing my own record-player, and was astonished by my ingenuity for up to ten minutes at a time—until the rubber band snapped, or the handful of change came unglued from the arm, and the damned thing broke all over again.

During the first week of September, it was my family's habit to rent a beach house on Ocean Isle, a thin strip of land off the coast of North Carolina. As youngsters, we participated in all the usual seaside activities—which were fun, until my father got involved and systematically chipped away at our pleasure. Miniature golf was ruined with a lengthy dissertation on impact, trajectory, and wind velocity, and our sandcastles were critiqued with stifling lectures on the dynamics of the vaulted ceiling. We enjoyed swimming until the mystery of tides was explained in such a way that the ocean seemed nothing more than an enormous saltwater toilet, flushing itself on a sad and predictable basis. 5

By the time we reached our teens, we were exhausted. No longer interested in the water, we joined our mother on the beach blanket and dedicated ourselves to the higher art of tanning. Under her guidance, we learned which lotions to start off with, and what worked best for various weather conditions and times of day. She taught us that the combination of false confidence and Hawaiian Tropic could result in a painful and unsightly burn, certain to subtract valuable points when, on the final night of vacation, contestants gathered for the annual Miss Emollient Pageant. This was a contest judged by our mother, in which the holder of the darkest tan was awarded a crown, a sash, and a sceptre. 6

Technically, the prize could go to either a male or a female, but the sash read "Miss Emol- 7 lient" because it was always assumed that my sister Gretchen would once again sweep the title. For her, tanning had moved from an intense hobby to something more closely resembling a psychological dysfunction. She was what we called a tanorexic: someone who simply could not get enough. Year after year, she arrived at the beach with a basecoat that the rest of us could only dream of achieving as our final product. With a mixture of awe and envy, we watched her broiling away on her aluminum blanket. The spaces between her toes were tanned, as were her palms, and even the backs of her ears. Her method involved baby oil and a series of poses that tended to draw crowds, the mothers shielding their children's eyes with sand-covered fingers.

It is difficult for me to sit still for more than twenty minutes at a stretch, so I used to interrupt my tanning sessions with walks to the pier. On one of those walks, I came across my father standing not far from a group of fishermen, who were untangling knots in a net the size of a circus tent. A lifetime of work beneath the coastal sun had left them with what my sisters and I referred to as the Samsonite Syndrome, meaning that their enviable color was negated by a hard, leathery texture reminiscent of the suitcase my mother stored all our baby pictures in. The men drank from quart bottles of Mountain Dew as they paused from their work to regard my father, who stood at the water's edge, staring at the shoreline with a stick in his hand. 8

I tried to creep by unnoticed, but he stopped me, claiming that I was just the fellow he'd been looking for. "Do you have any idea how many grains of sand there are in the world?" he asked. It was a question that had never occurred to me. Unlike guessing the number of pickled eggs in a jar, or the amount of human brains it might take to equal the weight of a portable television set, this equation was bound to involve the hateful word "googolplex," a term I'd heard him use once or twice before. It was an *idea* of a number and was, therefore, of no use whatsoever. 9

I'd heard once in school that if a single bird 10 were to transport all the sand, grain by grain, from the Eastern Seaboard to the west coast of Africa, it would take . . . I didn't catch the number of years, preferring to concentrate on the single bird chosen to perform this thankless task. It hardly seemed fair, because, unlike a horse or a seeing-eye dog, the whole glory of being a bird is that nobody would ever put you to work. Birds search for grubs and build their nests, but their leisure time is theirs to spend as they see fit. I pictured this bird looking down from the branches to say "You want me to do what?" before flying off, laughing at the foolish story he now had to tell his friends. How many grains of sand are there in the world? A lot. Case closed.

My father took his stick and began writing an 11 equation in the sand. Like all the rest of them, this one was busy with "x"s and "y"s resting on top of one another on dash-shaped bunks. Letters were multiplied by symbols, crowded into parentheses, and set upon by dwarfish numbers drawn at odd angles. The equation grew from six to twelve feet long before assuming a second line, at which point the fishermen took an interest. I watched them turn from their net, and admired the way they could smoke entire cigarettes without ever taking them from their mouths—a skill my mother had mastered, and one that continues to elude me. It involves a symbiotic relationship with the wind: you have to know exactly how and when to turn your head in order to keep the smoke out of your eyes.

One of the men asked my father if he was a 12 tax accountant, and he answered, "No, an engineer." These were poor men, who could no longer afford to live by the ocean, who had long ago sold their one-story homes for the valuable sand beneath them. Their houses had been torn down to make room for high-priced hotels and the A-frame cottages that now rented in season for a thousand dollars a week.

"Let me ask a little something," one of the 13 men said, spitting his spent cigarette butt into the surf. "If I got paid twelve thousand dollars in 1962 for a half-acre beachfront lot, how much would that be worth per grain of sand by today's standard?"

"That, my friend, is a very interesting ques- 14 tion," my father said.

He moved several yards down the beach and 15 began a new equation, captivating his audience with a lengthy explanation of each new and complex symbol. "When you say 'pie,'" one man asked, "do you mean a real live pie, or one of those pie shapes they put on the news sometimes to show how much of your money goes to taxes?"

My father answered their questions in detail, 16 and they listened intently—this group of men with nets, blowing their smoke into the wind. Stooped and toothless, they hung upon his every word while I stood in the lazy surf, thinking of the upcoming pageant and wondering if the light reflecting off the water might tan the underside of my nose and chin.

## Vocabulary

The following terms are identified by paragraph number. Make sure that you understand each term's meaning in its context. If you're not sure that you understand a term, look it up in a college-level dictionary.

| | | |
|---|---|---|
| transistor (1) | suspended animation (4) | emollient (6) |
| interminable (1) | ingenuity (4) | sceptre (6) |
| fickle (1) | dissertation (5) | dysfunction (7) |

| | | |
|---|---|---|
| gnomes (1) | trajectory (5) | reminiscent (8) |
| protruding (3) | dynamics (5) | symbiotic (11) |
| insufferable (3) | vaulted ceiling (5) | |

## Style and Strategy

1. What is the tone of this essay?
2. Provide a one-sentence description of the father, then a one-sentence description of the rest of the family.
3. What is the confusion over the word *pie* near the end of this essay?
4. How does the inclusion of the scene with the fishermen watching the father write in the sand add to the reader's sense of the father's value?
5. Does the author, after comparing the way his father is to the way the rest of the family is, come to an evaluative conclusion? In other words, does the author "choose" one side over the other? Explain your answer.
6. List at least five specific contrasts that Sedaris draws between his father and the rest of the family.
7. Does Sedaris tend more toward the point-by-point or the subject-by-subject approach?
8. Besides comparison/contrast, what other rhetorical strategies do you find here?

## Questions for Critical Thinking and Discussion

1. It is said that opposites attract. In your opinion, is this a good way to look for a life companion, or is it a recipe for trouble?
2. What are the implications that this essay raises for the future of the family's children? There are specific issues here (smoking, excessive exposure to the sun) as well as more general issues (frivolity versus seriousness, fun versus industry). What might you predict about the future of the Sedaris children?

## Suggestions for Writing

1. Do you know a couple in a long-term relationship who seem to be "opposites"? Write a 500-word essay contrasting these people and trying to explain why their relationship endures.
2. Which is better, living for the present or building for the future? Write a 500- to 750-word essay contrasting these two approaches to life.
3. Write a 500- to 750-word essay in which you explain how different you are from someone else in your family. Try to focus on a specific area of difference, such as your goals and aspirations or your tastes in music, food, clothing, or movies. Note that your essay should make a point, not just show areas of difference.

*Speaking Assignment*

Consider a common misconception about members of your age, of your ethnic or religious group, or of your sex. Then develop an oral presentation that counters this misperception by explaining the truth. (For more help with oral presentations, see Chapter 18.)

# From Outside, In

## BARBARA MELLIX

*In "From Outside, In," Barbara Mellix, a college instructor, writes about the gulf that separates her "at-home" language from the language she was and is expected to use in the outside world. The following is excerpted from Mellix's original essay, which first appeared in the* Georgia Review *in 1987.*

Two years ago, when I started writing this paper, trying to bring order out of chaos, my ten-year-old daughter was suffering from an acute attack of boredom. She drifted in and out of the room complaining that she had nothing to do, no one to "be with" because none of her friends were at home. Patiently I explained that I was working on something special and needed peace and quiet, and I suggested that she paint, read, or work with her computer. None of these interested her. Finally, she pulled up a chair to my desk and watched me, now and then heaving long, loud sighs. After two or three minutes (nine or ten sighs), I lost my patience. "Looka here, Allie," I said, "you too old for this kinda carryin' on. I done told you this is important. You wronger than dirt to be in here haggin' me like this and you know it. Now git on outta here and leave me off before I put my foot all the way down." [1]

I was at home, alone with my family, and my daughter understood that this way of speaking was appropriate in that context. She knew, as a matter of fact, that it was almost inevitable; when I get angry at home, I speak some of my finest, most cherished black English. Had I been speaking to my daughter in this manner in certain other [2] environments, she would have been shocked and probably worried that I had taken leave of my sense of propriety.

Like my children, I grew up speaking what I [3] considered two distinctly different languages—black English and standard English (or as I thought of them then, the ordinary everyday speech of "country" coloreds and "proper" English)—and in the process of acquiring these languages, I developed an understanding of when, where, and how to use them. But unlike my children, I grew up in a world that was primarily black. My friends, neighbors, minister, teachers—almost everybody I associated with every day—were black. And we spoke to one another in our own special language: *That sho is a pretty dress you got on. If she don' soon leave me off I'm gon tell her head a mess. I was so mad I could'a pissed a blue nail. He all the time trying to low-rate somebody. Ain't that just about the nastiest thing you ever set ears on?*

Then there were the "others," the "proper" [4] blacks, transplanted relatives and one-time friends who came home from the city for weddings, funerals, and vacations. And the whites. To these we spoke standard English. "Ain't?" my mother would yell at me when I used the term in the presence of "others." "You *know* better than that." And I would hang my head in shame and say the "proper" word.

I remember one summer sitting in my grand- [5] mother's house in Greeleyville, South Carolina, when it was full of the chatter of city relatives who were home on vacation. My parents sat quietly, only now and then volunteering a comment or answering a question. My mother's face took on a strained expression when she spoke. I could see that she was being careful to say just the right words in just the right way. Her voice sounded thick, muffled. And when she finished speaking, she would lapse into silence, her proper smile on her face. My father was more articulate, more aggressive. He spoke quickly, his words sharp and clear. But he held his proud head higher, a signal that he, too, was uncomfortable. My sisters and brothers and I stared at our aunts, uncles, and cousins, speaking only when prompted. Even then, we hesitated, formed our sentences in our minds, then spoke softly, shyly.

6    My parents looked small and anxious during those occasions, and I waited impatiently for our leave-taking when we would mock our relatives the moment we were out of their hearing. "Reeely," we would say to one another, flexing our wrists and rolling our eyes, "how dooo you stan' this heat? Chile, it just too hyooo-mid for words." Our relatives had made us feel "country," and this was our way of regaining pride in ourselves while getting a little revenge in the bargain. The words bubbled in our throats and rolled across our tongues, a balming.

7    As a child I felt this same doubleness in uptown Greeleyville where the whites lived. "Ain't that a pretty dress you're wearing!" Toby, the town policeman, said to me one day when I was fifteen. "Thank you very much," I replied, my voice barely audible in my own ears. The words felt wrong in my mouth, rigid, foreign. It was not that I had never spoken that phrase before—it was common in black English, too—but I was extremely conscious that this was an occasion for proper English. I had taken out my English and put it on as I did my church clothes, and I felt as if I were wearing my Sunday best in the middle of the week. It did not matter that Toby had not spo-

ken grammatically correct English. He was white and could speak as he wished. I had something to prove. Toby did not.

8    Speaking standard English to whites was our way of demonstrating that we knew their language and could use it. Speaking it to standard-English-speaking blacks was our way of showing them that we, as well as they, could "put on airs." But when we spoke standard English, we acknowledged (to ourselves and to others—but primarily to ourselves) that our customary way of speaking was inferior. We felt foolish, embarrassed, somehow diminished because we were ashamed to be our real selves. We were reserved, shy in the presence of those who owned and/or spoke *the* language.

9    My parents never set aside time to drill us in standard English. Their forms of instruction were less formal. When my father was feeling particularly expansive, he would regale us with tales of his exploits in the outside world. In almost flawless English, complete with dialogue and flavored with gestures and embellishment, he told us about his attempt to get a haircut at a white barbershop; his refusal to acknowledge one of the town merchants until the man addressed him as "Mister"; the time he refused to step off the sidewalk uptown to let some whites pass; his airplane trip to New York City (to visit a sick relative) during which the stewardesses and porters—recognizing that he was a "gentleman"—addressed him as "Sir." I did not realize it then—nor, I think, did my father—that he was teaching us, among other things, standard English and the relationship between language and power.

10    My mother's approach was different. Often, when one of us said, "I'm gon wash off my feet," she would say, "And what will you walk on if you wash them off?" Everyone would laugh at the victim of my mother's "proper" mood. But it was different when one of us children was in a proper mood. "You think you are so superior," I said to my oldest sister one day when we were arguing and she was winning. "Superior!" my sister mocked.

"You mean I'm acting 'biggidy'?" My sisters and brothers sniggered, then joined in teasing me. Finally, my mother said, "Leave your sister alone. There's nothing wrong with using proper English." There was a half-smile on her face. I had gotten "uppity," had "put on airs" for no good reason. I was at home, alone with the family, and I hadn't been prompted by one of my mother's proper moods. But there was also a proud light in my mother's eyes; her children were learning English very well.

Not until years later, as a college student, did 11 I begin to understand our ambivalence toward English, our scorn of it, our need to master it, to own and be owned by it—an ambivalence that extended to the public-school classroom. In our school, where there were no whites, my teachers taught standard English but used black English to do it. When my grammar-school teachers wanted us to write, for example, they usually said something like, "I want y'all to write five sentences that make a statement. Anybody git done before the rest can color." It was probably almost those exact words that led me to write these sentences in 1953 when I was in the second grade:

> The white clouds are pretty.
> There are only 15 people in our room.
> We will go to gym.
> We have a new poster.
> We may go out doors.

Second grade came after "Little First" and "Big First," so by then I knew the implied rules that accompanied all writing assignments. Writing was an occasion for proper English. I was not to write in the way we spoke to one another: The white clouds pretty; There ain't but 15 people in our room; We going to gym; We got a new poster; We can go out in the yard. Rather I was to use the language of "other": clouds *are,* there *are,* we *will,* we *have,* we *may.*

My sentences were short, rigid, perfunctory, 12 like the letters my mother wrote to relatives:

> Dear Papa,
>
> How are you? How is Mattie? Fine I hope. We are fine. We will come to see you Sunday. Cousin Ned will give us a ride.
> > Love,
> > Daughter

The language was not ours. It was something from outside us, something we used for special occasions.

But my coloring on the other side of that 13 second-grade paper is different. I drew three hearts and a sun. The sun has a smiling face that radiates and envelops everything it touches. And although the sun and its world are enclosed in a circle, the colors I used—red, blue, green, purple, orange, yellow, black—indicate that I was less restricted with drawing and coloring than I was with writing standard English. My valentines were not just red. My sun was not just a yellow ball in the sky.

By the time I reached the twelfth grade, 14 speaking and writing standard English had taken on new importance. Each year, about half of the newly graduated seniors of our school moved to large cities—particularly in the North—to live with relatives and find work. Our English teacher constantly corrected our grammar: "Not 'ain't,' but 'isn't.'" We seldom wrote papers, and even those few were usually plot summaries of short stories. When our teacher returned the papers, she usually lectured on the importance of using standard English: "I *am*; you *are*; he, she or it *is*," she would say, writing on the chalkboard as she spoke. "How you gon git a job talking about 'I is,' or 'I isn't' or 'I ain't'?"

In Pittsburgh, where I moved after gradua- 15 tion, I watched my aunt and uncle—who had always spoken standard English when in Greeleyville—switch from black English to standard English to a mixture of the two, according to where they were or who they were with. At home and with certain close relatives, friends, and neighbors, they spoke black English. With those less close, they spoke a mixture. In public and with strangers, they generally spoke standard English.

In time, I learned to speak standard English 16 with ease and to switch smoothly from black to standard or a mixture, and back again. But no matter where I was, no matter what the situation or occasion, I continued to write as I had in school:

Dear Mommie,

How are you? How is everybody else? Fine I hope. I am fine. So are Aunt and Uncle. Tell everyone I said hello. I will write again soon.

Love,
Barbara

## Vocabulary

The following terms are identified by paragraph number. Make sure that you understand each term's meaning in its context. If you're not sure that you understand a term, look it up in a college-level dictionary.

| | | |
|---|---|---|
| acute (1) | balming (6) | embellishment (9) |
| context (2) | reserved (8) | ambivalence (11) |
| cherished (2) | expansive (9) | implied (11) |
| propriety (2) | regale (9) | perfunctory (12) |
| articulate (5) | exploits (9) | envelops (13) |

## Style and Strategy

1. Mellix's thesis does not appear until paragraph 9. What is it?

2. Mellix uses a wealth of examples to develop her essay. In your opinion, what similarities and differences do these examples help develop?

3. Comment on Mellix's introduction. Why does it work so well, and what does it help her accomplish so early in the essay?

4. Besides comparison/contrast, what rhetorical options does Mellix use to develop her essay?

## Questions for Critical Thinking and Discussion

1. On one level, Mellix is contrasting black English and standard English. What else is she contrasting?

2. Mellix is writing about "the relationship between language and power" in the context of members of a minority group struggling for success in a society where the majority group makes the rules. In your experience, in what other contexts does the relationship between language and power become evident? For example, how might the relationship come into play in areas like school, the legal system, popular entertainment, and computer and other technology?

3. Consider this statement: "Fifty years from now, all this talk about a white establishment and 'official English' will be a historical artifact. America is becoming a nation of color, not just one dominant color." If this statement is true, what are some of its implications?

## Suggestions for Writing

1. Are there any advantages to having a "private self" that is very different from the "public self"? Write a 500- to 750-word essay contrasting the private you and the public you.

2. Write a 500- to 750-word essay that recounts a situation in which your cultural upbringing left you uncertain of how to handle the demands of a different culture or context. Possible areas include city versus country, native country versus foreign country, pool hall versus country club.

3. In an essay of at least 500 words, contrast two types of computer systems, search engines, satellite radio systems, cellular telephone carriers, mountain bikes, or other common products that you know well. If need be, use Internet or library research to gather more information about your subject.

4. In a 500- to 750-word essay, contrast the way in which a wedding or other social ritual is performed in this country with the way that it is performed in another country. You might also contrast weddings or other social rituals in different regions of the same country. As you plan your essay, try to focus on a limited number of points to cover, perhaps three or four of the same aspects of both. Again, you might profit from completing some research before you begin to write.

## Speaking Assignment

Develop an oral presentation in which you contrast the kind of language you might use in informal conversations with friends, classmates, or co-workers and the kind of language you might use in a more formal setting, such as a job or college interview, a business meeting, or a conversation with an instructor, a member of the clergy, a supervisor at work, or a government official. (For more help with oral presentations, see Chapter 18.)

· · · · · · ·
CATALYST 2.0

**MORE OPTIONS ONLINE**
If you would like to read additional comparison/ contrast essays, go to www.mhhe.com/ writingtoday.

# WRITING THE COMPARISON/CONTRAST ESSAY WITH A READER'S EYE

Students sometimes approach the comparison/contrast assignment as if it were merely an exercise instead of a great opportunity to communicate. All too often, this approach yields mechanical, boring essays that fulfill the assignment's requirements but do little else. Some of these essays seem to have been generated by an artificial intelligence program, not by a real, live human being with a history, with interests, and with ambitions. Your reader deserves more.

### Issues to Keep in Mind

As you work on your comparison/contrast essay, keep the following two issues in mind:

1. The need for balance between subjects in a comparison/contrast essay
2. The use of transitions to guide the reader through a comparison/contrast essay

### *Balanced Subjects*

Students sometimes write comparison/contrast essays that technically fulfill the requirements of this rather demanding option, but the essays are weak and ineffective because the two entities that they are contrasting are not "balanced"—in other words, not really suitable for comparison. Contrasting a cockroach with an elephant will almost certainly produce a pointless essay. Contrasting a roadside stand that sells carry-out smoked mullet with a gourmet restaurant is similarly pointless. However, contrasting an African elephant with an Indian elephant has promise, as does contrasting a gourmet French restaurant with a gourmet Chinese restaurant. Be aware of this need for balance; your reader is certainly aware of it.

### *Using Transitions*

Transitions provide the **coherence** that your reader needs to follow your comparisons and contrasts of the subjects. Very often, the difference between a weak essay and a strong one is the absence of transitions in the former case and their skillful use in the latter. Relevant transitions include the following (see also Chapter 3, page 73, for a chart that lists various transitions):

CONTRAST    **but, yet, however, on the other hand, nevertheless, nonetheless, conversely, in contrast, still, at the same time, whereas**

COMPARISON   **similarly, likewise, in the same way**

In the subject-by-subject approach to comparison/contrast, one subject is discussed, then the next subject. Writers using this approach tend to use transitions during the discussion of the second subject in order to establish connections to the first subject. For example, in the following passage the writer discusses one subject and then the other—the viewer's experience when watching a made-for-television movie and when watching a theatrical production—in order to show differences. Notice that although the writer looks at each subject separately, he does not analyze the subjects as if they were completely separate. Instead, as shown by the highlighted words, while discussing the second subject he reminds the reader of the first subject. The writer connects the two pictures he paints.

Made-for-TV movies have a secret attribute that becomes

painfully obvious the more you watch them: they are slaves to time.

The commercial breaks will arrive at severely structured intervals, and the drama or comedy that you are watching will disappear, replaced by whatever shilling needs to be done. The movie will be structured to accommodate those necessary interruptions. Transitions, moments of high drama, and cliff-hanging scenes are natural places to suspend narrative, so the entire production is designed around the commercial breaks, with logical stopping points built into the story. The effect is of paint-by-numbers drama—the movie has been packaged and trimmed to fit the needs of commercial television.

**An entirely different experience** awaits the theater-goer. Plays are live, representing an element of risk, and the audience is well aware of this possibility. However, if an actor makes a mistake, there's no going back. Literally, the show must go on. **And unlike dramatic productions made for TV,** plays are characterized by a certain natural, wonderful lack of balance. The play's acts won't be exactly the same length; the show won't start at the precise moment it was scheduled to. Even the audience can be a factor. I once attended a musical put on by a national touring company. The second act, after the intermission, begins with the main character's monologue. He was standing on stage about to speak when the exit door to his right opened and two society types rushed in front of him, oblivious to the fact that they were interrupting the performance. The performer was gracious yet funny: "Come on, ladies, take your drinks and have a seat." Then he continued. And, although the perpetrators of this type of "interaction" should be escorted to the back row of the balcony, it represents some of the theater's charm. **In contrast,** in a made-for-TV film, a mass murder/suicide could be in progress, and the idiot box would still break in to push products in the midst of the anguish and suspense.

In the point-by-point approach to organizing comparison/contrast, the two subjects are contrasted in terms of a particular quality or idea. Thus, the essay's body paragraphs must move from one subject to the next, back again, and so on. Appropriate transitions are essential here. The paragraph below is an excerpt from a comparison/contrast of library sources and Internet sources. The other paragraphs of this essay similarly develop other points. Notice the use of appropriate transitions, which are highlighted.

> The main issue that distinguishes library research from online research is trust. Scholarly journals found in a university library tend to be produced in much the same way: Academics submit papers, and the journal's editors send these manuscripts to a panel of experts, who then determine whether they should be published. Much of the scholarship online is similarly "vetted" by experts. **However,** a great many Internet postings are the electronic equivalent of vanity publishing. **In contrast to the process that occurs with traditional print publications,** an online "scholarly journal" could be assembled and posted by a crackpot. This seemingly authentic scholarly journal in fact represents no more authority than what is in the brain of said crackpot and perhaps the brains of his loony friends. **As opposed to the controls in the world of traditional publishing,** the world of the Internet has no mechanism to stop him or her. The unsuspecting researcher, then, may be accessing garbage and not realize it.

If you reread this paragraph without the boldfaced sections, you will see how much is lost.

**CATALYST 2.0**

**MORE OPTIONS ONLINE**
For more help with issues in writing the comparison/contrast essay, go to www.mhhe.com/writingtoday.

## Choosing a Topic

What kinds of topics should you consider? If your topics aren't already chosen for you, as in the vignette that opens this chapter, the list of possible topics for a comparison/contrast essay is virtually endless because there are so many different types of subjects to compare and contrast: individual people, groups of people, animals, college courses, and narrative experiences, to name only a few. When choosing a topic, then, your main concern won't be coming up with possibilities but with making sure that the possibilities you uncover are appropriate. The two most important considerations are the size of the topic and the likelihood that it will interest your readers:

1.  **Limit the size of your topic.** For example, "Democrats and Republicans" is much too broad a topic for an essay; it's the subject for a very large book, especially if it includes the historical dimension. What about "neoconservatives versus establishment Republicans"? This is perhaps

still a bit broad. But consider a more directed topic involving two politicians: Eileen X, who is a neoconservative, and Thomas Y, an establishment Republican. This topic should allow you to write a manageable analysis, one in which you will have a valuable opportunity to introduce definitions of "neoconservative" and "establishment Republican." The key is to avoid too large a topic, one that requires a very long essay or forces you to write only in generalities.

At the other end of the spectrum you'll find and need to avoid the severely limited, often strictly personal topic that (a) lacks broader implications and (b) tends to produce a mechanical, by-the-numbers essay. For example, a writer who contrasts a new skateboard with his or her previous one will almost certainly run this risk.

2. **Consider your audience.** When choosing a topic, always stop and think about your readers: Will your topic interest your audience? One important fact to keep in mind as you think about your audience is that readers love to be surprised, to have their expectations countered by a new idea. With a comparison/contrast essay, there are two very general types of topics that can enable you to surprise your readers.

The first type of topic is an exploration of differences between two subjects that the reader might expect to be similar. Consider this situation: two companies are leaders in the same industry, constantly battling each other for market share. One company is the type of place that most employees dream of, with flexible schedules, on-site day care, and a history of not laying people off to solve short-term corporate financial worries—in other words, a company run by people who have some sense of the needs of their employees. In contrast, the other company is a hellhole, where maniacal, profit-driven supervisors treat employees like slaves. Flexible schedules are nonexistent. Employees are expected to show up early and leave late. There are no child-care services; children are viewed as a "personal matter" and a "distraction." Management compensates for its blunders by periodically laying off huge numbers of workers and then driving the remaining few into the ground. In short, these equally successful companies have management philosophies that are radically different. Is there a good topic for a comparison/contrast essay here? We think so.

Or consider topics closer to home. In the introductory pages of this chapter, we discussed the case of the twin uncles who were quite dissimilar. Other topics of this type work equally well:

- Two of your siblings—one must have come home from the hospital in the wrong car
- Two of your best friends, possibly reflecting the fact that our friends meet different needs or correspond to different sides of our personality
- Two college courses that might seem to be "parallel," or at least related, but have furnished you with two very different experiences

With this type of topic, however, make sure that you have your reader in mind as you develop your essay in order to avoid the mechanical, "private" essay discussed above.

The second type of topic is an exploration of similarities between two subjects normally thought to be different. As mentioned in the introduction, focusing on similarities is the less common approach, largely because similarities tend sometimes to be less interesting. But interest isn't likely to be a problem if you're talking about similarities between subjects usually thought to be different. Consider, for example, these potential topics:

- American "southern food" can be found all over the country, whereas Cuban food is much more geographically limited; and, in general, most people don't think of these two cuisines as being very similar. But they are—amazingly so.
- The last twenty years have seen a growing interest in spiritualism— the so-called New Age movement. Whatever the name may imply and whatever people may think of this movement, a very similar phenomenon occurred at the end of the nineteenth century. Similarities between these two movements are well worth exploring.

## Prewriting

Comparison and contrast is a difficult rhetorical option. With that fact in mind, use several prewriting techniques to generate lots of ideas about your subjects. (For more on prewriting strategies, see Chapter 2.)

Freewriting may be the best method for you to choose when developing ideas for your comparison/contrast essay. If you are planning to use the subject-by-subject approach, freewrite on the first subject, then the second; this way, you will be able to review your response to the two subjects and see the points of comparison and/or contrast that link them.

If you are planning to use the point-by-point approach, you could start with an obvious area of comparison and then list or freewrite how each entity relates to that area. If, for example, you are contrasting two people, an obvious area of comparison is personality. You could freewrite on the personality of the first person, then the second. Reviewing your output would show you the major similarities or differences between the personalities of the two people.

If you're not yet sure whether to use a subject-by-subject or point-by-point organization, your prewriting can help you decide. If the results of your prewriting fall easily into categories of differences/similarities, then you should usually use point-by-point. If these areas or categories are not as obvious, use subject-by-subject.

Choosing the wrong strategy can be a dead end. Normally, when students make an inappropriate choice, they have elected the subject-by-subject method when point-by-point development would have worked better. Some writers perceive subject-by-subject to be "easier"—they think it's simpler to cover one subject at a time. In actuality, choosing an inappropriate method will lead to a first draft that is clearly unsuitable and thus to either a painful revision or an entirely new start. *Use the method that is best suited to your topic and the results of your prewriting.*

After you have generated ideas about your subjects, ask yourself these two questions:

1.  **Do I have enough material to support my topic?** If not, consider going to the library or on the Internet to look for additional support. (If you plan to research your topic, however, check with your instructor first.)
2.  **Can I generate a preliminary or working thesis from my material?** If not, think about your topic some more, and then try prewriting again. You need a working thesis before you begin organizing.

## Organizing

Once you have generated a sufficient number of points of comparison and contrast and developed your working thesis, the best way for you to organize this raw material is to arrange it into an outline. (Chapter 2 covers informal, sentence, and formal outline structures.) Sentence outlines work very well for developing the comparison/contrast essay; they establish sufficient structure but can be done quickly.

Whether you employ the point-by-point method or the subject-by-subject method, you should try to use an **emphatic** organization. To illustrate, in the point-by-point method, if you are comparing your two subjects in terms of three areas, your strongest area—the most significant (or startling) comparison or contrast—should be the third one in the body of your essay. In other words, build up to your most important point. If the three areas seem to be of equal importance, use the most logical order when organizing the body paragraphs of your essay. The writer of "Neighborhoods and Memories" (see pages 398–402 in the Drafting section) uses the logic of a **causal chain**, where one event causes another and that event causes a third, and so on (see also Chapter 9) to organize her essay: the friendly atmosphere of the neighborhood had changed, so people felt more distrustful and isolated, and, not surprisingly, property values declined.

If you are using the subject-by-subject method, consider which order of the two subjects will produce the stronger effect on your reader. A typical approach is to write about the more familiar subject first, then show how the second subject is surprisingly different. For example, the essay "Let the Unimportant Things Change" (see pages 398–402 in the Drafting section) explores two visits to a restaurant. The first visit took place when the writer proposed to his future wife, during a very nice evening. Six years later, the couple went back to the restaurant and found that everything about it had changed for the worse. The writer's purpose is to show that love and relationship stability are more important to him than the fate of someone else's restaurant.

Writers using the subject-by-subject method sometimes take the reverse approach. For example, a journalist might explore a degraded, polluted place, describing what a foul setting it has become. Then the writer will contrast this picture to the "old days," drawing upon the memories of current or former residents to develop a picture of a much more desirable past.

When deciding how to order a subject-by-subject essay, consider your purpose: What are you trying to accomplish? Answering this question will help you decide which order to follow.

## Drafting

In this section, we present two essays, both dealing with change. "Let the Unimportant Things Change" uses the subject-by-subject method to contrast two experiences and draw a full picture of how change has affected one element of the writer's world. "Neighborhoods and Memories" uses the point-by-point method to look at a before-and-after situation in terms of a set of issues and ultimately to evaluate the changes.

### The Introduction

The introductory paragraph or paragraphs of a comparison/contrast essay must establish sufficient context for your audience to appreciate what follows. All too often, students produce very brief introductions when writing this type of essay—sometimes only a pair of sentences. These students are putting all their efforts into the body of their essay and ignoring the importance of the background material that the reader needs. If it helps you, write your introduction after you have drafted the body of your essay.

Notice that the introductions to both of the following essays (1) give readers the necessary context for the essay and (2) state the thesis. In the case of the subject-by-subject essay, the thesis is general, pointing out that the essay will explore change—and the effects of change. In the case of the point-by-point essay, the thesis includes the three areas that will be covered (ambiance, security, and property values) and the nature of the evaluation (the changes are negative).

• *Consider Your Options*

Consider beginning a contrast essay by pointing out how similar your subjects appear on the surface. Consider beginning a comparison essay by pointing out how dissimilar your subjects appear on the surface.

**Essay A: Subject-by-Subject Approach**

Let the Unimportant Things Change

My wife and I have been married for more than five years now. I proposed to her almost six years ago. At that point I was just out of the Air Force, and Lois was a year past high school. I proposed to her at a suburban family restaurant, and recently, for fun, we went back to have dinner there. **Our experience showed us that time can be counted on to change almost everything.**

**Essay B: Point-by-Point Approach**

Neighborhoods and Memories

I grew up in the Bristol Park neighborhood, near the old armory. My childhood is still the source of some of my happiest memories, and Bristol Park's environment played a large role in creating these happy memories. However, I've been gone for ten years, and my picture of the old neighborhood has been based mainly on memories. Last summer I went back. My aunt Rita was undergoing cancer treatment, and I took care of her during the worst of it. While I cared for her, I got to experience Bristol Park again, and I found that its "quality of life" had changed dramatically. **To be specific, Bristol Park had undergone major, negative changes in three areas: ambiance, security, and property values.**

### The Body

The body paragraphs of the two essays offer fairly representative examples of the different kinds of development required by the subject-by-subject and point-by-point approaches. In Essay A, the first two paragraphs describe the experience that the writer and Lois had the evening he proposed, and then the following two paragraphs describe the "parallel" experience they had almost six years later. In Essay B, the writer analyzes her old neighborhood as it is now and as it once was, but this comparison/contrast is controlled by evaluative categories: ambiance, security, and property values. As you read each passage, note how the writer uses transitions to develop and link key ideas. Too often, students writing comparison/contrast essays—especially when using the subject-by-subject method—seem to be working in a vacuum: they are comparing two subjects, but *implicitly,* forcing the reader to make the connections that the writer should have provided. The writers of the two model essays establish these connections skillfully.

The comparison and contrast option allows for a wide range of internal strategies. In the two passages that follow, the writers use narration, description, exemplification, causal analysis, and process analysis to develop their respective thesis statements.

### Essay A: Subject-by-Subject Approach

Michael's Restaurant was—and is—located in a strip near the Railroad Mall. Six years ago, the strip had just been built, and Michael's was in its heyday. Our fateful night was a Thursday, normally a slow time for restaurants, but Michael's was hopping that night, an attractive, well-decorated place packed with couples and families.

Our server was attentive. I had filled her in on my nefarious plot—to propose to Lois after our dessert order—and the server was doing her part to make our night special. Lois must have wondered why we were treated like royalty, and perhaps she figured every-thing out after the server left with our dessert order and I produced a ring. I had a little money in those days, and the ring was impres-sive, if I do say so myself. When Lois gasped her acceptance, our server and her manager came over to congratulate us, and then led the room in applause. It was a perfect night.

What changes six years can bring. The Railroad Mall is now on the verge of being closed, and the surrounding area reflects decay, not hope. The strip where Michael's is located is mostly empty, and, at least on the night we returned, the parking lot was filled with trash.

When Lois and I visited recently, I noticed that the interior of the restaurant had not been redecorated in the years since our magic evening. The walls needed paint and the carpet was worn in spots. There weren't many people there, a stark contrast to the packed house of six years ago, and most of them were in the bar shouting at a football game. The server was from the group one sees so frequently these days: servers who have apparently never eaten in a restaurant and don't know that glasses need to be refilled and that all elements of a meal shouldn't be served at the same time. The food was mediocre: dry meat and microwaved vegetables. I would have complained to the manager had there been one around.

### Essay B: Point-by-Point Approach

The neighborhood I remember was characterized by its friendly atmosphere. Neighbors sat on each other's porches, exchanged recipes, borrowed a cup of flour, ended the day with a martini. We children played in the yards, in the empty fields behind the houses, up and down the sidewalk. The ambiance was friendly and commu-nal. However, the Bristol Park of today is a neighborhood of closed doors and warning signs. My aunt says that she doesn't know most of her neighbors, only third-hand bits of information and rumors about who so-and-so is and what he or she does. Children don't seem to live outdoors the way they used to, either. There are fewer children around, and they must spend their free time in front of a computer or the tube.

A related issue is security. When I was young, people didn't leave their doors unlocked or their car keys in the ignition (I'm not *that* old). However, crime perpetrated by people from outside the neighborhood was rare; we felt safe, and to a large degree we *were* safe. Today, on the other hand, Bristol Park suffers from burglaries and, scariest of all, home invasions. Nonresident cars cruise the streets, and I have to believe that at least some of the drivers are looking for an easy chance. Most of the houses feature burglar bars or yard dogs, in what is clearly becoming a war zone.

Not surprisingly, property values have declined. During the time my parents lived in Bristol Park, their house doubled in assessed value. Today, my old stomping ground is available for about 60 percent of that high-water mark. A similar trajectory is evident all over the neighborhood. This is an area going down, not up, and anyone with money is going to look for something a bit more appealing.

## The Conclusion

In the comparison/contrast option, summary is usually a weak way to end an essay. Instead, use the conclusion as an opportunity to draw your analysis together, to comment on the significance of what you have written. Note how the two writers of our example essays have taken advantage of this opportunity.

### Essay A: Subject-by-Subject Approach

I'm glad that Lois and I went back to Michael's on a whim, and not to "relive" our experience, for we would have been sorely disappointed by a trip into a rosy memory. Lois and I haven't changed very much. Our marriage is solid, and we are very much in love. Michael's, however, is a different story. But if one or the other needed to fail, I am glad it was Michael's. There will be other restaurants.

*Consider Your Options*

When writing a conclusion for a comparison/contrast essay, consider explaining how the reader might use the similarities or differences you have discussed. Another way to conclude—but only in a longer essay—is to summarize your main points, then rephrase your thesis for clarity and emphasis.

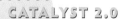
## ESSAY B: Point-by-Point Approach

It's obviously true that you can't go home again, and I'm glad I spent another summer in Bristol Park to confirm this idea. At least now I won't be tempted to go back and buy my parents' old house in this now unfriendly, dangerous, and declining neighborhood.

### EXERCISE 12.1

Write an outline of either "Let the Unimportant Things Change" or "Neighborhoods and Memories." (For help with outlines, see Chapter 2, pages 40–43.) How effective is the approach the writer has chosen (subject-by-subject or point-by-point)? Would the other approach have been a better choice? If so, why?

## Revising Your Draft

After you have completed a draft of your comparison/contrast essay, your next step is to revise it, using your own analysis and comments from classmates and friends. Use the peer review stage to make sure that your essay's structure and

## Questions for Reviewing a Comparison/Contrast Essay

1. Does the introduction give the reader enough context? Does it capture the reader's interest? How could the introduction be strengthened?

2. What is the thesis statement? Has the writer placed it in the best position within the essay? How could it be improved?

3. Does the essay have a clear and interesting general point? Is the writer doing more than mechanically comparing and contrasting two subjects?

4. Is the approach that the writer chose—point-by-point or subject-by-subject—appropriate for the topic and for the intended purpose?

5. If the essay uses the point-by-point approach, has the writer established coherence by using the appropriate transitions? Where are transitions needed?

6. If the essay uses the subject-by-subject approach, has the writer referred the reader to the contrasts and/or similarities between the two subjects? In other words, has the writer connected the second subject to the first, or do the two subjects seem separate and unrelated?

7. Regardless of the method used, is the analysis thorough and complete? Has the writer left out any obvious points or areas of discussion? If the essay is intended to paint two pictures, are the pictures vivid? If the essay has an evaluative purpose, is the coverage of the two subjects balanced?

8. Does the essay have an effective conclusion? How could it be improved?

content are sound. During peer review, answer the questions on page 402 about the draft you are reviewing, whether it is yours or another student's.

After reviewing for content, you need to go over your peer reviewers' responses to your essay and then revise for unity, coherence, language level, and tone (see Chapter 4). When you have revised your draft and are basically satisfied with it, read your draft for mechanical and grammatical errors. Concentrate on finding and correcting major sentence errors (fragments, comma splices, fused sentences), errors in pronoun agreement and subject-verb agreement, and spelling mistakes.

Now that you have made your corrections, *read your essay one more time* to catch any errors made during revision and find errors missed during your earlier reviews.

CATALYST 2.0

**MORE OPTIONS ONLINE**
For more help with revision, go to www.mhhe.com/ writingtoday.

## Student Essay

The following essay is Sam Leininger's response to a comparison/contrast assignment. The final draft is presented first. Then Sam's first draft is presented, with his comments about this draft and what he needed to do in the revision stage.

In this essay, Sam uses the point-by-point approach to contrast two very distinct kinds of moviegoers.

### Sam's Final Draft

### The Two Sides of the Aisle

Movie studios are concerned with target markets and audiences: they tailor certain movies for certain types of people. The advertising for the latest Vin Diesel adventure will appeal to different folks than the advertising for the new John Sayles drama. This process works well. When I go to the movies, I get myself ready in different ways, depending on the type of movie I am going to see. Most towns have an art-house theater that plays the independent and foreign releases and a few dozen multiplex theaters (often in malls) that play the big blockbusters, but with independent films gaining a margin of profitability, some of them are leaking on to one of the 37 screens at the local monsterplex. The local cinemas are becoming slightly homogenized, but the audiences are less so: The movie itself defines the crowd it draws. Crowds attending independent films have a few distinct characteristics that separate them from the average viewers of blockbusters.

Independent filmgoers tend to arrive early. The movie is more important to them, whereas it doesn't really matter if a viewer misses the first five minutes of a natural disaster movie—he or she can still identify the protagonist (that's the good guy, the one with the ruggedly handsome good looks and flimsy backstory) and the antagonist (the latest special effects creation that, although a natural phenomenon like lava or a tornado, somehow manages to chase the hero). 2

The trip to the concession stand is also a giveaway. The blockbuster crowd loads up on hot dogs, nachos, Twizzlers, and anything else they can carry, drag, or stuff in their or their girlfriends' purses (and, of course, I know men are stuffing things into their girlfriends' purses because the lone moviegoer doesn't happen at blockbusters: just as the movie is an event and not a piece of art, so is the experience an event and not a celebration of art). The independent film fan, however, is rarely there to eat. 3

Once in the theater, the two audiences have an equal propensity to be rude. The talking is directed differently, though. The independent audience members talk to each other, but loudly enough so that surrounding members can hear; the blockbuster audience tends to talk to the screen. Independent filmgoers are smart enough to realize that these fictional characters cannot hear them. 4

The major difference during the movie is in the laughter. The blockbuster audience tends to laugh as a single entity, and at obvious moments in the movie there are cues that let them know when to laugh. Independent films are a little more subtle, and not everyone understands the humor. To make up for their insecurities, audience members will sometimes laugh for no reason, at completely inappropriate times, to let others know that they are hip and get all the jokes. 5

As the movie ends, the differences between the audiences are similar to those at its beginning. The blockbuster crowd races out to 6 the parking lot as quickly as possible. In contrast, the independent moviegoer will often sit courteously through the credits and leave at a leisurely pace, talking with other moviegoers about the film.

Lately, moviegoers have been treated to an increasing number of cross-pollinations: some of the blockbuster crowd are taking a chance on the independent film that makes it to the Gigaplex 9000, and some independent fans are frequenting the latest Hollywood release during the slow time of the year. With any luck, this crossover will be a positive movement: the blockbuster audience may learn to respond to a film in more nuanced ways, and a few of them will even be exposed to higher-quality films. But, more likely, the independent fans may just give in to the ruder ways of the typical moviegoer, and the only place to watch any type of movie in relative peace will be at home—now if I could just get that big screen and film projector installed in the living room.

*Sam's First Draft*

### The Two Sides of the Aisle

Movie studios are concerned with target markets and audiences: they tailer certain movies for certain types of people. The advertising for the latest adventure flick will appeal to different folks than the advertising for the new British art film. And it works. When I go to the movies, I get myself ready in different ways. Most towns have an art-house theater and a few dozen multi-plex theaters that play the big blockbusters, but with independant films gaining a margin of profitability, some of them are showing up at the local multi-plex. Crowds attending independent films have a few distinct characteristics that separate them from the average viewer.

Independant filmgoers tend to arrive early. The movie is more important to them, whereas it doesn't really matter if you miss the first five minutes of a natural disaster movie. The trip to the concession stand is also a giveaway. The blockbuster crowd loads up on

7

1   This essay needed more detail—more of a sense of "reality" instead of just commentary.

2   I worked on the second and third paragraphs of the rough draft, turning them into five paragraphs.

anything they can carry, drag, or stuff in their or their girlfriends' purses. The independant film fan realizes that the concession money supports the movie theater and, not wanting to encourage them, will pass the counter frequently.

When I reread the second time, I focused on sentences, many of which were unclear and/or somewhat rough.

Once in the theater, audiences are relatively similar—both have the propensity to be just as rude. The talking is directed differently in the two theaters, though. The independant audience members must talk to each other, but loud enough so that surrounding members can hear; in the blockbuster theater, they tend to talk to the screen. The major difference, though, is laughter. The blockbuster audience tends to laugh as a single entity, and is given obvious moments in the movie that let them know when to laugh. Independant films are a little more subtle, and not everyone understands the humor. To make up for their insecurities, audience members will often laugh for no reason, at completely inappropriate times, to let others know that they are hip and get all the jokes. As the movie ends, the blockbuster crowd races out to the parking lot as quick as possible, while the independant moviegoer will often sit courteously through the credits and then talk with other moviegoers about the film.

Here is where I broke up the long third paragraph. I also added transitions and a bit more detail.

3

I added a final comment to strengthen the ending.

Lately, some of the blockbuster crowd have been taking a chance on the independant film that makes it to the giga-plex 9000, and independant fans are frequenting the latest Hollywood output. Hopefully, this will be a positive movement; the blockbuster crowds will be given an example of how to watch a film, and a few of them will even be exposed to higher quality films. But, more likely, the independant fans may just give in to the rude ways of the typical moviegoer, and the only place to watch any type of movie in relative peace will be at home.

4

## EXERCISE 12.2: REVISING

The following is the first draft of a student's comparison/contrast essay. Working in pairs or in small groups, review this essay. Using the Questions for

Reviewing a Comparison/Contrast Essay on page 402, decide what revisions you would suggest. If you have any questions that the student needs to consider, write these in the margin or on a separate sheet of paper. If your instructor directs you to, rewrite one or more paragraphs to make them stronger and to eliminate any grammatical or mechanical errors.

### My 2 Apartments

I recently moved to a new place, its much more closer to here. I find that my new apartment has many advantages over my old one; such as, environment, location and furnishings.

My old apartment was five miles from here on a busy highway; so it took me a halfhour to get to school each morning. My new apartment is located about only a mile from campus I could walk if I needed to.

My old apartment had a bad environment. The neighborhood was decaying and my neighbor's seemed to be mostly drug dealers and near do wells. My new apartment neighbors are mostly students. There're some great looking girls here.

My old apartment looked like a flop house inside. The carpet was awful, the couche was stained and wierd. The stove didnt work. The plumming was strange. My new apartment however everything is new. All the appliances work and every thing smells fresh and new.

I'm glad I moved. I feel safer and enjoy life more.

## Additional Writing Topics

1. As we get older, our cars tend to improve. Contrast your current vehicle to your first one. (As an alternative, you might contrast the kinds of clothes you wear now to those you once wore, or the kinds of music or movies you enjoy now to the kinds you used to prefer.)

2. How does the computer that you are now using differ from a computer that you used at some point in the past?

3. Have you ever looked forward to a first date, forming increasingly positive expectations of the person, and then found the reality of the date disastrous?

4. First impressions can be deceiving. They can cause us to misjudge a person and to form opinions about him or her that—positive or negative—are not true. Think about someone you have gotten to know well over a long

time. Is your appraisal of that individual's character different from what it was at the beginning of your relationship? Write a contrast essay in which you show how much your opinion has changed.

5. Write an essay in which you explain that your lifestyle is easier than, harder than, or just different from that of your parents or grandparents when they were your age. Focus on three or four major areas of discussion, such as educational or career opportunities, standards of living, family relationships, health—both physical and emotional—the influence of technology, and opportunities for travel, leisure, and entertainment.

6. Contrast the ways in which men and women of your generation complete a common task or ritual. For example, discuss differences in the ways they shop for groceries, clothes, and/or cars. Explain the ways in which men and women prepare for job interviews, get ready for big dates, or drive in heavy traffic. Then again, you might contrast the qualities that men and women look for in the ideal spouse.

7. **Writing on the job.** Contrast good customer service with poor service in a memo to your co-workers. (For help with writing a memo, see Chapter 17.)

## Comparison/Contrast and Visual Representations

In 1937 the Ohio River flooded near Louisville, Kentucky. Margaret Bourke-White took this photograph for *Life* magazine. The picture was taken at a time when racial segregation was still legal in the United States. The persons shown waiting for emergency assistance are all African Americans; white Americans would use a separate line.

The power of this photograph comes from the fact that the African Americans are waiting in line beneath a billboard that shows a radically different view of life in the United States. (By the way, this is not a staged photograph—Bourke-White was a journalistic observer of the tragedy as it unfolded.)

The photograph raises some uncomfortable issues. One of them is the question of whether the history of racial discrimination in the United States is just that, history, or whether this corrosive social problem remains with us today.

1. Write a response to this photograph. What are your thoughts and impressions? As you write, refer to Questions for Reviewing a Visual Representation.

2. Almost everyone would agree that today's social situation is much better than the one depicted in 1937 by Margaret Bourke-White. However, are there still some areas in which racial discrimination is prevalent? Think about this subject in terms of your own experiences, and then research it. Next, either write an essay explaining what you discovered (remember to document your sources—see also Chapter 21) or develop an oral presentation based on your research and conclusions (see also Chapter 18).

Photo by Margaret Bourke-White/Time Life Pictures/Getty Images MA.

## Questions for Reviewing a Visual Representation

- Is the representation forceful, passive, or something in between?
- What is the purpose of the representation—in other words, what is it trying to do to you, the reader/viewer?
- If the representation uses words, do they reinforce the visual image or in some way contradict it?
- What is the presumed audience for the representation—men, women, children, the elderly? Or does it have a broader appeal?
- If the representation is an advertisement, is it trying to sell a product or to get you to adopt a way of thinking?
- If the representation is an advertisement, does it try to persuade you in a fair manner, or do you feel manipulated?

## Responding to an Image

Tom McCarthy's *The Station Agent* (2003-R) tells the story of Fin McBride (played by Peter Dinklage), a dwarf who inherits property in a remote town in New Jersey (Newfoundland) and moves there to get away from the harassing stares and comments of the people of Hoboken. Fin is a very quiet and private man. In Newfoundland he meets Joe Aramis (played by Bobby Cannavale), a gregarious and almost needy man who wants Fin's friendship very badly.

© Miramax/Senart Film/Kobal Collection.

1. Write an informal response to the film still, in which Fin is indulging in one of his favorite pursuits: walking the railroad along with his friends Olivia and Joe, who don't seem quite as enthusiastic. What does this image tell you about the differences between these two men?

2. Watch the film. How does Fin work out the problems in his life, given that he is very different from the people he meets?

## Using the Internet

Search the Internet for insights and information to use when comparing and contrasting.

1. Pick a topic or issue that is related to your academic major or that has been discussed recently in a course you are taking. Find two Web sites that discuss this issue at length. Then write an essay that contrasts these two Web sites. Begin by describing their layouts and organizations and the ease with which they can be used. You can then evaluate the accuracy, completeness, and usefulness of the information presented. You might also evaluate the source or author of the information found in each Web site by researching these people on the Web. Finally, if you have chosen a current political, social, or moral issue—such as handgun control,

affirmative action, school choice, or police-community relations—you might compare or contrast the positions your Web sites take. The best way to organize this essay is point-by-point.

2. Go online to learn more about two technological advances or processes that were developed in the last three decades and that were designed to accomplish the same thing. For example, you might focus on a traditional telephone modem and a digital subscriber line (DSL) as ways to access the Internet, you might research the differences between the analog and digital versions of the cellular telephone, or you might find out about the differences between laser surgery and traditional surgery to correct someone's vision. The best way to organize this essay is subject-by-subject.

**DON'T VOTE**
UNLESS YOU CARE ABOUT
NATIONAL SECURITY • THE IRAQ WAR • TAXES
THE ECONOMY • IMMIGRATION • ENERGY POLICY
ETHICS • WAGES • ...MENT SPENDING
ABUSE OF POWER • ...HE ENVIRONMENT
SCANDAL • CRIM... ...EDERAL DEFICITS
TRANSPORTATI... ...• ABORTION
EDUCATION • JOB... ...AME-SEX MARRIAGE
STEM CELL RESEARCH... ...LLEGE TUITION COSTS
GOVERNMENT C... ...FGHANISTAN

### CHAPTER 13

# ARGUMENT

# Writing in Context

Just before lunch on Friday, Bob calls you into his office. "Have a seat," he says. "Thanks for putting together the preliminary billing for the Overton Presbyterian package. Just one problem: I've gone over our costs, and we'll need about seven hundred more to break even."

You are immediately angry but try not to show it: "With all due respect, we agreed to put together their project at a reduced rate—and at a firm price. We can't change the rules of the game on these people."

Bob grimaces—not a pretty sight. "I like the idea of us taking on the occasional charity case, but I refuse to lose money on that sort of deal. Get in touch with them and explain why we have to have the extra money."

You eat lunch with Todd, who lives three cubicles down. His take on the situation is not inspiring: "You could change Bob's mind—difficulty rating of 9.9. You could bite the bullet and tell those poor souls at Overton that we need seven hundred more clams. Or you could quit your job to make a point."

At least you'll have the weekend to think it over.

This situation is an example of the contexts in which argument occurs. Bob is not asking for a flat demand to the nonprofit Overton group; he knows that a reasoned, sincere appeal will have the best chance for success.

# HOW DOES ARGUMENT WORK?

An **argument** is a communication in which the writer takes a stand on an issue but indicates that he or she is aware that the "other side" has value as well. However, before we go on to elaborate about what constitutes an argument, let's first look at what argument is *not*.

If you and a friend have a screaming set-to, calling each other names and shouting imprecations, this is not an argument. It is a **quarrel**.

If you and a friend have decided to go to the movies this Saturday, perhaps the only issue left to decide is which film to see. You like the idea of *My Life as a Frog*. Your friend wants to see *Total Annihilation: The Day After*. You know little about this second film except that the title sounds certifiably moronic. However, your spiel goes something like this: "I heard that *The Day After* is really cheesy. Let's watch something made for adults for a change. It won't hurt you. I bet you'll like *My Life as a Frog*, and I know I'll hate another stupid disaster film." Here, you are not attempting to argue; instead, you're trying to **persuade** the other person in order to get your way.

However, persuasion is linked to argument in the sense that it is one of the *purposes* of argument. A writer who fairly argues an issue, acknowledging the valid points of the opposing side, may well have as his or her purpose the persuasion of the reader. But consider this situation: American newspapers, news magazines, and talk radio include some regular commentators who offer their opinions on the issues of the day. A great many of these pundits consistently favor either a right-wing or left-wing ideology. It is somewhat amazing, to be frank, that these people can look at any public event and turn it into a moral victory for their side and an alarming moral collapse for the other side. However, if you examine the "arguments" of these pundits, you'll find that they are not really arguments at all. They are statements of opinion meant to be persuasive. Typically, these commentators "bend" reality by simply ignoring inconvenient facts and hoping that the audience doesn't notice. These pundits are out to win, just as one person trying to change another person's movie preference is trying to win. After all, winning is pleasurable. But a writer's desire to "win" can override other concerns.

In this chapter, we address persuasion as a purpose of argument, not as a form of writing. Other purposes include arguing for causes of problems, overturning long-standing assumptions, and proposing solutions to problems. Argument is a complex rhetorical option, whereas persuasion is merely a goal.

A skillful arguer can advocate any position on an issue. Consider how debate teams (sometimes called forensics teams) work. These teams are frequently told to research an issue, but they do not know which stance ("pro" or "con") they will be arguing until the moment of the debate. This forces the teams to research the issue thoroughly; a well-prepared team is as conscious of the potential weaknesses of its own argument as it is of the other side's potential weaknesses.

Consider a scenario from the world of law. Susan J. Barrister, a criminal defense attorney, has just met a potential client, John A. Dubious. Mr. Dubious has been charged with a drug-trafficking offense. He has the money to pay for

Ms. Barrister's services, which will cost a great deal if the case goes to trial. And Mr. Dubious is smart. He tells his potential attorney the charges against him, then tells her a narrative about what happened. The narrative is close enough to the case that the police have prepared, but its implication is that Mr. Dubious is innocent.

Ms. Barrister has dealt with the likes of Mr. Dubious before. She suspects that he is (1) guilty but (2) smart enough not to let her know that. Although she hates representing people from the drug trade, Ms. Barrister has no valid reason to turn Mr. Dubious down. And once she accepts him as a client, her sworn duty as an attorney—as an officer of the court—is to gain the most favorable outcome for his case that she can without breaking the law or bending the code of ethics that lawyers must follow. After all, she reminds herself, the prosecutor will be doing the same thing, just with a different goal.

Some students dislike the idea of arguing for something in which they do not believe. They worry that such arguments are dishonest and morally suspect. But consider this scenario: you are taking a senior-level history class from a professor who is not known for brooking dissent to his well-established opinions. Your research paper will be on a topic on which you disagree with your professor—intensely, in fact. You have two choices: (1) try to work against his opinion or (2) toe the line. We aren't suggesting that you choose one or the other, just that similar scenarios are common in the working world. You will have to choose your approach, but in case you are more worried about your grade than about your true opinion, we believe that learning how to argue either side of an issue is a useful skill.

However, for most writing assignments, you will be encouraged to argue the side that you believe. You must be able to consider the evidence, weigh the opposing issues, and favor one side or the other. Obviously, this process is easier if you believe in the side for which you are arguing.

Not all issues are worthy of argument. Consider the following proposition:

> If a pedestrian sees that someone has planted a new flower garden, the pedestrian should attack the garden and dig up all the seeds and plants.

The response to this proposition is cut and dried: no. It's a ridiculous idea and will result in an open-and-shut argument. Instead, argument springs from issues about which intelligent people differ. This very fact bothers some students, who respond to an issue by showing the positive elements of each side, then leave the decision up to the reader. You should reject such an approach. Any issue that is worth arguing and that you care about should allow you to take a partisan stance—once again, with a thorough sense of the strengths and weaknesses of each side before you begin.

As the examples above suggest, you will be writing arguments throughout your college career as well as in your professional life. Assignments in almost any discipline can call for an argument. You might be asked to argue for your interpretation of a poem, play, or novel for a literature class; for or against a public policy for a government class; or for the implications of the results of an experiment in a biology or chemistry class. As part of your job, you may need to propose a solution to a company problem or argue for your evaluation of a product or service.

In the section that follows the professional essays, we talk about the elements—some of them conceptual and some mechanical—that go into an argument. A thorough treatment of argumentation is beyond the scope of this chapter and, in fact, this book. However, we will concentrate on some approaches to the argumentative essay that should help you.

## READING THE ARGUMENT ESSAY WITH A WRITER'S EYE

In the works that follow, Walter S. Minot argues that the recent upward trend in part-time employment by full-time college students is detrimental to these students' education; Caryl Rivers, while not asking for governmental censorship, argues that the anti-female bias in modern popular music is influencing young people in negative ways; and Michael Levin points out that torture, a cruel and unusual punishment, may be necessary in some extreme situations. The subject matter of these essays is diverse; argument, as a rhetorical option, can embrace almost any topic on which two reasonable people might disagree.

Following the essays, the second half of this chapter features strategies for writing the argumentative essay with a reader's eye (pages 426–437). If you decide to write on one of the topics that follow the three essays below, make sure that you have read the strategies section before you begin. Also note that additional writing topics are listed at the end of the chapter (page 443).

# Students Who Push Burgers

## WALTER S. MINOT

*Walter S. Minot is a professor of English at Gannon University. He is the author of* Rhetoric: Theory and Practice for Communication *(1981).*

*Minot published this essay in the* Christian Science Monitor *on November 22, 1988. Does any of his argument touch on an issue in your life as a student?*

A college freshman squirms anxiously on a chair in my office, his eyes avoiding mine, those of his English professor, as he explains that he hasn't finished his paper, which was due two days ago. "I just haven't had the time," he says. [1]

"Are you carrying a heavy course load?" [2]

"Fifteen hours," he says—a normal load. [3]

"Are you working a lot?" [4]

"No, sir, not much. About 30 hours a week." [5]

"That's a lot. Do you have to work that much?" [6]

"Yeah, I have to pay for my car." [7]

"Do you really need a car?" [8]

"Yeah, I need it to get to work." [9]

This student isn't unusual. Indeed, he probably typifies today's college and high school stu- [10]

dents. Yet in all the lengthy analyses of what's wrong with American education, I have not heard employment by students being blamed.

I have heard drugs blamed and television— that universal scapegoat. I have heard elaborate theories about the decline of the family, of religion, and of authority, as well as other sociological theories. But nobody blames student employment. The world seems to have accepted the part-time job as a normal feature of adolescence. A parochial school in my town even had a day to honor students who held regular jobs, and parents often endorse this employment by claiming that it teaches kids the value of the dollar. 11

But such employment is a major cause of educational decline. To argue my case, I will rely on memories of my own high school days and contrast them with what I see today. Though I do have some statistical evidence, my argument depends on what anyone over 40 can test through memory and direct observation. 12

When I was in high school in the 1950s, students seldom held jobs. Some of us baby-sat, shoveled snow, mowed lawns, and delivered papers, and some of us got jobs in department stores around Christmas. But most of us had no regular source of income other than the generosity of our parents. 13

The only kids who worked regularly were poor. They worked to help their families. If I remember correctly, only about five people in my class of 170 held jobs. That was in a working-class town in New England. As for the rest of us, our parents believed that going to school and helping around the house were our work. 14

In contrast, in 1986 my daughter was one of the few students among juniors and seniors who didn't work. According to the Bureau of Labor Statistics, more than 40 percent of high school students were working in 1980, but sociologist Ellen Greenberger and Laurence Steinberg in "When Teenagers Work" came up with estimates of more than 70 percent working in 1986, though I suspect that the figure may be even higher now. 15

My daughter, however, did not work; her parents wouldn't let her. Interestingly, some of the students in her class implied that she had an unfair advantage over them in the classroom. They were probably right, for while she was home studying they were pushing burgers, waiting on tables, or selling dresses 20 hours a week. Working students have little time for homework. 16

I attended a public high school, while she attended a Roman Catholic preparatory school whose students were mainly middle class. By the standards of my day, her classmates did not "have to" work. Yet many of them were working 20 to 30 hours a week. Why? 17

They worked so that they could spend $60 to $100 a week on designer jeans, rock concerts, stereo and video systems, and, of course, cars. They were living lives of luxury, buying items on which their parents refused to throw hard-earned money away. Though the parent would not buy such tripe for their kids, the parents somehow convinced themselves that the kids were learning the value of money. Yet, according to Ms. Greenberger and Mr. Steinberg, only about a quarter of those students saved money for college or other long-term goals. 18

How students spend their money is their business, not mine. But as a teacher, I have witnessed the effects of employment. I know that students who work all evening aren't ready for studying when they get home from work. Moreover, because they work so hard and have ready cash, they feel that they deserve to have fun—instead of spending all their free time studying. 19

Thus, by the time they get to college, most students look upon studies as a spare-time activity. A survey at Pennsylvania State University showed that most freshmen believed they could maintain a B average by studying about 20 hours a week. (I can remember when college guidebooks advised two to three hours of studying for every hour in class—30 to 45 hours a week.) 20

Clearly individual students will pay the price for lack of adequate time studying, but the problem goes beyond the individual. It extends to schools and colleges that are finding it difficult to demand quantity or quality of work from students. 21

Perhaps the reason American education has declined so markedly is because America has raised a generation of part-time students. And perhaps our economy will continue to decline as full-time students from Japan and Europe continue to outperform our part-time students. 22

## Vocabulary

The following terms are identified by paragraph number. Make sure that you understand each term's meaning in its context. If you're not sure that you understand a term, look it up in a college-level dictionary.

| | | |
|---|---|---|
| typifies (10) | parochial (11) | tripe (18) |
| scapegoat (11) | preparatory school (17) | markedly (22) |

## Style and Strategy

1. Minot clearly believes that he and the reader share an assumption. What is this assumption?

2. How does the author show that the issue has two sides?

3. What is Minot's internal rhetorical strategy—for example, narration, comparison/contrast, or process analysis?

4. Minot uses two specific examples of students who work or don't work—the anonymous unfortunate whose case opens the essay and Minot's daughter. Are more examples needed in an essay of this length?

## Questions for Critical Thinking and Discussion

1. As a student, what is your first priority? School? Social life? Work? Family?

2. Some commentators now see higher education as a place where "consumers" (part- or full-time students) "purchase" education on much the same basis as shoppers use to purchase anything—price, convenience, amenities. Others argue that students who take this approach may end up with degrees but will miss out on what the college experience has to offer and enter the work force at a disadvantage compared to their more studious colleagues. What do you think?

## Suggestions for Writing

1. Write a 500-word essay arguing that a specific group, office, or department fails to accomplish its stated goals because its members spend their time on other pursuits.

2. "American colleges should tighten up requirements for students. (a) More than one absence in a class—except in the case of provable emergency—should result in the administrative withdrawal of the student. (b) Tests and papers should never be accepted after their assigned date. (c) Students who arrive late to class should be openly reprimanded." Write a 500- to 750-word essay in which you agree or disagree with one or more of the statements above.

3. Minot argues that working—even part time—jeopardizes academic success. Can you argue that working part time (say fifteen hours or less per week) is advantageous because it teaches students skills and habits important to the world they will enter once they complete their studies? If so, write an essay of 500 to 750 words exploring this topic.

### Speaking Assignment

Develop a presentation in which you argue for a change in a school policy that will help students become more successful. Or argue for a change in a policy at work that will help make employees more efficient and/or productive. (For more help with oral presentations, see Chapter 18.)

# What Should Be Done About Rock Lyrics?

## CARYL RIVERS

*Caryl Rivers is a journalism professor at Boston University who has written a number of books on modern culture, including* More Joy Than Rage: Crossing Generations with the New Feminism *(1991) and* Slick Spins and Fractured Facts: How Cultural Myths Distort the News *(1996), along with three novels:* Virgins *(1984),* Intimate Enemies *(1987), and* Indecent Behavior *(1990).*

*The following essay was first published in 1985 in the* Boston Globe. *The questions that it asks are still fresh today.*

After a grisly series of murders in California, possibly inspired by the lyrics of a rock song, we are hearing a familiar chorus: don't blame rock and roll. Kids will be kids. They love to rebel, and the more shocking the stuff, the better they like it.

There's some truth in this, of course. I loved to watch Elvis shake his torso when I was a teenager, and it was even more fun when Ed Sullivan wouldn't let the cameras show him below the waist. I snickered at the forbidden "Rock With Me, Annie" lyrics by a black rhythm and blues group, which were deliciously naughty. But I am sorry, rock fans, that is not the same thing as hearing lyrics about how a man is going to force a woman to perform oral sex on him at gunpoint in a little number called "Eat Me Alive." It is not in the same league with a song about the delights of slipping into a woman's room while she is sleeping and murdering her, the theme of an AC/DC ballad that allegedly inspired the California slayer.

Make no mistake, it is not sex we are talking about here, but violence. Violence against women. Most rock songs are not violent—they are funky, sexy, rebellious, and sometimes witty. Please do not mistake me for a Mrs. Grundy. If Prince wants to leap about wearing only a purple jock strap, fine. Let Mick Jagger unzip his fly as he gyrates, if he wants to. But when either one of them starts garroting, beating, or sodomizing a woman in their number, that is another story.

I always find myself annoyed when "intellectual" men dismiss violence against women with a yawn, as if it were beneath their dignity to notice. I wonder if the reaction would be the same if the violence were directed against someone other than women. How many people would yawn and say, "Oh, kids will be kids" if a rock group did a nifty little number called "Lynchin," in which stringing up and stomping on black people were set to music? Who would chuckle and say, "Oh, just a little adolescent rebellion" if a group of rockers went on MTV dressed as Nazis, desecrating synagogues and beating up Jews to the beat of twanging guitars?

I'll tell you what would happen. Prestigious dailies would thunder on editorial pages; senators would fall over each other to get denunciations into the *Congressional Record.* The president would appoint a commission to clean up the music business.

But violence against women is greeted by silence. It shouldn't be.

This does not mean censorship, or book (or record) burning. In a society that protects free expression, we understand a lot of stuff will float up out of the sewer. Usually, we recognize the ugly stuff that advocates violence against any group as the garbage it is, and we consider its purveyors as moral lepers. We hold our nose and tolerate it, but we speak out against the values it proffers.

But images of violence against women are not staying on the fringes of society. No longer are they found only in tattered, paper-covered books or in movie houses where winos snooze and the scent of urine fills the air. They are entering the mainstream at a rapid rate. This is happening at a time when the media, more and more, set the agenda for the public debate. It is a powerful legitimizing force—especially television. Many people regard what they see on TV as the truth; Walter Cronkite* once topped a poll as the most trusted man in America.

Now, with the advent of rock videos and all-music channels, rock music has grabbed a big chunk of legitimacy. American teenagers have instant access, in their living rooms, to the messages of rock, on the same vehicle that brought them *Sesame Street.* Who can blame them if they believe that the images they see are accurate reflections of adult reality, approved by adults? After all, Big Bird used to give them lessons on the same little box. Adults, by their silence, sanction the images. Do we really want our kids to think that rape and violence are what sexuality is all about?

This is not a trivial issue. Violence against women is a major social problem, one that's more than a cerebral issue to me. I teach at Boston University, and one of my most promising young journalism students was raped and murdered. Two others told me of being raped. Recently, one female student was assaulted and beaten so badly she had $5,000 worth of medical bills and permanent damage to her back and eyes.

It's nearly impossible, of course, to make a cause-and-effect link between lyrics and images and acts of violence. But images have a tremendous power to create an atmosphere in which violence against certain people is sanctioned. Nazi propagandists knew that full well when they portrayed Jews as ugly, greedy, and powerful.

Violence against women, particularly in a sexual context, is being legitimized in two ways: by the increasing movement of these images into the mainstream of the media in TV, films, magazines, albums, videos, and by the silence about it.

Violence, of course, is rampant in the media. But it is usually set in some kind of moral context. It's usually only the bad guys who commit violent acts against the innocent. When the good guys

---

*Walter Cronkite (b. 1916):* the anchor of the *CBS Evening News* from 1962 to 1981.

get violent, it's against those who deserve it. Dirty Harry blows away the scum; he doesn't walk up to a toddler and say, "Make my day." The A Team does not shoot up suburban shopping malls.

But in some rock songs, it's the "heroes" who 14 commit the acts. The people we are programmed to identify with are the ones being violent, with women on the receiving end. In a society where rape and assaults on women are endemic, this is no small problem, with millions of young boys watching on their TV screens and listening on their Walkmans.

I think something needs to be done. I'd like to 15 see people in the industry respond to the problem.

I'd love to see some women rock stars speak out against violence against women. I would like to see disc jockeys refuse air play to records and videos that contain such violence. At the very least, I want to see the end of the silence. I want journalists and parents and critics and performing artists to keep this issue alive in the public forum. I don't want people who are concerned about this issue labeled as bluenoses and bookburners and ignored.

And I wish it wasn't always just women who 16 were speaking out. Men have as large a stake in the quality of our civilization as women do in the long run. Violence is a contagion that infects at random. Let's hear something, please, from the men.

## Vocabulary

The following terms are identified by paragraph number. Make sure that you understand each term's meaning in its context. If you're not sure that you understand a term, look it up in a college-level dictionary.

| | | |
|---|---|---|
| grisly (1) | denunciations (5) | cerebral (10) |
| torso (2) | purveyors (7) | propagandists (11) |
| gyrates (3) | moral lepers (7) | rampant (13) |
| garroting (3) | proffers (7) | endemic (14) |
| desecrating (4) | legitimizing (8) | bluenoses (15) |
| prestigious (5) | sanction (9) | |

## Style and Strategy

1. What contrast does Rivers draw in paragraphs 1–2 and then again in paragraph 3?
2. What rhetorical strategy does Rivers use in the "what-if" section (paragraphs 4–5)?
3. What is the process that Rivers describes in paragraphs 8–10?
4. In paragraphs 12–14, how does Rivers redefine violence in the media?
5. What solutions does Rivers suggest to deal with this problem?

## Questions for Critical Thinking and Discussion

1. Our era exhibits a great awareness of the need for sensitivity toward those who are different from us—due to race, sex, sexual orientation, religion,

disability, or country of origin. Yet some "differences" seem fair game. Which stereotypes still exist? Why?

2. The 1934 Frank Capra film *It Happened One Night* was the first movie to sweep the major Academy Awards. It was wildly popular, and it retains its appeal today. However, there is a significant problem in the film: the female lead, played by Claudette Colbert, is treated as a helpless idiot by the male lead, played by Clark Gable. Audiences in the 1930s found no problem here; after all, women had a subordinate status in that world. Today, however, audiences approach this film from a different frame of reference, and the treatment of Colbert's character seems, at times, abusive. How legitimate is it for people of today to impose their standards of political sensitivity on works of art and literature produced in accordance with the standards of another era?

3. "One hundred years from now, commentators will look back at us and disapprove of some of our most widely accepted attitudes and actions. At this point, we have no idea what they'll be criticizing us for." Comment on this statement.

## Suggestions for Writing

1. Popular music, like other forms of popular culture, such as films and television programs, is somewhat controlled by its audience. In other words, if the anti-woman message becomes too horrifying, consumers stop buying. But what about Internet sites, which are not subject to the same market controls? In a 500- to 750-word essay, argue for or against this statement: "The Internet contains a vast and dangerous collection of anti-female content that should be regulated."

2. Suppose, as some people argue, that censorship of popular media content should once again become the American norm. In other words, what people could read, watch, and view would be controlled by the standards of 1957. What do you think would happen? Argue your position in a 500- to 750-word essay.

3. Rivers asks us to break our silence about the portrayal of violence against women in rock lyrics. In what other ways might we fight this obnoxious trend? Write a 500- to 750-word essay that argues for steps to be taken by a variety of participants: the young people who buy this music, the parents of teenagers, the music industry, and—perhaps—even the government.

## Speaking Assignment

In a short presentation, argue that the television image of women, men, contemporary families, the police, or any other subject that you choose is inaccurate, insulting, and/or dangerous. Because time is limited, you might want to focus on one particular television series or even one episode in a series. (For more help with oral presentations, see Chapter 18.)

# The Case for Torture

## MICHAEL LEVIN

*Physical torture is both illegal and unconstitutional in the United States. But could there be times when Americans might regret that fact? Michael Levin thinks so. Levin, a philosophy professor at the City College of New York, originally published this essay as a Newsweek "My Turn" column on June 7, 1982.*

It is generally assumed that torture is impermissible, a throwback to a more brutal age. Enlightened societies reject it outright, and regimes suspected of using it risk the wrath of the United States.

I believe this attitude is unwise. There are situations in which torture is not merely permissible but morally mandatory. Moreover, these situations are moving from the realm of imagination to fact.

## Death:

Suppose a terrorist has hidden an atomic bomb on Manhattan Island which will detonate at noon on July 4 unless . . . (here follow the usual demands for money and release of his friends from jail). Suppose, further, that he is caught at 10 A.M. of the fateful day, but—preferring death to failure—won't disclose where the bomb is. What do we do? If we follow due process—wait for his lawyer, arraign him—millions of people will die. If the only way to save those lives is to subject the terrorist to the most excruciating possible pain, what grounds can there be for not doing so? I suggest there are none. In any case, I ask you to face the question with an open mind.

Torturing the terrorist is unconstitutional? Probably. But millions of lives surely outweigh constitutionality. Torture is barbaric? Mass murder is far more barbaric. Indeed, letting millions of innocents die in deference to one who flaunts his guilt is moral cowardice, an unwillingness to dirty one's hands. If *you* caught the terrorist, could you sleep nights knowing that millions died because you couldn't bring yourself to apply the electrodes?

Once you concede that torture is justified in extreme cases, you have admitted that the decision to use torture is a matter of balancing innocent lives against the means needed to save them. You must now face more realistic cases involving more modest numbers. Someone plants a bomb on a jumbo jet. He alone can disarm it, and his demands cannot be met (or if they can, we refuse to set a precedent by yielding to his threats). Surely we can, we must, do anything to the extortionist to save the passengers. How can we tell 300, or 100, or 10 people who never asked to be put in danger, "I'm sorry, you'll have to die in agony, we just couldn't bring ourselves to . . ."

Here are the results of an informal poll about a third, hypothetical, case. Suppose a terrorist group kidnapped a newborn baby from a hospital. I asked four mothers if they would approve of torturing kidnappers if that were necessary to get their own newborns back. All said yes, the most "liberal" adding that she would like to administer it herself.

I am not advocating torture as punishment. Punishment is addressed to deeds irrevocably past. Rather, I am advocating torture as an acceptable measure for preventing future evils. So understood, it is far less objectionable than many extant punishments. Opponents of the death penalty, for example, are forever insisting that executing a murderer will not bring back his victim (as if the purpose of capital punishment were supposed to be resurrection, not deterrence or retribution). But torture, in the cases described, is intended not to bring anyone back but to keep innocents from being dispatched. The most powerful argument against using torture as a punishment or to secure confessions is that such practices disregard the rights of the individual. Well, if the individual is all that important—and he is—it is correspondingly important to protect the rights of individuals threatened by terrorists. If life is so valuable that it must never be taken, the lives of the innocents must be saved even at the price of hurting the one who endangers them.

Better precedents for torture are assassination 8 and pre-emptive attack. No Allied leader would have flinched at assassinating Hitler, had that been possible. (The Allies did assassinate Heydrich.) Americans would be angered to learn that Roosevelt could have had Hitler killed in 1943—thereby shortening the war and saving millions of lives—but refused on moral grounds. Similarly, if nation A learns that nation B is about to launch an unprovoked attack, A has a right to save itself by destroying B's military capability first. In the same way, if the police can by torture save those who would otherwise die at the hands of kidnappers or terrorists, they must.

Idealism:

There is an important difference between terror- 9 ists and their victims that should mute talk of the terrorists' "rights." The terrorist's victims are at risk unintentionally, not having asked to be endangered. But the terrorist knowingly initiated his actions. Unlike his victims, he volunteered for the risks of his deed. By threatening to kill for profit or idealism, he renounces civilized standards, and he can have no complaint if civilization tries to thwart him by whatever means necessary.

Just as torture is justified only to save lives (not 10 extort confessions or recantations), it is justifiably administered only to those *known* to hold innocent lives in their hands. Ah, but how can the authorities ever be sure they have the right malefactor? Isn't there a danger of error and abuse? Won't We turn into Them?

Questions like these are disingenuous in a 11 world in which terrorists proclaim themselves and perform for television. The name of their game is public recognition. After all, you can't very well intimidate a government into releasing your freedom fighters unless you announce that it is your group that has seized its embassy. "Clear guilt" is difficult to define, but when 40 million people see a group of masked gunmen seize an airplane on the evening news, there is not much question about who the perpetrators are. There will be hard cases where the situation is murkier. Nonetheless, a line demarcating the legitimate use of torture can be drawn. Torture only the obviously guilty, and only for the sake of saving innocents, and the line between Us and Them will remain clear.

There is little danger that the Western democ- 12 racies will lose their way if they choose to inflict pain as one way of preserving order. Paralysis in the face of evil is the greater danger. Some day soon a terrorist will threaten tens of thousands of lives, and torture will be the only way to save them. We had better start thinking about this.

## Vocabulary

The following terms are identified by paragraph number. Make sure that you understand each term's meaning in its context. If you're not sure that you understand a term, look it up in a college-level dictionary.

| | | |
|---|---|---|
| impermissible (1) | hypothetical (6) | thwart (9) |
| throwback (1) | irrevocable (7) | recantation (10) |
| realm (2) | extant (7) | malefactor (10) |

excruciating (3)

barbaric (4)

deference (4)

flaunt (4)

precedent (5)

extortionist (5)

retribution (7)

dispatched (7)

pre-emptive (8)

flinched (8)

mute (9)

renounce (9)

disingenuous (11)

perpetrator (11)

murkier (11)

demarcating (11)

paralysis (12)

### Style and Strategy

1. In this essay Levin displays a *utilitarian* philosophy. Utilitarians believe that the greater good must be favored over the rights of a few—if the two sides happen to be in conflict. In the fourth paragraph, while admitting that torture is unconstitutional, Levin adds this: "But millions of lives surely outweigh constitutionality." Levin believes that his audience shares this assumption. Is he correct? To what degree would the audience of 1982 differ from today's audience?

2. In paragraphs 3, 5, 6, and 8, Levin paints four scenarios that would justify the use of torture. How does the fourth scenario differ from the first three? Does Levin acknowledge this difference?

3. One of the great strengths of "The Case for Torture" is the way its thesis controls the essay. Throughout, Levin makes sure that the reader knows exactly what he is arguing for—and, just as importantly, what he is *not* arguing for. List the instances when Levin pauses to make his focus clear.

### Questions for Critical Thinking and Discussion

Utilitarian philosophy raises many interesting and troubling questions. Consider and discuss the following statements and questions:

1. "Telling a lie is morally wrong unless doing so would cause less harm than would telling the truth."

2. "Allowing police to torture a terrorist in order to prevent a tragedy sounds like a good idea, but how would we ever know that torture wouldn't extend to other areas of police work?"

3. "The police used torture off and on in some parts of the United States until the 1950s, when the practice largely disappeared. But wouldn't we all be better off if torture allowed the courts to convict more obviously guilty criminals and get them off the streets?"

### Suggestions for Writing

1. Many people believe that every law has its exception. Write a 500- to 750-word essay arguing that a specific law or rule does or does not have an exception.

2. You work for a company that is part of a large, powerful chain. Your manager routinely ensures that each week, you and your co-workers get

paid for two fewer hours than you actually put in. One of your colleagues regularly tries to "even the score" by embezzling products and supplies roughly equal to the two-hour discrepancy. Is such behavior justifiable? Write a 500- to 750-word essay arguing your position.

3. Reread Levin's essay in light of the incarceration of terrorist suspects since September 11, 2001. Should we take Levin's advice in regard to these individuals? Why or why not? Express your opinions in an essay of between 500 and 750 words. Include library or Internet research.

4. In paragraph 12, Levin argues that "Paralysis in the face of evil" is more dangerous than inflicting "pain as one way of preserving order." Considering the current war on terror being waged by the United States, Great Britain, and other nations, do you agree or disagree with Levin? Write a 500- to 750-word essay in which you argue your case.

### Speaking Assignment

In paragraph 2, Levin acknowledges that torturing a terrorist is probably unconstitutional. Do you agree? Read the section of the U.S. Constitution that deals with cruel and unusual punishment. Then state your opinion, making clear and specific reference to the Constitution as needed. (For more help with oral presentations, see Chapter 18.)

# WRITING THE ARGUMENT ESSAY WITH A READER'S EYE

Argument is a complex rhetorical option that requires your understanding of issues that are not always present in the other options. The advice that follows will help you think like your reader as you consider your assignment and then prewrite, draft, revise, and edit your argument essay.

## Issues to Keep in Mind

You need to consider the following four issues as you work on your argument essay:

1. The language of argument
2. Supporting the essay's claims
3. Logical fallacies
4. Audience and purpose

### The Language of Argument

Argument has its own language, a set of terms deriving from historical philosophy and from formal logic. Understanding what these terms mean is more important than knowing the terms themselves; you don't actually use these terms in the course of an argument, but understanding these concepts is crucial to writing an effective argument.

An argument is made up of a series of **claims** (also known as **assertions**); these statements express the writer's belief that an issue should be decided one way and not another. A claim also represents a type of **appeal**, or means of convincing your audience. A writer can, categorically, appeal to **logic**, to **values** or **fairness**, and to **emotion**. However, many—perhaps most—arguments don't use all of these, concentrating instead on one or two types of appeals. The following scenario, the background for an essay that appears on pages 435–437, represents the rare instance in which all three types of appeals can be used:

> Currently, your university charges a good deal for parking. Students pay $100 per year; faculty and staff pay $150. Suddenly, seemingly out of nowhere, the university president announces that the two amounts will be switched, with students paying the lion's share.

The arguer's response to this situation is complex. There are three claims to make:

1. The shifting of responsibility is not fair. Students are frequently poor; however, faculty and staff have, by definition, ongoing income. This is an appeal to **values** or **fairness**.

2. The policy change is bad business. This university competes with other local providers of higher education, and area students are known to "shop" for the best value. The university is running the risk of driving students away. This is a **logical** appeal because it depends on analysis, common sense, and mathematics.

3. Student morale is already low. Because of a series of negative incidents over the past school year, students don't feel very good about the university and their relationship with it. Raising student parking fees while lowering faculty/staff fees just seems like a bit much. Students need good news right now, not more trouble. This is an **emotional** appeal.

Most argumentative essays depend on logical appeals and appeals to values or fairness. Be wary of the overuse of emotional appeals, which can produce an essay that seems manipulative.

Once you have made a claim, you must develop and substantiate it. One method is through **reasoning:** using logical processes to prove an assertion. Another method (which is usually combined with the first) employs **evidence** to back up an assertion (see the next section, "Supporting the Essay's Claims").

## Supporting the Essay's Claims

Two ways to substantiate an argumentative claim are by using **reason** and by using **evidence**.

*Reasoning*  People use two major forms of logic when they think and when they write: **deductive reasoning** and **inductive reasoning**. Deductive reasoning starts from a general principle and applies that principle to specific situations. Inductive reasoning requires you to look at specific examples and then move to a general conclusion. We'll look at deduction first.

The ancient philosopher Aristotle wrote that deductive reasoning takes the form of a **syllogism**, a combination that includes a major premise (a general principle), a minor premise (a specific situation), and the logical conclusion. For example,

- **Major Premise:** All tortoiseshell cats are female.
- **Minor Premise:** My cat is a tortoiseshell.
- **Conclusion:** Therefore, my cat is female.

If both premises are true, then the conclusion must be valid. However, if either premise is faulty, then the conclusion won't necessarily be sound. Notice the problem that occurs when the major premise is faulty:

- **Major Premise:** All computer programmers are solitary people.
- **Minor Premise:** Ed is a computer programmer.
- **Conclusion:** Ed is a solitary person.

The problem comes from the fact that the major premise is based on a stereotype, that of programmers being loners. There are many thousands of computer programmers; expecting all of them to have the same personality type is ludicrous.

Sometimes the problem is in the minor premise, as in the following example:

- **Major Premise:** All baseball players are athletes.
- **Minor Premise:** All jockeys are athletes.
- **Conclusion:** All jockeys are baseball players.

The subject of the minor premise must be the same type of thing as the subject of the major premise. Otherwise, the syllogism is faulty and, in this case, nonsensical.

Many students find deductive reasoning appealing, but it clearly has some drawbacks if improperly applied because the writer can easily end up with an essay built upon faulty conclusions. Many argumentative essays are built, instead, on inductive reasoning.

The inductive process reaches a conclusion by building upon specific information. For example, perhaps you are thinking about buying a car. You notice during your travels that one of the models you had been considering seems to be stranded beside the road alarmingly often. Also, recently the car company recalled that model for safety reasons. You would probably draw the inductive conclusion that this is a car to avoid. Such an approach—building upon facts to reach a conclusion—is an argumentative process that writers—and readers—tend to trust.

***Using Evidence***    For the most part, good argumentative essays depend on both abstract concepts and realistic evidence. Avoid writing an essay that depends upon abstractions without concrete evidence to back them up. Where can you find evidence to support your claims? The three basic types of evidence are the following:

1. Personal experience
2. Primary research sources
3. Secondary research sources

In a way, **personal experience** is self-explanatory. However, keep in mind that personal experience isn't limited to your own experience but can be drawn from those you know well and trust. Personal experience can be a very rich source of evidence for writers who pay attention to the world around them.

**Primary research sources** include sources that you develop through your own initiative. If you were planning to argue against a policy, you could gather information on the effects of that policy by conducting interviews, performing surveys, or distributing questionnaires. If your information gathering produces the results you have predicted, you would know that other people have experienced ill effects as a result of the policy, which would be evidence for your thesis. (Note that primary sources must be documented—see chapters 20 and 21.)

**Secondary research sources** include data, opinions, and other published commentary on a subject. By referring to facts, or data, you establish solid support for your claims. Referring to the published opinions or commentary by recognized authorities on a subject will also support your claims. (Note that secondary sources must also be documented—see chapters 20 and 21.)

## Logical Fallacies

**Fallacies** are errors in reasoning—whether deliberate or inadvertent—that weaken an argument and, of course, the quality of the essay that contains the argument. Fallacious arguments seem dishonest whether or not the writer intended them to be. The following list of common fallacies, with examples, is indicative of the types of errors to avoid:

1. *Appeal to strong emotion, belief, or prejudice.*

   Senator Craven has led the fight to preserve the integrity of the American flag. He is a true patriot. Reelect Senator Craven this November.

   The flag causes strong emotional responses in many American citizens, but besides his devotion to this long-time symbol of American values, what else has Senator Craven done? Is his love of the flag the best way to measure his worth?

2. *Appeal to the unknowable.*

   Yes, the film *Topocat* has careless, haphazard editing, but the director and the editor clearly did this on purpose.

   Unless evidence exists, how can a viewer know the intentions of the director and/or editor? How can the writer know?

**3.** *Appeal to tradition.*

Our city's practice of encouraging teenagers to steal cellular phones on the second week of each June is a tradition that shouldn't be questioned. We've always done this, and the tradition has popular support.

Does the fact that this "tradition has popular support" make it right?

**4.** *Appeal to the certain rather than the uncertain.*

The VCR is the best way to watch movies at home. Videocassettes throw a good image, and they last a long time. The entertainment industry is wasting its money if it tries to improve upon the VCR.

The writer argues that whatever is is preferable to whatever might be. Excuse us while we go hitch up the horses.

**5.** *Use of a red herring.*

Yes, Senator Craven is being questioned about his campaign finances. But his fight to preserve American morality will go on. There are forces in this country that would destroy the very basis of all we hold sacred.

Changing the subject is a very old strategy.

**6.** *Appeal to false authority.*

The Multitrust Investment Company group of mutual funds looks like a sure bet. Have you seen their commercials with Alice McDear, who plays the grandmother on *The Quiet Neighborhood*? She's probably the most trustworthy figure on TV.

Alice McDear, actress and investment wizard, couldn't be wrong, could she?

**7.** *Attack the person* (also known as *ad hominem attack*).

Senator Craven's new tax bill has some good points, but I must oppose it. Craven has led a life of depravity and dissolution. His struggles with alcohol are legendary. He has been divorced five times. He may be charged with fraud in the near future.

We weren't really thinking about having Senator Craven move in with us, but we were curious about what is in his new tax legislation. Sometimes, imperfect human beings have innovative ideas that are worth considering.

**8.** *Oversimplify the opponent's stand.*

**Senator Gravely:** It seems to me that our criminal justice priorities are wrong. We're letting murderers and armed robbers out of jail in order to make room for people convicted of simple drug possession. Illegal drug possession must be punished, but let's find a way to do it that keeps violent criminals—and drug dealers—in prison for their full sentences.

**Senator Craven:** Just like always, you're soft on crime, sir.

We're glad that Senator Gravely's argument wasn't any more complicated; clearly, Senator Craven does not want to deal with the reality of what Senator Gravely has to say. He simply chooses to make an easy political point.

**9.** *Beg the question.*

Sexual perversion is wrong because it's illegal. That's enough for me.

Or is it illegal because it's wrong? Perhaps the writer needs to reconsider the whole situation.

**10.** *Ask a loaded question.*

**Reporter:** Senator Craven, Senator Craven, are you still abusing alcohol?

If the answer is yes, the senator looks bad; if the answer is no, the senator still looks bad, if only a little less so.

**11.** *Use an either/or simplification.*

We should either build the new highway extension using the original plan, or we shouldn't build it at all.

Such a pair of choices leaves no room for other options. The dilemma presented is a false one because there almost always *are* more than two options in any given situation.

**12.** *Mistake correlation for causation* (also known as *post hoc, ergo propter hoc*).

Every time I wear my black sneakers, my basketball team wins. I'll wear them from now on.

Two events can happen simultaneously and coincidentally; this is **correlation**, not to be confused with **causation** (see also Chapter 9).

**13.** *Put forth a slippery-slope claim.*

If we let students wear T-shirts with obscene messages on them, the next thing we know they'll be smoking pot behind the gymnasium.

Someone who puts forward a slippery-slope claim sees one change as inexorably leading to a more drastic, horrible change when, in fact, the two events may be unrelated, or one event (stricter gun control) may not necessarily have a catastrophic result (total loss of Second Amendment rights).

**14.** *Make a hasty generalization.*

Jenkins failed in his first attempt to fix our computer network. Computer programmers usually don't know what they're doing.

Give Jenkins another chance or two before condemning him and his profession. One piece of evidence is not enough to support a generalization.

**15.** *Create a false analogy.*

Nature shows us through evolution that it continually improves plants and animals through natural selection. We don't have anything to do with this process. Therefore, I think we should tell the Department of

Family Services to leave the eastern part of our county alone. It's a new, fairly unsettled area, and those people will sort things out on their own.

Human society is not like natural evolution; the analogy is patently false.

16. *Use a non sequitur.* In this type of fallacy, a claim "doesn't follow" the evidence or the previous claim.

Eduardo's Embers is the best restaurant in the city, for the apple pie there is wonderful.

This argument is valid only for those on a strict apple-pie diet. Another example:

I should get a raise at the end of this evaluation period. After all, I got a raise at my last three evaluations.

This writer assumes that what has happened in the past will always happen in the future. If this writer were a machine working in a closed, uniform system, the claim might be valid. However, the writer may have not done enough quality work to justify a raise, slacking off from previous evaluation periods; newly hired colleagues may have raised the level of competition; the company may be experiencing short-term financial problems; the company may have been recently acquired by people who believe that the workers are paid too much already. These are the possible factors that could determine if the writer receives a raise, but he or she ignores them in this simple, flawed argument based on a non sequitur.

17. *Omit vital information.* This is a fallacy sometimes deliberately employed by writers who seek to persuade without offering enough reasons and evidence. "Winning" is key for these writers, not fairness.

**Scenario:** Townsend High and Parker High are about to have their traditional end-of-season football game. Two weeks ago, Townsend High ran all over Peabody Memorial, 63-7. However, last week Parker High, without the services of its star quarterback, Lance Archer, who was out with the flu, lost a squeaker against Peabody, 17-16. In the upcoming game against Townsend, Archer is expected to return at full strength. However, a local sports columnist has conveniently ignored this fact while arguing for Townsend's supremacy.

**Columnist:** "It seems clear we'll be seeing another blowout by Townsend. Two weeks ago they demolished Peabody Memorial, and I think we'll see the same result when they take on hated rival Parker, who couldn't even surmount lowly Peabody. Fans, this one should be a Townsend whitewash."

This practice of deliberately omitting critical information is highly annoying and unethical; it depends on the reader's lack of knowledge. Skilled, fair-minded arguers learn to avoid this fallacy.

## Consider Your Audience and Purpose

When you make an argumentative claim, consider the effect that it will have on your audience. Through the course of this book we have discussed various aspects of the writer-reader relationship, but in argument, this connection is especially important. In no other type of writing is purpose so inextricably connected to audience as in argumentation. As audiences become increasingly global, audience analysis becomes even more critical. As you plan and draft your argument, consider the following questions:

1.  **Do the reader and I have a common understanding of the central issues?** Successful arguments depend upon assumptions that the writer and the reader share. Most people share certain assumptions about the importance of fairness, equality, and responsibility. However, assumptions about politics, religion, morality, and other contentious areas can vary widely. For example, a writer who holds a very specialized or radical view of international relations—who believes, for instance, that the United States is a global bully that uses its economic and military powers to get its way with weaker countries—should not assume that such a view will be shared by a general audience. In this case, it is very likely that the writer and the reader will be at odds; the reader will not accept the argument because he or she does not accept the assumptions behind it. If the writer had carefully considered both audience and purpose, however, a different essay could have emerged, one that first tried to establish a common area of understanding with the reader, or at least tried to get the reader to understand his or her view. A writer and a reader can have widely varying political views, but it is still possible for them to find common ground.

2.  **Have I presented a fair, well-considered argument?** Your reader does *not* want to read a wishy-washy paper that argues both sides but refuses to back either one. However, your reader wants a sense that you have carefully considered the ramifications of your argument and have taken into account opposing views. An argument that stridently opposes a policy but fails to note the positive results of the policy is easy to criticize. A writer who argues that a social change should occur should not be fearful of acknowledging a valid opposing view. For example, we have read many student essays arguing that marijuana should be legal and for sale. These essays almost always have the following two flaws. First, they are written from a position of narrow self-interest. The writer likes marijuana. Pot is illegal, which makes its use inconvenient and dangerous, so the writer seeks to remove this obstacle. Second, the essays fail to address the enormous effect that legalizing marijuana would have on U.S. society, government, and commerce. The reader of such an essay frequently senses that it is just a plea, not a reasoned argument. A paper that acknowledged and/or recognized the validity of opposing views about legalizing marijuana would be a stronger argument. For example, the paper might acknowledge the fact that smoking marijuana impairs motor responses and judgment and that people driving cars or operating heavy machinery while under

the influence of marijuana should be arrested and prosecuted, just as drunk drivers are. It might also discuss the long-term health effects of using marijuana and suggest that warning labels like those for tobacco be used with marijuana. Doing so helps show that the writer has thought about this issue carefully, and it adds to the writer's credibility.

3. **Is my audience likely to agree with me already, be neutral, or oppose my claims?** When writing an argument, be careful to assess your audience carefully. Some readers might be quite receptive to your point of view. Others might not have an opinion at all, or they might be of a different mind and hold an opinion diametrically opposed to yours. In case of the latter, you might have to establish some common ground before stating your opinion explicitly.

**CATALYST 2.0**

**MORE OPTIONS ONLINE**
For more help with problem areas in the argument essay, go to www.mhhe.com/ writingtoday.

## Choosing a Topic

If your instructor lets you choose your own argumentation topic, consider these guidelines:

1. Avoid open-and-shut issues. If the point of your argument is a foregone conclusion—Why can't we all just get along?—then there's no use pursuing it. Choose an issue that has two or more viable positions; then concentrate on one of these.

2. Avoid narrow, personal topics. If your roommate is a slob and you want to argue that his slobbishness (slobdom?) threatens your ongoing living arrangement, then the only two people who are likely to be interested in this argument are you and your roommate. However, a more *general* topic—the threat that slobs pose to shared living quarters—could work quite well. In this approach, your roommate becomes an example: evidence that you can use.

3. Avoid topics that can't be proved. Students who argue on religious or spiritual topics sometimes find themselves backing up their claims by referring to their faith's authoritative text—the Bible or the Koran, for example. Or they may use their fervent personal beliefs as evidence. If you are writing for a general audience, though, neither approach is valid. Faith is faith, and logic is logic; the two have their own uses, but faith doesn't work as evidence to back up the claims of an argumentative essay. However, we're not stating that religion and religious issues are off-limits in argument. There are a vast number of potential topics in this intriguing category that don't have to be settled by referring to one's faith or to a denomination's doctrines.

## Prewriting

Writing an argumentative essay requires the generation of a great many ideas and pieces of evidence. Try this approach: use freewriting, brainstorming, or another prewriting method to generate your claims—the major assertions that you plan to make. Then work to generate reasons and evidence for these claims. How will you back up your claims? Will you need to do some research at the library or on the Internet? (See Chapter 20.) Focus on the types of evidence you will use (see also "Using Evidence," pages 428–429).

After this step, review your prewriting. (If you have produced more information than you can use, don't worry. This situation is always preferable to the opposite situation.) Can you turn your output into a coherent argument? Do you need to do more work before you start the organizing phase? Can you develop a preliminary or working thesis at this point?

## Organizing

At this point, organize your prewriting into an outline. (Chapter 2 covers informal, sentence, and formal outlines.) If you use a sentence outline, for example, be willing to revise it or construct a new one if, upon review, you decide that it won't work because it doesn't present your reasons in an effective order or it branches off in an irrelevant direction. Plan on organizing until you come up with a paragraph sequence that suits both your thesis and your purpose.

Consider this strategy: build a sentence outline with annotations. In other words, after you complete your outline, add notes (such as "transition here" and "relevance?") where needed. This way, you'll give yourself an extensive framework to use as you begin drafting.

## Drafting

To illustrate one approach to writing the argument essay, we have included the essay "Stuck Again."

### The Introduction

The introductory section of an argumentative essay explains the situation—the issue that your argument will address. Depending on the nature of your topic and the extent of your assignment, you may need more than one paragraph to introduce your argument. Be aware of the need for balance: although one paragraph may suffice to introduce a twelve-paragraph essay, a three-paragraph introduction is clearly too extensive for a seven-paragraph paper.

The following introduction sets up the essay on student parking fees versus faculty/staff parking fees that we mentioned earlier:

### Stuck Again

Parking is a sore subject on this campus. There is not enough to go around for both students and employees, and when talking to people who've been here a while, I learned that it's been many years since parking was *not* an issue. There seems to be no solution, either. Located as it is in a congested downtown area, the campus cannot acquire any more land. And the administration has been refused twice in its attempts to gain funds to build a parking garage. **However, the administration's latest decision—to lower the yearly rates for faculty/staff by $50 and to increase student rates by the same amount—is unfair, misguided, and cruel.**

• *Consider Your Options*

Be thorough in the introduction to an argument. Make sure that your reader understands exactly what you plan to argue. Good strategies include opening with an engaging anecdote or a provocative question. (For more on introductions, see Chapter 3.)

The first paragraph describes the situation, then concludes with the thesis: the writer's stance on the issue. From this introduction, the writer could either have gone on to present a one-sided rant against the university administration or develop a carefully balanced argument. Note how the essay continues.

### The Body

The first body paragraph reveals that the writer has a comprehensive grasp of the situation—he is not going to write a simple rant stemming from his wounded wallet. But after showing his understanding of "the other side," he needs to bring the focus of his writing back to his thesis, which he accomplishes with the first word of his second body paragraph. Read the following passage carefully:

> I understand that parking is a contentious issue for the administration. I also understand that the administration must deal with a lot of issues related to this situation that students don't hear about. And, on a cynical level, I suspect that the administration may be more worried about pleasing a "permanent" group (faculty and staff) than about displeasing a "temporary" group (students) while still increasing revenues, there being many more students at this campus than employees.
>
> **Nevertheless,** the administration's decision is patently unfair. Faculty and staff have incomes, whereas students may not. If I were employed here, I wouldn't like the fact that I would have to pay to park my vehicle next to my office, but I would at least have a biweekly paycheck, and I would know that I needed to budget for this expense. Students, on the other hand, tend to run short of funds. Many students are on near-starvation diets. Fifty dollars is a lot of money in that type of situation.

The writer's negative transition (*Nevertheless*) refocuses his argument in the direction indicated by his thesis. In this paragraph he offers a claim based on **values** and **fairness**—that the administration's decision is unfair—by using inductive reasoning to back up this appeal. The next body paragraph uses a different kind of claim:

> This administrative step is also misguided. This city is blessed with a number of institutions of higher learning; our university does not have a local or regional monopoly on college courses. On a practical level, the administration may literally be driving students away. (Excuse the pun.) Many students at this school also take classes elsewhere; more students can take this step.

In this paragraph the student uses a **logical** appeal: that the administrative decision is bad for business and therefore misguided. In the final body paragraph the student introduces an **emotional** appeal:

> Finally, the parking decision is just one more piece of bad news for students this year. Some people may have forgotten that the campus was haunted by a series of muggings during the fall term, two fraternity pledges were seriously injured in separate hazing incidents, asbestos was discovered in the women's dormitories, and our football and basketball teams both had atrocious seasons. Student morale is not at its highest level. For the administration to announce this decision at this time is just plain cruel.

### The Conclusion

The writer could summarize his argument at this point, but the essay is not long enough to require this step. Besides, summaries tend to sound perfunctory and boring. Instead, he takes a different approach, referring first to his second paragraph, then revisiting his thesis, and finally offering a possible solution to the overall problem:

> Although the administration has concerns other than the needs of the campus's students, the recent decision on parking fees seems horribly misguided. Rather than adding to students' financial burdens, surely the administration could choose a kinder, gentler course of action. At this point, most students would gladly accept a compromise: Why not make everyone pay the same price? This way, at least students wouldn't feel like they were subsidizing the parking costs of faculty and staff.

*Consider Your Options* •

For the conclusion to an argument, summarizing doesn't work as well as reinforcing your thesis. "Seal your case" at this point. (For more on strategies for concluding paragraphs, see Chapter 3.)

## EXERCISE 13.1

Write an outline of "Stuck Again." (For help with outlines, see Chapter 2, pages 40–42.) How has the writer organized his argument? Would a different organization have been more effective? Why?

## Revising Your Draft

After you have completed a draft of your argument essay, your next step is to revise it, using your own analysis and comments from classmates or friends. During peer review, answer the following questions about the draft you are reviewing, whether it is yours or another student's.

After reviewing for content, you need to go over your peer reviewers' responses to your essay and then revise for unity, coherence, language level, and tone (see Chapter 4). When you have revised your draft and are basically satisfied with it, read your draft for mechanical and grammatical errors. Concentrate on finding and correcting major sentence errors (fragments, comma splices, fused sentences), errors in pronoun agreement and subject-verb agreement, and spelling.

Now that you have made your corrections, *read your essay one more time* to catch any errors made during revision and find errors missed during your earlier reviews.

## Questions for Reviewing an Argument Essay

1　Does the introduction provide enough context to set up the rest of the essay?

2　Is there a clear thesis statement, and is the thesis adequately supported by the body paragraphs? How could the thesis or its support be improved?

3　Does the essay show a sufficient sense of its audience? In what ways has the writer demonstrated common ground with the audience? How could the writer strengthen the connection to his or her audience?

4　Has the writer organized the essay effectively? Does it seem coherent and complete?

5　Has the writer avoided using emotional appeals only? If any emotional appeals have been used, are they appropriate and effective?

6　Has the writer used logical reasoning? Are the essay's claims clear, and are they supported by appropriate evidence? Where is clarification or more support needed?

7　Has the writer avoided logical fallacies? Point out any fallacies that you find.

8　Has the writer indicated an awareness of other positions on the issue, and not just his or her stance? How has the writer dealt with these other positions?

9　Does the conclusion adequately reflect the body of the essay? Is it an effective and satisfying conclusion for the argument? What other strategy for concluding the essay might the writer consider?

## Student Essay

The following essay is Sam Leininger's response to an argument assignment. Sam's final draft is presented first. Then his first draft is presented, with Sam's comments about this draft and what he needed to do in the revision stage. Note that Sam's tone is somewhat ironic. While appropriate to his audience and purpose, it is not be the kind of tone you should use in most academic arguments.

*Sam's Final Draft*

### My Simple and Modest Plan

People make bad decisions on a daily basis: regular unleaded                    1
instead of high octane, fat-free ice cream instead of Ben & Jerry's,
the American rip-off *City of Angels* instead of the classic German
film *Wings of Desire*. Most of these decisions come from a lack of
taste, and nowhere is lack of taste more apparent than at the local
video store. People are not educated, and don't want to be educated, on the quality of movies. They want to be told what to
watch, but in a way that makes them feel like they have a choice. If
thirty copies of a particular historical boat movie are prominently
displayed on the most visible shelves, chances are likely that this
movie will be chosen over the British movie from 1958 that deals
with this very same historical boat (that is, if *A Night to Remember*\*
is even in the store). If people want some direction, it should be provided in a less subtle and more responsible manner; I propose that a
series of tests and levels of rental freedom be established to promote a true understanding of cinema as an art form.

I understand that taste is a subjective entity and that different                    2
people watch movies for different reasons. Some like to see car
chases and explosions (and feel that elements like dialogue and character development get in the way); others want to see the guy get
the girl, no matter what. I've even been known to watch *The Trouble with Mary* on occasion. I also abhor censorship and the thought of

---

\**A Night to Remember:* a film about the sinking of the *Titanic* in 1912.

controlling what people can and can't watch. Freedom with limitations is not freedom.

However, someone needs to raise the cultural level of society,                3
and we don't seem to be doing this on our own. Under my proposed
system, all new video-club members would take a test to determine
their existing cinema knowledge. The test would cover technical
aspects, film theory, history, and general aesthetics. The member
would then be assigned a level of membership based upon the test
results. The higher the score on the test, the more freedom the
member has. Someone who performs poorly on the test, for
instance, would need every movie to be verified by an employee as
suitable before rental. This person could never watch any Charlie
Sheen movies. Each member's rental history would be followed
closely, with rewards given to those with exemplary rental choices.
Watching *The General* (1927) and *Battleship Potemkin* (1925) would
earn even the lowest scoring members any Will Ferrell movie they
desire. Also, members can retake the test any time they feel able to
move up to a higher level of membership.

A few rules would also be established that would apply to all          4
members. First, every tenth movie must be foreign. People are often
scared away by subtitles, but some of the greatest films have come
from other countries. Repeat viewings would not be allowed on all
movies. Multiple viewings would be allowed only for films that have
a subtle, layered text with motifs and ideas that may not be understood on the first viewing. A member can rent *Kids* or *House of a
Thousand Corpses* only once, unless a valid, academic reason is supplied. Every member will get a set number of "guilty pleasure"
passes that allow him or her to rent any film without reproach,
because sometimes people need to see bad films to appreciate the
good ones. And, of course, anyone arguing with the decision of the
employee will have his or her membership revoked until a tribunal
can be set up to hear the member's argument.

This system would never work, however. If there is one thing                    5
that people like more than mind-numbing movies, it is screaming
about their right to watch mind-numbing movies. I just want to try
to pass on a little bit of the knowledge, admiration, and respect I
have for filmmakers who take their art seriously enough not to give
Ben Affleck a lead role in their films. You can't walk into an art
gallery and buy a velvet painting of dogs playing poker or a sculpture
of the fat Elvis, but you can walk into a video store and find more
bad films on the shelves than good ones. Until something is done to
change the way we view movies, both individually and as an art
form, cinema will never be recognized for the art that it is.

### Sam's First Draft

#### My Simple and Modest Plan

People make bad decisions on a daily basis: regular unleaded            1  This first draft is an
instead of high octane, fat-free ice cream instead of Ben & Jerry's,      example of me think-
                                                                          ing on paper—it's a
*City of Angels* instead of *Wings of Desire*. Most of these decisions come   very fast, rough draft.
from a lack of taste, and nowhere is lack of taste more apparent than
at the local video store. People are not educated on the quality of
movies. They want to be told what to watch, but in a way that makes
them feel good. If 30 copies of a particular historical boat movie are
available chances are likely that this movie will be chosen over *A
Night to Remember*. If people want this direction, I think it should be
done in a less subtle and more responsible manner; I propose that a
series of tests and levels of rental freedom be established.

I understand that taste is a subjective entity, and that different     2  When I write quickly, I
people watch movies for different reasons. Some like to see car           tend to lean on abstrac-
                                                                          tions, and this kind of
chases and explosions; others want to see the guy get the girl, no        argument better have
matter what. I also abhor censorship and the thought of controlling       specific support if it is
                                                                          going to work. In my
what people can and can't watch.                                          second draft I filled in
                                                                          the gaps.
However, someone needs to raise the cultural level of society.         3
Under my proposed system, every new member will take a test to

I added more details here about my proposed system.

determine their existing cinema knowledge. The member will then be assigned a level of membership based upon the test results. The higher the score on the test, the more freedom the member has. Someone who does bad on the test, for instance, will need every movie to be verified by an employee as valid before rental. Each member's rental history will be followed closely, and rewards given to those with exemplary rental choices. Also, members can re-take the test any time they feel able to move up.

A few rules would also be set that would apply to all members.  4 First, every tenth movie must be foreign. Repeat viewings will not be allowed on all movies. Multiple viewings should be saved for films that have a subtle, layered text. And, of course, anyone arguing with the decision of the employee will have their membership revoked until a tribunal can be set up to hear the member's argument.

I proofread my second draft carefully to tighten the language and look for grammatical errors, such as this pronoun agreement problem in the fifth sentence.

A classmate pointed out that watching movies isn't mentioned in the U.S. Constitution.

This system would never work, however. If there's one thing that  5 people like more than mind-numbing movies, it's screaming about their Constitutional rights to watch mind-numbing movies. I just want to try and pass on a little bit of the knowledge, admiration, and respect I have for filmmakers who take their art seriously. Until something is done to change the way we view movies, cinema will never be recognized for the art that it is.

### EXERCISE 13.2: REVISING

The following is the first draft of a student's argument essay. Working in pairs or in small groups, review this essay. Using the Questions for Reviewing an Argument Essay on page 438, decide what revisions you would suggest. If you have any questions the student needs to consider, write them in the margin or on a separate sheet of paper. If your instructor directs you to, rewrite one or more paragraphs to make them stronger and to eliminate any grammatical or mechanical errors.

"Clear Censor Ship"

Last Tuesday Morning I was asked to leave my Economics Class.

Its not that I was causing a disturbance, its the shirt I was wearing.

The Tshirt was a repro of a popular 1970's shirt with the words

"Makin' Bacon," it shows two pigs, well getting it own. My professor, dr. Silva found this offensive and told me to leave and to not return wearing this shirt.

First this is censor ship. I'm expressing myself by wearing this, who is dr. Silva to take offensce? Should we ware uniforms to school, so that dear dr. Silva wont feel threaten?

Second I pay my tuition and abide by the rules and nowhere in the rules is their a picture of my shirt with a notice telling me I cant wear it, if their was, I wouldnt be writing this and dr. Silva and I would not be at war as it is I might have to go over her head.

Im being treated like a child, censored against cause of what I wear and I think alot of students would agree with my gripe. Dr. Silva hasnt herd the end of this issue.

## Additional Writing Topics

1. In a few countries, such as Australia, adults are required by law to vote in national elections. Should the United States adopt such a law?

2. Nonpayment of child support is a massive problem for single mothers and their children. Should court-ordered child support become a payroll deduction for fathers who have been ordered to make such payments?

3. Should a person be allowed to marry someone of the same sex?

4. In most states, the minimum age at which a person can drive a motor vehicle without supervision is sixteen. However, teenagers are involved in far more than their share of serious car accidents. Should the minimum age be raised to nineteen?

5. Should public school students whose first language is not English and who have limited English proficiency be taught subjects such as history, science, and mathematics in their own languages until they become proficient in English? Or should they be mainstreamed into classes where only English is spoken?

6. Should taxpayer moneys be used to fund the education of students enrolled in parochial (church-run) schools? If so, why? And what form should this funding take? If not, why not?

7. **Writing on the job.** At the company where you work or where you used to work, what is one part of the company's procedure for dealing with customers or clients that is ineffective and needs to be changed? Write a memo to your manager arguing for this change. (See Chapter 17 for help with writing memos.)

### *Argument and Visual Representations*

In the United States, the rate of cigarette smoking by adults has declined substantially over the past few decades. However, if you were to go back in a time machine to the 1950s, for example, you might be very surprised by what you experienced. Most people smoked, and they did so virtually everywhere: on planes, trains, and buses; in doctors' and dentists' offices; in hospital rooms. The Surgeon General's warning that appears on cigarette packages went into effect in 1965, and it was not until 1971 that cigarette advertising was banned on television. Moreover, the laws that restrict or disallow smoking in various public places are largely creations of the 1990s and the early 2000s.

Back in the 1950s, cigarettes were just one more product to be marketed, and celebrities were often enlisted to give their testimonials, as you can see in the two print ads reproduced here. Before Ronald Reagan was the fortieth president of the United States, he was the governor of California, and before that he was an actor. He lent his celebrity endorsement to the Chesterfield brand. John Wayne was the most popular star in the history of American film. His

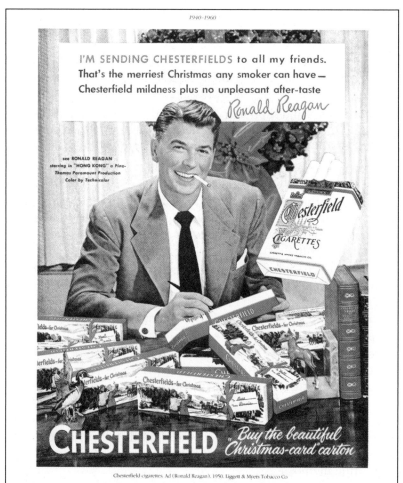

Chesterfield cigarettes. Ad (Ronald Reagan), 1950. Liggett & Myers Tobacco Co

The Advertising Archives.

usual role was as a rough-and-ready cowboy whose tough image was tempered by a self-deprecating sense of humor. He lent his support to the Camel brand.

Reagan died in 2004 of complications related to Alzheimer's disease; however, Wayne died in 1979 of lung cancer.

1. Write a response to these ads. What are your thoughts and impressions? As you write, refer to Questions for Reviewing a Visual Representation.

2. In the United States, tobacco companies do not have the same freedom to advertise as do companies selling other products. For example, tobacco companies cannot advertise on radio or television. However, they still find ways to market their products. Try to find five different tobacco-funded ads. What persuasive techniques do these ads use? As an alternative, research the marketing done by these same companies in other countries. Then either write an essay explaining what you discovered (remember to document your sources—see also Chapter 21) or develop an oral presentation based on your research and conclusions (see also Chapter 18).

The Advertising Archives.

*Questions for Reviewing a Visual Representation*

- Is the representation forceful, passive, or something in between?
- What is the purpose of the representation—in other words, what is it trying to do to you, the reader/viewer?
- If the representation uses words, do they reinforce the visual image or in some way contradict it?
- What is the presumed audience for the representation—men, women, children, the elderly? Or does it have a broader appeal?
- If the representation is an advertisement, is it trying to sell a product or to get you to adopt a way of thinking?
- If the representation is an advertisement, does it try to persuade you in a fair manner, or do you feel manipulated?

*Responding to an Image*

In the 1960s, the civil rights movement took to the streets. Protest marches gave the movement media exposure, with images appearing in national magazines and beamed through the airwaves of network television. In 1968 Ernest C. Withers took the photograph that appears below.

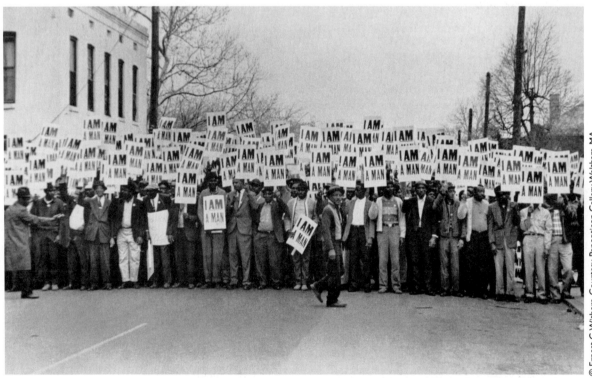

1. Write an informal response to the photograph. What do you notice? How does the image make you feel? How does the photograph use the argumentation option?

2. The photograph was taken at a time when African Americans were fighting for equal rights and treatment. Using a combination of library and online research, explore the public arguments that the civil rights movement prompted. Remember to narrow your topic so that you can adequately address it. Write a documented essay examining one of these arguments. (For more information on documented essays, see Chapter 21.)

## Using the Internet

Search the Internet for insights and information to use when developing arguments.

1. Practice spotting logical fallacies by searching for Web sites that present arguments on both sides of an important social, political, moral, or legal issue of your choice. Spend some time on this assignment by reading the perspectives and opinions that are presented on several different Web sites. Then review the material you have researched, and identify examples of at least five of the seventeen logical fallacies discussed on pages 429–432 in this chapter. In a short essay, explain how each of the examples you have chosen illustrates that particular fallacy.

2. Using information taken from the Web sites you visited in response to item 1, write an argument defending a position on the particular social, political, moral, or legal issue addressed in those Web sites. In the process, present and address arguments that oppose your own so that your reader will know that you have considered both sides of the issue.

   As always, combine the information and insights you have researched with your own ideas, but cite any material you quote, summarize, or paraphrase from another source. Use the Modern Language Association (MLA) format or the American Psychological Association (APA) format, explained in Chapter 21 of this textbook.

### CHAPTER 14

# THE BLENDED ESSAY

# Writing in Context

Bob has sent you an e-mail:

> It's review time. I'll be assessing your first ninety days with the company a week from Friday. Before then, I'd like you to send me an account of your experiences. What did you expect of your new position? What problems did you face? How did you deal with them? How do you think you performed during your probationary period?

Your first thought after absorbing this memo is that the biggest problem you faced was Bob, but you doubt that this fact will appear in your self-review. Beyond that, you find a jumble of impressions and memories. Certainly, there were expectations that weren't met, and a lot of surprises. There were long-running events that you'll want to briefly narrate, and there were situations whose causes you'll want to analyze and explain. You believe that your first ninety-day period was a success, and you think that Bob shares this belief. However, quite apart from the fact that you don't really trust Bob, in this self-review you should be making a case for yourself, so you'll need to have more than a hint of argument in your account.

In any case, you're going to have to integrate a number of strategies to put together an effective document.

The document Bob is asking for demands that you use multiple rhetorical options in order to explain various aspects of a complex situation: your performance at work. Many complex situations call for such an approach.

# HOW DOES THE BLENDED ESSAY WORK?

In the preceding nine chapters, we have discussed individual rhetorical options. Yet in each chapter we have also shown how writers use other strategies inside their essays to strengthen the essays' overall effectiveness. In reality, a writer would find it very difficult to write an essay of any length by using only one strategy. One *could* write a pure description or narration, but the reader might wonder about the essay's purpose. A good essay is one that "seizes" the reader, and it is able to do this precisely because it is generated through a more complicated process, involving multiple strategies. Every week and every month, you can read excellent essays in major newspapers and journals of opinion, and in many or most cases you would be hard-pressed to point out a dominant strategy. The writers organize their work according to the needs of their often complicated subjects.

Let's take what seems to be a simple topic and see what happens. If you were sent to visit a greenhouse as part of a field trip and asked to give an account of your visit, two obvious strategies come to mind: description and narration. But a more thorough approach would also use some or all of the following methods:

- **Definition:** explaining the specialized terms used in the greenhouse business
- **Classification:** discussing how the greenhouse's products are grouped
- **Process analysis:** recounting the steps or procedures used by the greenhouse manager
- **Causal analysis:** discussing why problems occur and what steps are taken to avoid them
- **Comparison/contrast:** examining successful plant species versus unsuccessful plant species, last year's business versus this year's, your expectations of the greenhouse versus its reality
- **Exemplification:** using specific examples to support the general points that you are trying to make

With these ideas in mind, you could write a very thorough account of your visit. There is no need to concentrate on one strategy when you can use several and thereby enhance your account. Notice also that by thinking in terms of these strategies, you might be better able to generate ideas.

You may well find such a combined approach useful when responding to writing assignments in your college classes. We have mentioned that your instructors' assignments sometimes point you toward an obvious strategy: by the wording of the assignment, your instructor is signaling what strategy he or she expects. However, in many instances the assignment is more open, as in the following example: "Describe the political environment in the years leading up to the passage of the Volstead Act."

Prohibition came into being after the passage of the Eighteenth Amendment to the U.S. Constitution. The Volstead Act, which was passed in 1919 to establish the guidelines for Prohibition, was an enormously controversial law. On one side was the temperance movement, whose supporters were concerned about drinking and its consequences—and this was before most people drove cars. On the other side of the debate were the business interests involved in the manufacture, distribution, and sale of alcoholic beverages, along with a large number of citizens who did not want their drinking privileges to disappear. The anti-alcohol forces won, and Prohibition lasted until President Franklin D. Roosevelt engineered its repeal in 1933.

The assignment asks the writer to "describe," but the word is not used in a literal sense here. What the instructor actually wants is for the writer to "tell me what you know, and show me how well you understand the big picture."

What approaches might the writer take? A successful response probably would include some or all of the following strategies:

- **Narration.** The assignment, after all, asks for a discussion of "the years leading up to . . .," so a chronological ordering would be hard to fault.
- **Exemplification.** Specific examples can back up any general statements that the writer makes.
- **Causal analysis.** What spurred the temperance movement? How did the liquor interests first react to the attempts to create a constitutional amendment restricting alcoholic beverages?
- **Process analysis.** How did the temperance movement convince the necessary number of state legislatures to ratify the amendment?
- **Comparison/contrast.** On the surface, the two opposing groups seem radically different, so this approach is an obvious one.
- **Classification.** Did everyone in the temperance movement believe in the same "party line," or were there factions?
- **Definition.** The word *temperance* means "moderation," not "abstinence." This historical irony could be explored.
- **Argument.** Could it be argued that Prohibition was inevitable, given the social, cultural, and political climate of the era? Or could it be argued that Prohibition was a poorly thought out solution to a complex social problem?

Being able to combine rhetorical options as needed is a valuable skill. However, keep in mind that this approach to the essay demands careful forethought, not a haphazard mixing of approaches. A typical blended essay depends on three or four rhetorical options—used as needed when the writer's purpose demands them. They serve the point that the writer is trying to make, not the other way around.

You have studied the dominant rhetorical options, have seen how published writers use them, and have written your own essays that concentrate on one of the rhetorical options. After reading the following essays and the rest of the chapter, you should be ready to write your own blended essay.

> *Consider Your Options*
>
> Reread the anecdote that opens this chapter. Have you faced circumstances on the job or in college that required you to produce a complex, multi-option document or oral response? How did you decide which options to use?

## READING THE BLENDED ESSAY WITH A WRITER'S EYE

In the following selections, Scott Russell Sanders explores different perspectives on male privilege, Anthony Bourdain gives the inside scoop on the restaurant business, and Elisabeth Kübler-Ross explores the inability of many

Americans to deal with the inevitability of death. As you read each essay, look for the strategies that the writer uses.

After each of these essays, we will ask questions about the various strategies used in the essay and suggest writing topics based on responses to the essay's content and approach. Additional writing topics are located at the end of the chapter (page 474).

# The Men We Carry in Our Minds

## SCOTT RUSSELL SANDERS

*With a bachelor's degree from Brown University, a doctorate from Cambridge University in England, a professorship at Indiana University, and several published books, Scott Russell Sanders would seem to be high up in the American social class system. Yet Sanders comes from a working-class background, and in the following essay, originally published in* Milkweed Chronicle *and collected in his* Paradise of Bombs *(1987), he describes how his background gives him a different outlook on the issue of male privilege.*

When I was a boy, the men I knew labored with their bodies. They were marginal farmers, just scraping by, or welders, steelworkers, carpenters; they swept floors, dug ditches, mined coal, or drove trucks, their forearms ropy with muscle; they trained horses, stoked furnaces, built tires, stood on assembly lines wrestling parts onto cars and refrigerators. They got up before light, worked all day long whatever the weather, and when they came home at night they looked as though somebody had been whipping them. In the evenings and on weekends they worked on their own places, tilling gardens that were lumpy with clay, fixing broken-down cars, hammering on houses that were always too drafty, too leaky, too small.

The bodies of the men I knew were twisted and maimed in ways visible and invisible. The nails of their hands were black and split, the hands tattooed with scars. Some had lost fingers. Heavy lifting had given many of them finicky backs and guts weak from hernias. Racing against conveyor belts had given them ulcers. Their ankles and knees ached from years of standing on concrete. Anyone who had worked for long around machines was hard of hearing. They squinted, and the skin of their faces was creased like the leather of old work gloves. There were times, studying them, when I dreaded growing up. Most of them coughed, from dust or cigarettes, and most of them drank cheap wine or whiskey, so their eyes looked bloodshot and bruised. The fathers of my friends always seemed older than the mothers. Men wore out sooner. Only women lived into old age.

As a boy I also knew another sort of men, who did not sweat and break down like mules. They were soldiers, and so far as I could tell they scarcely worked at all. During my early school years we lived on a military base, an arsenal in Ohio, and every day I saw GIs in the guardshacks, on the stoops of barracks, at the wheels of olive drab Chevrolets. The chief fact of their lives was boredom. Long after I left the Arsenal I came to recognize the sour smell the soldiers gave off as that of souls in limbo. They were all waiting—for wars, for transfers, for leaves, for promotions, for the end of their hitch—like so many braves waiting for the hunt to begin. Unlike the warriors of older tribes, however, they would have no say about when the battle would start or how it would be waged. Their waiting was broken only when they practiced for war. They fired guns at targets, drove tanks across the churned-up fields of the military reservation, set off bombs in the wrecks of old fighter planes. I knew this was all play. But I also felt certain that when the hour for killing arrived, they would kill. When the real shooting started, many of them would die. This was what soldiers were *for,* just as a hammer was for driving nails.

Warriors and toilers: those seemed, in my boyhood vision, to be the chief destinies for men. They weren't the only destinies, as I learned from having a few male teachers, from reading books, and from watching television. But the men on television—the politicians, the astronauts, the generals, the savvy lawyers, the philosophical doctors, the bosses who gave orders to both soldiers and laborers—seemed as removed and unreal to me as the figures in tapestries. I could no more imagine growing up to become one of these cool, potent creatures than I could imagine becoming a prince.

A nearer and more hopeful example was that of my father, who had escaped from a red-dirt farm to a tire factory, and from the assembly line to the front office. Eventually he dressed in a white shirt and tie. He carried himself as if he had been born to work with his mind. But his body, remembering the earlier years of slogging work, began to give out on him in his fifties, and it quit on him entirely before he turned sixty-five. Even such a partial escape from man's fate as he had accomplished did not seem possible for most of the boys I knew. They joined the Army, stood in line for jobs in the smoky plants, helped build highways. They were bound to work as their fathers had worked, killing themselves or preparing to kill others.

A scholarship enabled me not only to attend college, a rare enough feat in my circle, but even to study in a university meant for the children of the rich. Here I met for the first time young men who had assumed from birth that they would lead lives of comfort and power. And for the first time I met women who told me that men were guilty of having kept all the joys and privileges of the earth for themselves. I was baffled. What privileges? What joys? I thought about the maimed, dismal lives of most of the men back home. What had they stolen from their wives and daughters? The right to go five days a week, twelve months a year, for thirty or forty years to a steel mill or a coal mine? The right to drop bombs and die in war? The right to feel every leak in the roof, every gap in the fence, every cough in the engine, as a wound they must mend? The right to feel, when the lay-off comes or the plant shuts down, not only afraid but ashamed?

I was slow to understand the deep grievances of women. This was because, as a boy, I had envied them. Before college, the only people I had ever known who were interested in art or music or literature, the only ones who read books, the only ones who ever seemed to enjoy a sense of ease and grace were the mothers and daughters. Like the menfolk, they fretted about money, they scrimped and made-do. But, when the pay stopped coming in, they were not the ones who had failed. Nor did they have to go to war, and that seemed to me a blessed fact. By comparison with the narrow, ironclad days of fathers, there was an expansiveness, I thought, in the days of mothers. They went to see neighbors, to shop in town, to run errands at school, at the library, at church. No doubt, had I looked harder at their lives, I would have envied them less. It was not my fate to become a woman, so it was easier for me to see the graces. Few of them held jobs outside the home, and those who did filled thankless roles as clerks and waitresses. I didn't see, then, what a prison a house could be, since houses seemed to me brighter, handsomer places than any factory. I did not realize—because such things were never spoken of—how often women suffered from men's bullying. I did learn about the wretchedness of abandoned wives, single mothers, widows; but I also learned about the wretchedness of lone men. Even then I could see how exhausting it was for a mother to cater all day to the needs of young children. But if I had been asked, as a boy, to choose between tending a baby and tending a machine, I think I would have chosen the baby. (Having now tended both, I know I would choose the baby.)

So I was baffled when the women at college 8 accused me and my sex of having cornered the world's pleasures. I think something like my bafflement has been felt by other boys (and by girls as well) who grew up in dirt-poor farm country, in mining country, in black ghettos, in Hispanic barrios, in the shadows of factories, in Third World nations—any place where the fate of men is as grim and bleak as the fate of women. Toilers and warriors. I realize now how ancient these identities are, how deep the tug they exert on men, the undertow of a thousand generations. The miseries I saw, as a boy, in the lives of nearly all men I continue to see in the lives of many—the body-breaking toil, the tedium, the call to be tough, the humiliating powerlessness, the battle for a living and for territory.

When the women I met at college thought 9 about the joys and privileges of men, they did not carry in their minds the sort of men I had known in my childhood. They thought of their fathers, who were bankers, physicians, architects, stockbrokers, the big wheels of the big cities. These fathers rode the train to work or drove cars that cost more than any of my childhood houses. They were attended from morning to night by female helpers, wives and nurses and secretaries. They were never laid off, never short of cash at month's end, never lined up for welfare. These fathers made decisions that mattered. They ran the world.

The daughters of such men wanted to share 10 in this power, this glory. So did I. They yearned for a say over their future, for jobs worthy of their abilities, for the right to live at peace, unmolested, whole. Yes, I thought, yes yes. The difference between me and these daughters was that they saw me, because of my sex, as destined from birth to become like their fathers, and therefore as an enemy to their desires. But I knew better. I wasn't an enemy, in fact or in feeling. I was an ally. If I had known, then, how to tell them so, would they have believed me? Would they now?

## Vocabulary

The following terms are identified by paragraph number. Make sure that you understand each term's meaning in its context. If you're not sure that you understand a term, look it up in a college-level dictionary.

| | | |
|---|---|---|
| marginal (1) | limbo (3) | grievances (7) |
| stoked (1) | hitch (3) | scrimped (7) |
| tilling (1) | churned (3) | ironclad (7) |
| maimed (2) | toilers (4) | expansiveness (7) |
| arsenal (3) | savvy (4) | barrios (8) |
| stoops (3) | tapestries (4) | ally (10) |

## Style and Strategy

1.  How and where does Sanders use comparison/contrast? Give specific examples.

2.  Where does Sanders use (a) description, (b) narration, (c) definition, and (d) process analysis?

3.  What does the author's conclusion reveal about his purpose?

4.  How did Sanders's reaction to the "deep grievances of women" (paragraph 7) change over time? What understanding did he gain that made this change possible?

## Questions for Critical Thinking and Discussion

1.  What is your dominant perception of the role of men? Is it different from the one that Sanders describes himself as having had when he was young?

2.  What do you think marriage will be like in the future? Will there ever be true equality between men and women?

3.  Colleges and universities are frequently accused of being "ivory towers," places set apart from the realities of daily life to such an extent that the opinions of academics are seen to be somewhat dubious outside their areas of expertise. Regarding your college's faculty, what have been your experiences so far?

## Suggestions for Writing

1.  People's views on even the most important things are not always static. In fact, the thinking person realizes that in order to grow, people often need to revise their thinking and adopt a new vision. Write an essay of between 500 and 750 words in which you explain a change of opinion you came to about a significant subject, issue, or problem as a result of what you have learned within the last year.

2.  In the beginning of this essay, Sanders writes about men who worked at jobs that were both exhausting and dangerous. Pick an occupation that is physically or emotionally taxing: coal mining, farming, factory work, truck driving, law enforcement, marketing, corporate law, or finance, for example. In an essay of 500 to 750 words, explain why this occupation is so taxing. Rely on what you have learned about it from your own experience or from observation. Also include library or Internet research to support your conclusions.

## Speaking Assignment

In paragraph 7, Sanders says he was "slow to understand the deep grievances of women." Make an oral presentation in which you explain how you came to recognize, understand, and/or accept someone else's opinion on a significant issue. If appropriate, discuss an issue on which you once held a position diametrically opposed to that of the other person. (For more help with oral presentations, see Chapter 18.)

# Don't Eat Before Reading This

## ANTHONY BOURDAIN

*Anthony Bourdain is a long-time chef and the author of two novels,*
Bone in the Throat *(1995) and* Gone Bamboo *(1997). He pub-*
*lished the following article in* The New Yorker *on April 19, 1999.*
*The article's success prompted a publisher to ask Bourdain to use*
*it as the basis of a book, which appeared as the highly regarded*
Kitchen Confidential: Adventures in the Culinary Underbelly
*(2000). In 2001 Bourdain also published* A Cook's Tour: In Search
of the Perfect Meal. *He currently appears on the Travel Channel*
*as host of* No Reservations.

*"Don't Eat Before Reading This" is an essay in which an indus-*
*try insider lets the secrets out. As you read Bourdain's essay, notice*
*how he structures his various and fascinating confessions.*

Good food, good eating, is all about blood and
organs, cruelty and decay. It's about sodium-
loaded pork fat, stinky triple-cream cheeses, the
tender thymus glands and distended livers of
young animals. It's about danger—risking the
dark, bacterial forces of beef, chicken, cheese, and
shellfish. Your first two hundred and seven Well-
fleet oysters may transport you to a state of rap-
ture, but your two hundred and eighth may send
you to bed with the sweats, chills, and vomits.

Gastronomy is the science of pain. Professional
cooks belong to a secret society whose ancient rituals derive from the principles of stoicism in the
face of humiliation, injury, fatigue, and the threat
of illness. The members of a tight, well-greased
kitchen staff are a lot like a submarine crew. Confined for most of their waking hours in hot, airless
spaces, and ruled by despotic leaders, they often
acquire the characteristics of the poor saps who
were press-ganged into the royal navies of
Napoleonic times—superstition, a contempt for
outsiders, and a loyalty to no flag but their own.

A good meal has changed since Orwell's memoir of the months he spent as a dishwasher in
"Down and Out in Paris and London." Gas ranges

and exhaust fans have gone a long way toward
increasing the life span of the working culinarian.
Nowadays, most aspiring cooks come into the business because they want to: they have chosen this
life, studied for it. Today's top chefs are like star athletes. They bounce from kitchen to kitchen—free
agents in search of more money, more acclaim.

I've been a chef in New York for more than ten
years, and, for the decade before that, a dishwasher, a prep drone, a line cook, and a sous-chef.
I came into the business when cooks still smoked
on the line and wore headbands. A few years ago,
I wasn't surprised to hear rumors of a study of the
nation's prison population which reportedly found
that the leading civilian occupation among
inmates before they were put behind bars was
"cook." As most of us in the restaurant business
know, there is a powerful strain of criminality in the
industry, ranging from the dope-dealing busboy
with beeper and cell phone to the restaurant
owner who has two sets of accounting books. In
fact, it was the unsavory side of professional cooking that attracted me to it in the first place. In the
early seventies, I dropped out of college and transferred to the Culinary Institute of America. I
wanted it all: the cuts and burns on hands and
wrists, the ghoulish kitchen humor, the free food,
the pilfered booze, the camaraderie that flourished
within rigid order and nerve-shattering chaos. I
would climb the chain of command from *mal
carne* (meaning "bad meat," or "new guy") to
chefdom—doing whatever it took until I ran my
own kitchen and had my own crew of cutthroats,
the culinary equivalent of "The Wild Bunch."

A year ago, my latest, doomed mission—a
high-profile restaurant in the Times Square area—
went out of business. The meat, fish, and produce

purveyors got the news that they were going to take it in the neck for yet another ill-conceived enterprise. When customers called for reservations, they were informed by a prerecorded announcement that our doors had closed. Fresh from that experience, I began thinking about becoming a traitor to my profession.

Say it's a quiet Monday night, and you've just checked your coat in that swanky Art Deco update in the Flatiron district, and you're looking to tuck into a thick slab of pepper-crusted yellowfin tuna or a twenty-ounce cut of certified Black Angus beef, well-done—what are you in for?

The fish specialty is reasonably priced, and the place got two stars in the *Times.* Why not go for it? If you like four-day-old fish, be my guest. Here's how things usually work. The chef orders his seafood for the weekend on Thursday night. It arrives on Friday morning. He's hoping to sell the bulk of it on Friday and Saturday nights, when he knows that the restaurant will be busy, and he'd like to run out of the last few orders by Sunday evening. Many fish purveyors don't deliver on Saturday, so the chances are that the Monday-night tuna you want has been kicking around in the kitchen since Friday morning, under God knows what conditions. When a kitchen is in full swing, proper refrigeration is almost nonexistent, what with the many openings of the refrigerator door as the cooks rummage frantically during the rush, mingling your tuna with the chicken, the lamb, or the beef. Even if the chef has ordered just the right amount of tuna for the weekend, and has had to reorder it for a Monday delivery, the only safeguard against the seafood supplier's off-loading junk is the presence of a vigilant chef who can make sure that the delivery is fresh from *Sunday* night's market.

Generally speaking, the good stuff comes in on Tuesday: the seafood is fresh, the supply of prepared food is new, and the chef, presumably, is relaxed after his day off. (Most chefs don't work on Monday.) Chefs prefer to cook for weekday customers rather than for weekenders, and they like to start the new week with their most creative dishes. In New York, locals dine during the week. Weekends are considered amateur nights—for tourists, rubes, and the well-done-ordering pretheatre hordes. The fish may be just as fresh on Friday, but it's on Tuesday that you've got the good will of the kitchen on your side.

People who order their meat well-done perform a valuable service for those of us in the business who are cost-conscious: they pay for the privilege of eating our garbage. In many kitchens, there's a time-honored practice called "save for well-done." When one of the cooks finds a particularly unlovely piece of steak—tough, riddled with nerve and connective tissue, off the hip end of the loin, and maybe a little stinky from age—he'll dangle it in the air and say, "Hey, Chef, whaddya want me to do with *this*?" Now, the chef has three options. He can tell the cook to throw the offending item into the trash, but that means a total loss, and in the restaurant business every item of cut, fabricated, or prepared food should earn at least three times the amount it originally cost if the chef is to make his correct food-cost percentage. Or he can decide to serve that steak to "the family"— that is, the floor staff—though that, economically, is the same as throwing it out. But no. What he's going to do is repeat the mantra of cost-conscious chefs everywhere: "Save for well-done." The way he figures it, the philistine who orders his food well-done is not likely to notice the difference between food and flotsam.

Then there are the People Who Brunch. The "B" word is dreaded by all dedicated cooks. We hate the smell and spatter of omelettes. We despise hollandaise, home fries, those pathetic fruit garnishes, and all the other cliché accompaniments designed to induce a credulous public into paying $12.95 for two eggs. Nothing demoralizes an aspiring Escoffier faster than requiring him to cook egg-white omelettes or eggs over easy with bacon. You can dress brunch up with all the focaccia, smoked salmon, and caviar in the world, but it's still breakfast.

Even more despised than the Brunch People 11 are the vegetarians. Serious cooks regard these members of the dining public—and their Hezbollah-like splinter faction, the vegans—as enemies of everything that's good and decent in the human spirit. To live life without veal or chicken stock, fish cheeks, sausages, cheese, or organ meats is treasonous.

Like most other chefs I know, I'm amused 12 when I hear people object to pork on nonreligious grounds. "Swine are filthy animals," they say. These people have obviously never visited a poultry farm. Chicken—America's favorite food—goes bad quickly; handled carelessly, it infects other foods with salmonella; and it bores the hell out of chefs. It occupies its ubiquitous place on menus as an option for customers who can't decide what they want to eat. Most chefs believe that supermarket chickens in this country are slimy and tasteless compared with European varieties. Pork, on the other hand, is cool. Farmers stopped feeding garbage to pigs decades ago, and even if you eat pork rare you're more likely to win the Lotto than to contract trichinosis. Pork tastes different, depending on what you do with it, but chicken always tastes like chicken.

Another much maligned food these days is 13 butter. In the world of chefs, however, butter is in *everything*. Even non-French restaurants—the Northern Italian, the new American, the ones where the chef brags about how he's "getting away from butter and cream"—throw butter around like crazy. In almost every restaurant worth patronizing, sauces are enriched with mellowing, emulsifying butter. Pastas are tightened with it. Meat and fish are seared with a mixture of butter and oil. Shallots and chicken are caramelized with butter. It's the first and last thing in almost every

pan: the final hit is called *"monter au beurre."* In a good restaurant, what this all adds up to is that you could be putting away almost a stick of butter with every meal.

If you are one of those people who cringe at 14 the thought of strangers fondling your food, you shouldn't go out to eat. As the author and former chef Nicholas Freeling notes in his definitive book "The Kitchen," the better the restaurant, the more your food has been prodded, poked, handled, and tasted. By the time a three-star crew has finished carving and arranging your saddle of monkfish with dried cherries and wild-herb-infused *nage* into a Parthenon or a Space Needle, it's had dozens of sweaty fingers all over it. Gloves? You'll find a box of surgical gloves—in my kitchen we call them "anal-research gloves"—over every station on the line, for the benefit of the health inspectors, but does anyone actually use them? Yes, a cook will slip on a pair every now and then, especially when he's handling something with a lingering odor, like salmon. But during the hours of service gloves are clumsy and dangerous. When you're using your hands constantly, latex will make you drop things, which is the last thing you want to do.

Finding a hair in your food will make anyone 15 gag. But just about the only place you'll see anyone in the kitchen wearing a hat or a hairnet is Blimpie. For most chefs, wearing anything on their head, especially one of those picturesque paper toques—they're often referred to as "coffee filters"—is a nuisance: they dissolve when you sweat, bump into range hoods, burst into flame.

The fact is that most good kitchens are far less 16 septic than your kitchen at home. I run a scrupulously clean, orderly restaurant kitchen, where food is rotated and handled and stored very conscientiously. But if the city's Department of Health or the E.P.A. decided to enforce every aspect of its codes, most of us would be out on the street. Recently, there was a news report about the practice of recycling bread. By means of a hidden camera in a restaurant, the reporter was horrified to see returned bread being sent right back out to the floor. This, to me, wasn't news: the reuse of bread has been an open secret—and a fairly standard practice—in the industry for years. It makes more sense to worry about what happens to the left-over table butter—many restaurants recycle it for hollandaise.

What do I like to eat after hours? Strange 17 things. Oysters are my favorite, especially at three in the morning, in the company of my crew. Focaccia pizza with robiola cheese and white truffle oil is good, especially at Le Madri on a summer afternoon in the outdoor patio. Frozen vodka at Siberia Bar is also good, particularly if a cook from one of the big hotels shows up with beluga. At Indigo, on Tenth Street, I love the mushroom strudel and the daube of beef. At my own place, I love a spicy boudin noir that squirts blood in your mouth; the braised fennel the way my sous-chef makes it; scraps from duck confit; and fresh cockles steamed with greasy Portuguese sausage.

I love the sheer weirdness of the kitchen life: 18 the dreamers, the crackpots, the refugees, and the sociopaths with whom I continue to work; the ever-present smells of roasting bones, searing fish, and simmering liquids; the noise and clatter, the hiss and spray, the flames, the smoke, and the steam. Admittedly, it's a life that grinds you down. Most of us who live and operate in the culinary underworld are in some fundamental way dysfunctional. We've all chosen to turn our backs on the nine-to-five, on ever having a Friday or Saturday night off, on ever having a normal relationship with a non-cook.

Being a chef is a lot like being an air-traffic 19 controller: you are constantly dealing with the threat of disaster. You've got to be Mom and Dad, drill sergeant, detective, psychiatrist, and priest to a crew of opportunistic, mercenary hooligans, whom you must protect from the nefarious and often foolish strategies of owners. Year after year, cooks contend with bouncing paychecks, irate purveyors, desperate owners looking for the masterstroke that will cure their restaurant's ills: Live Cabaret! Free Shrimp! New Orleans Brunch!

In America, the professional kitchen is the last 20 refuge of the misfit. It's a place for people with bad pasts to find a new family. It's a haven for foreigners—Ecuadorians, Mexicans, Chinese, Senegalese, Egyptians, Poles. In New York, the main linguistic spice is Spanish. "*Hey, maricón! Chupa mis huevos*" means, roughly, "How are you, valued comrade? I hope all is well." And you hear "*Hey, baboso!* Put some more brown jiz on the fire and check your meez before the sous comes back there and fucks you in the *culo!,*" which means "Please reduce some additional *demi-glace,* brother, and reëxamine your *mise en place,* because the sous-chef is concerned about your state of readiness."

Since we work in close quarters, and so many 21 blunt and sharp objects are at hand, you'd think that cooks would kill one another with regularity. I've seen guys duking it out in the waiter station over who gets a table for six. I've seen a chef clamp his teeth on a waiter's nose. And I've seen plates thrown—I've even thrown a few myself—but I've never heard of one cook jamming a boning knife into another cook's rib cage or braining him with a meat mallet. Line cooking, done well, is a dance—a high-speed, Balanchine collaboration.

I used to be a terror toward my floor staff, par- 22 ticularly in the final months of my last restaurant. But not anymore. Recently, my career has taken an eerily appropriate turn: these days, I'm the chef de cuisine of a much loved, old-school French brasserie/bistro where the customers eat their meat rare, vegetarians are scarce, and every part of the animal—hooves, snout, cheeks, skin, and organs—is avidly and appreciatively prepared and consumed. Cassoulet, pigs' feet, tripe, and charcuterie sell like crazy. We thicken many sauces with foie gras and pork blood, and proudly hurl around spoonfuls of duck fat and butter, and thick hunks of country bacon. I made a traditional French pot-au-feu a few weeks ago, and some of my French colleagues—hardened veterans of the business all—came into my kitchen to watch the first order go out. As they gazed upon the intimidating heap of short ribs, oxtail, beef shoulder, cabbage, turnips, carrots, and potatoes, the expressions on their faces were those of religious supplicants. I have come home.

## Vocabulary

The following terms are identified by paragraph number. Make sure that you understand each term's meaning in its context. If you're not sure that you understand a term, look it up in a college-level dictionary.

| | | |
|---|---|---|
| distended (1) | purveyor (5) | patronizing (13) |
| rapture (1) | vigilant (7) | emulsifying (13) |
| gastronomy (2) | hordes (8) | definitive (14) |
| stoicism (2) | fabricated (9) | toque (15) |
| despotic (2) | mantra (9) | septic (16) |
| memoir (3) | philistine (9) | sociopath (18) |
| culinarian (3) | flotsam (9) | opportunistic (19) |
| acclaim (3) | credulous (10) | mercenary (19) |
| drone (4) | demoralize (10) | hooligans (19) |
| sous-chef (4) | faction (11) | nefarious (19) |
| pilfered (4) | ubiquitous (12) | misfit (20) |
| camaraderie (4) | trichinosis (12) | supplicants (22) |

## Style and Strategy

1. What is Bourdain's thesis, and where does it appear?
2. In which paragraphs does Bourdain use definition? What does this option contribute to his essay?
3. Where does the author use narration? What does this option contribute to his essay?
4. In paragraph 17, why does Bourdain include the passage about his after-hours eating habits? Does this inclusion add to or detract from his behind-the-scenes analysis? Explain.
5. The author contrasts two types of very different customers, one of which has various subtypes. What are the two types?
6. What other examples of contrast do you find in this essay?

### Questions for Critical Thinking and Discussion

1. Have you ever been involved in a process—during a job, say—that occurs largely away from the public eye? Describe the process, indicating what aspects would be likely to surprise people.

2. How safe are we when we entrust ourselves to strangers? For example, think of car repair, medical care, retail credit-card processing, and the keeping of personal records.

### Suggestions for Writing

1. Write a 500- to 750-word essay in which you evaluate the job at which you now work or any job at which you once worked. Discuss the employers, co-workers, vendors, and, if appropriate, customers with whom you came in contact. Also comment on the job's environment, your level of responsibility, the amount of work you did, and your treatment by your employer. You need not make this essay one-sided, so feel free to mention the positive aspects of a job you really dislike and vice versa.

2. Like Bourdain, can you tell outsiders secrets and other interesting—perhaps little-known—facts about a particular job you have held, a place where you have been employed, or an industry in which you have worked? If so, write a 500- to 750-word essay that does just that. Rely chiefly on your own knowledge, but, if necessary, include researched information to strengthen your essay.

### Speaking Assignment

Bourdain claims that restaurant workers ignore some health regulations. Think about the regulations that govern your college or workplace. Focus on one that you or others are in the habit of ignoring. Explain why this is so, and give a presentation in which you recommend whether this regulation should be rescinded. (For more help with oral presentations, see Chapter 18.)

# On the Fear of Death

## ELISABETH KÜBLER-ROSS

*A native of Switzerland, Dr. Elisabeth Kübler-Ross (1926–2004) was a pioneer in the study of aging and dying. Her books include the path-breaking* On Death and Dying *(1969);* Death: The Final State *(1974);* On Childhood and Death *(1985);* AIDS: The Ultimate Challenge *(1987);* On Life and Death *(1991);* The Wheel of Life: A Memoir of Living and Dying *(1997), her autobiography;* and Life Lessons: Two Experts on Death and Dying Teach Us About the Mysteries of Life and Living *(2000, with David Kessler).*

*In "On the Fear of Death," which is excerpted from* On Death and Dying, *Kübler-Ross contrasts "natural" approaches to death with "modern" approaches, pointing out that the latter approaches stem from a fear of death that pervades Western culture.*

Let me not pray to be sheltered from dangers but to be fearless in facing them.

Let me not beg for the stilling of my pain but for the heart to conquer it.

Let me not look for allies in life's battlefield but to my own strength.

Let me not crave in anxious fear to be saved but hope for the patience to win my freedom.

Grant me that I may not be a coward, feeling your mercy in my success alone; but let me find the grasp of your hand in my failure.

—Rabindranath Tagore, *Fruit-Gathering*

Epidemics have taken a great toll of lives in past generations. Death in infancy and early childhood was frequent and there were few families who didn't lose a member of the family at an early age. Medicine has changed greatly in the last decades. Widespread vaccinations have practically eradicated many illnesses, at least in western Europe and the United States. The use of chemotherapy, especially the antibiotics, has contributed to an ever decreasing number of fatalities in infectious diseases. Better child care and education have effected a low morbidity and mortality among children. The many diseases that have taken an impressive toll among the young and middle-aged have been conquered. The number of old people is on the rise, and with this fact come the number of people with malignancies and chronic diseases associated more with old age.

Pediatricians have less work with acute and life-threatening situations as they have an ever increasing number of patients with psychosomatic disturbances and adjustment and behavior problems. Physicians have more people in their waiting rooms with emotional problems than they have ever had before, but they also have more elderly patients who not only try to live with their decreased physical abilities and limitations but who also face loneliness and isolation with all its pains and anguish. The majority of these people are not seen by a psychiatrist. Their needs have to be elicited and gratified by other professional people, for instance, chaplains and social workers. It is for them that I am trying to outline the changes that have taken place in the last few decades, changes that are ultimately responsible for the increased fear of death, the rising number of emotional problems, and the greater need for understanding of and coping with the problems of death and dying.

When we look back in time and study old cultures and people, we are impressed that death has always been distasteful to man and will probably always be. From a psychiatrist's point of view this is very understandable and can perhaps best be explained by our basic knowledge that, in our unconscious, death is never possible in regard to ourselves. It is inconceivable for our unconscious to imagine an actual ending of our own life here on earth, and if this life of ours had to end, the ending is always attributed to a malicious intervention from the outside by someone else. In simple terms, in our unconscious mind we can only be killed; it is inconceivable to die of a natural cause or of old age. Therefore death in itself is associated with a bad act, a frightening happening, something that in itself calls for retribution and punishment.

One is wise to remember these fundamental facts as they are essential in understanding some of the most important, otherwise unintelligible communications of our patients.

The second fact that we have to comprehend is that in our unconscious mind we cannot distinguish between a wish and a deed. We are all aware of some of our illogical dreams in which two completely opposite statements can exist side by side—very acceptable in our dreams but unthinkable and illogical in our wakening state. Just as our unconscious mind cannot differentiate between the wish to kill somebody in anger and the act of having done so, the young child is unable to make this distinction. The child who angrily wishes his mother to drop dead for not having gratified his needs will be traumatized greatly by the actual death of his mother—even if this event is not linked closely in time with his destructive wishes. He will always take part or the whole blame for the loss of his mother. He will always say to himself—rarely to others—"I did it, I am responsible, I was bad, therefore Mommy left me." It is well to remember that the child will react in the same manner if he loses a parent by divorce, separation, or desertion. Death is often seen by a child as an impermanent thing and has therefore little distinction from a divorce in which he may have an opportunity to see a parent again.

Many a parent will remember remarks of their children such as, "I will bury my doggy now and next spring when the flowers come up again, he will get up." Maybe it was the same wish that motivated the ancient Egyptians to supply their dead with food and goods to keep them happy and the old American Indians to bury their relatives with their belongings.

When we grow older and begin to realize that our omnipotence is really not so omnipotent, that our strongest wishes are not powerful enough to make the impossible possible, the fear that we have contributed to the death of a loved one diminishes—and with it the guilt. The fear remains diminished, however, only so long as it is not challenged too strongly. Its vestiges can be seen daily in hospital corridors and in people associated with the bereaved.

A husband and wife may have been fighting for years, but when the partner dies, the survivor will pull his hair, whine and cry louder and beat his chest in regret, fear and anguish, and will hence fear his own death more than before, still believing in the law of talion—an eye for an eye, a tooth for a tooth—"I am responsible for her death, I will have to die a pitiful death in retribution."

Maybe this knowledge will help us understand many of the old customs and rituals which have lasted over the centuries and whose purpose is to diminish the anger of the gods or the people as the case may be, thus decreasing the anticipated punishment. I am thinking of the ashes, the torn clothes, the veil, the *Klage Weiber** of the old days—they are all means to ask you to take pity on them, the mourners, and are expressions of sorrow, grief, and shame. If someone grieves, beats his chest, tears his hair, or refuses to eat, it is an attempt at self-punishment to avoid or reduce the anticipated punishment for the blame that he takes on the death of a loved one.

This grief, shame, and guilt are not very far removed from feelings of anger and rage. The process of grief always includes some qualities of anger. Since none of us likes to admit anger at a deceased person, these emotions are often disguised or repressed and prolong the period of grief or show up in other ways. It is well to remember that it is not up to us to judge such feelings as bad or shameful but to understand their true meaning and origin as something very human. In order to illustrate this I will again use the example of the child—and the child in us. The five-year-old who loses his mother is both blaming himself for her disappearance and being angry at her for having deserted him and for no longer gratifying his needs. The dead person then turns into something the child loves and wants very much but also hates with equal intensity for this severe deprivation.

The ancient Hebrews regarded the body of a dead person as something unclean and not to be touched. The early American Indians talked about the evil spirits and shot arrows in the air to drive the spirits away. Many other cultures have rituals to take care of the "bad" dead person, and they all originate in this feeling of anger which still exists in all of us, though we dislike admitting it. The tradition of the tombstone may originate in this wish to keep the bad spirits deep down in the ground, and the pebbles that many mourners put

---

*Klage Weiber:** German for "wailing wives."

on the grave are left-over symbols of the same wish. Though we call the firing of guns at military funerals a last salute, it is the same symbolic ritual as the Indian used when he shot his spears and arrows into the skies.

I give these examples to emphasize that man has not basically changed. Death is still a fearful, frightening happening, and the fear of death is a universal fear even if we think we have mastered it on many levels. 12

What has changed is our way of coping and dealing with death and dying and our dying patients. 13

Having been raised in a country in Europe where science is not so advanced, where modern techniques have just started to find their way into medicine, and where people still live as they did in this country half a century ago, I may have had an opportunity to study a part of the evolution of mankind in a shorter period. 14

I remember as a child the death of a farmer. He fell from a tree and was not expected to live. He asked simply to die at home, a wish that was granted without questioning. He called his daughters into the bedroom and spoke with each one of them alone for a few moments. He arranged his affairs quietly, though he was in great pain, and distributed his belongings and his land, none of which was to be split until his wife should follow him in death. He also asked each of his children to share in the work, duties, and tasks that he had carried on until the time of the accident. He asked his friends to visit him once more, to bid good-bye to them. Although I was a small child at the time, he did not exclude me or my siblings. We were allowed to share in the preparations of the family just as we were permitted to grieve with them until he died. When he did die, he was left at home, in his own beloved home which he had built, and among his friends and neighbors who went to take a last look at him where he lay in the midst of flowers in the place he had lived in and loved so much. In that country today there is still 15

no make-believe slumber room, no embalming, no false makeup to pretend sleep. Only the signs of very disfiguring illnesses are covered up with bandages and only infectious cases are removed from the home prior to the burial.

Why do I describe such "old-fashioned" customs? I think they are an indication of our acceptance of a fatal outcome, and they help the dying patient as well as his family to accept the loss of a loved one. If a patient is allowed to terminate his life in the familiar and beloved environment, it requires less adjustment for him. His own family knows him well enough to replace a sedative with a glass of his favorite wine; or the smell of a home-cooked soup may give him the appetite to sip a few spoons of fluid which, I think, is still more enjoyable than an infusion. I will not minimize the need for sedatives and infusions and realize full well from my own experience as a country doctor that they are sometimes life-saving and often unavoidable. But I also know that patience and familiar people and foods could replace many a bottle of intravenous fluids given for the simple reason that it fulfills the physiological need without involving too many people and/or individual nursing care. 16

The fact that children are allowed to stay at home where a fatality has stricken and are included in the talk, discussions, and fears gives them the feeling that they are not alone in the grief and gives them the comfort of shared responsibility and shared mourning. It prepares them gradually and helps them view death as part of life, an experience which may help them grow and mature. 17

This is in great contrast to a society in which death is viewed as taboo, discussion of it is regarded as morbid, and children are excluded with the presumption and pretext that it would be "too much" for them. They are then sent off to relatives, often accompanied with some unconvincing lies of "Mother has gone on a long trip" or other unbelievable stories. The child senses that 18 something is wrong, and his distrust in adults will only multiply if other relatives add new variations of the story, avoid his questions or suspicions, shower him with gifts as a meager substitute for a loss he is not permitted to deal with. Sooner or later the child will become aware of the changed family situation and, depending on the age and personality of the child, will have an unresolved grief and regard this incident as a frightening, mysterious, in any case very traumatic experience with untrustworthy grownups, which he has no way to cope with.

It is equally unwise to tell a little child who lost 19 her brother that God loved little boys so much that he took little Johnny to heaven. When this little girl grew up to be a woman she never solved her anger at God, which resulted in a psychotic depression when she lost her own little son three decades later.

We would think that our great emancipation, 20 our knowledge of science and of man, has given us better ways and means to prepare ourselves and our families for this inevitable happening. Instead the days are gone when a man was allowed to die in peace and dignity in his own home.

The more we are making advancements in 21 science, the more we seem to fear and deny the reality of death. How is this possible?

We use euphemisms, we make the dead look 22 as if they were asleep, we ship the children off to protect them from the anxiety and turmoil around the house if the patient is fortunate enough to die at home, we don't allow children to visit their dying parents in the hospitals, we have long and controversial discussions about whether patients should be told the truth—a question that rarely arises when the dying person is tended by the family physician who has known him from delivery to death and who knows the weaknesses and strengths of each member of the family.

I think there are many reasons for this flight 23 away from facing death calmly. One of the most important facts is that dying nowadays is more

gruesome in many ways, namely, more lonely, mechanical, and dehumanized; at times it is even difficult to determine technically when the time of death has occurred.

Dying becomes lonely and impersonal because 24 the patient is often taken out of his familiar environment and rushed to an emergency room. Whoever has been very sick and has required rest and comfort especially may recall his experience of being put on a stretcher and enduring the noise of the ambulance siren and hectic rush until the hospital gates open. Only those who have lived through this may appreciate the discomfort and cold necessity of such transportation which is only the beginning of a long ordeal—hard to endure when you are well, difficult to express in words when noise, light, pumps, and voices are all too much to put up with. It may well be that we might consider more the patient under the sheets and blankets and perhaps stop our well-meant efficiency and rush in order to hold the patient's hand, to smile, or to listen to a question. I include the trip to the hospital as the first episode in dying, as it is for many. I am putting it exaggeratedly in contrast to the sick man who is left at home—not to say that lives should not be saved if they can be saved by a hospitalization but to keep the focus on the patient's experience, his needs and his reactions.

When a patient is severely ill, he is often 25 treated like a person with no right to an opinion. It is often someone else who makes the decision if and when and where a patient should be hospitalized. It would take so little to remember that the sick person too has feelings, has wishes and opinions, and has—most important of all—the right to be heard.

Well, our presumed patient has now reached 26 the emergency room. He will be surrounded by busy nurses, orderlies, interns, residents, a lab technician perhaps who will take some blood, an electrocardiogram technician who takes the cardiogram. He may be moved to X ray and he will overhear opinions of his condition and discussions and questions to members of the family. He slowly but surely is beginning to be treated like a thing. He is no longer a person. Decisions are made often without his opinion. If he tries to rebel he will be sedated and after hours of waiting and wondering whether he has the strength, he will be wheeled into the operating room or intensive treatment unit and become an object of great concern and great financial investment.

27 He may cry for rest, peace, and dignity, but he will get infusions, transfusions, a heart machine, or tracheotomy* if necessary. He may want one single person to stop for one single minute so that he can ask one single question—but he will get a dozen people around the clock, all busily preoccupied with his heart rate, pulse, electrocardiogram or pulmonary functions, his secretions or excretions but not with him as a human being. He may wish to fight it all but it is going to be a useless fight since all this is done in the fight for his life, and if they can save his life they can consider the person afterwards. Those who consider the person first may lose precious time to save his life! At least this seems to be the rationale or justification behind all this—or is it? Is the reason for this increasingly mechanical, depersonalized approach our own defensiveness? Is this approach our own way to cope with and repress the anxieties that a terminally or critically ill patient evokes in us? Is our concentration on equipment, on blood pressure, our desperate attempt to deny the impending death which is so frightening and discomforting to us that we displace all our knowledge onto machines, since they are less close to us than the suffering face of another human being which would remind us once more of our lack of omnipotence, our own limits and failures, and last but not least perhaps our own mortality?

28 Maybe the question has to be raised: Are we becoming less human or more human? . . . It is clear that whatever the answer may be, the patient is suffering more—not physically, perhaps, but emotionally. And his needs have not changed over the centuries, only our ability to gratify them.

---

*tracheotomy: a medical procedure in which a tube is inserted into a patient's neck, thus enabling him or her to breathe.

## Vocabulary

The following terms are identified by paragraph number. Make sure that you understand each term's meaning in its context. If you're not sure that you understand a term, look it up in a college-level dictionary.

| | | |
|---|---|---|
| eradicate (1) | deprivation (10) | euphemism (22) |
| morbidity (1) | sibling (15) | hectic (24) |
| malignancies (1) | embalming (15) | intern (26) |
| psychosomatic (2) | disfiguring (15) | electrocardiogram (26) |
| elicit (2) | sedative (16) | tracheotomy (27) |
| retribution (3) | infusion (16) | pulmonary (27) |
| unintelligible (4) | intravenous (16) | secretion (27) |
| omnipotence (7) | taboo (18) | excretion (27) |
| vestige (7) | pretext (18) | rationale (27) |
| bereaved (7) | emancipation (20) | impending (27) |

## Style and Strategy

*Paragraphs 1–2*

1.  What function do paragraphs 1–2 serve?

2.  Where is Kübler-Ross's thesis? Restate it in your own words.

*Paragraphs 3–7*

3.  How does Kübler-Ross use causal analysis in this section? Compare her use of causal analysis in paragraph 5 and in paragraph 6.

*Paragraphs 8–13*

4.  How does Kübler-Ross use exemplification in this passage?

5.  Where does Kübler-Ross restate her thesis? In your opinion, why does she do so?

*Paragraphs 14–19*

6.  Explain how Kübler-Ross uses description, narration, and causal analysis in this passage.

7.  What is your opinion of the anecdote in paragraph 15? In other words, does this "way to die" appeal to you, or does it affect you in some other way?

*Paragraphs 20–27*

8.  Explain how Kübler-Ross uses description, narration, exemplification, and comparison/contrast in this passage.

*Paragraph 28*

9.  Is Kübler-Ross's conclusion effective? In your opinion, what other issues might the author have covered here?

## Questions for Critical Thinking and Discussion

1.  How would you want the end of your life to occur?

2.  In the United States, many people have more medical resources expended for them in the last several days of their life than during the rest of their life altogether. In your opinion, is it a wise idea to expend so much for people who are clearly dying?

3.  What is your opinion on the issue of assisted suicide?

4.  Have you ever been to a funeral? If so, what were your impressions of what you observed and experienced?

## Suggestions for Writing

1.  In paragraph 24, Kübler-Ross says that in our culture, dying has become "lonely and impersonal." Write a 500- to 750-word essay that begins by summarizing her remarks about the way in which we approach dying. Then address each of the major ideas she puts forth and explain whether you agree or disagree with them. You might base your responses to Kübler-Ross on your own experiences and observations. Then again, you might include some researched material as well.

**2.** Write a 500- to 750-word essay that looks at the way we observe other important landmarks on the road of life. For example, critique the contemporary American wedding, the high school or college prom, a coming-of-age party, or a "special birthday" celebration.

### Speaking Assignment

What if you were to find yourself in a situation in which the only way to stay alive was through artificial means such as being put on a respirator? Would you want to be kept alive indefinitely? Why or why not? Develop a presentation to state your views. (For more help with oral presentations, see Chapter 18.)

# WRITING THE BLENDED ESSAY WITH A READER'S EYE

**CATALYST 2.0**

**MORE OPTIONS ONLINE**
If you would like to read additional blended essays, go to www.mhhe.com/ writingtoday.

Our discussion here is necessarily more general than in the preceding nine chapters. The decisions that you make when writing the blended essay require you to choose the best internal strategies to support your purpose and then to integrate those strategies to produce a unified essay.

## Prewriting

The prewriting stage is the point at which many writers realize that they *need* to use multiple options to write their essay. As you use any of the prewriting methods discussed in Chapter 2 to explore your topic and generate ideas, concentrate on finding the logical patterns that result. Look for the possibilities, keeping in mind the rhetorical options that you have learned in the preceding chapters. Keep your purpose in mind as you do so: you are not trying to use multiple strategies in some artificial exercise; your instructor will not grade you on successful and thorough inclusion of several internal options. Instead, you are planning an essay that will support its thesis throughout. Your instructor will be looking for thorough and effective development of each point that you make, no matter which strategy you have used to develop it.

At this point, you should be able to develop a preliminary thesis. Before proceeding, however, reconsider your thesis in terms of your purpose. Are they compatible? Keep in mind that you may need to revise or replace your thesis after your first draft.

## Organizing

When you are satisfied with the results of your prewriting and have developed your working thesis, the best way for you to organize this raw material is to arrange it into an outline. (Chapter 2 covers informal, sentence, and formal outlines.) If you use a sentence outline, for example, be willing to revise it or construct a new one if, upon review, you decide that the first one won't work. Plan on organizing until you come up with a paragraph sequence that suits both your thesis and your purpose.

A very useful strategy for organizing the blended essay is building a sentence outline with annotations. In other words, after you complete your outline, add notes (such as "transition here") where needed. This way, you'll give yourself an extensive framework to use as you begin drafting.

## Drafting

As you write your first draft, keep your thesis and purpose in the forefront of your thoughts. A blended essay presents complications, and all too often writers find themselves going astray—spending two paragraphs carefully developing a minor point that deserves only a few sentences, for example. Don't worry too much about this as you write your first draft, but be aware of the potential problem as you revise your draft.

As well, remember the crucial role of transitions in any essay. In a blended essay, transitions help link sections in which you are using different internal strategies; without transitions, the essay might read like three or four individual passages loosely connected to the thesis.

**CATALYST 2.0**

**MORE OPTIONS ONLINE**
For more help with problem areas in the blended essay, go to www.mhhe.com/writingtoday.

## Revising Your Draft

After you have completed a draft of your blended essay, your next step is to revise it, using your own analysis and comments from classmates or friends. Use the peer review stage to make sure that your essay's structure and content are sound. During peer review, answer the following questions about the draft you are reviewing, whether it is yours or another student's.

After reviewing for content, you need to go over your peer reviewers' responses to your essay and then revise for unity, coherence, language level,

## *Questions for Reviewing a Blended Essay*

1. Does the introduction give the reader enough context? Does it capture the reader's interest? How could the introduction be strengthened?

2. What is the thesis statement? Does it adequately reflect the essay's purpose and development? If necessary to do so, how could it be improved?

3. Is the essay organized in a logical and effective way? How could the organization be improved?

4. Do the internal strategies that the writer has chosen support the essay's main points and help the writer achieve his or her purpose?

5. Where are transitional words or sentences needed?

6. Are the body paragraphs fully developed? Where are additional details, or more specific details, needed?

7. Does the essay have an effective conclusion? How could it be improved?

and tone (see Chapter 4). When you have revised your draft and are basically satisfied with it, read your draft for mechanical and grammatical errors (fragments, comma splices, fused sentences), errors in pronoun agreement and subject-verb agreement, and spelling.

Now that you have made your corrections, *read your essay one more time* to catch any errors made during the revision and find errors missed during your earlier reviews.

## Student Essay

Today, Kevin Hunkovic, an accomplished young man, has a healthy level of self-esteem. As he points out in the following essay, which describes a situation that occurred more than ten years earlier, such was not always the case.

### Three Years Without Liberty

At age eleven I was just your average American child. I lived primarily between my hat and my heels. Because everything else was taken care of by my parents, I gave little thought to anything except for video games and television. In this fashion I was sheltered from the harsh realities of the world. **Little did I know that I was about to have an experience that would alter my outlook toward life forever: I experienced the microcosm of modern society called Liberty Middle School.**

In 1988 Liberty Middle School had a student body of about 1,700 students, give or take a few hundred. I was overwhelmed by the multitudes of diverse people around me. My classes were huge. There were 40-65 students per class. These numbers dwarfed me as I became a very small part of a whole. Soon after I started the sixth grade I began to notice a system underlying the way students and faculty interacted with each other. I later realized that it was a social class system. The highest members were the intellectuals, or nerds as they were called. They enjoyed special privileges that others did not have, such as getting to leave class and study alone in the library or move through the hallways without a pass. Then there was the middle class, those who weren't the best or the worst students. This group usually contained the athletes, cheerleaders, and the somewhat popular students. It constituted the majority of the student body. Next, there were the troublemakers, or the Future Criminals of America, as I called them. Those students tended to receive bad grades and get into trouble when they weren't causing it. Above all of this was the school faculty. Until I entered middle school, I thought the faculty were just the people who distributed the information to the students. At Liberty Middle School, however, the faculty took on all the functions of a small government: executives to run it, legislators to make the rules, and judges to punish wrongdoers with detentions. Finally, I noticed a class of outsiders, who for one reason or another did not fit into any category. They weren't mean enough to be in the lower class, or popular enough to converse with the middle class, or good enough at studying to be in the upper class. These students went unnoticed for the most part and were overlooked by teachers in an overcrowded classroom. The fourth class of people slipped through the cracks of the system, so to speak. In other words, they became victims of the institution.

In this milieu I'm afraid I ended up in the last group of people, mainly because of my shyness and my height. At age eleven I stood at 4 feet 5 inches. Most people my age were 5 inches to a foot taller than I. The older the student, the smaller I was by comparison. This happened to make me quite vulnerable to the lower class, or the Future Criminals of America. At least twice a day I was attacked by one bully or another. These attacks were never very brutal, although they usually left me holding my stomach and gasping for air. When I recovered from the pain, I'd stand up and attempt to locate where my books had been hidden. It was actually these frequent attacks that prompted me to realize the existence of the underlying system that divided people. Since the unfortunate encounters with a certain mean group of people made absolutely no sense, I tried to find some reason for them. This inspired me to observe closely my environment and the people in it. I eventually came to the conclusion that there were many factors involved. The category to which a student belonged, from bully to intellectual, seemed to be based on the institution's ability or inability to deal with that student. The people that the system could help were benefited by it. The intellectuals and the middle class were among those who did benefit. The others who did not benefit from the school became angry and lashed out at it, which caused the faculty to lash back. This cycle perpetuated itself into oblivion. Unfortunately, I was caught in the crossfire more than once.

Because I was very young at the time, every event that transpired seemed momentous and terrifying. Getting beat up almost every day might not have been enough to make me realize the situation and what it implied. I could have easily written the attacks off as the products of bad personalities. It wasn't until the authority figures themselves began to harass me as well that the entire system solidified in my mind. Once while I was waiting for the bus driver to drive me away from school, someone in the back of the bus threw an object that struck the bus driver at the base of her skull. She immediately left the bus, then promptly returned with an administrator. She then made inquiries as to who threw the object. Fearing punishment, a group of several miscreants all pointed at me in unison, while blaming me for the crime. Regardless of my spotless conduct record, I was called in to the office the following day. Because I was so young, I broke down into tears and protested that I was innocent. I proceeded to give a list of possible suspects, which would have had to be one of the kids who blamed me wrongly. After I left, the administrator had the idiocy to tell everyone that I accused everything I had said in my defense, including the fact that I had blamed him or her for the crime. Each suspect must have given a convincing

4

defense as well, because I was right back in the office the following day facing the same charges, but not before a group of ten students beat me up for telling the truth, with a promise to do it again at the end of the day. Now the criminals and the authority figures were after me simultaneously, all because I was minding my own business and waiting to go home.

Just as a doctor slaps a newborn baby, which causes it to cry and to breathe independently, this experience caused just enough mental stress to make me realize how contemporary society functions—and malfunctions. Everything I experienced in that school was a miniature version of the world at large. In essence, my three-year experience at Liberty Middle School woke me from my thoughtless childhood slumber. This realization remains with me to this day.

5

Let's look at the way Hunkovic constructed his essay and at the strategies he used.

## The Introduction

Hunkovic's first paragraph is devoted to description and definition. In providing the background for his essay, he **defines** himself at age eleven, **describing** what kind of boy he was at that age. His thesis, appearing in the final sentence of his first paragraph, indicates that his essay will be a **narration** but also something more than that.

*Consider Your Options*

What other methods of development might Hunkovic have used to introduce this essay?

## The Body

Hunkovic's first body paragraph is a complex **classification** of the people who inhabited Liberty Middle School: four classes of students and a faculty class. Hunkovic first discusses three of the categories of students: intellectuals, the middle class, and the troublemakers. He then classifies the functions of the faculty: executives, legislators, and judges. Finally, Hunkovic tells us about the fourth class of students: the "outsiders," destined to be "victims of the institution," at the mercy of all the other groups.

In his second body paragraph, Hunkovic characterizes himself as an unwilling member of the outsider class. This sets up a **contrast** between him and the "Future Criminals of America" and leads to **examples** of their ongoing persecution of him. He **describes** the characteristics that landed him in this group and the ongoing attacks he endured as a result. The second half of this paragraph is devoted to **causal analysis** as Hunkovic tries to ascertain what would lead the troublemakers to behave as they do.

**Consider Your Options**

Hunkovic's conclusion makes use of an analogy—"Just as a doctor. . . ." What other analogies might you suggest that could be used to conclude this essay?

The main part of the third body paragraph **narrates** the incident that led to an escalation of Hunkovic's problems and to his understanding more fully the system at Liberty Middle School. The anecdote is followed by an **analysis** of the **process** the school administrators used to get to the bottom of the situation.

### The Conclusion

Hunkovic's concluding paragraph confirms what the reader has sensed all along: that his essay has been a subtle **argument** against the unfairness of the school he attended as well as a claim that the school represents, in microcosm, the unfair world that faces us all.

## EXERCISE 14.1

Write an outline of "Three Years Without Liberty." (For help with outlines, see Chapter 2, pages 40–42.) How has the writer organized his essay? In what ways, if any, would you change the organization?

### Additional Writing Topics

1. Analyze and evaluate your life at this moment. Are you doing as well as you had hoped and planned?

2. What single mistake have you made in your life that you would correct if you could go back in time?

3. If you were granted the ability to write one piece of legislation to establish a new law or modify or nullify a current law, what would you propose?

4. What was your high school like? Discuss the building, the people, the curriculum, and the problems and challenges that you faced.

5. **Writing on the job.** For a self-evaluation, predict what your career will be like in ten years. Use your imagination, and be as specific as you can. Your audience is your immediate supervisor and the human resources manager at your company.

**CATALYST 2.0**

**MORE OPTIONS ONLINE**
For more help with the step-by-step development of the blended essay, go to www.mhhe.com/writingtoday.

### Blended Approaches and Visual Representations

Some products are clearly ahead of their time—the automobile developed by Preston Tucker in the late 1940s, for example. However, many people in the United States believe that certain innovative or revolutionary products are sure to be suppressed by the corporate giants that rely on existing products or technologies that would be made obsolete by the new inventions.

Such is the subject of Ben Katchor's "Goner Pillow Company," reproduced here. (First published in *Metropolitan* magazine, it was included in *The Best American Comics 2006*, edited by Harvey Pekar.) Read and examine "Goner" carefully; its message is subtle. As you read, note how many of the developmental options are blended here and how Katchor accomplishes a great deal in a relatively small space.

# The Goner Pillow Company by Ben Katchor

1. Write a response to this comic strip. What are your thoughts and impressions? As you write, refer to Questions for Reviewing a Visual Representation.

2. Are consumer products actually suppressed by big business, or is this idea just an urban legend? Research this issue. Then either write an essay explaining your findings and documenting your sources (see also Chapter

21) or develop an oral presentation based on your research and conclusions (see also Chapter 18).

## Questions for Reviewing a Visual Representation

- Is the representation forceful, passive, or something in between?
- What is the purpose of the representation—in other words, what is it trying to do to you, the reader/viewer?
- If the representation uses words, do they reinforce the visual image or in some way contradict it?
- What is the presumed audience for the representation—men, women, children, the elderly? Or does it have a broader appeal?
- If the representation is an advertisement, is it trying to sell a product or to get you to adopt a way of thinking?
- If the representation is an advertisement, does it try to persuade you in a fair manner, or do you feel manipulated?

## Responding to an Image

As World War II drew to a close, Allied soldiers took over areas formerly controlled by the Axis powers. In 1945 Toni Frissell took this photograph of a U.S. soldier examining a bombed church in Italy.

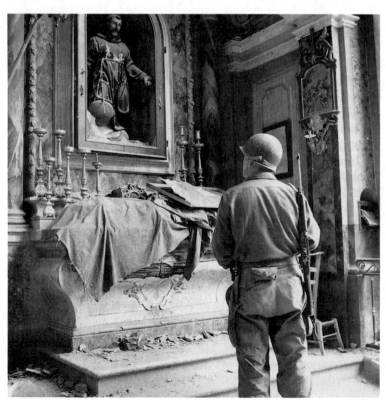

From the Collections of the Library of Congress.

1. Write an informal response to the photograph. What do you notice? How does the image make you feel? How does the photograph allow for multiple interpretations?

2. World War II cost the lives of millions of soldiers and noncombatants. It also caused the destruction of vast amounts of property, including many instances of fine architecture and artwork. Using a combination of library and online research, explore the destruction of a major building important for its architecture or the destruction or disappearance of a major collection of art. Write a documented essay that analyzes the importance of the architecture or artwork and then looks into what happened to it during the war and just after. (For more information on documented essays, see Chapter 21.)

## Using the Internet

Search the Internet for insights and information to use when developing essays that employ several options.

1. In paragraph 2 of "The Men We Carry in Our Minds," Scott Russell Sanders mentions the effects of the risks and dangers that working men he knew experienced on the job. Research and write an essay that explores the health hazards that people working in a particular industry, occupation, or profession face. For example, you might focus on the black lung that coal miners are at risk of developing, the carpal-tunnel syndrome experienced by office workers, or the long-term psychological or physiological risks of being a police officer.

    Learn more about your subject by reading about it online. In your essay you should use multiple strategies—for example, defining the health hazards, analyzing their causes, describing their physical and/or psychological effects, analyzing processes through which they may be avoided and treated, and providing pertinent examples of people or groups of people who have faced them.

2. Anthony Bourdain writes that there is "a powerful strain of criminality in the [restaurant] industry." Many people who have been paroled from prison find work in restaurants. Research and write an essay about the problems new parolees typically face. What do they have to do to keep from returning to prison?

**P**art 2 of this book examines the rhetorical options, the basic structures at the heart of the essay. As we point out, these options almost never occur as "pure" forms. Most essays, even if they rely primarily on a particular option, contain strategies derived from other options as well. The nine rhetorical structures covered in Part 2 are starting points that let writers develop essays suited to a specific purpose and audience.

Being able to write an essay in any one of the nine options is also a starting point. After the first-year composition course, writers find that the world of purposes and audiences expands dramatically. College courses, graduate and professional schools, and the business world dictate that writers build upon what they have learned. Good writers, in other words, think on their feet, improvising to meet the needs of the situation. Very often, whoever requests written work—a history professor, a production manager, a venture capitalist—doesn't care as much about format as about effective results.

Part 3 helps you take the next logical step—applying what you have learned to specific contexts: proposals, critiques, business documents, oral presentations, essay examinations, the research process and the research paper, and essays about literature.

Chapter 15 covers a very useful approach to writing: the proposal. This is a document that lets you "pitch" new ideas or your response to a call for proposals. In the business world, proposals are very important documents.

Chapter 16 examines the writing of critiques. This type of writing allows you to analyze the quality of a large range of subjects: a theatrical performance, a music CD, a business plan, or a new car. Critique writing is a useful skill to master.

Chapter 17 is devoted to the formats used in modern business: e-mail, memos, letters, and résumés. Often, students believe that writing is a peculiar requirement that their college, out of touch with the "real" world, persists in inflicting on them. They are frequently shocked when they get the job they've long dreamed of, only to find that it requires a great amount—and variety—of writing. In addition, supervisors have been known to express anger toward college-trained, entry-level workers who cannot produce coherent business letters. Finally, even getting a good job requires an effective résumé and a strong letter of application.

Chapter 18, "Group Projects and Oral Presentations," covers two major subjects that you will face in college. Group work and giving speeches are standard parts of today's higher education. These two activities are also ones that many students dislike. However, you will be asked to take part in group projects, and you will be asked to give presentations. This chapter offers you advice on how to become adept at each of these skill sets.

Chapter 19 discusses the essay examination. Too often, when faced with the time limits of an essay exam, students who ordinarily have a good grasp of the writing process will panic, writing as fast as they can whatever they remember in whatever order they remember it. Frequently, the result is a mess. You can avoid this problem, and Chapter 19 explains how to do so.

The research paper is a complicated task that most students dislike and/or fear. We offer a modified description: the research paper is a complicated yet straightforward task. As discussed in chapters 20 and 21, it is a rigorous project but not a mysterious one.

Today's student researchers must use both print sources and Internet sources. Chapter 20 discusses both, and it considers the value of the Internet as well as its potential pitfalls. Chapter 20 also discusses a mechanical process that many students find problematic: quoting text. Whether you are writing about literature, analyzing a psychological study, or writing a research paper, your ability to quote text accurately and appropriately will be a substantial factor in the ultimate quality of your document.

Chapter 21 builds on Chapter 20; it shows you how to use your research findings in a documented essay. We concentrate on the two formats most often required of undergraduates, the Modern Language Association (MLA) format and the American Psychological Association (APA) format. The former is normally used in English and other humanities courses; the latter is used in the social sciences. In addition to describing the steps and requirements of writing a research paper, we present a full-length documented essay written by a student using the MLA format.

Chapter 22 looks at writing that for many students is the next logical step after learning the rhetorical options. Writing about literature is an analytical process. "Book reports" and "appreciations" completed in high school are passé. Instead, instructors will ask you to read a short story, poem, or play and then explain some aspect of it, such as character development or theme. The successful student displays an understanding of the terminology of literary analysis, the ability to quote from the text and cite quotations correctly, and a strong understanding of the work's meaning. Actually, many students find that literary analysis is not as difficult as they feared. •

PART

3

APPLICATIONS

### CHAPTER 15

# WRITING PROPOSALS

## From Problem to Solution

A **proposal** is an argument that is written to address specific objectives or to solve specific problems. The ability to solve problems by applying critical thinking skills is important to almost any field of endeavor. Proposals are used in business, educational and other nonprofit organizations, public service, the military, the sciences and technologies, and the professions. Like other forms of argument, proposals assert opinions supported by factual evidence. However, they also attempt to persuade readers to adopt a plan of action.

BEFORE YOU DECIDE WHAT APPROACH TO TAKE in any proposal you are called on to write, you will have to determine your purpose—what you want to accomplish. In order to do that, you will also have to understand the problem's causes:

1. While creating a lesson on the U.S. Constitution, a student in a course on methods of teaching history has to devise a plan to make the lesson livelier and keep the students awake. The root of the problem is that some students dislike memorizing dates or lack interest in the ideas of men who wore powdered wigs and who died two centuries ago.

2. In order to deal with the problem of increasing product recalls, the quality control manager in a toolmaking factory has to recommend radical changes in the product inspection process or in the training of quality control personnel. The cause of the problem is that the inspection process as it now exists is just too complicated for employees who lack sufficient training in applying inspection criteria.

3. As a way to improve the city's medical emergency response system, the head of the health department proposes a program to improve the efficiency with which 911 operators gather critical information from people experiencing medical emergencies. The source of the problem is that many operators do not know the kinds of questions designed to get quick, accurate responses from patients—the kinds of responses that will prompt rapid responses from ambulance drivers and emergency medical technicians.

## PURPOSE: UNDERSTAND THE PROBLEM AND PROPOSE A SOLUTION

The purpose of a proposal is to suggest a way to solve a problem or address a concern. As indicated above, the first step is to recognize what the problem actually is. However, because of limitations on time, money, and personnel, as well as other constraints, you may find that you have to focus on a limited aspect of that problem.

For example, suppose the dean of students sends out via the college newspaper a request for proposals (RFP) to students, faculty, and staff, soliciting a plan that will make the first days of college less confusing, tiring, and stressful for new students than they have been in recent years. You think back to your first week on campus and recall spending hours in long lines at the registrar's office, the financial aid office, and the bookstore. You recall being referred to offices all over campus just to get signatures that would allow you into courses in which you thought you were already enrolled. You even had trouble finding a few of your classrooms on that first day. Finally, and most important, you came to the scary realization that you had enrolled for too many credits, especially in light of the fact that you had a demanding part-time job off campus. So you decide to respond to the dean's RFP.

# SCOPE: DECIDE HOW FAR TO GO AND CONSIDER ALTERNATIVES

As soon as you begin to plan your proposal, however, you are overwhelmed by the scope of the project and the amount of work that will surely be required to complete it. You decide to limit your proposal to a plan that will help prepare new students for "workload shock" by helping them construct realistic academic and work schedules. The scope of this project will be far more manageable than if you had taken on the task of trying to redesign the college's entire freshman registration program.

Earlier we said that writing proposals demands critical thinking. This skill is especially needed when you are deciding on the methods, approaches, and tools that you will recommend to solve the problem or attain the desired objective. Most objectives can be reached in a variety of ways, and most problems lend themselves to multiple solutions, but one approach or solution may not be as effective as another. You will usually need to consider various options before you decide on a specific plan. Therefore, it is a good idea to think through the steps in the process or plan that you are recommending. You might also map out a few other possible solutions in this way, just to see how they compare to your original. Doing so will help you predict which one might best solve the problem when it actually comes time to draft your proposal.

In addition, you will need to keep an open mind to new avenues of approach. Don't be satisfied with an approach that adapts old solutions to new problems. Indeed, as with any other type of writing, proposals demand creativity and the ability to be inventive; in short, you will want to approach or see the problem or situation you are addressing from a variety of perspectives.

# AUDIENCE: SEE THE PROBLEM FROM THE READER'S PERSPECTIVE

Like any other type of argumentative writing, proposals are designed to convince people of the validity of their arguments. However, as mentioned earlier, they are also intended to get people to act on those arguments. Remember that a proposal's audience comprises more than just readers. It also includes potential doers, the people who have the responsibility of enacting the recommendations they contain. Here are a few questions to ask yourself about the prospective audience for your proposal:

1. Do they agree that there is a problem?
2. How convinced are they that this problem is significant and needs attention or that the goal you are setting is worth reaching?
3. How familiar are they with the causes of the problem or with the specific benefits of reaching the desired goal?
4. How much do they already know about the techniques or approaches you might recommend to solve the problem or reach the goal?

**5.** Are they already considering or committed to a solution or approach other than the one you are proposing?

## Preparing to Write: Issues to Keep in Mind

In addition to the advice that you read earlier, consider the following issues as you plan your proposal:

**1.** Focusing on a topic: defining the problem or concern

**2.** Establishing the causes of the problem

**3.** Convincing your audience that the problem needs to be addressed or the goal needs to be achieved

**4.** Convincing your audience that what you propose is the best course of action

**5.** Convincing your audience that other solutions for the problem are not working or will not work and should be amended or abandoned in favor of a new course of action

### *Focusing on a Topic: Defining the Problem or Concern*

Sometimes the nature of a problem or concern is clear, and defining it can be relatively easy. On the other hand, writers of proposals sometimes mistake symptoms of a problem for the problem itself. Let's say that faculty at your college are concerned that many students are handing in substandard research papers. The reason, most faculty agree, is that students are failing to complete the kind of rigorous library research demanded at the collegiate level. Instead, they are relying more and more on Internet sites, but many of these sources are unreliable, inaccurate, misleading, or simply inappropriate for college work.

### *Establishing the Causes of the Problem*

At first, it may seem that the students find it more convenient to do their research online rather than to spend hours and hours in the library. However, the real reason is that, recently, the library's hours were significantly reduced. It now closes on weekdays at 9 P.M. rather than at 3 A.M. and on Saturdays at 5 P.M. rather than at midnight. It is closed on Sundays. But most full-time students have busy schedules, and many of them work part time at local malls or restaurants in the evenings. By the time they are able to return to campus to do their research (the malls close at 9 P.M. on weeknights), the library is shut tight. Of course, students can always access the library's periodical databases from their own computers, even at 3 A.M. However, they also need to use the library's reference section, which contains books that can't be checked out. In addition, some of the periodical resources they need can be found only in print, not in online databases.

In short, the new library schedule has severely limited the students' ability to complete the kind of research required in many of their classes. Even during those hours that the library is open, it is so crowded that few students have a chance of getting the individual help they need from the few professional librarians on duty.

### Convincing the Audience That the Problem Needs to Be Addressed

It is not enough to define the problem and its causes from your own perspective; you also need to make sure that your audience sees the problem as serious enough to be addressed. Take the problem discussed above, for example. When you first heard reports that students were having difficulty completing research because the library had decreased its hours, you dismissed the real problem by attributing it to a lack of planning on the part of a few malcontents. However, after speaking to several serious students you have come to respect and after having difficulty completing an important paper of your own, you now admit that the problem is real, and you decide to write a proposal to address it. However, at this point, you realize that you will also have to convince a skeptical audience—the college administration—that this is an important problem; you cannot assume that they will recognize its seriousness themselves.

But how will you do this? As with any other piece of persuasive writing, you will have to rely on evidence. For example, you might interview faculty to determine when they first noticed the drop in research paper quality. Did it occur about the time that the library began to curtail its hours? You might also distribute a questionnaire to students in classes that require research papers in order to get their views on the matter. Finally, you might find useful information in published research studies conducted at other colleges and universities.

### Convincing Your Audience That What You Propose Is the Best Course of Action

How you define the cause of the problem will determine the nature of the solutions you propose. Whatever you think about the causes of the problem, your solutions must be practical, convincing, relatively easy to implement, and cost efficient—not just possible. In other words, they will have to meet certain criteria relating to finances, logistics, and available personnel.

For example, to give busy students more access to your college library, you might suggest that the college hire additional professional librarians to staff the library late into the night and on Sundays. That solution seems easy; unfortunately, budgetary constraints make it unfeasible. So you need to find a compromise, perhaps by suggesting that the library be staffed during the expanded hours by work-study students. Although this solution does not provide students with access to highly trained librarians who can help them find materials and use library research tools, it does allow them more time to complete their research in an atmosphere that is far less stressful than the crowded conditions in which they must now work.

You will improve the credibility of your argument by being as specific as possible. You should indicate the number of extra hours that the library will be open, specifying days and times, as well as the number of work-study students the college will need to hire, the number of hours each will work, and the amount of money the college will need to budget for their salaries. You must also justify the number of people to be hired, the number of hours they will work, and so on. In other words, you need to prove that enough students will use the library during the expanded hours to justify the expenditure of personnel, time, and money. To convince readers that your predictions are accurate, you might present statistical evidence taken from studies—much like the marketing studies that retailers use.

In addition to feasibility, as you prepare your solution you also need to keep in mind the needs and concerns of the people who will evaluate your proposal and decide whether to implement it. In other words, you need to consider the proposal's effects on the organizational and political environment. For example, perhaps the professional librarians at your college belong to a faculty union or labor association that would consider the use of work-study students an infringement on librarians' employment rights. Your proposal could be seen as an attempt to replace faculty with lower-paid substitutes. It might even violate the current faculty labor agreement. If this is the case, you might suggest that the administration and the faculty union agree to a contract waiver limited to the purposes intended by your proposal.

As well, because work-study is a federally funded program with its own budget restrictions, you might have to convince your college's director of financial aid to devote some of Uncle Sam's money to your cause. If the work-study budget has already been determined, your job may be even harder, for you will have to persuade the director to take funds from other college programs and reallocate them to library staffing. This task might take some doing because you will need to show why your program is worthier of funding than the one from which the money would be taken. Then again, you might even have to consider an alternative to the use of work-study students to keep the library open longer. We didn't say writing proposals was easy!

If you are dealing with a reader who is especially hard to convince, logic and factual information may not be enough to win acceptance for your solution. You might need to start by appealing to the reader's interests and values. For example, let's say that a faculty committee has been organized to review your proposal on using work-study students to staff the library during expanded hours. You can appeal to their self-interest by explaining that your proposal will not affect the college budget and that it might improve student retention, thereby increasing job security for all college employees. In addition, it will help students write better papers—papers that the faculty will want to read. You can also appeal to their pride as educators by arguing that keeping the library open longer will strengthen the students' commitment to academic excellence, thereby enhancing the college's reputation.

### *Convincing Your Audience That Other Solutions Are Not Working or Will Not Work*

As with any other type of argument, writing proposals requires that you anticipate and deal with opposing arguments, in this case solutions other than the ones you are proposing. You can deal with this issue at any time in the process of writing your paper. However, you may find that the revising stage is the easiest time to address alternate solutions after you have explained the merits of your *own* position in your first draft.

In the part of your paper that discusses the causes of the library problem, for example, you may have explained that students have difficulty completing required research because the library's hours are limited and not because of an inability to manage their time or to plan, as some have claimed. Therefore, a possible alternate solution—such as having the counseling department hold time-management seminars for students—will not address the real causes of the problem. In explaining this alternate cause and showing the weakness of the possible solution, you are anticipating and answering an opposing argument.

Indeed, you might have to address several alternate proposals in your paper. Say that the college is planning to make arrangements for students to use a municipal library when the college library is closed. You could respond that the municipal library does not have the range of academic resources that students need, that it is open late only on Thursday nights, and that it is more than ten miles away, making it inaccessible to students without cars.

## Choosing a Topic: Determining Purpose and Scope

As with any piece of writing, the nature of a proposal's topic will determine the nature of your discussion. (For advice on choosing a topic, consult chapters 1 and 2.) However, focusing on the purpose of your writing may get a bit tricky. As indicated earlier, for example, the fact that students are not completing enough library research is not the problem. It is simply a symptom of the problem, which is that the library's hours are limited.

Here's another example. Let's say that some students in evening classes are bringing their children with them because they are having a hard time finding or affording child care. Unfortunately, the children disturb the classes by talking, running in and out of the room, and doing what little children simply have to do. The problem is, of course, that instruction is being affected. However, there is a larger problem: the students need to find available and affordable child-care services so that they can attend classes and concentrate on their work without worrying about their children. So you decide to write a proposal to the dean of students recommending that the college day-care center, which now closes at 6 P.M., be kept open at least until evening classes end.

As you begin to write your proposal, however, you notice that the child-care center could use a few more toys and books to keep the children occupied. Moreover, the center has only two computers, neither of which offers learning software appropriate to young children. Finally, you realize that the center's full-time nurse goes off duty at 6 P.M. and that the college cannot afford to hire an evening nurse. Most proposals like those you write in college will be from three to five pages long. Their scope—extent of coverage—is limited. Can you recommend ways to address all of the above concerns in such a report? Probably not—this is a job for a committee or task force charged with undertaking a long-term, comprehensive review of the problem. However, you can write a far more limited proposal that recommends extending the child-care center's hours to accommodate the children of evening students.

## Writing and Research

After considering your purpose, focus, and audience, you will need to gather information that will help you develop useful approaches or further develop those you have already decided upon. You can explore your problem and possible solutions by using various prewriting techniques discussed in Chapter 2. You will almost certainly need to complete some library and/or Internet research as well (see chapters 20 and 21).

As you think through your prewriting and research, you should review the general plan or approach you decided to take at the outset of the project, when you first determined the purpose and scope of your paper. It may be that the plan and the solutions you first envisioned and sketched out (in an outline or flowchart) now seem less appropriate than others that you have discovered as you have gathered more information and conducted research. You should not hesitate to revise your solution in response to your discoveries.

## Organizing

Proposals can be organized in a variety of ways. The format we suggest here is generic and is often used for business proposals. It will give you a good idea about the kinds of information that most proposals contain. However, remember that some organizations and corporations require writers to adhere to certain defined rules and observe certain specifications when submitting internal proposals. Indeed, when these entities are soliciting proposals from outside vendors or contractors, they usually publish those requirements in the form of a request for proposals in various newspapers and journals.

The type and complexity of your proposal will determine how many of the following elements you'll need to use. Some of them are boilerplate; others depend on your purpose and context. For example, if your proposal requires no expenditures, you won't need a "Costs" section. If you did no formal research, you won't need to have a "Sources" section. As well, the sections and proposed headings in the following list are suggestions. Follow the style of your company or the needs of your document's context.

1. **Address the proposal.** In the case of an internal proposal, if it is more than five pages, it should have a cover page, which indicates the title of the proposal, the person or group to which it is submitted, the date of its submission, and, of course, the author's or authors' names. If the proposal is short (up to five pages), you can simply use memorandum format with "To," "From," "Subject," and "Date" lines. For more on composing memoranda, refer to Chapter 17.

   In the case of an external proposal, you should include a cover letter briefly stating the reason that the proposal was written (Was it solicited directly? Are you writing in response to an RFP?), stating the problems or concerns being addressed, and including an invitation to meet with the addressees to discuss the proposal further.

2. **Write an abstract (executive summary).** Presented in the beginning paragraph(s), an abstract, also known as an executive summary, is the most important part of a proposal. If written clearly and engagingly, it will capture the readers' attention and induce them to read on. As its name indicates, it abstracts or summarizes the main points of the proposal and mirrors the organization of the proposal itself:

- Statement of problem or benefits to be derived
- Recommended solutions and procedures
- Estimated cost or funding requirements
- Time frame
- Statement of proposer's qualifications

The abstract also indicates whether the work will be followed by another report explaining the results of implementing the work recommended by the proposal.

3. **State the problem.** In this section, you will define the problem or the goal of the proposal, but you might also need to convince readers that this problem/concern is serious enough to demand attention or that this goal is worth achieving. This part of the proposal should be as concise as possible, but it should show that you have considered the problem or concern carefully and that you have limited its scope, as discussed earlier.

   In order to persuade readers of the urgency of the problem and the need for a solution, you will have to include convincing facts, statistics, and other concrete evidence gathered through research:

   - **Primary research** includes personal observations or experience as well as field research that you have designed and conducted yourself. An example of field research is the collection of data—via a written questionnaire—on the problems that new students encounter during registration.

   - **Secondary research** is information you have gathered from print or electronic sources that discuss the problem you are addressing.

4. **Describe the project.** This section explains how you will approach the problem. It discusses objectives, procedures and materials, staffing/administration, and evaluation.

   A. **Objectives.** Don't confuse goals and objectives. A clear understanding of goals can help define objectives, but goals are general and conceptual, whereas objectives are specific and measurable. Say you propose to expand the work of a student volunteer group that tutors inner-city children in reading. That is an admirable goal, but it is not a measurable objective. Instead, you might say that your objective is to increase the number of tutors from 20 to 25 during the first year and from 25 to 30 in the second year, thereby increasing the number of tutorial hours by 50 percent in two years.

      What you have just read is an example of a behavioral objective. There are three other types of objectives that you might consider as well:

      - A **product objective** results in the creation of something. Let's say that you are working in a homeless shelter teaching high school dropouts some basic computer skills. You realize that the technical manuals they have been given are far too challenging, so you propose to create a set of simpler, clearer instructions to be printed on an $8^1/_2 \times 11$ sheet of paper and then laminated.

- A **performance objective** aims at improving a person's skill or speed at an important task or function. For example, you might propose a plan to improve the response time of the city's four emergency medical units from an average of ten minutes to an average of four minutes.

- A **process objective** is aimed at measuring the best way to do something. For example, let's say you are working for a large cell phone maker. You might propose a plan to determine whether you should keep your technical services department at company headquarters, outsource this function to a company overseas, or allow your technical personnel to work from home using dedicated telephones and computers to address customer questions and complaints.

B. **Procedures and materials.** The kind of procedures you employ and the materials you use—if any—are determined by the nature of the problem and the objectives you wish to achieve. In discussing procedures, try to answer three questions:

- **How:** Discuss what you intend to do to address the problem step by step.

- **When:** Provide a schedule that explains when completion of each part of the procedures can be expected.

- **Why**: Explain why your methods are effective. If necessary, call upon the testimony of experts or use data, examples, and other evidence you have researched.

The proposed procedure section will probably be the longest part of the proposal and the one that demands the greatest amount of detail. In many cases, you will want to use a list format—often numbered—to explain what needs to be done and in what order the work will be completed. If equipment, supplies, or other materials are needed, make a list and, if appropriate, describe them under a subtitle in this section.

C. **Staffing needs.** The previous subsection lists tasks to be performed. If the project requires more than one person to complete, list the names of the staff members and indicate which tasks each person is assigned.

5. **Estimate the costs.** In this section you need to provide a fair estimate of the costs of your plan. This list should be specific and inclusive.

6. **Create a schedule for the completion of the project.** Divide the work into specific stages or tasks, and provide a completion date for each.

7. **State your credentials.** State your qualifications and the qualifications of those working with you—experience, education, awards—to convince your readers that you know what you are talking about and that your plan will meet the stated objectives.

8. **List references to secondary source materials.** If you have consulted or cited any secondary sources, you should list them at the end of the report using the format required by the organization or company to which the proposal is addressed.

## Other Aspects to Consider When Writing Proposals

1. In some cases, using the first person "I" or "we" is acceptable. However, many proposals use the more formal third person ("he," "she," or "they"). The style depends upon the guidelines for proposal writing specific to the organization for which you are writing.

2. Proposals exist in the realm of business and technical writing. Consider using lists—numbered or bulleted—whenever possible. You can also use the simple graphic elements available in any word processor—such as underlining, italic and bold type, and borders and shading—to make your proposal easier to read.

3. You can also make your proposal easy to read by using headings and subheadings that follow a logical layout and hierarchy, with the more general headings in a larger type size than less important ones. Don't forget to make such headings clear by positioning them so that they stand out and by putting them in capital letters or in bold type.

4. Including headings and subheadings is especially important if your audience is composed of multiple readers. It will enable them to read selectively, with each reader identifying sections of particular interest to him or her without having to read the entire document.

## SAMPLE INTERNAL PROPOSAL

**To:**       Members of the Dean's Advising Subcommittee
**From:**    Carly Rodriguez, President, Student Government Association (SGA)   *RC*
               Edwin Chan, Vice President, SGA   *EC*
**Subject:** Request for Proposals to Improve the Preregistration Process
**Date:**    November 14, 2008

Abstract

The request for proposals issued by your group outlined the common problems faced by students who are trying to register for the upcoming semester and asked for possible solutions. We believe that using a modified form of the electronic "status report" (now sent only to students approaching graduation) would have major benefits for all students. Our study of this idea leads us to believe that costs and operational difficulties would be minimal. We also believe that the system could be up and running by February 2009.

## Purpose

To investigate the use of software owned by both the Registrar's office and the Technical Support Center (TSC) to inform students of their comprehensive situation one week before the advising and registration period begins during each semester.

## Problem

Students frequently lack knowledge about their academic situation until they meet with their advisors during the registration period. As outlined in your request for proposals and as supplemented by our informal survey conducted during the past ten days, here are some of the problems that students face:

- Financial "holds" that prevent students from registering
- Changes in students' scholarship/financial aid status
- Lack of knowledge about course sequencing and degree completion requirements

The result is that many students meet with their advisors and learn for the first time information that should have been digested prior to the meeting. As well, many students complete the advising process but find that financial holds leave them unable to register, a very unpleasant outcome.

## Proposed Procedure

We propose that one week before registration begins, each student receive an official e-mail from the college that informs him or her of the following facts:

- Hours completed prior to the current semester
- Hours enrolled during this semester
- Hours remaining toward degree, subdivided into general education, major, and minor requirements
- Current GPA

- Name, office number, phone number, and e-mail address of the student's advisor
- Any financial issues, such as holds or financial aid changes, that would affect the student's ability to register for the upcoming semester or to pay for the upcoming semester
- Any "oddities" in the student's course progress—for example, notification that a student has taken a sequenced class out of order or that a fourth-year student still has not completed first-year classes.

## Implementing the Proposed Procedure

Before a student is allowed to graduate, the Bursar's office sends a report to the Registrar, who examines it for any financial issues that could affect the scheduled graduation date. The Registrar then sends a "status report" e-mail to the student, who is either cleared for graduation or told what steps need to be taken to be eligible to gain his or her degree. We propose using a modified form of the status report approach for each student in each semester of his or her residency.

On November 2, we interviewed Leon Lattimore, the technical manager of the TSC, to inquire about the viability of our plan. He responded favorably, pointing out the following:

- Only a "minor" modification would be required to the software that generates status reports for potential graduates.
- The programmer who wrote that software is still on staff.
- The proposed solution would end the "piecemeal" approach to the distribution of essential information to students.

## Potential Problems

1. **Universal coverage gaps.** Many students don't monitor their college-supplied e-mail account. We believe that in the area of advising and registration, this problem will be self-correcting. In satisfaction surveys, students

have consistently voiced their displeasure with the registration process, ranking it as one of their "least-satisfying" experiences while in residency. Therefore, we believe that once students realize what their status reports can provide, they will make an exception around registration time and look for this particular e-mail message.

2. **Costs.** This, we believe, is a minor area of concern. Two sets of "extra effort" will be needed:

- TSC will need to perform the initial software upgrade.

- The Registrar will have to have one of her staff send out the status report e-mails twice a year.

However, no new staff should have to be employed by the college.

### Schedule

Our conversation with Mr. Lattimore leads us to believe that the proposed system can be operational by February, giving the college plenty of time to try it out in the fall semester of 2009.

Please contact us at the SGA offices if you have any questions or desire further information.

## Revising Your Draft

As with any piece of writing, revising a proposal means reorganizing, focusing, adding to, and sharpening your ideas. After you have completed a draft, your next step is to revise your proposal, using your own analysis and comments from classmates and friends. As you know by now, a proposal is supposed to get people to act. You can make good use of the revising stage to do a variety of things, but this stage is one of the best times to add whatever it takes to convince the audience to act on your proposal. Use peer review to make sure that your proposal is specific and that you have anticipated and dealt adequately with objections and alternate solutions.

After reviewing for content, you need to go over your peer reviewers' responses to your essay and then revise for unity, coherence, language level, and tone (see Chapter 4). The revising stage is a good time to review the kind of language that your proposal uses. Generally, a positive tone is best. Note the following two examples:

> NEGATIVE     **If we do not keep the library open longer, students will continue to write substandard research papers.**

> POSITIVE     **Keeping the library open longer will give students the opportunity to do the kind of rigorous library research demanded in a collegiate setting.**

Which example do you find more convincing?

When you have revised your draft and are basically satisfied with it, read your draft for mechanical and grammatical errors (fragments, comma splices, fused sentences), errors in pronoun agreement and subject-verb agreement, and spelling.

Now that you have made your corrections, *read your document one more time* to catch any errors made during revision and find errors missed during your earlier reviews.

## Writing Topics

1. Write a proposal to the dean of students. Suggest ways to make the first month at your college or university less stressful for new students.

2. Write a proposal addressed to the municipal supervisor or mayor of the town or city in which you live. Recommend ways to improve traffic safety, especially in light of the increasing number of serious—even fatal—accidents involving people ages 18–25.

3. Write a proposal to your spouse, children, parents, or any other member(s) of your family. Recommend ways in which your family can save money on daily living expenses and thereby shrink the household budget.

## Using the Internet

Let's say that your college seeks to purchase a large number of laptop computers, which will be given to incoming freshmen next year. The cost will be passed on to students through a one-time tuition surcharge. Using the Internet as your research tool, write a proposal addressed to the purchasing office at your college. Your proposal should evaluate at least three popular laptop models and rank them in your order of preference.

If evaluating laptops doesn't interest you, write a proposal addressed to your fellow students in which you address various common problems faced by students. One example might be how to finance their college education.

## Reading Existing Proposals

Proposals come in many forms and are used for a variety of purposes. Use these links to read some formal proposals made by government agencies, businesses, and private individuals:

1. General Electric, Inc. "Ecomagination"

   http://ge.ecomagination.com

   Note: The sections on energy and infrastructure are particularly interesting.

2. Proposal to Create the Prince George's Community College Online Express

   http://academic.pgcc.edu/ole/proposalORIG.htm

3. Virginia Commonwealth University Proposal to Create a School of Public Health

   http://www.facultysenate.vcu.edu/soph_proposal.doc

4. A Proposal to Create a United States Postage Stamp Series: *America's Estuaries*

   http://www.longislandsoundstudy.net/archive/press/nepstamp.pdf

### CHAPTER 16

# WRITING CRITIQUES

## Reviewing, Evaluating, and Persuading

A **critique**—also known as a review—involves both analysis and evaluation. It is one of the most common forms of college writing. In fact, critiques of the type you might write in a composition course require a variety of observation and critical reading skills and persuasive techniques that you will use in many other college courses and in your career, whatever field you plan to enter.

The skills you might use to critique a proposal to merge departments, to relocate a plant, to launch a new marketing strategy, or to institute a new employee training program are the same skills you would use to construct a formal argument in any one of the academic disciplines. And they are the same skills you might use when deciding which graduate school to attend, which company to work for, which car to buy, or (dare we say it?) whom to marry!

# WHAT IS THE PURPOSE OF A CRITIQUE?

One purpose of a critique is to make the thing being evaluated—whether it is a work of art, a business plan, or a washing machine—more familiar and more understandable to the audience. In the case of a painting by the Spanish artist Salvador Dali, for example, you might explain something about the Surrealist movement and then state that one of Dali's purposes was to explore the subconscious on canvas. If you are evaluating a new hybrid automobile, you might explain that hybrid engines generate electrical energy that is used to help power the vehicle.

However, the main purpose of a critique is to evaluate the quality, accuracy, and/or usefulness of the object being critiqued and to render a judgment that the reader can use when deciding whether to see the film, read the novel, accept a proposal, buy a car, go to a particular restaurant, or spend time at an exposition of Surrealistic paintings (the list goes on and on).

Such information is often invaluable. For example, every year *U.S. News & World Report,* a respected weekly magazine, publishes an issue that rates U.S. colleges and offers advice to help students choose the one that is best for them. Each year *Money* magazine rates the best places to live in America, while *Forbes* magazine publishes a list of the best cities in America for singles. And millions of people rely on publications such as *Consumer Reports,* which rates everything from laptop computers to sports equipment and food processors. There are organizations that rate stocks, mutual funds, banks, discount department stores, politicians, government agencies, and charitable organizations (again, the list goes on and on).

Thus, whether they focus on plays, films, novels, paintings, computer games, pickup trucks, colleges and universities, public servants, business proposals, washing machines, restaurants, or even dog training academies, all successful critiques review, analyze, and evaluate.

# WHAT A CRITIQUE IS NOT

First, a critique is not a summary, a description, or a definition. Summary, description, and definition have their place in a critique, providing details that can help the reader better understand the thing being discussed. However, the purpose of a critique is to evaluate and, if appropriate, to recommend. Thus, while a movie reviewer may provide information about plot, setting, and character, his or her purpose is to convince the reader whether or not to shell out the $10 it will cost to see the film. And while an evaluation of the newest liquid crystal display (LCD) television might include the set's physical dimensions or briefly explain how LCD technology works, its purpose is to judge the quality of the picture and sound, to evaluate its compatibility with other home entertainment devices, to rate the manufacturer's technical support services, and, ultimately, to determine whether it is worth the consumer's money. Once again, then, a critique is a type of persuasive writing because it recommends a particular action or response. Indeed, most employers conduct periodic employee evaluations, which contribute to decisions regarding retention, salary increases, bonuses, promotions, demotions, and even terminations.

Finally, keep in mind that *critique* and *criticism* are not synonymous. A critique can and should identify strengths as well as weaknesses. Often, in fact, the most balanced and useful critiques are combination of both positive and negative comments.

# DECIDING ON CRITERIA FOR EVALUATION

One of the earliest steps in writing a critique is to decide on the criteria on which to judge the subject. The kinds of criteria you decide on will depend on the nature of the person, place, or thing being evaluated and the purpose of the critique.

Let's say you are reviewing the DVD of the Walt Disney animated film *Aladdin*. You might want to comment on the film's comic appeal to children, on the sophistication of its special effects, on the memorable qualities of its musical score, and even on the performance of Robin Williams, the voice of the Genie. But, given the movie's intended audience, would it be appropriate to point out that the dialogue between Jasmine and Aladdin does not contain the rich nuances exchanged between two young lovers in other films you have seen? And would it be fair to criticize the film as unrealistic because it contains genies and magic lamps?

Similarly, if you were trying to recommend the best car for a young family of four, you might consider cost of ownership, mechanical reliability, interior room, trunk space, fuel efficiency, length of warranty, and safety features. However, if you were evaluating sports cars, you would probably talk about horsepower, handling, sound systems, instrumentation displays, and interior appointments.

In some cases the audience—the readers of your critique—will affect the criteria you choose. For example, if you are writing an essay that recommends colleges, the criteria you use if you are addressing 18- to 22-year-old students might differ, in some ways at least, from the criteria you might use if your audience were made up of these students' parents.

Finally, remember that the criteria used will differ depending on the person or persons conducting the evaluation. This is especially true when it comes to critiquing works of art. For example, some critics raved about the film *Flags of Our Fathers* (see the *New York Times* review later in this chapter), whereas others were less enthusiastic. What accounts for this difference? In the case of this film, one side focused on the success with which the film addressed important philosophical and social questions, but the other objected to certain cinematic aspects. In other words, the reviewers were basing their evaluations on different criteria.

# PLANNING THE CRITIQUE

## Focus on a Topic

In college, you might enroll in humanities courses that require critiques of novels, plays, poems, paintings, and other works of art. You might also find yourself in economics or political science courses that require you to critique economic theories, practices, or policies. Then again, you might be in a class in which the choice is left up to you. If you are asked to choose your own topic, try to settle on something that you are interested in, that you know something about, and that you care about. For example, you might critique a new novel for your college literary magazine, review a new jazz CD to be broadcast on your college radio station, evaluate a local restaurant for your college newspaper, or compile a list of the best local employers, based on the extent to which they are student-friendly and willing to accommodate academic schedules.

## Decide on a Preliminary List of Criteria

The first step, as indicated earlier, is to determine a preliminary list of criteria on which you will judge the subject under discussion. Note that we say a *preliminary list*. Producing a critique is like any other writing task—it is a process, and the deeper you get into that process the greater will be your understanding of the subject. You might discover additional criteria to address as you outline, draft, or revise your paper. You may also want to change some criteria, and you might even want to eliminate others.

## Gather Information and Formulate a Thesis

Of course, you can always use freewriting, listing, or another prewriting technique to put down all you know about your subject. However, make sure that what you put down is accurate and thorough. This is especially true if you are reviewing sporting events, works of art, restaurants, and the like. For example, if you are critiquing a new television series that you last watched three weeks ago, make sure to watch the latest episode as well—just to sharpen your recollection. If you are writing a restaurant review, don't be afraid to take notes right at your table. If you are critiquing a film, play, or concert, make sure to write down your impressions immediately after the performance.

**• Consider Your Options**

When you are writing a critique, remember the importance of audience. It's one thing to critique a film, a television program, or a theatrical production, but it's quite another to critique a proposal or a process when you're at work. Someone at the office—or several someones—created that proposal or process, and you need to be careful with your tone and diction.

But don't stop there. Also try brainstorming with fellow students, friends, or colleagues who know and care about your subject—perhaps they have eaten at the same restaurant, seen the same play, driven the same car, or worked at the same place you are evaluating. Then find more information by completing library or Internet research if possible.

Finally, formulate a thesis statement that sums up your overall impression: "I will never eat at Bob's Botulism Bonanza again"; "Roberto Benigni's *Life Is Beautiful* is a tour de force that celebrates the human spirit better than any other film I have ever seen"; "The 2008 Wizbang 34i is a gas-guzzling rattrap that will endanger your wallet as well as your family." As always, you may want to modify your thesis as you progress through the writing process. But a preliminary thesis is always recommended.

## Develop Your Critique by Using Appropriate Methods

What are the best ways to develop an evaluation? They are the same as those you would use for any other piece of expository or persuasive writing:

- **Compare or contrast.** If you are writing an evaluation of the latest version of a popular word-processing software program, you might compare it with the previous version by commenting on its new features and capabilities and by explaining that some of the most common problems in the old version have been corrected.

- **Try examples.** If you are compiling a list of the best faculty on campus and one of your criteria is "accessibility to students," you might mention that Professor Capuana schedules fifteen office hours a week even though she is required to schedule only five. If you are picking the best values among places where students might spend spring break, you might mention particular hotels and restaurants and rate them on price, comfort, location, cleanliness, and service.

- **Use the cause-and-effect method.** If you are evaluating a city plan to reduce the costs of running the police department, you might do well to investigate the effects of a similar cost-cutting plan recently adopted by a city of about the same size and population and with a comparable crime rate. Another example comes from the pharmaceutical industry. Companies such as Merck, Pfizer, and Eli Lilly are required to publicize the side effects of their medications. Such information is invaluable to doctors when determining which medication is best for a particular patient.

- **Define and classify.** If you were rating the effectiveness of various treatments for osteoarthritis, you might first want to define osteoarthritis and distinguish it from the eight other types of chronic joint ailments. You might also have to define various types or classes of medications available, such as analgesics, biological response modifiers, and cortisone-related drugs.

- **Include statistical evidence.** One of the criteria on which automobiles are rated is their frequency-of-repair record, which is compiled from owner surveys. However, statistics can be used for any type of evaluation. For example, if you were writing a report that rated the best law schools in the nation, you might include statistics on the percentage of graduates from each school who passed the bar exam on the first try. You might also include statistics on the average starting salaries of graduates from each. If you were evaluating a hospital, you might check on its surgical mortality rates.

- **Rely on test data.** Such data can be obtained through research and often come in the form of statistics. For example, among the criteria that *Consumer Reports* uses to rate refrigerators and other appliances is energy efficiency. Such information is gleaned from controlled tests conducted by research facilities like those run by private organizations such as *Consumer Reports* and J. D. Power and Associates or by government agencies such as the National Highway Traffic Safety Administration and the Consumer Products Safety Commission.

- **Use summary (but sparingly).** If you are critiquing a novel or a film, you might have to summarize a few key events in order to support or clarify your opinions about the work. However, remember that your primary goal is to evaluate the artistic value of the work in order to persuade your audience that it is or is not worth reading or seeing.

## A Guide to Critiquing Written Texts

Critiquing written material begins with carefully reading the text and making appropriate notes. A second reading is always advisable, especially if is a relatively short piece such as a poem, short story, or newspaper article.

However you approach the object of the critique, make sure to gather relevant information and insights about the work as you experience it. One way to do this is to make notes based on a series of questions that you ask yourself. Such questions can be grouped into three categories based on the three activities common to all critiques: summarizing, analyzing, and evaluating.

Note that you will want to consider each of these questions, but you need not answer every single one when you write your critique. Indeed, some may simply not apply.

### Stage 1: Literal Reading

- What is the author's thesis or theme?
- What is the work's purpose if other than pure entertainment?
- What is the intended audience?
- If this is a novel, play, short story, or other work of art, what are its main components? For example, what major events make up the plot, if there is a plot? Is the play divided into acts and scenes? Is

the poem written in couplets, quatrains, and so on? (See also Chapter 22.)

- If this is an opinion piece or other commentary, what major arguments does the author use to support the thesis?

## Stage 2: Analysis

**If this is a literary or other artistic work (see also Chapter 22):**

- How do the plot, characters, setting, and other literary elements contribute to the development of the theme?
- Can more than one interpretation be assigned to an action, character, symbol, or other element in the piece? If so, what are those interpretations? If not, why not?
- How does the author create tone? How would you describe that tone? In what way does tone contribute to the overall effect of the work?
- Does the author use allusions or other references that help advance the work's purpose or theme? What are they, and how do they contribute to this end? How would you characterize the author's style?

**If this is an opinion piece:**

- What specific evidence or examples does the author use to develop the arguments presented in support of the thesis?
- Can you tell if the author has built the work on certain assumptions that he or she has made about the issue?
- Does the author use evidence from formal studies, surveys, and other expert or scholarly sources?
- What questions does the author ask about the issue being discussed? Are these questions rhetorical? Are they intended to be answered later in the opinion piece, or are readers simply expected to consider these queries as they read the piece? What answers, if any, does the author provide?
- Does the author use allusions or other references that help advance the thesis? What are they, and how do they contribute to this end?
- What techniques, such a startling remarks and statistics, thought-provoking images, and interesting examples, does the author use to keep your interest and advance the thesis?

## Stage 3: Evaluation

**If this is a literary or other work of art (see also Chapter 22):**

- Does the work keep the audience's interest?
- Is it unified and focused, or is the organization poorly planned or illogical?
- Are the plot, setting, dialogue, staging, and other aesthetic components executed in an intelligent and believable manner?

- How would you evaluate the author's use of language?

**If this is an opinion piece:**

- Are the essay's thesis and purpose clear and reasonable?
- Does the author focus on a limited topic, or does he or she attempt to cover too much?
- Are the ideas and information used to support the author's position logical and clearly related to the thesis?
- Are the facts on which the author bases the argument accurate? Is this information complete and used fairly, or has it been manipulated, taken out of context, or distorted to advance a particular point of view?
- Does the author use information from outside sources? Does he or she mention the authors or titles of these sources? Are these sources trustworthy, objective, and complete?
- Is the author impartial, or does he or she use language intended to appeal to the reader's emotions and self-interest? If the latter, is this language simply strong and moving, or is it unfair, biased, or inappropriate in any way?
- Does the essay or column you are critiquing lack important information that you know might contradict the work's thesis or one of its supporting ideas?
- Does the author raise important questions and answer them adequately? Does he or she include opposing arguments and address them fairly and completely?
- Is the essay well organized and unified? Or does it contain material that is out of place or irrelevant?
- Is the author's language appropriate to the intended audience?
- Does the essay keep your interest? Does it offer an effective introduction and a memorable conclusion?
- Is the author's tone appropriate to the intended audience and purpose? Should he or she have used less formal diction? Should the author have included rhetorical questions or tried to address the reader directly now and then? Or should the tone of the work have been more formal or more objective?

## Reading Critiques

This section includes reviews of Clint Eastwood's *Flags of Our Fathers* (2006) by *New York Times* film critic Manohla Dargis and of the first New York production of Tennessee Williams' *A Streetcar Named Desire* (1947) by noted drama critic Brooks Atkinson. It also contains two other critiques—one positive and one negative—of the Fox News Network. Questions for discussion follow the selections by Dargis and Atkinson as well as the two critiques of the Fox News Network.

# A Ghastly Conflagration,
# A Tormented Aftermath

## MANOHLA DARGIS

*Film critic Manohla Dargis began writing for the Village Voice in 1987 and became film editor of the L.A. Weekly in 1995. She began writing for the Los Angeles Times in 2002 and is now one of the two chief film critics of the New York Times. Flags of Our Fathers, a film by veteran actor and director Clint Eastwood, tells the story of the servicemen who raised the U.S. flag on Iwo Jima (the first Japanese home island to be captured) near the end of World War II.*

It seems hard to believe there is anything left to say about World War II that has not already been stated and restated, chewed, digested and spat out for your consideration and that of the Oscar voters. And yet here, at age 76, is Clint Eastwood saying something new and vital about the war in his new film, and here, too, is this great, gray battleship of a man and a movie icon saying something new and urgent about the uses of war and of the men who fight. "Flags of Our Fathers" concerns one of the most lethal encounters on that distant battlefield, but make no mistake: this is also a work of its own politically fraught moment.

The film distills much of the material covered in James Bradley and Ron Powers's affecting book of the same title about the raising of the American flag during the battle for Iwo Jima. Mr. Bradley's father, John Bradley, nicknamed Doc and played by an effectively restrained Ryan Phillipe, was one of six men who helped plant the flag (it was the second planted that day) on the island's highest point on the fifth day of the monthlong American offensive. An Associated Press photographer, Joe Rosenthal, immortalized the moment, and American politicians seized the day, sending the three surviving flag raisers—Doc, Ira Hayes (Adam Beach, delivering heart-break by the payload) and Rene Gagnon (Jesse Bradford)—on a hugely successful war-bond drive.

Collectively hailed as heroes from sea to shining sea, Rene embraced the spotlight, Doc settled into stoic unhappiness, while Ira, a Pima Indian shattered by Iwo Jima and its dead, sobbed and drank himself into oblivion. The efforts of Doc's adult son (Tom McCarthy) to tell his father's story years later give the film its scaffolding, but it is Mr. Beach's Ira, with his open face and vulnerability, who haunts it. Tears mixing with booze, he floods his scenes with raw emotion that serves as a rebuke to gung-ho fictions like "Sands of Iwo Jima," a 1949 bad joke in which John Wayne hands an American flag to the real Ira, Doc and Rene so they can raise Old Glory once more, this time over the sands of Southern California.

Mr. Eastwood's cinematic deconstruction takes a considerably darker view of the historical record. The Air Force had repeatedly bombed Iwo Jima before the American landing on Feb. 19, 1945; by D-Day, barely a blade of grass survived, even as more than 20,000 Japanese soldiers remained dug in. To replicate that scorched earth, Mr. Eastwood drains much of the color from the film's already muted palette, so much so that many of the scenes on the island look as if they were shot in black and white. It seems impossible that anything living could survive long in this charred, spooky place, and it isn't long after the invasion that American bodies begin piling up amid the orange-red explosions and dull-red sprays of blood.

During these anxious moments, Mr. Eastwood characteristically keeps his sights (and ears) on the troops and the choreographed chaos of their movements; the focus remains on them, not the filmmaking. When the men hit the shore, the cameras stick close to them, moving and then, during a sudden hailstorm of bullets, running alongside the men as if similarly searching for cover. Despite the occasional bird's-eye view that underscores the staggering scale of the operation—the hundreds of boats hugging the coast, the thousands of men dotting the land—the filmmaking retains a devastating intimacy, as in a quiet shot of dead soldiers lying facedown on the beach, the water under their bodies receding as if it were blood.

The scenes on Iwo Jima are harrowing, borderline surreal, and even after Doc, Ira and Rene leave the island, they never fully escape it. During the bond drive, the pop of a camera bulb, a flash of lightning and the bang of a backfiring car engine instantly return the three to the island and its horrors, a blurring between past and present that, with seamless, ruthless efficiency, Mr. Eastwood and his longtime editor, Joel Cox, turn into a dreadful memory loop. In Mr. Bradley and Mr. Powers's book, one Iwo Jima veteran describes seeing his dead friends while sitting in class at medical school; the flashbacks, he says, were "like a movie screen wrapped around me." We see a version of that movie here, and it is terrible.

Most war movies, even those that claim to be antiwar, overtly or implicitly embrace violence as either a political or cinematic means to an end. Few filmmakers can resist the thrill of the rocket's red glare and the spectacle of death; the violence is simply too exciting. There are plenty of big bangs in "Flags of Our Fathers," but because the screenplay, by William Broyles Jr. and Paul Haggis, oscillates among three separate time frames—Iwo Jima, the bond tour and, less successfully, contemporary scenes involving Doc and his son—and because the flag raisers were pulled off the field before fighting ended, the violence of their war remains at a frenzied pitch.

It doesn't build, evolve, recede; it terrifies and keeps terrifying.

What do we want from war films? Entertainment, mostly, a few hours' escape to other lands and times, as well as something excitingly different, something reassuringly familiar. If "Flags of Our Fathers" feels so unlike most war movies and sounds so contrary to the usual political rhetoric, it is not because it affirms that war is hell, which it does with unblinking, graphic brutality. It's because Mr. Eastwood insists, with a moral certitude that is all too rare in our movies, that we extract an unspeakable cost when we ask men to kill other men. There is never any doubt in the film that the country needed to fight this war, that it was necessary; it is the horror at such necessity that defines "Flags of Our Fathers," not exultation.

In this respect, the film works, among other things, as a gentle corrective to Steven Spielberg's "Saving Private Ryan," with its state-of-the-art carnage and storybook neatness. (Mr. Spielberg, whose company bought the film rights to "Flags of Our Fathers," is one of its producers.) Where "Saving Private Ryan" offers technique, Mr. Eastwood's film suggests metaphysics. Once again, he takes us into the heart of violence and into the hearts of men, seeing where they converge under a night sky as brightly lighted with explosions as any Fourth of July nocturne and in caves where some soldiers are tortured to death and others surrender to madness. He gives us men whose failings are evidence of their humanity and who are, contrary to our revolted sensitivities, no less human because they kill.

One view of Mr. Eastwood is that he has mellowed with age, or at least begun to take serious measure of the violence that has been an animating force in many of his films. In truth, the critical establishment caught up with the director, who for decades has been building a fascinating body of work that considers annihilating violence as a condition of the American character, not an aberration. "Flags of Our Fathers" is an imperfect addition to that body of work, though its flaws are minor and finally irrelevant in a film in which ambivalence and ambiguity are constituent of a worldview, not an aftereffect. Notably, Mr. Eastwood's next film, "Letters From Iwo Jima," set to open early next year, revisits the same battle, this time from the point of view of the Japanese.

"Flags of Our Fathers" is rated R (under 17 requires accompanying parent or adult guardian). The representation of war and its battlefield atrocities is extremely graphic. **11**

## Style and Strategy

1. Comment on this selection's introduction. Is it effective in capturing readers' attention and enticing them to read on? What is the effect of calling Clint Eastwood a "great, gray battleship of a man"?

2. Why does Dargis summarize actual historical events pictured in the movie? In what way does doing so help her support her rather positive view of this film? Why does she call the film a "cinematic deconstruction" (paragraph 4)?

3. Why does the critique contrast this movie with two other war films? Are those contrasts fair? How do they help her advance her thesis about this film? What do they tell us about her audience?

4. Why does Dargis mention Eastwood's next film, *Letters from Iwo Jima*?

## Questions for Critical Thinking and Discussion

1. What, according to Dargis, is Clint Eastwood trying to accomplish in *Flags of Our Fathers*? What does the film tell us about human nature and the nature of war?

2. What does your answer to question 1 reveal about the criterion or criteria that Dargis is using to evaluate a war film?

3. Dargis praises the way in which this film was put together—the cinematography, the screenplay, the use of flashbacks. Summarize what Dargis says about each of these. Is this a completely positive review, or does it find some weaknesses in the film?

4. Explain what Dargis means when, in paragraph 9, she tells us that Eastwood "gives us men whose failings are evidence of their humanity"?

## Suggestions for Writing

1. Make sure to see *Flags of Our Fathers*. Then rent and view *Sands of Iwo Jima* (1949) or *Saving Private Ryan* (1998), and write a critique of one of those two films (500 to 750 words) by contrasting it with *Flags of Our Fathers*.

2. Pick your favorite movie from another film genre, and write a critique of between 500 and 750 words. For example, you might pick a spy thriller, a romantic comedy, a cinematic recreation of an historic event, or even a documentary.

# First Night at the Theater: A Review of Tennessee Williams' *A Streetcar Named Desire*

## BROOKS ATKINSON

*Brooks Atkinson (1894–1984) was called "the most important reviewer of his time."*

*He served as theater critic for the* New York Times *on and off from 1925 to 1960. During the Second World War, Atkinson reported on front-line action in China. In 1945, he became the* Times' *chief correspondent in Moscow, winning the Pulitzer Prize in 1947 for his work there. He then returned to his post as theater critic, retiring in 1960, the year in which a Broadway theater was renamed in his honor.*

*Tennessee (Thomas Lanier) Williams (1911–1983) was a native of Mississippi and one the twentieth century's greatest playwrights. He won the Pulitzer Prize for drama for* A Streetcar Named Desire *in 1948 and for* Cat on a Hot Tin Roof *in 1955. Among his other plays are* The Glass Menagerie *(1945) and* The Night of the Iguana *(1961), both of which won the New York Drama Critics' Circle Award.*

*Atkinson reviewed the first New York production of* A Streetcar Named Desire *on its opening night, December 4, 1947.*

Tennessee Williams has brought us a superb drama, "A Streetcar Named Desire," which was acted at the Ethel Barrymore last evening. And Jessica Tandy gives a superb performance as a rueful heroine whose misery Mr. Williams is tenderly recording. This must be one of the most perfect marriages of acting and playwriting. For the acting and playwriting are perfectly blended in a limpid performance, and it is impossible to tell where Miss Tandy begins to give form and warmth to the mood Mr. Williams has created.     1

Like "The Glass Menagerie," the new play is a quietly woven study of intangibles. But to this observer it shows deeper insight and represents a great step forward toward clarity. And it reveals Mr. Williams as a genuinely poetic playwright whose knowledge of people is honest and thorough and whose sympathy is profoundly human.     2

"A Streetcar Named Desire" is the history of a gently reared Mississippi young woman who invents an artificial world to mask the hideousness     3 of the world she has to inhabit. She comes to live with her sister, who is married to a rough-and-ready mechanic and inhabits two dreary rooms in a squalid neighborhood. Blanche—for that is her name—has delusions of grandeur, talks like an intellectual snob, buoys herself up with gaudy dreams, spends most of her time primping, covers things that are dingy with things that are bright and flees reality.

To her brother-in-law she is an unforgivable liar. But it is soon apparent to the theatregoer that in Mr. Williams's eyes she is one of the dispossessed whose experience has unfitted her for reality; and although his attitude toward her is merciful, he does not spare her or the playgoer. For the events of "Streetcar" lead to a painful conclusion which he does not try to avoid. Although Blanche cannot face the truth, Mr. Williams does in the most imaginative and perceptive play he has written.     4

Since he is no literal dramatist and writes in none of the conventional forms, he presents the theatre with many problems. Under Elia Kazan's sensitive but concrete direction, the theatre has solved them admirably. Jo Mielziner has provided a beautifully lighted single setting that lightly sketches the house and the neighborhood. In this shadowy environment the performance is a work of great beauty.     5

Miss Tandy has a remarkably long part to play. She is hardly ever off the stage, and when she is on stage she is almost constantly talking—chattering, dreaming aloud, wondering, building enchantments out of words. Miss Tandy is a trim, agile actress with a lovely voice and quick intelligence. Her performance is almost incredibly true. For it does seem almost incredible that she can     6 convey it with so many shades and impulses that are accurate, revealing and true.

The rest of the acting is also of very high quality indeed. Marlon Brando as the quick-tempered, scornful, violent mechanic; Karl Malden as a stupid but wondering suitor; Kim Hunter as the patient though troubled sister—all act not only with color and style but with insight.

By the usual Broadway standards, "A Streetcar Named Desire" is too long; not all those words are essential. But Mr. Williams is entitled to his own independence. For he has not forgotten that human beings are the basic subject of art. Out of poetic imagination and ordinary compassion he has spun a poignant and luminous story.

## Style and Strategy

1. Write a brief outline of this review. What are the criteria that Atkinson uses to evaluate this performance of *A Streetcar Named Desire*?

2. Why does Atkinson spend so much time on Jessica Tandy's performance?

3. Comment on the length of Atkinson's paragraphs. Then talk about the kind of vocabulary he uses. What do these things tell us about his purpose and his audience?

4. Where does Atkinson make use of comparison and contrast? Where does he use plot summary? Where does he explain causes and effects?

## Questions for Critical Thinking and Discussion

1. What can we infer about the theme of this play from this review?

2. What does Atkinson mean when he claims that Williams "does not spare [Blanche] or the playgoer" (paragraph 4)?

3. Why does Atkinson believe that Williams is a great playwright?

4. Aside from the acting and the writing, what else does Atkinson praise?

5. Is this a balanced review? Should Atkinson's criticism of the play's length have received greater attention in this review?

## Suggestions for Writing

1. Obtain a copy of the filmed version (on videotape or DVD) of *A Streetcar Named Desire* directed by Elia Kazan and starring Jessica Tandy and Marlon Brando—the very production that Atkinson reviewed. Watch it, and then write your own review. In other words, use your own set of criteria to judge the play. Does it still speak to us sixty years after its first production? Are you as enthusiastic about it as Atkinson was? Why or why not?

2. Review a performance of a play now being staged at a high school, at a college or university, at a community playhouse, or at a professional theater. You might want to submit your work for publication in your

college newspaper, so assume that you are recommending or panning this play with a college audience in mind. Devise your own criteria against which to judge the play, but take your lead from Atkinson, and be sure to comment on the writing, the acting, and the production (staging effects, lighting, costumes, and/or props). If possible, also comment on the direction.

## IS FOX NEWS "FAIR AND BALANCED"?
## Two Critiques of the Popular News Network

The two critiques that follow come to diametrically opposed conclusions about whether the Fox News Network is as "fair and balanced" as it claims to be.

## Fox News: Enraging Liberals for 10 Years

### BRIAN C. ANDERSON

*Brian C. Anderson is a senior editor at the* City Journal. *He has also written for* The Public Interest, Wilson Quarterly, the New York Post, *the* New York Daily News, *the* New York Sun, *and the* Washington Times. *His latest book is* South Park Conservatives: The Revolt Against Liberal Media Bias (2005). *The essay that appears below was published in the* Los Angeles Times *on October 4, 2006.*

Fox News turns 10 this week, and it has every reason to celebrate. Launched by media tycoon Rupert Murdoch and former political consultant Roger Ailes as a refuge for viewers fed up with real or perceived liberal bias elsewhere in the media, Fox is the undisputed ratings champion of cable news. It's been trouncing CNN, MSNBC and CNBC for years, and it sometimes draws a fatter audience share than all its competitors combined, though viewership has slumped a little of late. Pugnacious Bill O'Reilly and conservative tough guy Sean Hannity have become two of the nation's most powerful broadcasters thanks to this kind of ratings pull. Fox is the news media success story of the last decade.

Liberals aren't celebrating the channel's birthday, though. Even before an angry Bill Clinton exploded at "Fox News Sunday" anchor Chris

Wallace a couple of weeks ago, accusing him of "a nice little conservative hit job" after getting pressed about his record on fighting Al Qaeda, Democratic pols and advocates have relentlessly attacked the cable network, accusing it of being a Republican propaganda mill. Al Gore has likened Fox to a right-wing "fifth column." Leftist groups, including MoveOn.org, funded the documentary "Outfoxed," which purports to expose the channel's nefarious Republican agenda, and petitioned the Federal Trade Commission to ban Fox's use of its famous "Fair and Balanced" slogan as deceptive advertising.

"When a news outlet is allowed to blur the lines between opinion and journalism and call it 'fair and balanced,' I think it's confusing to consumers of information in this country, and it's dangerous to democracy," fretted an official at Common Cause, one of the organizations joining the petition. Hollywood celebrities never miss an opportunity to bash "Faux News." Comedy Central's witty "Colbert Report" is a nightly satire of the channel and of O'Reilly in particular.

What explains all this hysteria? Success, of course.

The propaganda charge is unfair, at least 5 when it comes to the network's presentation of news. In the 2004 presidential race, Fox pollsters consistently underestimated President Bush's support. In its final preelection poll, Fox had Kerry winning by a couple of points, one of the only polls to show the Democrat on top. I'm not sure a right-wing fifth column would do that.

A recent comprehensive study by UCLA polit- 6 ical scientist Tim Groseclose and University of Missouri-Columbia economics professor Jeffrey Milyo found Brit Hume's "Special Report"—Fox's most straightforward news show—more centrist than any of the three major networks' evening newscasts, all of which leaned left.

The program is a model of smart news 7 television.

And although it's true that the network's 8 opinion shows (as opposed to its news shows) are, as they're supposed to be, noisily opinionated, it's equally true that Fox's biggest star, O'Reilly, is no mainstream Republican. He regularly charges the oil companies with price-gouging and attacks big business for squashing the little guy. And who can say what host Greta Van Susteren's politics are? She mostly zeroes in on lurid murder mysteries and scandals.

Liberals troop into and out of the Fox studios 9 every day—some of them, like host Alan Colmes and news analyst Marvin Kalb, affiliated with the channel. There's no doubt, of course, that Fox News is more conservative than CBS or CNN. But, after all, that was its founding mission.

Fox's real ethos is not Republican but anti- 10 elitist—a major reason it connects with so many Americans and annoys so many coastal elites. "There's a whole country that elitists will never acknowledge," Ailes once observed. "What people resent deeply out there are those in the 'blue states' thinking they're smarter."

This anti-elitism shows itself in Fox's pro-U.S. 11 stance in covering the Afghanistan and Iraq wars and its broadcasters' use of terms such as "terror-

ist" instead of "militant" to refer to . . . well, terrorists. Since the Vietnam War era, mainstream journalists have tended to see such blunt language and side-taking as unsophisticated, a betrayal of journalistic objectivity.

Another aspect of Fox's anti-elitism: Chris- 12 tians, far from being seen as lunatics or curiosities—as too often is the case in the mainstream media—actually get some respect.

"We regularly have on the Rev. Franklin Gra- 13 ham, Dr. James Dobson and other religious leaders, just as we put on Pat Ireland and Eleanor Clift," Hannity told me a while back. "Most Americans believe in God and have that as their foundation in life. So why shouldn't we have as guests people that they like, respect and want to hear from?"

What really frustrates liberals about Fox, 14 though, is simply that, along with talk radio and the conservative blogosphere, it has helped shatter the left's near-monopoly on news and information. Fox's opinion-driven programming gives conservatives and liberals a chance to get a hearing for their ideas. But Democratic politicians and activists who go on Fox also must defend their views, often against tough questioning, something that happens less often on the networks, where most journalists are left-of-center, survey after survey has shown.

Even more significant, Fox came on the scene 15 a decade ago as a professional news organization that could define and report news as something different from what the elite consensus says it is. To take one of many examples, the corruption of the United Nations' oil-for-food initiative in Iraq, initially downplayed by the mainstream media because of their sympathy for internationalism, was uncovered—deemed newsworthy—on Fox.

All this wouldn't matter if Fox News wasn't so 16 influential. But it is. According to the Pew Research Center, more than 20% of Americans now claim to get news from it, and lots of them (37%) are Democrats or independents. The network's success has also sparked a "Fox effect," leading some competitors to become more open to right-of-center opinions: MSNBC's "Scarborough Country," hosted by former Republican congressman Joe Scarborough, is a prime example. Until a few years ago, Democrats never had to deal with all these mediatized conservatives.

17    Nothing would please liberals more than to drag the nation back to the days when the New York Times and CBS News determined what was newsworthy. A group of congressional Democrats has warned Fox to end its supposed anti-Democratic bias—or else. Should Democrats retake Congress, an effort to shut down, or at least muzzle, Fox is far from inconceivable, creepy and illiberal as that sounds.

18    Something Fox News doubtless is keeping in mind as it pops the champagne corks this week.

# Still Failing the "Fair & Balanced" Test

## STEVE RENDALL AND JULIE HOLLAR

*Steve Rendall is a senior analyst with* Fairness & Accuracy in Reporting *(FAIR) and the host of the radio show* CounterSpin. *Julie Hollar is the communications director for FAIR. Their essay, which focuses on Fox's flagship news program,* Special Report, *first appeared on the FAIR Web site for July/August 2004.*

1    FAIR's latest study of Fox's Special Report with Brit Hume finds the network's flagship news show still listing right—heavily favoring conservative and Republican guests in its one-on-one interviews. And, according to the study, Special Report rarely features women or non-white guests in these prominent newsmaker interview spots.

2    In previous studies FAIR has found that looking at a show's guest list is one of the most reliable methods for gauging its perspective. In the case of Special Report, the single one-on-one interview with anchor Brit Hume is a central part of the newscast, and the anchor often uses his high-profile guests' comments as subject matter for the show's wrap-up panel discussion. If Fox is the "fair & balanced" network it claims to be, then the guest list of what Fox calls its "signature news show" ought to reflect a diverse spectrum of ideas and sources. FAIR has studied Special Report's guest list on two earlier occasions (Extra!, 7–8/01, 7–8/02).

3    FAIR's current study looked at 25 weeks of Special Report's one-on-one interview segments (6/30/03–12/19/03), finding 101 guests. FAIR classified each guest by political ideology, party affiliation (where applicable), gender and ethnicity. When FAIR first studied Special Report in 2001, the dominance of conservative guests was so overwhelming (71 percent of all guests) that we used just two ideological categories, "conservative" and "non-conservative." The latter included guests with no discernible political ideology.

4    When FAIR's second study in 2002 found conservative guests had dropped to less than half of the total, we added a "left of center" category for comparison purposes. Though the "left of center" category was more broadly defined than the "conservative" category—since many right-of-center guests were not counted as conservatives—conservatives still outnumbered those on the left, 14 to one.

For this study three ideological categories were used: conservative, centrist and progressive. Guests affiliated with openly conservative, centrist or progressive think tanks, magazines or advocacy groups, or who openly promote such views, are labeled as such. Guests who do not avow an ideology—such as military operations experts and journalists who decline to reveal their own political inclinations—were categorized as non-ideological. 5

As with earlier FAIR studies of Special Report, Republicans were not automatically counted as conservatives and Democrats were not automatically counted as liberals. For instance, Georgia Democratic Senator Zell Miller, who champions many conservative causes and openly campaigns for George Bush, is classified as an ideological conservative. Likewise, Georgia Democratic congressmember Jim Marshall, who has one of the most conservative voting records of any congressional Democrat, was classified as a "centrist," as was Democrat Susan Estrich, who was a member of Republican California Gov. Arnold Schwarzenegger's transition team and has implored Democrats to move to the center (e.g., "Let Clinton Be the Centrist Clinton," USA Today, 6/22/95). Dennis Ross, who has served under Republican and Democratic administrations and whose positions on the Middle East are center-right, was counted as a centrist for the purposes of this study. 6

In the past, Special Report featured interviews with moderate Republicans such as Christopher Shays, Christine Todd Whitman and David Gergen who were counted as "non-conservatives" under the earlier classification system. Only one Republican was counted as a "centrist" in the current study period: Noah Feldman, a legal expert who worked for the Bush administration in Iraq. 7

### Conservative & Republican

Fifty-seven percent of Special Report's one-on-one guests during the period studied were ideological conservatives, 12 percent were centrists and 11 percent were progressives. 8

Twenty percent of guests were non-ideological. Among ideological guests, conservatives accounted for 72 percent, while centrists made up 15 percent and progressives 14 percent. (The total exceeds 100 percent due to rounding.) Viewers were roughly five times more likely to see a conservative interviewed on Special Report than a progressive. 9

The five-to-one conservative-to-progressive imbalance is actually a marked improvement from FAIR's 2002 study, which found that "left-of-center" guests—three percent of the total—were outnumbered 14 to one. In the 2002 study, however, conservative dominance was less marked, at 48 percent of total guests. 10

Special Report's guest list shows a similarly heavy slant toward Republicans. Forty-two guests were current or former Democratic or Republican officials, candidates, political appointees or advisers. Guests who had past affiliations with both Republicans and Democrats were counted as nonpartisan; for example, Dennis Ross—having served under presidents Ronald Reagan, George H.W. Bush and Bill Clinton—was classified as nonpartisan. 11

Of the 42 partisan guests, 35 were Republicans and only seven were Democrats—a five-to-one imbalance. Furthermore, of the handful of Democrats that did appear, the majority were centrist or conservative, and frequently expressed views more typical of Republican guests. For example, centrist Rep. Jim Marshall (10/23/03) argued that the media weren't covering the "good news" in Iraq, while Sen. Zell Miller (11/4/03) talked about his dissatisfaction with the Democratic party and his fondness for George Bush. Thirty-four of the 35 Republicans who appeared were conservatives; only one, Noah Feldman, was classified as a centrist. 12

The five-to-one partisan imbalance represents a greater slant than FAIR's 2002 study, which found Republicans outnumbering Democrats by three to two, though it is still better than FAIR's 13

2001 study, which found Special Report's guest list favoring Republicans by more than eight to one (50 vs. 6). After the 2001 study, the show's anchor, Fox managing editor Brit Hume, told the New York Times (7/2/01) that, though he had yet to read the findings, "if it is a reasonable question, and we find that there is some imbalance, then we'll correct it."

### White & Male

Special Report continues to overwhelmingly favor white and male guests: As in 2002, only 7 percent of guests were women, and the percentage of people of color rose only slightly, to 11 percent from 7 percent in 2001 and 2002. In 2003, only one woman of color was featured in a one-on-one interview: National Security Adviser Condoleezza Rice.   14

As in past studies, those women and people of color who did appear on Special Report were remarkably conservative. Four of the seven appearances by women were by conservative Republicans and two were by centrist Democrat   15

Susan Estrich. No progressive women appeared in the study period. Of the seven guests of color (accounting for 11 appearances), five were conservative and only one was progressive, journalist Charles Cobb of allAfrica.com. The one person of color classified as non-ideological, Mansoor Ijaz, accounted for five appearances. Ijaz, a wealthy investment manager who has expressed support for Hillary Clinton, is also a frequent and vocal booster of neo-conservative causes and difficult to label ideologically.

In our second study of Special Report (Extra!, 8/02), FAIR remarked, "While Special Report can claim to have moderated its imbalance with regard to Republican and conservative guests, the show still falls short of reflecting the diverse ideas and communities of the United States." With current findings indicating that the show has tipped back toward increased imbalance, it becomes harder to defend Special Report from charges that it chooses its guests based on political sympathies, not news judgment.   16

### Style and Strategy

1.  Why does Anderson explain the liberal response to Fox News?

2.  What evidence does Anderson present to demonstrate that Fox News' reporting is fair and balanced? What evidence do Rendall and Hollar use to argue that it is not?

3.  How does Anderson's mentioning MSNBC's *Scarborough Country* in paragraph 16 help him advance his thesis?

4.  Rendall and Hollar categorize various guests appearing on *Special Report,* a news show hosted by Brit Hume, according to their perceived political philosophies: conservative, centrist, progressive. They then present statistics that reflect the frequency with which members of each group appear on Hume's show. What are the strengths and weaknesses of building a critique using this strategy?

5.  What is Anderson warning us about at the end of his critique? Given his subject, is this an appropriate way to conclude?

## Questions for Critical Thinking and Discussion

1. Explain the difference in connotation (if not denotation) between "terrorist" and "militant" as used in paragraph 11 of Anderson's essay.

2. Who are Rev. Franklin Graham and Dr. James Dobson, mentioned by Anderson in paragraph 13? How might their views differ from those of Pat Ireland and Eleanor Clift? Research these figures on the Internet, if necessary.

3. Is Fox's success an indication that it is, indeed, fair and balanced? If so, how?

4. Rendall and Hollar critique only one of the shows seen on the Fox News Channel. Would their essay have been more effective had they reviewed other Fox programs?

5. As you have learned, Rendall and Hollar work for Fairness & Accuracy in Reporting (FAIR). Research this organization via the Internet. Determine its mission and, if appropriate, its political slant. Do the same for the *Wilson Quarterly* and for the other publications Anderson has written for. What does such research tell you about the objectivity of these authors?

## Suggestions for Writing

1. Complete your own critique of a particular Fox News show (perhaps Brit Humes's *Special Report*). Watch the show every day for at least one week. Then determine if its approach to the news leans to the right or if it is "fair and balanced."

2. Review any other evening network news show. You can find several on NBC, ABC, CBS, MSNBC, and CNN. View the show every night. Then determine if it has a political bias or if its coverage is balanced.

3. Review any television or radio news show or any Internet news site. Watch, listen to, or read this news outlet for at least one week. Then write a critique based on three criteria: variety, depth, and accuracy of news coverage. If appropriate, also comment on the fairness with which the show or the site editorializes on important issues. If this assignment doesn't interest you, try critiquing a particular newspaper that you have read for a week.

## Additional Suggestions for Writing

1. Evaluate a teacher you had in high school. Begin by defining the criteria you believe make for excellence in teaching, especially in regard to the discipline or classes your subject teaches. Then explain how this teacher met or failed to meet these criteria. What advice, if any, would you give this instructor? Note: do not reveal the teacher's real name. Create an alias such as Dr. Warmheart, Ms. Algebra, or Mr. Motormouth.

2. Watch a children's television series such as *Sesame Street* or *SpongeBob SquarePants* for at least one week. Then pretend to have been contracted to write a critique of the show for a magazine called *A Parent's Guide to*

*Children's Television.* Would you recommend that parents allow their children to watch the show? Why or why not?

3. Critique a few television, radio, print, or Internet commercials that advertise a similar product or service. Which commercials pique your interest in the product or service? Which do not? In both cases, explain why.

4. In your college catalogue, look up the graduation requirements for a degree in your academic major or a major you might be interested in. Are these requirements up-to-date and appropriate to today's job market? Is there a balance between required general education courses and major courses? What would you change in the curriculum?

5. Critique your high school education by evaluating the extent to which it prepared you for college. Pay special attention to courses in English and mathematics, but don't forget other subjects, such as history, the sciences, and modern languages.

6. Evaluate a current government policy, practice, or program—local, state, or federal. For example, what are the strengths and weaknesses of the electoral college system, by which U.S. presidents are elected? What are the strengths and weaknesses of the Social Security system or of an all-volunteer military?

7. Critique a policy, process, requirement, or practice you have encountered in the workplace. Should it be maintained, eliminated, or modified? Why?

8. **Writing About Editorial Cartoons:** Critique two or three editorial cartoons on the same subject in a newspaper or magazine. Which one do you find most effective? Explain why the one you have chosen is more effective than the other(s).

9. **Using the Internet:** Find and critique two or three Web sites of organizations that have the same or similar missions. For example, you might critique the Web sites of two or three automobile manufacturers, of two or three environmental groups, or of two or three colleges or universities. Which one appeals to you most? Why?

# BUSINESS FORMATS

Carla works as an automobile designer. On a typical morning she arrives at work just before her design group's meeting. She checks her e-mail, but because there are so many messages, she prints them out to read during some dead time at the meeting. Her mailbox (the physical one) contains three letters and four memos, which she takes to the meeting as well.

AFTER THE MEETING, CARLA ANSWERS E-MAILS, writes letters, and writes a memo. She also attends to the "design" elements of her job.

Carla is astonished at how much writing her job requires. "I went to college to learn engineering," she says. However, the world of work requires strong communications skills, both oral and written, along with a sure sense of **audience**, crucial in dealing with colleagues, superiors, clients, and others.

This chapter covers four basic business documents: e-mail, the memo, the business letter, and the résumé, emphasizing standard formats and audience needs.

# E-MAIL, MEMOS, AND BUSINESS LETTERS

Electronic mail (e-mail) is a relative newcomer to business. For centuries, the two standard forms of written business communication were memos and letters. Memos are internal documents, sent within a business; letters go outside the business, to clients and vendors. Today, e-mail is used for both functions. However, e-mail has not replaced the memo or the letter. Each format still has a niche in business writing.

## E-mail

E-mail is a written message sent from one computer to another. It can be forwarded, saved, or deleted. E-mail saves businesses money when compared to the cost of long-distance telephone calls, and it also preserves a record of the communication automatically, which is normally not the case with a telephone call.

A true convenience, e-mail enables you to send a message to a colleague down the hall and or on the other side of the world. E-mail has other advantages as well. Let's say you make the following phone call: "Ed, the classroom change you requested has gone through. You're in Main Hall 214." Most people would thank you and hang up. Not Ed. He reiterates the reasons he needs the room change (of course, this is the third time you have heard them). He also rambles on about how much the scheduling office must hate him, for this is the third time in two years that he has made such a request. E-mail avoids this problem. Your two sentences are quickly sent to Ed, who probably feels isolated these days, for he receives no phone calls from anyone who can avoid him.

The main issues in writing and sending e-mails are the practical context and the rhetorical context, which includes audience analysis.

### The Practical Context

Note that it is very important to include in the subject line a phrase that will provide your reader with an immediate, specific, and accurate idea of the e-mail's contents.

The computer automatically inserts a date and time, so the writer doesn't need to add them. Moreover, like a memo, an e-mail has **To** and **From** lines at the top. Hence, there is no need for a salutation ("Dear Mark"). However, the **From** line might identify the sender as **Jennifer189,073@genericemail.com**, so it's always a good idea to add a "signature line," which usually includes your name and the name of your organization, at the bottom of any e-mail. Note how the practical context affects the following two e-mails, which otherwise contain the same message:

> From: Jennifer189,073@genericemail.com
> To: Mark47,751@genericemail.com
> Subject: Conference rescheduling
>
> Mark: Thank you for your note regarding the conference rescheduling. I was just about to make plane reservations, and you saved me a lot of trouble.
> Jennifer Lewis

> From: Jennifer_Lewis@Bindleburgbarns.com
> To: Mark_Pluta@Bindleburgbarns.com
> Subject: Conference rescheduling
>
> Thank you for your note regarding the conference rescheduling. I was just about to make plane reservations, and you saved me a lot of trouble.

In the second example, a salutation and "signature" are not necessary. However, are there times when they would be helpful? Read on.

### The Rhetorical Context

As you will see throughout this chapter, awareness of **purpose** and **audience** is crucial in business communication. The content of your message, as well as your tone, will depend on whether you are writing to your supervisor (up), your subordinates (down), or your colleagues (sideways). Often, in fact, a message is directed to more than one reader and going in more than one direction. Your content and tone will also be affected by your reason for writing.

If a copy of the e-mail from Jennifer to Mark was being sent to Jennifer's supervisor, for example, the rhetorical context would change. The boss might not know what Jennifer and Mark know, so Jennifer would need to include more information and perhaps make the tone more formal:

> From: Jennifer_Lewis@Bindleburgbarns.com
> To: Mark_Pluta@Bindleburgbarns.com
> CC: Ed_Rowe@Bindleburgbarns.com
> Subject: Conference rescheduling
>
> Thank you for your note regarding the conference rescheduling, from June 17-19 to June 24-26. I was about to make plane reservations when your message came through. I'll now make them for 4:00 p.m. on June 24.

### Memos

The **memo** (**memorandum**) is a staple of corporate and institutional life. Memos are *objective* and *quantitative;* they deal with day-to-day realities such as the following:

- Documenting the progress of projects
- Announcing changes in procedure and policy
- Accounting for time and money spent
- Giving orders
- Making requests

Most companies have policies regarding memo content, format, and distribution. However, the basic format and style of memos do not vary much. Figure 17.1 (page 518) is a memo written from a supervisor to her staff. The four lines at the top are standard. Some companies alter the wording or its order, but **DATE, TO, FROM,** and **SUBJECT** are generic. The handwritten initials of Angela de Jesus indicate her "ownership" of the memo. Memos are never signed, so the initials prevent a subversive employee from floating a document under someone else's name. The subject line ("Complaint messages") is specific and gets the reader's attention.

Traditionally, the text of a memo is divided into three parts—introduction, body, and conclusion:

1. A memo's **introduction** is usually brief. Functioning like an essay's **thesis statement**, it announces what the memo will cover. Be explicit: "This memo covers . . ." or "This memo explains . . ." saves readers time because it allows them to decide whether the memo is relevant to them before they even read it.

2. The memo's **body** is the reason the memo was written. The body of the memo in Figure 17.1 starts with "Identifying a Complaint Call" and continues through "Routing Complaint Calls." The supervisor outlines steps that customer support representatives should take with belligerent callers.

3. The memo's **conclusion** often restates important content from the body, in this case the supervisor's reasoning. It also fulfills an essential function: asking for a response, especially if clarification is needed. Had de Jesus neglected to ask for questions, an employee could have ignored her message and then tried to justify this act by claiming a lack of understanding.

### Formatting

A business writer must make documents easy to read because the audience is probably as busy as the writer. The following features of modern memos expedite the reader's task:

1. **Short paragraphs.** In an essay, paragraphs should be fully developed. Memos use shorter blocks of text. Some paragraphs may contain only one sentence.

2. **Paragraph format.** The preferred format is block style, single-spaced, with no first-line indentation but a full line space between paragraphs. (See Figure 17.2.)

3. **Headings.** If a writer divides a message into two or more sections, the body of the memo should include headings, normally styled in bold type. In Figure 17.1, the writer has two issues to address, so she separates them, enabling the reader to process the text more easily.

**Figure 17.1: Memo Written to Subordinates**

DATE:     18 November 2009
TO:       Customer Support Staff
FROM:     Angela de Jesus, Customer Support Manager
SUBJECT: Complaint messages

In our last meeting, we spoke about the difference between phone calls from customers needing technical support and phone calls that are really complaints. The following procedure, effective immediately, should be used to handle the latter.

IDENTIFYING A COMPLAINT CALL

Experience tells us that most complaint callers do not have a true complaint; they just need more technical assistance. Some are new users of networked systems and become frustrated when a problem occurs. Therefore, please follow these guidelines when in a situation that may require your supervisor's assistance:

- As indicated above, most complaint callers are more frustrated than angry. If you lead them through their problem step by step—even if you duplicate their first attempt to solve the problem—you may discover where the confusion lies.
- However, be alert to an angry tone, an abrupt or aggressive manner, or dismissive and judgmental comments. Pay special attention to threats of litigation.
- In any case, use your judgment. If you cannot help the client and the conversation worsens, call upon your supervisor.

ROUTING COMPLAINT CALLS

Route any phone message that indicates customer dissatisfaction to your supervisor or to me. If both of us are busy—which happens frequently during normal business hours—put the caller on hold, **but do not go to another call.** Angry people can become even more volatile when trapped on hold. Monitor the time the caller is "parked," and break in every 90 seconds to assure the caller that he or she will be connected to a supervisor soon.

We want satisfied customers. We also want you to find your work fulfilling and nonthreatening. The procedures above should make your job easier and our clients happier. If you have questions, please drop by my office or call me at 1104.

4. **Lists.** A newspaper's business section contains tables listing the values of hundreds of stocks and mutual funds. Each row in the table contains the same information for the different equities listed. Because the

paper is presenting parallel information, a table is the most efficient way to display these data. Similarly, a writer can use a list format to quickly and efficiently provide parallel information in business correspondence. (See Figure 17.2 below.) Lists can be either **numbered**, as in Figure 17.2, or **bulleted**, with a round (•), square, (▪), or diamond-shaped (♦) symbol before each item. Numbered lists show a sequence— a chronological list of steps to be followed or a list of items in order of their importance. Bullets are used when listed elements are equal in importance.

5. **Highlighting for emphasis.** In any memo, certain words, phrases, and sentences represent the reason that the memo exists. These can be highlighted—underscored, *italicized,* or **boldfaced**—to indicate their importance. The memo in Figure 17.1 contains a clause in bold type under "Routing Complaint Calls." "**Do not go to another call**" is the most important instruction in the procedure the supervisor is explaining.

   Note that highlighting works best when used sparingly. Memos filled with boldfaced and/or italicized terms are annoying.

**Figure 17.2: Memo Written to Co-Worker**

DATE:      April 19, 2008
TO:        Victor Espinoza
FROM:      Frank McGillis
SUBJECT: Completion of Second Presbyterian Project

As discussed in our phone conversation this morning, we know that Sara Bannion is steamed about the landscaping project's running late, but she also knows that we don't control the weather. Here is what we'll need to do:

1. We need to have Melton Environmental Services get back to work on Monday. Randy Melton tells me he has lost the subcontractor he was using because of scheduling overlaps caused by the storm, but he will reassign some of his own employees.
2. Randy says they'll be done by Wednesday. Let's go over there on Thursday. We both trust Randy, but time is tight.
3. The county inspector has agreed to view the site on Friday; all we have to do is call by noon on Thursday.
4. If anything goes wrong, Mr. Thompson has asked for a report and a meeting late in the week, but let's just take care of the situation ourselves.

**Further Thoughts**
I've asked Randy to call me on my cell phone if he needs to. I'll let you know if he calls.

*Examples of Business Memoranda*

Figures 17.1, 17.2, and 17.3 are examples of memos that might be used in the workplace. In Figure 17.1, a customer support manager outlines a new procedure to deal with complaint calls to her staff. The purpose is twofold: to make disgruntled customers happier and to help her subordinates do their jobs. Reread this memo, and answer the questions that follow.

*Questions*

1. What is the focus (the "thesis") of this memo?
2. Are there issues or details that need clarification? If so, what are they, and how would you clarify them?
3. How would you describe the author's tone? Does she come across as authoritarian, relaxed, or somewhere in the middle? Point to specific words, phrases, or sentences to support your answer.

The context for Figure 17.2, the first in a pair of memos, is a church landscaping project on which two employees are working together largely free of supervision. It is essentially a private communication in which Frank McGillis is writing to Victor Espinoza to outline tasks needed to get a job back on schedule. In this case, the writer knows that his reader shares the same information, so he need not explain the context to his colleague. Moreover, both men know that the "Mr. Thompson" referred to in the memo is their supervisor and that Sara Bannion is a member of the church finance committee. Therefore, McGillis doesn't need to identify them.

After you read both memos (Figures 17.2 and 17.3), answer the questions that follow on page 521.

Before sending the memo to Espinoza, McGillis remembers that he needs to send a copy to supervisor Bob Thompson. This change in audience changes the context as well. McGillis decides to revise the memo, for he realizes that Thompson knows only a little about the project and that he must provide more information, clarify details, and make his tone more formal in order to accommodate the boss.

**Figure 17.3: Memo Written to Co-Worker with Copy to Supervisor**

DATE: April 19, 2008
TO: Victor Espinoza
FROM: Frank McGillis
SUBJECT: Completion of Second Presbyterian Project

Regarding our phone conversation this morning, we both know that Sara Bannion of the church's finance committee is not happy that the landscaping project will conclude a week after its agreed-upon date, but she also recognizes that we didn't plan for a tornado and

*continued*

a resulting week of chaos. Here is what we'll need to do to finish up quickly:

1.  We need to have Melton Environmental Services get back to work on Monday. This was to be our last step before county inspection. Randy Melton tells me he has lost the subcontractor he was using because of scheduling overlaps caused by the storm, but he will reassign some of his own employees to get the job done and honor his contract.
2.  Melton says they will be done by Wednesday. If so, you and I should inspect the project on Thursday. We both trust Melton, but time is tight.
3.  The county inspector has agreed to view the site on Friday; all we have to do is call by noon on Thursday.
4.  If anything goes wrong, Mr. Thompson has asked for a report and a meeting late in the week, but if we can take care of the situation this week a meeting probably won't be necessary.

**Further Thoughts**
I've asked Randy Melton to call me on my cell phone if problems arise. You have promised Sara Bannion daily updates. Call me if you learn anything new, as I will do for you.

c: Robert Thompson

## Questions

1.  In which section(s) of the second memo does McGillis add more information that Thompson might need to know?
2.  In what ways has McGillis altered the tone of the memo?
3.  Identify specific lines in which more formal diction has been inserted.

## Writing Assignments

1.  For a team project, you and three classmates have been assigned to research the city's laws regarding the homeless. You are the group's coordinator. Write a memo to your colleagues to (a) assign responsibilities to each group member and (b) arrange a meeting time/place. Invent facts and details as needed.
2.  You are trying to be a full-time student, but your "part-time" job requires more and more of your attention. Write a memo to your supervisor requesting a meeting in which you will discuss ways to deal with the following problems:
    * Being required to work an increasing number of hours
    * Being asked to work the late shift, particularly on evenings preceding early-morning classes

- Being excluded from decisions about scheduling
- Being called in to work with little notice, especially at times when you need to be in class

3. What have you learned so far this semester? Write a progress report, in memo format, to your writing instructor. Use a list to discuss important concepts, practices, and techniques you have mastered. Develop each statement fully, but separate it from the next with a bullet or number.

## Business Letters

Although business letters serve a variety of needs, they fall into two broad categories: letters that **inquire** and letters that **respond.** For example, sales letters, letters requesting information, and letters of complaint can be categorized as inquiry letters. Letters of explanation or letters conveying information can be considered response letters. Unlike memos, letters are sent outside an organization or business to clients, vendors, and the public. They are normally more formal than memos.

### Formatting

The most common—and easiest to produce—style of business letter is full block. The lines are single-spaced, and none of the lines are indented; every paragraph starts at the left margin. Elements—including paragraphs—are separated by extra line spaces. Figure 17.4 on page 523 is an example of full-block style. The company's name, address, phone number, and e-mail address are centered because they are a part of the letterhead stationery.

Type a business letter in a standard font such as Times Roman, Courier, Palatino, Goudy, or Garamond, which are easy to read. Avoid gimmicky display fonts more suited for posters. Also avoid using all capital letters or a script font. Finally, use a type size no smaller than 12 point (or 10 characters per inch—CPI—if that is how your computer measures type). A letter in 10-point single-spaced type is difficult to read.

### Elements of the Letter

Include the following standard elements in a business letter (see Figure 17.4 on page 523 and Figure 17.5 on pages 524–525 for examples):

1. **Your address or your company's address, telephone number, and e-mail address.** In Figure 17.4, this information appears in the letterhead. If you are using stationery without a letterhead, type this information at the left margin as the first item on the page:

   Altacoma Integrated Digital Services, Inc.
   4197 Crestview Drive
   Altacoma, FL 39999
   904/555-4789
   altacomaids@genericemail.com

   Another option is to type the return address directly below your name, as in Figure 17.5.

*continued on page 525*

**Figure 17.4:  Letter Requesting Information**

Altacoma Integrated Digital Services, Inc.
4197 Crestview Drive
Altacoma, FL 39999
904/555-4789
altacomaids@genericemail.com

April 15, 2009

Traveler's Plaza Hotel
201 Peachtree Terminus
Atlanta, GA 30202

Dear Sir or Madam:

Our company is sending two managers, Ms. Sara Alvarez and Ms. Maria O'Connor, to Atlanta for three weeks (May 1 to May 21). We are interested in finding out about your hotel's arrangements.

Our representatives will be sharing a room—preferably a suite—and have requested the following:

1. Two double beds
2. A work area
3. Two phone lines and two data ports
4. A kitchen
5. Dry-cleaning service

Please also send us information about entertainment and restaurant options in the hotel's immediate area.

Because we are guaranteeing a three-week stay, we request a corporate package discount. We will be happy to pay in advance by credit card if details can be worked out. Thank you for your attention.

Sincerely yours,

*Michael Holgrove*

Michael Holgrove, Administrative Assistant
904/555-4789, ext. 2724
mholgrove_altacomaids@genericemail.com

c: Laura Bowen

**Figure 17.5: Letter of Complaint**

June 17, 2009

Mr. Miles Gonagle, Manager
Ocean View Mirage Motel
311 N. Ocean View Drive
Altacoma, FL 39999

Dear Mr. Gonagle:

On the weekend of June 7-9, my husband, Steve, and I celebrated our tenth anniversary at your establishment. Although we had been assured by your brochures that the Mirage is a resort, our stay there was quite disappointing.

First, although we had guaranteed reservations, when we arrived on Friday, June 7 at 6:00 p.m., we were told that our room would not be ready for another hour. Hungry, we decided to eat supper at the Mirage's "gourmet" restaurant, the Gilded Oasis. Several problems occurred with the food and the service:

1.  We had to wait seventy minutes between the arrival of our appetizers and the arrival of our entrées.
2.  However, the arrival of our "entrées" was really the arrival of only one entrée: my husband's. I was informed by Mike, the waiter, that the kitchen had run out of ingredients for my dinner and that I would need to order another. No matter—my husband had been brought the wrong entrée anyway, so we both had to reorder.
3.  When our suppers finally arrived, they were almost cold and tasted like cafeteria food.

Later that night, after we had turned out the lights and were attempting to sleep, two problems arose. One was the palmetto bugs that began dropping from the ceiling onto our bed. We notified the front desk, but the clerk responded that an exterminator would be sent in the morning; there was nothing else that he could do.

We killed the insects ourselves with a rolled-up newspaper, and once again we attempted to sleep. This proved impossible. That weekend, your other guests included the Southeast Convention of the Loyal Order of Field Mice, and their noisy, drunken antics went on into the night. When we called the front desk, the clerk said, "They'll wear out soon enough." Moreover, Mr. Gonagle, we were not told when we made reservations that a convention would be held during the weekend of our stay.

The next morning, Saturday, we checked out, two days early. Our total bill for this horrible night's stay and supper was $271.36, charged to my

*continued*

VISA card. In all fairness, I ask that you credit one-half of this amount to my account. Otherwise, I shall put the entire charge into dispute with VISA.

Please respond to my request by July 1.

Sincerely,

*Patricia Ogilvie*

Patricia Ogilvie
2801 Vine Street
Framingham, FL 39989
(305) 555-7843
paogilvie@genericemail.com

2. **The date.** Separate the date from other elements by two line spaces. The date should reflect the day the letter is mailed, not the day it is written.

3. **The inside address.** This is an essential element that is especially useful with "windowpane" envelopes. In Figure 17.4, the letter is addressed to a business, not an individual. In Figure 17.5, the letter is addressed to an individual, whose title is included after his name. If the title and name are too long, put the title on the second line by itself. If the addressee has a title signifying an academic degree, place those initials, such as *M.D.* or *Ph.D.,* preceded by a comma, after his or her name. Alternately, use abbreviations such as *Dr.* or *Prof.* before the name as appropriate. Do not use both abbreviations before a name and initials after a name:

| | |
|---|---|
| NOT | **Dr. Margaret Bander, Ph.D.** |
| BUT | **Dr. Margaret Bander** |
| OR | **Margaret Bander, Ph.D.** |

4. **The salutation.** The first word of the salutation is always *Dear,* followed by the appropriate designation before the addressee's surname. (Always try to find out the name of the person to whom you are writing. If you can't, use *Dear Sir* or *Dear Madam.*) Men are *Mr.* (or *Dr.* or *Rev.,* as the case may be); women who do not have professional titles should be addressed as *Ms.* unless you have discovered that the woman you are writing to prefers *Mrs.* or *Miss.* End the salutation with a colon, not a comma or a semicolon.

5. **The introductory paragraph.** Customarily, the first paragraph of a business letter is short—a few sentences indicating the letter's focus without going into details.

• *Consider Your Options*

When a financial transaction goes wrong—for example, a problem with a credit card statement or a telephone bill—it's tempting to pick up the phone and abuse a customer service representative. However, such an action will have no legal standing. You must write a letter (be sure to keep a copy) in order to make a legal objection to the disputed billing. Note how in Figure 17.5, Patricia Ogilvie is able to control her anger while stating her case.

6. **The body.** Organize the body according to your purpose. If your letter deals with a single issue, one paragraph may suffice. If it deals with more than one issue or a series of steps in a process, use multiple paragraphs (see Figure 17.5).

7. **The conclusion.** Like the introduction, a business letter's conclusion tends to be brief. You should normally thank the reader for his or her attention and request a response, if appropriate.

8. **The complimentary close and signature line.** The complimentary close has two appropriate forms: *Sincerely yours* or *Sincerely.* This line is followed by the writer's signature, followed by the writer's typed name. If a copy has been sent to another person, the last element in the letter will be a *c:* followed by the secondary recipient's name, as in Figure 17.4.

### Letters That Request Information or Adjustment

Figure 17.4 on page 523 is a letter requesting information to which the Traveler's Plaza Hotel should gleefully respond. Notice the level of specificity. The more specific your requests, the better the addressee will be able to respond. Note also the use of a list to enumerate the writer's needs. Had the writer used a narrative style, the result would have been wordy and confusing.

Figure 17.5 is a letter of complaint. It explains what went wrong and requests an adjustment: a refund or discount. In view of the Ogilvies' lost weekend at the Ocean View Mirage Motel, the request for a 50-percent refund seems reasonable. Notice that, despite Patricia Ogilvie's experience at the Mirage, the tone of her letter remains businesslike.

### Letters That Respond

Figures 17.6 and 17.7 exemplify the second type of letter: a response. They are alternative responses by Michael Delmonica of Altacoma Imaging to a complaint from a corporate customer, Helvetica Reprographics, Inc. The different contexts of these two letters call for different responses.

The letter in Figure 17.6, on page 527, was clearly the easier of the two to write. In it, Delmonica provides Ruth Vanmeter with what is bound to be good news: the problem was caused by a defective belt, which Altacoma will replace. Nonetheless, Delmonica takes care to use an extremely courteous tone, for even if a response letter is favorable, the addressee might be offended by a tone that seems insufficiently concerned and apologetic.

The letter in Figure 17.7 on page 528 is written in a different context. The malfunction is the result of an action by a Helvetica employee, so Altacoma is not responsible. However, Michael Delmonica has to break the bad news to Ruth Vanmeter without angering her; further, he wants to continue the two companies' business relationship. So he sweetens the deal by offering free installation of the replacement power supply and a reinstatement of the warranty. His letter should generate a positive response from Ruth Vanmeter.

**Figure 17.6: Letter Granting Favorable Response to Complaint**

Altacoma Imaging, Inc.
4107 N. Industrial Road
Altacoma, FL 39999
(904) 555-8575

November 14, 2009

Ruth Vanmeter
Vice President
Helvetica Reprographics, Inc.
11141 Hermes Street
Anniston, AL 33223

Dear Ms. Vanmeter:

Thank you for your phone call and e-mail regarding your MD 3080A photocopier's failure. We have determined that the problem was caused by
a defective belt. Please accept our apologies; we will make the situation right.

Because your machine is under warranty, we will send a technician with
a replacement belt on Friday, November 19. Your photocopier will be
operable by noon on Friday.

Once again, we are sorry for any production delays that our machine's
failure has caused. Please accept a one year's extension of your
warranty in consideration of your inconvenience. Also, please call or
write if you have additional questions or concerns.

Sincerely yours,

*Michael Delmonica*

Michael Delmonica
Technical Supply Manager

## Writing Assignments

1. You share a dorm room with another person. You are studious; your roommate
   likes loud music, loud conversation, and loud parties. You have not made any
   progress dealing with the situation. Write a letter to Student Housing outlining
   your problem and asking for help. Be specific in your request.

*continued on page 528*

**Figure 17.7: Letter Issuing Negative Response to Complaint**

Altacoma Imaging, Inc.
4107 N. Industrial Road
Altacoma, FL 39999
(904) 555-8575

November 14, 2009

Ruth Vanmeter
Vice President
Helvetica Reprographics, Inc.
11141 Hermes Street
Anniston, AL 33223

Dear Ms. Vanmeter:

As you know, we sent a technician to Helvetica after we learned from you about the breakdown of your MD 3080A photocopier. During her visit, the technician discovered that while attempting to dislodge a paper jam, someone ignored the safety directives attached to the copier and inadvertently ruined the power supply.

Unfortunately, this action voids the warranty supplied with the MD 3080A. However, we know the inconvenience that you are suffering, and we value our long-term business relationship. Thus, we would like to propose a compromise adjustment: if you will pay for the new power supply, we will be happy to install it for free and to reinstate the warranty on the entire system.

We hope this arrangement is acceptable. Please give me a call, and I'll send a technician the next day.

Sincerely yours,

*Michael Delmonica*

Michael Delmonica
Technical Supply Manager

2.  The Financial Aid office offers you a work-study position next semester in the biology lab. You have complications next semester and don't want the position, but you may want a similar position in the future. Write a letter responding to the offer.

# RÉSUMÉS AND LETTERS OF APPLICATION

Students go to college to prepare for a career; before they know it, they graduate and must launch that career. Being able to write an effective résumé and letter of application is an important skill. The résumé is a summary of the applicant's education and work history; the letter of application is a more personal, persuasive document tailored to the particular position the applicant desires.

## Elements of a Résumé

1. **Address, phone number, and e-mail address.** Note in Figure 17.8 on page 531 that Ronald Hauser lists two addresses and phone numbers—at school and at home—along with his e-mail address.

2. **Career objective.** This is a relatively new feature, for in the past people tended to have only one résumé. Today, most people produce their own résumés on computers, so the career objective can be changed to fit specific job advertisements.

3. **Education.** For young job-seekers, education normally precedes work experience, for they have had little of the latter; education is their main selling point. Too often, however, students mention only their major, their pending degree, and the date the degree is expected. Potential employers will read your résumé to determine how you are different from the next applicant. That's why Hauser mentions his experience as a research assistant and an intern. He points out that he has a high GPA in his major: 3.75. Presumably, his overall GPA isn't as impressive, so he accentuates the positive, always a good idea in a résumé.

4. **Experience.** You may have held part-time or seasonal jobs only. However, listing these will let the potential employer know you have worked successfully. Any job in which you held a position of responsibility—a lifeguard, for example, or a closer for a fast-food restaurant—is a plus. If you have completed a successful term in the military, by all means list this fact. Employers love hiring veterans. Describe your responsibilities using concrete "action" verbs: not *did*, but *arranged, closed, opened, monitored,* and so on.

5. **Computer skills.** List these if you have them.

6. **Languages.** If you are conversant to fluent in a foreign language, mention this important skill.

7. **References.** To guard the privacy of people who have agreed to vouch for you, use *Available upon request*. However, don't send out a résumé until at least three individuals have agreed to recommend you. The opinions of friends, relatives, and members of the clergy carry little weight with employers. Instead, ask for recommendations from professors and job supervisors.

## Submit Your Résumé Online

You can post your résumé online by using an Internet job-search service, such as Monster.com or Hotjobs.com. To do this, you will have to save your résumé as a plain-text file, which allows prospective employers to scan your résumé for key words and information without having to peruse the entire document, thereby saving them time and effort. Such a document is also known as a *scannable résumé*.

Plain-text files exclude most style elements such as bullets, symbols, underlining, bold type, and italics. Many Internet job-search services allow you to construct a plain-text résumé simply by typing information into fields provided for this purpose. However, you can also save an existing résumé as plain text. To do this, click on your file menu and choose the "Save As" option. Then select an appropriate choice. For example, Microsoft Word offers a "Plain Text Only" option.

Once your résumé is saved as a plain-text document, you will be able to select and paste it into the job-search service's template or text field. Many of these templates also allow you to provide key words or terms that prospective employers look for as they scan electronic résumés. This important information includes job titles, career objectives, degrees earned, and professional experience.

As is clear from Figure 17.8, the résumé is a dry, somewhat impersonal document, written in sentence fragments and avoiding the word *I*. But the résumé always travels with a letter of application, a much more personal communication.

## Elements of an Application Letter

1. **The salutation.** If you are writing to a named individual whose sex is unclear (is "Lee Meyers" male or female?), call the company and ask the receptionist or the personnel department so that you can avoid potential embarrassment.

2. **The introductory paragraph.** This brief paragraph serves only three functions: to announce your application, to tell the employer where you learned of the position, and to indicate your main qualification for the position.

3. **The body.** Normally, this entails two paragraphs, the first on your education and the second on your work experience. Stress how your education and experience have qualified you. However, don't list specific courses you have taken or other, similar information that might bore the reader and weaken the focus of your message.

   Note that a proliferation of the word *I* is inevitable. In Figure 17.9, Ronald Hauser avoids the problem of starting every sentence with *I* by putting transitions at the beginning of his sentences. Note also that in this section you should refer to your enclosed résumé.

*continued on page 533*

**Figure 17.8: Sample Résumé**

### Ronald S. Hauser

Bolton Hall, Room 648                 48 Sorghum Lane,
Franklin Southeastern University      Apt. 347
Coolmore, AL 35656                    Coolmore, AL 35659
(999) 555-2493                        (999) 555-8182

ronhauser3@genericemail.com

### Career Objective

A position in either business or research involving practical development
of alternative agricultural products.

### Education

2002-present    Franklin Southeastern University, Coolmore, AL
                B.S. in food science to be awarded in May 2008.
                Concentrated on aquaculture and food irradiation.
                Served three semesters as research assistant for
                director of aquaculture research center. Interned
                spring semester 2006 at Logan Biograde, a food irradi-
                ation company. GPA in major: 3.75.

### Experience

2005-2006       Lorenzo Catfish, Inc., Lorenzo, MS
                Pond developer/harvester. Coordinated the work of
                17 part-time/seasonal employees. Was responsible for
                maintaining health of crop and maximizing acreage
                yield. Won Employee of the Month award on three
                occasions.

2001-2003       Wal-Mart, Inc., Coolmore, AL
(summers)       Stocker. Worked both part time and full time between
                the warehouse and the store. In 2002, coordinated
                store's fund drive to aid children of two employees
                who were killed in an auto accident.

### Computer Skills

MS Office, MS Word, Quattro Pro, Quark.

### References

Available upon request.

**Figure 17.9: Letter of Application**

March 17, 2009

Mr. Wade Michaels, Director
Agrisearch Analytical Association
1442 Gidney Avenue
Bloomington, IN 47999

Dear Mr. Michaels:

I am writing to apply for the position of Innovative Farm Products Coordinator, Southeast Region, advertised on March 12 in the *Atlanta Constitution*. I will graduate this spring with a B.S. in food science from Franklin Southeastern University. My blend of education and experience uniquely qualifies me for this position.

At Franklin, I concentrated in aquaculture and food irradiation. As my résumé indicates, I worked for three semesters as a research assistant for Dr. Herman Lovelace, the director of the aquaculture research center. I also completed a semester internship at Logan Biograde, a company specializing in the development of food irradiation techniques. My GPA in my major is 3.75.

My degree at Franklin has taken me six years to complete, for I took a year and a half off to earn future tuition. I spent that time working directly in aquaculture at Lorenzo Catfish, a massive operation in Lorenzo, Mississippi. Thus, I believe I have learned a great deal about the aquaculture business.

I welcome the opportunity to discuss further my qualifications for this position. If you are amenable, I will travel to Bloomington for an interview at your convenience.

Cordially,

*Ronald Hauser*

Ronald Hauser
Bolton Hall, Room 648
Franklin Southeastern University
Coolmore, AL 35656
ronhauser3@genericemail.com

Encl.: résumé

4.  **The concluding paragraph.** Here, restate your main qualifications for the position, and request an interview. The correct wording is some variation of "I am available for an interview at your convenience." In other words, don't set limitations on your availability.

## Writing Assignments

1.  Write your résumé. After you're done, ask yourself what makes your résumé better than that of one of your peers. What can you do during the rest of your college program to make yourself stand out?

2.  What would be your ideal part-time job while in college? Write a letter applying for this position. Invent specific details as needed.

### CHAPTER 18

# GROUP PROJECTS AND ORAL PRESENTATIONS

In years past, undergraduate classes rarely included group projects and oral presentations. However, instructors have become increasingly aware of the educational value of both of these activities, along with the blending of the two: the group oral presentation.

The topics covered in this chapter are essential survival skills for the modern college student. We'll begin with a discussion of group work, then address oral presentation skills, then look at how these two subjects can work together.

# WORKING IN GROUPS

Being involved in a group project can bring out the best in some people and the worst in others. Here are some common pitfalls you should watch out for when engaging in group work:

1. *Unclear roles.* It is impossible for each member of a group to contribute effectively if roles are not clearly defined.

2. *Lack of a firm schedule.* Groups that do not schedule their meetings throughout the allotted time for the project run the risk of having to do too much work at the last minute.

3. *Freeriding.* Unfortunately, some students do not contribute to their group project. Realizing that they can depend on the contributions of other, more dependable group members, these students contribute little, "freeriding" on their peers' labors.

4. *A refusal to share responsibilities.* This is the opposite of freeriding. Here, one person takes the "it's easier to just do it myself" approach, effectively freezing out the other group members. This approach defeats the entire purpose of group work.

*"With your kind permission, I've taken the liberty of putting Marvin on 'mute.'"*

How can you avoid these potential problem areas and do effective group work? Think of the endeavor as a process, a series of steps. Follow through with each of these steps, and your group will be able to work efficiently.

## Define Your Group's Purpose

Your group's first meeting is the time and place to establish clearly your group's goals. If your group has been formed in response to an assignment, use the time to examine the assignment and to identify any possible problem areas. Although instructors take great care in preparing assignments, discrepancies and ambiguities might still be present. Look for these, and if they exist, ask your instructor for clarification. Then nail down exactly what the assignment will require from your group—the "pieces" of the project and the steps that will have to be taken to assemble those pieces.

## Assign Tasks

Dividing up responsibilities is essential to balancing the workload in a group project. It ensures that no one will do too much or too little. When deciding each group member's tasks, try to consider both the interests and the strengths of each individual. Also, keep in mind that the heart of group work is *collaboration*—don't make assignments so rigid that there is no opportunity for peer support or group input.

What kind of tasks might need to be assigned? Keeping in mind that all groups and all projects are different, you will want to ensure that one person or a small team is responsible for:

- *Scheduling meetings* and giving the requisite reminders via phone or e-mail.
- *Researching* the subject your group has chosen.
- *Drafting* the paper or report your group is responsible for producing.
- *Editing* any materials your group creates. (Note that editing is a task that is usually best performed by multiple people—often, the more eyes on a piece of work, the better.)
- *Creating graphics* to accompany your project or presentation.

Again, the specifics of what will need to be done depend largely on the particular goals of the group. What is essential is that you identify the necessary steps to completing your group's goals, and then divide this work—fairly and wisely—across all the group members.

## Help Keep Your Group on Track

Once group members have been assigned their roles, it is important to ensure that everyone follows through and completes his or her tasks. Establishing redundancy in group roles can be good insurance against the process becoming derailed. *Redundancy* is a term that sounds negative, but in certain contexts it is not. Having an extra ink-jet cartridge has saved many a last-minute project from disaster, for example.

The process works as follows: each person assigned to a role "reports" to a second person. If anything happens to the first person that limits or ends his or her contributions, the second person is in the best position to take up the work that the first person has accomplished and to present it to the group as roles are reassigned. Sound complicated? It's actually not, and although it's one extra step in a process that can involve a daunting number of steps, establishing role redundancy is worth the trouble and time.

Another way to help maintain group accountability is peer evaluation. In this approach, each group member writes his or her sense of the amount and quality of work produced by each of the other group members. In some group assignments, the instructor will require this step in order to avoid the freeriding problem, discussed above. However, even if peer evaluation is not required, it's still a good idea. If your group is suffering from the depredations caused by a freerider, and he or she is not responsive to your requests for better performance, you may want to visit your instructor.

## EXERCISE 18.1

1. What strengths do you bring to group work? What are your strongest skills? In what areas do you want to improve? How would you evaluate your work ethic?

2. Choose a group project that you worked on in the past—perhaps in high school or in the workplace. What went right during this process? What problems did your group encounter?

# DEVELOPING EFFECTIVE ORAL PRESENTATIONS

Polls of people in the United States have shown, year after year, that they rank giving a speech as scarier than dying violently. Some people literally have phobias about this subject. Others, frustrated by their fear of public speaking and needing this skill to help with their business or professional career, have joined organizations such as Toastmasters, whose members meet for a common purpose: to conquer their fears and hone their speaking skills. Let's concentrate on the skills part.

## Creating a Script

Nothing sinks the spirit of a listening audience more than hearing a speaker read from a prepared text. Speakers who take this route haven't created a script; they're actually reading an essay aloud. A speech is a dynamic, interactive encounter with an audience; an essay is a collection of sentences and paragraphs frozen on paper.

Let's look at the other extreme: speakers who use no "text" at all. These people are living dangerously—what happens if they "lose their place" or "freeze" because of nervousness?

*"And so, while the end-of-the-world scenario will be rife with unimaginable horrors, we believe that the pre-end period will be filled with unprecedented opportunities for profit."*

Surely there is a safer, more effective middle ground. Actually, there are two approaches that most seasoned speakers use: index cards or an outline.

Whether or not you use an outline during your actual presentation, it's a good idea to create a preliminary outline during your preparation. A preliminary outline will help you establish the basic parts of your speech:

1. Introduction (brief)
2. Body (lengthy)
3. Conclusion (brief)

This three-part model is at the heart of most structured communication. In a speech, the introduction tells the audience what they are about to hear. The body of the speech is just that: the main content of the presentation, the reason you are standing before the audience. The conclusion sums up the presentation, reminding the audience of your main points and delivering your final thoughts on the topic. Developing a preliminary working outline will help you structure your speech. This outline does not have to be a formal document; think of it as more of a personal guide as you progress through the process of preparing your presentation.

## EXERCISE 18.2

Develop a preliminary outline on this topic: "How to Use (or Do) _____."
You fill in the blank. Here is the scenario: you are expected to speak for five minutes, with no visual aids such as slideshows. In other words, you are alone speaking to an audience for five minutes. Work up an outline that would let you
develop this topic fully and produce a high-quality five-minute presentation.

## Developing the Final Script

Again, we strongly recommend avoiding the approach of reading your presentation from a prepared text or the "winging it" approach, in which you work
only from memory. Instead, if you develop your final script in the form of an
outline or on index cards, you are more likely to produce an interesting,
dynamic speech.

Good speeches involve a speaker who looks at the audience, making eye
contact. The speaker has a confident demeanor because he or she has mastered
the material and practiced its delivery. If someone in the audience asks a question, the speaker is ready to respond to it and then resume the presentation
without becoming flustered. Working with a final script that consists of index
cards or an outline will help you deliver an effective presentation.

Typically, both the index card model and the outline model contain the
same information: each main point, along with some detail, that the speaker
plans to cover. Speakers using outlines will typically use enlarged typefaces
(24- to 28-point) so that they can easily see the outline entries as they glance
down. The following example of the beginning of a presentation is typical of
outline form:

**VOLUNTEERING AT ANIMAL SHELTERS**

(INTRO)

1. Local animal shelters always need volunteers.
2. Now, the need has become acute.
   a. Local human population increases.
   b. Downturn in local economy.

**WE NEED YOUR HELP!**

This example includes the speech title, the label of the speech part (the introduction), two main points (numbered), two supporting points, and then,
finally, the main point that the speech will develop in the body ("We need
your help!"). Someone using index cards would write the same information,
but arrange it on one or more cards.

A speaker who has practiced extensively will not need to refer very often
to the outline or index cards. These become a safety device for the prepared
speaker. The speaker can very briefly check the outline or cards as he or she
progresses through the speech to ensure that all of the content has been

covered. If the speaker hits a rough spot or "freezes" during the speech, he or she has a ready reminder of where to go next.

Here are some other tips to keep in mind as you develop your presentation:

### Cite Your Sources

If all of your speech is developed from your own experience or from common knowledge (see Chapter 21, pages 577–578), then sources are not an issue. However, if you are developing your speech by relying on any outside source, you need to let your audience know this fact. If you quote someone (in other words, use exact language—see Chapter 20), say who the source is. If you paraphrase or summarize someone else's words (see Chapter 21, pages 577–578), inform the audience of this fact. You can do an adequate citation without interrupting your speech. Consider these examples:

> Samuel Clemens once wrote that "the difference between the right word and the almost right word is like the difference between lightning and the lightning bug."

> In *The Forgotten Americans*, John Schwarz and Thomas Volgy examine the working class and their shrinking American Dream. People in the working class live on an increasingly dicey economic margin.

These examples show acceptable and effective ways to document a source while giving a speech. However, please keep in mind that textual citations are a different matter. When you write an essay, you will be expected to follow a formal, established system designed to document your use of sources. Chapters 20 and 21 cover documentation and the question of "fair use" in essays.

### Practice, Practice, Practice

A great many speeches go badly because of a simple fact: the speaker neglected to give the presentation a dry run before standing in front of an audience. There are two good ways to practice a speech. One is in front of a mirror. This allows you to get a sense of how you will come across to an audience. However, a better approach is to practice your speech in front of another person or persons, then ask for feedback from your preliminary audience. Ask your roommate, a friend, a classmate, or anyone else who can spare a small amount of time. You may be quite surprised by how much valuable feedback you can get from this process.

### Be Physically Ready

If at all possible, get a good night's sleep before a morning presentation. And before any presentation, day or night, make sure that you give your stomach a chance to cooperate with your speech. Make sure that you have had something to eat, but also avoid eating greasy foods that might upset your stomach.

*"As you can see, ladies and gentlemen, the available
data clearly suggest six more weeks of winter."*

## EXERCISE 18.3

Finish and practice the oral presentation that you began in Exercise 18.2.
Make sure that you have developed a final script and that you are ready to
perform at your instructor's request.

## Using Visual Aids

Today, it's uncommon for someone to give a presentation that does not include
some form of visual aid. The use of such features makes a speech more
dynamic, cuts down on the possibility of audience boredom, and takes some
of the focus off the speaker—for people who are nervous or uncomfortable
when speaking in public, this last issue is particularly significant.

However, visual aids are misused almost as often as they are used effectively. The following sections look at the opportunities and pitfalls that visual
aids present.

### Handouts

Giving each audience member a page or set of pages containing information
related to your speech may seem like a good idea. However, if you provide this

material at the beginning of your presentation, you're giving people the chance to ignore you. If you want to use handouts, consider giving them to your audience at the end of your speech. This way, you provide a textual reminder of your subject and avoid audience distraction.

### Posters

Creating a poster or set of posters to use as display material is usually worthwhile, provided the answers to the following questions are *yes:*

1. Can you create an attractive, relevant, and coherent poster?
2. Will the poster be legible to everyone in the room? In a large room, the use of posters can be problematic.
3. Can you safely transport the poster to the site of your speech? This is not a trivial concern.

Posters may be going out of fashion. Compared to slideshows (discussed below), they might seem unsophisticated. However, in the right context, they can still be effective adjuncts to an oral presentation. For example, if you plan to refer to a document or diagram at many different points during your speech, blowing it up to poster size for display is often a good idea.

### Slideshows

Technology such as Microsoft's PowerPoint has radically changed the nature of presentations. Slideshows can provide text ("bullet points"), still images, and even moving images to be displayed during a presentation. Some speeches use slideshows effectively, and some don't. Follow these guidelines to make the most of slideshows:

1. Don't create a slideshow that duplicates your script. Few things are more depressing to an audience than watching a speaker who turns on a slideshow and then begins reading it aloud. "We can read!" is the silent cry from the audience. This is the digital equivalent of reading a script verbatim. Remember that any visual aid should be used to add value to your speech; it should not duplicate it. Slides can be used effectively to introduce your main points, to show support for your ideas as you discuss them, and to summarize your key messages as you finish. Regardless, your spoken words should be fully developed, not just responses to what appears on your slides.
2. Be careful with visual images and moving images. Too often, speakers provide still images that are more decorative than relevant, and these distract the audience. Moving images have a built-in distraction factor. Use them judiciously.
3. Be sure to cite your sources. If your slideshow includes quotations, indicate the source. In the case of a visual image, include the citation at the bottom of the frame. (Note: check with your instructor on this issue so that you know exactly what is expected of you.)

4. Avoid wasted time due to technical problems. If you are planning to give an oral presentation supplemented by a slideshow and you want to use the classroom's computer, ask your instructor if you can try out the system beforehand so that you're comfortable with its operation.

5. Proofread! A typo on a large slide leaps out at the viewer. Your instructor will be gauging your entire performance, and sloppy text on your slides will hurt your grade.

## EXERCISE 18.4

Add visual elements to the presentation that you worked on in Exercise 18.3. Practice this speech, and be ready to deliver it at your instructor's request.

# THE GROUP ORAL PRESENTATION

Presentations delivered by two to five people can be extremely effective, but thorough planning is necessary. As in any group endeavor, roles, redundancy, scheduling, and preparation are the essential elements.

1. *Roles.* Will all of your group's members be required to speak? If so, then you and your colleagues will need to decide who takes which section. Will each person develop the section that he or she will deliver, or will your group have one person develop the script, another person revise it, and others deliver it? These are the questions that you and your colleagues need to answer. Assign roles and then meet regularly to assess the results.

2. *Redundancy.* As we pointed out on pages 536–537, having backup for each group role ensures that if one member of a group is unable to show up on speech day, all is not lost. If each person has secondary responsibility for another person's role, it's still possible to deliver a quality performance in the face of the unexpected.

3. *Scheduling.* Make a firm schedule for meetings to assess your group's progress. This is an essential step for a group presentation.

4. *Preparation.* Practicing a group speech is even more important than practicing a speech that you give on your own. The coordination of all the group members' efforts needs to be established during practice sessions.

As we mentioned earlier in the chapter, it is a good idea for members of your group to evaluate one another's contributions, even if your instructor does not require this step. The knowledge that peer evaluation is going to take place and be recorded should help all group members stay focused and motivated for the entire process of preparing and delivering the presentation.

### CHAPTER 19

# ESSAY EXAMINATIONS

In the semesters to come, you will find that some instructors rely on objective tests whereas others prefer essay exams. Essay exams have the advantage of indicating more about what the student knows and how the student thinks. They measure not only knowledge but also analytical and organizational skills.

Many students are concerned with only one feature of the essay exam: the time limit. This focus is understandable but potentially dangerous. Writing essays for English classes can be a relatively leisurely task for students, who can take their time drafting, revising, and proofreading. In contrast, having only fifty or seventy-five minutes to complete an exam can be daunting. Some test takers rush through the exam without using what they learned in composition classes; others plan, prewrite, draft, and revise. The latter course is obviously preferable.

## STUDY FOR THE EXAM

Before the day of the essay exam, you can improve your chances of success by the amount of time you devote to studying for it. Studying for an essay exam is no different than studying for a short-answer test. Both processes are hard work. However, essay exams often require you to state an idea or opinion or take a position and then to support that statement with information that demonstrates your knowledge of the subject. The facts, opinions, and other information you include will be of your own choosing, yet they will have to relate directly to the question. As such, essay exams require a firmer grasp of the material than do short-answer exams. They also require different approaches, as discussed below.

## READ THE DIRECTIONS

Students often get themselves in trouble on essay exams because they misinterpret or fail to read directions. Directions indicate the instructor's expectations.

- **Answer only what you are asked:** If the directions ask you to "write a fully developed paragraph in response to *seven* of the following twelve questions," writing on all twelve probably won't help your grade. Most instructors will grade only your first seven responses.

- **Meet or exceed minimum expectations:** If the test asks you to write "fully developed paragraphs" and your responses are two sentences long, don't expect a good grade. It's almost impossible to develop an informative paragraph by using only two sentences, and your instructor may view such an effort as slacking. A professor of film studies showed us a student's exam in which each of five questions was to be answered by a minimum of eighty-five words. All five of the responses were between eighty-six and ninety-one words. Obviously, the student cared less about displaying his command of the subject than about crossing the minimal threshold.

The test's directions may ask for "short answers," "paragraphs," or "essays." Therefore, an important part of reading the directions is to distinguish among these three types of responses.

## Short Answers

Students frequently equate "short answer" with "single sentence." Most instructors want a bit more. Compare the following two responses to this exam question used in a sports history class:

What is the significance of the year 1912 to American golf?

Student X: That was the year Snead, Nelson, and Hogan were born.

Student A: Ben Hogan, Byron Nelson, and Sam Snead were all born in 1912. This trio dominated American golf for thirty years, spanning the era from the retirement of Bob Jones to the arrival of Arnold Palmer and Jack Nicklaus.

Note that student A has added information, not simply words. She displays a far wider grasp of and appreciation for the question than student X does.

## Paragraphs

A paragraph written in response to an exam question is no different from a paragraph written for an English composition. It needs a topic sentence, internal supports, and evidence. The following response to a political science exam question could have appeared in the text of an out-of-class paper as well:

The electoral college was put in place by the Founding Fathers to ensure stability in presidential elections. Since then, the electoral college—not the popular vote—has determined the results of five presidential elections, the most recent being the Bush-Gore struggle in 2000. For its detractors, the electoral college system, whereby each state sends a predetermined number of electors to reflect the state's vote total, denies the overall will of the nation's voters. For example, Al Gore's national vote total was greater than George W. Bush's. However, the supporters of the electoral college point out that without this system, candidates would concentrate their campaigns in the heavily populated states—New York, Illinois, California, Texas, and Florida, along with a few others—and ignore the rest. Indeed, a map showing who won what in the 2000 race indicates that "most of the country" (in a geographic sense) voted for Bush. The only heavily populated states not won by Gore were Texas (Bush's home state) and, controversially, Florida.

This response is thoughtful and fully developed. The paragraph begins with a topic sentence that is supported by the example of the 2000 presidential election and by a discussion of the Gore-Bush results. More important, it presents specific facts, clearly revealing the student's strong grasp of the material.

## Essays

How much longer is an essay than a paragraph? The answer depends on a number of variables, some of which are physical. If the instructor gives you a page and a half of writing space, you should be able to estimate how much text you can fit into it. If the instructor has indicated how long you should spend on each section of the exam and you are given thirty minutes for the essay part, you should plan accordingly. The main requirement, no matter what length is expected, is that you produce an essay with all of its components: introduction, including thesis; body paragraphs with as much development as you can muster; and a conclusion, even if it is a brief one. (See the sample essay at the end of this chapter, pages 550–551, for a sense of how this type of response can be developed.)

# ALLOCATE YOUR TIME

Begin by reading all of the directions and all of the questions. As you read them, think about how you will allocate your time:

- **Decide what to do first and what to leave for last.** If the exam asks you to respond to five questions and you are comfortable with four, do these four first. Save the remaining time for the fifth. Otherwise, you might waste time on a question on which you're probably not going to do well anyway.
- **Don't get too comfortable with just one part of the exam.** Many students who are thoroughly prepared for an exam start on the first section—paragraph-length responses—and do so well that they forget that the essay-length section follows. The high marks they make on the paragraphs are brought down by low marks on the essay section. Poor planning, not a lack of study and skills, is the culprit here.
- **Avoid trying to finish early.** When you take an objective test, you answer all questions, you check your work, and then you're done. However, an essay exam is more dynamic—many things can go wrong. Careful students use all the time allotted to them.

# INTERPRET KEY WORDS

The rhetorical options you learned about in Part 2 can be used in the essay exam as well. However, the instructor probably won't ask for a specific approach; you will need to interpret key words in test directions to decide on the correct option or options. To see how this works, read through these sample test questions and the analysis that follows each one:

1. *Outline Jean Piaget's theory of psychological development. Use examples to illustrate each stage.*

   Here, the student is asked to discuss stages of development—that is, development over time. Thus, *stage* is a key word that clearly suggests **narrative**. Also, because stages together make up a process, with each stage building on the previous one, both **process analysis** and **causal analysis** will work here as well. Finally, the question calls for examples, so **exemplification** is another obvious strategy.

2. *Describe Picasso's* Guernica *and its effect on the viewer.*

   There are two key words here—*describe* and *effect*—that direct the student's response.

3. *In the early 1950s, congressional Democrats were split into three factions. Name these groups, and explain how they came to exist.*

   **Classification** is the overriding strategy here, but either **process analysis** or **causal analysis** will be needed to fulfill the second part of the question.

4. *No one has been drafted into the U.S. military for thirty years. Is the decision to have an all-volunteer army a good one?*

   This question asks for the student's opinion, so **argument** is the obvious choice. As with all argumentative essays, however, specific **examples** will strengthen this response.

5. *Explain the role of mitochondria in cell division.*

   Mitochondria have a role (part) in cell division, which is a process. **Process analysis** (informative, not instructional) is required here.

6. *In 1919 the Volstead Act instituted Prohibition, which lasted until 1933. What was a major unanticipated consequence of Prohibition?*

   *Consequence* means "effect"; hence, the best approach is **causal analysis**, focusing on effects.

7. *In 1980, U.S. voters were asked to choose as their president either Jimmy Carter or Ronald Reagan. What political traditions and outlooks did the two candidates represent?*

   Clearly, the student is being asked to concentrate on the differences between Carter and Reagan. **Comparison/contrast** is the likely option, developed point by point.

8. *In the 1950s, how did the Polaroid Company market its revolutionary camera?*

   The key word is *how;* the emphasis is on **process analysis**.

9. *Historians rank Franklin D. Roosevelt as one of our greatest presidents. Why did fifty years go by before an appropriate national monument was established?*

   The key word is *why;* the best approach is **causal analysis**, focusing on causes.

10. *Describe the "ideal Victorian woman" and compare her to the "ideal woman of today."*

    Here, *describe* is used loosely. An analytically minded student will realize that *define* is more apt. In addition to **defining** the ideal Victorian woman and the ideal contemporary woman, the student must shift gears and use **contrast**. This approach naturally calls for a subject-by-subject organization: after the first part of the essay defines the Victorian ideal and the contemporary ideal, the second part portrays—in detail—the differences between the modern ideal and its earlier counterpart.

# PREWRITING ESSAY RESPONSES

We often hear students claiming "I don't have time to prewrite; I barely have enough time to *write*." However, time pressure makes prewriting even more important. We're not referring to formal outlines or lengthy freewriting, just quick, down-and-dirty prewriting that gives focus to your essay and helps ensure that you won't get stuck at one point or another with nothing left to say.

Consider example 6 in the previous section, which asks the student to explain "a major unanticipated consequence of Prohibition." The following is an example of the fast prewriting that will help the student write an essay response:

Option—cause/effect, use effect

Intro—What was Prohib?

2nd ¶—what act. happened: people kept drinking

3rd ¶—problem-how to get booze

4th ¶—unorganized crime

5th ¶—organized crime

Conc.—org. crime still with us today

Running out of time often induces nervousness, if not panic. Having a guide to follow can help control this reaction and keep you working in a systematic way rather than scribbling down random ideas as they come to mind. In addition, such prewriting is an aid to memory, invaluable when you are under stress.

> *Consider Your Options*
>
> This prewriting provides clues on how to develop each paragraph. Notice the variety of options you would use to develop the intended essay:
> - Develop the introduction using definition and cause/effect.
> - Develop paragraph 2 using narration.
> - Develop paragraph 3 using process analysis.
> - Develop paragraphs 4–5 using description, exemplification, and contrast.
> - Develop the conclusion using exemplification.

# DRAFTING ESSAY RESPONSES

In some ways, a good response on an essay exam resembles an essay written out of class; in others, it does not. For example, both the introduction and the conclusion of a response to an exam question tend to be shorter than those found in formal essays. The body of the exam essay gets the major emphasis because the grader wants to see (1) how much the student knows and (2) how well the student can organize this information. Moreover, because of time constraints, an exam essay will likely not have as much structure as one written out of class.

In most ways, however, the two are essentially similar. One feature that should not be altered or omitted is a clear statement of intent. In other words, both exam essays and essays written out of class must be controlled by a clearly stated thesis, and both must contain clear topic sentences in each body paragraph. You don't need to impose a great deal of structure when writing an exam essay, just enough to help your reader process your response. Of course, you also need to include enough supporting detail to make your response credible and to reveal the full extent of your knowledge.

## Sample Essay Exam Response

The essay below was written in response to the following question on a midterm exam in an introductory sociology class:

*What are two theories about the individual self and social interaction?*

Introduction and thesis.

How a person defines the self and presents the self in social interactions are two separate but related issues.    1

First theory discussed.

Process analysis used to explain first theory.

In one theory, the individual defines the self in terms of the world in which she lives. Charles Horton Cooley put forth the theory of the "looking-glass self" to explain the process of self-definition. This is an imperfect process, but essentially the individual uses others as a mirror (looking-glass) from which to begin to perceive the self. Three steps take place. First, the individual tries to imagine how her appearance, personality, and overall persona are perceived by others. (Am I fat? Am I sullen? Am I likable?) Next, the individual tries to determine how others *judge* this impression. Third, the individual develops a self-concept based on the first two factors.    2

Cause and effect used to explain a problem with the process.

As mentioned, the process is imperfect. If in step one the individual is mistaken about others' perceptions, then step two is corrupted because the individual thinks she is being "judged" according to a set of perceptions that do not in fact exist. Also, it seems that Cooley's theory can be extended in the sense that we can develop    3

Example used to illustrate a complication of the first theory.

different self-concepts in different contexts. For example, Jane works in a highly competitive, large office. She is not the brightest of her peers or the most pretty. She has a "low" self-concept at work. However, one night a week Jane volunteers at a soup kitchen for homeless women. Here she realizes that she is perceived as pretty and smart. Her self-concept is "high" in this context.

A second, more dynamic theory is put forth by Erving Goffman. He believed that in public, people are actors, rarely revealing their "true selves." Public is the "front stage," according to Goffman, where people "act" according to the needs of the situation. Home is the "back stage," where we can be ourselves.

What complicates the "front stage" is that everyone is aware of the fact that everyone is "acting," so people are alert to the possibility of a poor performance, in which someone falls out of his or her role. People are graded on the quality and consistency of their "impression management," their ability to control how they are perceived. Goffman called the ongoing dynamic and its study "dramaturgical analysis."

Both theories have been attacked for being too simplistic or reductive. However, they are definitely a starting point for understanding the self in society.

*4 Second theory discussed.*

*Analogy used to explain second theory.*

*5*

*Effects of social interaction as acting discussed.*

*6 Conclusion.*

## EXERCISE 19.1

Do you have an upcoming essay exam? If so, try to predict from your studying what questions might be asked. Take one of these projected questions, establish a time limit for yourself, and use this chapter's guidelines to write a practice exam essay.

### CHAPTER 20

# THE RESEARCH PROCESS

Many students see the research paper as a complicated, daunting assignment. However, it helps to see it instead as a series of steps, for viewing the research paper as a process is much easier than worrying about the whole picture. This chapter concentrates on the process of focusing on a topic and thesis, finding and taking notes from appropriate sources, and including that information as you plan, write, and revise your paper.

CHAPTER 21 EXPLAINS HOW TO INCORPORATE RESEARCHED MATERIAL using either Modern Language Association (MLA) style or American Psychological Association (APA) style. In addition, Chapter 21 includes a sample student research paper to illustrate MLA guidelines.

Research can take many forms. If you are in the market for a new car, stereo system, or computer, you might find information about competing models in a consumer magazine. If you want to find a restaurant that will impress your friends yet fit your budget, you might look in the newspaper's entertainment section or in a restaurant guide for your city or state. Academic research is a little more complex. It usually involves finding multiple sources of information and opinion in print and electronic publications located in your college library and on the Internet. In addition, you might have to interview experts on your topic or use information from a variety of other sources, including DVDs, musical recordings, and even paintings.

The process of writing a paper that uses research is more complex than that of writing other papers. However, as with all other types of writing, you will need to start by focusing on a working topic. Of course, your instructor might ask you to write on a predetermined topic. Whether you are given a general topic or are allowed to choose your own, you will need to focus on a question or aspect of the topic that you can manage to discuss thoroughly given the kind and length of paper you have been asked to write.

In addition, you need to fulfill three responsibilities when completing a research paper that are not necessary when completing other essays:

- Research information relevant to your topic in primary and/or secondary sources and take notes from these sources in an efficient and easy-to-retrieve manner. (See page 555 for a discussion of primary and secondary sources.)

- Incorporate this information into your paper in a way that logically supports your own ideas and conclusions, that is easy to comprehend, and that is placed naturally and correctly.

- Document the sources of this information properly, using an accepted style such as the one recommended by the Modern Language Association (MLA), the American Psychological Association (APA), or another professional organization, as assigned by your instructor. You can find out more about these formats in Chapter 21.

# NARROWING YOUR TOPIC AND FRAMING A RESEARCH QUESTION

If you have a pre-assigned, focused topic, you will find it relatively easy to get started. Such topics often come with the instructor's assurance that they can be researched in your college library or on the Internet. However, topics that you choose for yourself may be more interesting to you personally. As a matter of fact, you may already have a storehouse of information about your topic gained from your own experiences or reading. This information may serve as a foundation to which you can add researched information from primary and secondary sources.

If your instructor wants you to narrow a broad topic that he or she has assigned or to choose your own topic, you will have to limit that topic so that it can be discussed in a paper of the assigned length. This is one of the most important steps in the research process. In many ways, a broad topic is far more difficult to research than a limited one simply because a narrow topic makes it easier to identify sources that are relevant to your task. For example, the following topics are far too broad for a 2,500- to 3,000-word paper:

Teenage suicide

Environmental risks

Alternative fuel sources

Computer programming

Vegan diets

Instead, try one of the following:

Peer pressure as a cause of teenage suicide in American females

The environmental risks of oil drilling in the Great Lakes

The use of ethanol as an alternative fuel source for cars

Job and salary prospects for computer programmers in the United States, 2010–2020

The benefits and dangers of following a vegan diet

Once you have established a workable topic, turn it into a general question in order to clarify your purpose and better direct your research efforts. Unless your instructor tells you otherwise, you ought to choose questions whose answers might serve as a thesis that you can support and argue for as you draft your research paper. For example, the topics above might be turned into the following questions:

- To what extent does peer pressure contribute to teenage suicide in American females?
- Are the environmental risks of drilling for oil in the Great Lakes too great for the anticipated return?
- Will ethanol replace or partially replace gasoline as an automotive fuel?
- Do U.S. job and salary prospects make computer programming an attractive major for college students in 2010 through 2020?
- Do the benefits of following a vegan diet outweigh the dangers?

However you frame your question, remember that it is only a starting point. You can refine it at any time as you conduct your research. Remember, too, that the research you do is intended to help you arrive at an answer to that question, an answer that will serve as the thesis of your paper. For example, after doing extensive research on job and salary prospects for computer programmers, you might come up with the following thesis statement: *Quali-*

*fied computer programmers will have little trouble finding high-paying, satisfying jobs in the second decade of the twenty-first century.*

### EXERCISE 20.1

Choose a possible topic for a research paper of approximately 1,250 to 2,000 words. Then narrow that topic and frame a question on which you could base your research. Use one of the sample research questions above as your model.

## BEGINNING WITH TOOLS FROM THE REFERENCE ROOM

The reference section of your library contains general reference works such as dictionaries and encyclopedias as well as more specialized books, guides, and encyclopedias intended to provide an overview of a discipline or a subject. Those devoted to specific fields of study, such as the *Encyclopedia of World Art* and *The McGraw-Hill Encyclopedia of Science and Technology,* are good places to start your research. They provide background information, define technical terms, and include valuable bibliographies of even more specific sources that you might want to research. However, such books are sometimes too general to serve as sources for productive note taking. Check with your professor before using information from such sources.

## USING PRIMARY AND SECONDARY SOURCES

**Primary** sources are original works containing firsthand information and insights that you might make the focus of a research paper or that you might use to support or develop ideas about other works or related subjects. A work of literature; a painting or musical composition; a government, historical, or intellectual document such as the Declaration of Independence or Newton's *Mathematical Principles;* the report of a government or corporate agency; the Bible, the Koran, or other religious document; a contemporary newspaper account; or any other original document or work of art is a primary source. However, information you discover yourself can also be used as a primary source. For example, information that you obtain from interviewing an expert on your topic is also considered primary, as are data collected through questionnaires or surveys that you design and distribute.

    **Secondary** sources provide data, analyses, opinions, and ideas from experts other than yourself. For example, if you were writing a research paper on Arthur Miller's *Death of a Salesman,* that play would be your primary source. However, you might also include information about the play from scholarly studies and critiques such as Gerald Weales's book *American Drama Since World War II* and Alan Seager's article "The Creative Agony of Arthur Miller." Secondary sources include written materials—books, journal and magazine articles, pamphlets, Internet sites, and the like.

Only some research papers that you will be assigned in college require the use of primary sources, but virtually all require secondary sources. For example, if you write a research paper on the Great Depression, you might or might not use primary sources such as newspaper accounts written at the time, but you would certainly use secondary sources such as historians' assessments of the causes of this economic calamity. Similarly, a paper arguing for an increased reliance on solar energy might not rely on primary sources such as the records of scientific experiments conducted at a solar observatory, but it would surely include information from reports of such experiments published in journals such as *Scientific American,* which are more accessible to the lay reader.

Your college library is the perfect place to start research. In it, you will find both primary and secondary sources on your topic. However, you can also find a wide range of sources on the Internet. If you have trouble locating any source or need to request an interlibrary loan for a title in another library, seek the help of the librarians. It is their job to help students become proficient at using library resources, and the vast majority are more than happy to do so.

# CREATING A WORKING BIBILIOGRAPHY

Before you begin taking notes, you should create a working bibliography. This document will differ from your Works Cited section (MLA style) or References page (APA style) in that a working bibliography contains records of *all* of the books, periodical articles, Web sites, and other sources you search to find information. Works-cited and references sections list only works from which you have taken information for incorporation into your paper.

You can begin your working bibliography by listing titles you have obtained from your background reading in reference texts. Then, as you go along, you can add titles of promising books found in your search of the library's book catalogue, as explained below. Additional entries can be made as you begin to find magazine, journal, or newspaper articles and Web sites that seem relevant.

You may not use every source you record, but the record you keep of your sources will be invaluable. In any case, your working bibliography will be an asset as you prepare your essay's works-cited or references section. Make sure that you record the appropriate information for each type of source. (Chapter 21 discusses the format and content of works-cited and reference entries.) Note that the information you will need to record for a book is different from what you will need for a journal article or for a source from the Internet. Indeed, the content and format for two different kinds of books vary significantly, as do the content and format for materials found in journals or on the Internet. For now, be sure to include the following information for any sources you list:

**Book:**

Author(s)

Editor and translator (if appropriate)

Title and subtitle

Publisher

Date and place of publication

Volume number or edition number (if appropriate)

Page numbers

**Periodical article or work found in an anthology (collection of articles):**

Author(s)

Editor of the anthology

Translator (if appropriate)

Title of article

Title of journal, magazine, newspaper, or anthology

Date of publication, publisher, and place of publication of anthology

Volume number, issue number, date (for example, 7 July 1999 or Fall 2000 or March 2002)

Page numbers

**Electronic source:**

Author(s)

Editor or translator (if appropriate)

Publication information if source appeared in print before being published in electronic format

Title of the Web site or CD-ROM

Sponsor of the Web site or service company publishing the CD-ROM

Title of the online journal, newspaper, or magazine publishing the article, along with any standard publication data for a periodical, such as volume and issue number

Date the work was published electronically or was most recently updated

Date you accessed the work

Complete URL

### EXERCISE 20.2

In your college library, find at least one general or subject reference book relating to the research question you framed in Exercise 20.1. Consult the bibliography of these reference works to find at least five focused sources—books and periodical articles—relating to your research. Copy down all information listed for these five sources. You will use it as you begin to compile a working bibliography.

## LOCATING BOOKS AND ARTICLES ON YOUR TOPIC

Most libraries have computerized their book catalogues to save space and to make searching easier for users. In fact, most card catalogues have been removed from the reference room and put in storage.

---

*Consider Your Options*

You can record bibliographic (publication) information for all sources in a list on a piece of paper. Another way to store bibliographical information for a source is to record it on a bibliography index card (one for each source), then store these cards in a separate file or box.

A third way to preserve important information about your sources is to photocopy articles in their entirety or relevant sections of a book. Include the title page, copyright page, and table of contents of the publication. Sites found on the Internet can be printed out or saved to a disk. Another way is to record this information in a computer file. Also, online databases and catalogues allow you to e-mail source information as you continue with your research.

## Online Book Catalogues

In addition to indicating call number, author, title, subject, edition, publication information, and the number of copies the library owns, online catalogues tell whether a book is "checked out" or "not on shelf." Some libraries have joined with others to form consortia, or groups, to share resources. In such cases, the catalogue will indicate from which member library or libraries a book can be obtained.

The book's call number is a crucial piece of information. A **call number,** which is also printed on the book's spine, refers to the place on the library shelves (stacks) where the book is stored. Some libraries use Dewey Decimal System call numbers; others use Library of Congress call numbers. If your library has open stacks, you can use the call number to find the book yourself. If your library has closed stacks, you can use the call number to order the book at the circulation desk.

Online catalogues can be used to search for books by keyword, author, title, and subject. Most catalogues provide search directions; they usually appear on an online help menu or in written form near the monitor. Let's say you want to find books for a research paper on air pollution. You might conduct a keyword search simply by typing *air pollution* in the search box. This will probably yield a large list of books, depending on the size of the collection you are searching. To limit your search and make it more manageable, you might add the word *industrial* or *urban* to your search phrase.

The following is an example of the first screen you would see if you were to type *air pollution* in the search box of LMxAC, the electronic book catalogue

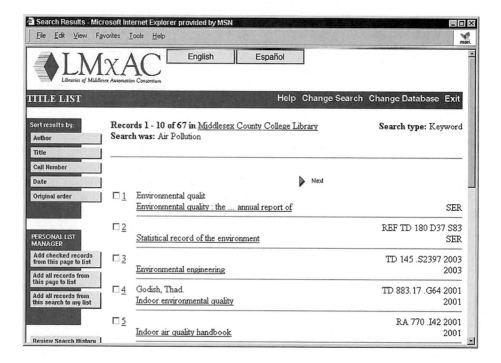

of the Libraries of Middlesex Automation Consortium, the system for the college libraries in Middlesex County, New Jersey. It lists the first ten entries containing that keyword, with fifty-seven others to follow.

After reading over the entire list of books, you might decide to find more information about several of them. A click of the mouse will usually do the trick (again, you must follow directions appropriate to the system you are using). Here is the entry you would see if you chose one of the books listed—Thad Godish's book *Air Quality*. The entry includes publication information about the book as well as the branch it can be found in, its call number, and its status ("Not Checked Out").

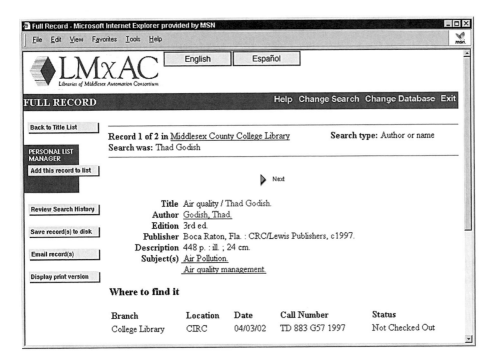

## The Traditional Card Catalogue

You may come upon a library that still uses a traditional card catalogue. Such a catalogue usually consists of alphabetically arranged cards indexed by author, subject, and title. Information for each entry is printed on a card, as in the example on page 560; cards are stored in long, narrow drawers.

### EXERCISE 20.3

Continue the preliminary bibliography you began in Exercise 20.2. Using your college library's book catalogue, locate five books that relate to the research question you chose in Exercise 20.1. Record their pertinent publication information (see the list for books on pages 556–557) in your working bibliography.

Sample Subject Card from a Traditional Book (Card) Catalogue

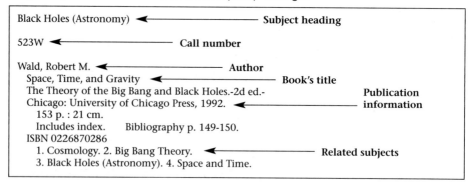

## Periodical Indexes

**Periodicals** are publications that come out at regular intervals—daily, weekly, bi-weekly, monthly, quarterly, semi-annually, and so on. The information in periodicals is often more up to date than that found in books, and the publications provide a forum for the research, opinions, and commentary of experts. Periodical indexes are lists of magazine, journal, and newspaper articles—often arranged by author, title, and subject. They can be found in both bound and online versions in the library's reference area. These indexes are limited to information about articles published annually or during another specified period. Some indexes are general, listing articles from a variety of periodicals that appeal to a wide readership. Others focus on articles published in journals and magazines devoted to specific disciplines or fields of interest. You will likely find many indexes in both printed form and as electronic databases. As always, check with your librarian if you are having trouble finding an index.

Let's look at three types of periodical sources and at the indexes in which you can find the sources listed.

**Magazines,** such as *U.S. News & World Report, Time, Atlantic Monthly,* and *Business Week,* contain articles written for general audiences. Magazine articles are researched and written by journalists who might or might not be experts in the fields on which they report. The best-known index for finding magazine articles is the *Readers' Guide to Periodical Literature.*

The *Readers' Guide,* now available in both bound and online versions, contains information from more than 400 magazines of interest to the general public. Arranged by subject and author, each volume of the bound version provides suggestions for using the *Readers' Guide* as well as a legend to abbreviations used. Here is an excerpt from a page in the bound version; the subject is *black holes:*

**BLACK HOLES (ASTRONOMY)**

Biggest black hole in the universe? J. Horgan. il *Scientific American* 265:32 Jl '91

A black hole found at last? il *Astronomy* 19:22 F '91

Black holes in galactic cores: the research mounts [research by John Kormendy] il *Sky and Telescope* 82: 344-5 O '91

Black holes swarming at the galactic center? [Granat satellite data]
   M. M. Waldrop il *Science* 251-166 Ja 11 '91

**What the first entry contains:**

**Title of article:** Biggest black hole in the universe?

**Author:** J. Horgan

**Note that article is illustrated:** il

**Magazine in which article appeared:** *Scientific American*

**Volume number/page number:** 265:32

**Publication date (July 1991):** Jl '91

Here is an entry on black holes found in the online version of the *Readers'
Guide,* made available by subscription from the H. W. Wilson Company:

| | |
|---:|:---|
| **Title:** | Black holes in all sizes |
| **Personal author:** | Talcott, Richard |
| **Journal name:** | Astronomy |
| **Source:** | Astronomy v. 28 no. 12 (December 2000) p. 26-8 |
| **Publication Year:** | 2000 |
| **Physical Description:** | Illustration |
| **ISSN:** | 0091-6358 |
| **Language of Document:** | English |
| **Abstract:** | Astronomers have discovered a new variety of black hole. The black hole, which is midway in size between the 2 types of hole identified so far, was discovered lying about 600 light-years from the center of M82, in Ursa Major. The breakthrough finding came when astronomers using the Chandra X-ray Observatory compared high-resolution images of M82 with optical, radio, and infrared maps of the same region. The discovery both opens a whole new field of research and raises the possibility that the Milky Way might contain midsized black holes. |
| **Full Text:** | Full Text HTML |
| **Subject(s):** | Black holes (Astronomy) |
| **Document Type:** | Feature Article |
| **Abstract Indicator:** | Y |
| **Full Text Indicator:** | Y |
| **Update Code:** | 20010329 |
| **Date Entered:** | 20001121 |
| **Date Indexed:** | 20001205 |
| **Database:** | General Science; Readers' Guide (Current Events) |
| **Accession Number:** | 200033604350003 |
| **Persistent URL:** | HTML: http://vnweb.hwwilsonweb.com/hww/jumpstart.jhtml?recid=0bc05f7a67b1790e7008f4f7781ac18794b79b40addf0747875697dcbed954f68df84a3c98a328ef&fmt=H |

Note that the online version provides an abstract (summary) of the article, which
you can use to determine whether the article is relevant to your research project
and worth reading in its entirety, as well as a way to access the article in its entirety.

**Journals** contain articles devoted to specific disciplines or fields of interest, and they are aimed at limited audiences, usually experts in those fields. Among the most famous are the *New England Journal of Medicine,* the *Harvard Business Review,* and *Publications of the Modern Language Association.* Often, journals are published by colleges and universities and by professional organizations. Articles in such journals are written by experts in the field.

Many different library indexes list information on journal articles. Like the materials they reference, these indexes focus on specific disciplines. Many are published by professional or educational organizations. They are usually bound annually, and some are available online or in electronic format. Many of those published electronically also include abstracts. Among commonly used journal indexes are the *Applied Science and Technology Index,* the *Business Periodicals Index,* the *Arts and Humanities Citation Index,* the *Education Index,* the *Educational Resources Information Center* (ERIC), the *Engineering Index,* the *Guide to Nursing and Allied Health,* the *Index Medicus,* the *Index to U.S. Government Periodicals,* the *Modern Language Association International Bibliography,* the *Music Index, Psychological Abstracts,* and the *Social Sciences Citation Index.*

Here is a sample entry taken from the *Modern Language Association International Bibliography,* an index published by a professional organization made up of teachers of modern language, literature, linguistics, and folklore:

*Cather, Willa*
[8429] Saposnik-Noire, Shelley. "The Silent Protagonist: The Unifying Presence of Landscape in Willa Cather's *My Ántonia.*" MQ. 1990 Winter; 31(2): 171-179.

**What this entry contains:**

**Subject heading:** Cather, Willa

**Entry number:** [8429]

**Author:** Saposnik-Noire, Shelley.

**Title of article:** "The Silent Protagonist:
The Unifying Presence of Landscape
in Willa Cather's *My Ántonia*"

**Title of journal (*MQ = Midwest Quarterly*):** MQ

**Year/quarter of publication:** 1990 Winter

**Volume/issue numbers:** 31(2)

**Pages on which article appears:** 171-179

**Newspaper** articles can be found by using a variety of indexes. One of the most famous is the *New York Times Index,* which lists articles published in that newspaper. In addition, electronic databases such as the Newspaper Source of EBSCO, offer publication information and abstracts of articles appearing in the *Christian Science Monitor,* the *New York Times,* the *Wall Street Journal,* and the *Washington Post* (see also page 563).

## Electronic Databases

In the last fifteen years, computerization has revolutionized library research. Not only have most libraries computerized their catalogues, but they also buy and subscribe to lists of books, articles, and other documents that are delivered via the Internet or stored on computer disks or other portable media. Some of these databases list bibliographical information only—the title, author's name, date of publication, and so on. Others include abstracts (summaries) of articles. Other databases offer copies of whole articles. In some cases, in fact, you can even get copies of entire books—usually classics—on the Internet at no cost.

Here is a partial list of online databases to which your library might provide you access. As always, check with your librarian to find out exactly what your library offers.

1. **ABI INFORM:** Provides full texts of articles in business and management. It draws articles from more than 2,900 academic and professional journals and trade magazines published worldwide.

2. **Academic Search Premier:** The world's largest multidisciplinary database, which provides the full texts of articles from more than 4,400 publications.

3. **Anthropological Index Online:** Provides access to articles published in current periodicals found in the Anthropological Library at the British Museum.

4. **Applied Science and Technology Index:** Contains abstracts of articles published in about 760 professional journals in aeronautics, computer science, engineering, and related scientific and technical disciplines.

5. **Cumulative Index to Nursing and Allied Health Literature (CINAHL):** References nearly 1,850 scholarly journals in the health sciences. It also contains information on books, dissertations, and educational software in the health professions.

6. **ERIC** (Education Resources Information Center): Includes journal articles, reports, and speeches on education.

7. **Humanities:** Offers citations and abstracts of journal articles in art, classics, history, language, literature, music, philosophy, religion, and other humanities. In addition, it provides the full text of some articles.

8. **JSTOR:** A scholarly journal archive, JSTOR stands for Journal Storage. It makes available back issues of important journals in the humanities, social sciences, and sciences.

9. **CGP:** The Catalog of U.S. Government Publications, which indexes documents published by the federal government.

10. **Newspaper Source:** A service of EBSCO. This index includes citations and abstracts of articles published in the *Christian Science Monitor*, the *New York Times*, the *Wall Street Journal*, and the *Washington Post*.

11. **Project Muse:** Contains citations to articles appearing in more than 300 diverse journals published by Johns Hopkins University Press and 60 other scholarly presses.

12. **PsycINFO:** Indexes and abstracts books, journal articles, and dissertations in psychology and related disciplines, and also offers full-text links via PsycARTICLES.

For an example of what you might find if you used one of these online indexes, look at this sample page from the Academic Search Premier. The keywords *air pollution, prevention,* and *automobiles* were used for this search.

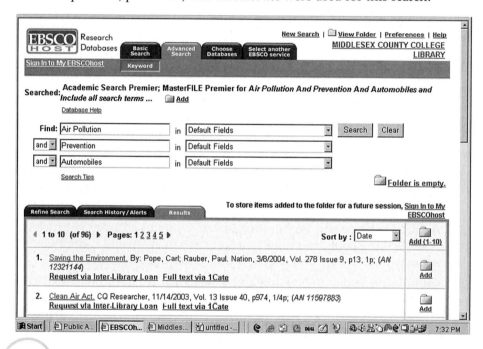

### EXERCISE 20.4

Continue the working bibliography you began in Exercise 20.2. Using resources like those discussed above, locate five periodical articles that relate to the research question you chose in Exercise 20.1. Record their pertinent publication information (see the list for periodical articles on page 557) in your working bibliography.

## SEARCHING THE INTERNET

The **Internet**, including the World Wide Web, is a system that connects computers at various research, educational, corporate, personal, and other types of institutions around the world. It can provide you with a rich trove of databases, which can yield much valuable information. (In fact, the twelve library databases listed above can be accessed via the Internet.) Students can access whole books, articles from online magazines and scholarly journals, government and organization position papers, government documents, pamphlets, brochures, and a host of other information sources.

However, before you begin to learn to use the Internet as a research tool, you need to realize that the Internet is valuable only if approached with caution and discrimination:

- The contents of the Internet are ever-changing. On one hand, this is an advantage because the Internet can provide access to the most current information on a topic. On the other hand, what you find on the Internet one day might not be there the next, a fact that you should take into account when evaluating your sources. After all, the reliability of such information might be questionable.

- College libraries are run by professionals who can be counted on to order materials prepared by qualified and reputable authors and publishers. Often, specific books, journals, and other materials are requested directly by college faculty. In general, then, you can have confidence that the materials in your college library are reliable, although you still need to read them critically and evaluate their usefulness and relevance to your topic. On the other hand, anyone with access to a server can create a Web site and post information on it. Therefore, when using the Internet you will have to take steps to assure yourself of the credibility, expertise, and reliability of any electronic sources you want to include. For example, if you searched for information about the Greek goddess Aphrodite on the Web, you might find materials by Joseph Campbell, a noted expert on ancient mythology. Then again, you might come up with a research paper on Aphrodite posted on the personal Web site of a college student who wants to show his parents how hard he has been working.

- Unscrupulous people and groups can and do take advantage of the ease of publishing on the Web. For example, hate mongers, racial supremacists, and the like sometimes post false and defamatory information about public figures and about ethnic, religious, or other groups. On occasion, the material is presented in such a devious manner that it seems to be coming from a legitimate news source or a think tank (a professional organization that researches and publishes papers on issues affecting the public). In such cases, it is especially important for you to discover and evaluate the sources of information that you intend to use.

A fuller discussion of how to evaluate Internet sources appears on pages 572–573.

**Browser:** Software that allows you to access the Internet. Microsoft Internet Explorer and Netscape Navigator are browsers.

**E-zine:** Name given to magazines published on the Internet. *Salon.com* is an example of such a magazine. (Many print magazines and newspapers also provide material on the Internet.)

## A Brief Glossary of Internet Terms

**FAQ:** An abbreviation for "frequently asked questions." Most Internet browsers, services, and search engines provide a list of such questions so that users experiencing common problems can find solutions quickly.

**Home page:** The main organizational/navigational page of a Web site. A home page contains hyperlinks that will take you to other parts of the Web site as well as to related sites. For example, the home page of a professional organization might have hyperlinks to a list of its members, its online publications, and Web sites for other departments as well as to Web sites of other professional organizations in the same or related disciplines.

**HTML** (Hypertext Markup Language): A computer "language" that allows you to create a Web site.

**Hyperlink:** A word, phrase, icon, or object found on a Web page that, when clicked, takes you to another page in that site or to another Web site.

**Keyword(s):** Used in searching the Web and in conducting electronic research, a word or phrase that focuses a search so that you can more efficiently retrieve information on a limited topic.

**Mailing list:** An electronic discussion group focused on a particular subject or task. Students taking online courses often communicate with their professors and classmates via electronic mailing lists.

**Newsgroups:** Online forums dedicated to a particular topic on which participants can post comments.

**Online:** Connected to the Internet.

**Search engine:** Software that allows you to search for information on a topic by entering keywords. Many search engines provide suggestions that can help make your search more productive.

**URL** (Uniform Resource Locator): The address of a Web site. Typing a URL into the address box of your browser allows you to connect directly to the site without using a search engine.

## Internet Search Tools: URLs, Directories, and Search Engines

If you know the **URL** (Uniform Resource Locator) of a Web site, you can connect to that site directly by typing the URL into the address box of your browser. It is always wise to keep a record of the URLs of Web sites you have accessed; you can do this simply by printing out the site's home page or copying the URL and pasting it into your working bibliography, using your computer's cut-and-paste function.

If you are just beginning your search for information on a topic, however, you will probably want to start by using an Internet browser such as Microsoft Internet Explorer or a **search engine** such as AltaVista, Google, or Lycos. Many Internet browsers and search engines display **directories**, or listings of search categories that will bring you to relevant sites. For example, Yahoo! lists "Arts and

Humanities," "Business and Economy," and "Education" among many other categories. Searching for information by using these categories will lead you to sites that people running the search engine have determined are the most useful to their most frequent users. However, such searches might not always produce results that are useful to you. In addition, remember that many Web site creators pay a fee to register their sites with certain search engines. This entitles them to be listed among the sites that come up when you use the search engine's directory. Again, these sites might not be the most appropriate for your search.

Chances are that you will have to conduct your own keyword search via a search engine, which looks through many databases for the keywords you have indicated. Any Web browser can provide you with access to more search engines than you will ever need. However, not all search engines access the same sites. Therefore, searching for the same topic via different search engines might very well produce different results. For future reference, it is a good idea to "bookmark" or include in your list of "favorites" those search engines you find most useful.

Search engines offer users several different ways to limit and refine their searches. With many search engines, for example, if you type in the keywords *AIDS education,* you will find sites relevant both to *AIDS* and to *education.* In some cases, you might be able to refine your search simply by typing your keywords in quotation marks, thereby significantly limiting your yield to sites on topics dealing only with "educational efforts aimed at dealing with AIDS." Fortunately, most search engines provide their users with advice on how to best use their services. For example, using Google's advanced search function can help you refine a search for information on *AIDS education* (see the screens on page 568). To make your search efficient, spend a few minutes reading these suggestions, at least those offered by the search engine you use most often. (See pages 569–570 for tips on using search engines.)

## A Brief List of Popular Search Engines

**AltaVista** (http://www.altavista.com): A useful search engine for academics, it provides access to more than thirty million pages of information.

**Excite** (http://www.excite.com): This search engine conducts concept as well as word or phrase searches. Thus, if you were to type *AIDS education* in the search box, it might return links to articles on HIV infection and on AIDS prevention as well as links to information on AIDS education.

**Google** (http://www.google.com): Google provides access to more than eight billion Web pages, and it includes a number of special features to improve searches. It ranks Web sites according to the number and quality of pages that link to them. This is a very powerful and widely used search engine.

**Hotbot** (http://www.hotbot.com): Developed by a joint venture of the Inktomi Corporation and Hotwired, this search engine allows you to use several configurations of keywords. It searches several different aspects of the Web site, not just its title or metatag (the device created by the Web site designer to enable the search engine to index the site).

**Library of Congress World Wide Web Homepage** (http://www.lcWeb .loc.gov): This search engine provides information on the contents of the United States Library of Congress, perhaps the largest collection in the world. Its home page offers databases of state and federal government publications. The THOMAS database, named after Thomas Jefferson, provides information on bills under consideration in the U.S. House and Senate.

**Ask.com** (http://www.search.ask.com): This search engine combines Ask Jeeves with Teoma. It uses what it calls "subject-specific-popularity" to evaluate a site "based upon the number of same-subject pages that reference it, not just general popularity."

**WebCrawler** (http://www.webcrawler.com): Now part of the Excite system, WebCrawler searches for keywords in the text of a Web site, not just in its title or metatag.

**Multi-Search Engines:** Such resources access other search engines and can therefore expand your search significantly. However, because their range is so wide, they work more slowly than other search engines. Examples of multi-search engines are DogPile (http://www.dogpile.com), Metacrawler (http://www.metacrawler.com), and Vivísimo (http://vivisimo.com).

## EXERCISE 20.5

Using three different search engines, look up a subject such as one of the following:

1. College literacy standards
2. Ethanol as an alternative fuel
3. Advantages of vegan diets
4. Bilingual education
5. U.S. immigration policy
6. Reducing teenage pregnancy rates

Decide which one finds the greatest number of useful sites and which one is easiest to use.

As discussed earlier, all search engines offer specific on-screen help; however, here are three general strategies you might find helpful:

1. **Try a Boolean Search:** Boolean searches use AND, OR, and NOT with keywords and phrases so as to limit searches and make them more efficient. If you typed *victim* AND *crime* AND *compensation*, you would gain access to more sites that contain information about compensating victims of crime, and you would eliminate sites relating to, for example, *compensation for corporate executives* or the *victimization of women in the workplace*. If you searched for *virus* NOT *computer*, you would limit your search to viruses known to medicine.

# Three Tips on Using Search Engines

2. **Use a Wild Card:** A *wild card* is a character, often an asterisk, that is used with a keyword to search for variations of that word as well as the word itself. For example, typing the keyword *crim\** might produce sites containing the words *crime, criminology, criminals,* and *criminality.*

3. **Include Quotation Marks** (" "): Quotation marks tell the search engine to look for the words you have typed in the exact order they appear in the search box. For example, if you wanted to find sites that discuss "standard of living," you would put quotation marks around those words.

### EXERCISE 20.6

Continue the working bibliography you began in Exercise 20.2. Using resources like those discussed above, locate five Internet documents that relate to the research question you chose in Exercise 20.1. Record their pertinent publication information (see the list for electronic sources on page 557) in your working bibliography.

## EVALUATING SOURCES

As you add more and more sources that you believe are relevant to your research topic and question to your working bibliography, you will realize that some of the sources you have gathered will not be worth using. They may be too general, irrelevant, or even inaccurate. The fact that a book or article has been published does not guarantee the reliability or even the authenticity of its information. The guidelines that follow will help you avoid wasting hours taking notes that will be useless when it comes time to draft your paper.

### Tips on Evaluating Sources for Your Research Paper

1. Before you even start taking notes from a work, preview it. Does the work seem to contain enough information relevant to your topic and research question to make it worth your time to read it and take careful notes? Check the index and table of contents of a book, and read its preface or introduction. Skim a periodical article or electronic source. Read subheadings as well as the article's introduction and conclusion. Examine any charts, graphs, or other visual elements that are included.

2. Evaluate the content of the source. Does the author support opinions with facts, reliable statistics, and other trustworthy data, or does he or she rely heavily on unsupported ideas and opinions? Does the author make his or her case logically? Does the work seem balanced, or does the author provide only part of the evidence—the part that supports his or her thesis? Does the work rely on well-documented research, and do

the sources of this research seem reputable? For example, contrast these two claims:

People under the age of 30 make high-risk drivers. They cause and are involved in the greatest number of fatal automobile accidents.

According to the authors of "The Insurance Dilemma," an eleven-year study (1990–2000) of automobile accidents published by the Allied Auto-mobile Institutes of North America, "drivers under age of 30 were involved in 45% of all serious collisions (with repair or replacement costs of over $5000) and accounted for 60% of fatalities in such accidents" (44).

3. Does the material presented seem objective, or could it be biased? For example, information on the efficacy of a drug taken from a publication of the National Institutes of Health is likely to be objective, whereas information from a pamphlet published by the manufacturer of that drug will probably be biased in favor of the drug. Most pharmaceutical manufacturers are trustworthy and will provide accurate information, but they are in business to make a profit. Therefore, the perspective from which they provide information is not disinterested.

4. Consider the publication date. For topics in the sciences and technologies as well as in the social sciences, the more current the publication, the better.

5. Consider the author. What are his or her credentials, such as education, years of experience, and professional affiliation? Is he or she a college or university professor or a well-known reporter, commentator, scientist, or other professional in a field related to your topic? Is he or she a member of a respected research institution? Has the author published articles or books on the same or related topics? Are these sources available in college libraries?

   You might want to verify an author's credentials by searching for more information about him or her on the Internet, in your college library, or in *Books in Print,* which would list other book-length works he or she might have written. If you cannot verify his or her credentials, find other sources of information. In addition, you should ask yourself whether the author has a political, artistic, or other bias that makes his or her viewpoint less than objective. If so, is the information still useful if used with caution, or is it so tainted that using it would harm the integrity of your work?

6. Consider the publisher. Is this a respected commercial or academic publisher? Or is this a "vanity" press, which is willing to print a manuscript that other publishers have rejected on the condition that the author agrees to cover all or part of the publication costs? Is the publisher known for putting out inflammatory, biased, or other material that is inappropriate to scholarly research? You can find out about various publishing houses by reading *Literary Marketplace* or *Editor & Publisher,* or by consulting your college librarian or professor.

## Tips on Evaluating Electronic Sources
## for Your Research Paper

The logic, principles, and good sense that you would apply to a print source are the same as those you apply to all sources, including those found on the Internet. However, remember that the sources you find in the library have already been screened through a process that involves professionals—college faculty and librarians—ordering materials that they believe will best support the curriculum. Moreover, no publisher with a reputation to maintain can afford to print a text that is poorly prepared, inflammatory, biased, fraudulent, or unfair. You can be fairly confident, then, that most of the print sources available in your college library are appropriate for college research. In the case of articles in scholarly journals, in fact, submissions are often juried or peer-reviewed—that is, judged for quality by reviewers who are themselves experts in the discipline.

On the other hand, any organization or any person—regardless of education, experience, bias, or intent—can publish on the Internet. No screening process exists for such material. Consider the following *additional* criteria as you decide whether or not an Internet source is appropriate:

1. Who sponsors the Web site or publishes the CD-ROM? Is it a college or university, a research institution, a professional journal, a reputable magazine, or a respected think tank? Is it just a personal Web site that the creator has published by renting space on a commercial server? If the latter, find other sources of information.

2. What is the purpose of the site? Consider the Web address (URL). Addresses for sites sponsored by educational institutions usually end in "edu." Those for city, state, and federal government sites end in "gov." Sites whose addresses end in "org" (organization) need careful scrutiny. As a general rule, groups such as the League of Women Voters, the United Way, or the Girl Scouts provide information that is unbiased; of course, you will have to read the mission or purpose statements of such organizations for yourself to be sure. Other groups, such as the Americans for Democratic Action, the American Civil Liberties Union, and the Young Republicans, also publish a great deal of reliable information, but you must remember that the overall purpose of these organizations may make their views on an issue less than disinterested. Then there are organizations that are so biased that you should never rely on information from their Web sites unless you are trying to expose that bias or analyze its causes and effects. Many Web sites are simply organs of propaganda put on the Web by fringe groups who are trying to advance a political, social, medical, or other type of agenda that would not have been disseminated were it not for the relatively cheap and easy means of publishing on the Web.

   Still another type of address ends in "com," for commercial. Corporations usually use such addresses. If you are considering material posted on a corporate Web site, you need to ask yourself if the material presented is simply informational and objective or if its purpose is to sell you something.

3. What information about the Web site can you find by going to the home page, which may provide more and better information about the author and the sponsor than any single Web page can? You can get to a site's home page by clicking on the home page link. You can also learn more about a site doing a WHOIS search (www.networksolutions.com/whois).

4. Is the material well written, well presented, and well developed? Is the Web site constructed logically and coherently? Is it updated regularly? Does it include links to other sites? What sites are they? Do they seem reputable? If the answer to these questions is no, find other sources of information.

5. Was the document published in a print version as well as on the Internet? If not, could it have been? If the document does not meet the criteria for evaluating all sources of information (see the list above), you can't rely on the information that it contains, and you need to find other sources.

**CATALYST 2.0**

**MORE OPTIONS ONLINE**
For a source evaluation tutor, go to
**www.mhhe.com/
writingtoday.**

### EXERCISE 20.7
Evaluate the sources in the working bibliography you have been developing. Remove sources that are not appropriate according to the criteria for print and nonprint sources discussed above. Do you have enough sources left for you to start taking notes, or should you try to find more sources? If in doubt, consult your instructor.

## TAKING NOTES

When you read, you will want to keep a record of information that is potentially important for your research paper. This is best done by recording notes on index cards (4" × 6" cards are recommended). Use one index card for each fact, idea, opinion, or group of supporting data that you take from a source. This method enables you to organize your notes easily and efficiently once you have finished your research and are ready to begin outlining and drafting.

As an alternative to traditional note cards, you might consider keeping your notes in a computer file or annotating photocopies and printouts of your source material.

- **Taking notes on a computer:** As with note cards, you'll need to take notes in a way that will allow you to organize your information easily. Start each note from a source on a new page, and identify the source of each piece of information. Writing your quotations, summaries, and paraphrases (see pages 574–576) in a computer file can save you time once you begin your paper because you can simply cut and paste information into your draft.

- **Taking notes on photocopies or printouts:** If your paper is brief, and you are not using many sources, this system can work very well. You can highlight key points in your sources on the printout and write notes and ideas in the margins.

**Note:** Avoid recording information in a notebook or on looseleaf paper. Doing so makes organizing your notes far more difficult later on.

After taking your notes on cards, in a computer file, or on printouts, read over these notes carefully. As you do, general points or major ideas that you might use in your paper will start to emerge. Next, arrange the cards or printouts in a separate pile for each of those ideas. Arranging your notes in this way gives you a preliminary notion of how your paper will be organized—at least in general. Now read over the notes in each pile and arrange the cards or printouts in that pile in the order that will best present the information. If you have taken a lot of notes, you may have to spread your notes on a large table or even on the floor. Doing so allows you to begin to see your paper take form. Once you review your initial "layout," however, you can change the positions of notes, add or delete notes as needed, and make other changes easily and logically. You might even see the need to do more research. In any event, you can then use this arrangement of cards as a model from which to outline your paper.

**Note:** You can easily keep track of your sources by beginning your note taking with a 3" × 5" "bibliography card" for each source. On it, record all of the publication data you will need to include in that particular source's entry in the works-cited or references section, the list of the sources you used in your paper. You can also transfer this information to your working bibliography. (You will learn more about works-cited and references entries in Chapter 21.)

Bibliography Card

> *"Are School Vouchers Un-American?"*
>
> *Gary Rosen, Pages 25-28*
>
> <u>*Commentary*</u>
>
> *Vol. 10    Issue 2*
>
> *Date   Feb 2000*

Then, at the top of each of your "content" cards, you can simply write the author's last name and the relevant page number(s). If no author is given, use a shortened version of the source's title.

Notes take three forms: direct quotations, summaries, and paraphrases:

**Direct quotations** use the exact words of the source. Sometimes you will read a passage with insights that are so precise, clear, or moving that you will want to repeat them exactly. A direct quotation is a word-for-word copy of the original, as in the example on page 575. Place quotation marks (" ") around passages you may want to quote as you take notes. The quotation marks will remind you that the information was copied exactly and that you will have to place quotation marks around the passage in your paper. (See pages 579–580 in this chapter for more guidelines on quoting.)

You can use summaries and paraphrases to present borrowed information, insights, and ideas using your own words and your own sentence patterns. Summaries and paraphrases convey insights and information that you can use as major ideas or as support for those ideas.

Direct Quotation Note Card

<u>Rosen 26</u>

"By any measure, public education in America's cities is in deep trouble, and has been for some time. On any given day in Cleveland, almost one of every six students is likely not to show up. In Washington, D.C., a majority of tenth graders never finish high school. And in Los Angeles, school officials recently retreated from a plan to end the practice of 'social promotion,' realizing that it would have required holding back for a year more than half of the district's woefully unprepared students."

**Summaries** condense information into a shorter form while expressing the main idea. Simply try to focus on the main point or idea the author is making in a passage or paragraph, and state that idea in one or two sentences that use your own words only. Compare this paragraph from Ernest Albrecht's *The New American Circus* (page 1) with the summary that follows it:

> The circus had truly become the best (and often the only) entertainment bargain in town, a display of profligacy that has not been seen outside that wildly prosperous period the United States enjoyed between 1870 and 1915. So abundant were its demonstrations of skill and daring that it required not just three rings to contain them all but four elevated stages as well. Pageants of splendor and inflated grandiosity wound their way around the hippodrome track that encircled the giant tent. In its enormity the American circus had become the glorious embodiment of America's unofficial motto: "All New This Year: Bigger and Better than Ever."

Summary Note Card

<u>Albrecht 1</u>

In the period of economic growth that spanned the end of the nineteenth and the beginning of the twentieth centuries, the American circus grew into a huge, flamboyant, and extravagant enterprise that met the nation's growing desire for more exciting and lavish spectacles.

A **paraphrase** is like a summary except that it can be about as long as the original. Once again, use your own words while capturing the writer's main idea. Compare an idea from Vicki Goldberg's essay "Death Takes a Holiday, Sort Of," from page 29 of *Why We Watch,* a collection of essays on violence, with the paraphrase that follows it.

> In the eighteenth century, the popular print, still limited in number, came into its own. The last years of the century saw new and revived graphic techniques, including wood engraving (incising an image on the harder end piece of the wood), which would be vital to the nineteenth-century illustrated press, and lithography. Both permitted much, much larger illustrated press runs. The introduction of photography, in 1839, riveted the eyes of the world on pictures, and by 1851, an easy means of duplicating photographic prints made them cheaper and readily available.

Paraphrase Note Card

> <u>Goldberg 29</u>
>
> At the end of the 1700s, new methods enabled printers to mass-produce illustrations more clearly than before. Thus, illustrations began to appear more frequently in printed materials. One of these methods was lithography. Another was engraving, carving images on wooden blocks, used in the illustrated newspapers and magazines of the next century. In the 1800s, the invention of photography and of inexpensive methods to reproduce photographs further increased the presence of visuals in printed materials.

**Note:** You might want to include some words from the original in a paraphrase. If so, be sure to put quotation marks around them.

Paraphrase Note Card That Includes Quoted Material

> <u>Goldberg 29</u>
>
> At the end of the 1700s, new methods enabled printers to mass-produce illustrations more clearly than before. Thus, illustrations began to appear more frequently in printed materials. One of these methods was lithography. Another was engraving, carving images on wooden blocks, used in the illustrated newspapers and magazines of the next century. In the 1800s, the invention of photography, which "riveted the eyes of the world on pictures," and of inexpensive methods to reproduce photographs further increased the presence of visuals in printed materials.

EXERCISE 20.8

Find and begin taking notes on one of the sources in your working bibliography. Make sure you have a bibliography card, as well as at least one card that contains a direct quotation, one that contains a paraphrase, and one that contains a summary.

# AVOIDING PLAGIARISM

Schools, colleges, and universities insist on the integrity of their students' work. **Plagiarism,** which is the use of someone else's words or ideas without giving the source appropriate credit, is a serious offense. It violates the very purpose of education, which is, essentially, the search for truth, and it is usually punished severely. Indeed, penalties for plagiarism can range from failure in the course to dismissal from the college or university.

Most often, intentional plagiarism involves copying something from a source, usually word for word, and using it without quotation marks. However, students who are just learning to write research papers sometimes commit unintentional plagiarism, which can result from any of the following actions:

1. Forgetting to put quotation marks around quoted material when taking notes or forgetting to include quotation marks when placing those notes in the text of the paper.

2. Using material that has been summarized or paraphrased and forgetting to tell readers the source of that material.

3. Paraphrasing or summarizing incorrectly. Inadvertent plagiarism includes accidentally adopting the sentence and/or paragraph structure of the original or including many of the words from the original (except for proper nouns). Note that while this is not done intentionally, it is still a serious problem and may result in a substantially lower grade than the paper could have earned.

Contrast a direct quotation from Frank Ancona's book *Myth* with a partially plagiarized paraphrase. Then look at a legitimate paraphrase and summary of the same material.

### Original
In *The Interpretation of Dreams*, Freud recognized the difficulty inherent in trying to communicate with the unconscious. He attributed the problem to what he called a "censor." He believed that some elements of consciousness did not want the messages from the unconscious to surface. (23)

### Plagiarized Paraphrase
In *The Interpretation of Dreams*, Freud **recognized** how **difficult** it was **to communicate with the unconscious.** He theorized that the problem was caused by something **he called a "censor." He believed that some** parts of **consciousness did not want messages from the unconscious to** come out.

### Legitimate Paraphrase

To Freud, a "censor" within the conscious mind kept the unconscious mind from communicating with it. In his book *The Interpretation of Dreams*, he theorized that an aspect of the conscious mind prevented troublesome ideas from emerging.

### Legitimate Summary

Freud theorized in *The Interpretation of Dreams* that something within the conscious mind attempts to keep out information buried within the unconscious.

The plagiarized paraphrase contains words taken directly from the original. In this case, the student needs to rephrase the note or simply to put the author's original wording in quotation marks.

Keep in mind that you are allowed to "use" the work of another, within reason, as long as you acknowledge and credit this source. On the other hand, a research paper shouldn't be just an unbroken string of direct quotations, paraphrases, and summaries from other sources. Exactly what needs to be cited?

1. A direct quotation of another person's writing or speech, even if only a few words

2. A paraphrase or summary of another person's writing or speech

3. An opinion expressed by another person

4. Statistical data produced by another person

5. Graphic or audiovisual material produced by another person

What kind of information does *not* need to be cited? Only the following categories fall into this group:

1. Common knowledge: U.S. citizens are expected to pay taxes on their income; water freezes at 32 degrees Fahrenheit; most gasoline bought in the United States is imported.

2. "Background" knowledge generated from your research. (Be careful not to interpret this category too broadly.) If you are researching an essay on prison overcrowding in your state, for example, and twelve sources in a row indicate that the problem is serious, you have no need to cite a source for this opinion. However, if one of these sources claims that prison overcrowding is the *most* serious problem afflicting your state, and you express this opinion in any way, you must credit its source. Similarly, if you are researching an article on the salaries paid to Major League Baseball players in the 1980s and find source after source mentioning the continuing escalation in salaries, you have no need to cite a source. However, if a source points out that salaries increased fivefold during the 1980s, you need to cite this source if you include this information.

**CATALYST 2.0**

**MORE OPTIONS ONLINE**
For more information on how to avoid plagiarism, go to www.mhhe.com/ writingtoday.

If you are not sure whether to cite information, be conservative: credit the source. The consequences for being too careful are minimal compared to the damage that plagiarism wreaks.

# QUOTING TEXT

Chapter 21 discusses the research paper, and Chapter 22 covers writing about literature. Whether you are writing a research paper or a literary analysis (or a combination of the two), you need to know how to quote text properly and how to incorporate the text into your work.

Why is this issue so important? Being able to choose and include the proper quotation is essential in a number of different contexts. Along with writers of research papers, attorneys preparing written arguments ("briefs") and journalists writing news articles know that including a key quotation—and doing so properly—can dramatically improve the impact of a document.

In Chapter 21, we explain how to *cite* quotations using the Modern Language Association (MLA) format or the American Psychological Association (APA) format. In this chapter, we concentrate on how to *quote* text, along with how to handle basic citations of page numbers. We'll start with the MLA guidelines and then show how the same text example would be treated in the APA system. However, we begin with some general advice about quoting.

## General Principles for Quoting Text

1. **Quote accurately.** Too often, original text such as "Your sensibilities are what are in question, Mr. John" becomes "You're sensabilities are what is in question, Mr. Johnson." Check your transcription to avoid introducing errors.

2. **Preserve the integrity of your sources.** Later in the chapter we indicate how to elide, or remove, unnecessary text from a quotation. However, never omit text in a way that changes the meaning of a quotation; if a quotation doesn't support your point, don't try to "reshape" it so that it does.

3. **Give full credit to your sources.** On pages 577–578 in this chapter and page 596 in Chapter 21, we explain how to avoid **plagiarism,** or the use of someone else's work without giving proper credit. Follow those guidelines.

4. **Don't try to merge text from different parts of a source into one quotation.** For example, connecting a sentence from page 5 with one from page 16 by using an ellipsis (see page 583 and page 589) is intellectually dishonest. Instead, introduce and quote the first sentence, followed by its citation; then introduce and quote the second one, followed by its citation, as in the following example (which follows MLA guidelines):

   Rodriguez points out that the winters in his boyhood were difficult: "I grew up in some of the worst weather in the twentieth century" (5). Later, he reiterates his point: "My grandmother told me that she had never seen winters so cold" (16).

5. **Use the correct documentation system for your context.** English and the humanities use MLA; the social sciences use APA. If you try to use APA style in a paper analyzing a poem, for

example, you will run into an insurmountable problem: the APA *Publication Manual* offers no guidelines for citing poetry.

6. **When you are writing an essay using quotations, don't refer to them as such.** *Quote* is a verb, not a noun. If you need to refer to text that you have quoted, call it a *statement* or a *passage,* not a *quote* or a *quotation.*

7. **Note that a comma does not precede every opening quotation mark.** In the following sentence, the comma is not needed:

INCORRECT   Olsen's discussion of, "biosocial ethics" (499) is thorough and informative.

CORRECT   Olsen's discussion of "biosocial ethics" (499) is thorough and informative.

The writer probably wouldn't have considered using a comma if *biosocial ethics* had not been enclosed in quotation marks.

## INCORPORATING DIRECT QUOTATIONS: MLA GUIDELINES

The examples in this section are quotations from the following paragraph, which comes from George Orwell's "Shooting an Elephant." (This essay is part of a collection titled *Shooting an Elephant and Other Essays;* the passage is found on page 165.)

> The orderly came back in a few minutes with a rifle and five cartridges, and meanwhile some Burmans had arrived and told us that the elephant was in the paddy fields below, only a few hundred yards away. As I started forward practically the whole population of the quarter flocked out of the houses and followed me. They had seen the rifle and were all shouting excitedly that I was going to shoot the elephant. They had not shown much interest in the elephant when he was merely ravaging their homes, but it was different now that he was going to be shot. It was a bit of fun to them, as it would be to an English crowd; besides they wanted the meat. It made me vaguely uneasy. I had no intention of shooting the elephant—I had merely sent for the rifle to defend myself if necessary—and it is always unnerving to have a crowd following you. I marched down the hill, looking and feeling a fool, with the rifle over my shoulder and an ever-growing army of people jostling at my heels. At the bottom, when you got away from the huts, there was a metalled road and beyond that a miry waste of paddy fields a thousand yards across, not yet ploughed but soggy from the first rains and dotted with coarse grass. The elephant was standing eight yards from the road, his left side towards us. He took not the slightest notice of the crowd's approach. He was tearing up bunches of grass, beating them against his knees to clean them and stuffing them into his mouth.

Note this sentence early in the paragraph: "They had seen the rifle and were all shouting excitedly that I was going to shoot the elephant." Here are three ineffective or incorrect ways and three effective, correct ways to quote and cite this sentence:

### WEAK: QUOTATION TREATED AS DIALOGUE

**Orwell writes, "They had seen the rifle and were all shouting excitedly that I was going to shoot the elephant" (165).**

This writer is using the same method that fiction writers and journalists use to report dialogue:

He said, ". . . ."

She writes, ". . . ."

In a research paper, however, using an introductory phrase or clause will give the quotation more emphasis and context:

### EFFECTIVE: QUOTATION PRECEDED BY INTRODUCTORY PHRASE OR CLAUSE

**According to Orwell, "They had seen the rifle and were all shouting excitedly that I was going to shoot the elephant" (165).**

**As Orwell notes with annoyance, "They had seen the rifle and were all shouting excitedly that I was going to shoot the elephant" (165).**

### INCORRECT: FLOATING QUOTATION

**The tension builds as Orwell receives the gun. "They had seen the rifle and were all shouting excitedly that I was going to shoot the elephant" (165).**

Quotations must be *connected* to your text, not detached from it. One way to connect a quotation and add variety to your quoting style is to use subordination:

### EFFECTIVE: QUOTATION SUBORDINATED

**As he starts out, Orwell realizes that "They had seen the rifle and were all shouting excitedly that I was going to shoot the elephant" (165).**

The key word is *that,* which *subordinates* Orwell's sentence to the writer's introduction. (For more on subordination, see chapter 4.) **Note:** You can also change "They" to "[t]hey." (For more on using brackets, see page 584.)

### INCORRECT: COMMA SPLICE

**The tension builds as Orwell receives the gun, "They had seen the rifle and were all shouting excitedly that I was going to shoot the elephant" (165).**

This writer has tried to join the quoted sentence with the preceding, introductory sentence but has created a comma splice. (For more on comma splices, see chapters 4 and 25.)

### CORRECT: QUOTATION INTRODUCED BY COLON

**The tension builds as Orwell receives the gun: "They had seen the rifle and were all shouting excitedly that I was going to shoot the elephant" (165).**

The colon at the end of the first sentence indicates that the sentence is introducing the quotation. Remember that you must have a complete sentence followed by a colon (*not* a semicolon) before the quoted text begins. After the colon, you may quote one or more complete sentences, as in the example above, or a word or phrase, as in this example:

> Orwell's phrasing echoes his title: "to shoot the elephant" (165). This task becomes increasingly significant to him as the narrative continues.

These three methods of quoting from sources will help you integrate source material successfully and add variety to your writing. In addition to these methods, the following guidelines will help you use source material accurately and effectively.

1. **Quoting text containing dialogue.** On page 164 of "Shooting an Elephant" this sentence appears:

> There was a loud, scandalized cry of "Go away, child! Go away this instant!" and an old woman with a switch in her hand came round the corner of a hut, violently shooing away a crowd of naked children.

To indicate the quotation within this sentence, you need to change Orwell's double quotation marks to single quotation marks:

> According to Orwell, "There was a loud, scandalized cry of 'Go away, child! Go away this instant!' and an old woman with a switch in her hand came round the corner of a hut, violently shooing away a crowd of naked children" (164).

However, if you are quoting only the woman's speech, you can use double quotation marks:

> The woman seemed both angry and scared: "Go away, child! Go away this instant!" (164).

2. **Using quotation marks with exclamation points and question marks.** In the example above, the quoted sentence ends with an exclamation point. Note that the exclamation point precedes the closing quotation marks, the page citation, and the added period:

> instant!" (164).

A quotation that ends with a question mark is treated similarly:

> instant?" (164).

If the exclamation point or question mark is not part of the quotation but ends your sentence that contains the quotation, it follows the closing quotation mark and page reference:

> Ironically, Orwell notes that he "had no intention of shooting the elephant" (165)!

The writer, not Orwell, is exclaiming here.

3. **Eliding (omitting) text.** Well-chosen quotations can add authority and interest to your writing, but you do not need to quote text that is irrelevant to your point. One way to quote economically is to **elide** (remove) superfluous text. Note this sentence:

They had seen the rifle and were all shouting excitedly that I was going to shoot the elephant.

You might want to remove the end of the sentence:

Orwell writes that "They had seen the rifle and were all shouting excitedly . . ." (165).

The three dots, called an **ellipsis**, indicate that you have removed the end of the sentence.

If you are eliding text *within* the sentence, the ellipsis takes the place of the missing words:

The villagers' reaction was immediate: "They . . . were all shouting excitedly that I was going to shoot the elephant" (165).

However, *do not* use the ellipsis if you are removing the beginning of a single quoted sentence:

The villagers "were all shouting excitedly that I was going to shoot the elephant" (165).

You may start a quotation at any logical point in a sentence, but don't omit words in a way that will change the meaning of the sentence you are quoting.

In some situations, you may want to quote two adjacent sentences and elide part of one of them. Note how this procedure is done:

| ORIGINAL PASSAGE | As I started forward practically the whole population of the quarter flocked out of the houses and followed me. They had seen the rifle and were all shouting excitedly that I was going to shoot the elephant. |
| --- | --- |
| QUOTED WITH AN ELLIPSIS | "As I started forward practically the whole population of the quarter flocked out of the houses and followed me. . . . shouting excitedly that I was going to shoot the elephant" (165). |

4. **Quoting only a few words.** If you want to quote only a few words from a sentence, don't use the ellipsis; instead, embed the quotation within your sentence:

The concept of an elephant "merely ravaging" (165) a home is a terrifying understatement.

Note that the page reference can also appear at the end of the sentence, before the period:

The concept of an elephant "merely ravaging" a home is a terrifying

understatement (165).

5.  **Using square brackets to interpolate your own text.** The next-to-the-last sentence in Orwell's paragraph is "He took not the slightest notice of the crowd's approach." Sentences that begin with pronouns can be difficult. (He who?) Note the following solution:

According to Orwell, "He [the elephant] took not the slightest notice

of the crowd's approach" (165).

The square brackets indicate that you are adding clarifying information. However, you might try an alternate approach:

According to Orwell, the elephant "took not the slightest notice of

the crowd's approach" (165).

Again, you may start quoting at any logical point in the sentence.
   Square brackets are also used to indicate an error—either a misspelling or an obvious factual problem—in text that you are quoting. Note the following examples:

As Bohannon writes, "When President Kennedy was killed in 1964

*[sic]*, the nation was horrified" (419).

Rodgers uses this ancient chestnut: "It is better to give than recieve

*[sic]*" (37).

Kennedy was killed in 1963; *receive* is spelled with the *e* preceding the *i*. The use of *[sic]*, meaning "thus" ("that's the way I found it"), tells your reader that you know the source is incorrect.

6.  **Using block quotations.** According to MLA guidelines, any passage that (a) consists of more than one paragraph or (b) takes up more than four lines in *your* text must be set off as a block quotation, or extract. Here are guidelines for displaying a block quotation:
    - Don't add quotation marks before or after the quotation or alter any quotation marks that appear within the quotation.
    - Start the extract on a new line with a block indent of one inch from the left margin. Most word-processing programs have a default tab indent of half an inch, so use a double-left indent. If you are quoting more than one paragraph, indent the first line of each paragraph an additional half-inch.
    - Don't indent the right side of the quotation or attempt to center the extract.
    - Double-space the extract, and leave only a double space above and below it.

- Place the page reference at the very end of the extract, after the terminal punctuation. Note the following example:

Orwell writes of the building excitement:

> The orderly came back in a few minutes with a rifle and five cartridges, and meanwhile some Burmans had arrived and told us that the elephant was in the paddy fields below, only a few hundred yards away. As I started forward practically the whole population of the quarter flocked out of the houses and followed me. They had seen the rifle and were all shouting excitedly that I was going to shoot the elephant. (165)

Use block quotations sparingly. Never use them as a way to lengthen your paper.

7. **Citing page numbers.** In all of the examples above, note that only a number appears in the parentheses to indicate the page in the source on which the quoted text appears. Do *not* add *page, pg., p.,* or *pp.* If a passage begins on one page and continues to another, then you should indicate the page break this way:

. . . last word" (41-42).

. . . last word" (161-62).

Note that the second hundreds digit is dropped if it is the same as the first one: 161–162 becomes 161–62.

## EXERCISE 20.9

1. The following passage is excerpted from an article written by John Vardamus Doe and published in a regional magazine. The full article appears on pages 22–23 of the magazine. A student wrote an analysis of Doe's article; part of this analysis appears after the excerpt.

   First, read the excerpt. Then read the student's response, which contains ten errors in quoting from Doe's article. Don't try to edit or "smooth out" the response, but look for instances in which the student did not follow proper quoting procedures, and correct the student's errors.

   [from page 22] The debate over Internet content rages on. The defenders of "freedom of choice" make up one side, and those who would protect young people and traditional standards of morality make up the other.

   In the early days of widespread Internet access, several lessons were learned. For example, Wynton's, an upscale grocery chain, offered free Internet access at each of its stores. The practice was stopped when several instances of shoppers' children accessing porn sites brought objections from both the parents and other concerned shoppers. In another instance, the Fresnell County Library system chose to radically restrict the range of Internet access it provided after complaints of hard-core porn images beaming into the face of every patron who walked past the terminals. According to an assistant librarian, "It was like **[page 23 begins here]** walking through an adult bookstore."

Do we want to let adults make adult decisions? Certainly.

Do we want to protect children from clearly inappropriate subject matter? Certainly.

The Internet offers a whole new world of information and communication, but it offers serious problems as well. How will we reconcile these two issues?

### Excerpt of Student's Analysis of Doe's Article

Doe's writing is on the debate between the free speech crowd and the morality groups. He states, "How will we reconcile these two issues" (23). Parents want to protect their children, and adults want to protect their own personal rights to access adult material.

It's true that Internet content can pose problems in public places, libraries, for instance. Before a local library changed its policy, Doe quotes the assistant librarian as describing the situation this way, "It was like walking through an adult bookstore" (23). However, the rights of adults need to be considered as well. The main downfall of Doe's writing is he refuses to take a stand. "Do we want to let adults make decisions? Certainly. Do we want to keep children from clearly inappropriate subject matter? Certainly" (23).

Doe seems to back the morality groups, and to discount the needs of, "defenders of "freedom of choice'" (22). However, he needs to state his case more forcefully and not be afraid to take a stand.

**2.** After correcting the quoting errors in the student's response, revise it so that it is a more effective, coherent, and unified analysis of the passage.

# INCORPORATING DIRECT QUOTATIONS: APA GUIDELINES

The examples in this section are quotations from the following paragraph, which comes from George Orwell's "Shooting an Elephant." (This essay is part of a collection titled *Shooting an Elephant and Other Essays* [1950]; the passage is found on page 165.)

The orderly came back in a few minutes with a rifle and five cartridges, and meanwhile some Burmans had arrived and told us that the elephant was in the paddy fields below, only a few hundred yards away. As I started forward practically the whole population of the quarter flocked out of the houses and followed me. They had seen the rifle and were all shouting excitedly that I was going to shoot the elephant. They had not shown much interest in the elephant when he was merely ravaging their homes, but it was different now that he was going to be shot. It was a bit of fun to them, as it would be to an English crowd;

besides they wanted the meat. It made me vaguely uneasy. I had no intention of shooting the elephant—I had merely sent for the rifle to defend myself if necessary—and it is always unnerving to have a crowd following you. I marched down the hill, looking and feeling a fool, with the rifle over my shoulder and an ever-growing army of people jostling at my heels. At the bottom, when you got away from the huts, there was a metalled road and beyond that a miry waste of paddy fields a thousand yards across, not yet ploughed but soggy from the first rains and dotted with coarse grass. The elephant was standing eight yards from the road, his left side towards us. He took not the slightest notice of the crowd's approach. He was tearing up bunches of grass, beating them against his knees to clean them and stuffing them into his mouth.

Note this sentence early in the paragraph: "They had seen the rifle and were all shouting excitedly that I was going to shoot the elephant." Here are three ineffective or incorrect ways and three effective, correct ways to quote and cite this sentence:

### WEAK: QUOTATION TREATED AS DIALOGUE

**Orwell (1950) writes, "They had seen the rifle and were all shouting excitedly that I was going to shoot the elephant" (p. 165).**

This writer is using the same method that fiction writers and journalists use to report dialogue:

He said, ". . . ."

She writes, ". . . ."

In a research paper, however, using an introductory phrase or clause will give the quotation more emphasis and context.

### EFFECTIVE: QUOTATION PRECEDED BY INTRODUCTORY PHRASE OR CLAUSE

**According to Orwell (1950), "They had seen the rifle and were all shouting excitedly that I was going to shoot the elephant" (p. 165).**

**As Orwell notes with annoyance (1950), "They had seen the rifle and were all shouting excitedly that I was going to shoot the elephant" (p. 165).**

### INCORRECT: FLOATING QUOTATION

**The tension builds as Orwell (1950) receives the gun. "They had seen the rifle and were all shouting excitedly that I was going to shoot the elephant" (p. 165).**

Quotations must be *connected* to your text, not detached from it. One way to connect a quotation and add variety to your quoting style is to use subordination:

### EFFECTIVE: QUOTATION SUBORDINATED

**As he starts out, Orwell (1950) realizes that "they had seen the rifle and were all shouting excitedly that I was going to shoot the elephant" (p. 165).**

The key word is *that,* which *subordinates* Orwell's sentence to the writer's introduction. (For more on subordination, see Chapter 4.)

**INCORRECT: COMMA SPLICE**

**The tension builds as Orwell (1950) receives the gun, "They had seen the rifle and were all shouting excitedly that I was going to shoot the elephant" (p. 165).**

This writer has tried to join the quoted sentence with the preceding, introductory sentence but has created a comma splice. (For more on comma splices, see chapters 4 and 25.)

**CORRECT: QUOTATION INTRODUCED BY COLON**

**The tension builds as Orwell (1950) receives the gun: "They had seen the rifle and were all shouting excitedly that I was going to shoot the elephant" (p. 165).**

The colon at the end of the first sentence indicates that the sentence is introducing the quotation. Remember that you must have a complete sentence followed by a colon (*not* a semicolon) before the quoted text begins. After the colon, you may quote one or more complete sentences, as in the example above, or a word or phrase, as in this example:

Orwell's phrasing echoes his title: "to shoot the elephant" (1950, p. 165). This task becomes increasingly significant to him as the narrative continues.

These three methods of quoting from sources will help you integrate source material successfully and add variety to your writing. In addition to these methods, the following guidelines will help you use source material accurately and effectively.

1.  **Quoting text containing dialogue.** On page 164 of "Shooting an Elephant" this sentence appears:

    There was a loud, scandalized cry of "Go away, child! Go away this instant!" and an old woman with a switch in her hand came round the corner of a hut, violently shooing away a crowd of naked children.

    To indicate the quotation within this sentence, you need to change Orwell's double quotation marks to single quotation marks:

    According to Orwell (1950), "There was a loud, scandalized cry of 'Go away, child! Go away this instant!' and an old woman with a switch in her hand came round the corner of a hut, violently shooing away a crowd of naked children" (p. 164).

    However, if you are quoting only the woman's speech, you can use double quotation marks:

    The woman seemed both angry and scared: "Go away, child! Go away this instant!" (Orwell, 1950, p. 164).

2.  **Using quotation marks with exclamation points and question marks.** In the example above, the quoted sentence ends with an exclamation

point. Note that the exclamation point precedes the closing quotation marks, the page citation, and the added period:

instant!" (Orwell, 1950, p. 164).

A quotation that ends with a question mark is treated similarly:

instant?" (Orwell, 1950, p. 164).

If the exclamation point or question mark is not part of the quotation but ends your sentence that contains the quotation, it follows the closing quotation mark and page reference:

Ironically, Orwell (1950) notes that he "had no intention of shooting the elephant" (p. 165)!

The writer, not Orwell, is exclaiming here.

3. **Eliding (omitting) text.** Well-chosen quotations can add authority and interest to your writing, but you do not need to quote text that is irrelevant to your point. One way to quote economically is to **elide** (remove) superfluous text. Note this sentence:

They had seen the rifle and were all shouting excitedly that I was going to shoot the elephant.

You might want to remove the end of the sentence:

Orwell (1950) writes that "They had seen the rifle and were all shouting excitedly" (p. 165).

You might want to remove the beginning of the sentence:

The villagers "were all shouting excitedly that I was going to shoot the elephant" (Orwell, 1950, p. 165).

You may start a quotation at any logical point in a sentence, but don't omit words in a way that will change the meaning of the sentence you are quoting.

Note that if you are using APA style, you may elide the beginning of a single quoted sentence and/or the end without indicating that you have done so, unless—perhaps to avoid misinterpretation—you need to let readers know that you are not using the whole sentence. To indicate an omission, you will need to use an ellipsis (see below).

If you are eliding text *within* the sentence, an **ellipsis** (three spaced dots) takes the place of the missing words:

The villagers' reaction was immediate: "They . . . were all shouting excitedly that I was going to shoot the elephant" (Orwell, 1950, p. 165).

The ellipsis indicates that you have removed words from the sentence. APA requires that you use an ellipsis if you elide text within a sentence or if you quote two sentences and elide text from the end of the first sentence and/or the beginning of the second one, as in the following example:

ORIGINAL PASSAGE   As I started forward practically the whole population of the quarter flocked out of the houses
and followed me. They had seen the rifle and
were all shouting excitedly that I was going to
shoot the elephant.

QUOTED WITH   "As I started forward practically the whole
AN ELLIPSIS   population of the quarter flocked out of the
houses and followed me. . . . shouting excitedly that I was going to shoot the elephant"
(Orwell, 1950, p. 165).

4. **Quoting only a few words.** If you want to quote only a few words from a
sentence, don't use the ellipsis; instead, embed the quotation within your
sentence:

The concept of an elephant "merely ravaging" (Orwell, 1950, p. 165)

a home is a terrifying understatement.

5. **Using square brackets to interpolate your own text.** The next-to-the-
last sentence in Orwell's paragraph is "He took not the slightest notice of
the crowd's approach." Sentences that begin with pronouns can be
difficult. (He who?) Note the following solution:

According to Orwell (1950), "He [the elephant] took not the slightest

notice of the crowd's approach" (p. 165).

The square brackets indicate that you are adding clarifying information.
However, you might try an alternate approach:

According to Orwell (1950), the elephant "took not the slightest

notice of the crowd's approach" (p. 165).

Again, you may start quoting at any logical point in the sentence.
    Square brackets are also used to indicate an error—either a misspelling
or an obvious factual problem—in text that you are quoting. Note the
following examples:

As Bohannon (2001) writes, "When President Kennedy was killed in

1964 *[sic]*, the nation was horrified" (p. 419).

Rodgers (1999) uses this ancient chestnut: "It is better to give than

recieve *[sic]*" (p. 37).

Kennedy was killed in 1963; *receive* is spelled with the *e* preceding the *i.*
The use of [*sic*], meaning "thus" ("that's the way I found it"), tells your
reader that you know the source is incorrect.

6. **Using block quotations.** According to APA guidelines, any passage that consists of more than one paragraph or contains more than forty words must be set off as a block quotation, or extract. Here are guidelines for displaying a block quotation:

   - Don't add quotation marks before or after the quotation or alter any quotation marks that appear within the quotation.
   - Start the extract on a new line with a block indent of one-half inch from the left margin, which is the default tab indent of most word processing programs. If you are quoting more than one paragraph, indent subsequent paragraphs one-half inch.
   - Don't indent the right side of the quotation or attempt to center the extract.
   - Double-space the extract, and leave only a double space above and below it.
   - Place the page reference at the very end of the extract, after the terminal punctuation. Note the following example:

   Orwell writes of the building excitement:

   > The orderly came back in a few minutes with a rifle and five cartridges, and meanwhile some Burmans had arrived and told us that the elephant was in the paddy fields below, only a few hundred yards away. As I started forward practically the whole population of the quarter flocked out of the houses and followed me. They had seen the rifle and were all shouting excitedly that I was going to shoot the elephant. (165)

   Use block quotations sparingly. Never use them as a way to lengthen your paper.

7. **Citing multiple page numbers.** Note that if a passage begins on one page and continues to another, then you should indicate the page break this way:

   . . . last word" (pp. 161-162).
   . . . last word" (pp. 41-42).

## EXERCISE 20.10

1. The following passage is excerpted from an article written by John Vardamus Doe and published in a regional magazine in 1998. The full article appears on pages 22–23 of the magazine. A student wrote an analysis of Doe's article; part of this analysis appears after the excerpt.

   First, read the excerpt. Then read the student's response, which contains ten errors in quoting from Doe's article. Don't try to edit or "smooth out" the response, but look for instances in which the student did not follow proper quoting procedures, and correct the student's errors.

**[from page 22]** The debate over Internet content rages on. The defenders of "freedom of choice" make up one side, and those who would protect young people and traditional standards of morality make up the other.

In the early days of widespread Internet access, several lessons were learned. For example, Wynton's, an upscale grocery chain, offered free Internet access at each of its stores. The practice was stopped when several instances of shoppers' children accessing porn sites brought objections from both the parents and other concerned shoppers. In another instance, the Fresnell County Library system chose to radically restrict the range of Internet access it provided after complaints of hard-core porn images beaming into the face of every patron who walked past the terminals. According to an assistant librarian, "It was like **[page 23 begins here]** walking through an adult bookstore."

Do we want to let adults make adult decisions? Certainly.

Do we want to protect children from clearly inappropriate subject matter? Certainly.

The Internet offers a whole new world of information and communication, but it offers serious problems as well. How will we reconcile these two issues?

### Excerpt of Student's Analysis of Doe's Article

Doe's writing (1998) is on the debate between the free speech crowd and the morality groups. He states, "How will we reconcile these two issues" (p. 23). Parents want to protect their children, and adults want to protect their own personal rights to access adult material.

It's true that Internet content can pose problems in public places, libraries, for instance. Before a local library changed its policy, Doe quotes the assistant librarian as describing the situation this way, "It was like walking through an adult bookstore" (p. 23). However, the rights of adults need to be considered as well. The main downfall of Doe's writing is he refuses to take a stand. "Do we want to let adults make decisions? Certainly. Do we want to keep children from clearly inappropriate subject matter? Certainly" (p. 23).

Doe seems to back the morality groups, and to discount the needs of, "defenders of 'freedom of choice'" (p. 22). However, he needs to state his case more forcefully, and not be afraid to take a stand.

**2.** After correcting the quoting errors in the student's response, revise it so that it is a more effective, coherent, and unified analysis of the passage.

# THE RESEARCH PAPER

The end of the semester is near, and the English composition instructor is grading a stack of research papers. The instructor opens the first one and starts reading. Here is the third paragraph:

"Students of legal age vote at a surprisingly low rate." (Anderson, pg. 7). According to Anderson, "The franchise given to eighteen-
year-olds in 1972 has apparently decreased in value." (Anderson,
page 7). "Most people don't become fully engaged in the political
process until their late twenties." (pg. 8). And some wait until even
later. "Many observers talk of the "senior stranglehold" over the
political process." (Anderson, page 8, Fox & Snow, pg. 9).

THE INSTRUCTOR MIGHT BE EXCUSED for throwing this "research paper" away
and requesting another attempt from the student. The most interesting
point is that this paragraph was written *after* the instructor lectured for several
class periods about the research paper assignment, showing the class what to
do and what not to do—in other words, providing his or her exact expectations. This student clearly didn't get the message or chose to ignore it.

Students' problems with research papers sometimes arise from their tendency to view the research paper with dread. They envision a huge project that
is somehow unrelated to what they have already learned. However, you should
keep this definition in mind: a research paper is simply a documented essay.
The only real distinguishing feature of a documented essay is its use of sources
and its need to account for that use in an acceptable manner.

Writing a research paper *is* a complicated process, but this process
becomes much easier to approach when it is looked at as a series of steps. For
this reason, the first section of this chapter focuses on the steps that can be
taken in approaching any research paper. The next two sections explore the
guidelines for producing a documented essay provided by the Modern Language Association (MLA) and the guidelines provided by the American Psychological Association (APA). We also include a sample student research paper
that follows MLA guidelines and that illustrates various issues students face
during this process. However, keep in mind that your professor might want
you to use another style, so always clarify this point before you start drafting
the paper.

Chapter 20 covers the process of researching, taking notes, and including
researched material as you draft and revise your paper. Here, we show you how
to use your research to develop an essay that uses secondary sources.

## GENERAL STRATEGIES FOR THE RESEARCH PAPER

Use these strategies for any documented essay that you write:

1. **Read and follow the assignment.** Each research assignment is different,
   and each instructor will specify what he or she wants to see. When grading
   your paper, if the instructor realizes, for example, that instead of using ten
   sources (five print sources and five Internet sources, as specified), you have

used eight Internet sources and no print sources, your essay is at great risk. The same is true if your instructor asked for a minimum of 1,500 words and you produced 975 words, or if your instructor stated that no more than 25 percent of your essay should be taken up by quotations, summaries, and paraphrases, and half of your essay is material taken from secondary sources.

2. **Don't be afraid to ask for clarification.** During your college career you will be asked to write research papers in a range of courses. Many instructors will spell out the guidelines for these assignments; other instructors might be more vague. Some years ago, one of our students asked a history instructor exactly what he was looking for in his research paper assignment. "You know, a research paper," he responded. "You've taken composition; you know what a research paper is."

   The student pressed for clarification: "I know how to do an MLA-style paper with parenthetical documentation. Will that work?" The instructor answered in the affirmative, and the student was then able to approach the assignment with more confidence.

3. **Use your time wisely.** Most instructors give plenty of time for a research paper to be completed; however, some students don't start the process of researching and writing until insufficient time remains. In other words, instructors see the research paper as a series of steps, but some students begin the process the day before the essay is due.

   Consider this hypothetical situation: if either author of this textbook were given an assignment at 6:00 P.M. on a Monday evening to research and write a 2,000-word essay analyzing Thomas Hardy's "Convergence of the Twain," using no fewer than eight sources, all of them from print publications, with the finished essay due at 10:00 A.M. the next day, the writer would (bleary-eyed, no doubt) turn in a good research paper at or before the assigned time. Keep in mind, though, that we have been studying and/or teaching college English for a very long time. We have learned a few things along the way. Even so, with more time to conduct research, plan, and draft, a "good" effort can become an excellent paper.

   Don't even consider trying to write a research paper the night before it is due. Instead, use your time wisely. If you have three weeks to write a paper, consider scheduling approximately a week for research, a week for drafting, and a week for revision. Better yet, if you have twenty-one calendar days, allot about five days for each of these three steps, leaving a six-day window in case of unexpected problems. For example, sometimes you will need to go back to the library after your first draft. More frequently, the demands of your other classes, your family, your relationships, or your job will find a way to cut into your time. If you become ill during the semester, the illness may well occur toward the end of the term, when, unfortunately, research papers tend to be assigned.

4. **Consider the "shape" of your research paper.** During this semester you have been learning to write essays using various rhetorical options: definition,

causal analysis, and so on. Can you organize your essay around one of these frameworks? Probably, but check the wording of your assignment. If your instructor asks you to explore the reasons for the entry of the United States into the Spanish-American War, causal analysis is an obvious strategy. If your instructor asks you to explain how the World Bank decides to lend money to developing nations, process analysis will be your choice. Any topic that asks for "the best" or "the ideal" will need both definition and argument. Some research paper topics will require using a blended option in which you combine various approaches (see Chapter 14).

5. **Prepare carefully.** As Chapter 20 indicates, after you have done the bulk of your research, you will have note cards full of information and language that you will want to incorporate into your research paper. However, this information will be of little use if you do not plan how to organize your essay so that you use your researched material to your best advantage. You need to develop a tentative thesis statement at this point. (For more on developing a working thesis, see Chapter 2.) Although your final thesis may vary somewhat from your earliest version, developing this "guiding principle" will help you focus your efforts. Next, you will need to outline your essay. We suggest using a sentence outline. As you saw in Chapter 2, a sentence outline lists, in order, the proposed thesis statement and the proposed topic sentence of each following paragraph. This outline is not carved in marble; you may need to alter it during the writing process. However, a sentence outline gives you a focus and a tentative organization. Such an outline also lets you write the parts of your essay out of order without worrying about a loss of coherence.

6. **Use your sources carefully, and cite them accurately.** The term *research paper* is perhaps misleading. A better term is *essay that uses research for support.* The essay that you turn in should be guided by your point of view and your assertions, backed up by logic, examples, and the support provided by your sources. Your essay should *not* be a hodgepodge of quotations and paraphrases, with your voice occasionally emerging. What you draw from your sources is secondary to what you write in your own voice.

   Some students are troubled by the thought of exploring a subject and then determining what information needs to be cited. Their concern is valid: using someone else's work without giving proper credit can invite a charge of **plagiarism,** which will have decidedly unpleasant consequences for a student's academic standing. Think of the protocol this way: you are allowed to "use" the work of another, within reason, as long as you acknowledge and credit this source. For specific guidelines on what types of information must be cited, see Chapter 20, page 578.

7. **Separate the drafting process from the revision process.** Once you have your essay written, put it aside for a day or two. The essay will look quite different if you give your brain time to concentrate on something else. Revision and writing require two very different sets of skills. Allow yourself time to regroup, psychologically speaking, before you start to review your draft.

**CATALYST 2.0**

**MORE OPTIONS ONLINE**
To learn more about how to avoid plagiarism, go to
www.mhhe.com/ writingtoday.

# THE MLA-STYLE RESEARCH PAPER

The following discussion is based on the sixth edition of Joseph Gibaldi's *MLA Handbook for Writers of Research Papers,* published by the Modern Language Association (2003). It is widely used by writers in the humanities.

MLA uses a **parenthetical** documentation system, also known as an in-text citation system. It involves citing sources in parentheses in the text of the paper. This approach eliminates the need for footnotes and endnotes, except those needed for further explanation of concepts or citations in the text. Thus, an MLA-based research paper ends with a works-cited section, an alphabetical list of all sources actually used—and cited—in the paper. Each entry in this list contains all the bibliographic data that a reader needs in order to find in the original source the information you have cited. Note that any source cited in the essay must also appear in the works-cited list and that any entry in the works-cited list must be cited in the essay.

## Parenthetical (In-Text) Citations

A parenthetical (in-text) documentation system such as the one used by MLA identifies quickly and unobtrusively the source of any quotation, paraphrase, or summary used in the research paper. Here is an example of such a citation:

> Johnson writes that "the 1998 influx of tourists strained Central
>
> Florida's highways to the breaking point" (22).

The author cited is Johnson; the page from which the quotation has been taken is 22. Alternatively, the author's name can appear with the page number in parentheses following the quotation, paraphrase, or summary. (Note that the period follows the citation.)

> One commentator writes that "the 1998 influx of tourists strained
>
> Central Florida's highways to the breaking point" (Johnson 22).

In general, the first method is preferable because the source is named within the text (for more on strategies for quoting text, see Chapter 20). In either case, however, the reader can expect, upon scanning the works-cited entries, to find an entry such as this:

> Johnson, Karen. "Area Infrastructure Not Keeping Up." <u>Central
>
> Florida in Review</u> Mar. 1999: 21-24.

The citation and the works-cited entry match, and the entry provides the reader with full information about the source.

Parenthetically citing summaries and paraphrases requires the same approach, with the exception that no quotation marks are used:

> Johnson indicates that the region needs an extra 2,000 miles of
>
> roadway (24).

When using a paraphrase or a summary, you should introduce the author's name first and finish with the page reference. Otherwise, the reader will not be able to tell when the paraphrase or summary begins and ends.

### Special Cases

Often, you will need to modify these basic citation forms slightly. Here are some examples:

**1. Citing two or more sources by the same author.** This situation is very common in essays dealing with business or technical topics because writers in those disciplines specialize in an area or have the area assigned as their "beat" by the publication for which they work. In such a case, your in-text citation would include a short title to make clear which article by Johnson is being cited, as in the following examples:

> According to Johnson, "Rapidly shifting demographics in south and east Lake County have upset the formerly tranquil nature of local government" ("Clermont" 28).

> As one observer writes, "Commuters in northwest Orange County are most affected" (Johnson, "Area" 21).

The works-cited entries for such a situation are shown on page 609.

**2. Combining direct quotations with your own sentence.** To integrate a direct quotation in this way, you need to place quotation marks in the proper places, making certain that the quotation works naturally and correctly with your own language. Include a parenthetical citation that contains the author's name and the page number if the author's name is not mentioned in the text, or just the page number if the author's name *is* mentioned.

> Aletha Huston explains that the government could well end up satisfying "the short-term goal of reduced welfare costs while leading to long-term social problems of school failure and delinquency for children who experience unsafe and inadequate care during their early years" (16).

Chapter 20 has detailed coverage of the process of integrating quotations into your text.

**3. Using a direct quotation longer than four lines.** MLA format requires that quotations longer than four typed lines be double-spaced and indented one inch from the left margin. Because the quotation is indented, no quotation marks are used except in cases where quotation marks appear in the original:

> In *India: Myths and Legends,* Donald MacKenzie explains the importance of priests in Indian literature and religion:
>
>> Priests were poets and singers in early Vedic times. A Rishi was a composer of hymns to the gods, and several are named in the collections. Every great family appears to have had its bardic priest and its special poetic anthology which was handed down from generation to generation. Old poems might be rewritten and added to, but the ambition of the sacred poet was to sing a new song to the gods. The oldest Vedic hymns are referred to as "new songs," which suggests that others were in existence. (33)

**Note:** For a long (block) quotation, the parenthetical citation comes after the period. For a short quotation, which is not set off, the period comes after the citation.

**4. Using a source with two or three authors.** Name all of the authors in the text of the paper (use last names only):

> Kelemen and Callahan argue that the "financial crises experienced by many American cities have more to do with poor fiscal planning than with demographic factors" (67).

> Spano, Del Vecchio, and Price indicate that "the need for developmental courses in reading is increasing in four-year and two-year colleges alike" (85).

> Research into the spread of Spanish influenza now proves that "the disease killed more people than were killed in all of World War I" (Swanicke, Szilagyi, and De Lisi 14).

**5. Using a source with more than three authors.** In such cases, you can simply use the name of the first author listed followed by the abbreviation *et al.,* a Latin abbreviation for "and others."

> The history of medicine traces the "derivation of many modern pharmaceuticals to herbs and other natural sources" (Coleman et al. 44).

**6. Citing information from a corporate or organizational author.**
If your source has as its author the Southeastern Maritime Commission, for
example, treat it no differently than a source written by a named person. If the
corporate author appears with the page number in a parenthetical citation,
include its full name:

> (Southeastern Maritime Commission 574)

You can use common abbreviations, such as *Natl.* for *National,* to shorten the
name of a corporate author given in parentheses.

**7. Citing a source with no author named.** If a print source lists neither a
person (by name) nor a corporate author, cite the title of the source along with
the page number. Never cite "Anonymous," "Staff," or "Wire Reports." Use the
full title in the text, but shorten the title to a few words if it appears in the
parenthetical citation:

> According to the article "Homeless Focus Shifts to South Patterson,"
>
> "area authorities want to build a homeless shelter near a subdivision
>
> despite residents' objections" (23).

> According to a recent article, "area authorities want to build a
>
> homeless shelter near a subdivision despite residents' objections"
>
> ("Homeless Focus Shifts" 23).

**8. Including a quotation found in another source.** If you are using a
quotation that your source has taken from yet another source, use "qtd. in" for
"quoted in" in the parenthetical citation:

> According to Burke, "The greater the power, the more dangerous the
>
> abuse" (qtd. in Frary 18).

**9. Including information from a selection in an anthology.** An
anthology is a collection of works (poems, essays, plays, stories, and the like)
put together by an editor. Cite information from such a selection by the name
of the author, not the name of the editor. For example, *The Best American Essays
1997,* which is edited by Ian Frazier, contains an essay called "Black Swans" by
Lauren Slater. Here's what a citation to this essay might look like:

> Slater celebrates a child's fascination with snow: "There is some-
>
> thing satisfying and scary about making an angel, lowering your
>
> bulky body into the drowning fluff, stray flakes landing on your
>
> face" (144).

The format for a works-cited entry for a work in an anthology is shown on page 610.

**10. Using ideas from an entire work.** Indicate the author's name in the text or parenthetical citation. Obviously, no page number can be given. Take this example from *A Drinking Life,* the autobiography of Pete Hamill:

> A Drinking Life chronicles the life of its author, but it also provides
>
> insight into the events and people who made history in America from
>
> the 1940s through the 1960s (Hamill).

**11. Using material from two different authors with the same last name.** Simply include both the first names and last names of the authors in the citations or the text:

> Greek sculpture illustrates the "endless struggle between the flesh
>
> and the spirit" (Edith Hamilton 65).

**12. Including information from two sources in the same sentence.** Use a semicolon to separate the authors and page numbers in the parenthetical citation:

> There were important differences in the ways the ancient Greeks
>
> and Romans worshipped even though their gods were virtually the
>
> same (Romero 52; Christiansen 184).

**13. Including material from a work in more than one volume.** If you take information from one volume in a multivolume work, indicate the volume number in the parenthetical citation. Separate the volume and page numbers with a colon and a space:

> In the Encyclopedia of Philosophy, Wooldruff explains that the British
>
> chemist and physicist Michael Farraday began his career as a book-
>
> binder (3: 18).

**14. Including material from printed works that are not paginated or from online sources.** In the case of printed sources, you can use paragraph numbers if they appear in the the source; otherwise, you need to cite the entire work (see guideline 10). For online sources, cite the author's name if no page numbers are available. If the source lists no author, cite the title of the online source in quotation marks. As in guideline 7 above, if you place a long title in a parenthetical citation, shorten it to a few words—enough so that your reader can match the title to the appropriate works-cited entry.

**15. Using content endnotes.** Use such notes only if you need to provide explanations that go beyond what you can place within parentheses. Indicate an endnote by using a superscript number (most word-processing programs have an automatic function for this). At the end of your text—before the list of works cited—type the heading *Note* or *Notes,* depending on the number of notes that you have, and use a superscript number again to begin the note, as in the following example:

> There is always the sense, when one reads Percy's novels, of a conscious avoidance of Faulkner, and when Percy does get a bit too close—as in the depiction of Ed Barrett in The Second Coming—the effect is eerie.[1]

This endnote appears at the end of the text:

Note

[1]Although Faulkner was an occasional guest of Will Percy, Walker Percy never met him there. When Percy and Foote were undergraduates, they once traveled through Oxford, but when Foote stopped to visit Faulkner, Percy claims to have stayed in the car. Although Percy later professed to be somewhat embarrassed by what he saw as callow behavior (see "A Talk with Walker Percy" [85]), his conscious "avoidance" of his predecessor was obviously a lifelong habit.

Chapter 20 includes additional guidelines for quoting, especially quotations that relate to writing about literature. Refer to them as needed.

## The Works-Cited List

The last element of your research paper is the works-cited section, a list of entries that tells your reader the sources you have used and cited in the paper. Entries are alphabetized by the last name of the source's author. Sources with more than one author should be alphabetized by the last name of the first author appearing in the work's byline. Sources that don't have named authors, either human or corporate, are alphabetized by the first major word in the title, as shown in the following alphabetized list:

Harper, Leo

Lefou, Ariel

Le Franc, David

Maritime Fisheries Commission

"The Nature of Wax Beetles"

Roth, Michelle

Roth-Lynn, Leo

Rothman, Thomas

1. For alphabetizing purposes, articles (*the, a,* and *an*) are disregarded. "The Nature of Wax Beetles" is alphabetized using the word *Nature*.

2. Le Franc is treated as one word, so it follows Lefou.

3. Roth has fewer letters than Roth-Lynn, and the hyphen is disregarded in Roth-Lynn so that "Rothl" precedes "Rothm."

## *The Basic Works-Cited Format*

Most works-cited entries include author, title, and publishing information. Here is a basic entry for a book by one author:

Peters, Elizabeth. <u>Night Train to Memphis</u>. New York: Warner, 1994.

Note the following:

1. The author's name is inverted, with the last name appearing first.

2. The first line of the entry starts on the left margin. Succeeding ("turnover") lines are indented half an inch.

3. The first letter of the first word in the title is always capitalized. The first letters of all other words in the title are capitalized except for articles (*a, an, the*) and prepositions and conjunctions of fewer than five letters (*and, but, to, of, with,* and so on). If the title has a colon, the first letter of the first word after the colon is capitalized. Titles of books and periodicals are underlined (or italicized).

4. Works-cited entries, like the rest of the essay, are double-spaced.

The rest of this section lists and describes standard MLA works-cited entries. For more information, refer to the *MLA Handbook for Writers of Research Papers,* sixth edition. However, before you begin looking at the works-cited entries, examine the following pages, which will help you find the information that you will use to create these entries.

### Article in an Online Magazine

Author's name                                              Article title

Saletan, William. "Girl, Interrupted: The Power to Shrink Human Beings."

Magazine        Date of        Date of
title              posting        access                                    URL

<u>Slate</u> 20 Jan. 2007. 22 Jan. 2007. <www.slate.com/id/2157861/?nav=tap3>.

## Book with One Author

Author's name                     Book title and subtitle

Fussell, Paul. <u>Abroad: British Literary Traveling Between the Wars</u>.

City of          Publisher      Year of
publication                     publication

New York: Oxford UP, 1980.

*British Literary Traveling Between the Wars* by Paul Fussell, Oxford University Press, 1980. Used with permission.

Copyright © 1980 by Paul Fussell

Library of Congress Cataloging in Publication Data

Fussell, Paul, 1924-
Abroad.

Bibliography: p.
Includes index.
1.   English prose literature—20th century—History and criticism.   2.   Voyages and travels in literature.
3.   Authors, English—20th century—Journeys.
4.   British in foreign countries.   I.   Title.
PR808.V68F8   1980      820'.9'355      80-12810
ISBN 0-19-502767-1

Grateful acknowledgment is made to the following for permission to quote material in copyright:
B. H. Blackwell Ltd., for excerpts from "When It's Over," © 1917 from *A Lap Full of Seed* by Max Plowman. Jonathan Cape for excerpts from *The Road to Oxiana* by Robert Byron, © 1937; for excerpts from *One's Company: A Journey to China* by Peter Fleming, © 1934. Chatto & Windus Ltd., for excerpts from "It

# ABROAD

## British Literary Traveling
## Between the Wars

### PAUL FUSSELL

New York   Oxford
OXFORD UNIVERSITY PRESS
1980

*British Literary Traveling Between the Wars* by Paul Fussell, Oxford University Press, 1980. Used with permission.

## Article in a Journal with Consecutive Pagination

Author's name           Article title

Myers, Martha A. "Gender and Southern Punishment After the Civil War."

Journal    Volume, year, and
title      page range

Criminology 33 (1995): 17-46.

# CRIMINOLOGY

## AN INTERDISCIPLINARY JOURNAL

### THE OFFICIAL PUBLICATION OF THE AMERICAN SOCIETY OF CRIMINOLOGY

99827

VOLUME 33          NUMBER 1          FEBRUARY 1995

# GENDER AND SOUTHERN PUNISHMENT AFTER THE CIVIL WAR*

MARTHA A. MYERS
The University of Georgia

*Recent scholarship raises two questions about the historical relationship between gender and official responses to criminality. First, to what extent has the formal social control of women changed in the past two centuries? Second, to what extent can changes in the presence of women within the criminal justice system be traced to the same factors that account for the changing presence of men? To address these questions, I focus on women incarcerated for felonies in a southern state (Georgia) between 1870 and 1940. Along with a comparable sample of male offenders, this population forms the basis of a time-series analysis that compares, and seeks to account for, trends in admission rates. The analysis yields little evidence that women disappeared from formal systems of punishment. Instead, there were gender similarities in punishment trends and in explanations for those trends. Concluding the paper is a discussion of its implications for further research on gender differences in punishment.*

Criminality among women is actually infrequent and we may expect its gradual disappearance. Delinquency on the distaff side is bad news for the human race.

> —Miriam van Waters (1941:123)

Over half a century ago, Miriam van Waters, superintendent of the Reformatory for Women in Framingham, Massachusetts, lamented the negligible attention the research community paid to female criminality (van Waters, 1941). Although interest has been slow to shift, the same charge would be less justifiable today. Since the 1970s, social scientists have examined gender differences in crime, in explanations for criminality, and in the nature and severity of official reactions to criminality (see, e.g., Harvey et al., 1992; Steffensmeier and Allan, 1995; Steffensmeier et al., 1993). Of more recent vintage are studies of the past, particularly crime and responses to crime in the 18th and 19th centuries. This paper fixes attention on an unfamiliar context, the American South, to address two familiar issues raised by these studies. The first issue is the extent to which temporal changes in punishment differed for women and men, and the second is the existence of gender differences in factors that account for

---

* This paper is a revised version of a paper presented at the annual meetings of the American Society of Criminology, October 27–30, 1993, Phoenix, Arizona.

### Newspaper Article

Author's name       Article title       Newspaper title

James, Joni. "Session Strikes a Deal." St. Petersburg Times

Date of publication    Edition    Page range

22 Jan. 2007, Tampa ed.: 1A+.

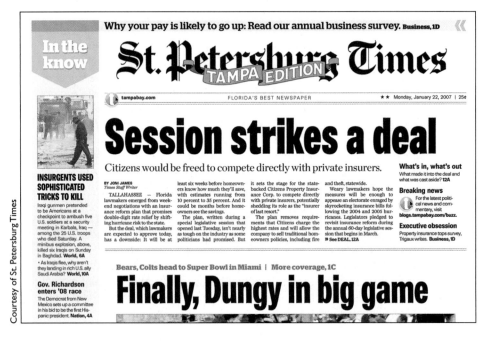

Courtesy of St. Petersburg Times

### MLA Citations—Books

### Book with One Author

Percy, Walker. The Moviegoer. New York: Knopf, 1961.

The publisher's full name is Alfred A. Knopf, Inc. As in this entry, use a shortened version of the publisher's name, and never include *Inc.*

### Book with Two Authors

Brooks, Tim, and Earle Marsh. The Complete Directory to Prime Time

Network and Cable TV Shows: 1946-Present. New York: Ballantine, 1995.

Note that the second author's name is not inverted.

### Book with Three Authors

Vander, Arthur, James Sherman, and Dorothy Luciano. Human Physiology:

The Mechanics of Body Function. 8th ed. New York: McGraw, 2000.

This is an eighth edition, as noted after the title.

## Book with More Than Three Authors

You may type the first author's name, last name first, followed by a comma and *et al.* This is an abbreviation for *et alia,* the Latin for "and others." (If you wish to include all of the names, however, you may do so.)

> Malikin, David, et al. <u>Social Disability: Alcoholism, Drug Addiction, Crime,</u>
>
> <u>and Social Disadvantage</u>. New York: New York UP, 1973.

This publisher is New York University Press. Any university press should be designated by *UP.*

## Two or More Works by the Same Author

> Johnson, Karen. "Area Infrastructure Not Keeping Up." <u>Central Florida in</u>
>
> <u>Review</u> Mar. 1999: 21-24.
>
> —-. "Clermont Council at Impasse." <u>Central Florida in Review</u> June 1999:
>
> 28-29.

Note that the two entries are alphabetized by title, with "Area" preceding "Clermont." The three hyphens mean "ditto," Karen Johnson again.

## Book with Corporate or Organizational Author

> American Psychological Association. <u>Publication Manual of the American</u>
>
> <u>Psychological Association</u>. 5th ed. Washington, DC: American
>
> Psychological Association, 2001.

## Book with an Editor

If you are using information from a book's editor (editors often introduce and comment on work they are presenting), use the abbreviation *ed.* or *eds.,* as in the following:

> Garrod, H. W., ed. <u>Keats: Poetical Works</u>. London: Oxford UP, 1970.

This means that you have taken information from Garrod, not from Keats.

If you are using information from the author of a book that has been edited by someone else, place the author's name first, followed by the title, followed by the abbreviation *Ed(s).,* followed by the name of the editor(s).

> Twain, Mark. <u>A Connecticut Yankee in King Arthur's Court</u>. Ed. Allison E.
>
> Ensor. New York: Norton, 1982.

## Book in a Later Edition

> Gibaldi, Joseph. <u>MLA Handbook for Writers of Research Papers</u>. 6th ed.
>
> New York: Modern Language Association, 2003.

### Book in More Than One Volume

> Daiches, David. <u>A Critical History of English Literature</u>. 2nd ed. 2 vols.
>
> New York: Ronald, 1970.

This is the works-cited format used when you are referring to all volumes of a multivolume work. In the text of the paper, you would cite page numbers by volume: (2: 107), for example. However, if you are citing only one of the volumes of a multivolume work, here is the format for the works-cited entry:

> Daiches, David. <u>A Critical History of English Literature</u>. 2nd ed. Vol. 2.
>
> New York: Ronald, 1970.

In the text, you would need to cite page numbers only.

### Book in a Series

> Knapp, Bettina L. <u>Voltaire Revisited</u>. Twayne's World Authors Ser.: French
>
> Lit. New York: Twayne, 2000.

You can use *Ser.* for *Series* and other common abbreviations such as *Lit.* for *Literature*.

### Book of Collected Essays or an Anthology

> Montaigne, Michel Eyquem de. <u>The Complete Essays of Montaigne</u>. Trans.
>
> Donald M. Frame. Palo Alto: Stanford UP, 1958.
>
> Frazier, Ian, ed. <u>The Best American Essays 1997</u>. Boston: Houghton, 1997.

Use this format when you want to refer to a whole collection of essays, not an individual essay.

### Essay in an Anthology or a Collection
See also page 600.

> Montaigne, Michel Eyquem de. "Of Constancy." <u>The Complete Essays of</u>
>
> <u>Montaigne</u>. Trans. Donald M. Frame. Palo Alto: Stanford UP, 1958. 30-31.
>
> Ozick, Cynthia. "A Drugstore Eden." <u>The Best American Essays 1997</u>. Ed. Ian
>
> Frazier. Boston: Houghton, 1997. 98-110.

Use this format when you want to refer to one essay in a collection, not the whole collection. The translator's or editor's name follows the title.

### More Than One Essay in an Anthology or a Collection

> Frazier, Ian, ed. <u>The Best American Essays 1997</u>. Boston: Houghton, 1997.
>
> Ozick, Cynthia. "A Drugstore Eden." <u>The Best American Essays 1997</u>.
>
> Frazier 98-110.

When you need to cite more than one essay from the same anthology or collection, MLA allows you to use the shortened format shown above. List the book, and then list each essay as demonstrated in the Ozick example.

### Translation

> Dostoyevsky, Fyodor. <u>Crime and Punishment</u>. Trans. Sidney Monas.
>
> > New York: New American Library, 1980.

## MLA Citations—Periodical Articles

The three types of articles are journal (academic) articles, magazine articles, and newspaper articles.

### Article in a Journal with Consecutive Pagination

> Jones, Karen. "Second-Hand Moral Knowledge." <u>Journal of Philosophy</u> 96
>
> > (1999): 55-78.

Like most academic journals, this one starts the first issue of each year on page 1 and then numbers consecutively throughout the year. The volume number for 1999 is 96.

### Article in a Journal Paginated by Issue

> Lützeler, Paul. "Goethe and Europe." <u>South Atlantic Review</u> 65.2 (2000):
>
> > 95-113.

This journal starts each issue on page 1. This is volume 65, issue number 2 (65.2).

### Article in a Magazine Published Monthly

> Codman, Ogden, Jr. "The Decoration of Town Houses: Renovating a
>
> > Manhattan Residence." <u>Architectural Digest</u> Oct. 1997: 164-71.

Entries for magazine articles don't include volume numbers, just dates of publication. Note that all months except May, June, and July are abbreviated.

### Article in a Magazine Published Weekly

> Branson, Louise. "Children of the Tunnels." <u>Maclean's</u> 8 Nov. 1993: 29-30.

Note the inverted date.

### Magazine Article Without Author

> "Flour Power." <u>Harper's Bazaar</u> Dec. 1989: 200+.

The page listing (200+) indicates that the article "jumps"; it starts on page 200 but continues after an interval of some pages.

### Essay in an Anthology or Collection

See page 610.

### Article in a Daily Newspaper

> Tanner, Lindsey. "Study Shows Men Listen with Half a Brain." <u>Lakeland
>
> Ledger</u> [Florida] 29 Nov. 2000: A4.

The *Lakeland Ledger* is a local newspaper, so the state (Florida) needs to be added for exact identification. However, newspapers with the city's name in the title or nationally published newspapers such as the *Wall Street Journal* do not need further identification.

### Article Unsigned in a Daily Newspaper

> "Mexican Drug Cartel May Be Linked to 3 US Dead." <u>Los Angeles Times</u>
>
> 12 May 2000: 5.

Simply start with the title of the article.

### Editorial in a Daily Newspaper

> "The Gun Windmills." Editorial. <u>Wall Street Journal</u> 13 Dec. 1999: A34.

Since editorials are normally unsigned, you can use the same format as you would for an unsigned article except that you must include the word *Editorial* immediately after the title.

### Review in a Magazine or Newspaper

> Lane, Anthony. "Blown Away." Rev. of <u>Arlington Road</u>, dir. Mark Pellington, and
>
> The Lovers on the Bridge, dir. Leos Carax. <u>New Yorker</u> 19 July 1999: 98-99.

> Preston, William J. "The Politics of Hysteria." Rev. of Many Are the
>
> <u>Crimes: McCarthyism in America</u>, by Ellen Schrecker. <u>Los Angeles
>
> Times</u> 31 May 1998: Book Reviews 6.

### MLA Citations—Online Sources

Online documentation is evolving. The following is based on the most recent MLA guidelines.

### Online Document Retrieved from an Information Database, Online Project, or Professional Web Site

Information databases and online projects are sponsored by a number of organizations, including news and media corporations, professional groups, and educational institutions. Your college or university library may subscribe to several of these resources. They contain abstracts of articles, articles in their entirety, books, chapters of books, poems, and a variety of other materials you might find useful. Cite such sources as follows:

1. Name of author, last name first
2. Title of the work in quotation marks or, if it is a book, underlined
3. Name of the database, project, or Web site, underlined
4. Electronic publication data, including the date of the electronic publication or of the most recent update; the name of the database or project sponsor; and the version number (if available)
5. The date you accessed the material
6. The uniform resource locator (URL) in angle brackets. If the URL must be divided between lines, divide it after a slash.

> O'Hanlon, Larry. "Extreme Measures: The Art of Analyzing Natural
>
> Disasters." 25 Feb. 2000. <u>Discovery Channel Online</u>. Discovery
>
> Channel. 17 Sept. 2000 <http://www.discovery.com/news/features/
>
> disasters/disasters.html>.

The title of the database is *Discovery Channel Online*. The work was published electronically on February 25, 2000. The sponsor of the database is the Discovery Channel. The date the student accessed the material is September 17, 2000. The URL appears in angle brackets.

### Online Article from a Scholarly Journal

> Loranger, Carol. "'This Book Spill Off the Page in All Directions': What Is
>
> the Text of <u>Naked Lunch</u>?" <u>Postmodern Culture</u> 10.1 (1999). 27 Aug.
>
> 2000 <http://muse.jhu.edu/journals/pmc/v010/10.1loranger.html>.

*Postmodern Culture* is an online scholarly journal. Note that the information that is given is similar to information that would appear in an entry for a print journal article (see page 611).

### Online Article from a Weekly or Monthly Magazine

> Saletan, William. "Electoral Knowledge." <u>Slate</u> 28 Nov. 2000. 30 Nov. 2000
>
> <http://slate.msn.com/framegame/entries/00-11-28_94258.asp>.

### Online Article from a Newspaper or News Service

> Babinek, Mark. "Railroad Killer Gets Death Penalty." <u>San Francisco</u>
>
> <u>Examiner</u> 22 May 2000: 3 pp. 27 May 2000 <http://examiner.com/
>
> ap_a/AP_Railroad_Killer.html>.

As in the example above, provide the number of pages if this information is available.

### Article Accessed Through an Online Library Service (Information Database)

Hannon, Kerry. "The Joys of a Working Vacation." U.S. News & World

Report 10 June 1996: 89-90. OCLC First Search. College of Lake

County Lib. 22 Oct. 2001 <http://newfirstsearch.oclc.org/WebZ/

FSPag...-64142-ct4j2jzt-cqj0po:entity pagenum=111:0>.

College and university libraries, as well as some public libraries, usually subscribe to at least one online access service. These services allow researchers quick access to periodical articles that are available online. Note that the information from the author through the page range is the same as it would be for a works-cited entry of the print version of the article. This information is followed by the underscored name of the access service, the library, the date accessed, and the URL, which is provided by the access service.

### Article Published by an Online Scholarly Project

"Jane Austen's Brothers and Sister." Jane Austen Information Page. Ed.

Henry Churchyard. 6 Sept 2000. 30 March 2007 <http://

www.pemberley.com/janeinfo/janelife.html#janesibl>.

### Article Published on a Professional Web Site

Dockray, Keith. "The Wars of the Roses: The Political History of the Wars."

The Richard III Society Web Site. 6 Dec. 2006. 17 Feb. 2007 <http://

www.richardiii.net/begin.htm>.

### E-Mail Message

Start with the name of the sender, followed by the title of the e-mail (if any) in quotation marks. Next, indicate the kind of document being cited and its recipient. End with the date the e-mail was sent.

Cornell, Pamela J. "Re: Tips on Toddlers." E-mail to the author. 29

Aug. 2002.

### Online Book Previously Published in Print Form

Melville, Herman. The Piazza Tales. 1856. ESP: Electronic Scholarly

Publishing. 21 Oct. 2000 <http://www.esp.org/books/melville/

piazza>.

Melville's book is available in print form and online. The entry for the digital version shows author, title, original publication date, provider, date of access, and URL.

### Part of Online Book Previously Published in Print Form

Melville, Herman. "Benito Cereno." <u>The Piazza Tales</u>. 1856. <u>ESP:</u>

<u>Electronic Scholarly Publishing</u>. 24 Oct. 2000 <http://www.esp.org/

books/melville/piazza/contents/cereno.html>.

"Benito Cereno" is one of the stories that make up *The Piazza Tales*.

### Posting to a Forum, Newsgroup, or Discussion Group

**Forum message:** Start with the author's name, last name first. In quotation marks, provide the title of the posting (if available), followed by the words *Online posting* and the date the message was posted. Provide the name of the "thread" or subject being discussed (if available) and the title of the forum sponsoring the discussion. End with the date you accessed the message, and the URL.

Harrington, J. K. "Publishing." Online posting. 19 May 2000. The Writing Life:

Inkspot Writers' Community Forums. 25 May 2000 <http://writers-bbs.

com/inkspot/threads.cgi?action=almsgs&forum=writinglife>.

**Newsgroup posting:** Begin with the author's name, followed by the subject of the discussion in quotation marks. Follow this with the words *Online posting,* the date of the posting, the date you accessed the message, and the URL.

**Discussion group message:** Begin with the author's name, followed by the subject of the discussion in quotation marks. Follow this with the words *Online posting,* the date of the posting, the name of the discussion group if available, the date you accessed the message, and the URL.

Note that such resources may be open to anyone who has access to the Internet, whether or not he or she is an expert on the subject being discussed. Therefore, be extra careful about the validity of the information you take from forums, discussion groups, and the like.

## MLA Citations—Miscellaneous Sources

### Dictionary Entry

"Carpe Diem." <u>The Random House Dictionary of the English Language</u>.

9th ed. 1966.

### Encyclopedia Entry

"Athabascan." <u>Concise Columbia Encyclopedia</u>. 3rd ed. 1994.

### Government Publication

United States. Bureau of Labor Statistics. <u>Employment and Earnings</u>.

Washington, DC: GPO, 1992.

*GPO* stands for "Government Printing Office."

### Published Interview

Johnson, Paul. "Live with TAE: Interview with Paul Johnson." <u>American</u>

<u>Enterprise</u> Sept./Oct. 1998: 20-23.

Begin with the name of the person interviewed. Follow with the title of the interview, if any, in quotation marks. If the interview has no title, simply include the word *Interview* after the subject's name.

### Personal, Telephone, or E-Mail Interview

Rodriguez, Dr. Myra S. Personal interview. 6 Sept. 2000.

### Personal Letter

Cornell, Matthew Robert. Letter to the author. 9 June 1998.

Begin with the writer's name, followed by *Letter to the author* and the date the letter was written.

### Sound Recording

Puccini, Giacomo. <u>La Bohème</u>. Perf. Luciano Pavarotti, Mirella Freni,

Elizabeth Hardwood, and Gianni Maffeo. Opera of Berlin Chor. and

Berlin Phil. Orch. Cond. Herbert von Karajan. London, 1972.

Begin with the name of the composer, speaker, or singer, followed by the title of the work. Then, if appropriate, include the names of the leading performers, the orchestra, and the conductor. Conclude with the name of the recording company and date of the recording. Note that in this case London is the name of the recording company, not the place in which the recording took place.

### Film

<u>Strictly Ballroom</u>. Dir. Baz Luhrmann. Perf. Paul Mercurio and Tara Morice.

Miramax, 1992.

### Television or Radio Program

"Mountain Wedding." <u>The Andy Griffith Show</u>. CBS. 29 Apr. 1963.

CATALYST 2.0

**MORE OPTIONS ONLINE**
For more help with
formatting works-cited
entries, go to
www.mhhe.com/
writingtoday.

## MLA Research Paper Format

Double-space the essay on white 8½" × 11" paper, using text margins of one inch at the top, bottom, and sides. Use a standard text font, such as Times, Courier, Palatino, Garamond, or Goudy, in 12-point type. Indent one-half inch for the beginning of paragraphs, but don't leave extra space between paragraphs.

Unless your instructor asks for a title page, start your essay with this format:

Your Name

Professor _____

Course Name and Section

23 October 20__

Title of Your Research Paper

First line of your research paper.

Notice that all elements are double-spaced, with no extra space between them. For page numbering, use the "header" function on your computer. The header appears at the upper right corner of each page, one-half inch from the top of the page, and consists of your last name and the page number:

Surname 1

The page numbering continues through the end of the document, which will be your works-cited section.

Start the works-cited section on a new page immediately after the end of your text. Center the words *Works Cited*. Then start the first entry on the next line after the head. As with the rest of your essay, this section is double-spaced, with no extra space added.

Once again, follow your instructor's directions if they differ from the above guidelines.

## Sample Research Paper in MLA Format

The documented essay that appears on the following pages was written by Valerie Richfield. Her class was researching the condition of the working poor in the United States. Ms. Richfield selected and developed a related topic—subsidies for day care—and then wrote an argumentative research paper that criticizes current U.S. policies.

Valerie Richfield

Dr. Pharr

ENC 1102.37

25 April 2001

Child Care and the Working Poor

The idea of the "working poor" seems to be a bit contradictory. If people <u>work</u>, then the assumption is that they are
making money. In the United States, then, why are so many
working people <u>poor</u>? The answer lies in the fact that many
people lack the skills necessary for a well-paying job; therefore, these people have limited job opportunities, and the
majority of the available jobs provide very low salaries.

The difference between the working poor and the welfare
poor is not as distinct as some may believe. A huge overlap
actually exists. Both of these groups endure a very uncertain
economic life. The welfare poor and the working poor could
definitely benefit from a larger job market with higher wages
and the availability of affordable health insurance and child
care. However, the welfare poor receive money from the government every month, while the working poor depend primarily on themselves.

Of the world's major, industrialized countries, the United
States offers a unique situation. As Barbara R. Bergmann points
out,

> The countries of Western Europe have programs in place
> that work to shield children and their families. . . . They

*Black quote*

have built programs and devoted large sums of taxpay-
ers' money to this effort. On a per capita basis, these
countries spend a great deal more money than Americans
do for programs benefiting children. They provide
income supplements and housing assistance; all of their
children have access to medical care under national
health insurance schemes; some of these countries provide government-sponsored child care that is free or
highly subsidized. The availability of such low-cost child
care enables many single parents to take jobs and free
themselves from total dependence on government cash
grants. (5)

*[handwritten annotations: "Only I quote in into", "page # of source"]*

The United States takes a more laissez-faire approach that
leads to the survival of the fittest. The poor, especially the
working poor, are largely expected to fend for themselves.

In this country, one of the many problems the working poor
must face is the issue of child care. Since they have such low-
paying jobs, the working poor just barely get by, using almost
all of their money to pay for the necessities of life such as
shelter and food. It is virtually impossible for them to be able
to afford the expenses of child care after their vital bills are
paid. If the government wants people working in order to
escape from welfare, then it is essential that the working poor
receive help with the cost of child care, only until they can
finance it themselves. Some people argue over how poor parents have to be to receive government assistance. A thoroughly

Author's name
introduces block
quotation, so
there is no
need to include
it in the paren-
thetical citation.

Widely available
information
about the work-
ing poor does
not need to be
documented.

**619**

reasonable response is that as long as the parents are working at minimum wage and are unable to completely support
their family, it is crucial that government assist with the
problem of financing their child care.

Government support for families needing child care is critical for several reasons. The number of women working these
days is growing; therefore, the availability of child care is crucial in maintaining their employment. Michele Friedman claims
that in the middle decades of the twentieth century, less than
20 percent of mothers were in the work force, but by the end
of the twentieth century, the number had increased to 65 percent of mothers with children six or younger. Subsequently,
child care is necessary for the increasing number of women
who are trying to sustain their job(s). Moreover, because many
of the women belong to the working poor, it is imperative that
they receive assistance with financing their children's care.
Another reason that child care aid is so important is that people
who earn the minimum wage cannot possibly afford child care
expenses. Friedman gives an example:

> Child care expenses can range anywhere from $4,000 to
> $10,000 a year per child. . . . In 1997, the median annual
> income of the average female-headed household was
> $17,256. At such earning levels, child care expenses can
> easily consume one third or more of the household budget.

In this instance, the expenses of child care would leave very
little money for other needs. Therefore, many people are

---

**Thesis statement.**

**Paraphrased information from a Web site does not include a page number.**

**Quotation introduced with a colon. Ellipsis indicates that words have been omitted.**

forced to stay home because of their family responsibilities, and they are thus unable to escape from this cycle of economic dependency. The working poor need assistance in order to improve their lives.

The role that the government actually plays in helping the working poor is an important issue. Each state can use the money the federal government grants it in different ways. Harrell R. Rodgers explains how states use this money:

> The states might use some of the funds to subsidize providers of child care services to low-income families. The states would have the option of providing more lucrative incentives to public or private agencies offering child care services to specific low-income parents, such as single parents. (<u>Poor Women, Poor Families</u> 129)

In terms of the issue of financial assistance from the federal government, two questions are crucial: (1) How much help is needed? (2) To whom should it be directed? Many people move back and forth from employment to welfare, making it very difficult at any given time to differentiate between those on welfare and the working poor. Child advocates Theresa Feeley and Deborah Stein maintain that income, not receipt of welfare benefits, should be the deciding factor. If a family's income is below the poverty level, that family should receive benefits. One example of how this process works comes from La Petite Academy, a well-known child care company with centers throughout the United States. The company is affiliated with

Two works by the same author are listed in Works Cited, so the title appears in parentheses.

An idea from a source is paraphrased and credited.

the government program called Community Coordinated Care for Children (4-C). This program screens families according to their level of income. As Sue Taff, a La Petite director, states,

> If child care is 200 dollars a week, 4-C determines how much government assistance a family will receive depending on their income level. Say the government decides to give that family 75 percent; then it will pay 150 dollars, and the family will have to come up with the difference, which in this case is 50 dollars.

The federal government also offers other support services. The JOBS program is a way for a parent to receive government assistance so that he or she does not have to apply for welfare. Rodgers explains that the "federal government has significantly expanded funding for child care where the parent is enrolled in a JOBS program, where the working parent needs child care help to avoid becoming eligible for AFDC" (<u>Poor Women, Poor Children</u> 159). Such aid is extremely important for the families of the working poor.

Unfortunately, several problems emerge in the administration of government aid for child care. Not enough families receive support from the government, creating a major problem because of the necessary role that child care plays in keeping parents employed. According to one report, less than a third of working-poor families get help with financing care for their children, while almost 40 percent of "non-working poor and middle-income families" do (<u>Child Care for Low Income</u>

---

A quotation from an interview with on expert in the topic of the paper.

Because the Works Cited list contains two works by Rodgers, the writer specifies the source she is referencing here.

Phrase from source is enclosed in quotation marks; source does not have an author, so title appears in parentheses.

Families). If child care for the working poor were more readily available, parents would be able to maintain their jobs without being put on a waiting list for over a year, a situation mainly caused by cutbacks in government funding. As Steve Burghardt and Michael Fabricant of the University of Michigan's School of Social Work explain, "While economic insecurity is driving more and more women into an already discriminatory job market, fiscal cuts in child care programs are marginalizing more and more poor women in their attempts to attain meaningful employment" (97). This lack of funding creates a huge predicament for the working poor as they struggle to become self-sufficient.

Writer includes authors' credentials for added authority.

The situation leads to another major dilemma for the working poor: What about their future? Helping people who are unable to afford child care will benefit them at that particular moment, but their future, along with the future of their children, will still appear to be bleak. The working poor lack the adequate education and job skills that are necessary for them to better themselves by obtaining a well-paying job. For example, the TANF (Temporary Aid for Needy Families) program "creates added hardship for families while not offering the range of long-term supports that would allow welfare clients to become self sufficient" ("Working Families" 4).

The quotation is integrated smoothly into the student's sentence.

These problems are stressful for parents, of course, but the uppermost focus should be on the problems that the children must endure. Their parents serve as role models. Because the parents lack many skills required to become self-sufficient, their children often will not pick up the skills <u>they</u> need to join the labor force (Levitan, Gallo, and Shapiro 64). This syndrome causes a never-ending poverty cycle, which becomes extremely arduous to break.

A source with three authors is cited in parentheses.

This vicious cycle also affects the problem of delinquency. Without proper supervision after school, young people are more likely to become involved with drugs, crime, and sex. Aletha Huston explains that the government could well end up satisfying "the short-term goal of reduced welfare costs while leading to long-term social problems of school failure and delinquency for children who experience unsafe and inade-quate care during their early years" (16). Although this out-come is not necessarily the case all the time, inadequate child care and lack of supervision are obvious pitfalls for young, developing children.

Thoughtful solutions to their child-care problems can help the working poor and eventually benefit our economy as a whole. One solution is the federal government program Head Start. This program is beneficial because it provides child care for the work-ing poor. However, the feature that distinguishes Head Start from other government assistance agencies is that it doubles as an education provider. As Levitan, Gallo, and Shapiro explain, "Head Start combines child care assistance for poor workers with an enriched educational environment for preschoolers. The program stresses the latter, but the program also serves as a child care provider for half of Head Start working parents" (80).

Another solution would be for employers of the working poor to become more understanding about their employees' schedules. Flexible supervisors can improve a working parent's chances of successful employment. Terry Adams and Greg Duncan stress that flexible hours, also known as <u>flextime</u>, along with sufficient child care, can enable single mothers to work longer hours (89). Flextime greatly benefits parents with family responsibilities because they are still able to maintain their jobs.

These are just a few of the several different types of solutions that are now helping, or could help, to improve government assistance for the working poor and help break the cycle of poverty. Although it is unlikely that the United States will suddenly adopt the sweeping programs of Western Europe, some steps are quite feasible. For example, an increase in the minimum wage could help working parents bring themselves out of economic insecurity. Ann Tickamyer explains that higher minimum wages, along with "extending the earned income tax credit, and dealing with child care problems, [will] address this issue and may well have a discernible effect on the fortunes of poor and low-income persons" (60). In the long run, it is imperative that everyone have access to child care so that people can improve their lives and the lives of their children. In order to achieve this goal, the federal government needs to increase its funding, but more importantly, it needs to increase its overall commitment to child care.

A word in brackets allows the student to fit a quotation into her sentence.

Conclusion refers back to the thesis.

## Works Cited

Adams, Terry K., and Greg J. Duncan. "Long-Term Poverty in
Rural Areas." Rural Poverty in America. Ed. Cynthia M.
Duncan. New York: Auburn House, 1992. 63-93.

Bergmann, Barbara R. Saving Our Children from Poverty: What
the United States Can Learn from France. New York: Russell
Sage Foundation, 1996.

Burghardt, Steve, and Michael Fabricant. Working Under the
Safety Net. Newbury Park: Sage, 1987.

Child Care for Low Income Families: Summary of Two Workshops.
Ed. Deborah A. Phillips. Washington, DC: National Academy Press, 1995. 4 Apr. 2001 <http://www.nap.edu/
readingroom/books/childcare/chap4d.html>.

Feeley, Theresa J., and Deborah L. Stein. "Stretching the
Limits: How States Are Using Welfare Flexibility to
Support Children." Jan. 1999. National Association
of Child Advocates 6 Apr. 2001 <http://
www.childadvocacy.org/publicat.html>.

Friedman, Michele. "Child Care." Almanac of Policy Issues 6
Apr. 2001 <http://www.policyalmanac.org/social_
welfare/childcare.shtml>.

Huston, Aletha C., ed. Children in Poverty. New York: Cambridge
UP, 1991.

Levitan, Sar A., Frank Gallo, and Isaac Shapiro. Working but Poor.
Baltimore: Johns Hopkins UP, 1987.

Title centered.

Hanging indent
of one-half inch.

Entries are
double-spaced.

Source without
an author.

Rodgers, Harrell R., Jr. <u>Poor Women, Poor Children: American</u>
<u>Poverty in the 1990s</u>. 3rd ed. New York: Sharpe, 1996.

—. <u>Poor Women, Poor Families</u>. New York: Sharpe, 1990.

Taff, Sue. Telephone interview. 9 Apr. 2001.

Tickamyer, Ann R. "The Working Poor in Rural Labor Markets:
The Example of the Southeastern United States." <u>Rural</u>
<u>Poverty in America</u>. Ed. Cynthia M. Duncan. New York:
Auburn House, 1992. 41-61.

"Working Families." <u>HandsNet</u> 4 Apr. 2001 <http://www.igc.org/
handsnet/body_a.html>.

More than one
work by a
source is cited.

Interview con-
ducted by the
author is cited.

## Checklist for MLA-Style Research Papers

1.  Check your quotations for accuracy. Make sure that you have transcribed correctly.

2.  Make sure that all of your primary and secondary sources have been properly credited. Check to be sure that you have not created an ambiguous situation for your reader.

3.  Credit your paraphrases and summaries the same way as direct quotations. Make sure that you have not forgotten to cite a source.

4.  Use ellipses properly. If you have elided part of any quotation, make sure that (a) you follow the guidelines of Chapter 20, page 583, for using ellipses and (b) you have not altered the meaning of the original passage.

5.  Format any quoted passage that is the equivalent of more than four lines of *your* paper as a block quotation. Check your essay to make sure you have followed this guideline.

6.  Check to make sure that all sources cited in your essay appear in your list of works cited and that all entries in your list of works cited are cited at least once in your essay.

7.  Alphabetize and double-space your list of works cited. Do not number this list.

# THE APA-STYLE RESEARCH PAPER

The following discussion is based on the fifth edition of the *Publication Manual of the American Psychological Association* (2001). This style guide is widely used by writers working in the social sciences.

APA uses a **parenthetical** documentation system that differs from MLA primarily in its inclusion of the date of publication as part of the parenthetical citation. Like MLA, APA relies on parenthetical citing and discourages the uses of notes, except for further explanations of concepts or citations included in the text. The last element in an APA-style research paper is the references list, an alphabetical listing of the sources actually used—and cited—in the essay. Any source used in the essay must appear in the references section; any entry that appears in the references must be cited in the essay.

## In-Text Citations

The parenthetical documentation system used by APA identifies quoted sources by giving the author(s), date, and page number of the quoted text, as in this example:

> Johnson (1999) writes that "the 1998 influx of tourists strained Cen-
>
> tral Florida's highways to the breaking point" (p. 22).

The source is Johnson (1999); the page from which the quotation was taken is 22. An alternate approach delays mentioning the author's name and the date until the end, including them with the page number in a parenthetical citation:

> One commentator writes that "the 1998 influx of tourists strained
>
> Central Florida's highways to the breaking point" (Johnson, 1999, p. 22).

In either case, the reader can expect, upon scanning the reference entries, to find a listing such as this one:

> Johnson, K. (1999, March). Area infrastructure not keeping up. *Central*
>
> *Florida in Review, 24,* 21-24.

The citation and the entry match, and the entry provides full publication information for the source.

When you are citing summaries and paraphrases in your text, APA requires only the author(s) and date:

> Johnson (1999) indicates that the region needs an extra 2,000 miles of roadway.

### Special Cases

Often, you will need to modify the basic in-text citation form shown above.

**1. Citing two or more sources by the same author.** Because APA citations (in contrast to MLA citations) include publication dates, using two or more sources by the same author will usually not cause confusion for readers. The year makes clear to which source in the references page the citation refers.

> Johnson, K. (1999, March). Area infrastructure not keeping up. *Central*
>
> *Florida in Review, 24,* 21-24.
>
> Johnson, K. (2000, June). Clermont council at impasse. *Central Florida in*
>
> *Review, 25,* 28-29.

The older of the two entries comes first. If, however, you need to cite two works written in the same year by the same author(s), attach letter suffixes to the year—for example, 1993a and 1993b—which are determined by checking the alphabetical order of the two titles:

> Shinzato, L. (1999a). Core beliefs.
>
> Shinzato, L. (1999b). Normal expectations.

**2. Citing information from a corporate or organizational author.** Treat this source no differently than a source written by a named person; however, if such an author appears in a parenthetical citation, include the entire name with a suggested abbreviation the first time you use it:

> (Southeastern Maritime Commission [SMC], 1991, p. 574)

Thereafter, you can refer to *SMC* in your parenthetical citations and avoid repeating the lengthy full title.

**3. Citing a source with no author named.** If a print source lists neither a person nor a corporate author, cite the title of the source, normally a periodical article. (Never cite "Staff" or "Wire Reports," but note that "Anonymous" should be used if that is how the source is actually credited.) Use the full title if you mention it outside the parenthetical citation. Shorten the title to a few words if it appears within the parenthetical citation:

> According to the article "Homeless Focus Shifts to South Patterson,"
>
> "area authorities want to build a homeless shelter near a subdivision
>
> despite residents' objections" (2000, p. 23).

> According to a recent article, "area authorities want to build a
>
> homeless shelter near a subdivision despite residents' objections"
>
> ("Homeless Focus Shifts," 2000, p. 23).

**4. Citing an online source.** If an online source has page or paragraph numbers, cite them to direct your reader more specifically to the source of a quotation. (Use *p.* to refer to a page and ¶ or *para.* to refer to a paragraph; also include the date of electronic publication.) However, because most online sources do not have page or paragraph numbers, you will usually cite the author's name only. If the source lists no author, cite the title of the online source in quotation marks. As in guideline 3 above, if you place the title in a parenthetical citation, shorten long titles to a few words—enough so that your reader can match the title to the appropriate reference entry.

**5. Using a source with multiple authors.** In the social sciences, many works are written by two or more authors. If a work you are citing was written by a pair of authors, link the two with an ampersand (&) if you are giving the names in parentheses:

> (McPherson & Rico, 1989, pp. 237-238)

However, if you refer to the authors outside the parentheses, don't use an ampersand; use *and*.

If a source has three to five authors, cite all of them the first time you use the source:

> (McPherson, Rico, Maze, & Carter, 1988)

For subsequent citations, either within your text or in parentheses, use the last name of the first author followed by *et al.* ("and others"), as in this example:

> (McPherson et al., 1988)

If a source has six or more authors, use the first author's last name plus *et al.* for any citation, including the first.

**6. Using an ellipsis in a quotation.** APA uses the ellipsis only in the middle of quoted text, not at the beginning or end, unless it is needed to prevent confusion.

**7. Using a quotation longer than forty words.** If you are quoting a passage that is forty words or more (not including the citation), set it off as a block. Indent the block one-half inch from the left margin, and double-space the quotation.

**8. Using content notes.** Although APA emphasizes parenthetical documentation, you may occasionally need to provide explanations about sources or content that go beyond what you can appropriately place within parentheses in the text. In such cases, use a note with a superscript number (most word-processing programs have an automatic function for superscript type), and place the note on a separate page with the title *Footnote* or *Footnotes*. The first line of each note should be indented one-half inch, and the note or notes should be double-spaced.

**9. Citing personal communication.** APA format includes personal communication (personal/telephone interviews, e-mails, and the like) in parenthetical citations only, not in the references list. To write such a citation, include the initials and last name of the person with whom you communicated and the date.

> (M. R. Cornell, personal communication, June 9, 1998)

## The References List

The last element of your research paper is the references section. This is a list of entries that tells your reader the sources you have used and cited in your essay. These entries are alphabetized by the last name of the source's author. Sources with more than one author are alphabetized by the name of the first author listed. Sources that don't have named authors, either human or corporate, are alphabetized by title. Some complications may occur, as shown in the following list:

Harper, Leo

Lefou, Ariel

Le Franc, David

Maritime Fisheries Commission

The nature of wax beetles

Roth, Michelle

Roth-Lynn, Leo

Rothman, Thomas

1. For alphabetizing purposes, articles (*the, a,* and *an*) are disregarded. "The Nature of Wax Beetles" is alphabetized using the word *Nature.*

2. Le Franc is treated as one word, so it follows Lefou.

3. Roth has fewer letters than Roth-Lynn, and the hyphen is disregarded in Roth-Lynn so that "RothL" precedes "Rothm."

### The Basic References Format

Most entries include author, title, and publishing information. Here is a basic entry for a book by one author:

Peters, E. (1994). *Night train to Memphis.* New York: Warner Books.

Note the following:

1. The author's name is inverted, with the last name appearing first. First and middle names are always shortened to initials. If more than one initial is listed, a space separates the initials: Chesterton, G. K.

2. The first line of the entry starts at the left margin. Succeeding ("turnover") lines are indented one-half inch, as in the example below.

3. The only letters that are capitalized in titles are the first letter of the first word, the first letter of the first word after a colon (if any), the first letter of a proper noun, and acronyms (such as IBM). For example,

Kendall, D. (1998). *Sociology in our times: The essentials.* Belmont, CA:

Wadsworth.

4. Note that titles of books, as well as titles of periodicals, are italicized. (Titles of articles in periodicals are not italicized.)

5. Use a shortened version of the publisher's name (for example, Alfred A. Knopf is shortened to Knopf), and never include *Inc.* However, include *Press* or *Books* if it is part of the publisher's name (see the basic entry above).

6. The location of the publisher is indicated by the city and state (represented by the postal service abbreviation):

Cheyenne, WY

San Jose, CA

However, for large, easily identifiable cities (New York, London, Philadelphia, Chicago, Los Angeles), the state is not needed. If the publisher lists more than one city on the title page, use only the first one.

7. References entries, like the rest of the essay, must be double-spaced.

The rest of this section lists and describes standard APA reference entries. For more information, consult the *Publication Manual of the American Psychological Association,* fifth edition. However, before you begin looking at the reference entries, examine the following pages, which will help you find the information that you will use to create these entries.

### Article in an Online Magazine

Author's name        Date of posting                    Article title and subtitle

Saletan, W. (2007, January 20). Girl, interrupted: The power to shrink

Magazine
title            Date of access                    URL

human beings. *Slate*. Retrieved January 27, 2007, from www.slate.com/

id/2157861/?nav=tap3.

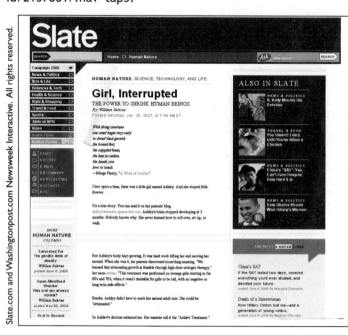

## Book with One Author

Author's    Year of
name    publication                    Book title and subtitle

Fussell, P. (1980). *Abroad: British literary traveling between the wars.*

City of
publication            Publisher

New York: Oxford University Press.

# ABROAD

British Literary Traveling

Between the Wars

PAUL FUSSELL

New York   Oxford
OXFORD UNIVERSITY PRESS
1980

## Article in a Journal with Consecutive Pagination

Author's name　Year of publication　　　　　Article title

Myers, M. A. (1995). Gender and Southern punishment after the

Journal title　Volume and page range

Civil War. *Criminology, 33,* 17-46.

# CRIMINOLOGY

### AN INTERDISCIPLINARY JOURNAL

#### THE OFFICIAL PUBLICATION OF THE AMERICAN SOCIETY OF CRIMINOLOGY

99827

VOLUME 33　　　　NUMBER 1　　　　FEBRUARY 1995

# GENDER AND SOUTHERN PUNISHMENT AFTER THE CIVIL WAR*

MARTHA A. MYERS
  The University of Georgia

*Recent scholarship raises two questions about the historical relationship between gender and official responses to criminality. First, to what extent has the formal social control of women changed in the past two centuries? Second, to what extent can changes in the presence of women within the criminal justice system be traced to the same factors that account for the changing presence of men? To address these questions, I focus on women incarcerated for felonies in a southern state (Georgia) between 1870 and 1940. Along with a comparable sample of male offenders, this population forms the basis of a time-series analysis that compares, and seeks to account for, trends in admission rates. The analysis yields little evidence that women disappeared from formal systems of punishment. Instead, there were gender similarities in punishment trends and in explanations for those trends. Concluding the paper is a discussion of its implications for further research on gender differences in punishment.*

Criminality among women is actually infrequent and we may expect its gradual disappearance. Delinquency on the distaff side is bad news for the human race.

—Miriam van Waters (1941:123)

Over half a century ago, Miriam van Waters, superintendent of the Reformatory for Women in Framingham, Massachusetts, lamented the negligible attention the research community paid to female criminality (van Waters, 1941). Although interest has been slow to shift, the same charge would be less justifiable today. Since the 1970s, social scientists have examined gender differences in crime, in explanations for criminality, and in the nature and severity of official reactions to criminality (see, e.g., Harvey et al., 1992; Steffensmeier and Allan, 1995; Steffensmeier et al., 1993). Of more recent vintage are studies of the past, particularly crime and responses to crime in the 18th and 19th centuries. This paper fixes attention on an unfamiliar context, the American South, to address two familiar issues raised by these studies. The first issue is the extent to which temporal changes in punishment differed for women and men, and the second is the existence of gender differences in factors that account for

---

* This paper is a revised version of a paper presented at the annual meetings of the American Society of Criminology, October 27–30, 1993, Phoenix, Arizona.

## Newspaper Article

Author's  Date of
name  publication    Article title  Newspaper title

James, J. (2007, January 22). Session strikes a deal. *St. Petersburg*

     Edition   Page range

  *Times* (Tampa ed.), pp. 1A, 12A.

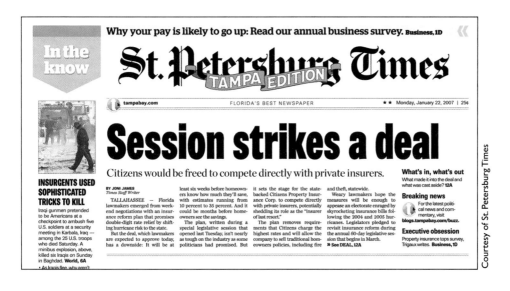

Courtesy of St. Petersburg Times

## *APA Citations—Books*

### Book with One Author

Percy, W. (1961). *The moviegoer.* New York: Knopf.

### Book with Two Authors

Brooks, T., & Marsh, E. (1995). *The complete directory to prime time*

  *network and cable TV shows: 1946-present.* New York: Ballantine.

### Book with Three to Six Authors

Vander, A., Sherman, J., & Luciano, D. (2000). *Human physiology: The*

  *mechanics of body function* (8th ed.). New York: McGraw-Hill.

**Note:** If a book has more than six authors, type *et al.* after the sixth name, and follow this with the date.

### Book with Corporate or Organizational Author

American Psychological Association. (2001). *Publication manual of the*

  *American Psychological Association* (5th ed.). Washington, DC: Author.

Note the use of *Author* in the publisher position.

### Book with an Editor

If you are using information from a book's editor (editors often introduce and comment on work they are presenting), use the abbreviations *Ed.* or *Eds.,* as in the following:

> Garrod, H. W. (Ed.). (1970). *Keats: Poetical works.* London: Oxford
>
> University Press.

This means that you have used information from Garrod, not from Keats.

If you are using information from the author of an edited book, begin with the author's last name:

> Twain, M. (1982). *A Connecticut Yankee in King Arthur's court* (A. Ensor,
>
> Ed.). New York: Norton. (Original work published 1889)

### Book in a Later Edition

> Boorstin, D. J. (1985). *The discoverers: A history of man's search to know*
>
> *his world and himself* (2nd ed.). New York: Vintage.

### Multivolume Book

> Daiches, D. (1960). *A critical history of English literature* (Vols. 1-2).
>
> London: Secker and Warburg.

### Multivolume Book in a Later Edition

> Daiches, D. (1970). *A critical history of English literature* (Vols. 1-2). (2nd
>
> ed.). New York: Ronald.

### Book in a Series

> Knapp, B. L. (2000). *Voltaire revisited.* New York: Twayne.

APA does not require the series title and the name of the series editor.

### Book of Collected Essays or an Anthology

> Frazier, I. (Ed.). (1997). *The best American essays 1997.* Boston: Houghton.
>
> Lynch, R. E., & Swanzey, T. B. (Eds.). (1981). *The example of science: An*
>
> *anthology.* Englewood Cliffs, NJ: Prentice-Hall.

Use this format when you want to refer to a whole collection of essays, not an individual essay.

### Essay in an Anthology or Collection

> Thomas, L. (1981). Ceti. In R. E. Lynch & T. B. Swanzey (Eds.), *The example*
>
> *of science: An anthology* (pp. 9-13). Englewood Cliffs, NJ: Prentice-Hall.

Use this format when you want to refer to one essay in a collection, not the whole collection.

### Translation

> Dostoyevsky, F. (1980). *Crime and Punishment* (S. Monas, Trans.). New
>
> York: New American Library. (Original work published 1866)

## APA Citations—Periodical Articles

Compared to MLA, APA style makes fewer distinctions between journal articles and magazine articles. Volume numbers are required for both types.

### Article in a Journal with Consecutive Pagination

> Jones, K. (1999). Second-hand moral knowledge. *Journal of Philosophy,*
>
> *96,* 55-78.

Like most academic journals, this one starts the first issue of each year on page 1, then numbers consecutively throughout the year. The volume number for 1999 is 96.

### Article by Two Authors in a Journal with Consecutive Pagination

> Benson, J. J., & Loftis, A. (1980). John Steinbeck and farm labor
>
> unionization: The background of *In dubious battle. American*
>
> *Literature, 52,* 194-224.

Note that both authors' names are inverted and separated by a comma and an ampersand (&).

### Article by Three to Six Authors in a Journal with Consecutive Pagination

> Magnusson, W. E., da Silva, E. V., & Lima, A. P. (1987). Diets of Amazonian
>
> crocodiles. *Journal of Herpetology, 21,* 85-95.

Note that all three authors' names are inverted and separated by commas, with an ampersand (&) preceding the last author's name. If an article has more than six authors, type *et al.* after the sixth name, and follow this with the date.

### Article in a Journal Paged by Issue

> Lützeler. P. (2000). Goethe and Europe. *South Atlantic Review, 65*(2), 95-113.

This journal starts each issue on page 1. This is volume 65, issue 2. Notice that the issue number is not italicized.

### Article in a Magazine Published Monthly

> Codman, O., Jr. (1997, October). The decoration of town houses:
>
> Renovating a Manhattan residence. *Architectural Digest, 54,* 164-171.

As with an article in a journal paged by issue, the volume number is given, but instead of an issue number following the volume number, the month of publication follows the year: (1997, October). Note that the complete page number is provided for both numbers (164–171) as opposed to the MLA style (164–71).

### Article in a Magazine Published Weekly

Branson, L. (1993, November 8). Children of the tunnels. *Maclean's, 106,* 29-30.

This entry differs from that for a monthly magazine only in that the exact date of publication appears: (1993, November 8).

### Magazine Article Without Author

Flour power. (1989, December). *Harper's Bazaar, 122,* 200, 213-214.

The entry begins with the article title. Also note the full listing of the pages. (MLA would indicate the pages in this discontinuous article as 200+; APA requires a full listing of the article's pages.)

### Article in a Daily Newspaper

Tanner, L. (2000, November 29). Study shows men listen with half a brain.

*The Lakeland Ledger,* p. A4.

Note that for newspaper articles, APA requires "p." before the listed page. If the article had "jumped" to a new page for its conclusion, the page listing would look like this: pp. A4, A16.

### Essay in an Anthology or Collection
See page 638.

### Article or Chapter in an Edited Book

Junod, M. (1987). Visiting Hiroshima: 9 September 1945. In J. Carey (Ed.),

*Eyewitness to history* (pp. 638-640). New York: Avon.

### Review in a Magazine or Newspaper

Lane, A. (1999, July 19). Blown away [Review of the motion pictures *Arlington Road* and *The lovers on the bridge*]. *The New Yorker, 75,* 98-99.

Preston, W. J. (1998, May 31). The politics of hysteria [Review of the book *Many are the crimes: McCarthyism in America*]. *The Los Angeles Times,* Book Reviews, p. 6.

### APA Citations—Online Sources
Online documentation is evolving. Here are some of the most recent APA guidelines.

## Online Document Retrieved from an Information Database, Online Project, or Professional Web Site

Information databases and online projects are sponsored by a number of organizations, including news and media corporations, professional groups, and educational institutions. Your college or university library may subscribe to several of these resources. They contain abstracts of articles, articles in their entirety, books, chapters of books, poems, and a variety of other materials you might find useful. Cite such sources as follows:

1. Name of author, last name first, followed by initial(s).

2. Date of electronic publication in parentheses.

3. Title of the work. Capitalize the first major word and proper nouns only.

4. If the work appears in a periodical, indicate the periodical's title and any available publication data appropriate to that type of periodical, including volume, issue, and page numbers. If the work is a section or chapter in a book, indicate the book's title and pertinent publication information. If the work is part of a Web site, indicate the title of the Web site in italics.

5. The date you retrieved the work, followed by a comma and the URL or the name of the database or project from which you retrieved it. Do not add a period after the URL.

6. The item or access number of the work (optional).

> O'Hanlon, L. (2000, March 25). Extreme measures: The art of analyzing natural
>
> disasters. *The Discovery Channel online.* Retrieved September 17, 2000,
>
> from http://www.discovery.com/newsfeatures/disasters/disasters.html
>
> Brown, T. (1998, October). Problems and solutions in the management of
>
> child abuse allegations [Electronic version]. *Family & Reconciliation*
>
> *Courts Review, 36.* Retrieved May 11, 2002, from EBSCOhost
>
> database, item 1121380.

O'Hanlon's article was written for the Discovery Channel's Web site. Brown's article first appeared in print and then became part of a database, as indicated by the words *Electronic version.*

## Online Article from a Scholarly Journal

> Loranger, C. (1999). "This book spill off the page in all directions": What is the
>
> text of *Naked lunch? Postmodern Culture, 10*(1). Retrieved August 27,
>
> 2000, from http://muse.jhu.edu/journals/pmc/v010/10.1loranger.html

*Postmodern Culture* is an online scholarly journal. Note that the information through the volume and issue number is the same as that which would appear for a print journal article.

### Online Article from a Newspaper or News Service

> Babinek, M. (2000, May 22). Railroad killer gets death penalty. *San Francisco Examiner*. Retrieved May 27, 2000, from http://examiner.com/apa/AP_Railroad_Killer.html

### Online Article in a Weekly or Monthly Magazine

> Saletan, W. (2000, November 28). Electoral knowledge. *Slate*. Retrieved November 30, 2000, from http://slate.msn.com/framegame/entries/00-11-28_94258.asp

Note the date of posting: (2000, November 28).

### Article Accessed Through an Online Library Service

> Hannon, K. (1996, June 10). The joys of a working vacation [Electronic version]. *U.S. News & World Report, 120*, 89-90. Retrieved October 22, 2001, from OCLC First Search database.

College and university libraries usually subscribe to at least one online access service. These services allow researchers quick access to periodical articles that are available online. Note that the information from the author through the page range is the same as it would be for an entry of the print version of the article. The entry ends with the name of the access service. No URL is needed.

### Article Published on a Professional Web Site

> Dockray, K. (2006, December 6). The wars of the roses: The political history of the wars. *The Richard III Society Website*. Retrieved February 17, 2007, from http://www.richardiii.net/begin.htm

### Online Book Previously Published in Print Form

> Melville, H. (2000). *The piazza tales.* (Original work published 1856). Retrieved October 21, 2000, from http://www.esp.org/books/melville/piazza

Melville's book is available in print form and online. The entry for the digital version shows author, title, original publication date, date of access, and URL.

### Part of Online Book Previously Published in Print Form

> Melville, H. (2000). Benito Cereno. *The piazza tales.* (Original work published 1856). Retrieved October 24, 2000, from http://www.esp.org/books/melville/piazza/contents/cereno.html

"Benito Cereno" is one of the stories that make up *The Piazza Tales*.

## Messages Posted to Newsgroups, Online Forums, Discussion Groups, and Electronic Mailing Lists

1.  Begin with the author's name, followed by the exact date of the posting.
2.  Type the subject or "thread" name of the posting, followed by any other identifying information in brackets.
3.  Close with *Message posted to* and the URL.

> Harrington, J. K. (2000, May 19). Publishing [The Writing Life Inkspot
>
> Writers' Community Forums, Msg. 3]. Message posted to http://
>
> writers-bbs.com/inkspot/threads.cgi?action=*almsgs&forum=*
>
> *writinglife*

Note that such resources may be open to anyone who has access to the Internet, whether or not he or she is an expert on the subject being discussed. Therefore, be extra careful about the validity of the information you take from forums, discussion groups, and the like.

## APA Citations—Miscellaneous Sources

### Encyclopedia or Dictionary Entry

> Earthquake. *Concise Columbia encyclopedia* (3rd ed.). (1994). New York:
>
> Columbia University Press.

If the encyclopedia has an editor, then use the format for a book listed by editor.

### Government Publication

> U.S. Bureau of Labor Statistics. (1992). *Employment and earnings*.
>
> Washington, DC: Government Printing Office.

### Film or Television Program

> Miall, T. (Producer), & Luhrmann, B. (Director). (1992). *Strictly ballroom*
>
> [Motion picture]. Australia: Miramax.

> Fritzell, J., & Greenbaum, E. (Writers). (1963, April 29). Mountain
>
> wedding [Television series episode]. In A. Ruben (Producer), *The*
>
> *Andy Griffith show*. New York: Columbia Broadcasting System.

### Personal Communications

In APA style, personal communications appear in parenthetical citations only, not in the references section. Such communications include personal/telephone interviews, e-mails, and other messages that are not archived.

CATALYST 2.0

**MORE OPTIONS ONLINE**
For more help with formatting APA-style references, go to
www.mhhe.com/writingtoday.

Checklist for
APA-Style
Research
Papers

1.  Check your quotations for accuracy. Make sure that you have transcribed correctly.

2.  Make sure that all of your primary and secondary sources have been properly credited. Check to be sure that you have not created an ambiguous situation for your reader.

3.  Credit your paraphrases and summaries the same way as direct quotations. Make sure that you have not forgotten to cite a source.

4.  Make sure that you have used ellipses properly.

5.  Format any quoted passage that is forty or more words as a block quotation. Check your essay to make sure you have followed this guideline.

6.  Check to make sure that all sources cited in your essay appear in your references list and that all entries in your references are cited at least once in or essay.

7.  Alphabetize and double-space your list of references. Do not number this list.

## APA Research Paper Format

Double-space the essay on white, $8\frac{1}{2}$" × 11" paper, using text margins of one inch at the top, bottom, and sides. Use a standard text font, such as Times, Courier, Palatino, Garamond, or Goudy, in 12-point type.

The APA format requires a title page. Center the title both horizontally and vertically on the page. The title is followed on the next line by your name (also centered); the last line of the title page is your course and section number (also centered). Your instructor may also require you to include his or her name and the date.

Number all pages of your essay. Use the "header" function of your word-processing program to include a shortened version of your essay's title followed by five spaces (one-half inch) and then the page number, all flush right at the top margin, such as in this example:

Electromagnetic Variations    1

Note that each page is numbered, including the title page.

The last element of your essay will be your references section. Start this section on a new page. At the top of the page, center the word *References*. Then start the first entry on the next line after the head. Like the rest of your essay, this page is double-spaced, with no extra space added anywhere.

## Sample Research Paper in APA Format

You can access a sample paper in APA style written by Joel Darulla, a student in a technical communication course, at the *Writing Today* Web site: www .mhhe.com/writingtoday.

# WRITING ABOUT LITERATURE

At some time in your college career, you will probably be asked to write about literature. Sophomore literature surveys, humanities courses, and some freshman composition classes often include such an assignment. In order to write about literature effectively, you will have to learn how to analyze it; to understand, appreciate, and use varying interpretations of the same work; and to synthesize the work of scholars with your own opinions and insights.

IN THIS CHAPTER, WE CONCENTRATE ON THE TYPE OF ANALYSIS that readers use to understand literature and the organizational strategies that writers use to respond to topics about literature. We also look at some specific mechanical issues that arise in this type of writing. We start with a short story and then move on to a poem. Note that the *Writing Today* Web site (www.mhhe .com/writingtoday) includes a section that discusses how the techniques used to write about stories and poems need to be modified when a writer analyzes a play or a film.

Whatever type of work you are reading, you need to approach it in a systematic and careful manner. Reading a novel or a book of short stories for the sheer pleasure of it is certainly worthwhile. However, reading literature assigned in a college course is often a far more demanding and time-consuming task than reading the latest best-seller. The very purpose of reading literature in college is to prompt analytical, interpretive, and evaluative responses from students, thereby improving their ability to think critically and to discuss sophisticated ideas intelligently.

To approach a work of literature and to write about it require the same attention to the rules of academic reading and writing that you apply in any other discipline. In addition, you should adhere to the following guidelines.

## General Guidelines for Reading and Writing About Literature

### Reading Literature

- Reading, like writing, is a process. To understand and appreciate a short story, play, or poem, you may have to read it more than once. The same is true for a novel, but time constraints might permit you to give multiple readings only to selected passages or chapters.

- As with any text, don't be afraid to underline significant lines or passages or to make marginal notes that will help you construct a coherent analysis of the piece later on. The most common types of notes that students make when reading a short story or play are descriptions or analyses of particular characters, descriptions of setting, or ideas that lead to a fuller understanding of the **theme**—the vision or message about human experience that the author is trying to convey. The most common types of notes students make when reading poetry relate to word choice and figurative language (see Chapter 4), to tone, and to meter and rhyme scheme.

- Make your notes and markings in pencil so you will be able to revise, erase, or replace notes when you read the work a second or third time.

- Adopt an active stance. Reading sophisticated literature demands intellectual curiosity and a willingness to engage the text. For example, to discover the deeper meaning of a short story, you need to do more than simply follow the plot. You need to understand the ironic twists in the plot caused by pure coincidence, setting, or the motives of a particular character. You also need to consider how setting informs tone and how tone, in turn, contributes to the story's theme. All of these tasks require you to draw conclusions and to interpret what is happening, what is being said, where and when the action is taking place, who is involved, and how one event or character affects another.

- When analyzing literature from another culture, try not to make assumptions based upon what you know of your own culture.

After you have decided on an aspect of the short story or poem to write about and have developed a plan, or outline, for your essay, you are ready to draft your paper. The following guidelines apply to all types of literary analyses.

Writing About Literature
_____

- If you quote directly, summarize, or paraphrase from a primary or secondary source, provide citations for those sources. The piece of literature you are reading and analyzing is one type of primary source. A book, journal article, or other scholarly commentary about that piece of literature is a type of secondary source. The system that is normally used to cite such sources is the one recommended by the Modern Language Association and found in Joseph Gibaldi's *MLA Handbook for Writers of Research Papers,* sixth edition (2003). MLA style is also discussed in chapters 20 and 21 of this textbook.
- Double-check to make sure that you are quoting, summarizing, or paraphrasing accurately. You can find out more about using direct quotations, summaries, and paraphrases in chapters 20 and 21.
- Whether you are analyzing a story, novel, poem, play, or film, use the present tense (sometimes called the *literary present*). For example, at the beginning of John Updike's short story "A&P," the main character, Sammy, *is* a clerk at a grocery store. He *had been* a high school student. Note that the past perfect tense is used for narrative events that happened before the time that you are discussing.
- Refer to authors by their last names.

# WRITING ABOUT FICTION

Short stories and novels are called **fiction.** Although they are narratives, they differ from narrative essays, which are based on real events and are considered nonfiction. Short stories and novels are products of the author's imagination or are imaginative re-creations of real events.

Many first-year English classes that cover fiction have students read short stories rather than novels. When instructors assign a critical essay on a short story, they are normally looking for an essay about a feature or an issue associated with that work—for example, the personality and motives of a character, the use of a particular type of symbol, or the effect of setting on the characters and theme. These instructors want more than a simple recounting of the narrative, point by point, event by event—a practice that is unnecessary and that fails to address the assignment.

## Useful Terms for Writing About Fiction

In order to analyze a short story and then to use this analysis as the basis of a critical essay, you will need to learn a few literary terms and the way they work together. The following terms will improve your understanding of the elements of a short story as you read and analyze it.

**antagonist**   The character, force, or situation that opposes the *protagonist,* the main character.

**character**   A person involved in the action of a story. In a more particular sense, *character* refers to the personality and motivations of a person.

**characterization**   The way that a *character* is developed by the author.

**climax**   The moment at which the events in the narrative reach a crisis, usually near the end of the narrative.

**conflict**   The struggle that shapes a narrative. Three broad areas of conflict are individual versus society, individual versus nature, and individual versus himself or herself.

**denouement**   The period after a narrative's *climax* in which final questions and details are addressed.

**dramatic irony**   A device created when characters in a short story, novel, play, or film discuss an issue at cross-purposes; each character has incomplete information about the issue but not the same incomplete information. Furthermore, the characters do not realize that each is referring to a different set of facts. Only the audience knows all of the truth. The device's power is due to this gap between the audience's knowledge and the characters' knowledge. See also **irony.**

**epiphany**   A profound revelation experienced by a character as the result of a narrative's events.

**foreshadowing**   The writer's use of hints in a narrative to suggest an upcoming event in the plot.

**image**   A description meant to evoke a mental picture for the reader: "A drowned dog floated by, or was it a bad piñata?" The image of the piñata reinforces the image of the disfigurement caused by drowning.

**imagery**   Images working together to create a desired effect.

**irony**   A discrepancy between appearance and reality: "That the people of the 1920s believed the first world war was the final global battle is ironic when the events of the late 1930s are considered." (See also **dramatic irony.**)

**metaphor**   A figure of speech in which one thing is represented by or is compared to another without using *like* or *as.* Thus, "The club scene is a black hole for my wallet" uses the metaphor of *black hole* to describe the financial losses suffered by the writer as a result of club crawling.

**motif**   A recurring word, musical phrase, or visual object with thematic significance: "Each major character in *Death of a Salesman* has his or her 'own' music that announces the character's stage entrance; this motif engages an audience in a very interesting way."

**narration**   The telling of a story.

**narrative**   A story.

**narrator**   The storyteller. The narrator and the author are not synonymous. The narrator might even be a character in the story.

**parody**   A literary work that imitates another literary work in order to ridicule it.

**plot**   The events that make up a narrative.

**point of view**   The perspective from which the story is narrated. In **first-person narration**, the narrator (storyteller) is a character in the story who uses *I*. Novels using first-person narration are *Great Expectations, Moby-Dick, Huckleberry Finn,* and *Invisible Man.* The *I* narrator does not have to be the main character; *The Great Gatsby* is told by Nick Carraway, a secondary figure.

Third-person narration does not use an *I* narrator. However, the writer can have the reader experience the plot through the eyes of one character, a technique called **third-person limited omniscience.** A good example is Stephen Crane's *The Red Badge of Courage.* The author can also tell the story from multiple points of view, letting the reader see events from the perspectives of several characters, but again without using an *I* narrator. This approach is called the **third-person omniscient** point of view.

**protagonist**   The main character of a narrative: "Ruby Turpin is the protagonist of Flannery O'Connor's 'Revelation.'" The protagonist is not necessarily heroic, just the main character. See also **antagonist.**

**satire**   A work that ridicules either for entertainment or to suggest reform: "Voltaire's *Candide* is a wide-ranging satire of the Enlightenment's belief systems."

**setting**   The time and place of a narrative. Given the differences among cultures, countries, regions, and eras, knowing both when and where a narrative is set is crucial to understanding it.

**simile**   A figure of speech in which one thing is represented by or compared to another by using *like* or *as*. The Scottish poet Robert Burns wrote that "My love is like a red, red rose."

**symbol**   An object used to suggest something else, usually an abstract concept. For example, a broken pair of eyeglasses could symbolize a character's loss of moral perception.

**theme**   The "point" of the story—its controlling idea or message.

Keeping these elements in mind and remembering the general guidelines for reading literature presented earlier, read the following short story, and then consider the two student responses that follow it.

# The Answer Is No

## NAGUIB MAHFOUZ
Translated by Denys Johnson-Davies

*Naguib Mahfouz (1911–2006) was the author of almost forty novels and fourteen short-story collections. Much of his work is set in his homeland, Egypt. He was awarded the Nobel Prize for literature in 1988.*

The important piece of news that the new head- 1 master had arrived spread through the school. She heard of it in the women teachers' common room as she was casting a final glance at the day's lessons. There was no getting away from joining the other teachers in congratulating him, and from shaking him by the hand too. A shudder passed through her body, but it was unavoidable.

"They speak highly of his ability," said a col- 2 league of hers. "And they talk too of his strictness."

It had always been a possibility that might 3 occur, and now it had. Her pretty face paled, and a staring look came to her wide black eyes.

When the time came, the teachers went in 4 single file, decorously attired, to his open room. He stood behind his desk as he received the men and women. He was of medium height, with a tendency to portliness, and had a spherical face, hooked nose, and bulging eyes; the first thing that could be seen of him was a thick, puffed-up mustache, arched like a foam-laden wave. She advanced with her eyes fixed on his chest. Avoiding his gaze, she stretched out her hand. What was she to say? Just what the others had said? However, she kept silent, uttered not a word. What, she wondered, did his eyes express? His rough hand shook hers, and he said in a gruff voice, "Thanks." She turned elegantly and moved off.

She forgot her worries through her daily tasks, 5 though she did not look in good shape. Several of the girls remarked, "Miss is in a bad mood." When she returned to her home at the beginning of the Pyramids Road, she changed her clothes and sat down to eat with her mother. "Everything all right?" inquired her mother, looking her in the face.

"Badran, Badran Badawi," she said briefly. 6 "Do you remember him? He's been appointed our headmaster."

"Really!" 7

Then, after a moment of silence, she said, "It's 8 of no importance at all—it's an old and long-forgotten story."

After eating, she took herself off to her study 9 to rest for a while before correcting some exercise books. She had forgotten him completely. No, not completely. How could he be forgotten completely? When he had first come to give her a private lesson in mathematics, she was fourteen years of age. In fact not quite fourteen. He had been twenty-five years older, the same age as her father. She had said to her mother, "His appearance is a mess, but he explains things well." And her mother had said, "We're not concerned with what he looks like; what's important is how he explains things."

He was an amusing person, and she got on 10 well with him and benefited from his knowledge.

How, then, had it happened? In her innocence she had not noticed any change in his behavior to put her on her guard. Then one day he had been left on his own with her, her father having gone to her aunt's clinic. She had not the slightest doubts about a man she regarded as a second father. How, then, had it happened? Without love or desire on her part the thing had happened. She had asked in terror about what had occurred, and he had told her, "Don't be frightened or sad. Keep it to yourself and I'll come and propose to you the day you come of age."

And he had kept his promise and had come 11 to ask for her hand. By then she had attained a degree of maturity that gave her an understanding of the dimensions of their tragic position. She had found that she had no love or respect for him and that he was as far as he could be from her dreams and from the ideas she had formed of what constituted an ideal and moral person. But what was to be done? Her father had passed away two years ago, and her mother had been taken aback by the forwardness of the man. However, she had said to her, "I know your attachment to your personal independence, so I leave the decision to you."

She had been conscious of the critical posi- 12 tion she was in. She had either to accept or to close the door forever. It was the sort of situation that could force her into something she detested. She was the rich, beautiful girl, a byword in Abbasiyya for her nobility of character, and now here she was struggling helplessly in a well-sprung trap, while he looked down at her with rapacious eyes. Just as she had hated his strength, so too did she hate her own weakness. To have abused her innocence was one thing, but for him to have the upper hand now that she was fully in possession of her faculties was something else. He had said, "So here I am, making good my promise because I love you." He had also said, "I know of your love of teaching, and you will complete your studies at the College of Science."

She had felt such anger as she had never felt 13 before. She had rejected coercion in the same way as she rejected ugliness. It had meant little to her to sacrifice marriage. She had welcomed being on her own, for solitude accompanied by self-respect was not loneliness. She had also guessed he was after her money. She had told her mother quite straightforwardly, "No," to which her mother had replied, "I am astonished you did not make this decision from the first moment."

The man had blocked her way outside and 14 said, "How can you refuse? Don't you realize the outcome?" And she had replied with an asperity he had not expected, "For me any outcome is preferable to being married to you."

After finishing her studies, she had wanted 15 something to do to fill her spare time, so she had worked as a teacher. Chances to marry had come time after time, but she had turned her back on them all.

"Does no one please you?" her mother asked 16 her.

"I know what I'm doing," she had said gently. 17

"But time is going by." 18

"Let it go as it pleases, I am content." 19

Day by day she becomes older. She avoids 20 love, fears it. With all her strength she hopes that life will pass calmly, peacefully, rather than happily. She goes on persuading herself that happiness is not confined to love and motherhood. Never has she regretted her firm decision. Who knows what the morrow holds? But she was certainly unhappy that he should again make his appearance in her life, that she would be making of the past a living and painful present.

Then, the first time he was alone with her in 21 his room, he asked her, "How are you?"

She answered coldly, "I'm fine." 22

He hesitated slightly before inquiring, "Have 23 you not . . . I mean, did you get married?"

In the tone of someone intent on cutting 24 short a conversation, she said, "I told you, I'm fine."

*Analysis*

Here is the topic assigned after discussion of the story:

> Write a 400- to 550-word essay in response to the following statement:
>
> "The Answer Is No" takes place in a traditional culture. The protagonist is an oddity, the rare young woman who is allowed to make her own decisions. As a result, she scorns Badawi's offer of marriage—a daring choice. In effect, she takes the prerogative of a man. However, when Badawi becomes the headmaster of the school at which she teaches, she loses her "male prerogative" and suffers as a "traditional" woman.
>
> Do you agree? (Hint: read the end of the story very carefully.)

Two student responses follow. We have broken each essay into its component paragraphs, accompanied by our comments. The first essay illustrates several errors you ought to avoid. The second is an example of a far more effective response to the question.

## First Student Response to "The Answer Is No": Needs Improvement

The Answer Is No[1]

In this story[2] the narrator[3] is a young woman who was sexually abused by a math tutor at the age of fourteen.[4] Years later he becomes the headmaster of the school where she teaches. She loses her male prerogative[5] and lives in fear of him.

**Comments**

1.  Instead of using the title of the story as the essay's title, the writer needs a title that reflects the essay's focus. The writer of the second student response (see page 654) provides insight into her essay's contents and point of view by titling it "An Ongoing Equilibrium." Note that this is a far more intriguing title and serves to draw the reader into the text.

2.  The essay starts with "In this story. . . ." A better first sentence would begin with "In 'The Answer Is No,' Naguib Mahfouz portrays. . . ." The title of the story needs to be identified within the text.

3.  The young woman is *not* the narrator; the narrator tells the story. She is, instead, the *protagonist,* or main character.

4.  After the first sentence, the reader might ask "Who was fourteen, the woman or the math tutor?"

5.  To write that a woman "loses her male prerogative" is to repeat part of the question without explaining what that phrase means. Also, *does* the woman "live in fear" of Badawi? Finally, is "loses her male prerogative" an effective thesis?

The story begins with the arrival of the new headmaster, Badran.[1]

The narrator is shocked at this unexpected turn of events. She dis-

cusses the situation with her mother and worries about implications.[2]

**Comments**

1. The headmaster should be referred to by his last name, Badawi, not by his given name, Badran.
2. This paragraph is plot summary, but the audience—the instructor—already knows the plot.

The narrator thinks back to the events that had caused her such

sorrow. She was fourteen, he twenty-five.[1] Their student-tutor rela-

tionship was going well. Then one day, he apparently raped her. He

tried to make up for this by promising to marry her when she was old

enough. However, she refused when he reappeared when she turned

eighteen.[2, 3]

**Comments**

1. This information is inaccurate. When the protagonist is fourteen, Badawi is thirty-nine.
2. The statement that eighteen is the age of majority is an assumption; eighteen might be the magic number in the United States, but Egypt is a different culture.
3. The paragraph contains almost nothing but plot summary.

When the narrator again meets Badran, with him as her boss, she

is fearful.[1] The rest of her working life will be spent under a man[2]

who has two reasons for revenge. Her "male prerogative" is gone.[3]

**Comments**

1. Another reader of this short story might question the word *fearful* and see the protagonist's response as *measured*. Of course, people can have two very different interpretations, both of which are valid. The key is to establish that validity. Thus, the writer of this essay might make reference to the text to support his contention that the protagonist is *fearful*.
2. The phrase *under a man* is unfortunate. Perhaps *being supervised by a man* would work better.
3. A conclusion can serve a variety of purposes, but summarizing plot is not one of them. Perhaps a better conclusion might have explained how the protagonist's losing her "prerogative" makes her a victim. Another interpretation might explain that her reactions to her new situation reveal strength of character. Still another use of the conclusion might be to reveal the protagonist as a splendid oddity, a woman of independent means with

a self-directed future, living in a world where men traditionally make decisions. Indeed, there are many conclusions that could be reached about the character of the protagonist and of the nature of her predicament. That's why forgoing these opportunities simply to retell the story seems wasteful.

The student's essay also suffers from more general concerns. It doesn't answer the question in the writing assignment. This essay is simply a personal response to the story, a useful approach in an informal journal, perhaps, but not what the assignment requested.

Moreover, the essay reflects a lack of understanding of the elements of a short story and the terms used to designate them. Like other areas of study, literary analysis has its own technical terminology. Being able to use these terms will improve your literary analyses (see pages 648–649).

Another weakness of this essay is the absence of direct quotations from the text. Quoting is an invaluable way to support your assertions about a short story. Chapter 20 discusses how to incorporate direct quotations in your essay.

### Second Student Response to "The Answer Is No": More Effective

Here is a student's response to the topic that offers a valid thesis and supports it with evidence from the story:

An Ongoing Equilibrium

In Naguib Mahfouz's "The Answer Is No," the unnamed protagonist is an Egyptian woman schoolteacher who learns that an old nemesis has returned to her world. When the protagonist was fourteen years old, her math tutor, Badran Badawi, had raped her. Years later she learns that he has been appointed headmaster of the school where she now teaches. The story analyzes her complex reaction to this news.

*This is an appropriate plot summary. It is long enough to demonstrate an overall grasp of the story without boring the reader. What follows in subsequent paragraphs is analysis.*

The protagonist cannot be seen as an "average" Egyptian woman. In that traditional, Islamic country, the future of a woman is more likely to involve marriage and children than a professional position. Yet the protagonist has brains, money, a liberal family, and a ruthless streak of independence: "It had meant little to her to sacrifice marriage. She had welcomed being on her own, for solitude accompanied by self-respect was not loneliness" (544). It is a mistake, then, to read "The Answer Is No" as a harbinger of a dismal future for her. Her peace of mind has been disturbed, but unlike so

*In this paragraph, the student makes good use of a direct quotation that relates directly to and supports an important point.*

many other women, she is not trapped. She can either deal successfully with Badawi or move on.

The depiction of the rape shows an interesting contrast in perception. The protagonist is the daughter of a wealthy couple, who
are able to procure a math tutor for her. However, the math tutor
ravishes his pupil as if the right were divinely given: "She had asked
in terror about what had occurred, and he had told her, 'Don't be
frightened or sad. Keep it to yourself and I'll come and propose to
you the day you come of age'" (544). Badawi obviously equates
"woman" with "peasant," regardless of the woman's social standing.
Thus, he is almost casual about his crime.

Again, the student
makes excellent use of
direct quotation. In
addition, she draws a
valid, if rather harsh,
conclusion about
Badawi's vision of
women.

Badawi keeps his word, however, and returns to "make things
right." Unfortunately, he misjudges the character of his potential
"bride": "She had felt such anger as she had never felt before. She
had rejected coercion in the same way as she rejected ugliness"
(544). Her answer, obviously, is no.

In the years that follow, the young woman devotes her life to her
career, never marrying but learning to appreciate her solitude. The
news of Badawi's appointment as headmaster comes as a nasty surprise. The man to whom she had once said "For me any outcome is
preferable to being married to you" (544) is now her boss. The situation is a tricky one for Badawi as well. He tries to make small talk to
her, asking about the intervening years, but finds that his former
pupil has an icy wall that will not allow him entrance.

Although these para-
graphs contain some
recounting of plot,
they concentrate on
character analysis and
help to explain the
dynamics of the rela-
tionship between the
protagonist and her
rapist/suitor.

Ironically, the person the protagonist has become is a reaction to
her childhood assault by Badawi. To see him appointed as her supervisor, however, is intolerable. In effect, she has spent her life avoiding gender domination, and now fate has put her on a strange path.
But the protagonist is fortunate in one major respect: she can move
on, and many women do not enjoy that kind of independence and
mobility.

The conclusion is
appropriate in that it
clearly responds to the
assignment. The writer
disagrees that the pro-
tagonist "loses her
'male prerogative'
and suffers as a 'tradi-
tional' woman."

**EXERCISE 22.1**

Reread "The Answer Is No." Write a 400- to 550-word essay on the following topic:

> Evaluate the character of Badran Badawi. What does the story tell you about him? In your opinion, does his character change over the years covered by the narrative? What is your sense of this man?

Quote from the story to support your assertions, and cite the appropriate page number(s).

# WRITING ABOUT POETRY

Although some poems are narratives, most are not. When you read poetry, you need to pay attention to language, interpretation, and imagery more than to plot and characterization.

A further distinction can be made between types of poetry. Traditional poetry follows patterns of rhyme and meter. On the other hand, modern poetry, which dates from about the time of the nineteenth-century American writer Walt Whitman (1819–1892), has slowly moved away from rhyme schemes and fixed rhythms. By the middle of the twentieth century, many serious poets were writing **free verse**, poetry without intentional rhyming and rhythmic patterns. When analyzing traditional poetry, you need to be aware of the techniques the poet uses to accommodate the needs of his or her chosen form. For example, in the sonnet "On First Looking into Chapman's Homer," John Keats ends by mentioning *Darien,* an archaic name for Panama:

> Much have I traveled in the realms of gold,
>     And many goodly states and kingdoms seen;
>     Round many western islands have I been
> Which bards in fealty to Apollo hold.
> Oft of one wide expanse had I been told          5
>     That deep-browed Homer ruled as his demesne;
>     Yet did I never breathe its pure serene
> Till I heard Chapman speak out loud and bold:
> Then felt I like some watcher of the skies
>     When a new planet sweeps into his ken;          10
> Or like stout Cortez when with eagle eyes
>     He stared at the Pacific—and all his men
> Looked at each other with a wild surmise—
>     Silent, upon a peak in Darien.

The reader might believe that Keats was being willfully obscure unless he or she understands that *Darien* fits Keats's rhyme scheme in this sonnet; *Panama* does not. Keats seems to have been trying to find a word that fit.

In analyzing modern poetry, the reader needs to concentrate more on the role of the speaker, on the use of language, figurative or otherwise, and on the creation of tone, mood, and imagery. Whatever "type" of poetry you analyze, it is always helpful to know something about the literary and historical context in which it was written as well as about the life of the poet. Moreover, knowing the appropriate terminology for the elements of poetry is invaluable. Learning these concepts and the terms for them will help you derive more meaning from the poems you analyze.

## Useful Terms for Writing About Poetry

**alliteration**   The repetition of initial consonant sounds in nearby words: "The crow's cackling caw." (See also **consonance**.)

**allusion**   An indirect reference to a well-known person, work of art, or event. Describing a current baseball player as "the new Sultan of Swat" is an allusion to Babe Ruth, the original Sultan of Swat.

**assonance**   The repetition of vowel sounds: "The trees freeze in the breeze."

**caesura**   A stop, pause, or break, often signaled by a period, within a line of poetry.

**character**   A figure within any creative literary work. (See also **antagonist** and **protagonist** from the list on pages 648–649.)

**consonance**   The repetition of internal consonant sounds or ending consonant sounds in nearby words: "The brick clicked." (See also **alliteration**.)

**figurative language**   (See **metaphor, personification**, and **simile**; see also Chapter 4.)

**free verse**   Poetry without a rhyme scheme or fixed meter.

**image**   A description meant to evoke a mental picture for the reader: "A drowned dog floated by, or was it a bad piñata?" The image of the piñata reinforces the image of the disfigurement caused by drowning.

**imagery**   Images working together to create a desired effect.

**irony**   A discrepancy between appearance and reality: "That the people of the 1920s believed the first world war was the final global battle is ironic when the events of the late 1930s are considered."

**metaphor**   A figure of speech in which one thing represents or is compared to another without using *like* or *as*. Thus, "The club scene is a black hole for my wallet" uses the metaphor of *black hole* to describe the financial losses suffered by the writer as a result of club crawling. In one of his sonnets, Shakespeare compares trees in winter to "Bare ruined choirs where late the sweet birds sang." (See also **personification** and **simile**; see also Chapter 4.)

**meter**   A patterned rhythm of stressed and unstressed syllables found in traditional poetry. The meter of a poem is partly determined by the type of *feet* (combinations of syllables) used:
- Iambic: *collapse* (two syllables with stress on the second)
- Trochaic: *apple* (two syllables with stress on the first)

- Dactyl: *tenderly* (three syllables with stress on the first, and the next two syllables unstressed)
- Anapest: *unappeased* (three syllables with the first two unstressed and the third stressed)

The meter of a poem also depends on the number of feet per line. The terms *trimeter, tetrameter, pentameter,* and *hexameter* refer to lines of three, four, five, and six feet, respectively. When the type of foot is connected to the number of feet, the meter is identified. Here is a line in iambic tetrameter: "I put a hat upon my head." The line has eight syllables constituting four feet. The rhythm is iambic—the stressed syllables are two, four, six, and eight.

**metonymy**   A figure of speech in which a noun is used to evoke associated meaning: "Live by the sword, and die by the sword" probably doesn't refer to a person who owns a sword. Rather, the word *sword* is used to suggest "violence."

**motif**   A recurring word, musical phrase, or visual object with thematic significance: "Each major character in *Death of a Salesman* has his or her 'own' music that announces the character's stage entrance; this motif engages an audience in a very interesting way."

**narrator**   The teller of the story. Note that *narrator* does not equal *author.* Frequently, the narrator of a story, novel, or poem is a character within the narrative.

**onomatopoeia**   The use of a word that sounds like what it describes: *squeak, screech, hoot,* and so on.

**parody**   A literary work that imitates another literary work in order to ridicule it.

**personification**   A figure of speech in which human characteristics are ascribed to nonhuman entities: "The full moon smiled kindly at us." The moon can't smile. However, the writer uses personification to build a pleasant tone and illustrate the scene. (See also **metaphor** and **simile**; see also Chapter 4.)

**prosody**   The technical study of poetry. See also **meter** and **rhyme scheme**.

**rhyme**   Matching sounds at the end of two or more lines of poetry: "He stands upon his *feet* / before he takes a *seat.*" See also **rhyme scheme**.

**rhyme scheme**   The pattern of rhyming found in a poem. Some rhyming poetry uses *couplets,* pairs of lines that rhyme. Other rhyme schemes include those used in the English sonnet and the Italian sonnet. (See also **sonnet.**) Traditionally, a rhyme scheme is charted by assigning a letter, starting with *a,* to the sound at the end of a line. Note the following four lines:

I put a hat upon my head,          (a)
I walked out in the street.          (b)

There my boss I chanced to meet,     (b)

I wished I'd stayed in bed.     (a)

This doggerel has a rhyme scheme of abba (head, street, meet, bed). If this poem were to continue—thankfully, it does not—the next new line-ending sound would be assigned the letter *c*.

**satire**   A work that ridicules either for entertainment or to suggest reform: "Voltaire's *Candide* is a wide-ranging satire of the Enlightenment's belief systems."

**setting**   The time and place of a narrative or poem. Given the differences among cultures, countries, regions, and eras, knowing both when and where a narrative or poem is set is crucial to understanding it: "Peter Straub's novel *Ghost Story* is set in upstate New York in the early 1970s."

**simile**   A figure of speech similar to a **metaphor.** However, similes use *like* or *as* to create comparisons. Note the difference between these two lines:

METAPHOR     **My love is a red, red rose.**

SIMILE     **My love is like a red, red rose.**

(See also **metaphor** and **personification;** see also Chapter 4.)

**sonnet**   A fourteen-line poem in iambic pentameter (see also **meter**). The **English** (or **Shakespearean**) sonnet's rhyme scheme (see also **rhyme scheme**) is abab cdcd efef gg. Lines 13 and 14 are called the *couplet.* The **Italian** sonnet has two parts. The first eight lines, called the *octave,* always follow this pattern: abba cddc. The final six lines, called the *sestet,* can use a variety of rhyme schemes. In both types of sonnet, the poet typically uses the first part of the poem (lines 1–12 in the English and lines 1–8 in the Italian) to frame an argument, present a situation, or ask a question. The remaining lines "confirm" or "solve" the situation or problem presented. Thus, for example, a poet writing an Italian sonnet might ask a question in the octave and provide the answer in the sestet.

**stanza**   Two or more lines grouped together and sometimes separated from other stanzas by a line space.

**symbol**   An object used to suggest something else, usually something abstract. For example, a broken pair of eyeglasses could symbolize a character's loss of moral perception.

**synecdoche**   A figure of speech in which a part stands for the whole or in which a general term is used to describe a more specific actor or action: "Five sails approach the harbor" refers to five ships." "Run! It's the law!" actually means "Run! It's a police officer!"

The poem on page 660 is William Wordsworth's "Composed upon Westminster Bridge, September 3, 1802." The model student essay that follows it, "Beauty in a Strange Context," was written in response to this assignment: "Pick one Wordsworth poem from the group assigned, and explain why it is different from the rest."

## Guidelines for Quoting Poetry

Chapter 20 explains how to use the MLA style of quoting text. Those guidelines also apply to quoting poetry, with three modifications:

1. Cite line numbers, not page numbers. Include *line* or *lines* with your first reference, as the student paper does on page 661.

2. If you are quoting two or three lines of a poem, separate the lines with a slash (/), as in the following example:

   > Wordsworth emphasizes his overwhelmingly positive sense of London at daybreak: "Never did sun more beautifully steep / In his first splendour, valley, rock, or hill; / Ne'er saw I, never felt, a calm so deep!" (9–11).

   Note that the slash is preceded and followed by a space.

3. If you are quoting more than three lines, set off the quotation as a block, as in the following example:

   > Wordsworth emphasizes his overwhelmingly positive sense of London at daybreak:

   > This City now doth, like a garment, wear
   >
   > The beauty of the morning; silent, bare,
   >
   > Ships, towers, domes, theatres, and temples lie
   >
   > Open unto the fields, and to the sky;
   >
   > All bright and glittering in the smokeless air. (4–8)

   Note that the block quotation matches the poem line for line and that no quotation marks are added.

### Composed upon Westminster Bridge, September 3, 1802

Earth has not any thing to show more fair:
Dull would he be of soul who could pass by
A sight so touching in its majesty:
This City now doth, like a garment, wear
The beauty of the morning; silent, bare,                    5
Ships, towers, domes, theatres, and temples lie
Open unto the fields, and to the sky;
All bright and glittering in the smokeless air.
Never did sun more beautifully steep
In his first splendour, valley, rock, or hill;              10
Ne'er saw I, never felt, a calm so deep!
The river glideth at his own sweet will:
Dear God! the very houses seem asleep;
And all that mighty heart is lying still!

Beauty in a Strange Context

William Wordsworth's "Composed upon Westminster Bridge, September 3, 1802" takes a traditional Romantic enthusiasm, the love of nature's beauty, but finds a strange source for this beauty in industrial London. Wordsworth confounds our expectations by praising a sight we would expect him to abhor.

Thesis: the point about the poem that the writer will support.

The Industrial Revolution was in full swing in 1802. London was filled with industry, homes, and air pollution spawned by a reliance on soft coal as a fuel. It was an enormous, filthy place, hardly to be mentioned in the same breath with the natural, untouched beauty of Wordsworth's beloved Lake District, in the western part of England. However, the poet catches the city just before it awakes; the resulting picture is surprising and gains value because of that surprise.

"Westminster Bridge" is an Italian sonnet. The octave is regular; the sestet follows the CDCDCD pattern. The iambic rhythm is not perfect; especially in the second half of the poem, Wordsworth strives for a conversational rhythm rather than a strict one. The result is an informal effect—the poet has seen something that amazes him, and the poem reflects this growing surprise.

The writer shows how Wordsworth modifies the traditional approach to the form he is using.

In the first line, Wordsworth defines the city's visual beauty by using the negative: "Earth has not any thing to show more fair." It is a "sight . . . touching in its majesty" (line 3). He then uses a simile to show the temporary nature of this sight: "This City now doth, like a garment, wear / The beauty of the morning . . ." (4-5). The poet then uses one of his frequent techniques, listing, to show the power of the scene: "Ships, towers, domes, theatres, and temples" (6) are revealed as a majestic vista, "All bright and glittering in the smokeless air" (8). The key word is "smokeless." The factories are not running; the home fires are banked. Briefly, the city is not corrupted by pollution.

The writer indicates omitted words with an ellipsis.

The writer uses well-chosen quotations to demonstrate how Wordsworth portrays the beauty of the city.

The writer explains what the sonnet form contributes to Wordsworth's poem.

Thus ends the octave, whose traditional purpose in the Italian sonnet is to pose a problem, present an argument, or ask a question. Here, Wordsworth sets up a proposal and then uses the sestet to give his summation or evaluation. He points out that never in a rural area did he see the sun "steep" a landscape, using "steep" in the same sense as "brew" (9). Nor has he ever before experienced "a calm so deep!" (11). His conclusion is "And all that mighty heart is lying still!" (14). At first light, London presents a scene of beauty that will surely disappear as the workday begins.

William Blake, Wordsworth's fellow Romantic, believed that even a grain of sand could indicate infinity. In "Westminster Bridge," Wordsworth takes a similar approach: Nature can overpower the stinking industrial hell that London had become by 1802. The reader's surprise at this paradox helps to stimulate the imagination when experiencing the sonnet.

The conclusion refers back to the thesis by mentioning the reader's surprise.

CATALYST 2.0

**MORE OPTIONS ONLINE**
To learn how to write about drama and film, go to
www.mhhe.com/ writingtoday.

## EXERCISE 22.2

Reread "On First Looking into Chapman's Homer" (page 656). Write a 400- to 600-word essay on the following topic:

This poem is about quest and discovery. What, exactly, has Keats discovered, and how does he indicate his astonishment at what he has found?

Quote from the poem to support your assertions, and cite the appropriate line number(s).

**Thinking of grammar as dry and** perhaps mundane, students rarely want to study English at the level of sentences. But the truth is that students who can't write effective sentences also can't write effective essays. Essays are, after all, collections of sentences.

The good news is that American English is highly systematic in most areas. In other words, once you learn a particular concept, you will be able to apply it to various writing situations. In addition, once you learn some basic sentence concepts, learning others will become easier.

Chapter 23 focuses on the parts of speech and the way they function. Chapter 24 moves to the working parts of sentences and then explains how you can design whole sentences so that they achieve a specific function.

Chapter 25 analyzes major sentence errors, the ones that cause the greatest grief for most students, and explores several ways to avoid these errors. Chapter 26 discusses the correct use of verbs.

Chapter 27 covers problems with pronouns while Chapter 28 deals with the use of modifiers—various types of adjectives and adverbs, their forms, and their placements.

Chapter 29 explains how to punctuate sentences using a comma or commas. As a follow-up, Chapter 30 discusses using other marks of punctuation. Chapter 31 covers mechanics. Chapter 32 explains diction and word choice: the problem of nuance, of "weasel words," and of idiom. This chapter concludes with a look at spelling problems. Chapter 33 is a glossary of usage, discussing often-confused words and distinctions of meaning.

PART

4

# GRAMMAR AND MECHANICS

Chapters 23 through 32 are filled with examples and illustrations of the concepts that we discuss. Each of these chapters also contains several exercises so that you can practice "making things right." Our emphasis, as always, is on function. We believe that the logical and most useful response to a student who says, for example, "I think this is a comma splice" is "How are you going to correct it?" •

# PARTS OF SPEECH

### CHAPTER 23

As a writer, you don't need to know the part of speech of every word in every situation, but one fact is unavoidable: when instructors discuss grammar, they have to refer to parts of speech. Therefore, the more you know about this topic, the easier it will be to understand grammar.

The two main parts of speech are nouns and verbs. In this chapter we will discuss first nouns and the parts of speech that relate to them, and then verbs and the parts of speech that relate to them.

## 23a NOUNS

**Nouns** name a

| **person** | **thing** | or | **place** |
|---|---|---|---|
| Moses | wheat | | Wyoming |
| Gandhi | computer | | Prague |
| technician | college | | the South |
| teacher | strength | | Suffolk County |
| woman | spiritualism | | Pakistan |

1. **Proper nouns** refer to a specific person, place, organization, religion, title, or brand name; their first letter is capitalized:

   David

   Philadelphia

   *The Matrix*

   Kleenex

   Judaism

2. **Common nouns** name someone or something that is more general; they are not capitalized:

   police officer

   city

   film

   tissue

   religion

   The trend in American English is to see nouns as common that were once seen as proper:

   the mayor

   the president

   However, when attached to a person's name, the common noun becomes a proper noun:

   Mayor Sanders

   President Polk

   For more on capitalization, see Chapter 31.

   Some common nouns are **abstract;** they refer to concepts:

   | | |
   |---|---|
   | maturity | suffering |
   | love | excitement |
   | democracy | intellect |
   | selfishness | perseverance |

Other common nouns are **concrete**; they refer to tangible items:

| | |
|---|---|
| cats | desks |
| computers | trees |
| dust | buildings |
| sofa | shoes |

3.  **Count nouns** refer to items that are normally enumerated. They form their plurals by adding *-s* or *-es*. Typically, these are concrete nouns:

horses

boxes

cars

vacuums

However, some count nouns are irregular and retain the same spelling, whether singular or plural:

| | |
|---|---|
| one moose | seventeen moose |
| one sheep | forty sheep |
| one deer | eight deer |

4.  **Noncount nouns** refer to concepts or to things that are normally not counted but are otherwise identified or measured:

| | |
|---|---|
| spirituality | oxygen |
| justice | equipment |
| rice | poetry |
| dust | music |

Generally, the articles *a* and *an* are not used with noncount nouns:

**NOT**   a rice

**BUT**   the rice *or* rice

We *weigh* rice; we don't *count* it as we would biscuits: "I made six biscuits and half a pound of rice."

> However, note that some nouns are either count or noncount depending on context and meaning:

Jennifer thought that **love** was a fascinating topic.
Francisco has many **loves** in his life.

In the first example, *love* is an emotion (noncount and abstract); in the second, *loves* refers to people or things (count and concrete).

5.  **Nouns and their sentence functions.** Nouns function as subjects, objects, and complements.

> The **subject** of a sentence controls the verb:

**Parker** read the novel.
**Justice** prevails.

The **direct object** of a verb receives its action:

Serena kicked the **door.**

gr
23b

An **indirect object** is the word or words for which the action is completed:

           i.o.          d.o.

John mailed **Joan** the **present.**

*Joan* is the indirect object; *present* is the direct object.

A **complement** appears when the sentence contains a **linking verb,** such as *be, feel, seem,* or *appear* (see page 678) The linking verb connects the subject to its complement.

Alejandro is my **friend.**

A **gerund** is a noun that is formed by adding *-ing* to a verb. Gerunds name activities. For example, adding *-ing* to the verb *play* results in the noun *playing:*

**Playing** soccer is my young son's favorite activity.

Note that when you add *-ing* to a verb, the result is not always a gerund. In the sentence "My son is playing soccer," *playing* is a participle (see 23k).

## EXERCISE 23.1

Underline the nouns in the following paragraph.

Traveling by bus provides a fascinating peek into an aspect of America that many people have not seen. Buses take the back roads, stopping at small towns that time seems to have forgotten. "Good Food" and "Eat" appear in the neon signs of old restaurants. People wave to each other from their cars, and they turn to see who is getting off the bus. Dogs sleep in the streets. Indeed, time seems to stand still. However, the observer has not entered a time warp. Unless the town is very small and isolated, a Wal-Mart store (or a similar competitor) is likely to be nearby. The Internet also provides a link to the larger world. As well, cable and satellite TV services allow small-town residents access to HBO and Bravo, among other options. The world of the small town may look different, but perhaps it is not so different after all.

## 23b PRONOUNS

**Pronouns** replace nouns or other pronouns. The noun or pronoun that is replaced is called an *antecedent,* "the word that comes before."

        antecedent                       pronoun

The **parents** wished the best for **their** son.

Pronouns are used to create emphasis and avoid repetition. There are eight classes of pronouns: personal, indefinite, reflexive, intensive, relative, interrogative, demonstrative, and reciprocal.

1.  **Personal pronouns** refer to specific people, places, and things. They are classified by **case,** the role they play in the sentence:

I [subjective case] found the letter.
The letter was found by **me** [objective case].
The letter is **mine** [possessive case].

Here are the personal pronouns:

| Subjective Case | Objective Case | Possessive Case |
|---|---|---|
| I | me | my, mine |
| you | you | your, yours |
| he | him | his |
| she | her | her, hers |
| it | it | its |
| we | us | our, ours |
| they | them | their, theirs |

Remember to use the correct case and to avoid careless sentences like this one:

INCORRECT   **Bill came over to Martha and I, asking if we had heard about the tornado.**

Take out *Martha and,* and the sentence sounds absurd. You would never write *Bill came over to I.* The correct form is *me,* not *I,* for *me* is the object of the preposition *to.*

As shown in the chart above, personal pronouns indicate **number**—that is, singular or plural (*she* is singular; *they* is plural). They also indicate gender (*he* is masculine; *she* is feminine; *it* is neuter). Finally, they indicate person (*I* and *we* are first-person; *you* is second-person; *he/she/it* and *they* are third person).

2. **Indefinite pronouns,** as their name suggests, refer to unspecified persons or things. Some are always singular, some are always plural, and some are singular or plural depending on context.

| Always Singular | Always Plural | Singular or Plural Depending upon Context |
|---|---|---|
| another | both | all |
| anybody | few | any |
| anyone | many | either |
| anything | several | enough |
| each | | more |
| every | | most |
| everybody | | neither |
| everyone | | none |
| everything | | some |
| no one | | |
| nobody | | |
| nothing | | |

**Always Singular**

one

somebody

someone

something

Almost **everyone** in my class **is** here for the game.
**Few have** stayed behind.
**All** of the pizza **is** disappearing as we approach the kickoff.
**All** of our football players **are** ready to do their best.

3. **Reflexive pronouns** refer to the self and always end in -*self* or *selves:*

The farmer checked **himself** for deer ticks.

Here are the reflexive pronouns:

| | |
|---|---|
| myself | yourself |
| herself | yourselves |
| himself | ourselves |
| oneself | themselves |
| itself | |

Use reflexive pronouns only when they are appropriate. "David and myself made the dessert" should be "David and I. . . ." Also, avoid nonstandard forms, such as *hisself, theirself,* and *theirselves.*

4. **Intensive pronouns** are spelled the same as reflexive pronouns but have a different purpose—to provide emphasis:

Joan's young daughter baked the cake **herself.**
We **ourselves** have replaced the plumbing in our home.

5. **Relative pronouns** introduce dependent (subordinate) clauses that act as adjectives. Clauses that begin with relative pronouns refer to an earlier noun or pronoun in the sentence. Remember that *who, whom, whoever,* and *whomever* always refer to people.

| | |
|---|---|
| who | that |
| whoever | what |
| whom | whatever |
| whomever | which |
| whose | whichever |

Martha is the only gymnast **who** had a perfect score.

Here is the car **that** I want to buy.

The elderly man, **whatever** his relationship to you, is a gentleman.

6. **Interrogative pronouns** are used to form questions:

| | |
|---|---|
| what | whatever |
| which | whichever |
| who | whom |
| whoever | whomever |
| whose | |

**Which** is the correct road?
**What** is the answer?
To **whom** does the future belong?

7. **Demonstrative pronouns** (*this, these, that, those*) are used to show "which one":

**This** is the hat Carlotta will wear to the wedding.
**That** is the same problem Judy mentioned.
**These** are not my shoes.
**Those** were the paintings we saw in the gallery.

8. **Reciprocal pronouns** (*each other, one another*) refer equally to individual parts of a plural antecedent:

Juan and Maria love **each other.**
The three brothers consulted **one another** regularly.

Use *each other* to refer to a plural antecedent made up of two entities; use *one another* to refer to a plural antecedent made up of three or more entities.

## EXERCISE 23.2

In the following paragraph, underline the pronouns. Then identify each pronoun by writing the correct number above it: (1) personal, (2) indefinite, (3) reflexive, (4) intensive, (5) relative, (6) interrogative, (7) demonstrative, or (8) reciprocal.

My friend Gene and I talk to each other frequently. Gene is a successful accountant. However, he has confided to me that he wants to separate himself from his middle-class world and join a carnival. What is wrong with him? Nothing, as far as I can tell. Gene has harbored this fantasy for years, which is why I find myself surprised to learn that I am the only other person who knows about it. Anyone who keeps this type of secret must eventually doubt his or her sanity, and I was quick to assure Gene that everybody has a harmless reverie. I myself sometimes dream about becoming an international hip-hop star, which is a much stranger idea to me than joining a traveling carnival.

## 23c ADJECTIVES

An **adjective** modifies a noun or pronoun; in other words, it makes the noun or pronoun more specific by describing, limiting, evaluating, clarifying, and so on. In English, most adjectives *precede* nouns:

> A **large, brown** dog ran along the **dusty** road into a **small** shack that sat at the foot of a **flower-covered** hill.

> The **rusty old** car belongs to Joshua.

Note that nouns can sometimes be used as adjectives:

> a **computer** class        a **Ford** dealership        a **rock** concert

In **compound adjectives**, the first adjective describes the second and is connected to it with a hyphen. Collectively, the resulting term modifies the noun:

> a **coal-black** fish

Adverbs may be part of such a formation:

> an **all-too-common** problem

Adjectives can act as **complements** in sentences with linking verbs (*be, feel, seem,* and so on—see page 678).

> **SUBJECT COMPLEMENT**   I [subject] feel [linking verb] tired [subject complement].

> **OBJECT COMPLEMENT**   His tone [subject] made us [direct object] nervous [object complement].

In the preceding sentence, the linking verb is implicit:

> His tone made us [feel] nervous.

Do not follow a linking verb with an adverb used as a subject complement, as in the following sentence:

> **INCORRECT**       I feel badly.

> **CORRECT**        I feel bad.

Any adjective can be used in its **positive** (base) form as well as in its **comparative** and **superlative** forms. The comparative form is used when comparing two persons or things; the superlative is used with three or more persons or things:

> **POSITIVE**       John is **tall.**

> **COMPARATIVE**      Betty is **taller** than he.

> **SUPERLATIVE**      Calogero is the **tallest** of the three soldiers.

You can find more about creating comparatives and superlatives in Chapter 28.

### EXERCISE 23.3

In each of the following sentences, choose the correct word from the choices in the parentheses.

1. This new cologne smells (bad, badly).
2. Of the two paintings, the older one is clearly (better, best).
3. Terry is the (taller, tallest) member of his extended family.
4. Sara is very happy with her new (macintosh, Macintosh) computer.
5. Juan is (tall, taller, tallest).

## 23d ARTICLES

**Articles** modify nouns, much as adjectives do (see page 672). Usually, articles are not attached to pronouns, except in sentences such as the following:

> Are you **the** one I've been hearing about?

The **indefinite articles** (*a* and *an*) can be used with count nouns that are not specific (see page 667 for a discussion of "count" and "noncount" nouns):

> **a** car     **a** unit     **an** insect     **an** actor

Note that *a* is used before words beginning with consonant sounds; *an* is used before words beginning with vowel sounds. The key term here is *sounds*. Although *unit* begins with a vowel, the *u* is voiced as *y*, so *a* is needed instead of *an*.

When an indefinite article is separated from the noun by one or more adjectives or adverbs, use *a* or *an* according to the initial sound of the modifier nearest to the indefinite article:

> **an** indefinite article
>
> **a** commonly used article of clothing

Indefinite articles are rarely used with proper nouns. Here is an exception:

> There is **a** Robert Kendall here to see you, Dr. Fernandez.

The **definite article** (*the*) indicates a specific noun: **the** *college,* **the** *elephant,* **the** *unit:*

> **The** woman [specific person] arguing with **the** store manager [specific manager] is not **a** friend [any particular friend] of mine.

The definite article is sometimes used with proper nouns, but rarely with names:

> **the** Mississippi River          **the** Porsche Boxster
>
> Bennigan's Restaurant          Marisa Tomei

For more on using articles, see pages 757–759.

### EXERCISE 23.4

In each of the following sentences, the article is highlighted. Decide if each article is used correctly. If not, revise the sentence so that it is correct.

1. We stopped at **an** highway sign along Route 17.
2. My uncle paid twenty dollars for **a** Uriah Heep album.

**3.** This soup is horrible; I'm going to complain to **a** restaurant's owner.

**4.** Her car accident was surely the result of **a** uncommon situation.

**5.** Let's eat lunch at **the** Subway.

## 23e PREPOSITIONS

**Prepositions** connect nouns and pronouns to other words in a sentence. They normally indicate time, place, position, contrast/similarity to, direction, or some other kind of relationship between the noun or pronoun and the words to which the preposition is connecting the noun or pronoun. Many prepositions are single words; others are compound words.

### Single-Word Prepositions

| | | | |
|---|---|---|---|
| about | below | for | through |
| above | beneath | from | to |
| across | beside | in | toward |
| after | between | including | under |
| against | beyond | inside | underneath |
| along | by | into | until |
| amid | despite | like | up |
| among | down | near | upon |
| as | during | of | via |
| at | except | on | with |
| before | excluding | over | within |
| behind | following | since | without |

### Compound-Word Prepositions

| | | |
|---|---|---|
| according to | except for | in spite of |
| along with | in addition to | instead of |
| as to | in front of | on account of |
| because of | in place of | with regard to |
| by means of | in reference to | up to |

We received a letter **from** our insurance agent.
Mike lives **near** the river.
**According to** this map, Glenwood is just a few miles farther.
The baseball team won **in spite of** its five errors.

The noun, pronoun, or gerund (a noun ending in *-ing,* which is made from a verb and names an activity) that follows a preposition is called the preposition's **object;** combined, the structure is called a **prepositional phrase.** Occasionally, writers wonder how to structure a difficult prepositional phrase or which preposition goes with a verb to make a verb phrase. Certain objects and verbs "take" specific prepositions; in other words, the correct wording is dictated by custom, not by logic. See Chapter 32, pages 818–820, for a list of many of the troublesome phrases in English. The following are some common phrases:

Angelo and Mark **agreed on** a plan.
Angelo and Mark **agreed to** a meeting.
Angelo and Mark **agreed with** their boss.

The umpire expected the players to **conform to** (not **with**) the rules.

The police have **joined in** the investigation.
The police have **joined with** the FBI in the investigation.

The Murcias **live on** this street.
The Murcias **live in** this house (community, town, county).

Marissa **looked in** the Bible for an appropriate quotation.
Marissa **looked at** the Bible sitting on the altar.
Marissa **looked for** the Bible she had misplaced.
Marissa **looked to** the Bible for guidance.
Marissa **looked on** as the Bible was placed on the podium.

The protestors **marched in** the parade.
The protestors **marched to** the courthouse.
The protestors **marched on** Washington.

Mary **rode on** a bus (train, boat).
Mary **rode in** a car.

The children are **sleeping on** the couch.
The children are **sleeping in** their beds.

Arnold is **working on** a new project.
Arnold is **working in** Tulsa.

Jeff **sat** quietly **at** his desk.
Jeff **sat** quietly **in** his chair.
Jeff **sat** quietly **on** the barstool.

We **parked on** the street.
We **parked in** a municipal lot.

Prepositions are also used with verbs to form multiword (or phrasal) verbs, such as *run into, call off,* and *pick up.* When prepositions are used in this way, they are called **particles**.

## EXERCISE 23.5

In each of the following sentences, fill in the blank with the appropriate preposition. In some cases, more than one answer may be correct.

1. Karen was pleased _____ the quality of her employees' presentation.
2. Franco has lived _____ this condo _____ his elderly father _____ six years.
3. I need to ask you some questions _____ the lunch break.
4. The winner _____ the race was the best _____ many qualified athletes.
5. Go _____ this door to get _____ the security building.

## 23f CONJUNCTIONS

**Conjunctions** join words, phrases, and clauses. There are four types: coordinating conjunctions, correlative conjunctions, conjunctive adverbs, and subordinating conjunctions.

1. The seven **coordinating conjunctions** are *and, but, for, so, yet, or,* and *nor.* Of these seven, *and, but, yet, or,* and *nor* are used to connect words, phrases, and clauses of equal grammatical weight:

   Carlos **and** Luisa are getting married.

   Finding a house **or** renting an apartment is our next project.

   The rescue worker didn't want to inspect the wreckage again, **nor** did she want to risk missing any survivors.

   As conjunctions, *for* and *so* are used only between independent clauses:

   Brenda's mechanic retired, **so** she had to find a new one.
   Alan will stay home tonight, **for** he needs to study.

   **Note:** Use the mnemonic FANBOYS (<u>f</u>or <u>a</u>nd <u>n</u>or <u>b</u>ut <u>o</u>r <u>y</u>et <u>s</u>o) to remember the seven coordinating conjunctions.

2. **Correlative conjunctions** are pairs of conjunctions that emphasize relationships—*both/and, not only/but also, either/or, neither/nor:*

   **Both** Larry **and** Gayle are late.
   Lori is **not only** cooking the food **but also** serving the meal.
   **Either** turn down the radio **or** listen to music elsewhere.

   When you use correlative conjunctions, make sure not to omit part of a pair. For example, don't link *not only* with *but* alone; the expression needs both words: *but also.*

3. **Conjunctive adverbs** (also known as transitional expressions) link independent clauses to show one sentence's relationship to the previous sentence. Like coordinating conjunctions, conjunctive adverbs join items of equal weight:

   | | |
   |---|---|
   | **WITH COORDINATING CONJUNCTION** | Sara wanted to go ice skating, **but** the rink was closed. |
   | **WITH CONJUNCTIVE ADVERB** | Sara wanted to go ice skating; **however,** the rink was closed. |
   | **WITH COORDINATING CONJUNCTION** | Hungary and Finland are in Europe, **but** their languages are not Indo-European. |
   | **WITH CONJUNCTIVE ADVERB** | Hungary and Finland are in Europe; **nonetheless,** their languages are not Indo-European. |

   Read the two preceding pairs of sentences again. Note that conjunctive adverbs can often provide greater emphasis. In addition, conjunctive adverbs, along with transitional expressions (their grammatical equals), allow writers to show precise relationships, whereas coordinating conjunctions have more general meanings. For a list of conjunctive adverbs and transitional expressions, see Chapter 25, pages 703–704.

Conjunctive adverbs can also be used to introduce a new sentence, as in the following example:

Sara wanted to go ice skating. **However,** the rink was closed.

In this instance, the writer decided to use two sentences instead of one. Note that conjunctive adverbs can appear *within* a sentence as well:

Sara wanted to go ice skating. The rink, **however,** was closed.

Conjunctive adverbs can also function as simple adverbs:

**However** isolated a person may be in our world, civilization is never far away.

4. **Subordinating conjunctions** show that one clause of a sentence (the dependent clause) is less important than and is dependent upon the other clause (the independent or main clause). For example, you might write the following:

We ate dinner; we saw a movie.

This sentence works fine if you wish to place equal emphasis on each clause or if the relationship between the two ideas in these clauses is not important. But what if you want to create emphasis or indicate a relationship? Here are two ways to do so. As you learned earlier, you can use a **conjunctive adverb:**

We ate dinner; **then** we saw a movie.

However, for variety's sake, you might also use a **subordinating conjunction:**

**After** we ate dinner, we saw a movie.

Here are some more examples:

| | |
|---|---|
| INDEPENDENT CLAUSES | Ishmael was sent into the desert. His name has come to mean "outcast." |
| ONE CLAUSE SUBORDINATED | Because Ishmael was sent into the desert, his name has come to mean "outcast." |
| INDEPENDENT CLAUSES | James Monroe was James Madison's secretary of state for a brief period. At the same time, he was Madison's secretary of war. |
| ONE CLAUSE SUBORDINATED | James Monroe was James Madison's secretary of state for a brief period while he was also serving as Madison's secretary of war. |

**Common Subordinating Conjunctions**

| | |
|---|---|
| after | in order to |
| although | since |
| as long as | unless |
| as soon as | until |
| as though | when |
| because | whenever |
| if | while |

For a more complete list of subordinating conjunctions, see Chapter 25, pages 703–704.

### EXERCISE 23.6

Each of the following sentences needs a coordinating conjunction, a correlative conjunction, a subordinating conjunction, or a conjunctive adverb/transitional expression. Supply an appropriate conjunction. More than one answer may be correct.

1. John returned home, he learned that his accountant was running behind on preparing tax returns.
2. Wanda wanted to see a movie; George was tired and wanted to stay home.
3. The bookstore was out of the novel that I wanted, I tried to find it online.
4. The prices here are ridiculous; the service is terrible.
5. Ed won't start college this fall, he didn't mail his application on time.

## 23g VERBS

**Verbs** show action (*walk, tell*) or a state of being (*do, seem*).

### 23g.1 VERB TYPES

There are four types of verbs: transitive, intransitive, linking, and helping (auxiliary) verbs.

1. A **transitive verb** shows action taken by a subject upon an object. A transitive verb always needs a *direct object,* which receives the action and makes the sentence a complete thought.

           t.v.     d.o.

   Melissa **hit** the **ball.**

2. An **intransitive verb** does not act upon an object:

           i.v.

   Jason **laughed.**

   Note that some verbs can be both transitive and intransitive depending on the context:

   Joe just **opened** a new ice cream shop.
   The new ice cream shop just **opened.**

3. Unlike most verbs, a **linking verb** does not indicate an action but expresses a relationship or a description. A linking verb connects the subject to its *complement,* a word or words that describe the subject:

   Tapioca **is** <u>an interesting dessert.</u>
   Your CD player **sounds** <u>strange.</u>

   Common linking verbs are *appear, be, become, feel, remain, seem, smell, sound,* and *taste.* (Note that some of these verbs can also function as action [transitive] verbs: *Maria tasted the peaches.*)

**4.** A **helping (auxiliary) verb** "qualifies" the main verb by showing its tense and mood (see the discussion of tense, page 681, and mood, page 682):

Theresa **is** studying tonight.
Theresa **will** study all of this weekend.
Theresa **has been** studying all week.

All forms of *be, do,* and *have* can function as helping verbs.

**5.** **Modal auxiliaries**, a subclass of auxiliary verbs, further "qualify" a main verb:

My friends **might** see a movie.
My friends **could** see a movie.
My friends **should** see a movie.

**6.** **Phrasal verbs** consist of a verb plus one or more prepositions. Some phrasal verbs are **separable;** in other words, an object may appear either within the verb phrase or after it:

Go **pick up** a large pizza for dinner.
Hoshi **picked** Susana **up** an hour before the concert.

Other phrasal verbs are **inseparable.** Their parts must remain together:

The car **broke down** three miles from Ashland.
We are **looking forward** to your arrival.

### 23g.2 VERB FORMS

Verbs often change spelling to indicate tense (time). The verb tenses include present, past, and future; present, past, and future perfect; and the six progressive tenses. You will learn about them in the next section. The change in spelling is minor in regular verbs, more pronounced and harder to predict in irregular verbs.

Regular verbs form their past tenses by adding *-ed* or *-d,* their present participles by adding *-ing,* and their past participles by adding *-d* or *-ed.* They form their future tenses by using *will.* For example, here are the forms for the regular verb *to paint:*

I like **to paint** alone. (base form)

I **paint** alone, but she **paints** with a friend. (present tense)

I **painted** alone. (past tense)

I **am painting** alone. (present progressive tense)

I **have painted** alone. (present perfect tense)

I **had painted** alone. (past perfect tense)

I **will paint** alone. (future tense)

Although most verbs are **regular,** some are **irregular.** The spelling of the principal parts of irregular verbs deviates from the regular pattern, such as with the irregular verb *go: go, goes, went, going, gone.* Check your dictionary. If the principal parts are not listed, the verb is regular. For now, here is a brief list of irregular verbs to use as a reference:

| IRREGULAR VERBS | | | |
|---|---|---|---|
| Present | Past | Present Participle | Past Participle |
| arise | arose | arising | arisen |
| awake | awoke | awaking | awaked, awoke |
| beat | beat | beating | beaten, beat |
| bring | brought | bringing | brought |
| catch | caught | catching | caught |
| choose | chose | choosing | chosen |
| cling | clung | clinging | clung |
| come | came | coming | come |
| do | did | doing | done |
| draw | drew | drawing | drawn |
| drive | drove | driving | driven |
| eat | ate | eating | eaten |
| fall | fell | falling | fallen |
| fly | flew | flying | flown |
| forgive | forgave | forgiving | forgiven |
| get | got | getting | gotten |
| go | went | going | gone |
| hang (to suspend) | hung | hanging | hung |
| hang (to execute) | hanged | hanging | hanged |
| keep | kept | keeping | kept |
| know | knew | knowing | known |
| lay (to place) | laid | laying | laid |
| lie (to recline) | lay | lying | lain |
| lie (to speak falsely) | lied | lying | lied |
| lose | lost | losing | lost |
| ride | rode | riding | ridden |
| rise | rose | rising | risen |
| run | ran | running | run |
| see | saw | seeing | seen |
| sit | sat | sitting | sat |
| speak | spoke | speaking | spoken |
| teach | taught | teaching | taught |
| tear | tore | tearing | torn |
| throw | threw | throwing | thrown |
| write | wrote | writing | written |

## EXERCISE 23.7

Each of the following sentences contains an irregular verb in parentheses. Provide the correct form of the verb.

**1.** The gold dollar (lie) on the ground for three hours before someone spotted it.

**2.** Mark had (get) fired from three jobs before he finally settled down.

**3.** The police believe that the suspect is (lie) about her whereabouts on the night of the robbery.

**4.** The carpenter discovered that he had (tear) his overalls during the morning.

**5.** Have you (eat) breakfast yet?

Three major features of verbs are their tense, mood, and voice.

## 23h VERB TENSE

Basically, **tense** refers to the time that a verb indicates. There are five basic categories of tense: present, past, future, the perfect tenses, and the progressive tenses.

The **present tense** indicates events occurring at the moment or that happen on a recurring basis:

The race **starts** now.
I **eat** sushi every week.

The **past tense** conveys action that has been completed:

The race **started** on time last year.
I **ate** sushi at Natalia's wedding last Sunday.

The **future tense** conveys future action:

The race **will start** when the referee blows her whistle.
I **will eat** sushi at dinner tonight even if it kills me.

The **perfect tenses** show action spanning different periods of time.

The **present perfect tense** refers to an action in the recent past and/or an action that is occurring in the present and is ongoing:

Eduardo **has spoken** about this issue many times.
The band **has played** for two hours.

The **past perfect tense** is used to refer to a time frame *before* a past time frame:

Luis **had dated** his fiancée before he **entered** the Air Force.

The past perfect in this sentence is indicated by the auxiliary verb *had;* the simple past is indicated by *entered* without *had.*

The **future perfect tense** refers to a future time before a fixed future time:

By the time our vacation has ended, we **will have driven** 2,500 miles.

The **progressive tenses** show ongoing activity. There are six types of progressive tenses:

| | |
|---|---|
| PRESENT PROGRESSIVE | Reina **is working** as fast as she can. |
| PAST PROGRESSIVE | Miguel **was visiting** Paris when he died. |
| FUTURE PROGRESSIVE | Phil **will be jogging** across the state in a charity marathon this week. |
| PRESENT PERFECT PROGRESSIVE | Angelo **has been collecting** money at our church. |
| PAST PERFECT PROGRESSIVE | Ingrid **had been trying** to get away when the police arrested her. |
| FUTURE PERFECT PROGRESSIVE | By next year, the company **will have been conducting** business in Moline for fifty years. |

### EXERCISE 23.8

Each of the following sentences contains a verb or verb phrase in parentheses. Given the context of the sentence, provide the correct form of the verb or verb phrase. More than one answer might be possible.

1. The Latino Association (has host) a lecture series for the past five years.
2. Ellen (has be run) every week for three years now.
3. Luis (has qualify) for his current rank two years before he applied for promotion.
4. By the end of the year, Andros (will has serve) over 5,000 pancakes.
5. To pick out Ray at the airport, remember that he (will is wear) a red hat.

### 23i  VERB MOOD

The **mood** of a verb tells the reader how to interpret a particular statement. Verbs occur in three moods: indicative, imperative, and subjunctive.

The **indicative mood,** the most common, is used in declarative and interrogative sentences to convey facts and ask questions:

Mivette **votes** in every election.
My sister **drove** an SUV across the country.
**Does** Ed **belong** to a labor union?

The **imperative mood** is used for commands, requests, and directions:

**Walk** carefully on this trail.
Always **back up** the computer's hard drive.
Please **pass** the salt.
**Turn** right at the next light.

The **subjunctive mood** indicates hypothetical situations, wishes, and conditions contrary to fact. It is also used to make recommendations. Sentences in the subjunctive often contain or begin with *if* and/or *were*:

If I **were** to go to tonight's training seminar, I might impress my boss.

I wish I **were** wealthy so that I could buy my parents a new car.

If cows **were** able to fly, air traffic would be horrendous.

In the first sentence, the writer hasn't decided whether to go or not, so the situation is hypothetical. The second sentence expresses a wish. The third sentence refers to an impossible situation, one contrary to reality.

Note that when the subjunctive appears in the present tense, the base form of the verb is used, as in this sentence, which recommends something:

The auditing committee recommends that the bank **fire** its CFO.

## EXERCISE 23.9

In each of the following sentences, examine the highlighted verb. Decide if it is used correctly. If not, revise the sentence.

1. If Kyle **was** more polite, he might have more friends.
2. If cats had thumbs, we **will** never live in safety again.
3. I suggested to my uncle that he **purchase** supplemental health insurance.
4. It is important that you **are** ready to start college this fall.
5. My nephew wishes that he **was** eighteen, not twelve.

## 23j VERB VOICE

Verbs have two voices: active and passive. The **active voice** is the more common:

     s.     v.       o.

John washed the car.

In the active voice, the subject acts. However, in the **passive voice**, the subject is acted upon:

     s.          v.

The car was washed by John.

Overusing the passive voice is a common error. The active-voice example above is simple and direct. The passive-voice example is indirect and wordy. Use the passive only when you have a good reason to do so:

The bank **was robbed** last night. [The culprit is unknown.]

Mistakes **were made** in the planning stages. [The writer doesn't wish to embarrass the person responsible.]

The door **was left** open. [By whom? It probably doesn't matter.]

The room **had been** vandalized. [This version is more direct than using the active voice. Writing "Vandals had torn the room apart" does not add any more information, and it contains an additional word.]

Otherwise, avoid the passive voice. The active voice is more forceful and economical.

gr
23k

### EXERCISE 23.10

Each of the following sentences uses the passive voice. Decide if the sentence is acceptable. If not, rewrite the sentence so that it uses the active voice.

1. Marisa's car was stolen last week.
2. The cat was chased by the dog for almost a hundred yards.
3. It was believed by Michael that late marriage was better than none at all.
4. After the party, we discovered that the front gate had been left unlatched all night.
5. Irregularities were discovered during the IRS auditor's examination of Ellen's tax returns.

## 23k VERBALS

**Verbals** are formed from verbs but function as other parts of speech. The three types of verbals are gerunds, participles, and infinitives.

A **gerund** is an *-ing* form of a verb that functions as a noun:

**Walking** is good exercise.
**Sleeping** has become a chore for me.

**Participles**—both present and past—function as adjectives:

The **winning** team will receive a trophy.
The **troubled** young man wandered the streets.

Note that the present participle and past participle can have different meanings:

Lucas is a very **tired** man.
Lucas is a very **tiring** man.

The past participle is normally used to describe how a person or thing has been *affected,* such as in "tired man." The present participle describes the effect the modified noun has on *others.* Lucas is "a very tiring man" because he exhausts others.

Keep in mind that some past or present participles cannot be used as adjectives:

CORRECT        The **doomed** prisoner was led to the execution chamber.

INCORRECT      The prisoner was thinking about the day that he heard the **dooming** news.

The second sentence is not idiomatic. Although *doom* has a present participle, *dooming,* it should not be used as an adjective.

An **infinitive** is the base form of the verb preceded by *to.* An infinitive can function as an adverb, an adjective, or a noun:

They went to Turkey **to study** Roman ruins. (adverb)
Jason is the person **to fix** your car. (adjective)
**To sacrifice** is noble. (noun)

## EXERCISE 23.11

Each of the following sentences contains a highlighted verbal. First, identify the verbal as a gerund, a present participle, a past participle, or an infinitive. Then indicate the function that the verbal serves—as adjective or as noun, for example.

1. Mr. Walters was a **broken** man after his business failed.
2. This pasta is **disgusting.**
3. **To play** a violin has long been her dream.
4. **Finding** fish is only half the battle on this river.
5. The **tired** racehorse fell back in the stretch.

## 23l  ADVERBS

**Adverbs** modify verbs, adjectives, or other adverbs by limiting their meaning, describing them, or evaluating them. Adverbs answer questions such as "how," "how often," "when," "where," and "to what extent."

Most adverbs are formed by adding *-ly* to an adjective:

| Adjective | Adverb |
|-----------|--------|
| nice | nicely |
| cruel | cruelly |
| terrible | terribly |

Notice the spelling change between *terrible* and *terribly.* The final *e* is dropped frequently but not always. For example, *definite* becomes *definitely.* A college-level dictionary will show you which spelling to use. Look up the adjective; then go to the end of the entry to find the adverbial spelling.

However, not all words that end in *-ly* are adverbs—*family, friendly,* and *portly,* for example. And keep in mind that not all adverbs end in *-ly. Well, too, very,* and *almost* are all adverbs.

In addition, some words can act as both adjectives and adverbs:

adj.                                      adv.
Ron owns a **fast** car, but he drives it too **fast.**

adj.                                   adv.
The **early** train will get us there **early.**

## 23m  PLACEMENT OF ADVERBS

Finding the correct position for an adverb can be complicated. Adverbs do not always appear next to the word they modify. The following guidelines will help:

1. When an adverb modifies an adjective or other adverb, it precedes the word it modifies: *very rich, **extremely** hungry, **really** too much, **almost** totally destroyed.*

    An exception *may* occur when an adverb modifies a present or past participle. In the following sentence, the adverb can either precede or follow the past participle:

gr
23n

The ballet was **beautifully** performed.
The ballet was performed **beautifully**.

However, in most situations, the adverb precedes the adjective or adverb that it modifies.

2.  When an adverb modifies a verb, the adverb might appear in several different positions without affecting the meaning of the sentence:

Veronica realized **slowly** that her computer was infected.
Veronica **slowly** realized that her computer was infected.
**Slowly,** Veronica realized that her computer was infected.

Often, however, changing the position of a verb modifier alters the meaning of a sentence—or makes the meaning unclear. Therefore, always position the adverb so that it clearly refers to *one* verb. Note these alternatives, in which the placement of *frequently* changes the sentence's meaning:

People who **frequently** use discount coupons save money.
People who use discount coupons save money **frequently**.

For more on adverbs and their placement, see Chapter 28.

### EXERCISE 23.12

Each of the following sentences is followed by an adverb in parentheses. Place the adverb in the *best* position in the sentence.

1.  The food at Mongolian Paradise is delicious. (absolutely)
2.  To read is better than not to read at all. (slowly)
3.  Dr. Taylor teaches advanced courses. (thoughtfully)
4.  Franklin began thinking about studying law. (seriously)
5.  Completing this course will require a great deal of work. (successfully)

### 23n  INTERJECTIONS

**Interjections** are short words or phrases that indicate surprise, disappointment, joy, or some other strong emotion:

**Oh, no,** I've overdrawn my checking account again.
**Alleluia!** Aunt Martha is finally leaving.

Interjections are connected to the rest of the sentence or sometimes stand alone, as in the second example.

### CHAPTER 24

# SENTENCE PARTS AND SENTENCE TYPES

To be a **sentence,** a group of words must contain a subject and a predicate and must express a complete idea. Of course, most sentences contain additional parts of speech grouped together in clauses and phrases. Sentences can be constructed in several forms: simple, compound, complex, and compound/complex. They can also be classified according to purpose: declarative, interrogative, imperative, and exclamatory.

# SENTENCE PARTS

## 24a SUBJECTS

The **subject** of a sentence is a noun, pronoun, or group of words that (1) completes an action, (2) is acted upon, or (3) is described or explained.

| | |
|---|---|
| SUBJECT THAT ACTS | **Laura Thompson** battles forest fires. |
| SUBJECT ACTED UPON | **The orphanage** was destroyed by fire. |
| SUBJECT DESCRIBED/ EXPLAINED | **The wonderful old cathedral** is more than four hundred years old. |

In the last example sentence above, *cathedral* is the **simple subject**; the **complete subject** is *the wonderful old cathedral*. **Compound subjects** contain more than one subject linked by *and:*

| | |
|---|---|
| COMPOUND SUBJECT | **Leslie and Jack** arrived an hour after the party began. |

Note that **gerunds** (nouns that end in *-ing* and that name an activity) and **gerund phrases** (see 24e) can also be subjects:

**Smoking** is prohibited in all campus buildings.

**Looking for antiques and shopping for curtains** took up their entire day.

Sometimes, subjects are quite long:

**The fact that no one ever checked Mark's résumé before we hired him** worries me.

## 24b PREDICATES

A **predicate** is a word or group of words that contains the sentence's verb and any of its modifiers. A predicate makes a statement about the subject. In the following sentences, the complete predicate is in italics; the verb appears in bold.

| | |
|---|---|
| PREDICATE THAT CONVEYS ACTION | In 1859, Joshua A. Norton *unabashedly **proclaimed** himself emperor of the United States.* |
| PREDICATE THAT DESCRIBES | Norton ***had** an obviously deranged set of beliefs.* |

## 24c OBJECTS

In addition to acting as subjects, nouns and pronouns can act as direct objects, indirect objects, and objects of prepositions.

A **direct object** receives the action of a predicate:

d.o.

In 1939, Germany attacked **Poland**.

d.o.
Seamus Heaney writes **poetry.**

An **indirect object** is a noun, pronoun, or group of words *for which* an action is completed:

i.o.      d.o.
The attacks of September 11, 2001, sent **the United States a horrifying message.**

i.o.    d.o.
Bonaparte gave the **French a unique set of laws** known as the Napoleonic Code.

The **object of a preposition** has the same function as an indirect object, except that it is introduced by a preposition such as *by, for, of,* or *to:*

o.p.
**To the French,** Bonaparte gave a unique set of laws known as the Napoleonic Code.

## 24d COMPLEMENTS

A **subject complement** is a word or group of words that provides information about a subject and follows a linking verb:

s.c.
Shirley Jackson's "The Lottery" is a **masterpiece of short fiction.**

An **object complement** comes after a direct object (see 24c) and describes or explains it:

d.o. o.c.
I call **him** a **genius.**

### EXERCISE 24.1

In each of the following sentences, a word or a group of words is highlighted. Identify the word or words as (1) subject, (2) predicate, (3) direct object, (4) indirect object, (5) object of a preposition, (6) subject complement, or (7) object complement.

1. **John's sister** is a nationally known dance critic.
2. In the **end,** you'll see that the training program is worth the trouble.
3. Mark gave **Helen** diamond earrings for their anniversary.
4. Tomoko is **a brilliant painter.**
5. Waiter, the salmon **seems to be a bit off today.**
6. Charles was angry after his boss called him a **moron.**
7. The police officer closed the **door** and sat in a chair.
8. **The bad news that the early mail supplied** was enough to ruin Dr. Le's day.
9. The family **plans to drive to Nebraska and visit their old neighbor.**
10. When I first visited the physical therapist, I didn't think much of **him.**

gr
24e

## 24e PHRASES

Phrases do not have both a subject and a predicate. A **phrase** is any related group of words that functions as a unit in a sentence but is not a clause. There are nine types of phrases, and each has a specific function.

1.  An **absolute phrase** is a clause without a verb; it modifies an entire sentence (see 24f for more on clauses):

    | CLAUSE | Her head was aching. |
    | --- | --- |
    | REDUCED TO ABSOLUTE PHRASE | **Her head aching,** Myra tried to steer her car through the snowstorm. |
    | CLAUSE | Its ancient tires were almost flat. |
    | REDUCED TO ABSOLUTE PHRASE | **Its ancient tires almost flat,** the car rested in the shadow of the barn. |

2.  An **appositive phrase** appears directly after a noun, renaming or otherwise identifying it. Most appositive phrases are set off by commas:

    Softball, **a sport derived from baseball,** is played in many elementary schools.

    My brother, **a stockbroker,** is vacationing in Alberta.

    Our class loved discussing Hemingway's *A Moveable Feast,* **his memoir of Paris in the 1920s.**

    Note that an appositive that specifically identifies a noun is not set off by commas (see also pages 766–768):

    Rita McAlester **the fashion designer** is not the same person as Rita McAlester **the international fugitive.**

3.  A **verbal phrase** is a group of words that begins with a past or present participle or an infinitive (see 23k), but that acts as another part of speech:

    **Dancing on the piano** is prohibited. [noun]

    **Having danced on the piano,** they were thrown out of the club. [adjective]

4.  A **gerund phrase** includes a gerund (an *-ing* form of a verb used as a noun) plus any other words that modify the gerund. Gerund phrases act as nouns and can be subjects or direct objects:

    **Driving to work** can take me up to two hours. [subject]

    Rita enjoyed **dancing with José.** [direct object]

5.  An **infinitive phrase** is made up of an infinitive (*to* plus the base form of a verb) and any other words that modify the infinitive:

    Jason is the best person **to fix your car.** (adjective)

    Lesya stopped at the diner **to eat lunch.** (adverb)

    **To live well** is the best revenge. (noun)

6. A **noun phrase** includes a noun and its modifying words and phrases:

   <u>Success</u> **by accident** is a feature of Tom's career. (subject)

   The speaker used **several convincing** <u>statistics</u> **taken from government sources.** (object)

   The result of the explosion was **an unforgettable** <u>shower</u> **of sparks and flames.** (complement)

7. A **participial phrase** includes either a present or past participle (see 23k) plus any accompanying words. It frequently describes a noun.

   Mr. Johnson is the man we see **walking beside the lake.**

   Nicholas, a man **shattered by the horrors of war,** is the soldier in the photograph.

8. A **prepositional phrase** consists of a preposition such as *by, in, over,* or *with* and its object as well as any modifying words:

   We decided never to go **to the mall.**

   **Beside the couch,** Jim had piled copies of the Sunday papers.

   The supervisor rarely showed interest in projects **under her control.**

   English depends heavily on the idiomatic use of prepositional phrases. For a list of "difficult" phrases involving prepositions along with verbs and adjectives, see Chapter 32, pages 818–820.

9. **Verb phrases** contain main verbs preceded by auxiliary verbs:

   I **have been thinking.**

   He **does believe** in you.

   We **will be considering** your proposal.

## EXERCISE 24.2

Underline each phrase in the following sentences. Then identify the phrase as (1) absolute, (2) appositive, (3) verbal, (4) gerund, (5) infinitive, (6) noun, (7) participial, (8) prepositional, or (9) verb.

1. Breaking slowly from the gate, the horse was seven lengths behind the rest of the pack.
2. My neighbor, a copywriter for an ad agency, has always believed in extraterrestrial life.
3. "Creativity by design" is our company's latest attempt at a motto.
4. The old man was hurt by the loss of his wife and son in the same year.
5. The fish jumping near the old stump is one that I have hooked and lost three times in the past two months.
6. His foot swollen to twice its normal size, Walter struggled up the hill to his car.
7. I've always wanted to go to Japan; reading about its culture fascinates me.

8. The Coen brothers' movie *Fargo* is one of the best films of the 1990s.

9. When people are troubled, tossing and turning can keep them up all night.

10. Michael is the one over there talking to Lisa.

## 24f CLAUSES

A **clause** is a group of words containing a subject and a verb. Clauses are either independent or dependent. An **independent (main) clause** can function alone as a sentence or be part of a compound, complex, or compound/complex sentence. A **dependent (subordinate) clause** cannot function alone; it must be part of a larger sentence that contains an independent clause.

All clauses, whether independent or dependent, must contain a subject and a predicate. A **subject** is the noun, pronoun, phrase, or clause that functions as the "actor" in the sentence. The subject "acts" through the verb or verb phrase that is the basis of the **predicate**, the verb along with its modifiers.

Having a subject and a predicate distinguishes clauses from phrases, which have a subject but not a predicate, or a predicate but not a subject:

| | |
|---|---|
| **SUBJECT WITHOUT PREDICATE** | the stock market indexes |
| **PREDICATE WITHOUT SUBJECT** | rose sharply |
| **CLAUSE** | The stock market indexes rose sharply. |

### 24f.1 INDEPENDENT CLAUSES

An **independent clause** is so named because it can stand alone as a sentence. An independent clause can be brief or lengthy:

Go!
Karen rested.
Buenos Aires is the capital of Argentina.
The *Ramayana*, a classic of Sanskrit literature, was written in India in the third century B.C.E.

The third and fourth examples are longer than the first two, but all of the examples include a subject and a predicate. (In the first example, an imperative sentence, the subject—*you*—is implied.)

### 24f.2 DEPENDENT CLAUSES

A **dependent (subordinate) clause** differs from an independent clause; it cannot stand alone as a sentence. A dependent clause by itself is a **sentence fragment** (see Chapter 25). Dependent clauses consist of four types: noun clauses, adjective (relative) clauses, adverb clauses, and elliptical clauses.

1. **Noun clauses** begin with *how, that, what, whatever, when, where, whether, which, whichever, who, whoever, whom, whomever, whose,* or *why*. The resulting clause functions as a subject or object:

   | | |
   |---|---|
   | SUBJECT | **How a two-year-old could program a VCR is a mystery.** |
   | DIRECT OBJECT | I wish Mike would watch **what he is doing.** |
   | OBJECT OF PREPOSITION | We decided to stop at **whichever gas station was closest.** |

2. **Adjective (relative) clauses** begin with **relative pronouns** (*that, which, who, whom, whose*) and function as adjectives, modifying nouns and pronouns:

   She is the woman **who was falsely accused of murder.**
   Here is the couple **whose baggage was lost.**
   The Italian and English sonnet forms, **which were developed during the Renaissance,** both contain fourteen lines.

3. **Adverb clauses,** which function as adverbs, begin with a subordinating conjunction, such as *after, although, as soon as, because, in order to, until,* or *when*. (For a more extensive list of subordinating conjunctions, see page 697 in this chapter.)

   | | |
   |---|---|
   | ADVERB CLAUSE | **After the mechanic fixed the radiator** |

   As with other dependent clauses, in an adverb clause, something is missing—the rest of the sentence:

   **After the mechanic fixed the radiator,** the car was ready to roll.

4. In **elliptical clauses,** a word or words are not present, but the meaning is obvious anyway. Normally, elliptical clauses appear in comparisons:

   Tariq has more money **than I** [have money].

   Bob is as rich **as Geena** [is rich].

## EXERCISE 24.3

In the following sentences, underline each dependent clause. Then identify the clause as (1) a noun clause, (2) an adjective clause, (3) an adverb clause, or (4) an elliptical clause.

   1. Whoever built this house must have had the plans upside down when he first started.
   2. My uncle is a man who was once famous for his yodeling skills.
   3. After you finish backing up the hard drive, see if you can find out who was responsible for opening that infected e-mail.
   4. Whenever you want to eat lunch is all right with me.

5. When Richard bought his new car, he got a five-year loan because he wanted to keep his payments low.

6. Some financial advisors are known for pushing whichever mutual fund has the highest commission.

7. I know Gene is tall, but is he as tall as Jared?

8. Take off your work boots before you come in the house.

9. This is the painting that was stolen in the 1975 burglary.

10. Robert cleaned the gutters so that his overworked father wouldn't have to do the chore on Saturday.

# SENTENCE TYPES

Sentences can be classified according to purpose:

| | |
|---|---|
| DECLARATIVE | The officer asked for Jana's driver's license. [states a fact or an opinion] |
| INTERROGATIVE | May I see your driver's license? [asks a question] |
| IMPERATIVE | Give me your driver's license. [gives an order/direction or makes a request] |
| EXCLAMATORY | Oh, my gosh, I have lost my driver's license! [expresses strong emotion or emphasis] |

Within each type, the way that you construct a sentence affects how your reader processes your intended meaning. Your aim is to emphasize the parts of the sentence that are most important and to create sentence variety. Doing so will help communicate your message better and keep your reader's interest.

1. A **simple sentence** contains one main (independent) clause, but it may contain phrases as well. The main clause in the following sentence is highlighted:

   Bordering Honduras and Costa Rica, **Nicaragua is located in Central America.**

2. A **compound sentence** contains two main (independent) clauses connected by a coordinating conjunction (*and, but, for, nor, or, yet, so*) or by a semicolon:

   Some Nicaraguans work in gold and tungsten mines, **but** most are farmers.

3. A **complex sentence** contains a main (independent) clause and at least one subordinate (dependent) clause. In the following sentence, the subordinate clause is highlighted:

   **Although Nicaragua had been part of Guatemala and then of the Mexican Empire,** it became a republic in 1838.

**4.** A **compound/complex sentence** contains two main (independent) clauses and at least one subordinate (dependent) clause:

i.c.                 i.c.

Anastasio Somoza took power in 1937, and he continued to rule until 1979,

d.c.

when his regime was overthrown by the Sandinista National Liberation Front.

In this sentence, two independent clauses are followed by a dependent clause.

## 24g CREATING EMPHASIS AND VARIETY: COMPOUND SENTENCES

Simple sentences can be used to convey information effectively, but a steady diet of them will make it difficult for you to emphasize the ideas you want to stress. More important, it will bore your readers. You need to be able to use compound sentences for emphasis and variety. Here are three main ways to join two independent clauses to make a compound sentence: (1) comma plus coordinating conjunction, (2) semicolon alone, and (3) semicolon plus conjunctive adverb or transitional expression:

> The interstate was flooded, **and** the side streets were slick.
> Mark hates yearly reviews; Gail also hates them.
> My relatives are visiting this evening; **consequently,** I need to leave work early.

All three methods work, but which one is best? It depends on context. Using a comma plus a coordinating conjunction is frequently effective. However, some stylists see this technique as a bit too informal to depend on in academic writing. There is a second problem as well: the seven coordinating conjunctions convey a limited range of meaning. Note the problem in the following sentence:

> Andrew was furious about the errors in his credit-card statement, **and** the statement got to him a week late.

Here, the information is adequately conveyed, but only adequately; emphasis is lost. The sentence works much better if a conjunctive adverb is used in place of the coordinating conjunction:

> Andrew was furious about the errors in his credit-card statement; **moreover,** the statement got to him a week late.

Conjunctive adverbs and other transitional expressions have a greater range of meaning than do the coordinating conjunctions; therefore, they allow you to write sentences that are much more focused and precise. (See Chapter 25, page 703, for a list of conjunctive adverbs and transitional expressions.)

For more on using compound sentences in your writing, see Chapter 4.

### EXERCISE 24.4

Combine each of the following pairs of sentences by using a comma plus a coordinating conjunction, a semicolon, or a semicolon plus a conjunctive adverb or other transitional expression. Be prepared to defend your choice. You can find examples of coordinating conjunctions, conjunctive adverbs, and transitional expressions in Chapter 25, pages 703–704.

1. Laura was sad. Her friend David was being transferred across the country.
2. The first car we looked at cost $32,000. The next model was only $17,500.
3. This college has a lot of problems. The parking situation is terrible.
4. We won't need you anymore today. Make sure that you check in tomorrow.
5. The software instructions seemed clear enough. The program wouldn't come up on my screen.
6. The plane was overbooked. Mr. Robbins decided to take the airline up on its offer for discounts.
7. Ed opened the door. He noticed that the office seemed strangely quiet.
8. Andrea is not happy today. She's just gotten some bad news about her tax return.
9. Jane cleaned off her desk. She started to answer her e-mail.
10. My nephew likes swimming. His sister hates it.

## 24h CREATING EMPHASIS AND VARIETY THROUGH SUBORDINATION

Consider the following sentence:

John opened his mail, and he got a bad shock.

This is a **balanced** sentence, a compound sentence in which two actions (John *opened his mail* and *he got a bad shock*) receive equal weight. But are those two actions equal? Surely, the most important information here is in the second clause. People open their mail six days a week, but they are usually not shocked by its contents. To emphasize the information in the second clause, the writer needs to use **subordination**:

**When** John opened his mail, he got a bad shock.

An even more effective choice is to place the independent clause first:

John got a bad shock **when** he opened his mail.

Note that all three sentences are grammatically correct; however, the second and third sentences communicate their meaning more accurately and effectively.

You can introduce a subordinate clause with a subordinating conjunction or a relative pronoun.

| Subordinating Conjunctions | Relative Pronouns |
|---|---|
| after | that |
| although | what |
| as | whatever |
| because | which |
| before | whichever |
| even if | who |
| even though | whoever |
| if | whom |
| in order that | whomever |
| once | whose |
| provided that | |
| rather than | |
| since | |
| so that | |
| so (that) | |
| that | |
| though | |
| unless | |
| until | |
| when | |
| whenever | |
| where | |
| whereas | |
| wherever | |
| whether | |
| while | |

**Because we failed to make reservations,** we were not able to get a table.
He will not march in the graduation line **unless he passes chemistry.**
**When he was a young man,** my father owned a bookstore.
The soldiers **who were honored last night** were part of an airborne division.

In addition to indicating on which idea or part of the sentence you want to place emphasis, subordination can also supply extra information about a subject. In the following sentence, the subordinate clause is highlighted:

Joan was eventually transferred to St. Louis, **which was at least near the town where her sister lived.**

However, note that too much subordination weakens a sentence:

Michael walked to his office, *which* **is on Third Street,** *which* **is the oldest paved street in the city,** *which* **itself is the fourth-oldest municipality in the state.**

Readers of this sentence may feel as though they are being led through doorway after doorway for no purpose. Subordination should not be used to attach stray thoughts or extra facts; rather, it should establish focus and add valuable—albeit secondary—information.

For more on using subordination for variety and emphasis, see Chapter 4.

. . . . . . . .

CATALYST 2.0

**MORE OPTIONS ONLINE**
For more exercises,
go to
www.mhhe.com/
writingtoday.

## EXERCISE 24.5

Combine the sentences in each item by using subordination. You may want to rearrange details as you do so.

**1.** Hispaniola is a subtropical island in the West Indies. Haiti and the Dominican Republic share the island.

**2.** The Delaware Indians lived in the woodlands of the eastern United States. They spoke the Algonquian language.

**3.** Martin Luther disagreed with many of the practices of the Roman Catholic church. He broke with Rome and founded a sect of Protestantism that bears his name.

**4.** The Persian Wars of the fifth century B.C.E. lasted for over fifty years and resulted in a victory for the Greek city-states. They began when the cities of Ionia revolted against Darius I.

**5.** Romulus was the legendary founder of Rome. He and his twin brother, Remus, were suckled by a she-wolf and were later raised by a shepherd.

# MAJOR SENTENCE ERRORS

### CHAPTER 25

The first two sections of this chapter concentrate on three of the most damaging sentence-level errors. To receive good grades on college essays, you must avoid sentence fragments, fused sentences, and comma splices. The last section of this chapter discusses three other sentence-level issues: parallelism, appropriate comparisons, and mixed constructions.

# SENTENCE FRAGMENTS

As its name suggests, a **sentence fragment** is an incomplete sentence; it "acts" as a sentence, but it is missing a subject, a verb, or a complete thought.

## 25a PHRASES AS FRAGMENTS

A phrase, by definition, cannot be a complete sentence. Here are some typical phrasal fragments:

### Incomplete Verb Form

| | |
|---|---|
| FRAGMENT | The doctor **thinking** that the patient looked better. |
| REVISED | The doctor **was thinking** that the patient looked better. |

### Prepositional Phrase Used as Sentence

| | |
|---|---|
| FRAGMENT | You'll find the hammer out back. **Beside the rotary saw.** |
| REVISED | You'll find the hammer out back, beside the rotary saw. |

### Infinitive Phrase Used as Sentence

| | |
|---|---|
| FRAGMENT | We drove to town. **To buy a new hammer.** |
| REVISED | We drove to town to buy a new hammer. |

### "Illustration" Phrase Used as Sentence

| | |
|---|---|
| FRAGMENT | Alcoholics can develop many health problems. **For example, cirrhosis of the liver.** |
| REVISED | Alcoholics can develop many health problems—for example, cirrhosis of the liver. |
| FRAGMENT | They were troubled by the motel's location. **Also, the condition of the room they were shown.** |
| REVISED | They were troubled by the motel's location and also by the condition of the room they were shown. |

As you can see, many fragments are phrases that clearly belong with an adjacent sentence but that are acting as stand-alone sentences:

| | |
|---|---|
| FRAGMENT | **Wishing that finals week were over.** Jan reluctantly turned back to her studies. |
| FRAGMENT | **To meet our June 1 deadline.** We've got to work hard during the next two weeks. |
| FRAGMENT | **Near the end of its useful life.** The old bridge seemed to sag as heavy trucks strained its rotted timbers. |
| FRAGMENT | Rosa ran to hug her child. **Her eyes filling with tears.** |

Of course, you can always correct such fragments by making complete sentences out of them:

CATALYST 2.0

**MORE OPTIONS ONLINE**
If you would like to test your knowledge of major sentence errors before reading this chapter, go to
www.mhhe.com/ writingtoday.

CORRECT        Jan wished that finals week were over. She reluctantly turned back to her studies.

However, a steady diet of such short, choppy thoughts gets boring. Try these other remedies as well:

1. Treat the fragments as elements of the adjacent sentences:

    CORRECT        Wishing that finals week were over, Jan reluctantly turned back to her studies.

    CORRECT        To meet our June 1 deadline, we've got to work hard during the next two weeks.

    CORRECT        Near the end of its useful life, the old bridge seemed to sag as heavy trucks strained its rotted timbers.

    CORRECT        Rosa ran to hug her child, her eyes filling with tears.

2. Turn the fragments into subordinate (dependent) clauses and combine them with the sentences they adjoin:

    CORRECT        **Although** she wished finals week were over, Jan reluctantly turned back to her studies.

    CORRECT        We've got to work hard during the next two weeks **if** we are going to meet our June 1 deadline.

    CORRECT        **Because** the old bridge was near the end of its useful life, it seemed to sag as heavy trucks strained its rotted timbers.

    CORRECT        As Rosa's eyes filled with tears, she ran to hug her child.

3. Turn the fragments into independent (main) clauses and combine them with the sentence they adjoin to make a compound sentence:

    CORRECT        Jan wished that finals week were over; nonetheless, she reluctantly turned back to her studies.

    CORRECT        We have to meet our June 1 deadline, so we've got to work hard during the next two weeks.

    CORRECT        The old bridge was near the end of its useful life, and it seemed to sag as heavy trucks strained its rotted timbers.

    CORRECT        Rosa's eyes filled with tears; she ran to hug her child.

Students frequently write phrasal fragments because they erroneously believe that long sentences are "run-ons" and therefore wrong. But long sentences are just that: long sentences. They may be grammatically correct or incorrect depending on how they're written and punctuated, not depending on their length.

Note that revising some phrasal fragments involves more than merely attaching the phrase to a nearby sentence:

| | |
|---|---|
| FRAGMENT | The Secret Service is located in Washington, D.C. **A branch of Alcohol, Tobacco, and Firearms.** |
| INCORRECT REVISION | The Secret Service is located in Washington, D.C., a branch of Alcohol, Tobacco, and Firearms. |

The fragment is now a modifier, but it is in the wrong position, making the reader wonder how Washington, D.C., could be a branch of a federal agency. The writer needs to place the modifier near the word or words it describes.

| | |
|---|---|
| CORRECT REVISION | The Secret Service, a branch of Alcohol, Tobacco, and Firearms, is located in Washington, D.C. |

For more on misplaced modifiers, see 28a.

## EXERCISE 25.1

In each of the following pairs of items, one is a complete sentence; the other is a fragment. Combine them to eliminate the fragment. You may need to add, delete, or reorder words.

1. Maria decided to wait before buying a new computer. Hoping to find one on sale after Christmas.
2. Believing that tomatoes were poisonous. Many people in the nineteenth century refused to eat them.
3. The afternoon rain caused traffic back-ups all over Ft. Lauderdale. A common occurrence there.
4. Will and Jennifer went to the Humane Society shelter and then went home. Having adopted a Siamese kitten.
5. Samantha skied carefully down the icy slope. To maintain her balance and avoiding falling.
6. Many people who are planning a camping trip don't buy sufficient supplies. For instance, insect repellent and rain gear.
7. The firefighters left the scene. Believing that they had extinguished the blaze.
8. Marisa was considering some important issues. Such as whether to quit her job and whether to apply for more school loans.
9. Plymouth is a few miles from here. Just past Martinsville.
10. The bank will lend us all we need minus about four thousand dollars. A troublesome situation, if I do say so myself.

## 25b DEPENDENT CLAUSES AS FRAGMENTS

In the box on pages 703–704, the subordinating conjunctions appear in the middle column. Any single-clause sentence, such as *She had danced all night,* can be changed to a dependent subordinate clause by placing one of these conjunctions before it:

> **after** she had danced all night
> **because** she had danced all night
> **even though** she had danced all night
> **if** she had danced all night

However, the resulting dependent clause is no longer a sentence and must be attached to an independent clause; if not, it is a fragment.

> **After** she had danced all night, Vanessa slept for eight hours.
>
> Vanessa was exhausted **because** she had danced all night.
>
> **Even though** she had danced all night, Vanessa was able to complete a full day at work the next day.
>
> **If** Vanessa had danced all night, she would not have gone to work the next day.

## Sentence Connectors

| Conjunctive Adverbs/ Transitional Expressions | Subordinating Conjunctions | Coordinating Conjunctions |
|---|---|---|
| accordingly | after | and |
| additionally | although | but |
| also | as | for |
| as an illustration | because | nor |
| at the same time | before | or |
| besides | even if | so |
| certainly | even though | yet |
| consequently | if | |
| conversely | in order that | |
| finally | once | |
| for example | provided that | |
| for instance | rather than | |
| furthermore | since | |
| hence | so that | |
| however | so (that) | |
| in addition | than | |
| in brief | that | |
| in conclusion | though | |
| in contrast | unless | |
| in short | until | |
| in summary | when | |
| in the same way | whenever | |
| indeed | where | |
| instead | whereas | |

## Sentence Connectors (continued)

| Conjunctive Adverbs/ Transitional Expressions | Subordinating Conjunctions | Coordinating Conjunctions |
|---|---|---|
| likewise | wherever | |
| meanwhile | whether | |
| moreover | while | |
| namely | | |
| nevertheless | | |
| next | | |
| nonetheless | | |
| of course | | |
| on the other hand | | |
| otherwise | | |
| similarly | | |
| specifically | | |
| still | | |
| subsequently | | |
| then | | |
| therefore | | |
| thus | | |
| to be sure | | |

Subordinate (dependent) clauses that begin with the relative pronouns *which, who, whom,* or *whose* can also be fragments unless they are connected to main clauses:

**FRAGMENT**   The method of measurement based on the meter is the metric system. Which was first adopted in France in 1899.

**CORRECT**   The method of measurement based on the meter is the metric system, which was first adopted in France in 1899.

**FRAGMENT**   In Norse mythology, the fates were known as the Norns. Who spun out the destinies of human beings.

**CORRECT**   In Norse mythology, the fates were known as the Norns, who spun out the destinies of human beings.

**FRAGMENT**   The Norns are probably related to the three witches. Whom we meet in Shakespeare's *MacBeth.*

**CORRECT**   The Norns are probably related to the three witches whom we meet in Shakespeare's *MacBeth.*

For more on relative clauses, see 24f. For help with punctuating sentences with subordinate clauses, see 29b and 29c.

An incorrectly used semicolon can cause what is sometimes called an **internal fragment**:

INCORRECT    **Although the stadium is old; it has character.**

INCORRECT    **Katie was close to tears; feeling that she had been manipulated.**

In each sentence, a semicolon has been used incorrectly in place of a comma. Keep this idea in mind: in such cases, a semicolon functions as an *internal period;* what comes before or after it must be an independent clause.

## EXERCISE 25.2

Read each group of sentences below. Revise as needed to eliminate fragments.

1. The new classroom building was almost a year behind on its construction schedule. Because the contractor had submitted a timetable that was absurd.

2. Once Lucas realized his mistake. He called the branch office again. So that he could catch Ella Hassamin before closing time.

3. The language of the contract was difficult; although the summary at the end made the details clear.

4. I realized that I had been fooled again. After I opened the last envelope in the stack.

5. Whenever a production delay happens. Call the shift manager.

6. After losing his calculus text, missing a biology quiz, and getting a parking ticket, Cameron went home; feeling bitter.

7. The map was old; even though Tina had once lived in the area, the map didn't correspond to her memory of the place.

8. On Friday, the dealership refused to sell Bianca the new van. Even though they had worked out the details on Thursday. To avoid time delays on the busy weekend.

9. Lia married a man from Arkansas. Who owns seven office-supply stores.

10. New students at this university seem to be a bit overwhelmed; whereas sophomores have the air of those who have seen it all.

11. The front door is standing open. Which bothers me.

12. Eddie is a selfish young man. Whose sole purpose in life is to have fun.

13. Here is my great-grandfather's diary from the early twentieth century. Some of which is fascinating reading.

14. The new candidate for mayor is an interesting person. Who I think will give the incumbent a run for his money.

15. Lora was furious; because she had arrived before the financial aid office was supposed to close and found the door locked.

## 25c INTENTIONAL FRAGMENTS

Professional writers who use **intentional fragments** know that they are break-ing the rules, but they do so for dramatic effect. Advertisements often use this strategy. Nonetheless, when you are writing for college courses, using intentional fragments can be risky. What you see as intentional may be considered an error by your instructor. However, you can be secure about using an intentional frag-ment when answering a rhetorical question (a question to which the answer is obvious). Such questions are usually asked to draw the reader into the text:

> CORRECT     **Should senior citizens be faced with new taxes? Of course not.**

Writing dialogue for a narrative essay might provide another context in which the use of intentional fragments would be acceptable. Otherwise, avoid frag-ments altogether in college writing.

### EXERCISE 25.3

Rewrite the following paragraph to correct fragments.

> Martin joined the U.S. Navy. To learn a trade and earn some money for college. Which he dearly wanted to attend. Although he was short on funds. Martin had applied for scholarships; hoping to pay for college that way. He could get only about half of what he needed for school. While his friend David got a free ride to a state university. Consequently, Martin spent four years in the Navy. Visiting different countries and meeting a variety of peo-ple. Some of whom became his close friends. Therefore, although joining the Navy had not been Martin's first choice. It turned out to be a worthwhile experience. Both personally and financially.

# AVOIDING "RUN-ONS": FUSED SENTENCES AND COMMA SPLICES

A **fused sentence** occurs when two independent clauses are joined with no punctuation:

> FUSED SENTENCE     **I may be wrong I may be right.**
>
> FUSED SENTENCE     **Ed tried to buy a new car however he couldn't get decent financing.**

A **comma splice** occurs when two independent clauses are joined with a comma:

> COMMA SPLICE     **I may be wrong, I may be right.**
>
> COMMA SPLICE     **Ed tried to buy a new car, however he couldn't get decent financing.**

As you can see, fused sentences and comma splices are related. Although both are serious errors, they are easy to correct once you find them. The following sections discuss three methods for eliminating fused sentences and comma splices.

## 25d  USE A "FULL STOP" (PERIOD, SEMICOLON, OR COLON) BETWEEN THE INDEPENDENT CLAUSES.

**1.** If the two independent clauses are not closely related, use a period and form two sentences:

| | |
|---|---|
| FUSED SENTENCE | Mark drove in from seventy miles away Zoe brought salmon quesadillas. |
| REVISED | Mark drove in from seventy miles away. Zoe brought salmon quesadillas. |
| COMMA SPLICE | The site exploration team arrived at the hotel, meanwhile, the company's officers made plans that would change the scope of the project. |
| REVISED | The site exploration team arrived at the hotel. Meanwhile, the company's officers made plans that would change the scope of the project. |

Note that in the last sentence, the presence of the transitional adverb *meanwhile* has nothing to do with the sentence's being a comma splice. Using this transitional word between the two clauses helps the reader process the sentence, but it doesn't cause or prevent the comma splice.

**2.** If the two independent clauses are closely related, connect them with a semicolon:

| | |
|---|---|
| FUSED SENTENCE | Zoe brought salmon quesadillas Brian made chicken. |
| REVISED | Zoe brought salmon quesadillas; Brian made chicken. |
| COMMA SPLICE | Zoe hates chicken, Brian won't eat fish. |
| REVISED | Zoe hates chicken; Brian won't eat fish. |

**3.** If the ideas in the two independent clauses are closely related but a transition is needed, connect the two clauses with a semicolon plus a conjunctive adverb/transitional expression followed by a comma:

| | |
|---|---|
| FUSED SENTENCE | Zoe is a frequent guest however, we rarely see Mark. |
| REVISED | Zoe is a frequent guest; however, we rarely see Mark. |
| COMMA SPLICE | Mark drove in from far away, Zoe lived next door. |
| REVISED | Mark drove in from far away; however, Zoe lived next door. |

You can find a list of conjunctive adverbs/transitions in the box on pages 703–704.

**4.** If the idea in the second clause is introduced by the first or is caused by the first, consider connecting them with a colon. *Use this method sparingly.*

| | |
|---|---|
| FUSED SENTENCE | Now came the moment we all feared the building exploded and collapsed. |
| REVISED | Now came the moment we all feared: the building exploded and collapsed. |
| COMMA SPLICE | Juan knew one thing, he had to find a way out of his deathtrap job. |
| REVISED | Juan knew one thing: he had to find a way out of his deathtrap job. |

## EXERCISE 25.4

The following sentences are either comma splices or fused sentences. First, identify the error. Next, revise the sentence by using a period, a semicolon, or a colon. Be prepared to justify your choice of revision method.

**1.** The company manufactures many interesting home appliances, it also offers factory tours.

**2.** Vacuum the carpet, then mop the floor.

**3.** It's not that Jason lacks talent it's that he is late for work three days out of four!

**4.** The door opened to admit the last person we wanted to see, Sergeant Albertson stood there with a sadistic grin as he watched our discomfort.

**5.** We had hoped to take a big vacation this summer however, our finances didn't really allow us to do so.

## 25e USE A COMMA AND COORDINATING CONJUNCTION (*AND, BUT, FOR, NOR, OR, SO, YET*) TO CONNECT THE TWO INDEPENDENT CLAUSES.

| | |
|---|---|
| FUSED SENTENCE | Supper wasn't ready my sister practiced her piano lesson. |
| REVISED | Supper wasn't ready, **so** my sister practiced her piano lesson. |
| COMMA SPLICE | Ed thought the film was wonderful, Maria didn't agree. |
| REVISED | Ed thought the film was wonderful, **but** Maria didn't agree. |

Note that the proper pattern is always comma plus coordinating conjunction.

Although using a coordinating conjunction is an easy way to fix a comma splice or fused sentence, remember that such connectors describe a limited number of relationships. Overusing this technique can (1) give your writing a monotonous rhythm and (2) fail to express subtle shades of meaning. Frequently, using a semicolon plus a transitional expression produces a more accurate sentence. However, when the context is appropriate, a comma plus a coordinating conjunction works well.

## EXERCISE **25.5**

The following sentences are either comma splices or fused sentences. First, identify the error. Next, revise the sentence by adding the appropriate coordinating conjunction preceded by a comma if one is not already present.

**1.** Tuesday was a gloomy day, Wednesday was equally bad.

**2.** Vito loves bananas Eddie hates them.

**3.** When did you find out, why didn't you tell me?

**4.** James committed the crime, James is lying.

**5.** We can't go outside let's watch a DVD.

## 25f  CHANGE ONE OF THE TWO INDEPENDENT CLAUSES TO A DEPENDENT CLAUSE OR TO A PHRASE.

**1.** **Use subordination.** Subordination reduces one of the main (independent) clauses to a subordinate (dependent) clause. You can subordinate a clause by using one of the subordinating conjunctions from the box that lists sentence connectors (pages 703–704).

| | |
|---|---|
| FUSED SENTENCE | Enrico left the party early he wasn't in the mood to carouse. |
| REVISED | Enrico left the party early **because** he wasn't in the mood to carouse. |
| COMMA SPLICE | Anita studied very hard, she still made a low score on the chemistry exam. |
| REVISED | **Although** Anita studied very hard, she still made a low score on the chemistry exam. |
| REVISED | Anita studied very hard, **although** she still made a low score on the chemistry exam. |

Note that when a dependent clause follows an independent clause, a comma is usually not necessary, unless the subordinator is negative, such as *although* in the last sentence. (For more on commas, see Chapter 29.)

Another way to use subordination is to turn one of the main clauses into a relative clause—a clause introduced by *that, which, who, whom,* or *whose.*

| | |
|---|---|
| FUSED SENTENCE | The Toltec arrived in Meso-America even before the Aztec they are among the first inhabitants of Mexico. |
| REVISED | The Toltec, **who** arrived in Meso-America even before the Aztec, are among the first inhabitants of Mexico. |

fs/cs
25f

2.   Change one of the independent clauses into a phrase:

COMMA SPLICE   John believes he will do better in economics, he plans to change his major.

REVISED   **Believing** that he will do better in economics, John plans to change his major.

FUSED SENTENCE   On a winter day, we watched the eagles they soared over the Mississippi River.

REVISED   On a winter day, we watched the eagles **soaring** over the Mississippi River.

Note that when the phrase follows the independent clause, a comma is usually not necessary. (See Chapter 29 for more help with commas.)

## EXERCISE 25.6

The following sentences are either comma splices or fused sentences. First, identify the error. Next, use one of the strategies covered in this section to revise the sentence.

1.   History is important, history is not as crucial as some would have us believe.
2.   The flood tore through the valley it created a new lake near Walston Road.
3.   Danny washed his car he took it for a spin.
4.   This is my cat, he is a very strange creature.
5.   Tax time is over I'll feel more like a human being again.
6.   Walston Industries is a very profitable company, it manufactures kites, gliders, and rockets.
7.   Karen reviewed her options once more she made her decision.
8.   This Web site is quite useful, it has an enormous number of links.
9.   Leo believed his upcoming work schedule was hopeless, he felt that his course assignment deadlines weren't much better.
10.  Yoshi was interested in Web page design, Yoshi took a class at the local technical college.

Choosing a revision strategy to eliminate comma splices and fused sentences depends upon context. One method will be clearly superior to another in any given situation. Exercise 25.7 asks you to find the best revision method for each defective sentence.

## EXERCISE 25.7

Mark each of the following sentences **C** (correct), **CS** (comma splice), or **FS** (fused sentence). Then choose the best strategy to revise each comma splice and fused sentence. Be prepared to defend your decision.

1. Cheating has become a major issue for American colleges therefore various security strategies are being studied.

2. Mammals are warm-blooded whereas reptiles are not.

3. Load the software, then run the start-up disk.

4. Rain can be a blessing, acid rain, however, is something of a mixed blessing.

5. Ramona couldn't attend her son's recital she certainly wanted to.

6. What brand is that, where did you buy it?

7. The professor is a very well-known scholar, she has the respect of her peers throughout the world.

8. That's not a squirrel it's a rat!

9. Sarah shut down her laptop and cleaned out her desk; thus, she said good-bye to seven years at Wentworth Industries.

10. This is not a question of which movie we want to see, it's a question of whether we really want to leave the house in this weather.

## COMBINATION EXERCISE

The following passage contains fragments, comma splices, and fused sentences. Rewrite the passage to correct these problems by using the strategies you have learned in this chapter. Reword and combine sentences as needed.

The world has known many calendars. Methods by which to track the passage of time. Today, most of the world uses the Gregorian calendar for business purposes and for conducting international affairs. Indeed, with its twelve months from January to December. This solar calendar is probably the most widely known method of tracking days, weeks, months, and years, it contains 365.25 days per year. One day being added every fourth or leap year. Years in the Gregorian calendar are counted from the birth of Christ, with B.C. (the abbreviation for "Before Christ") being added to years that preceded Christ's birth. A.D. (the Latin abbreviation for "Year of our Lord") being added to years that follow it.

The Gregorian calendar was established in 1583 during the papacy of Gregory III. Scientists and historians realized that the Julian calendar, then in use, was not accurate and needed to be revised, named after the Roman general Julius Caesar, it had been used in Europe since 45 B.C. While the Gregorian calendar was more accurate, it did not receive acceptance throughout Europe for many years, in fact, it was not adopted by the British Empire until 1752. Sweden followed suit in 1753, however, numerous countries in eastern Europe did not adopt the Gregorian calendar until the early twentieth century. In many countries, ordinary people continued to follow the Julian calendar long after the Gregorian calendar had been introduced, this resulted in people using different dates for the same event. In such cases. Events that were recorded according to the Julian method were followed by O.S. ("Old Style") those recorded according to the Gregorian calendar were followed by N.S. ("New Style").

Like the Gregorian calendar, first used in Christian countries and now adopted worldwide. The Islamic calendar has twelve months, it begins in Muhharram and ends with Dhu-al Hijjah. Unlike its European counterpart, however, the Islamic calendar is a lunar instrument, each month begins when the lunar crescent is first seen after the new moon. Years in the Islamic calendar are counted beginning from the Hijra, this is a term referring to the flight of Mohammed to Mecca, whose date corresponds to the year 622 A.D. in the Christian calendar, therefore, dates in the Muslim world are followed by an abbreviation signifying "year of the Hijra." It is interesting to note that because the Christian calendar is based on the movements of the sun and the Islamic calendar is based on the movements of the moon. The latter is about eleven days shorter.

The Jewish calendar has thirteen months, beginning with Nissan and ending with Adar II. With the number of days in each month varying from 29 to 30. Unlike the first month in the Christian calendar, which comes in the winter in northern latitudes. Nissan occurs in the spring. The season of Passover, an important Jewish holiday. The Jewish New Year falls in the seventh month, Tishri, it is at that time that the number of the year advances. The numbering of years in the Jewish calendar is based upon the number of years since the Creation, as recorded in the Scriptures when referring to years in the Gregorian calendar, however, the Jews do not use A.D. or B.C. instead they attach C.E. ("the common era") and B.C.E. ("before the common era") to their dates.

# OTHER SENTENCE-LEVEL PROBLEMS

## 25g PROBLEMS WITH PARALLELISM

When you give equal emphasis to two or more things, actions, ideas, or activities, use **parallel** wording: nouns with nouns, verbs with verbs, prepositional phrases with prepositional phrases, and so forth. A sentence that uses parallel structures is both rhythmic and effective. Note the difference between the following examples:

> NOT PARALLEL    Jessica likes several outdoor activities, including swimming, hiking, and to sail.
>
> PARALLEL    Jessica likes several outdoor activities, including swimming, hiking, and sailing.

For a reader, the second sentence is more effective than the first, which is awkward. The first sentence uses two gerunds followed by an infinitive (*to sail*). The second, parallel sentence uses three gerunds (*swimming, hiking, sailing*). Most of the time, you can avoid writing sentences like the first one without a great deal of trouble. The following guidelines will help:

1. Group nouns with nouns:

   | NOT PARALLEL | Edwin has arthritis, and he also suffers from a cracked vertebra as well as a nerve that was pinched. |
   | PARALLEL NOUNS | Edwin has arthritis, a cracked vertebra, and a pinched nerve. |

2. Group verbs with verbs:

   | NOT PARALLEL | At the conference, our project team went to workshops, had a comparison of notes, and then dinner. |
   | PARALLEL VERBS | At the conference, our project team went to workshops, compared notes, and then ate dinner. |

3. Group verbals (infinitives, gerunds, and participles) with the same kind of verbals:

   | NOT PARALLEL | On the weekends, the district manager likes to walk, golfing, and plays cards. |
   | PARALLEL INFINITIVES | On the weekends, the district manager likes to walk, to golf, and to play cards. |
   | NOT PARALLEL | Jenn loves dancing, partying, and to go out on the town. |
   | PARALLEL GERUNDS | Jenn loves dancing, partying, and going out on the town. |

4. Group prepositional phrases with prepositional phrases:

   | NOT PARALLEL | You can find these vases in Austin and San Antonio, and you can also find them in Fort Worth. |
   | PARALLEL PREPOSITIONAL PHRASES | You can find these vases in Austin, in San Antonio, and in Fort Worth. |

5. Be careful with correlative conjunctions. Correlative conjunctions are pairs of conjunctions (*both/and, not only/but also, either/or, neither/nor*) that emphasize relationships. (For more on correlative conjunctions, see 23f.) Note the following sentence:

   | NOT PARALLEL | Failing to dress appropriately for the weather can not only ruin a person's day but also leads to health problems. |

   The two main verbs—*ruin* and *leads*—are not parallel. Now note the revision:

   | PARALLEL | Failing to dress for the weather can not only ruin a person's day **but can also lead** to health problems. |

When you use a pair of correlative conjunctions, make sure that you use parallel structures within the elements they connect.

For more on parallelism, see Chapter 4.

## 25h AVOIDING FAULTY COMPARISONS

Faulty comparisons are in many ways a kind of faulty parallelism. In an inexact comparison, the writer is sometimes trying to compare two things that cannot be logically compared:

> INCORRECT    The new software company has sold more of its e-mail virus patches than any other software company.

*E-mail virus patches* are not comparable to *any other software company.* Note the revision:

> CORRECT    The new software company's e-mail virus patches have sold better than those of any other software company.

Faulty comparisons can also be the result of an omitted word:

> INCORRECT    Jenkins does more work than any member of her division.

Isn't Jenkins *in* her division? Adding a word clears the matter up:

> CORRECT    Jenkins does more work than any **other** member of her division.

Some faulty comparisons are truly ambiguous:

> INCORRECT    Some people use Internet searches more than librarians.

> CORRECT    Some people use Internet searches more than librarians **do.**

> ALSO CORRECT    Some people use Internet searches more than **they consult** librarians.

As Chapter 4 discusses, avoid omitting key words, especially in comparisons.

## 25i AVOIDING MIXED CONSTRUCTIONS

In a **mixed construction**, the writer starts a sentence with a structure that leads the reader to expect a particular type of sentence. Then, however, the writer goes in a different direction, leaving the reader baffled: the two parts of the sentence are not compatible. Note the following examples:

> INCORRECT    Because he broke his ankle was the reason that Christian gave up basketball.

> REVISED    Because he broke his ankle, Christian gave up basketball.

> INCORRECT    The reason for my anger is because of your habitual lack of punctuality.

> CORRECT    The reason for my anger is your habitual lack of punctuality.

| | |
|---|---|
| INCORRECT | By studying harder improves anyone's chance of success. |
| CORRECT | Studying harder improves anyone's chance of success. |
| INCORRECT | When Einstein relocated to Princeton was a very special honor for that university. |
| CORRECT | Einstein's relocation to Princeton was a very special honor for that university. |

All the incorrect examples above are typical "first-draft" mistakes that often happen because writing and thinking do not occur at the same speed. Writers frequently start a sentence in one direction, then change their minds in midcourse. The revision stage is the point at which careful writers find and correct these errors.

## EXERCISE 25.8

Each of the following sentences suffers from mixed constructions, faulty comparisons, or a lack of parallelism. Revise each sentence to eliminate the error. In some cases, more than one answer is possible.

1. Mia gives better presentations than anyone in this company.
2. Because dogs like humans is the only reason that the two species coexist so well.
3. One idea concentrates on the possibility of humans living until age 150 is being taken seriously by many researchers.
4. Liberals tend to like a powerful federal government more than conservatives.
5. I want rest, relaxation, and to plan.
6. Veronica is attractive, funny, and she has lots of talent.
7. These pickles are more popular than any other brand.
8. After the mudslide is when the police chief left town.
9. Ronald likes sardines more than Wanda.
10. A person who repeatedly fails to wear sunblock can suffer both feeling serious pain and skin cancer.

· · · · · · · ·
CATALYST 2.0

**MORE OPTIONS ONLINE**
For more exercises,
go to
www.mhhe.com/
writingtoday.

### CHAPTER 26

# PROBLEMS WITH VERBS

Verbs are among the most important parts of a sentence; therefore, your ability to use them correctly is crucial. Two common problem areas are subject-verb agreement and shifts in tense, voice, and mood.

# SUBJECT-VERB AGREEMENT

Properly written sentences have a structural balance: singular subjects are matched with singular verbs, and plural subjects with plural verbs; singular nouns are matched with singular pronouns, plural nouns with plural pronouns. This balance is called **agreement.**

Agreement is in one way different from many other grammatical and mechanical concerns: even professional writers make agreement errors in their first drafts. To make sure that your subjects and verbs agree, you will need to check for agreement problems when revising and editing. Look, for example, at the following sentence:

INCORRECT    There **is** a number of reasons for my choice.

CORRECT    There **are** a number of reasons for my choice.

Because the verb comes before the subject in this sentence—not the most common order—the writer might easily choose the incorrect verb form. Catching problems such as these in the revision stage will help you keep your final draft free of agreement problems. The sections in this chapter show you where agreement problems are likely to occur and how to correct them. For now, keep the following in mind:

- A subject must agree in *number* with its verb. For example, a singular verb is needed for a singular noun, as in this sentence:

  The **house** that we have owned for many years **sits** on two acres.

- A plural noun requires a plural verb:

  The **houses** that we saw in Tennessee last week **are** well constructed.

Most writers have few problems with basic subject-verb agreement. In the sentence "John (work, works) for a large company," the choice is straightforward: *John works*. However, beware of verbs that end in *-ist;* because the verb already has an *-s* sound near the end, it's easy to forget that in the sentence "The last surviving member of the species (exist, exists) in a zoo," the correct verb is *exists*. Writers must also deal with many situations that are not basic; one of the chief problems in subject-verb agreement is determining whether the subject is singular or plural.

## 26a SUBJECTS CONNECTED BY *AND*

Two or more nouns or pronouns joined by *and* are called **compound subjects.** These constructions are normally plural:

Walter **and** Luisa **plan** to get married.

Five rabbits, a hamster, **and** a cat **are** the pet shop's remaining inventory.

Going to school **and** working twenty hours per week **have** become difficult for Maureen.

**CATALYST 2.0**

**MORE OPTIONS ONLINE**
If you would like to test your knowledge of verb problems before reading this chapter, go to www.mhhe.com/ writingtoday.

However, if any word or phrase other than *and* joins two parts of a subject, the verb is singular if both parts of the subject are singular:

Walter, **as well as** Luisa, **has** been nominated for chairperson.

Volvo, **along with** Mazda, **is** owned by Ford Motor Company.

Going to school **plus** working twenty hours a week **is** too much for Maureen.

A case of pneumonia, **in addition to** several double shifts at work, **has** put Louise into the hospital.

## 26b COMPOUND SUBJECTS TREATED AS SINGULAR CONSTRUCTIONS

Sometimes, two singular subjects joined by *and* are really one entity—person or thing—and they take singular forms:

*Track and field* **is** Amelia's best sport. (Track and field is one type of athletic activity.)

He believed that *rock and roll* **was** an abomination. (Rock and roll is one kind of music.)

My best *friend and confidant* **is** coming for a visit. (In this sentence, the writer is referring to the same person.)

Two **gerund phrases** linked with *and* can also sometimes be singular:

Going downtown and playing snooker **is** my grandfather's secret vice.

Here, the subject (*going downtown and playing snooker*) is essentially one activity. On the other hand, the following sentence has a compound gerund phrase that clearly indicates two separate activities:

Getting dressed and driving to my date's home **are** the last two steps in the ritual.

### EXERCISE 26.1

In the following sentences, decide if the highlighted verb is correct in number. If it is not, supply the correct form of the verb, or restructure the sentence so that the existing verb form is correct. Not all sentences contain errors.

1. Martha and John **has** signed up for our study group.
2. Tossing and turning all night **are** my response to stress.
3. Harriet, as well as her sister Jane, **is** expected to attend the public lecture.
4. Health and safety **were** my least-favorite class in high school.
5. Moss and lichens **grows** on many different varieties of trees.

## 26c  SUBJECTS CONNECTED BY *OR, NOR, EITHER . . . OR, NEITHER . . . NOR,* AND *NOT ONLY . . . BUT ALSO*

These connectors join subjects, but the resulting subjects do not act as a compound subject. Therefore, these connectors need a special series of rules for subject-verb agreement:

1.  If both subjects joined by one of these connectors are singular, the verb is singular:

    **Neither Jane nor he is** expected to apply.

2.  If both subjects are plural, the verb is plural:

    **Neither cats nor dogs are** able to fly.

3.  If one subject is singular and the other is plural, the verb agrees in number with the closer noun:

    **Vitamins or exercise is** what Jessica needs right now.
    **One CD or two magazines are** all Wayne can afford right now.

    This rule also applies if three or more subjects are connected by *or;* the subject *closest* to the verb determines the verb's number:

    Cherries, grapes, or **cake is** all we can offer you for dessert.

    If a sentence is correct but sounds strange, you can eliminate the awkwardness by rearranging the nouns:

    Cake, cherries, or **grapes are** all we can offer you for dessert.

## EXERCISE 26.2

In the following sentences, choose the correct word. Rewrite the sentence if the result is awkward.

1.  Neither bananas nor grapes (contains, contain) all the vitamins that a human needs.
2.  Either Ed or the Johnsons (has, have) bought a new car.
3.  Not only floods but also drought (has, have) been a problem in this region.
4.  Neither the Walker brothers nor Ellen Hastings (was, were) sent an invitation.
5.  Two ducks, a fox, or three turkeys (is, are) what I shall paint today.

## 26d  SUBJECTS THAT ARE INDEFINITE PRONOUNS

A **definite pronoun** refers to a specific person: *he, she,* and so on. An **indefinite pronoun,** such as *someone* or *anybody,* refers to a "generalized other." Indefinite pronouns fall into three categories, as shown in the following box.

## Indefinite Pronouns

| Always Singular | Always Plural | Singular or Plural Depending upon Context |
|---|---|---|
| another | both | all |
| anybody | few | any |
| anyone | many | either |
| anything | several | enough |
| each | | more |
| every | | most |
| everybody | | neither |
| everyone | | none |
| everything | | some |
| no one | | |
| nobody | | |
| nothing | | |
| one | | |
| somebody | | |
| someone | | |
| something | | |

### 26d.1 INDEFINITE PRONOUNS THAT ARE ALWAYS SINGULAR

Many of the words in the first column *seem* plural, such as *everyone* and *everybody,* but in practice they are always singular. Also remember that when *each* or *every* precedes a subject, it makes that subject singular:

**Everyone** in the study group **is** invited to participate.

**Each** of the four defendants **was** tried separately.

**Every** detective and lawyer in North America **has** been jolted by the news of McNamara's prison break.

However, when **each** *follows* a plural subject, the verb is plural:

At the ceremony, the **players each thank** the coach for his dedication.

### 26d.2 INDEFINITE PRONOUNS THAT CAN BE SINGULAR OR PLURAL

The words in the third column of the above box are indefinite pronouns, but they do not determine a subject's number; instead, the nouns that they are linked with determine whether the verb should be singular or plural:

All of the **work** on the garage **is** complete.

All of the clerical **tasks,** such as typing, collating, and filing, **are** done by Chris.

Some of the **damage is** severe.

Some of the **computers are** still working.

**Either (Neither)** the players **or (nor) the coach is** being fined.

**Either (Neither)** the coach **or (nor) the players are** being fined.

In the last example, the first sentence uses a singular verb because the subject closer to it, *coach,* is singular. The second sentence uses a plural verb because the subject closer to it, *players,* is plural.

## EXERCISE 26.3

In the following sentences, choose the correct verb. Treat the sentences as a continuous passage.

1. Everyone (is, are) expected to stand in line, Steve.
2. Either success or failure (await, awaits) us.
3. Most (believes, believe) that they will get to the window before the office closes.
4. Some of the procedure (is, are) explained in the company's personnel manual.
5. Neither the deadline nor the three different entry fees (has, have) been announced.

## 26e  SUBJECTS THAT ARE COLLECTIVE NOUNS

Collective nouns, such as *family, team, couple, pair, trio, group, panel,* and *committee,* refer to groups. They often cause subject-verb agreement problems. In American English, these words are usually treated as singular depending on context:

The **team is** coming out of the locker room.

The **jury is** still deliberating.

Her **family is** back together again.

However, they are sometimes treated as plural:

The **choir raise** their voices in song.

The **couple are** saying their wedding vows.

What's the distinction? In the first three examples, the collective noun (*team, jury, family*) is acting as a unit. In the last two examples, the elements that make up the collective nouns (*choir, couple*) are acting separately *within* the unit. To test this distinction, you might try to treat the collective nouns in the last two examples as singular:

The choir raises its voice in song.

The couple is saying its wedding vows.

The effect is awkward. One solution is to add the word *members* after the collective noun, making the construction automatically plural, as in *choir members*. However, this strategy doesn't work in all contexts. You would never say *the couple members*. In the second example, changing to a compound subject would produce a more natural-sounding sentence: *The bride and groom are saying their wedding vows.*

## EXERCISE 26.4

In each of the following sentences, choose the correct word.

1. The legislature (has, have) passed a resolution praising the governor.
2. After standing to acknowledge the applause of the audience, the orchestra took (its, their) (seat, seats).
3. The hockey team (is, are) arguing among (itself, themselves) about the coach's decision.
4. The family (is, are) planning to go to Manitoba for (its, their) vacation.
5. The awards committee (is, are) still deliberating.

## 26f OTHER COLLECTIVE NOUNS THAT CAUSE AGREEMENT PROBLEMS

Problems sometimes occur because of a difference between informal English and formal English; other problems represent highly specific developments in English over time.

1. **News:** This word is always treated as a singular noun:

   The news **is** good.

2. **Media:** In informal English, *media* is frequently used as a singular noun. In formal English, however, *media* is always plural. When you refer to the news or entertainment media, you are talking about a collection made up of each specific *medium,* such as print, radio, and television. Hence, *media* should always take a plural verb:

   The news media **are** reporting that the wildfire is being brought under control.

3. **Data:** This word is the plural form of the rarely used *datum.* Although in informal usage a singular verb is often used with *data,* formal English requires a plural verb:

   The data **are** consistent.

4. **Subjects or activities that end in -*s*** (physics, statistics, politics, ethics, economics, sports): These words are singular when they refer to a concept,

activity, subject, or academic course but plural when they refer to a specific "set" of individual items:

Physics **is** my least favorite course.
The physics of outer space **are** fascinating.

Statistics **is** my least favorite course.
The statistics from the two studies **are** consistent.

Sports **is** her future.
Team sports **are** dominating the intramural schedule.

5. **Company names:** The name of a single company or institution is always singular, even if it sounds plural:

Johnson and Johnson **makes** pharmaceutical supplies.

Ibbotson Research Associates **is** a new company in this area.

The Organization of American States **is** having an emergency meeting.

6. **Mathematical expressions:** Mathematical expressions are usually treated as singular:

Notice that 16 plus 24 **is** 40.

In fact, $(4 \times 2 + 3x)^3$ **is** the resulting polynomial.

7. **Distances and measurements of time:** When a distance or measurement of time is treated as one unit, it is singular:

Seven hundred miles **is** a long drive.

Two hours **seems** like a long time to wait for a doctor.

However, when a distance or measurement of time is seen as the sum of its individual units, it is plural:

Five miles of rough road **are** still in front of us.

Four hours **have** crawled by minute by minute.

In these two examples, five miles will be experienced *mile by mile,* and four hours have been suffered *minute by minute.*

8. **Word as word/number as number:** When you refer to a word *as* a word or a number *as* a number, the noun is singular:

*Hieroglyphics* **is** a very hard word to spell.

Eight **is** my lucky number.

9. **The number/a number:** *The number (of)* is singular; *a number (of)* is plural:

The number of guests for our upcoming party **has** been reduced; a number of people **have** called to cancel.

### EXERCISE 26.5

In the following sentences, choose the correct verb.

1. The United Nations (has, have) survived decades of political turmoil.
2. The sports media often (fail, fails) to cover events in swimming and water polo.
3. "Eight thousand maniacs" (refers, refer) to the people waiting to buy concert tickets.
4. The number of people who buy umbrellas (is, are) surprisingly small.
5. Statistics (indicates, indicate) that drunken driving is a leading cause of highway fatalities.

## Special Situations

## 26g SUBJECTS SEPARATED FROM THEIR VERBS

Don't be misled by intervening words, words that come between the subject and the verb:

> Lake Superior, the largest of the Great Lakes, (is, are) a vast body of water.

The subject of the sentence is *Lake Superior,* which is singular, so *is* is the correct verb. However, the word immediately preceding the verb is *Lakes,* and some writers, fooled by the closeness of this word, might want to use *are* instead. Remember to check for the number of the *subject,* not the number of the nearest noun or pronoun. Here are more examples:

> A **bouquet** of lilies, mums, and irises **makes** a stunning centerpiece.
>
> **Ford,** a company that owns many automobile brands, **is** expected to explore various alternative-fuel options.
>
> The **computer,** which has revolutionized both business and personal communications, **was** first used by the military.

### EXERCISE 26.6

In the following sentences, choose the correct verb in parentheses.

1. Excitement in all of its sordid varieties (is, are) the principal attraction of the Adelphi Nightclub.
2. The batter for the Washington Nationals (has, have) played for seven different teams.
3. Peanuts, an agricultural mainstay of the South, (is, are) a versatile food source.
4. William, one of five brothers, (owns, own) a car dealership.
5. All voters, regardless of their party affiliation, (seem, seems) interested in debating the bond issue.

## 26h  SUBJECTS AND LINKING VERBS

Linking verbs, especially forms of *be* as well as words like *taste, feel,* and *smell,* connect a subject to a word or words that describe it, called its complement. They cause a unique problem in subject-verb agreement:

|  | singular | plural | plural |
|---|---|---|---|
| INCORRECT | The main **problem** at the plant **are** production errors. | | |

|  | singular | singular | plural |
|---|---|---|---|
| CORRECT | The main **problem** at the plant **is** production errors. | | |

The subject can sometimes be plural and the complement singular, or vice versa. A common error is to make the verb agree with the complement, but, as always, the *subject* determines whether the verb is singular or plural. If a sentence is correct but sounds strange, remember that you can switch the subject and the complement. Then the verb will change number to match the new subject:

> The main problem **is** production errors.
> Production errors **are** the main problem.

### EXERCISE 26.7

In the following sentences, choose the correct verb.

1. Penguins (is, are) a tourist attraction in the Antarctic.
2. The problem with this drug (is, are) its side effects.
3. Errors in the programming language (is, are) our focus today.
4. Walking and biking (is, are) good exercise.
5. Driver's licenses (is, are) one item most people carry at all times.

## 26i  SUBJECTS THAT FOLLOW VERBS: INVERTED SENTENCE STRUCTURES

Some English sentences do not use the standard pattern of subject then verb. In a question, for example, the subject comes after the verb. In such instances, make sure that the verb agrees with the number of its subject:

> What **are** the **causes** of the problem?
> **Is this** a good reason for your behavior?

A similar situation occurs in declarative sentences beginning with *here, there,* and *what.* The subject is delayed until after the verb:

> **Here comes** my **aunt,** strolling down the aisle.
> **Here come** my **aunts,** strolling down the aisle.

> What **is** clearly an animal **track** was lifted by the police forensics specialist.

> What **are** clearly animal **tracks** were lifted by the police forensics specialist.

A third type of inverted sentence pattern happens when a writer deliberately switches the normal order for effect:

> Above the mountains **rises** a blinding **sun.**

Here, as always, identifying the subject and its number is crucial.

## EXERCISE 26.8

In the following sentences, choose the correct form of the verb.

1. Which (is, are) the correct instructions, this batch or the one over there?
2. Here (is, are) a few interesting questions to contemplate.
3. Through the busy shoppers (moves, move) Bettina, her Christmas buying almost finished.
4. On the barren ridge above the old house (sit, sits) a wolf and her pups.
5. There (is, are) many reasons not to go cave diving.

# VERB SHIFTS

As noted earlier, writers frequently need to project themselves into the reader's role and ask "I understand what I mean, but will my reader understand as well?" When writers change verb usage in a sudden or unexpected way (when they make a "shift"), they often cause problems for readers. This section will help you avoid three kinds of shifts—of tense, of voice, and of mood.

## 26j TENSE SHIFTS

Before we talk about incorrect shifts of verb tense (see also Chapter 23), it is important to note that a writer may correctly change tenses when such a change is called for. For example, a sentence or a paragraph may mention events that happened at different times. Therefore, changing tenses can be logical and necessary. Note the following example:

> In 1946 my father **was** in a quandary. Before World War II he **had been** a college student; however, in 1946 he **wasn't** sure what to do. He felt that the world **was becoming** a much more complicated place. Today, I **feel** the same way.

Four tenses (past, past perfect, past progressive, and present) are used in this paragraph, but this mix is acceptable. However, a sudden tense shift for no apparent reason is not acceptable:

| INCORRECT | Bobby **rode** up on his Harley, and he **starts** talking a mile a minute. (The action in the sentence either happened in the past or is happening now; the use of both tenses confuses the reader.) |
|---|---|
| CORRECT | Bobby **rode** up on his Harley, and he **started** talking a mile a minute. (In this version, both verbs are in past tense.) |

A special situation occurs when you are writing about literature, television, or film (you can read about such papers in Chapter 22). In this situation the **literary** present tense is used:

| CORRECT | In *Pulp Fiction,* Jules and Vincent **are** two of the major characters. |
|---|---|

## 26k VOICE SHIFTS

For most purposes, the **active voice** ("Kevin hit the wall") is preferable to the **passive voice** ("The wall was hit by Kevin"). In any case, mixing voices within a sentence is usually not the best choice:

| ORIGINAL | The criminal fled the scene, but he was arrested by the police that afternoon. |
|---|---|

The first independent clause is in the active voice; the second one is in the passive voice. Note how much more direct and forceful the revised sentence is:

| REVISED | The criminal fled the scene, but the police arrested him that afternoon. |
|---|---|

As you can see, in the active voice, the subject acts on a direct object. In the passive voice, the subject is acted upon. (To learn more about voice, see Chapter 23.) Here's another example:

| ORIGINAL | As Sean ran up the stairs, laughter could be heard. |
|---|---|
| REVISED | As Sean ran up the stairs, he could hear laughter. |

## 26l MOOD SHIFTS

Verbs can have one of three **moods** (see also Chapter 23). The **indicative** mood is the most common; it is used to state facts, make assertions, and ask questions. The **imperative** mood gives commands. The **subjunctive** mood describes hypothetical situations, wishes, or conditions contrary to fact, as in "If I **were** to flap my arms and fly out the window, everyone would be surprised." An inappropriate shift in mood occurs when the writer starts in the subjunctive mood but then switches to the indicative:

| INCORRECT | If I **were** wealthy, I **am going to buy** a sports car. |
|---|---|
| CORRECT | If I **were** wealthy, I **would buy** a sports car. |

The original sentence shifts from the subjunctive mood to the indicative; the revised sentence uses the subjunctive in both clauses. In the next example, the writer shifts from the imperative to the indicative:

INCORRECT    **Study hard tonight, and then you should rest.**

CORRECT      **Study hard tonight, and then rest.**

### EXERCISE 26.9

Each of the following sentences contains a shift of tense, voice, or mood. Revise each incorrect sentence.

1. It is believed by scientists that the epidemic will not occur, and parents welcome the good news.
2. American business always concentrated on efficiency, and some of today's firms are models of streamlining.
3. Jeremy is surviving a day in which he had seen his job almost lost, his car almost wrecked, and his house almost torched.
4. If Maria were able to finish college a year early, she will go immediately to graduate school.
5. *Damnation Boulevard* is a good movie, but everyone died in the end.
6. Instruments of the violin family are played with a stringed bow, but guitars, mandolins, and lyres would be played by hand.
7. Part of the German protectorate of Togoland from 1886 to 1914, Togo was administered by the French until 1982, when it becomes a republic.
8. In 1620, the Pilgrims establish Plymouth Colony, which was followed by the Massachusetts Bay Colony. By the 1700s, Massachusetts begins to prosper and had become part of the triangle trade, which involved the selling of molasses, rum, and slaves.
9. President Kennedy establishes the Peace Corps in 1961, and more than forty years later, people with technical skills who are willing to work in underdeveloped countries are still attracted to its mission.
10. White settlements in the mineral-rich hills of South Dakota were opposed by the Sioux Indians under Crazy Horse. With other Indian leaders, Crazy Horse defeats U.S. troops under George Custer at the Little Bighorn in 1876.

### COMBINATION EXERCISE

The following passage contains sentences with verb problems. Fix any errors that you see.

If someone says that he or she is going to be on time, one hopes that will be the case. If I were to make an appointment with you, you are sure that the appointment will be kept and that I will be prompt. Last Monday I made a tee time for 7:30 a.m. at the Hidden Value Estates

Golf Club. My friends Ed and Luis, along with Mike, who is one of Ed's friends, is supposed to meet me at Hidden Value. The course, which is owned by Golf Management Specialists, are located east of the city. I got there first and suspected that traffic problems was the issue, for I waited and waited.

Waiting for latecomers and still remaining patient is not my strong suit. Ed, as well as Luis, are constantly late, and I have no idea about Mike's problems. I sat and listened to the television news, which were bad, as usual. Statistics were indicating that the recent downturn in the North American economies were caused by a number of factors. Either the job market, inflationary trends, or European trade were the main culprit, according to the report. An opposing view countered that the real problem were the billions of dollars in U.S. Treasury bonds owned by the Japanese banks. In my opinion, neither trade issues nor foreign debt are the main issue; I feel that the investor class have just gotten scared of an overheated stock market.

Meanwhile, I was about to lose our tee time—or, should I say, Ed, Luis, and Mike was going to lose it for me. Thirty minutes are not a long time to wait, but the starter and his assistant was beginning to glare in my direction. Golf Management Specialists are not a patient group; it does not hesitate to cancel tee times and then a charge for a missed appointment is levied. Finally, with only a few minutes to spare, my three cohorts arrive in one car. Luis's facial expression and body language was not positive (he had waited for the other two), but we got off at 7:29, as planned.

CATALYST 2.0

**MORE OPTIONS ONLINE**
For more exercises,
go to
www.mhhe.com/
writingtoday.

### CHAPTER 27

# PROBLEMS WITH PRONOUNS

**Pronouns** take the place of and refer to nouns or other pronouns, called **antecedents.** The word *antecedent* signifies that such nouns and pronouns usually come before the pronouns that refer to them. Keep the advice in this chapter in mind when you revise or edit your papers so that you use pronouns correctly and make them relate clearly and correctly to their antecedents.

# PRONOUN-ANTECEDENT AGREEMENT

Pronoun-antecedent agreement follows the logic of subject-verb agreement (see Chapter 26). The pronoun agrees in number with its antecedent. Singular antecedents require singular pronouns; plural antecedents require plural pronouns:

> **Karen** asked that I call **her.**

> The Williams **brothers** were annoyed; the hotel had lost **their** reservations.

In addition, pronouns must be in the correct case (subjective, objective, possessive) and must agree with their antecedents in gender (male and female):

> **She** is my Aunt Lil Mcgill; I telephone **her** every week. (The pronoun *she* is in the subjective case; it is the subject of the first clause. The pronoun *her* is in the objective case; it receives the action of telephoning.)

> **Lil** is a name **she** took on **her** twenty-first birthday, but **she** is known as Nancy. (The pronouns in this sentence are all female, for they all refer to Lil.)

# DETERMINING WHETHER THE ANTECEDENT IS SINGULAR OR PLURAL

As with the subject in subject-verb agreement, there are many situations in which the writer's main problem is determining the number of the pronoun's antecedent.

## 27a ANTECEDENTS THAT USE *AND* AND OTHER CONNECTORS

1.  **Compound nouns and phrases with *and:*** Antecedents joined by the word *and* usually form a plural compound. Thus, pronouns referring to such antecedents must also be plural:

    > **Luis and Martina** have bought a new home; **they** are delighted to have a home of their own.

    > **Chile and Argentina** are in South America; **they** border each other.

    > Sally enjoys **planting** flowers and **reading** mysteries because **they** help relax her.

2.  **Compound nouns and phrases with other connectors:** Using other connectors (*as well as, along with, in addition to, plus*) to join two nouns can result in problems:

    > INCORRECT    Karen, along with her friend Ed, is coming to the fund drive; **they** will bring a couch for the auction.

In this sentence, *they* has no antecedent because *along with* does not connect *Karen* and *her friend Ed.* The solution here is simple—change *along with* to the coordinating conjunction *and.*

CORRECT   Karen **and** her friend Ed are coming to the fund drive; **they** will bring a couch for the auction.

3.  **Compound words treated as singular constructions:** Sometimes, two singular words connected by *and* are actually the same entity. When such words act as an antecedent, refer to them with a singular pronoun:

**My best friend and most exacting critic** is my sister; **she** plans to visit next week.

Whenever I hear **rock and roll,** I have to sing or dance to **it.**

4.  **Gerund phrases linked with *and*:** In the following sentence, the subject (*going downtown and playing poker*) is essentially one activity. It should be referred to by using a singular pronoun.

**Going downtown and playing poker** is my grandfather's secret vice; he does **it** three days a week.

On other hand, the following sentence has a compound gerund phrase that clearly indicates two separate activities:

**Getting dressed and driving to my date's home** are the last two steps in the ritual, and **they** are the two easiest steps.

## EXERCISE 27.1

In the following sentences, decide if the highlighted pronoun is correct in number. If it is not, supply the correct pronoun or rewrite the sentence. Not all sentences contain errors.

1.  Lately, my wife has complained about my tossing and turning all night; **they** are keeping her awake as well.
2.  When Bob and Leo went fishing, **he** decided to bring a radio.
3.  When a Major League Baseball player leaves the game, **they** can normally expect paid retirement.
4.  When Elrod and Lurine got **their** first assignment in the Navy, **they** were shipped to Alaska.
5.  When running water and electricity came to our rural cabin, **it** surely made our lives easier.

## 27b ANTECEDENTS JOINED BY *OR, NOR, EITHER . . . OR, NEITHER . . . NOR, AND NOT ONLY . . . BUT ALSO*

As in subject-verb agreement, using these connectors to join nouns can cause problems in pronoun-antecedent agreement. Note the following basic guidelines:

1. If both antecedents (nouns or pronouns) joined by these words or phrases are singular, the pronoun is also singular.
2. If both antecedents joined by these words or phrases are plural, the pronoun is also plural.
3. If one antecedent is plural and the other is singular, the pronoun agrees in number with the antecedent closer to it.

The first two guidelines are fairly straightforward:

> Either Michael or Edgar left **his** car keys on the counter.

> Either the Parkers or the Robbins left **their** car keys on the counter.

The third guideline is more complex. When a singular noun is connected by *or* to a plural noun, the pronoun's number is determined by *the noun that is closer to the pronoun:*

> Neither my mother nor my sisters found **their** way to my cabin.

But note the problem posed by this sentence:

> Either the Robbins or Edgar left **his** car keys on the counter.

This sentence is technically correct; however, it does not say what its writer intends. To revise, the writer could reverse the order of the two nouns, allowing the pronoun to change number:

> Either Edgar or the Robbins left **their** car keys on the counter.

Remember that *you* control the sequence of your nouns in these situations; make sure that your sentences are logically correct as well as technically correct.

Note also that you can often solve problems by eliminating the pronoun altogether:

> Either the Robbins or Edgar left **a set of** car keys on the counter.

## EXERCISE 27.2

In the following sentences, choose the best term from the parentheses. In some sentences, more than one set of choices may be correct.

1. If you see Jane or Nancy, ask (her, them) to bring some plates.
2. For supper, I think that I'll have either (fishsteaks or pizza, pizza or fishsteaks); (it, they) really (appeal, appeals) to me.
3. (Neither Lance nor Marie) (Both Lance and Marie) (will admit) (refuse to admit) (that she is wrong) (that they are wrong).
4. The specials tonight include not only pork loin but also quesadillas; (it, they) (sounds, sound) wonderful.
5. After a hard night at the casino, (neither the Parkers nor their daughter Ellen) (neither Ellen Parker nor her parents) wanted to risk any more of (her, their) money.

## 27c ANTECEDENTS THAT ARE INDEFINITE PRONOUNS

An **indefinite pronoun,** such as *each, everyone, no one,* and *somebody,* refers to a nonspecific person or thing. You can find a chart of indefinite pronouns in Chapter 26, page 720.

### 27c.1 INDEFINITE PRONOUNS THAT
### ARE ALWAYS SINGULAR

Such pronouns include *anybody, everyone,* and *something,* as well as many others:

> **Something** must have spoiled in the refrigerator. **It** is probably the fish I left in there last August.

> **Everyone** must vote according to **his or her** conscience.

A little more than half the people in the world are female. Unfortunately, English has no single word that can refer to an "indefinite" person of either sex. An informal solution is to write *Everyone must vote their conscience.* However, *their* is plural whereas *everyone* is singular. A better solution is to use the *his or her* construction (as above) or to recast the sentence into the plural:

> All **citizens** must vote according to **their** consciences.

The same approach will work when using words such as *any, each,* and *every:*

> Any **student** who wants to do well in Dr. Oshiro's physics class must make sure that **he or she** is prepared to study.

> **Students** who want to do well in Dr. Oshiro's physics class must make sure that **they** are prepared to study.

Another way to fix this problem is to get rid of the pronoun altogether if possible:

> Anybody who forces **his or her** child into show business should be prosecuted.

> Anybody who forces **a** child into show business should be prosecuted.

### 27c.2 TROUBLESHOOTING

1. Some contexts require singular forms. Consider this situation: your college offers the Landstar Scholarship to a single student. All students are eligible. Hence, the winner will be either male or female. A carefully worded requirement of the scholarship might read like this:

   > **The student** who is awarded the scholarship must present proof of **his or her** completion of thirty semester hours.

   A plural context won't work here: only one winner will be selected. Therefore, using *his or her* is necessary.

2. If you have to use a singular indefinite pronoun, use *he or she* or *she or he.* Avoid *s/he* and *[s]he.* These are not considered acceptable style; furthermore, they can't be spoken.

3. If your context refers to an all-male or an all-female population, use the appropriate singular pronoun to refer to an "indefinite" person. Any

player in the National Hockey League can, at this time, be safely referred to as *he*. Any golfer in the LPGA can be referred to as *she*.

## EXERCISE 27.3

In the following sentences, choose the correct pronoun. If the result is awkward, rewrite the sentence so that a more natural-sounding sentence results.

1. Anyone who wants to participate in the contest better have (his, her, their, his or her) cooking utensils.

2. A knight in the Middle Ages owed (his, her, his or her, their) allegiance to a feudal lord.

3. Everybody who is scheduled for writing conferences must file (his, her, their, his or her) proposal with the instructor.

4. Each car mechanic and technician is responsible for (his, her, their, his or her) own certification.

5. All the people at this meeting have pledged at least $100 of (his, her, their, his or her) money toward the reelection campaign.

## 27d ANTECEDENTS THAT ARE COLLECTIVE NOUNS

Words such as *family, team, couple, pair, trio, group, panel,* and *committee* are called **collective nouns.** They are normally singular, but sometimes they are plural, according to context:

> The **team** emerged; **it** was ready for action.

> The **couple** said **their** vows.

When you use a collective noun, you need to ask the following question: Is the collective noun functioning as one entity, or are the individual members acting separately? In the first example, the team is acting as one entity. In the second example, each of the two people in the wedding ceremony speaks separately; the two people are effectively plural. As noted in the section on subject-verb agreement (see 26e and 26f), you can avoid problems with most collective nouns by adding the word *members.* Consider the following sentence, which is correct and sounds correct:

> The committee has not yet reached its decision.

However, this sentence is correct but *sounds* incorrect:

> The committee are arguing among themselves.

Adding the word *members* helps avoid awkwardness:

> The committee **members** are arguing among themselves.

This strategy works most of the time, except with the collective nouns *couple, pair,* and *duo.* If you use these words alone, you must decide if the context makes them singular or plural when choosing a pronoun.

The pair walked hand in hand, discussing **their** future.

This pair [of pants] is worn out; throw **it** away.

## 27e OTHER COLLECTIVE NOUNS THAT CAUSE AGREEMENT PROBLEMS

In the section on subject-verb agreement, we list a number of collective nouns that cause special problems in agreement (see Chapter 26, pages 722–723). Here is a shortened version of that list—most of these words cause fewer problems in pronoun-antecedent agreement:

1. **News** is singular:

   I heard the news; **it** is good.

2. **Media** is plural:

   A problem with the media is **their** belief that people will never tire of hearing about scandals.

3. **Data** is plural:

   I've checked the data, and **they** seem realistic.

4. **Physics, statistics, politics, ethics, economics,** and **sports** are all singular if they refer to a concept, subject, or academic course:

   Physics is my favorite course; **it** fascinates me.

   My grandfather wants me to go into politics, but **it** is not for me.

   They are plural if they are referring to a "set" of individual items:

   We examined the statistics on car thefts; **they** show a clear pattern.

   Gary has tried various sports, but **they** don't interest him.

5. **Company names** are singular:

   Betty's Wondrous Roses has failed; **it** is bankrupt.

6. **Mathematical expressions** are singular:

   The result we come up with is $(4x + 3)^3/1.5x$; **it** now needs to be tested.

7. **Measurements of distance and time** are singular when treated as one unit:

   Seven hundred miles is a long drive; **it** wears me out.

   They are plural when treated as the sum of units:

   Five years passed slowly. **They** seemed to drift by like a bad dream.

8. **Words treated as words and numbers treated as numbers** are singular:

   When I try to spell *hieroglyphics,* **it** gets twisted around in my memory.

   Eight is my lucky number; **it** always has been.

9. **The number of . . .** is singular:

   The number of attendees was small; **it** was under fifty.

10. **A number of . . .** is plural:

    A number of people canceled; **they** didn't want to brave the weather.

## EXERCISE 27.4

In the following sentences, choose the correct word or words.

1.  An example of a controversial organization is the United Nations; (it, they) can inspire a number of reactions among people in the United States.

2.  Golf and swimming are my two sports; (it, they) can keep me occupied in my spare time.

3.  When you see the term "teeming millions," (they, it) (mean, means) the bulk of the population.

4.  When I drove up to Farber and Associates, (it, they) (was, were) closed.

5.  We've rerun the data several times; (it, they) (keeps, keep) coming back the same way.

6.  The commission (has, have) announced (its, their) new guidelines.

7.  The winning (team, team members) divided the bonus money among (itself, themselves).

8.  Tamara and Juan, a newlywed couple, (is, are) planning to spend (its, their) vacation in New Mexico.

9.  The Dining and Entertainment Planning Committee (is, are) made up of seven members; (it, they) will make new recommendations next week.

10. When I last saw the baseball team, (it, they) (was, were) taking batting practice.

# PRONOUN REFERENCE

If the pronoun's antecedent (the noun or pronoun it replaces) is vague or ambiguous—or if no antecedent exists—readers may have a difficult time understanding your meaning. Indeed, they may see two or more possible meanings in a particular sentence. The following sections will help you avoid unclear pronoun reference.

## 27f  PRONOUNS WITHOUT APPROPRIATE ANTECEDENTS

A pronoun must have an antecedent, and the antecedent must be an appropriate noun or pronoun, not another word that merely seems like an antecedent.

1.  **Don't use an inappropriate noun or an entire clause as an antecedent.**

    AMBIGUOUS     Caleb loved the idea of farming, but he had never been on one.

    What does *one* refer to? Obviously, the writer means to link *one* to *farm*, but the word *farm* is not in the sentence—*farming* is.

    REVISED     Caleb loved the idea of farming, but he had never been on a farm.

In the revised version, the noun *farm* replaces the ambiguous pronoun *one*.

| AMBIGUOUS | The moving truck collided with an SUV, **which** left debris all over my front lawn. |
| REVISED | The collision of the moving truck with the SUV left debris all over my front lawn. |

In this example, the pronoun *which* has no noun to which it can logically refer. In the revision, the sentence is recast to eliminate the pronoun altogether.

2. **Don't use an adjective or a possessive as an antecedent.**

| INCORRECT | Ever since being introduced to Japanese art, Jeff has wanted to visit it. |
| REVISED | Ever since being introduced to Japanese art, Jeff has wanted to visit Japan. |
| INCORRECT | Decades after Franklin D. Roosevelt's death, the country has finally decided to erect a memorial to him. |
| CORRECT | Decades after Franklin D. Roosevelt's death, the country has finally decided to erect a memorial to the thirty-second President. |

In the last example, the writer is trying to link *him* to *Roosevelt*. However, *Roosevelt* is not in the sentence; *Roosevelt's* is, and it is possessive. Technically, then, *him* has no antecedent. This is a fine point, but revision is your best option.

3. **Make sure that the pronoun *it* has an antecedent.** You would be absolutely correct if you wrote this sentence:

Maria wants to buy my old car, but she can't afford **it.**

Here there is an obvious link between *it* and *car*. Also, you would be correct if you used *it* to refer to the weather:

**It** has been raining all day.

However, when you begin a sentence with *it,* you run the risk of failing to include an antecedent, as in the following sentence, thereby leaving out important information:

| AMBIGUOUS | **It** is generally believed that the Sumerians developed cuneiform writing. |

In reading such a sentence, the reader might ask "Who believes this?"

| REVISED | Historians generally believe that the Sumerians developed cuneiform writing. |

Writers can also cause ambiguity by using *it* to mean different things in the same sentence:

AMBIGUOUS    **It** was raining that afternoon, and **it** was clear that the party would need to be moved inside or **it** would have to be rescheduled.

REVISED    Rain was falling that afternoon, and I realized that the party would need to be moved inside or be rescheduled.

In the revised sentence, *it* has been eliminated. However, don't get the impression that you should avoid *it* altogether; just avoid conflicting uses of this word. Note the following sentence:

This is my laptop; I bought **it** a year ago, and **it** is worth the high price I paid for **it.**

The word *it* occurs three times in this sentence, but all three instances clearly refer to the laptop computer, so the sentence is not ambiguous.

4. **Don't skip the antecedent altogether.**

INCORRECT    During the musical *A Chorus Line,* **they** tell their own stories.

REVISED    During the musical *A Chorus Line,* the **dancers** tell their own stories.

INCORRECT    In the latest issue of *Newsweek,* **it** said the election would be close.

REVISED    In the latest issue of *Newsweek,* **a reporter** said the election would be close.

REVISED    The latest issue of *Newsweek* said the election would be close.

5. **Avoid using the pronoun *you* when you mean a more general word, such as *one, anyone,* or *someone.*** Using the pronoun *you* is appropriate if you are addressing the reader directly:

We ask that **you** remit your payment of $150 by December 20.

However, when you really mean the more impersonal *one* or an equivalent pronoun, *you* is inappropriate:

INCORRECT    As you enter the execution chamber, you notice that everything is white and sterile.

In the sentence above, the writer presupposes that the reader will actually visit an execution chamber.

REVISED    As an observer enters the execution chamber, he or she notices that everything is white and sterile.

## EXERCISE 27.5

In each of the following sentences, decide if the highlighted pronouns have appropriate antecedents. If not, revise the sentence to eliminate the problem.

1. Jeremy hadn't heard from home lately; he wondered if he should call **them.**

2. When **you** have a baby, **you** soon realize that **your** life is no longer **your** own.

3. He dreamed of studying at Oxford University, **which** was about to come true.

4. It occurred to Miguel that **it** was possible for **it** to rain that afternoon.

5. **They** said on the radio that school was canceled.

## 27g PRONOUNS WITH UNCLEAR ANTECEDENTS

Follow these suggestions to make sure that pronouns refer clearly to their antecedents:

1. **Make sure that the pronoun has only one possible antecedent.** Sometimes, a writer asks the reader to connect a pronoun to its antecedent when there is more than one possible antecedent. The writer's meaning then becomes unclear:

   AMBIGUOUS    When Larry and Gus went fishing, **he** took a lantern.

Who? Larry or Gus? Consider this revision:

   CLEAR        Gus took a lantern when **he** went fishing with Larry.

Most writers who have trouble with pronouns tend to use them too often. When in doubt, repeat the noun or revise the sentence so that the pronoun clearly links to its antecedent.

Connectors such as *as well as, along with, in addition to,* and *plus* can cause problems:

   AMBIGUOUS    Peter, as well as Michael, believes in high ethical
                standards; **he** says that his business ethics class taught
                **him** a great deal.

After the semicolon, *he* seems to indicate Peter, but the reader can't be sure. Here are two possible revisions:

   CORRECT      Peter and Michael believe in high ethical standards; Peter
                says that **his** business ethics class taught **him** a great deal.

   CORRECT      Peter and Michael believe in high ethical standards;
                **they** say that **their** business ethics class taught **them**
                a great deal.

A related problem involves careless use of *which, this,* and *that.* Note the following ambiguous sentence:

   AMBIGUOUS    I spent the afternoon waxing the car and buffing it, **which**
                is difficult.

Is buffing difficult? Or waxing? Or, as seems more likely, is the combined task difficult? Here is a possible revision:

REVISED    I spent the afternoon waxing and buffing the car, **which** is a difficult process.

As is so often the case with ambiguous pronouns, the writer is simply not using *enough* words to get his or her meaning across.

A similar problem occurs when the writer asks *which, this,* or *that* to carry too much weight. Note the following:

The guest speaker could not keep still. She walked back and forth constantly, and her hands flew around like deformed birds. She also laughed suddenly and inappropriately at several points. **This** drove me crazy.

"This" what? The laughter or the entire experience? The writer probably means the latter, so the final sentence of the passage should be clarified:

**This bizarre performance** drove me crazy.

2. **Don't start a paragraph with a pronoun.** The beginning of a paragraph is an ideal place to establish or reestablish an antecedent. If you use a pronoun to start a paragraph, you are asking your reader to think back to the previous paragraph and "retrieve" the antecedent.

3. **Remember that pronouns aren't your only choice.** Use articles—*a, an,* and especially *the*—instead. Rather than using the indefinite *someone,* use (if possible) *people.* This way, you can avoid ambiguity while also avoiding the use of *he or she,* or *his or her.*

WITH PRONOUN    **No one** wants to be frustrated when **his or her** car overheats in traffic.

WITH ARTICLE    **No one** wants to be frustrated when **the** car overheats in traffic.

WITH INDEFINITE PRONOUN    **Everyone** should be concerned about this threat to **his or her** health.

WITH *PEOPLE*    **People** should be concerned about this threat to **their** health.

## EXERCISE 27.6

In the following sentences, determine whether the highlighted pronoun is ambiguous. If so, revise the sentence to eliminate the ambiguity. You may be able to use more than one revision method.

1. Eddie told John that **he** was fifth in the batting order.
2. The door was open, and the light was broken; **this** worried me.
3. The bedroom has an aquarium and a small filter, **which** I plan to replace.
4. Our manager, Ms. Shinzato, seems to think we're running late, although she hasn't actually said **that.**
5. Elrod and Lurine were very pleased when **they** finally bought a house.

## EXERCISE 27.7

The following passage is filled with ambiguous pronouns. Revise each sentence as needed.

> Some teams in the local softball league have started to have problems with couples on the teams. They are untrustworthy. A problem that couples are having can cause one or both of them to miss an important game or practice. This makes it hard on the rest of the team; they have to pick up the slack. It is hard to play a schedule when it depends on each team holding together.
>
> For example, take the case of Jim and Laura. She is normally reliable, but he is not. His boss frequently makes him stay late at work, finishing some project, or he gets exhausted, which causes him to miss practices and games. He also has an anger-management problem. This is not a pretty sight to behold.
>
> He does his best, and she helps him. That's good. Otherwise, our team members would have more frustrations than triumphs, and they would be without a solution. For they're our best two players. One night when it was raining, it was clear that we would lose a weather-shortened game unless Jim got on it and made it to the game. This he did. He hit two home runs in the fourth and fifth innings, and they made the difference.

## 27h AVOIDING SHIFTS OF PERSON

Personal pronouns can be first person, second person, or third person, as the following list indicates:

| First Person | Second Person | Third Person |
|--------------|---------------|--------------|
| I | you | she |
| me | your | her |
| my | yours | hers |
| mine | | he |
| we | | him |
| us | | his |
| our | | it |
| ours | | its |
| | | they |
| | | them |
| | | their |
| | | theirs |

To use pronouns appropriately and consistently, follow these guidelines:

**1.** Use *I* to refer to yourself within an essay. In the past, writers were told to avoid the use of *I*, but this restriction is fading.

**2.** Use *we* to refer to you and your audience when you share values or experiences:

CORRECT    As Americans, **we** share a long history.

CORRECT    At the end of *The Sound and the Fury,* **we** realize the mixture of desolation and faint hope that Faulkner has developed.

**3.** Use *you* sparingly, only when referring to the reader directly (as in an instructional process analysis, discussed in Chapter 8):

CORRECT    After **you** have tightened the lugs, check the edges of the seal.

Do not use *you* to mean "a person" or "someone":

INCORRECT    When **you** shoot heroin, **you** are taking a great risk.

CORRECT    When **a person** shoots heroin, **he or she** is taking a great risk.

CORRECT    When **people** shoot heroin, **they** are taking a great risk.

**4.** Use the third-person pronouns to refer to people, places, things, and ideas:

CORRECT    People who follow a strict exercise regimen may become bored; **it** can seem like a prison to **them.**

To avoid inappropriate shifts when you are using personal pronouns, follow the above guidelines. You also need to understand how to use indefinite pronouns (see 27c, page 734). The following sentence incorrectly shifts from second to third person. It also has problems with pronoun-antecedent agreement:

INCORRECT    When **a person** sees a student standing outside a locked faculty office at 5:15 P.M. with a blank look on **their** face, **you** know that **they** are seriously adrift.

REVISED    A student standing outside a locked faculty office at 5:15 P.M. with a blank look on **his or her** face is seriously adrift.

REVISED    Students standing outside a locked faculty office at 5:15 P.M. with blank looks on **their** faces are seriously adrift.

To avoid shifts in person, use the word *you* carefully, and remember the advice from 27c: whenever possible, don't refer to *a person, a student, a swimmer,* and so on when you can use *persons, students,* or *swimmers* instead. You will then automatically avoid this common—and serious—pronoun problem in your writing.

## EXERCISE 27.8

Revise the following paragraph so that it uses pronouns appropriately and avoids shifts in person.

When a student first attends college, no matter how much advice you have received and preparation you have endured, you will be

case
27i

surprised. The student may find that their roommate is new, as the expected roommate has found another place for their domicile. Your classroom may have changed, or you might locate the right classroom but notice that the instructor is not who they're supposed to be. My current roommate is on the men's golf team, and he told me that at the start of this year's practice season, each golfer learned that their coach had suddenly resigned. If you ask me, all this seems to be part of a vast plan to prepare you for the uncertainties of your adult life.

# PRONOUN CASE

Consider this sentence: "He gave she a present for they anniversary." Something is obviously wrong. *He* is correct, but *she* should be *her,* and *they* should be *their:* "He gave her a present for their anniversary." This example illustrates pronoun **case**, which means that pronouns have different spellings according to their function in a sentence. In the correct version, *He* is in the **subjective case**, functioning as a subject; *her* is in the **objective case**, functioning as an object; and *their* is in the **possessive case**, indicating ownership. (Note that objective-case pronouns can be direct objects, indirect objects, and objects of prepositions.)

## 27i THE SUBJECTIVE CASE, THE OBJECTIVE CASE, AND THE POSSESSIVE CASE

Here are the subjective, objective, and possessive forms of the personal pronouns:

| Subjective | Objective | Possessive |
| --- | --- | --- |
| I | me | my, mine |
| you | you | your, yours |
| she | her | her, hers |
| he | him | his |
| we | us | our, ours |
| they | them | their, theirs |
| it | it | its |

The pronouns *who* and *whoever* also have different forms according to their function:

| Subjective | Objective | Possessive |
| --- | --- | --- |
| who | whom | whose |
| whoever | whomever | |

Remember to use the correct pronoun case when you write. Avoid careless sentences such as this one:

**INCORRECT** Jamal came over to Nancy and **I,** asking if we had a copy of the assignment.

REVISED        Jamal came over to Nancy and **me**, asking if we had a copy of
               the assignment.

The correct form is *Nancy and me* because *me* is the object of the preposition *to.*
If you take out *Nancy and,* the sentence sounds absurd. You would never write
*Jamal came over to I.* Here are a few more examples:

       O.C.  S.C.         O.C.

Kavan asked **me** if **I** would e-mail **him** the meeting's agenda.

                     S.C.                      O.C.

Theresa and Ron are my closest friends; **I** have the utmost respect for **her**

  O.C.      S.C.                  O.C.

and **him.** OR: **I** have the utmost respect for **them.**

S.C.                                        O.C.

**We** had a bad scare last night; a police officer almost arrested **us** in a
case of mistaken identity.

    O.C.                       S.C.

To **whom** is the letter addressed? **Who** is involved here?

S.C.                           O.C.

**We** Americans are a diverse group, but to **us** Americans, certain issues
cause little disagreement.

In the last example, the pronoun is the same case as the noun that follows it.
The sections that follow will help you avoid pronoun case errors.

## 27j PRONOUNS THAT ARE SUBJECT COMPLEMENTS

A personal pronoun connected to the subject by a linking verb—normally a
form of *be*—is a subject complement and is in the subjective case:

          S.C.

John called; **it** was **he** who left the message yesterday afternoon.

                  S.C.

The speaker has arrived; that is **she** over by the podium.

As you can see, following this rule can cause some stilted and strange constructions. Note how the second example sentence can be recast for a more natural
sound:

The speaker has arrived; **she** is the one over by the podium.

## 27k PRONOUNS IN COMPARISONS

When writers use *as* or *than* to compare people or things, they frequently omit
the verb in the second part of the comparison.

Harley is taller than Mike [is].

Melissa is at least as talented as Gayle [is].

When the second part of the comparison uses a personal pronoun instead of a noun, the pronoun should be in the subjective case:

> Harley is taller than **I** [not **me**].
>
> Melissa is at least as talented as **I** [not **me**].

Do these sentences sound awkward? Then "fill out" the comparison:

> Harley is taller than I **am.**
>
> Melissa is at least as talented as I **am.**

## 271 PRONOUNS THAT ARE SUBJECTS OF CLAUSES

When an entire clause is the object of a sentence, the subject of the clause is still in the subjective case:

> I hope that **Ron will do well as an intern at Mercy Hospital.**

Note that *Ron* is the subject of the objective clause. If a personal pronoun is used to replace *Ron,* that pronoun must be in the subjective case:

> I hope that **he** will do well as an intern at Mercy Hospital.

The pronoun is the subject of the subordinated clause even though the clause is an object; therefore, the pronoun (*he*) should be in the subjective case.

*Who* and *whom* are troublesome pronouns. Note the difference between the following two sentences:

> CORRECT   I must say that the person **who** is responsible for this mess won't have a job tomorrow morning.
>
> CORRECT   Please find out to **whom** I should send this letter.

In the first sentence, *who* is the subject of the dependent clause (*who is responsible . . .*). In the second sentence, *whom* is the object of the preposition *to;* it is not the subject of the dependent clause.

### EXERCISE 27.9

Choose the best form of each pronoun in the following sentences.

1. We realize that (we, us) members of the Widget Club must take our responsibilities seriously.
2. Marina and Miguel are here; see if (he and she, him or her, they, them) want something to eat.
3. Lisa can run faster than (I, me).
4. With (who, whom) has the FBI communicated about the recent kidnapping?
5. Disha is talented; I hope that (she, her) is given a promotion.
6. Rob and (me, I) will be ready soon.

7. It is (I, me) who will be your guide.

8. To (who, whom) is the letter addressed?

9. (Whoever, Whomever) is responsible better start apologizing.

10. Roger has progressed more quickly than Amanda; he is at least as qualified as (she, her).

## 27m REFLEXIVE PRONOUNS AND INTENSIVE PRONOUNS

**Reflexive pronouns** show that a subject is taking action toward itself:

> The beetle righted **itself.**
> On the hike, Karen made a practice of checking **herself** for ticks.
> The ballplayers viewed **themselves** as the country's finest.

The correct forms of these pronouns are *herself, himself, itself, myself, oneself, ourselves, themselves, yourself,* and *yourselves.* Avoid *hisself, theirself, theirselves,* and *ourself.* Also, don't use a reflexive pronoun when it is not needed:

INCORRECT    Jason and myself went to the psychic fair.

CORRECT    Jason and I went to the psychic fair.

INCORRECT    The gift is for Bob and yourself.

CORRECT    The gift is for Bob and you.

When reflexive pronouns are needed, they're essential; when they're not needed, their inclusion is incorrect.

**Intensive** pronouns are spelled the same way as reflexive pronouns but have a different purpose—they are used to emphasize a point:

> I checked that report **myself.**
> Jay **himself** admits that the process has flaws.

## EXERCISE 27.10

In the following sentences, correct any misuse of reflexive or intensive pronouns. Some sentences may be correct.

1. The four-course Italian dinner was prepared by Carl and myself.

2. Alton Brown hisself couldn't have done any better.

3. You should check out the gourmet cooking yourself.

4. Carl and I couldn't always agree between ourself about certain parts of the recipe.

5. Carl prides himself on his cold antipasto, eggplant Siciliano, and baked ziti.

## COMBINATION EXERCISE

Rewrite the following paragraph to correct pronoun problems.

It is certain that hepatitis is an inflammation of the liver. Anyone who gets this disease will know it, for they will become jaundiced, lose their appetites, and suffer a loss of energy and a fever. The disease comes in many types, but the most common forms are hepatitis A and hepatitis B. Either form is very dangerous; in fact, they can be fatal. You get hepatitis A from contaminated food and water, but they seem to be able to treat this type with some success. Hepatitis B, on the other hand, can be transmitted when surgical instruments are not adequately sterilized. This is why practicing asepsis is crucial in a hospital and why they work so hard to maintain a sterile environment in operating rooms. Many people have also contracted hepatitis B when receiving transfusions of tainted blood, which is how my cousin Rudy got it. It was him who nearly died in the automobile accident that made the front page of the local paper three years ago. When they brought him into the hospital emergency room, you could see that he had lost a lot of blood. Unfortunately, it was not known that the two pints they gave him were tainted. The donor had not been properly screened for hepatitis; they may have contracted the disease through drug or alcohol abuse.

CATALYST 2.0

**MORE OPTIONS ONLINE**
For more exercises, go to
www.mhhe.com/writingtoday.

### CHAPTER 28

# PROBLEMS WITH MODIFIERS

A **modifier** is a word or group of words that describes, evaluates, limits the meaning of, or provides more information about another word or group of words in a sentence. Generally speaking, modifiers can be classified as adjectives and adverbs, parts of speech discussed in 23c and 23l.

THIS CHAPTER DISCUSSES PROBLEMS that you may have with the logical use and placement of modifiers in sentences, the incorrect substitution of adjectives for adverbs, the use of comparative and superlative forms, the sequencing of adjectives, the question of split infinitives, and the proper use of articles.

## 28a MISPLACED AND AMBIGUOUS (SQUINTING) MODIFIERS

You will confuse your reader if you place modifiers in the wrong position or if you place modifiers in an ambiguous position. The first situation creates a **misplaced modifier;** the modifier does not refer to what the writer intended:

MISPLACED     Brice solved the problem, a proven leader.

What did the writer mean for *a proven leader* to do, modify *Brice* or *the problem*? Obviously, the answer is *Brice*. Note the revision:

CORRECT       Brice, a proven leader, solved the problem.

MISPLACED     A zoologist said that polar bears are the most effective predators **on television.**

CORRECT       A zoologist said **on television** that polar bears are the most effective predators.

A common problem occurs with the modifiers *only* and *just*. Read the following two sentences:

MISPLACED     I **just** have five dollars.

CORRECT       I have **just** five dollars.

The first version suggest that the only thing going on in the writer's life is his or her possession of five dollars, an absurd statement. The second version is correct; *just* modifies *five dollars.*

MISPLACED     Frank **only** worked in Philadelphia for five months.

CORRECT       Frank worked in Philadelphia for **only** five months.

In the first version, *only* modifies *worked,* a structure that suggests that Frank did absolutely nothing else in Philadelphia, such as eat, breathe, and walk, during those five months. In the second version, *only* relates clearly and directly to *five months.*

If a sentence contains the second type of error, an **ambiguous** or **squinting modifier,** the reader must "squint" (look carefully) to determine what the writer intended, as the following example shows:

AMBIGUOUS     Friends who ride in car pools together **frequently** become angry with one another.

Here, *frequently* can refer to either *ride* or *become angry,* but which one? The sentence must be rewritten to make the meaning clear:

CORRECT        Friends who ride in car pools together become angry with
               one another **frequently.**

CORRECT        Friends who **frequently** ride in car pools together become
               angry with one another.

Misplaced and squinting modifiers sometimes occur at the beginning of a
sentence:

INCORRECT        **Staggering on the sidewalk, the police officer**
                 **approached the drunkard outside the bar.**

To fix the sentence, you can (1) place the word that the modifier refers to
immediately before or after the modifier or (2) add a subject and verb to the
modifier, turning it into a dependent clause:

CORRECT        **The police officer approached the drunkard staggering**
               **on the sidewalk outside the bar.**

CORRECT        **As the drunkard staggered on the sidewalk outside the bar,**
               **the police officer approached him.**

In the example above, the reader can assume that it is the drunkard who is
staggering and not the police officer, even if the incorrect sentence seems to
say otherwise. In some cases, though, placing a modifier incorrectly may make
it impossible for the reader to make such a distinction. In other words, misplaced or ambiguous modifiers cloud meaning:

INCORRECT        **Alex found useful books and other resources in**
AND              **the town library that had been donated by a local**
UNCLEAR          **corporation.**

Did the corporation donate the books and resources, or did it donate the entire
library? To make the message clear, the sentence needs to be restructured:

CORRECT        **In the town library, Alex found useful books and other**
               **resources that had been donated by a local corporation.**

CORRECT        **In the town library, which had been donated by a local**
               **corporation, Alex found useful books and other resources.**

## EXERCISE 28.1

The following sentences contain misplaced and squinting modifiers. Correct
them.

1. I only have a week to write this paper.
2. Thrashing the water furiously, the angler hooked the trout.
3. Jim just bought a special gift for his wife, a coffee grinder.
4. The coach only said that she would consider our request.
5. Ella claimed that she was very happy in the restroom.
6. Last Saturday, we went to a French restaurant and then walked home,
   a rare treat.

7.  Spinning out of control, Ed watched in horror as the car slammed into the bridge.

8.  They sat through a four-hour meeting and then went out for dinner with their boss, a true horror.

9.  Perched on the stone gargoyle, we watched the young pigeons.

10. The old man opened the letter, weary and ailing.

## 28b DANGLING MODIFIERS

A sentence has a **dangling modifier** when there is nothing in the sentence to which the modifier can actually refer:

> INCORRECT  **After studying the problem, it became clear that a lot of money would be needed.**

The subject of the sentence is implied, but the reader needs more. Who studied the problem? To whom did it become clear that . . .?

> CORRECT  **After we studied the problem, we realized that a lot of money would be needed.**

When writers use the passive voice, as in the example above, a dangling modifier is sometimes the unintended result. Using the passive voice reverses the normal English sentence structure and removes an active subject: "The midfielder kicked the ball" becomes "The ball was kicked by the midfielder" or, more simply, "The ball was kicked." (For more on passive voice, see chapters 4, 23, and 26.)

> DANGLING  **Arresting the suspect, handcuffs were placed on his wrists.**
>
> DANGLING  **Looking over the river, the city's skyline could be seen.**

Here's how to fix these dangling modifiers: first, change the passive to the active voice; second, make sure that the modifier refers to a *stated* subject, not an *implied* one:

> CORRECT  **Arresting the suspect, the police placed handcuffs on his wrists.**
>
> CORRECT  **Looking over the river, we could see the city's skyline.**

Dangling modifiers can also occur even if the sentence is in the active voice:

> DANGLING  **Before any strenuous physical exercise, a few warm-up activities are necessary.**
>
> CORRECT  **People must do a few warm-up activities before any strenuous physical exercise.**
>
> DANGLING  **After years of abusing alcohol and drugs, liver disease can develop.**
>
> CORRECT  **After years of abusing alcohol and drugs, one can develop liver disease.**

CORRECT        Abusing alcohol and drugs for years can result in liver disease.

## EXERCISE 28.2

Each of the following sentences contains a dangling modifier. Rewrite each sentence, supplying a subject as needed.

1. Feeling bad about the interview, it became clear that more work was needed before the next job application.
2. After a long night, the rosy daybreak was greatly appreciated.
3. Drinking hot coffee, the cup slipped from my hand.
4. Running a small business and investing wisely, great wealth was amassed.
5. When growing older, priorities need to be reexamined.

## 28c INCORRECT SUBSTITUTION OF ADJECTIVES AND ADVERBS

Remember that adjectives describe or modify nouns and pronouns. Adverbs describe or modify verbs, adjectives, and other adverbs. Don't use one when the other is called for.

INCORRECT ADJECTIVE     Sam was **real** sorry for the trouble he caused last week.

CORRECT ADVERB     Sam was **really** sorry for the trouble he caused last week.

In the example above, the adjective *sorry* should be modified by the adverb *really,* not the adjective *real.*

INCORRECT ADVERB   Angela was **quickly** to praise her boss.

CORRECT ADJECTIVE   Angela was **quick** to praise her boss.

Here, *quick,* an adjective, is needed to modify *Angela,* a noun.
    Note that some adjective/adverb pairs have radically different spellings:

| Adjective | Adverb |
|-----------|--------|
| few | less |
| good | well |
| many | much |

When *good* and *well* are used to describe one's personal health, well-being, and/or appearance, they have an idiomatic pattern:

He looks **good.** (appearance)

I feel **well.** (health)

She is finally **well** after her long recuperation. (health)

Otherwise, do not substitute *good* for *well:*

adj/
adv

28d

| INCORRECT | I played really **good** today. |
| CORRECT | I played really **well** today. |

Finally, never use *firstly* and *secondly*; the adjective forms, *first* and *second,* are correct.

### EXERCISE 28.3

Revise the following sentences to correct problems with adverbs and adjectives.

1. Iron conducts heat and electricity extremely good.
2. Firstly, Miguel wanted to thank his supporters for their contributions and hard work.
3. Andrea feels well about her chances of finding a better job.
4. On an extreme cold Christmas Eve, Washington's army crossed the Delaware nearly silent as they prepared to attack the Hessian troops, who were contentedly and comfortably in their Trenton barracks.
5. The American prisoners of war were not treated kind or humane by our World War II enemies. The United States suffered much casualties as a result.

## 28d  PROBLEMS WITH COMPARATIVES AND SUPERLATIVES

Adjectives and adverbs come in positive (base), comparative, and superlative forms. **Comparatives** are used to compare two people, places, or things. **Superlatives** are used to compare three or more people, places, or things. Here are the three ways that the comparative and superlative forms occur:

1. **The suffixes -*er* and -*est* are added to adjectives and some adverbs of one or two syllables:**

| Positive | Comparative | Superlative |
|---|---|---|
| dark | dark**er** | dark**est** |
| happy | happi**er** | happi**est** |
| fast | fast**er** | fast**est** |

However, note what happens with the three-syllable adjective *terrific:*

| INCORRECT | terrific | terrificer | terrificest |

2. *More* **and** *most* **are used with adjectives of three or more syllables and most adverbs:**

| CORRECT | terrific | more terrific | most terrific |

   Unfortunately, some adjectives of one or two syllables won't work with -*er* or -*est* suffixes either. The word *common* follows the *more/most* pattern of larger adjectives: *more common, most common*. However, note that if you can attach a suffix to an adjective (such as *dark + er*), don't also use *more* or *most:*

| INCORRECT | The cave seemed to be getting **more darker.** |
| CORRECT | The cave seemed to be getting **darker.** |

**3.** **Irregular adjectives** change their spellings or form in the comparative and superlative:

| Positive | Comparative | Superlative |
|----------|-------------|-------------|
| bad | worse | worst |
| good | better | best |
| little | less | least |
| many | more | most |
| much | more | most |
| some | more | most |

If you are not sure which form to use in a comparison, say the word with an -*er* or -*est* ending. If it sounds strange, it's probably wrong. However, your best approach is to look up the word in a college-level dictionary. If -*er* or -*est* suffixes are appropriate, they should be indicated somewhere in the entry.

## EXERCISE 28.4

In the following sentences, the highlighted words are used incorrectly. Revise to eliminate errors.

**1.** Robert is obviously **badder** at nine-ball than George is.

**2.** The lecture on Egyptian art was the **more valuabler** of the two we attended.

**3.** Among this season's five snowfalls, the **later** was the **worse**.

**4.** Laura looked **more sadder** after she heard the news.

**5.** Of the two families, the Agrigentos are the **richest**.

## 28e  PROBLEMS WITH ADJECTIVE ORDER

**Cumulative adjectives** are a group of adjectives that come before a noun; each successive adjective modifies the adjective(s) and noun that follow (*an old black shoe*). **Coordinate adjectives** modify the noun separately and are separated by commas (*expensive, beautiful shoes*). See 29e for more on punctuating groups of adjectives. Adjectives that precede a noun follow a traditional pattern:

**Determiner:** a, an, the, this, those, my, their, many, four

**Evaluation:** great, boring, beautiful, sad

**Size:** big, small, huge

**Shape:** circular, square, triangular

**Age:** old, new, ancient

**Color:** red, yellow, amber

**National or geographic origin:** British, German, African

**Religion:** Catholic, Jewish, Taoist

**Material:** steel, paper, silk

Noun acting as adjective: garden wall, car phone, school bus, bird house

EXAMPLE   In **the large square glass** case, the visitors saw **a wonderful old Japanese silk** kimono.

## EXERCISE 28.5

Rewrite the following sentences to correct problems with adjective order.

1. The rectangular large truck delivered a load of antique Italian beautiful furniture to Miriam's red-brick new home.
2. Henry II of England (1133–1189) gained vast French rich lands when he married Eleanor of Aquitaine in 1152.
3. Are radio high-frequency waves harmful to one's health?
4. Katmandu, the capital of Nepal, sits 4,500 feet above sea level in a fertile stunningly beautiful valley, which has a great deal of historical significance.
5. An unbroken honor centuries-old code binds the members of our organization together.

## 28f PROBLEMS WITH SPLIT INFINITIVES

In most cases, avoid splitting an infinitive. An **infinitive** is a verbal made up of *to* plus the base form of the verb. An infinitive is "split" when an adverb is placed between the two parts of the infinitive:

to **boldly** go

to **wildly** dream

to **slowly** realize

to **carefully** consider

Splitting an infinitive used to be considered unacceptable. Today, however, most style experts recognize that certain sentences are less awkward with a split infinitive. Consider these two sentences:

The thing Jan wants most is **to quickly conclude** this deal.

The thing Jan wants most is **to conclude quickly** this deal.

The first sentence contains a split infinitive; however, this sentence works a lot better than the second one. Then again, you could write this sentence:

The thing Jan wants most is **to conclude** this deal **quickly.**

By moving the adverb, *quickly,* away from the verb and after the object, *deal,* you can avoid both a split infinitive and awkwardness; moreover, the sentence is not ambiguous.

## EXERCISE 28.6

Each of the following sentences contains a split infinitive. Revise each sentence to eliminate it. Reword as needed.

1. In this time-enhanced sequence, the caterpillar is going to slowly change into a butterfly.

2. After waiting for several hours, the parents decided to finally go home.

3. The directions tell us to carefully place the glass inside the wire holder.

4. The evidence led the detective to instantly decide that the perpetrator was known by the victim.

5. I don't think it's possible for a person to actually fall in love at first sight.

## 28g PROBLEMS WITH ARTICLES

**Articles** modify nouns in much the same way that adjectives do. However, articles can pose very specific and serious modification problems, as the following guidelines indicate:

1. When you are using an indefinite article (*a* or *an*), choose *a* when the next word starts with a consonant sound; choose *an* when the next word starts with a vowel sound:

   **a** tire

   **a** unit

   **a** precise analogy

   **an** uncle

   **an** awful surprise

   Note that the *sound* at the beginning of the next word is key here—thus, *a unit* but *an uncle*.

2. When you use a singular count noun, precede it with an article. A count noun, as its name suggests, denotes something that is normally counted instead of measured:

   **a** dog    **the** monster    **an** aviator    **the** mayor

   Note that either an indefinite article (*a, an*) or the definite article (*the*) can be used, depending on the context. But also note that if you are using a plural count noun, only the definite article (or no article at all) can be used:

   | INCORRECT | **A dogs** ran down the street. |
   |---|---|
   | CORRECT | **Dogs** ran down the street. |
   | ALSO CORRECT | **The dogs** ran down the street. |

3. When you use a noncount noun, do not precede it with an indefinite article. A noncount noun denotes something that is normally not counted but is otherwise identified or measured:

   machinery (not **a** machinery)

   sugar (not **a** sugar)

However, note that the definite article can be used with noncount nouns in some contexts:

Linda became interested in the design of **machinery** after she read a book about **the machinery** used to build dams.

4. You can use *the* before any common noun, but in some contexts it is inappropriate. Trouble occurs with nouns that represent general qualities or concepts. When a word such as *wisdom* or *age* is used in a general context—with no specific connection to another noun or concept—don't precede it with *the*.

| | |
|---|---|
| CORRECT | This library contains **the** wisdom of the ages. (*Wisdom* is identified by the phrase *of the ages*.) |
| INCORRECT | **The** wisdom is a good quality to achieve. (*Wisdom* is a general concept.) |
| CORRECT | Wisdom is a good quality to achieve. |
| CORRECT | Julia is at **the** age at which the world looks rosy. (*Age* is identified by the phrase *at which the world looks rosy*.) |
| INCORRECT | Martin is fifty years old but looks as if he were thirty-five; he doesn't have to worry about **the** age. (*Age* is a general concept.) |
| CORRECT | Martin is fifty years old but looks as if he were thirty-five; he doesn't have to worry about age. |

5. When you use a proper noun, remember that it may sometimes need a definite article, but usually not if the noun is a person's name, a place name, or a day of the week or month of the year:

Reese Witherspoon

Nebraska

October

Friday

the Ohio River

the Toyota Corolla

**Exception:** the United States

The cases in which definite articles are used with names are infrequent and usually involve a sentence like this one:

Is he **the** Wayne Smith who held so many appointed positions in the eighties and nineties?

Indefinite articles can precede singular proper nouns in special contexts:

Ms. Walker, **a** Lisa Androz is on the phone.

We need to go to Wal-Mart; I believe there is **a** Wal-Mart on University Avenue.

Someone has double-parked **a** Ford Ranger outside the front door.

## EXERCISE 28.7

A blank line precedes each noun or noun phrase in the following paragraph. Write *a, an, the,* or *X* (no article) for each situation. In some cases, more than one answer is possible.

Last _____ Saturday, _____ Jeremy had _____ dinner with _____ head of his _____ department at _____ work. After _____ appetizers and _____ soup, they enjoyed _____ main course of _____ Peking duck and _____ wild rice. _____ conversation was not about _____ work; instead, the occasion was meant to be _____ get-acquainted evening following _____ company's new policy. Indeed, _____ evening went well. When _____ Jeremy returned to _____ office on _____ Monday, he felt _____ inkling of _____ hope for his future with _____ company.

## COMBINATION EXERCISE

Rewrite the following paragraphs to correct modifier problems.

Ever since the breakup of the communist former state of Yugoslavia in the 1990s, most people have had hard time distinguishing the small various countries that emerged in the Balkan peninsula. One of these, of course, is Serbia, which had been the larger of the many regions of the old Yugoslavia. It occupies the west and south. Containing beautiful mountains and rich in timber and agriculture, the capital city is a Belgrade. Serbia's official language is Serbo-Croatian. Writing in this language, it appears in Cyrillic, for the Serbs use the same alphabet used in Russia and in some other parts of the eastern Europe. Being members of the Eastern Orthodox Church, the majority of a Serbian population is Christian.

Neighbors to the Serbs, the language of Croatia is also Serbo-Croatian, but the Croats use the Latin alphabet. Being Roman Catholics, connections with the West seem stronger in Croatia than with the Serbs, where there is natural tendency to look toward Russia and the East. The second larger of the former many Yugoslavian regions, Croats make their home in the northwest. A region rich in coal, oil, and timber, it is also well-known for its Adriatic beautiful beach resorts because of which a tourist lucrative trade was once enjoyed. Tourism has significant decreased since the wars that near destroyed Croatia in the early 1990s.

Bosnia/Herzegovina is found in the central part of the old Yugoslavia, a joint province. Despite having rich mineral deposits, a poverty continues to plague it. With Sarajevo as its capital, Bosnians have been witnesses to great events in history. A most famous is the art

28g

········

CATALYST 2.0

**MORE OPTIONS ONLINE**
For more exercises,
go to
www.mhhe.com/
writingtoday.

assassination of Austrian Archduke Francis Ferdinand in 1914 by a Serbian revolutionary who wanted to free the region from Austro-Hungarian control, a event that sparked the World War I. More recently, civil war that engulfed the country killed tens of thousands. Bosnian Serbs, supported by their neighbors in Serbia and Montenegro, fought a bloody conflicts with the Bosnian Muslim population minority, which ended after only international intervention that resulted in a multi-ethnic government.

# PUNCTUATING SENTENCES WITH COMMAS

### CHAPTER 29

Much misinformation surrounds the use of the comma **(,)**. Many students dread dealing with commas; however, in most cases, comma usage is logical and systematic. The comma appears in six main contexts: in certain compound sentences, after introductory elements, to distinguish nonessential elements, in series, between coordinate adjectives, and by convention—in dates and addresses, for example.

## 29a COMMAS WITH INDEPENDENT CLAUSES

An easy way to connect two independent clauses and make a compound sentence is by using a comma plus one of the seven coordinating conjunctions (*for, and, nor, but, or, yet, so*—many students use the mnemonic FANBOYS to remember the coordinating conjunctions).

When you combine two independent (main) clauses with a coordinating conjunction and a comma, remember that the comma comes *before* the conjunction:

The sun slid behind the mountain, **and** night was upon us.

Laura refused to study any longer, **for** she had already put in more than twelve hours.

We tried to start the car, **but** the battery was dead.

Ben didn't like the restaurant, **nor** did he like my cousin.

You can try my computer, **or** you can call customer support about yours.

I worked hard last week, **yet** I didn't get enough done.

The dog couldn't get anyone's attention, **so** he gave up and fell asleep.

Compound sentences can be questions or commands:

What did Melissa say, **and** when did she say it?

Boot the computer, **but** don't turn the printer on yet.

Here are some problem areas that you should keep in mind:

1.  Coordinating conjunctions are frequently used to connect two nouns or adjectives:

    John **and** Mary

    poor **but** honest

    young **or** old

    Don't put a comma between these words automatically; make sure that the conjunction links two independent clauses before using a comma.

2.  Watch out for sentences with **compound predicates**, two or more verbs and their related words, joined by *and:*

    We **raked the leaves and cut the grass.**

    This sentence is not compound; it has only one subject, so no comma is needed before *and*. However, note what happens if we add the second subject:

    We raked the leaves, **and** we cut the grass.

    Look for two independent clauses, not just the suggestion of them.

3.  Remember that using the comma to join compound sentences works *only* with coordinating conjunctions. In the following sentence, the writer has

incorrectly assumed that *next*, a conjunctive adverb, can be used in place of a coordinating conjunction:

COMMA SPLICE  **We talked for a while about the new assignment, next we made arrangements to meet again.**

REVISED      **We talked for a while about the new assignment; next, we made arrangements to meet again.**

The revised sentence uses the correct punctuation pattern for a compound sentence joined by a conjunctive adverb/transitional expression: semicolon plus conjunctive adverb plus comma. (For more help in correcting comma splices, see Chapter 25.)

The following sentence is also incorrectly punctuated. Can you tell why?

INCORRECT    **Maria opened the door, so Bob could bring in the packages.**

The sentence certainly *looks* correct (two apparently independent clauses connected by a comma and *so*). However, in the sentence above, the comma plus *so* can be replaced by the subordinating conjunction *so that*. (See the sentence connectors chart on pages 703–704.) Often, when writers need to use *so that*, they drop the *that* and use *so* alone. The resulting sentence is *not* a compound sentence but a complex sentence, so no comma is needed:

REVISED      **Maria opened the door so Bob could bring in the packages.**

## EXERCISE 29.1

Insert commas or delete commas as needed in the following sentences. Some sentences may be correct.

1. The mayor has not announced her bid for reelection yet many people believe that it's only a matter of time.
2. The new dessert is tasty, and low in fat.
3. Martin, and his brother John are going to college on basketball scholarships.
4. Roll up your sleeve, and get ready for a little discomfort.
5. I'm going to have to find a new Internet service provider for the one I use now is as slow as mud.
6. Neither Alice, nor Edna knows how to drive.
7. Jarrod wasn't able to study last night so he's nervous about today's chemistry exam.
8. You need to drive to town, and get some bread and milk.
9. Ed worked two jobs so his daughter could go off to college.
10. Did the defendant stay at home that night or was he instead at the scene of the crime?

## 29b COMMAS WITH INTRODUCTORY CLAUSES, PHRASES, AND WORDS

A variety of clauses, phrases, and words can precede an independent clause. In almost all cases, put a comma after these introductory elements.

### 29b.1 COMMAS AND INTRODUCTORY DEPENDENT CLAUSES

A **dependent clause** is an independent clause with a subordinating conjunction at its beginning. Thus, *John learned to swim* is an independent clause, but *After John learned to swim* is a dependent clause. When a dependent clause precedes an independent clause, use a comma to separate the two clauses:

> **Because the puppy had grown so quickly,** we had to buy a new carrier.

> **Even though Martina was ill,** she attended her classes.

> **When we swim,** we get excellent exercise.

When the dependent clause *follows* the main clause, a comma is normally not used unless the subordinating conjunction is negative, as in the second example below:

> We had to buy a new carrier **because the puppy had grown so quickly.**

> Martha attended her classes, **although she was severely ill.**

A dependent clause can also be *embedded* within a sentence, as in the following example:

> The lecture lasted much longer than scheduled, but **because Michael had nothing else planned that day,** he stayed until the end.

This sentence begins with an independent clause (*The lecture lasted much longer than scheduled*) and then uses a comma plus *but* to connect it to the second independent clause. However, a dependent clause (highlighted) is embedded after the coordinating conjunction *but*, so a comma separates the embedded dependent clause from the second independent clause (*he stayed until the end*).

### EXERCISE 29.2

In the following sentences, insert commas or delete commas as needed. Some sentences may be correct.

1. After Gerald Ford became president upon the resignation of Richard Nixon he named Nelson Rockefeller his vice president.

2. My cat doesn't like going to the vet, because she is afraid of dogs.

3. Because the two sides couldn't agree the trial was postponed.

4. Michael naps, whenever he can.

5. The race lasted three hours and although they needed to be in Pensacola by 5:00 they stayed to the end.

6. Andrea took this class so she could get a pay raise at work.
7. While John is a reader his brother Mike is obsessed with computers.
8. The neighbors argued among themselves, while our problems grew.
9. After you leave for town I'll start dinner.
10. Mayra emigrated from Hungary to the United States; after she found a job here she felt good about her choice.

### 29b.2 COMMAS AND INTRODUCTORY PHRASES

When a phrase precedes an independent clause, a comma is *usually* needed:

**A lifelong nonsmoker,** Jean led the fight to make her company tobacco-free.

**Feeling good about the progress of his group project,** Curtis took the night off.

**Loved by all,** the comedian was box office magic.

**In the last years of his long reign,** the king wondered who would succeed him.

You may choose to omit a comma after a very short prepositional phrase if the absence of a comma does not interfere with communication:

**During the afternoon** we went to a number of stores.

**In 1999** people worried about computers crashing because of Y2K.

**For years** Internet retailers have struggled with security issues.

However, notice the need for commas in the following sentences:

**In 1994,** 438 cases were filed at the county courthouse.

**For dinner,** four choices are available.

**During class,** work options were discussed.

The best advice is to use a comma in borderline situations, especially if you see any chance that a comma's absence might impede the reader's understanding.

## EXERCISE 29.3

In the following sentences, insert commas as needed.

1. That year our company earned more money than it had in the previous four years put together.
2. After a long day at the office Linda turned off the computer.
3. Looked at realistically Gerald's conduct at the last meeting was abominable.
4. Next week or the week after I will have to prepare my tax returns.
5. For much too long Felicia has gotten away with bad behavior.

### 29b.3 COMMAS AND INTRODUCTORY WORDS

Simple adverbs, participles, conjunctive adverbs, and other transitional expressions frequently precede the independent clause. These terms are almost always followed by a comma, with one exception: *then*.

> **Cautiously,** the burglar crept along the ledge and approached the open window.
>
> **Delighted,** Sally thanked the crowd for the warm reception they gave her singing.
>
> **For example,** consider the role of the Federal Reserve.
>
> **However,** your appeal has been denied.
>
> **Therefore,** the contract was signed.
>
> **Then** the lawyers went home.

When transitional expressions appear inside a sentence rather than at the beginning, they still require commas (except for *then*):

> Your appeal**, however,** has been denied.
>
> Consider**, for example,** the role of the Federal Reserve.
>
> The contract**, therefore,** was signed.
>
> The lawyers **then** went home.

Finally, use a comma after words or phrases used to address the reader directly:

> Your Honor, my client is innocent!
>
> Peter, we have had enough of your nonsense.

### EXERCISE 29.4

In the following sentences, insert or delete commas as needed. Some sentences may be correct.

**1.** Thus the day ended.

**2.** Mr. Brooks your client is, nevertheless, implicated.

**3.** Lisa talked to the class for ten minutes; then it was Juan's turn.

**4.** On the other hand the new tax proposal does have some merit.

**5.** Occasionally an estate will auction off some beautiful antique jewelry.

## 29c COMMAS AND NONESSENTIAL ELEMENTS

Sentences can contain two types of modifiers. **Essential modifiers** (sometimes called **restrictive modifiers**) are, as their name suggests, necessary for understanding a sentence's meaning. Commas are not used with these modifiers:

> My sister **Lucie** and my sister **Andrea** are both coming to visit.

In this context, each essential modifier answers a question: which sister? Obviously, the writer has more than one.

> Quentin Tarantino's film *Jackie Brown* represents a new maturity in the director's work.

Tarantino has directed more than one film; the title *Jackie Brown* answers this question: Which film are you writing about?

On the other hand, **nonessential (nonrestrictive) modifiers** are *not* necessary for understanding a sentence's meaning; instead, they offer extra, explanatory information:

> Ken's only brother**, Chadwick,** will soon become a father.
>
> Jeremy found his driver's license**, which he thought he had lost,** under the couch.

In both examples, the modifier is *not* essential—there is no "which one" question to answer. In the first sentence, the writer refers to Ken's *only* brother; in the second, it is natural to assume that, like most of us, Jeremy has only one driver's license.

In these and similar contexts, the presence or absence of commas can make a difference in the sentence's meaning. Consider the following pair of sentences:

> My grandmother **who lives in Phoenix** is coming for a visit.
>
> My grandmother**, who lives in Phoenix,** is coming for a visit.

In the first sentence, both of the writer's grandmothers are alive. The modifier *who lives in Phoenix* serves to answer the question "Which grandmother?" No commas are used. In the second sentence, the writer has only one surviving grandmother, so commas are placed around the useful—but not essential—information that she lives in Phoenix.

In all of the nonessential modifier examples examined so far, *pairs* of commas set off the modifier because the sentence continues after the modifier is finished. If the modifier is the final element in the sentence, however, only one comma is needed:

> I'd like you to meet my grandmother, **who has come all the way from Phoenix.**
>
> Lois, have you met my only brother, **Chadwick?**

Here is an easy way to decide whether an element is essential or nonessential: if you can remove the word or words from the sentence without changing the sentence's meaning, you can be sure that those words are nonessential and need to be set off with commas:

> Eric's wife, **Catherine,** is the executive of a tire company.
>
> Our current governor, **James Fallon,** is considering a run for the Senate.
>
> Chicago, **the largest city in Illinois,** was once destroyed by fire.

The highlighted elements in each of these sentences add information, but they do not identify the nouns that come before them. Eric has only one wife, we have only one current governor, and there is only one major city named Chicago.

In modifiers that describe people, as the previous examples show, *who* is the relative pronoun of choice, whether or not the modifier is essential. But note the difference within each of the following pairs:

There is the car **that I'm going to buy.**
There is my car**, which is a Ford.**

The fish **that the turtle caught** was eaten quickly.
The fish**, which I caught this afternoon,** is cooking on the stove.

When not referring to people or named animals (pets, celebrity beasts, famous racehorses), writers use *that* (without a comma) to indicate essential modifiers:

There is the car **that I'm going to buy.**

The modifier *that I'm going to buy* answers the question "Which car?"

Writers use *which* (preceded by a comma) to indicate nonessential information:

There is my car**, which is a Ford.**

The car has already been identified (*my* car), so the modifier offers only extra information.

### EXERCISE 29.5

In the following sentences, insert or delete commas as needed. Some sentences may be correct.

1. We traveled to Albany which is the capital of New York.
2. Ernest Hemingway who is credited with popularizing the term *lost generation* lived much of his life outside the United States.
3. I want you to meet my sister Louise, who coordinated this event.
4. Parker Enterprises is the company, that wanted to buy my uncle's firm.
5. Find me the armadillo that has the virus.
6. No, I mean Joe Morgan the local architect, not Joe Morgan the baseball analyst.
7. Practice and repetition, hallmarks of the serious athlete require dedication and grit.
8. Is he the one, who was recently arrested?
9. Jason told me that the answer was 44 which is incorrect.
10. Over there is my wife Edwina.

### 29d  COMMAS AND ITEMS IN A SERIES

Words, phrases, and even clauses can appear in **series**—three or more words or word groups serving a similar purpose:

The barn was **old, crooked, and weathered.**

> The energetic pup **raced around the mailbox, ran through the door, and jumped into his owner's lap.**

> The cold weather lasted until May, the flowers bloomed later than usual, and **the spring rains caused the creek to flood its banks.**

The commas you see between the items above are necessary to separate one item from the next. But what about the last comma, the one that appears before *and* or *or* in the examples? Some writers—especially journalists—omit it, but in formal writing *using this final comma can help your reader.* Consider the following scenario: you are giving a dinner party and are preparing a list of names of couples and individuals to invite. After the list is completed, you give it to a friend, who will write invitations. The last part of your list reads as follows:

> . . . Anne, Mark and Bob and Wanda

Your friend is confused: "Wait a minute. Who's who?"

You explain that Anne and Mark aren't a couple and will arrive separately. Bob and Wanda are a couple, however. They need just one invitation. Adding a comma before *and* would prevent this confusion:

> . . . Anne, Mark, and Bob and Wanda

Remember, when your choice in punctuation is between giving your reader less "guidance" or more, give more—in this case, remember to use that last comma.

When series items themselves contain commas, use **semicolons** instead of commas to separate those items (see also Chapter 30, pages 779–780). Note the following example, which uses commas only:

> We had a wonderful dinner at the new restaurant: appetizers, including salad and bread, two entrées, veal and salmon, shared between us, and a fascinating dessert.

Readers have trouble with a sentence such as this one because they have to determine the role of each comma. Note the aid provided by semicolons used in place of the series commas:

> We had a wonderful dinner at the new restaurant: appetizers, including salad and bread; two entrées, veal and salmon, shared between us; and a fascinating dessert.

## 29e COMMAS WITH COORDINATE ADJECTIVES

Writers frequently use more than one adjective to modify a noun or pronoun. When each adjective is working alone to modify its noun or pronoun, the result is a set of **coordinate adjectives,** separated by commas:

> The children brought home an **old, brown, weary** cat.

> Yesterday's hero has become a **bruised, battered, discouraged** man.

How can you decide if the adjectives are coordinate—that is, each modifying the noun separately? Try inserting *and* before the last one. If the result is logical, the adjectives are indeed coordinate and should be separated by commas:

an old, brown, weary cat

an old, brown, and weary cat

**Noncoordinate** (or **cumulative**) adjectives serve a different function:

the **new antique** store

my **former insurance** agent

her **ragged, old softball** glove

Try the test we used for coordinate adjectives:

the new and antique store

The result is nonsensical. Clearly, *new* modifies *antique store*, not just *store*. The same applies to the second example. However, the third example has both coordinate adjectives and a noncoordinate adjective:

her ragged and old softball glove

*Old* and *ragged* are coordinate adjectives, but *softball* is not.

## EXERCISE 29.6

In the following sentences, insert or delete commas as needed. Some sentences may be correct.

1. The steep winding road rose through the mountains fell through the valleys and leveled off in the plains.
2. Working hard playing hard and sleeping light are the three methods I use to deal with modern life.
3. A modern, high school should be well administered.
4. When I'm hungry, I dream about a warm, flavorful hot dog.
5. The results were poor, disappointing and infuriating, leading Mr. Perkins to reevaluate the contractor's efforts.

## 29f COMMAS WITH OTHER EXPRESSIONS

Sentences may contain other words or expressions that need to be set off by commas. Some expressions, such as *by the way*, briefly interrupt a sentence's main idea: *Shannon, by the way, has decided not to go to the movie tonight.* Other expressions name a person directly or add information. Transitions, such as *for example* and *on the other hand*, help connect one idea to another (see also 29b). With the exception of a few transitions, such as the word *then*, the following kinds of expressions should be separated from the rest of the sentence by commas:

1. "Not" phrases

   Sheila asked the waiter for ham, **not hamburger.**

   A need for less stress, **not more money,** led Walter to seek a new career.

2. "Echo" questions

   Clare won't be able to attend the graduation, will she?

3. Interjections

   Oh, what a wonderful idea!

## 29g COMMAS AND CONVENTIONAL USES

### 29g.1 DATES

If a full date is given, two commas are needed, one after the numerical day of the month and one after the year. However, if the numerical day is not present, no commas are used:

> January 15, 2008, is today's date.
>
> January 2008 is the current month.

Note that no comma is used when the day comes first: 15 January 2008.

### 29g.2 ADDRESSES

When city and state appear together, each is followed by a comma:

> Orlando, Florida, is where I live right now.
>
> Spokane, Washington, is her place of birth.

Placing the comma after the name of the state is seen by many to be old-fashioned; however, this comma is still necessary in today's usage.

### 29g.3 NUMERALS

Starting with the numeral 1,000, use commas to denote thousands, millions, billions, and so on:

> 1,435     2,000,000     25,289,074,745

An exception is calendar years: 2007, 1995.

### 29g.4 DIALOGUE

Reported speech is preceded or followed by a comma, according to context:

> Jeffrey exclaimed, "Marcia, you look heavenly this evening."
>
> "Thanks, Jeffie. It's just an old outfit," Marcia countered.

However, apart from dialogue, other quoted material may not need to be set off with a comma or commas:

no ʌ
29h

The words "Bye, bye, Miss American Pie" have a nostalgic ring for
people who grew up in the early 1970s.

In situations such as this one, the need for commas depends on whether the
words in quotation marks are essential or nonessential to the meaning of the
sentence (see section 29c).

### 29g.5 SALUTATIONS AND COMPLIMENTARY CLOSES

In personal letters, the salutation is traditionally followed by a comma, as is
the complimentary close:

Dear Aunt Lisa,

Sincerely yours,

In business letters, the complimentary close is followed by a comma, but the
salutation is followed by a colon:

Dear Professor Walker:

Sincerely,

### EXERCISE 29.7

In the following sentences, insert commas or delete commas as needed.
Some sentences may be correct.

1. June 15, 2009, will be his fiftieth birthday.
2. Wanda moved from Saint Louis Missouri to Providence Rhode Island.
3. It was a dislike of people not a fear of crowds that kept her indoors most
   of the time.
4. Oh I guess this will be acceptable Leo.
5. October 2008 is the target date.

## 29h  UNNECESSARY COMMAS

Read the following pair of sentences, both of which are correct:

As I recall, Marcy, although tiny, devoured the plate of nachos, which
was immense.

The dog stretched its rangy legs and ran down the hill just as I realized
that she was coming to attack me and my family while we sat contentedly beside a quiet brook that ran through a stand of ancient pine.

The first sentence has fourteen words and four commas; the second sentence
has forty-one words and no commas. The need for commas is not determined
by sentence length, the "need for a pause," or a desire to provide a dramatic
effect. The following examples explain when *not* to use commas:

1. Never use a comma to separate the subject from the verb unless another
   rule causes you to do so:

   **INCORRECT**      **Walking through the woods, is my favorite type of exercise.**

Although sentence subjects are usually nouns or pronouns, they can be phrases as well:

REVISED **Walking through the woods is my favorite type of exercise.**

This problem frequently occurs when the subject is a noun or pronoun followed by several modifiers. In such cases, writers often think that a "grammatical pause" is appropriate, but it isn't:

INCORRECT **The boy who grew up in a rustic cabin in the middle of the wilderness, eventually became President.**

REVISED **The boy who grew up in a rustic cabin in the middle of the wilderness eventually became President.**

As mentioned, however, a comma may be required by another rule. For example, a nonessential modifier may follow the sentence's subject.

REVISED **Walking through the woods, an activity I recently started, is my favorite type of exercise.**

The intervening nonessential modifier should be set off with a pair of commas. (See section 29c.)

2. Connect two items with a comma and a coordinating conjunction *only* when you are joining two independent clauses to form a compound sentence:

INCORRECT **Leanne showed Rafael the proposal, and asked for his opinion.**

REVISED **Leanne showed Rafael the proposal and asked for his opinion.**

REVISED **Leanne showed Rafael the proposal, and she asked for his opinion.**

3. When joining two independent clauses to form a compound sentence, place a comma before, not after, the coordinating conjunction:

INCORRECT **Larry ate lunch that day in the cafeteria and, Heather decided to join him.**

REVISED **Larry ate lunch that day in the cafeteria, and Heather decided to join him.**

An exception occurs when a nonessential modifier follows the coordinating conjunction:

CORRECT **Larry ate lunch that day in the cafeteria, and, proving that miracles still occur, Heather decided to join him.**

4. In most cases, do not place a comma before a subordinate conjunction that comes after an independent clause:

INCORRECT **Jeremy was excited about going to the play, because his best friend had the lead role.**

no ‸
;

29h

| | |
|---|---|
| REVISED | Jeremy was excited about going to the play because his best friend had the lead role. |

If the subordinate clause is not essential to the meaning of the sentence, though, set it off with a comma. (See section 29c.)

| | |
|---|---|
| CORRECT | Jeremy enjoyed the play, even though he had seen it before. |

5. Do not use commas to set off essential elements (see also section 29c):

| | |
|---|---|
| INCORRECT | He is the man, who received last year's Outstanding Community Servant award. |
| REVISED | He is the man who received last year's Outstanding Community Servant award. |

6. Do not place a comma between a series containing only two items joined by a coordinating conjunction:

| | |
|---|---|
| INCORRECT | John, and Mary have moved to Tulsa. |
| REVISED | John and Mary have moved to Tulsa. |
| INCORRECT | Ed wasn't sure if he'd rather be eating, or sleeping. |
| REVISED | Ed wasn't sure if he'd rather be eating or sleeping. |

7. In a series of three or more items, make sure that you place the series comma *before* the coordinating conjunction, not *after* it:

| | |
|---|---|
| INCORRECT | Your choices are coffee, espresso or, cappucino. |
| REVISED | Your choices are coffee, espresso, or cappucino. |

An exception occurs when another rule comes into play:

| | |
|---|---|
| CORRECT | To get there, you may fly, drive, or, if you'd like, walk. |

In this example, the nonessential element *if you'd like* needs to be set off by a pair of commas. As well, do not put a comma after a series unless another rule requires you to do so:

| | |
|---|---|
| INCORRECT | Many architects admire the Empire State Building, the Chrysler Building, and the Hoover Dam, as examples of Art Deco design. |
| CORRECT | Many architects admire the Empire State Building, the Chrysler Building, and the Hoover Dam as examples of Art Deco design. |

8. Do not place a comma after *like, as,* or *such as*:

| | |
|---|---|
| INCORRECT | Jason prefers old-style heavy metal bands like, Metallica. |
| REVISED | Jason prefers old-style heavy metal bands, like Metallica. |
| INCORRECT | Small children are likely to engage in such activities as, public displays of emotion. |

REVISED    Small children are likely to engage in such activities as public displays of emotion.

INCORRECT    Vera enjoys visiting Latin American countries such as, Brazil and Argentina.

CORRECT    Vera enjoys visiting Latin American countries, such as Brazil and Argentina.

**9.** Do not place a comma next to a dash or a question mark.

Sometimes, rules of punctuation can come into conflict with each other, as in the following sentence:

INCORRECT    Mark, who has trouble getting up in the morning, took a second-shift job,—a very bad move,—and then he compounded the error by registering for early-morning classes.

Dashes always *replace* other marks of punctuation (see also Chapter 30, pages 783–784):

REVISED    Mark, who has trouble getting up in the morning, took a second-shift job—a very bad move—and then he compounded the error by registering for early-morning classes.

Question marks sometimes need to appear within a sentence, but they should never be followed by commas:

INCORRECT    Guillen's latest novel, *Where to Next?*, is a humorous account of two slackers on the run.

IMPROVED    *Where to Next?* is Guillen's latest novel, a humorous account of two slackers on the run.

Note that in the improved sentence, the words have been reordered.

**10.** In a set of coordinate adjectives, do not place a comma after the last adjective:

INCORRECT    The only item left in the abandoned playground was an old, damaged, swing set.

REVISED    The only item left in the abandoned playground was an old, damaged swing set.

## EXERCISE 29.8

*Some* of the commas in the following sentences are unnecessary. Delete these commas, but retain those that are used correctly.

**1.** Cooking a huge supper for her mammoth family, was a chore that Ms. Van Meter had come to dread.

**2.** Voting, or not voting is a choice that we, as citizens, have to face.

**3.** She walked all the way downtown, and stopped at Cloisonné, her favorite shop.

4.  The legislature should pass this measure, because the people's long-term well-being will be improved, if it is passed.

5.  Tall, dark, and handsome, the hero of the movie we saw last night, was a virtual cliché.

6.  All I had to eat today was an old, bruised, apple.

7.  The new breakfast spot has coffees from many countries, such as, Kenya, Colombia, and Ecuador.

8.  Knowing the consequences of failure, can put a student under tremendous stress.

9.  The singer's first number,—absolutely guaranteed to please the audience,—was his first hit, from way back in 1965.

10. This was the moment, that Constance had been waiting for.

## COMBINATION EXERCISE

Add or delete commas as necessary in the following two paragraphs.

1.  Although China is an ancient country it has few great buildings that date to a time before the Ming Dynasty which ruled the country from the fourteenth to the seventeenth centuries. Of course the most obvious exception is the Great Wall of China. Originally built to keep out northern invaders like the Mongols, and the Manchus the Wall stretches for 1500 miles from the Yellow River to the Province of Gansu. Because it is so large no one person or royal dynasty can claim to have built it. It is instead a stringing together of many walls some of which date back to the third century B.C.E. In its present state the Wall has existed about 700 years. Unfortunately it never lived up to its purpose for in the fourteenth century the Mongols did successfully invade China making it the center of their empire which stretched as far as eastern Europe. In the seventeenth century the Manchus also invaded China and they established a dynasty that lasted until 1912.

2.  The United Nations, and the League of Nations have much in common. Among the most prominent similarities, that the UN shares with the now defunct League, is a mission to maintain world peace. The League was founded shortly after World War I which lasted from 1914 to 1918. Because "the Great War" as it was then called was the most destructive war in history many world leaders decided to create an organization, that would make World War I, "the war to end all wars." At the outset the League was conceived by leaders of the United States Great Britain Italy and France whose countries had been victorious.

. . . . . . . . .

CATALYST 2.0

**MORE OPTIONS ONLINE**
For more exercises,
go to
www.mhhe.com/
writingtoday.

# PUNCTUATING SENTENCES WITH OTHER PUNCTUATION MARKS

### CHAPTER 30

You learned in Chapter 29 that correct use of the comma will help you arrange words in a sentence so that your readers will process your message quickly, efficiently, and accurately. The same applies to other marks of punctuation. Learning how to use all of them is essential to controlling sentence structure and communicating clearly.

## 30a PERIODS (.)

**Periods** are used to end sentences and to indicate abbreviations, initials, and decimals.

1. **To end sentences.** The major function of the period is to end a complete declarative or imperative sentence:

    DECLARATIVE **Illinois is the birthplace of Carl Sandburg.**

    IMPERATIVE **Look for the gas station on the left side of the road.**

2. **To indicate abbreviations.** Only a few terms are always shown in abbreviated format:

    | | |
    |---|---|
    | A.M. or a.m. (ante meridian) | C.E. (common era) |
    | P.M. or p.m. (post meridian) | B.C.E. (before common era) |
    | A.D. (anno Domini) | i.e. (*id est*—"that is") |
    | B.C. (before Christ) | e.g. (*exempli gratia*—"for example") |

    Most other commonly abbreviated terms should first be spelled out, with the abbreviation in parentheses following the full name—for example, *National Football League (NFL)*—and subsequently referred to by the abbreviation. Some abbreviations take periods; others do not. Usually, titles and college degrees are abbreviated with a period:

    | | |
    |---|---|
    | Dr. Martin | M.A. |
    | Mr. Sanchez | M.B.A. |
    | Ms. Ishigotu | M.S. |
    | Mrs. Janowitz | Ed.D. |
    | B.A. | B.S. |
    | Ph.D. | J.D.D. |

    Abbreviations for addresses and geographical areas tend to use periods as well:

    | | |
    |---|---|
    | 21 Parker Rd. | Boston, Mass. |
    | 1497 Summerlin Ave. | Atlanta, Ga. |

    However, *USA* is the accepted abbreviation for *United States of America,* and *U.S.* is the shorter form. Most writers use the abbreviations recommended by the U.S. Postal Service when referring to states—for example, *CO* for *Colorado* and *GA* for *Georgia.*

    You need to decide whether to add periods to abbreviations in the names of companies and organizations on a case-by-case basis. If you are unsure whether to use the period when abbreviating common terms, however, consult a college-level dictionary.

3. **In initials.** When you refer to people by their initials, put a period after each initial, and insert a space after each period:

    E. L. Williamson          G. V. W. Vance IV

**30b**

**Exception:** If a company's name is based on the initials of its founder, follow the company's chosen style—for example, JC Penney or E. F. Hutton.

4. **In decimals.** The period is also used to indicate decimals in mixed numbers:

The inflation rate of 3.2 percent was very close to the previous year's rate.

## 30b SEMICOLONS (;)

**Semicolons** are used to separate independent (main) clauses in a sentence and to separate items in a series when those items contain commas.

1. **To separate independent (main) clauses.** The following sentences both contain two independent clauses connected with a semicolon:

Poland was once controlled by the Soviet Union; it is now an independent member of the world community.

Juan's dentist was ill; consequently, Juan needed to change his appointment.

When a semicolon is used in this way, *it acts as an internal period*. The semicolon has the same "weight" as a period, but it allows you to keep both clauses in the same sentence, a choice that is often very effective. For instance, in the second example, the second clause tells readers of something that happened because of the situation explained in the first clause. The two clauses are related; one states a cause, the other an effect.

Because it can separate two independent clauses, a semicolon is one way to correct a comma splice or fused sentence:

| COMMA SPLICE | My sister became seriously ill, therefore, I had to postpone my vacation. |
| FUSED SENTENCE | My sister became seriously ill therefore, I had to postpone my vacation. |
| CORRECT | My sister became seriously ill; therefore, I had to postpone my vacation. |

A semicolon should never be used to separate a dependent clause from an independent clause, however.

| INCORRECT | When I did get to take my vacation; I couldn't decide where to go. |
| CORRECT | When I did get to take my vacation, I couldn't decide where to go. |

2. **To separate items in a series when those items contain commas.** The following example contains items separated only by commas:

| CONFUSING | Our trip to Italy included visits to several historic sites: the Colosseum, the Vatican, and the Spanish Steps in Rome, the ancient streets, taverns, and private homes of Pompeii, |

and the many temples, amphitheaters, and catacombs in Segesta, Agrigento, and Siracusa, Sicily.

Readers have trouble processing a sentence such as this one because they have to determine the role of each comma. To make it easier to read the sentence, add a semicolon between each major entry or item:

CLEARER    **Our trip to Italy included visits to several historic sites: the Colosseum, the Vatican, and the Spanish Steps in Rome; the ancient streets, taverns, and private homes of Pompeii; and the many temples, amphitheaters, and catacombs in Segesta, Agrigento, and Siracusa, Sicily.**

## EXERCISE 30.1

Insert periods or semicolons as appropriate in the following sentences. You may have to remove other marks of punctuation.

1. Florida is an important state for example, the vote in Florida decided the 2000 presidential election.

2. Amy isn't an MD, she's a Ph.D.

3. V J Harris planned on attending medical school, therefore, he took many biology and chemistry classes.

4. Martha wanted to explore the new lamp store that just opened on Stockholm Street however, it was closed.

5. We should work hard and save, we should also be kind to those who are less fortunate.

6. The college has changed its policy on drop/add, now the period has been extended to four days.

7. Mr and Mrs Rogers didn't go to Ontario this summer, instead they went to New Brunswick.

8. Don't hold the shift key down just hit enter twice.

9. It's been very hot this summer, in fact, we had four days that set new temperature records.

10. Starting preschool is stressful for children for some, it is a very painful separation.

## 30c QUESTION MARKS (?) AND EXCLAMATION MARKS (!)

**Question marks** are normally used to end direct questions:

How is it that Congress can waste so much money?

Can you put down two bucks on the four-horse, Lefty?

However, question marks can also sometimes appear within sentences:

The salmon had returned to their river of birth (who knows how?) and proceeded upstream.

An error to watch for is the question mark used incorrectly to end an implied question:

INCORRECT    **She asked if we'd be done by noon?**

CORRECT    **She asked if we'd be done by noon.**

Another error is the question treated as a declarative sentence:

INCORRECT    **What might have happened if Laura had stayed home that day.**

CORRECT    **What might have happened if Laura had stayed home that day?**

**Exclamation marks** are used to express strong emotion or to emphasize a point:

Put that gun down!

Then he had the nerve to ask for a raise!

In some instances, an exclamation mark can appear *within* the sentence, usually at the end of a sentence in parentheses or set off by dashes:

We saw *Volver* that night (what a film!) and saw *Dreamgirls* the next afternoon.

Use the exclamation mark judiciously. It is a very forceful mark of punctuation, and readers can become annoyed if they see it too often ("And the battle was over! General Lee had finally lost!").

Exclamation marks and question marks can appear inside or outside of quotation marks, depending on the sense of the sentence:

Did Jennifer say that "the committee has already met"?

Jennifer asked, "Has the committee already met?"

The first sentence is a question about a statement. Therefore, the question mark relates to the entire sentence, not just to the quotation. The second sentence is a statement about a question. The question mark relates only to the question, which appears in quotation marks.

The same logic applies when dealing with exclamation marks and quotation marks:

I can't believe that Roxanne has voted to "abstain"!

"Give me liberty," declared Henry Patrick, "or give me a salami on rye with lots of mustard!"

You can find more about using quotation marks in 30h–30j.

## EXERCISE 30.2

In the following sentences, add or delete periods, question marks, and exclamation marks where appropriate.

**1.** Walter asked if we needed any lunch?

2. Is the meeting in the morning or in the evening.

3. "Roger," she shouted, "you are an absolute idiot"

4. The boss has scheduled another meeting (will this madness never end) for Thursday.

5. A restaurant in New York charges over $40 for a hamburger. People who eat there have rocks in their heads.

## 30d COLONS (:)

**Colons** are used to introduce a list or an example and to show cause-and-effect relationships, as in these sentences:

> Bring the following supplies to the first class: watercolors, bonded paper, and notebooks.
>
> Shaun is what our organization needs most: an excellent programmer.
>
> Ms. Thompson's constant carping has had one very bad effect on our office: no one feels like doing any more than is strictly necessary.

Notice that in each case, the colon means the same as *namely*. If you can substitute a comma plus *namely* for the colon, the colon is logical.

Capitalizing the first word of a complete sentence following a colon is optional. Whether or not you choose to capitalize, be consistent throughout your document.

Colons also appear in the salutations of business letters:

> Dear Dr. Gonzalez:
>
> Dear Personnel Director:

The colon is sometimes useful in sentences that have too many commas:

| CHOPPY | Albeit talented, Roderigo, one of my former classmates, is lacking in one area, persistence. |
| SMOOTHER | Albeit talented, Roderigo, one of my former classmates, is lacking in one area: persistence. |

Colons are useful, but remember to employ them only when they are needed. They are not needed after introductory phrases like *such as, for instance,* and *for example:*

| INCORRECT | Woody Allen has directed many fine films, such as: *Annie Hall* and *The Purple Rose of Cairo.* |
| CORRECT | Woody Allen has directed many fine films, such as *Annie Hall* and *The Purple Rose of Cairo.* |

Note that this rule applies even when introducing block quotations (see chapters 20 and 21).

Never insert a colon after a linking verb (*be, seem, feel, appear,* and so on):

| INCORRECT | The only make of car he buys is: Toyota. |

| | |
|---|---|
| CORRECT | The only make of car he buys is Toyota. |
| CORRECT | He buys only one make of car: Toyota. |

Never use more than one colon per sentence:

| | |
|---|---|
| INCORRECT | Our History of Eastern Europe class began our trip by visiting Poland's two major cities: Warsaw and Krakow, and then we went on to the capitals of Hungary and the Czech Republic: Budapest and Prague. |
| CORRECT | Our History of Eastern Europe class began our trip by visiting Poland's two major cities: Warsaw and Krakow. Then we went on to the capitals of Hungary and the Czech Republic: Budapest and Prague. |

## 30e DASHES (—)

Consider this sentence, which is swimming in commas:

> Browsing through the store, I stopped to listen to the cologne seller's pitch, a stupid choice on my part, and then, somewhat chastened, I headed through the accessories, women's, and home decorating departments.

Although this sentence is correctly punctuated, the reader can't tell which part of it should be emphasized. Adding a pair of dashes helps organize the ideas in the sentence:

> Browsing through the store, I stopped to listen to the cologne seller's pitch—a stupid choice on my part—and then, somewhat chastened, I headed through the accessories, women's, and home decorating departments.

The strongest statement here is *a stupid choice on my part*. Therefore, setting it off with dashes instead of commas makes its significance clear.

Dashes call attention to part of the sentence. They set off nonessential parts of a sentence, as commas do (see Chapter 29, pages 766–768), but they provide much more emphasis than commas. Moreover, as in the example above, they can tighten a sentence's focus.

Here are some guidelines for using dashes:

1. When you are producing a handwritten essay, draw the dash as a continuous line approximately twice as long as a hyphen (see Chapter 31, pages 803–804). The dash should touch both words that surround it; don't add a space in front of or after it. When writing on a computer, use the solid dash if your software supplies it; if not, use two hyphens. In either case, do not insert spaces before and after the dash.

2. Dashes take the place of other punctuation, so a dash should never appear next to a comma, for example:

| | |
|---|---|
| INCORRECT | The Marine on the left,—the one wearing all the medals,—is Phil's brother. |
| CORRECT | The Marine on the left—the one wearing all the medals—is Phil's brother. |

3. Commas are used in pairs to set off nonessential modifiers unless the modifier comes at the end of the sentence. Dashes are used in exactly the same way:

John's funny speech—an abrupt departure from his previous tirade—caught the audience by surprise.

Our group made only seventeen dollars from Saturday's car wash—a major disappointment.

4. Don't overuse dashes. Too many dashes produce choppiness:

| | |
|---|---|
| CHOPPY | Valerie's research paper on *anorexia nervosa*—the one that received an A+—was used as a model for writing in *Becoming Writers*—a booklet of exemplary student prose that has been published by the English Department every semester since 1979. |
| SMOOTHER | Valerie's research paper on *anorexia nervosa*—the one that received an A+—was used as a model for writing in *Becoming Writers*, a booklet of exemplary student prose that has been published by the English Department every semester since 1979. |

## 30f PARENTHESES ( )

Dashes emphasize information, but **parentheses** are much more subtle, or "quiet." They are used to remind the reader of a fact or a name or to add an interesting comment. Parentheses are always used in pairs:

Luis works for ML Silicone (formerly known as ML Southeast).

A health maintenance organization (HMO) has made us an attractive offer for our group health insurance needs.

We ate at the Salmonella Diner (as always, a bitter disappointment), and then we went to the movies.

Parentheses can replace commas that enclose nonessential elements, but other commas may still be needed, as in the third example sentence above. Without parentheses, this sentence would have been punctuated as follows:

We ate at the Salmonella Diner, as always, a bitter disappointment, and then we went to the movies.

When the commas before and after *as always, a bitter disappointment* are replaced with parentheses, the sentence still consists of two independent clauses joined by *and,* a coordinating conjunction. Therefore, a comma is still needed before *and,* as shown in the example above.

Whole sentences can appear in parentheses, as can independent clauses that the writer wants to embed within a sentence:

Susan's testimony seemed to clear Mark of any wrongdoing. (However, as we learned later in the day, Susan hadn't told all that she knew.)

Jason heroically offered to pay for the education of his two new stepchildren (but he worried about how he would manage to come up with the money).

Finally, you can use parentheses to enclose a short definition within a sentence:

We installed an anemometer (a device to measure wind speed) on the roof.

## 30g BRACKETS ([ ])

**Brackets** have two uses. The most common use is to insert an explanation, comment, or additional material in a quotation:

According to one report, "It [the Porsche Boxster] is the most interesting new European design in years."

Two years ago, a news story claimed that "[Anna] Sadowski and [Samuel] Entremonte [were] the county's highest paid employees."

In the second example above, the writer has added the first names of the employees and changed the tense of the verb in the quotation from present to past in order to fit the context of the sentence. You can also use brackets to indicate a problem within a quotation:

According to Marshall, "When President Kennedy was assassinated in 1964 *[sic]*, the country was in turmoil."

The sentence above has a factual error: Kennedy was killed in 1963. Using *sic* (meaning "thus" or "so"—in other words, "don't blame me") shows that the writer recognizes the error. You can also use this device when quoting text that contains a misspelled word. (See, as well, Chapter 20.)

Another, less common use of brackets is to take the place of parentheses that are needed *inside* other parentheses:

Magra South Ventures (a privately held health maintenance organization [HMO]) is establishing a branch office near our area.

## EXERCISE 30.3

The following sentences are punctuated with commas only. Reading the sentences as a continuous passage, insert colons, dashes, and parentheses as appropriate. Be prepared to defend your choices.

1. Our city's downtown section, a perennial topic of conversation, is not improving as hoped.

**2.** The mayor, a Republican, had promised in her election campaign to try to attract new business to the area.

**3.** She believed that she knew just what area businesses wanted, tax breaks.

**4.** However, her plan was voted down by the city council, made up of five Democrats and a Republican.

**5.** Therefore, the downtown area, formerly just shabby, has gotten worse, a real eyesore.

**6.** In fact, the building on the corner of Third and Vine, formerly the site of Mammoth Family Shoes, has started to crumble.

**7.** The result is inevitable, and the building will have to be demolished.

**8.** Its owner, a hideous man, has threatened the city with a lawsuit if his building is condemned.

**9.** Go to the stoplight at Monroe and Parker, about three blocks down.

**10.** From there, you can see the building owner's office, a true architectural eyesore.

## 30h  DOUBLE QUOTATION MARKS (" ")

**Double quotation marks** have four main uses:

**1.** To give special emphasis or ironic emphasis to a word or phrase, as in these examples:

> The governor's "Look Forward" program is a model of innovation.
>
> Jeremy's "car" is an alarming collection of rusty parts.

**2.** To show that text from a source is being used verbatim:

> According to McPherson, "The decomposition coefficient remains constant at low temperatures."
>
> The lawyer's claim that "the behavior of the police was more criminal than the offense for which my client is charged" will open some eyes in the district attorney's office.

For an in-depth discussion of quoting from secondary sources, see chapters 20 and 21.

**3.** To report dialogue:

> Alice said, "I don't want to disrupt my life right now, John."
>
> John replied, "I hope that you don't see me as a disruption."

Note that when you report dialogue *indirectly,* you should not use quotation marks:

| INCORRECT | Did Diego say that "he was going home"? |
|-----------|------------------------------------------|
| CORRECT | Did Diego say that he was going home? |

4. To enclose the titles of short stories, poems, articles or essays, chapters, songs, and television episodes or parts of television anthologies. Longer works, such as books, plays, magazine or journal titles, CD titles, film titles, and names of television programs, along with the names of ships and aircraft, are italicized or underlined (see also Chapter 31, pages 800–801).

   Here is an easy test to determine whether a title should be in quotation marks or italicized (underlined): you can buy a copy of *Newsweek* magazine, but you can't buy a single article from it. You can buy a book, but not Chapter 7 of that book. You can buy a newspaper, but not an opinion column within that paper. Thus, large, "whole" titles are italicized or underlined; *parts* of a "whole" title are enclosed in quotation marks.

| *Italicized Title* | "**Part**" **Title** |
|---|---|
| *Sixty Degrees of the Blues* (CD title) | "Fourth Street Hammer" (song title) |
| *Newsweek* (magazine title) | "Washington Adrift" (article title) |
| *My Life* (book-length collection of essays) | "The War Years" (title of essay) |

## 30i SINGLE QUOTATION MARKS (' ')

**Single quotation marks** have only one purpose: to replace double quotation marks when the word or words that need to be enclosed in quotation marks are part of a larger quotation:

| INCORRECT | According to Walker, "Melville's "After the Pleasure Party" is a dense, almost opaque poem." |
|---|---|
| CORRECT | According to Walker, "Melville's 'After the Pleasure Party' is a dense, almost opaque poem." |

Note that magazine and newspaper designers frequently use single quotation marks in unconventional ways, as do the creators of advertisements. Keep in mind that such decisions are made for *visual* impact, not editorial correctness.

## 30j QUOTATION MARKS WITH OTHER PUNCTUATION

Many writers are uncertain about what to do when it is time to add a closing quotation mark. Where does the period go? What about a semicolon? The following guidelines should help:

1. Periods and commas always *precede* the closing quotation mark, as in the following examples:

The title of her essay is "Facing Home."

You've read "Pied Beauty," haven't you?

2.  Colons and semicolons always *follow* the closing quotation mark:

There is a powerful underlying message in Hemingway's "Soldier's Home": the need to bury personal horror.

Yesterday on the radio, I heard "Maxwell's Silver Hammer"; I had almost forgotten that strange Beatles song.

3.  Question marks and exclamation marks should be placed inside the closing quotation mark if they are a part of the quotation or title; they should be placed outside the closing quotation mark if they are punctuating the sentence as a whole:

The title of her article is "They Stole My Children!"

Have you read "Shiloh"?

4.  If a closing single quotation mark and a closing double quotation mark appear together, they should not be separated by a punctuation mark:

Baines writes that "Maria's career is encapsulated in 'Jamaica Town.'"

5.  If a question mark or an exclamation mark appears within a closing quotation mark at the end of a sentence, a period is not needed:

| INCORRECT | The title of her article is "They Stole My Children!". |
| CORRECT | The title of her article is "They Stole My Children!" |

When a question mark or an exclamation mark appears within a sentence, an additional comma is unnecessary:

| INCORRECT | When asked "Did you know that the contribution was illegal?," the mayor declined comment. |
| CORRECT | When asked "Did you know that the contribution was illegal?" the mayor declined comment. |

As an alternative, you can rephrase the original sentence or recast the quoted question as an indirect question:

The mayor declined comment when asked "Did you know that the contribution was illegal?"

When asked if he knew that the contribution was illegal, the mayor declined comment.

## EXERCISE 30.4

In the following sentences, add double quotation marks, single quotation marks, and underlining as needed.

1.  Are you coming to the game, Eliot? Maria asked.

2.  According to Schellen, Faulkner's mastery in That Evening Sun is illustrated by the almost tossed-away quality of the short story's conclusion.

**30H**

3.  If you're going to the grocery store, bring back some coffee, a copy of Vogue, and a copy of the New York Times.

4.  After I saw the film, I actually had a chance to acquire some salvage from the real Titanic.

5.  Jane, your little fling, as you call it, may turn out to have serious consequences, commented Lawrence.

## 30k APOSTROPHES (')

**Apostrophes** have several functions. Their main function is to signal possession. They are also used with some plurals and in contractions.

### 30k.1 POSSESSIVES

A possessive is an *of* structure in reduced form. Consider the following passage:

> Wanting to see my friend Ed, I went to the house of Ed. Ed did not answer the door, but the wife of Ed said that Ed was in the garage of Ed, working on the 1965 Ford Mustang of Ed.

Fortunately, people don't talk or write this way. Instead, they reduce the *of* structures into more efficient possessive forms. Personal pronouns simply change form to reflect possession: *I/my* or *mine; you/your* or *yours; he/his; she/her* or *hers; it/its; we/our* or *ours; they/their* or *theirs.* However, nouns do not change form. Instead, writers show the possessive forms of nouns by adding an apostrophe (') and *-s* or just an apostrophe (') at the end of the noun.

1.  To make any singular noun possessive, add *'s* to the end of the word, even if it ends in *-s, -ss, -x,* or *-z.*

    the car's hood

    the dictionary's cover

    Bob's friend

    Morris's friend

    Harriss's friend

    Moskowitz's report

2.  To make a plural noun that ends in *-s* possessive, add an apostrophe after the *-s.*

    the cats' dish

    the boys' secret

    the clouds' darkness

    the Harrisses' friend

3.  To make a plural noun that does not end in *-s* possessive, treat the noun as if it were singular and add *-'s* to its end.

    the men's department

    the women's golf team

the children's hour

the people's choice

the geese's nesting area

These three rules have no exceptions, so why do many writers struggle with the spelling of possessive nouns? One reason may be the errors that people see every day. For example, if you go to your nearest department store, odds are that you will see these signs: *Mens, Womens.* You know what these signs mean, but in fact *Mens* and *Womens* are misspelled versions of *Men's* and *Women's.* Constant exposure to such errors does not help the student of English keep apostrophe rules straight.

Another reason that forming possessive nouns can be difficult has to do with the often complex spelling patterns of English. Consider the word *company,* meaning business or firm:

**singular:** company

**singular possessive:** company's

**plural:** companies

**plural possessive:** companies'

To form the plural possessive of *company,* a writer needs to use the "drop the *-y,* add *-ies*" rule, then place the apostrophe correctly. (For more on spelling, see Chapter 32, pages 820–822.) For many writers, these rules can seem tricky or confusing.

Note that writers often forget to include possessives in constructions such as the following:

John spent a **week's** salary on dinner.

To some people, a good **night's** sleep is an absolute gift.

Years ago, a **quarter's** worth of candy would get you through an entire movie.

In addition, note that nouns and pronouns preceding gerunds are possessive:

**Andrea's diving** was the only thing we really wanted to see.

The committee seemed unwilling to listen to **his complaining** about the meeting's agenda.

## EXERCISE 30.5

In the following sentences, make any changes necessary to produce correct possessive forms. Not all sentences contain errors.

1. Jeans truck won't start.
2. The four kittens mother has vanished.
3. Please look in the childrens room.
4. The Subaru's reputation for dependability is well-founded.
5. The Barretts house needs a coat of paint.

   **6.** Give me five dollars' worth of gasoline, please.

   **7.** The mens choir is practicing tonight.

   **8.** For Ryan, it's always somebody elses problem.

   **9.** When I look back, I am astonished by my parents patience.

**10.** A security guards' hat was found near the bridge.

## 30k.2 PLURALS OF NUMERALS, LETTERS, AND ACRONYMS

Traditionally, the plurals of numerals are formed by adding *'s,* as in the following example:

   The judges gave the first diver two **8's** and a 9.

Similarly, individual letters form the plural by adding *-'s:*

   Janine earned four *A***'s** and one *B* during fall semester.

   An apostrophe may be used to form the plural of an **acronym**, an abbreviation formed from the first letters of a name:

   The Pentagon expressed concern over the maintenance of the nation's **ICBM's.**

Recently, however, the trend has been to drop the apostrophe in the plural form of acronyms. In the previous example, *ICBMs* would also be acceptable. Whatever you choose to do, be consistent.

   Another recent trend has been to form the plural of a decade without an apostrophe: *1990s.* However, *1990's* is still acceptable. Note that when you drop the century number, you should avoid using numerals at all. Don't refer to the *'80s;* use the *eighties* instead.

   As you have seen, the apostrophe is used to form plurals in a few special situations. However, *do not* use the apostrophe to form the plurals of nouns, no matter how great the temptation and no matter how strange the plural noun looks without an apostrophe. Remember that regular nouns become plural with the addition of *-s* or, in a few instances, the addition of *-es*. Notice the correct forms of the following nouns:

| Singular | Plural |
|----------|--------|
| ski | skis |
| Subaru | Subarus |
| camera | cameras |
| potato | potatoes |
| tomato | tomatoes |

## 30k.3 CONTRACTIONS

Some contractions consist of shortened forms of verbs and the word *not.* The apostrophe takes the place of the deleted *o* in *not.*

   is not = isn't

   are not = aren't

cannot = can't

could not = couldn't

A few negative contractions are irregular:

will not = won't

shall not = shan't (now uncommon)

Some verb contractions do not involve negatives, but, as in negative contractions, the apostrophe replaces the deleted letter:

I am = I'm

he is = he's

she has = she's

we are = we're

we have = we've

they are = they're

they have = they've

let us = let's

A few contracted forms are idiomatic noun constructions:

o'clock = of the clock

jack-o'-lantern = jack of the lantern

*Always remember* the important difference between *it's* and *its. It's* is a contraction of *it is* or *it has:*

*It's* cold outside.

*It's* been a year since we saw him.

*Its* is a possessive pronoun:

The horse had lost *its* way in the blizzard.

Also note the difference between *they're* and *their:*

*They're* about to put *their* house up for sale.

## EXERCISE 30.6

Add, move, or delete apostrophes in the following sentences. Not all sentences contain errors.

1. Lets ask the security guard if we can stay late tonight; she frequently let's us do so if her supervisor is'nt on the grounds.
2. This parking lot is full of Volvo's.
3. The 1970s were kind to my aunt; she made her fortune then.
4. Robbie vowed to make all As next semester.
5. As we began to eat, we realized that the spaghetti hadnt been cooked long enough.

## 30I SLASHES (/)

The **slash** has two primary functions: to separate lines of poetry that appear within text and to connect nouns that have a dual role or nature:

1. **To separate lines of poetry:**

   Shakespeare's Sonnet 116 begins with "Let me not to the marriage of true minds / Admit impediments; love is not love / Which alters when it alteration finds. . . ."

2. **To connect nouns:**

   agent/manager

   owner/driver

Hyphens are also used to connect nouns; for more information, see Chapter 31, pages 803–804.

### COMBINATION EXERCISE

The following passage has problems with the kinds of punctuation marks discussed in this chapter. Revise the passage to correct those errors.

Last Sunday at about 11 am, I was given the companies car and told to take a pair of client's to a baseball game. There are worse assignment's. Theres nothing like going a ball game on a Sunday afternoon, even though you know the home team's players hitting and fielding could be stronger. The Montgomery Eagle's are'nt the strongest team in the league, but their local. Besides, my boss—the person I rely on for my livelihood,— told me to make sure that our client's got they're fill of baseball.

It is rare that I would pay eight dollars to park, however, it was'nt my money, so I forked it over. The ticket's were waiting for us, so in we went to what one local sports writer has labeled "one of the strangest ballparks in the major leagues"! Why is it that the inside of Mountaintop Stadium looks like a malls food court. As I walked around, I wondered where I had seen more places to eat at a stadium? The game started after five minutes worth of delay, for something was wrong with the second basemens glove, and the prima donna refused to use another one!

The Mountaintops manager's must have a strange idea about baseball fans—that we get easily bored—that we need more stimulation than a baseball game can provide—and that we need constant entertainment. Almost every inning had it's attraction: such as trivia contest's, activity's meant for children, and music; music; music.

My clients' seemed to enjoy the game, but they're attention was mostly on the food courts offerings. Im a little worried about the expense report I will have to file because my spending over one hundred and fifty dollar's on beer, hot dogs, and other assorted goodies is sure to raise my boss eyebrows. I hope my companies budget for entertainment it is only a few thousand dollars can take this hit. Perhaps we should have budgeted for antacid's as well. Im sure my client's stomachs could have used them.

### CHAPTER 31

# MECHANICS

This chapter discusses some important practical issues: when to capitalize letters, how to use italics, when to use a written number and when to use a numeral, and how to use hyphens.

## 31a CAPITALIZATION

cap
31a

In the eighteenth century, when the Declaration of Independence was written, capitalization was haphazard. Writers sometimes capitalized words for emphasis, and sometimes they capitalized words for no apparent reason. Today, however, the conventions governing capitalization are well established, and a relatively small number of guidelines cover most situations.

1. **Geographical features.** Capitalize the first letter of each word in the names of cities, counties, states, countries, and geographical landmarks:

   | | |
   |---|---|
   | Nashville | Painted Desert |
   | Robertson County | Ohio Valley |
   | Tennessee | Stone Mountain |
   | United States | |

   Besides mountains, deserts, and valleys, geographical landmarks include lakes, rivers, and other bodies of water:

   Lake Tahoe      the Missouri River      Walden Pond

   Also capitalize the first letter of a section of a country:

   Darla grew up in the Midwest.

   The South varies greatly from state to state.

   But don't capitalize directions, such as *east, west, southeast,* and *north,* or adjectival forms—*midwestern, southern*—unless the form is part of the term for an era, study, event, or cultural entity: *Western civilization* or *Eastern customs,* for example.

   **Exceptions:**
   - **Geographical terms treated as plurals:** the Missouri and Mississippi rivers.
   - **Place names with conventionally accepted lowercase words:** Rio de Janeiro.

2. **Months, days of the week, and holidays.** Capitalize the first letters of names of months, days, and the official names of holidays:

   | | |
   |---|---|
   | June | Independence Day |
   | Tuesday | Thanksgiving |

   Do not capitalize first letters of the seasons. For example,

   **Memorial Day** is the unofficial opening of **summer,** but **Halloween** ushers in the **fall** holiday season.

3. **Countries, nationalities, languages, and religions.** Capitalize the first letters of the names of nationalities, religions, and languages and of adjectives made from those nouns:

   | | | |
   |---|---|---|
   | Italy | Italian | Italian painting |
   | Russia | Russian | Russian wolfhound |

| | | |
|---|---|---|
| Japan | Japanese | Japanese automobiles |
| Catholicism | Catholic | Catholic nuns |
| Buddhism | Buddhist | Buddhist priests |

An exception is *french fries*. Also, note that when *catholic* is used to mean *universal,* the first letter is not capitalized.

4. **Sacred books.** Capitalize the first letters of sacred texts and of many adjectives made from such nouns. The titles of these books are not italicized (underlined):

| | |
|---|---|
| the Bible | Biblical authority |
| the Gospels | Gospel writers |
| the Talmud | Talmudic scholars |
| the Vedas | Vedic studies |
| the Koran (Qur'an) | Koranic references |

5. **Historic events, cultural/intellectual movements, and philosophies.** Capitalize the first letters of the names of historic events, of cultural/ intellectual movements, and of some philosophies, as well as the first letter of many adjectives made from those nouns:

| | |
|---|---|
| The Middle Ages | medieval |
| The Renaissance | Renaissance |
| Impressionism | Impressionistic |
| existentialism | existentialist |
| Romanticism | Romantic |

A college-level dictionary will indicate correct capitalization of such terms.

In general, do not capitalize nouns that name political and economic movements unless they are used to name official organizations:

| | |
|---|---|
| democracy | the Democratic Party |
| republicanism | the Republican Party of the State of New York |
| socialism | the Socialist Workers' Alliance |

However, in terms such as *Jeffersonian democracy,* the *J* is capitalized because *Jeffersonian* is derived from a person's name.

6. **Course titles.** Capitalize the first letters of major words in the title of academic courses, but do not capitalize words that simply describe a course or that name an academic discipline:

At Wassamatta University, Statistics 101 is a prerequisite for Calculus 240.

*But*

At Wassamatta University, science classes require students to use their knowledge of statistics and calculus.

In the first sentence, *Statistics 101* and *Calculus 240* are the official names of courses as listed in a college catalogue. In the second sentence, *statistics* and *calculus* refer to the disciplines or fields of study.

Iago got an *A* in English Literature.

> *But*

Iago has always been fascinated by English literature.

The first sentence in the example above refers to a college course titled *English Literature;* the second example refers to a discipline. Note that *English* is capitalized in both cases because it is an adjective derived from the name of a language.

7. **Names of buildings, ships, air/spacecraft, and animals:**

the Wrigley Building

the Alamo

the *Andrea Doria*

HMS *Hood*

the *Challenger*

Lassie

Dumbo

8. **Names of companies, organizations, and trademarks.** Capitalize the first letter of names of companies, organizations, and trademarked products. However, do not capitalize names of generic products:

> Union Carbide Corporation is headquartered in Danbury, Connecticut.
>
> Alcoholics Anonymous has chapters virtually throughout the world.
>
> Johnson and Johnson controls the "Band-Aid" trademark; competitors call their own products "bandages."
>
> Only Coca-Cola Bottlers can tempt you to drink "Coke"; other soft-drink makers sell "colas."

9. **Names of people and supernatural entities.** Capitalize the first letter of the names of people, religious figures, and supernatural entities, except when convention requires the use of lowercase letters or when the person in question prefers lowercase letters:

| | | |
|---|---|---|
| Sinead O'Connor | God | Eve |
| Eamon De Valera | Yahweh | Gabriel |
| Alexis de Tocqueville | Jesus | Ariel |
| bell hooks | Vishnu | Lucifer |
| e. e. cummings | Muhammad | |

Note that the *De* in Eamon De Valera (the first president of the Irish Republic) is capitalized and that the *de* in Alexis de Tocqueville (nineteenth-century French historian) is not. Such distinctions reflect family tradition or conventions developed in different countries. However, bell hooks (contemporary social scientist) and e. e. cummings (twentieth-century poet) chose to represent their names without capital letters, and these choices must be honored. If you are not sure how to spell the name of a prominent figure, look it up in a good encyclopedia or dictionary.

10. **Job and affiliation titles.** When a job or affiliation title immediately precedes a name, capitalize the first letter of the title:

Officer Preston          Uncle Rey

President Carter         Senator Louis

However, when a job title is used alone, don't capitalize it:

The corporation I work for just chose a new president.

Walker is a long-time senator; she is a close friend of Representative Suzuki.

Be aware that you can capitalize *President* when used alone if you are referring to the President of the United States:

The President was greeted by members of the House and Senate with thunderous applause.

Also note that acronyms formed from job titles appear in all-capital letters:

Michael is now the chief financial officer (CFO) of Tri-State Data Transport.

Titles representing family affiliation are capitalized only if they appear with the family member's name or are used in direct address:

Did **Uncle Ed** serve in Vietnam?

"Hey, **Mother**," announced Jackie, "I just got engaged!"

*But*

Andrea's **uncle** served in Vietnam.

"I just got engaged!" Jackie announced to her **mother.**

Also, family affiliations are not capitalized if accompanied by another adjective: *My uncle Ed served in Vietnam.*

11. **Titles of essays, articles, poems, plays, films, books, and periodicals.** For media titles, follow these guidelines:

* Capitalize the first letter of all nouns, verbs, pronouns, adjectives, and adverbs.

* Begin all articles and conjunctions with lowercase letters, unless those words begin or end a title. The same is true for prepositions of fewer than five letters:

*Gone with the Wind*          *The Old Man and the Sea*

**Exception:** Some publishers use lowercase letters for all prepositions, regardless of length. Whichever method you adopt, be consistent.

Suppose that you need to cite in a research paper the following title of a magazine article:

OSPREY IS PRESSING ON WITH EXPANSION WITHOUT FEAR OF
SAGGING ECONOMY

The title appears in capital letters because the magazine's designer prefers it that way. However, here is how the title should appear if you are referring to it in your writing.

Osprey Is Pressing on with Expansion Without Fear of Sagging Economy

Note that *Is* begins with a capital letter because it is a verb, even though it is a short word. *With* is a preposition of fewer than five letters, so it is not capitalized. *Without* is a preposition of seven letters, so it is capitalized.

- The first word of a title and the first word of a subtitle (following the colon separating the title from the subtitle) are always capitalized. Note that this rule overrides rules 1 and 2:

A Worst-Case Scenario: To Succeed in Business Requires Virtual Isolation

## Capitalizing Within Sentences

The following guidelines reflect current U.S. standards for capitalizing words within a sentence:

1. Capitalize the first letter of the first word of each sentence.

2. When a sentence appears in parentheses, capitalize the first word only if the parentheses are not embedded in another sentence:

| INCORRECT | After using the transponder, store it in a cool, dark place. (this step keeps humidity from affecting the lithium diodes.) |
| CORRECT | After using the transponder, store it in a cool, dark place. (This step keeps humidity from affecting the lithium diodes.) |

3. If a sentence contains a colon but the text that follows the colon is not an independent clause, do not capitalize the first word following the colon unless the word is a proper noun:

| INCORRECT | The injured man knew what he faced: A long period of rehabilitation. |
| CORRECT | The injured man knew what he faced: a long period of rehabilitation. |

4. If a sentence contains a colon and the text that follows the colon is an independent clause, either capitalize the first word following the colon or leave it in lowercase, but be consistent throughout your paper:

CORRECT       Our softball game was quickly terminated by an unex-
               pected event: Rain came down hard and steadily.

CORRECT       Our softball game was quickly terminated by an unex-
               pected event: rain came down hard and steadily.

## EXERCISE 31.1

In the following sentences, change lowercase letters to uppercase letters as needed, and vice versa. Some sentences may be correct.

1. the caloosa river splits harbin county in half.
2. my cousin roy works for Eddlestone industries.
3. his brother mike is the chief operating officer (coo).
4. i once had the honor of meeting president carter.
5. the headline in the *rockport times* was interesting: "State To Ban Cow Tipping In Rural Areas."
6. juan orosio drives a volkswagen passat.
7. orosio lives on bennington street in rockport.
8. Orosio used to live in the Southern part of our State.
9. The poetry of e. e. cummings can be difficult to understand.
10. We drove until we almost reached our destination (The Crafton city limits were now only a few miles away).

## 31b ITALICS AND UNDERLINING

Most word-processing software allows you to use *italic style,* a style of type in which the letters slant upward and to the right. As an alternative, if italics are not available or you are following a style that requires it, you can use <u>underlining</u>. Italics or underlining can be used in the following situations:

1. To indicate titles of long works or the names of ships or aircraft:

   *The Scarlet Letter* (novel)

   *The Day Lincoln Was Shot* (nonfiction book)

   *Chicago Tribune* (newspaper)

   *U.S. News & World Report* (magazine)

   *Academic Questions* (professional journal)

   *Romeo and Juliet* (play)

   *The Pianist* (film)

   *Law and Order* (television show)

   *The Barber of Seville* (opera)

   *Leaves of Grass* (long poem)

   *Andrea Doria* (ship)

**Note:** By convention, the word "the" is not capitalized or italicized when the title of a newspaper or magazine such as the *New York Times* or the *New Republic* appears within text.

Remember that parts or chapters of longer works such as those mentioned above are not underlined or placed in italics. Instead, they are put in quotation marks:

"The Prison Door" (title of chapter in the novel *The Scarlet Letter*)

"Allies Land in Normandy" (headline of a newspaper article)

"Great Books in the Undergraduate Curriculum" (title of article published in the professional journal *Academic Questions*)

"When Lilacs Last in the Dooryard Bloom'd" (short poem published in a collection titled *Drum-Taps*)

2. To indicate that a word or letter is being used as a word or letter:

   *Accommodate* contains two *c*'s and two *m*'s.

3. To show emphasis:

   The ship sank in only *twelve minutes*.

## EXERCISE 31.2

Rewrite the following sentences, using italics and quotation marks as appropriate.

1. Karl Zinmeister, editor of The American Enterprise magazine, wrote an article titled How America's SWAT Team Helped Swat Saddam.

2. Jonathan's reading for the week included A History of the Middle Ages by Joseph Dahmus as well as two plays by Shakespeare: Hamlet and Love's Labor's Lost.

3. My high school English teacher recommended that I read the Los Angeles Times each day.

4. Phil and Marna couldn't agree on which Al Pacino movie to rent: The Godfather or City Hall.

5. One of the essays in David Quammen's book The Flight of the Iguana is The Face of a Spider.

## 31c NUMBERS AND NUMERALS

Rules on the use of numbers and numerals vary from discipline to discipline; however, the rules below work well in the humanities and social sciences.

Spell out the following:

1. Numbers one through ninety-nine (see exceptions on page 802).

2. The first word of a sentence. This rule overrides all others.

3. Large, whole numbers, such as *one thousand* and *three million*.

Use numerals for the following:

1.  **Numbers higher than 99,** except for large, whole numbers, as noted above.

2.  **Fractions and decimals,** such as 1/7 and 3.14.

3.  **Numbers appearing with percentage signs or the word** *percent,* such as 8%.

4.  **Street addresses:** 6 Maple Avenue.

5.  **Dates:** September 17, 2007.

6.  **Sums of money:** He earns $14.38 per hour.

7.  **Volume, chapter, and page numbers:** The information you want appears in Volume 3, Chapter 14, page 67.

8.  **Exact times and dates:** 7:43 P.M., 92 C.E.

9.  **Speeds:** Do not exceed the speed limit: 55 mph.

10. **Sports scores:** The Mets won by a score of 3 to 2.

11. **Statistics:** Students in my high school miss an average of only 8 days per year for illness. Faculty average only 4 sick days per year.

12. **Numbers used as numbers:** In the snow, someone had written a large 3.

**Exceptions:**

1.  If one number in a sentence must be expressed as a numeral, use numerals for all other numbers in that sentence:

    Of Dr. Moore's 114 students, 7 withdrew for medical reasons, and 28 withdrew for academic reasons.

2.  When two numbers appear together, one number should appear as a numeral:

    The judges gave the diver **three 8's** and **two 9's.**

Use hyphens between compound numbers that you write out from twenty-one to ninety-nine:

Harriet was twenty-nine when she began teaching and sixty-five when she retired.

## EXERCISE 31.3

Revise the following sentences to correct problems with numbers.

1.  80 percent of the first-year class this year say they are confident about their academic success.

2.  Of his 12 "guidelines for success," four are nonsense, and 8 are plagiarized.

3.  My score on the exam was eighty-eight point six.

4.  She lives at Ninety-Six Columbus Street.

5.  Of the 368 entries, only seven got past the first review.

## 31d HYPHENS

Dashes (see Chapter 30, pages 783–784) are used to *separate* words; **hyphens** are used to *connect* words. Hyphens are used in several different contexts:

1.  Hyphens appear in the dictionary entries for spellings of common compound words such as *well-known, cave-in,* and *up-to-date.* If you think that a compound word should be hyphenated, don't guess; look it up in a college-level dictionary.

2.  Common prefixes such as *non, pre, post, anti,* and *pro* are sometimes followed by hyphens and sometimes not. Generally, the trend in modern American English is to avoid the hyphen and to use solid word forms: *predetermined,* for example. College-level dictionaries almost always contain many such words, sometimes in list format, to show you whether a prefix needs a hyphen when attached to a given common noun. However, if your dictionary offers no guidance about a specific word, follow this rule of thumb: use the hyphen only if its absence would cause an awkward spelling or make a word difficult to identify. For example,

    | Without Hyphen | With Hyphen |
    |---|---|
    | nonessential | non-European |
    | antiwar | anti-establishment |
    | pregame | pre-engineered |

    In the right-hand column, the hyphens make the term easier to comprehend.

3.  Hyphens are used when numbers larger than twenty but not a multiple of ten are written out:

    twenty-one    thirty-seven       eighty-four

4.  Hyphens are used when simple fractions are written as words:

    one-half    two-thirds       three-sixteenths

5.  Hyphens are used in typography to even out or "justify" the right margin of a page. Note that you will almost never be asked to produce right-justified pages when writing an essay or a research paper; the major style guides, such as MLA and APA, invariably specify that a manuscript paper should not be justified. But, if you do need to right-justify and hyphenate, your word-processing program will do this task for you. The computer may hyphenate some words incorrectly, however. In American English, words are hyphenated by *sound;* thus, words such as *present, record,* and *attribute* cause problems. Each of these can be either a noun or a verb and will be pronounced differently according to which part of speech they are.

    | Hyphenated as Noun | Hyphenated as Verb |
    |---|---|
    | pres-ent | pre-sent |
    | rec-ord | re-cord |
    | attri-bute | attrib-ute |

If you are producing a right-justified document, check to make sure that your software is dividing words such as these properly.

6. Hyphens are also used to form **compound adjectives** *when they precede a noun.* In compound adjectives, the first adjective describes the second and is connected to it with a hyphen. Collectively, the resulting term modifies the noun:

coal-black fish

three-bedroom apartment

late-night snack

country-music awards

student-rights activist

As you can see from the following examples, however, compound adjectives are not always hyphenated:

She wore a **hot-pink** dress.

The dress was **hot pink.**

In the first sentence, the compound adjective precedes the noun, so a hyphen is used for clarity. In the second, the adjective is a complement and appears after the noun it modifies, so the hyphen is not used. Also, simple adverb/adjective combinations do *not* use hyphens.

INCORRECT  **an easily-confused clerk**

CORRECT  **an easily confused clerk**

However, various three-word adverb/adjective constructions are hyphenated when they *precede* a noun that they modify:

We witnessed an **all-too-frequent** collapse of our baseball team late in the season.

The late-season collapse of our baseball team is **all too frequent.**

## COMBINATION EXERCISE

Rewrite the three paragraphs that follow to correct problems with capitalization and mechanics.

the First inhabitants of new zealand are thought to be the maori, polynesian people who came to the two-islands of this country in the 14th century and who spoke a tahitian like language. They now make up about eight % of the country's population. The first europeans to come to new zealand were dutch, who arrived in the 17th century and named the place after zeeland, a province in holland.

Eighteenth century english explorer captain james cook visited new zealand in his ship *endeavor.* However, nearly a century had to pass before the first permanent european settlement was established at wellington. At that time, the country was still part of the australian colony of new south wales, and the british fought several wars with the maori to gain control of both the Northern and Southern islands. As a result, the maori population dropped to below 100,000. (an academy award winning film, the piano, released in 1995, explores relations between the europeans and the maoris during the early days of colonization.) Today, however, the Native population has recovered, and the maori number well over 400,000.

In nineteen hundred and seven, new zealand was granted commonwealth nation status; in nineteen thirty one, it became an independent country. In both world war I and world war II, the country supplied troops and materials to the allies. Today, new zealanders enjoy one of the strongest economies in the far east. They have also made contributions to the arts, as illustrated by keri hulme's winning of the booker prize for her novel the bone people, which reveals much about maori life in the 2nd half of the 20th century. However, new zealand remains one of most sparsely-populated countries in the world. Indeed, there are far more sheep in this two island nation than there are people.

CATALYST 2.0

**MORE OPTIONS ONLINE**
For more exercises,
go to
www.mhhe.com/
writingtoday.

### CHAPTER 32

# DICTION, USAGE, AND SPELLING

**Diction** can be defined as "the words you choose." Being alert to the potentials and pitfalls of diction can help you avoid dull, inaccurate, or verbose writing and produce lively, vivid, and accurate language instead. This chapter examines four issues important to clear writing: using the right word, choosing the appropriate language level, using the correct idiom, and improving your spelling.

## 32a USING THE RIGHT WORD

Over the past six decades, written communication has lost some of its dominance to more visual forms of communication—photographs, drawings, and moving images—and to oral communication. Written communication is still crucial; after all, contracts are not yet written using cartoon figures. Nevertheless, popular culture has edged away from the written word. One result of this trend is that many people today are less familiar with written communication than earlier generations were.

This reduced level of familiarity has two major effects. One is a smaller vocabulary. People who don't read very much tend to learn only the words they hear. Frequent readers encounter a greater variety of words because, on the whole, written English employs many words heard less often in conversation. A second effect of the trend away from reading is an unfamiliarity with the way that words "look." Students sometimes turn in essays filled with word forms reflecting the way they *hear* the words, not the way that the words are correctly spelled.

An example of the first problem—reduced vocabulary—is seen in the following sentence:

> INCORRECT     The movie was dreadful; Rob was **disinterested** in seeing the sequel.

> CORRECT     The movie was dreadful; Rob was **not interested** in seeing the sequel.

The correct form here is *not interested*. Rob doesn't care to see the sequel; the film has bored him. *Disinterested* means "without bias." A judge in a legal proceeding should be disinterested; the judge should pay attention to but not favor either side. The meaning of *disinterested* does not fit the context, something a person who reads a great deal would be more likely to know.

The second type of error, illustrated by the following sentences, shows a writer's almost complete dependence on spoken English:

> INCORRECT     My self of steam suffered that year.

> INCORRECT     He attacked the task with avengince.

> INCORRECT     It is no adsaduration to call him the best guitarist of his error.

> INCORRECT     Love of money is the rude of all evil.

All four of these sentences appeared in the writing of students in a composition course. Each student understands what he or she is communicating; however, college writing demands a precision that the "phonetically transcribed" approach to spelling will never attain.

Two strategies can help you make sure you are using the right word in the right form:

**1.** Try to read a wider variety of writing than you encounter in your classes and at work. For example, in addition to reading what is assigned, read a related article or book as well. The more you read, the less you will depend upon "heard" English and the more you will be comfortable with "seen" English.

2. Make a dictionary your constant, much-used companion. Learn how dictionary entries work. Use electronic dictionaries as well; they might be even more helpful than print versions. If you can't find your spelling of the word in a dictionary, you may have to look up other combinations. However, incorrectly spelled words such as *adsaduration* pose special difficulties. For example, a computer spell-checker will offer no alternatives to this spelling. In such cases, try looking up synonyms, such as *overstatement,* which the dictionary defines as "exaggeration," thereby providing you with the correct spelling.

## 32b  DENOTATION AND CONNOTATION

A word's **denotation** is its dictionary definition. However, words also have associations not covered by dictionary definitions. What a word *suggests* is its **connotation.** Note the differences between the following pairs of synonyms:

| | |
|---|---|
| thrifty | cheap |
| complain | grumble |
| activist | radical |

The words on the left are neutral; those on the right have negative connotations. Being aware of connotation can help you make your writing vivid and emphatic; ignoring connotation can get you into trouble. For more on denotation and connotation, see Chapter 4.

## 32c  GENERAL VERSUS SPECIFIC NOUNS AND VERBS

When writers use specific nouns, they can create more vivid pictures:

GENERAL     David drove up in his **new truck.**

SPECIFIC     David drove up in his **red 2009 Toyota Tacoma.**

The reader of the first sentence gets basic information; the reader of the second gets a mental picture.

A related problem occurs with "weak" verbs, which create boring statements:

WEAK     Ms. Gutierrez **spent** several years as an office manager.

STRONGER     Ms. Gutierrez **managed** an office for several years.

WEAK     My cousin **is** a truck driver.

STRONGER     My cousin **drives** an eighteen-wheeler.

The second item in each pair is more interesting and emphatic than the original. For more on using specific nouns and verbs, see Chapter 4.

## 32d WRITING LEAN SENTENCES

As writers think through concepts on paper or on a computer screen, they often use more words than they have to. As a result, first drafts frequently express the writer's thoughts but are not in a finished, polished form.

Of course, the shortest version of a sentence might not be the best one. You will often need to clear up ambiguities by adding words as you revise your writing. Nonetheless, you should eliminate useless and wordy structures. Compare these sentences:

> There is a car coming down the street.

> A car is coming down the street.

The only difference between these two sentences is the number of words; the sentences mean the same thing. Starting the first sentence with the empty expletive *There is* adds nothing but words. A similar problem is caused by overusing *it:*

> It is a certainty that the proposal will be adopted.

> The proposal will certainly be adopted.

These two sentences have the same meaning and emphasis; the only difference is length.

Should you always avoid starting a sentence with the expletive *there* or *it*? No, but if you use these words, ask yourself if they serve a purpose. If not, use a basic subject/predicate structure instead.

As you revise, also weed out bloated phrasing, in which several words are used when one or two suffice:

> BLOATED **Due to the fact that** the stock market is shaky, Sarah is investing in a bond fund instead.

> LEAN **Because** the stock market is shaky, Sarah is investing in a bond fund instead.

Look as well for unnecessary verb or verbal phrases, and reduce them to simple verbs:

> BLOATED Joan, I think we need to hold a meeting.

> LEAN Joan, I think we need to meet.

Other problems to look for when you are revising for diction are repetition and redundancy. **Repetition** occurs when a word is repeated in the same sentence or in a nearby sentence. It can make your writing tedious:

> REPETITIVE Of the ten apple pies in the bake-off, my grandmother's apple pie was the best.

> REVISED Of the ten apple pies in the bake-off, my grandmother's was the best.

**Redundancy** is the result of using two or more words that mean the same thing. In effect, redundancy means saying the same thing twice:

> REDUNDANT The dead corpse lay in the narrow alley.

> REVISED The corpse lay in the alley.

All *corpses* are dead; all *alleys* are narrow.

REDUNDANT    The wealthy tycoon recalled the past history of the company's rise in a very unique industry.

REVISED    The tycoon recalled the history of the company's rise in a unique industry.

By definition, *tycoons* are wealthy, *history* is made up of past events, and anything that is *unique* is one of a kind already, so using *very* is unnecessary. For more on how to write efficient sentences, see Chapter 4.

## EXERCISE 32.1

The following sentences suffer from the diction problems that have just been discussed. Revise each one.

1. Some people think the business world has a doggy-dog mentality.
2. The recipe called for a well-beeten egg and two cups of flower.
3. The bride took the groom's love for granite as she walked down the isle.
4. We need to undertake an investigation of the cost overruns.
5. It is clear that the sun will rise tomorrow.
6. There is reason to believe that a large number of persons who have immigrated to this country are having problems with the English language.
7. What this is is an electronic signal locator.
8. In all probability, the profits for the third quarter will be in the neighborhood of $30 million.
9. The doctor provided a diagnosis of my condition.
10. Manuel has proved to be a political activist because of his letters complaining about the county commissioners' policies.
11. The tone of our supervisor's memo infers that he is not very happy about the remodeling costs.
12. Last Wednesday, the geologist lead his party into a newly discovered cave.
13. Harriet was to excited to speak.
14. Ask the waiter if their are any desert specials.
15. I hope to rise my GPA this semester.

## 32e AVOIDING SEXIST LANGUAGE

Words can sting. The use of overtly malicious language to describe women is rarer and rarer these days; however, **sexist language** still appears in speaking and writing because of insensitivity or ignorance. Consider this sentence:

SEXIST    The consultant entered with his assistant, an attractive blonde of about thirty, who helped him set up the presentation.

The sentence suggests a hidebound and offensive social dichotomy: men are functional, women decorative. This dichotomy is no longer acceptable. Note the revision of the sentence above:

ACCEPTABLE  **The consultant entered with his assistant, who helped him set up the presentation.**

Remember these guidelines when you write:

1. Avoid job titles that imply gender. In the 1920s and 1930s, the famous pilot Amelia Earhart was labeled in the media as an "aviatrix," as opposed to an "aviator." Still with us today are the hard-to-get-rid-of *waiter/waitress* distinction and a distinction that plagues film and theater: *actor/actress*. Note this list of old-fashioned job titles and their modern equivalents:

| Gender-Linked Title | Gender-Free Title |
|---|---|
| repairman | technician |
| mailman | letter carrier |
| fireman | firefighter |
| policeman | police officer |
| chairman | chair |
| congressman | representative |

   Keep in mind that you do not need to use such bizarre terms as *waitperson* and *ombudsperson; server* and *mediator* will suffice.

2. When you write about both men and women, treat each sex equally. What's wrong with the following passage?

SEXIST  **The two candidates, William Rogers and Sara Gonzalez, were introduced to the audience. In his preliminary remarks, Rogers said that he would focus on lower taxes. Ms. Gonzalez, however, spoke on improving local roads.**

The writer is being inappropriately polite, identifying the male candidate as "Rogers" but the female candidate as "Ms. Gonzalez."

REVISED  **The two candidates, William Rogers and Sara Gonzalez, were introduced to the audience. In his preliminary remarks, Rogers said that he would focus on lower taxes. Gonzalez, however, spoke on improving local roads.**

In the revised version, the writer refers to both candidates by their last names.

   A similar problem occurs when a writer identifies groups containing both males and females as if they included males alone:

SEXIST  **At the convention, the doctors and their wives enjoyed the best the Sunset Resort had to offer.**

We doubt that the female doctors brought their "wives":

REVISED  **At the convention, the doctors and their spouses enjoyed the best the Sunset Resort had to offer.**

3. Use pronouns fairly and accurately. English lacks a single pronoun to refer to an indefinite person of either sex. This shortcoming causes problems with accuracy and *agreement* (see also chapters 26 and 27). Writers need to avoid using *he* or *she* alone or plural pronouns such as *they, them,* and *their* to refer to singular indefinite pronouns, such as *anyone, everybody,* or *someone,* or to nouns used in a general sense, such as *any doctor* or *the average teacher:*

SEXIST  **Everyone** must vote according to **his** conscience.

SEXIST  **Any student** who wants to do well in Dr. McDonald's economics class must be sure that **he** is prepared to study.

INCORRECT  **Everyone** must vote according to **their** conscience.

INCORRECT  **Any student** who wants to do well in Dr. McDonald's economics class must be sure that **they** are prepared to study.

The preferred pronoun forms are, instead, *he or she, him or her,* or these forms in reverse order:

CORRECT  **Everyone** must vote according to **his or her** conscience.

CORRECT  **Any student** who wants to do well in Dr. McDonald's economics class must be sure that **she or he** is prepared to study.

The pronouns and antecedents in the two sentences above agree in number, and the revisions avoid sexism. However, an essay that is filled with *he or she, him or her,* and *his or her* becomes tiresome. On the other hand, almost all sentences with indefinite pronouns can be revised with plural nouns, as in the following example:

CORRECT  **All citizens** must vote according to **their** conscience.

The same approach will work with nouns used in a general sense:

CORRECT  **Students** who want to do well in Dr. McDonald's economics class must be sure that **they** are prepared to study.

You should use *he, him,* or *his* alone or *she* or *her* alone only when the context is male only or female only, as in the following:

A British cavalry officer of the 1850s could be sure that **his** future depended not only on **his** abilities but also on the politics of the chain of command.

Any member of this sorority who violates the finals-week quiet hours will have **her** room assignment voided.

The possibility that a nineteenth-century British cavalry officer *could* have been a woman disguised as a man or that a male college student *might* be passing as a sorority member is negligible and not worth considering.

For more on pronoun-antecedent agreement, see Chapter 27.

## EXERCISE 32.2

In each of the following sentences, determine whether the highlighted term is acceptable. If it is not, replace it with a more appropriate word or rewrite the sentence.

1. Joan has broken another line-class record for sea trout; she is the best **fisherperson** I've ever had the pleasure to know.

2. Each officer to be honored must wear **his** dress uniform.

3. A grandmother must be careful not to compete with **her** grandson's parents for **his** affection.

4. An employee of a defense plant must show **his** ID upon entering.

5. The American coal miner of the 1830s saw the potential end of **his or her** life about twice weekly.

## 32f USING FIGURATIVE LANGUAGE AND AVOIDING CLICHÉS

**Figurative language** is a way to amplify the description of a subject by comparing the subject to something else that is not *literally* like the subject but is like it in a compelling way. As Chapter 4 points out, using figurative language effectively is a matter of degree. Make sure your language is fresh, and try to avoid clichés, overused and worn-out figures of speech. (You will read more about clichés later in this section.)

As discussed in Chapter 4, there are three main categories of figurative language:

1. A **metaphor** compares two things directly by claiming that the subject and its description are one:

   The Internet startup company proved to be a huge vacuum cleaner that sucked up its investors' money.

2. A **simile** compares two things by using *like* or *as:*

   Jason says that after his back surgery, he looked **like a defective banana.**

   Robbins turned as green **as turtle soup** when he heard about the burglary.

3. **Personification** attributes human characteristics to nonhuman entities:

   The forest **whispered** of a simpler, more peaceful existence.

   The darkening sky **wore the garments of doom.**

A well-turned figure of speech is highly effective and can be the difference between good writing and memorable writing. However, a straightforward sentence without figurative language is better than a sentence that is labored or strained:

| | |
|---|---|
| STRAINED | The dog pulled at its leash like a hound of hell. |
| STRAIGHT-FORWARD | The dog pulled urgently at its leash. |

The first example might be appropriate in some contexts, but the second would work in all contexts.

Two other problems can occur when you are using figurative language: a **mixed metaphor** and a **cliché**. A **mixed metaphor** results when a writer uses two unrelated figures of speech in the same sentence:

| | |
|---|---|
| MIXED METAPHOR | On a motorcycle, Andrew becomes an angry bulldog who rockets through town like a missile. |
| REVISED | On a motorcycle, Andrew becomes an angry bulldog, snarling and growling as he races through town. |
| MIXED METAPHOR | The arena of love can be a snarl of confusing roads. |
| REVISED | Love can be a snarl of confusing roads, with signs that lead in different directions. |

In each of the revised versions, two figures of speech are used, but they are clearly related.

A **cliché** is a worn-out phrase that readers have heard many times. Including such figures of speech can make your writing flat and boring:

| | |
|---|---|
| CLICHÉ | My salary increase was **the icing on the cake**; being assigned to a new department was all I had requested. |
| FRESHER | My salary increase was a real bonus; being assigned to a new department was all I had requested. |

Most people have read *icing on the cake* numerous times. In the revised version, a more straightforward construction and avoids sounding hackneyed and stale.

## EXERCISE 32.3

In each of the following sentences, replace the highlighted expression with a more effective word or phrase. Different answers are possible.

1.  Using too many clichés is an illness whose symptoms include dullness; avoid them **like the plague**.

2.  The exploratory committee **kicked the bucket** after its first suggestions **went south**.

3.  During the shoe sale, customers **swarmed** into the store **like bees** in a **barroom brawl**.

4.  **In a nutshell,** we should have reviewed **the bottom line** before **jumping in feet first.**

5.  **It will be a cold day in Hell** before Wanda Jane becomes a church member.

## 32g AVOIDING FILLERS, EUPHEMISMS, AND JARGON

Empty language and language offered without a sense of audience are a waste of effort both for the writer and the reader. Three varieties of misguided language are fillers, euphemisms, and jargon.

1.  **Fillers** are well-known but essentially empty expressions used when a more basic expression—or none at all—would suffice:

    all in all

    needless to say

    first and foremost

    golden opportunity

    safe and sound

2.  **Euphemisms** are sensitive or "safe" terms used to refer to unpleasant realities that reflect bodily functions, sexual activities, and death, to name a few. The deceased are sometimes said to have "passed on" or to have "met their Maker." People who have lost their jobs are said to have been "downsized." These are weasel words, language designed to avoid reality:

    UNNECESSARY    **Jane is in a family way.**
    EUPHEMISM

    REVISED           **Jane is pregnant.**

    In addition, euphemisms can be misleading by masking the seriousness of a condition or situation:

    UNNECESSARY    **Subjects in the psychological study were high-strung.**
    EUPHEMISM

    REVISED           **Subjects in the psychological study suffered from anxiety disorders.**

    With the subjects of bodily functions and sexual relations, however, a polite level of euphemism is expected. "I need to go to the restroom" is always preferable to an explicit account of what one plans to do there. "The young couple made love for the first time" raises no eyebrows. The key is to avoid language that fears its subject or that seeks to lie about the true nature of its subject.

3.  **Jargon** is the specialized language used in a particular field or discipline. It is language used among engineers, chemists, accountants, and other specialists. Jargon is perfectly acceptable—in fact, useful—as long as it is not used outside the field or discipline to which it belongs. Only when a specialist speaks to nonspecialists does jargon become an issue.

| JARGON | The publisher warned the author that the book's **front-matter** was too long. |
| REVISED | The publisher warned the author that the book's **introductory section** was too long. |

If you need to use a word or phrase that you know will be jargon, define the term the first time it appears. Then use it as needed. However, this approach has its limits. If you define several such terms, you risk overwhelming your reader.

## EXERCISE 32.4

Look for fillers, clichés, euphemisms, and jargon in the following sentences. Replace each inappropriate word or phrase.

1. The company's accountants input new data into the computer in order to complete the product's projected-cost assessment.

2. The guests flocked to the buffet table, swooping down and tackling anyone in their way.

3. Please eliminate that stupid fly.

4. The new testing center has nipped the cheating problem in the bud.

5. All in all, the commission found that the rules and regulations that the company had put into place over the specified period of time were appropriate.

## 32h USING THE APPROPRIATE LANGUAGE LEVEL

Writers vary their level of language according to the nature of their audiences. When you write a letter or an e-mail to a lifelong friend, you probably use informal language and a friendly tone. However, if you were to write a proposal seeking funding for a research project, you would avoid such informality.

Language level is determined in part by the level of formality of the words used. Dictionaries commonly identify three levels of formality:

1. **Formal** words are used in scholarly or legal contexts. Typically, these words have Latin or Greek roots. A resident of North America might seldom hear these words spoken; they are far more common in print. Here are two examples:

propinquity (existing close together)

censorious (highly critical)

2. **Standard** words make up the text of popular magazines and daily newspapers, as well as most college writing. These words are of a level most likely to be understood by the average reader. For example, the standard alternative to the more formal *propinquity* would be *nearness*. The alternative to *censorious* might be *negative*.

3. **Informal** words are found in conversation and in conversational writing, such as e-mail messages. They are not appropriate in college writing. Here's an example:

When I started college a year ago, I bought a new computer. (Actually, my parental unit bought it for me.) It had all the bells and whistles, top of the line. Now—just one year later!—it's like it has suffered some weird aging disease. It's slow against the Net, and the word processing gizmos are, like, ancient. I need a new box!

Informal language often includes colloquial language and slang.

**Colloquial** language is informal language that is peculiar to a geographical region. For example, in parts of New England, long sandwiches are known as *grinders,* but in other parts of the country they are known as *submarines* or *heros.* In the South, you might hear someone tell you to beware of a "pig in a poke." In other words, never buy a product without seeing it first.

**Slang** consists of temporary, stylish language forms that reflect popular culture and are traditionally used more by young people than by older people. (The example above is filled with slang.) Like colloquial language, slang is usually inappropriate in college-level writing because (1) your audience might not understand it and (2) slang has no fixed, permanent meaning.

Note the difference among language levels for the following terms:

| Formal | Standard | Informal | Slang |
|---|---|---|---|
| altercation | quarrel | fight | rumble |
| unsophisticated | rough | rube | scrub |
| comely | attractive | cute | hot |

When you write for your college classes, use standard English. (For more on levels of language, see Chapter 4.)

## 32i USING A CONSISTENT LANGUAGE LEVEL

Sometimes, college students stray from general English in a paper. They might suddenly slip into informal English; later, their vocabulary might suddenly become quite elevated, as if they had just discovered a thesaurus. Remember the importance of using standard English consistently. Sometimes, you'll need a more formal word, and sometimes—when quoting dialogue, for instance—you might have to use slang, but these should be exceptions, not common occurrences.

### EXERCISE 32.5

The following sentences are written in general English but stray from that category. Revise as needed.

1. Jan had not expected to receive so much calumny because of turning in her research notes beyond the deadline.

2. The small town was populated largely by rubes.

3. Worrying about a math exam won't get you anywhere; you need to chill a bit, then form a study plan.

4. Mr. Banks is a good supervisor but a real hard-nose about punctuality.

5. The smell coming from the restaurant was truly odoriferous.

## 32j USING THE CORRECT IDIOM

Many English phrases are **idiomatic**; that is, certain combinations of words are acceptable, but similar phrases are not. *On the contrary* is standard, but *in the contrary* is meaningless. Unfortunately, when you are trying to decide which construction is correct, logic won't help.

Most troublesome idioms in English involve prepositions. The following list includes combinations that commonly cause problems:

accuse of: She was **accused of** embezzlement.

accustom to: I'm not **accustomed to** luxury.

adhere to: We **adhere to** a code of ethics.

adjacent to: The restaurant is **adjacent to** a dry cleaner.

advice on: I need some **advice on** this mutual fund.

advise of: The detective **advised** us **of** the new developments.

advise to: Dr. Sanchez **advised** me **to** take microeconomics.

agree on: Let's **agree on** a plan.

agree to: I'll **agree to** her demands on one condition.

angry with: Cathy is **angry with** Rob.

apologize for: We need to **apologize for** our loud party.

apply for: He **applied for** the management position.

assent to: The administration **assented to** the students' demands.

benefit from: We have **benefited from** her advice.

blame for: I took the **blame for** my brother's antics; I **blame** him **for** getting me into trouble.

bored by: James was **bored by** Karen's constant talking.

bored with: I'm **bored with** staying home and watching television.

capable of: Cats are **capable of** great mischief if left unattended.

compliment on: The judge **complimented** the jury **on** their promptness.

comply with: Please **comply with** our guidelines, Mr. Roberts.

concerned about: Janet was **concerned about** her children.

concur with: I **concur with** Jane; we must change our level of customer service.

confide in: Laura **confides** only **in** her mother.

confide to: Laura **confided** the secret **to** me.

confident of: The incumbent is **confident of** success in the upcoming election.

conform to: This design **conforms to** the county building code.

consent to: I **consented to** the new regulations.

decide on: Have you **decided on** which film to see tonight?

derive from: The recipe was **derived from** an eighteenth-century cookbook.

despair of: Wayne **despaired of** ever finishing his degree.

deviate from: This type of orchid **deviates from** the norm.

devoid of: The musical's cast was **devoid of** talent.

different from: Baseball is **different from** cricket.

discourage from: The new legislative guidelines **discourage** students **from** changing majors.

disdain for: Julie has a great **disdain for** unmotivated students.

embark on: Today, we **embark on** a new chapter in our company's story.

foreign to: This kind of fish is **foreign to** my taste.

hinder from: Working part-time can **hinder** a student **from** studying properly.

hindrance to: Too much background noise can be a **hindrance to** careful thought.

implicit in: His motives are **implicit in** his actions.

in accordance with: We have drawn up the contract **in accordance with** our notes from the meeting.

independent of: The French researcher reached her findings **independent of** the Russian scientist.

in search of: We are **in search of** the truth.

insight into: The lab report should give us some **insight into** the patient's condition.

interfere in: Veronica loves to **interfere in** her friends' lives.

interfere with: My love of partying **interfered with** my studies.

involve in: How did you get **involved in** this mess?

involve with: Are you **involved with** that organization?

mistrustful of: Sometimes it's too easy to be **mistrustful of** a friend.

neglectful of: The new security guard was **neglectful of** the compound's perimeter.

oblivious of (*or* to): Middle-class people are frequently **oblivious of (to)** the plight of the homeless.

opposition to: My **opposition to** rezoning is well-known.

partial to: I am **partial to** chicken cooked in any manner.

peculiar to: This orchid is **peculiar to** only one very small part of Brazil.

preferable to: Success is **preferable to** failure.

prevent from: The police **prevented** me **from** parking near my house.

protest against: I must **protest against** this madness, sir!

receptive to: Oddly, Mr. Younger was **receptive to** my plan.

renege on: The bank **reneged on** our original agreement.

responsible for: The captain is **responsible for** the people on the ship.

responsible to: She is **responsible to** her supervisors.

rich in: The dessert was **rich in** carbohydrates.

sensitive to (about): Jason is **sensitive to** (or **about**) questions regarding his past.

similar to: This car is **similar to** my old one.

superior to: This wine is **superior to** others of its type.

suspect (*verb*) of: He has long been **suspected of** embezzlement but has never been caught.

unaware of: Dr. Vershinsky was **unaware of** his class's boredom.

variance with: These specs show a large **variance with** our original blueprints.

void of: This movie is **void of** any redeeming qualities.

wary of: Be **wary of** telephone sales pitches.

yield to: Don't **yield to** temptations too early; think before acting.

## EXERCISE 32.6

The following sentences contain unidiomatic expressions. Reword as necessary.

1. The factory management has consented with the request for the installation of more safety equipment and will not interfere on meetings called by union officials.
2. Juan has an education that he will benefit with in his new job.
3. Michael embarks in a new career; he will be involved with matters related to national security.
4. The new coach was not concerned for the future of the team.
5. Rita always wants to be different than everyone else in her dorm.

## 32k IMPROVING YOUR SPELLING

Modern English is derived from a hodgepodge of languages. As a result, English spelling is not always predictable. Some lucky writers process language *visually;* they "see" words as they think them. However, most people process language orally, and to spell correctly, they must depend on phonetics and their memory.

For any writer who is uncertain about how to spell a word—and this includes a lot of us—a dictionary provides invaluable help. If you make a point of looking up words when you are unsure of their spelling, eventually you will remember them. Keep a list of "corrected spellings" for your reference. Also, remember that most good spellers are habitual readers.

The following guidelines will help, but they almost always include exceptions. Use your dictionary whenever you are not sure about how to spell a word.

1. *ie* or *ei:* Use *i* before *e* except after *c* and except in words pronounced without the long *e* sound (as in *see* or *beat*).

| | | | |
|---|---|---|---|
| field | ceiling | neighbor | foreign |
| grief | conceit | sleigh | height |
| niece | conceive | vein | heir |
| relief | deceive | weigh | stein |

Exceptions are *fiery, neither, seize, species,* and *weird.*

2. Final *e:* Drop a silent final *e* before suffixes beginning with a vowel; keep a silent final *e* before suffixes beginning with a consonant:

| | | |
|---|---|---|
| guidance | virtuous | nineteen |
| wasting | lovely | sincerely |

Exceptions are *dyeing* (fabric), *ninth, truly,* and *courageous.*

3. Changing *y* to *i:* When adding a suffix, change a final *y* to *i* except before a suffix beginning with *i:*

cry, crying, crier

forty, fortieth

rely, reliance

4. Forming plurals: Most plurals are formed by adding *-s* to the singular form; plurals of nouns ending in *s, ch, sh,* or *x* add *-es.*

| | | | |
|---|---|---|---|
| bassists | cars | foxes | lunches |
| cables | handfuls | dishes | mosses |

An exception is *stomachs.*

Singular nouns ending in *y* preceded by a consonant form the plural by changing the *y* to *i* and adding *-es.*

berries, caddies, lobbies

Singular nouns ending in *o* preceded by a consonant usually add *-es,* but note the exceptions:

heroes, potatoes, tomatoes, zeroes

ghettos or ghettoes, mosquitos or mosquitoes

**Exceptions:** hippos, jumbos, pros

Here is a list of eighty commonly misspelled words:

| | | | |
|---|---|---|---|
| accommodate | a lot | argument | category |
| acquaintance | altogether | athletic | cemetery |
| aggravate | amateur | bureaucracy | competition |
| all right | analysis | calendar | condemn |

sp
32h

| | | | |
|---|---|---|---|
| conscience | feasible | loneliness | proceed |
| conscientious | February | maintenance | prominent |
| conscious | gauge | maneuver | psychology |
| consistent | government | mischievous | questionnaire |
| continuous | grammar | necessary | receive |
| criticize | guard | noticeable | recommend |
| definitely | harass | occasionally | repetition |
| desperate | hurriedly | occurred | rhythm |
| develop | hypocrisy | parallel | schedule |
| disappoint | imitation | personnel | separate |
| disastrous | independent | possess | succeed |
| dissatisfied | intelligence | preceding | susceptible |
| embarrass | irrelevant | predominant | temperament |
| environment | irresistible | prejudice | unanimous |
| exaggerate | knowledge | prevalent | undoubtedly |
| existence | license | privilege | villain |

## EXERCISE 32.7

Sixteen of the following words are misspelled. Provide the correct spellings.

1. definatly
2. paralel
3. wholly
4. personell
5. accomodation
6. independent
7. resistence

8. seperate
9. occurrance
10. mispell
11. catagory
12. cematery
13. aggrivate
14. bureaucracy

15. disasterous
16. goverment
17. develope
18. hypocrisy
19. predominent
20. mischievious

# A GLOSSARY OF USAGE

### CHAPTER 33

The following glossary contains words that are commonly misused or misspelled, along with pairs or groups of words that are commonly confused.

**a, an** These are the two indefinite articles. Use *a* before a word beginning with a consonant sound; use *an* before a word beginning with a vowel sound. For example, *one* starts with a consonant sound: a one-term president. *Hour* starts with a vowel sound: an hour.

**absolutely** Avoid using this word to produce redundant expressions such as *absolutely perfect* and *absolutely unique.*

**accept, except** *Accept* is a verb: "Will they **accept** our proposal?" *Except* is normally a preposition: "Everything is finished **except** the letter."

**access, excess** *Access* means "entry," "entrance," or "availability to": "Susan was denied **access** to sensitive files." *Excess* means "too much of," "surplus," or "redundancy": "When buying meat, have the butcher trim off the **excess** fat."

**adapt, adopt** *Adapt* means "to alter to fit": "The armadillo has **adapted** to life in Florida." *Adopt* means "to take in" or "accept": "We **adopted** our new dog at the humane shelter."

**adverse, averse** *Adverse* means "unfavorable" or "hostile." *Averse* indicates "unwillingness," "reluctance," and even "repugnance." "She is not **averse** to going sailing as long as we don't encounter **adverse** weather."

**advice, advise** *Advice* is a noun; *advise* is a verb: "I did not like my boss's **advice,** for she **advised** me to find other employment."

**affect, effect** *Affect* is almost always a verb: "The weather forecast **affected** our plans." In the social sciences, *affect* is sometimes used as a noun to mean "normal human responses": "The psychopath showed a chilling lack of **affect.**" *Effect* is almost always a noun: "The **effect** of the storm was profound." However, *effect* can also be used as a verb, as in "to **effect** change," meaning to cause change to happen.

**again, back** Avoid using these words to create redundant phrases such as *reiterate again* and *return back.*

**aggravate** This word is often confused with *irritate* and *annoy.* However, *aggravate* means "to worsen": "The symptoms of my cold were **aggravated** because I was able to get only three hours' sleep." "Children can **irritate** [*not* **aggravate**] their parents by making unreasonable requests."

**a half a** Avoid; use either *half a* or *a half,* according to context: "I had **half a** [*not* **a half a**] cantaloupe; then I drank **a half** [*not* **a half a**] quart of water."

**ahold** Not a word—use *hold* instead: "The diver tried to get **hold** of the side of the rescue boat."

**ain't** This is a nonstandard contraction of *am not, are not,* or *is not.* Avoid it unless reporting dialogue.

**all ready, already** *All ready* indicates that everyone or everything is prepared: "They were **all ready** to go." *Already* is an adverb meaning "at this time" or "before this time": "Laura had **already** finished eating when her son called."

**allude, elude** *Allude* is a verb meaning "to mention indirectly": "The senator **alluded** frequently to the *Iliad.*" Note that *allude* does not have the same meaning as *refer,* which means "to mention directly." *Elude* means "to avoid capture or censure": "The escaped convict **eluded** the police for three days."

**allusion, illusion** An *allusion* is an indirect "reference": "In *Paradise Lost,* Milton makes **allusions** to the classics and to the Bible." An *illusion* is a "mirage," a "fantasy," or a "misperception": "Anna is under the **illusion** that everyone is capable of doing good and avoiding evil."

**alot** Avoid—use *a lot,* meaning "much" or "many," or *allot,* a verb meaning "to divide among."

**alright** Avoid—the correct spelling is *all right*.

**alternately, alternatively** The first word means "in turn," "in sequence," or "in rotation": "Meetings of the committee are held once per month **alternately** in Hightstown and Princeton." *Alternatively* refers to a "choice": "You can pay full tuition; **alternatively,** you can join the work-study program and have your payments reduced by 20 percent."

**altogether, all together** *Altogether,* an adverb, means "completely": "We were **altogether** disgusted with the new film." *All together* is a phrase meaning "in a group" or "in a collection": "My family was **all together** this Christmas."

**alumnus, alumna, alumni, alumnae** Use *alumnus* to refer to a college graduate of either sex; use *alumni* for more than one graduate. Avoid *alumna* and *alumnae,* which are outdated and sexist.

**among, between** Use *among* to connect more than two; use *between* to connect two: "**Between** you and me, Dr. Justino is **among** the best three surgeons in the state."

**amoral, immoral** *Amoral* means "without moral principles": "Jerry believes there is no right and wrong in this world; he has a thoroughly **amoral** philosophy." *Immoral* has an even stronger negative connotation and means "sinful," "evil," or "depraved": "The Holocaust was the manifestation of an utterly **immoral** philosophy."

**amount, number** Use *amount* to refer to entities that are normally weighed or measured, not counted, such as rice, sugar, and sunshine. Use *number* for entities that are normally counted, such as peaches and people: "The **amount** of fog made driving on the highway unsafe; the **number** of people trapped in their cars was astounding." See also **fewer, less.**

**ampersand (&)** Do not use this symbol to mean "and" in college writing unless it is part of a company's name or is required by a particular documentation style.

**an, a** See **a, an.**

**and etc.** Avoid this redundancy; in fact, *etc.* alone should be used with caution. See also **etc.**

**and/or** Avoid this clumsy construction except in legal and scientific writing.

**and so, and therefore** Redundant phrases—use *so* or *therefore* instead.

**angry at** This is a nonstandard form. Use *angry with* instead.

**angry, mad** *Angry* refers to an emotional state. In college writing, use *mad* to mean "insane" or "deranged": "How can you be **angry** with someone who has obviously gone **mad**?"

**any, any other** Using *any* instead of *any other* can sometimes create illogical comparisons: "Anna is better at mathematics than **any** student in her class." This sentence claims that Anna is even better than herself, an absurdity! The correct version is "Anna is better at mathematics than **any other** student in her class."

**anyone, any one** *Anyone* is an indefinite pronoun meaning "a person." *Any one* is a phrase referring to an individual singled out from a group: "**Anyone** is eligible; **any one** of us could win."

**anyways** Not a word—use *anyway* instead.

**appraise, apprise** *Appraise* means "to set a value on"; *apprise* means "to inform": "The jeweler **apprised** her clients that their ring had been **appraised** at $100,000."

**apt, likely** These words are synonymous. However, don't confuse *likely* with *liable* (see also **liable**).

**around** *Around* refers to position. Avoid using it to mean "near" or "about" in formal writing: "**Around** the fort, the remains of which are **near** Santa Clara, were amassed **about** one thousand enemy soldiers."

**as, like** When comparing, use *like*: "Joan is **like** her sister." When subordinating an independent clause, use *as* (or *as if, as though*): "Ed was late, **as** we knew he would be." Avoid using *as* in place of *because* or *while*: "He was late **because** [*not* **as**] he had to wait **while** [*not* **as**] the mechanic fixed his car."

**as regards** Avoid—use *concerning* instead.

**assure, ensure, insure** *Assure* means to "affirm" or "pledge." *Ensure* means "make sure" or "make certain." *Insure* means "to guarantee against destruction, loss, or harm": "We **assure** you that enough monies have been put aside to **ensure** his release." "Reggie is an executive with a company that **insures** businesses against loss by theft, fire, or natural catastrophes."

**awful, awfully** *Awful* means "awe-inspiring." However, it has taken on the popular meaning of "horrible" or "dreadful." In speech, *awfully* sometimes replaces *very*. Avoid both of these popular uses in college writing: "News of the **appalling** [*not* **awful**] conditions in the city's hospitals spread through the media **very** [*not* **awfully**] fast."

**awhile, a while** *Awhile* is an adverb: "We ran **awhile**." *A while* functions as a noun and is often used as the object of a preposition: "I thought for **a while** about Bianca's proposal."

**bad, badly** *Bad* is an adjective: "Edwin is not a **bad** man, and I'm sure he feels **bad** about losing his temper." Note that the second *bad* is used as an adjective complement, a word that describes the subject *he*. *Badly* is an adverb: "We played **badly** all day at the new golf course."

**basically** Do not use this word as a filler, as in "**Basically**, we feel sorry for Mike because of his wife's illness."

**being as (being that)** Do not use to mean "because": "I believe that my sixteen-year-old daughter is ready for college **because** [*not* **being as** or **being that**] she has compiled an outstanding academic record in high school."

**beside, besides** *Beside* is a preposition that means "adjacent to": "The parking lot is **beside** the store." *Besides* is an adverb that means "in addition to" or "except for": "**Besides** her regular job, Karen does freelance work; Andre, on the other hand, has no other sources of income **besides** his printing business."

**between** See **among, between.**

**both** Avoid redundant expressions such as "they both agree" or "both together."

**breath, breathe** *Breath* is a noun: "Slow down and take a **breath**." *Breathe* is a verb: "'**Breathe** deeply,' said the doctor."

**broke** This word is informal for "insolvent," "without money." Avoid this use of *broke* in college writing.

**but** Do not join this word with other negative conjunctions, as in *but yet* and *but however*.

**can, may** *Can* refers to ability or possibility: "**Can** the helicopter make it to the accident scene in time?" *May* refers to permission: "No, you **may** not put your feet on my sofa!" *May* is also used as a synonym for *might*: "We **may** get this project finished on time; it's too soon to tell."

**cannot** The verb *can* plus *not* is usually spelled as one word. However, if you need to stress the *not*, separate the two words and underline (italicize) *not*: "You **can *not*** drive from Los Angeles to San Francisco in two hours."

**can't hardly** Avoid this double negative; use *can hardly* instead.

**can't help but** This is an informal construction. Instead, use *can't help:* "I **can't help** loving you!"

**capital, capitol** *Capital* is the noun for a city that is the governmental center of a county, state, province, or country. However, it can also refer to money or financial resources. *Capitol* refers to the building in which lawmakers and other government officials meet: "Arriving in the **capital** by train, the senators proceeded directly to the **capitol**, where they presented a bill to cut **capital** spending."

**censor, censure** To *censor* is to remove from a document materials that are considered offensive. To *censure* means to "condemn," "admonish," or "strongly criticize": "Let's hope that the courts will **censure** the government if it attempts to **censor** the press."

**center around** Inaccurate—use *center on* instead.

**childish, childlike** The first of these words carries a negative connotation: "Though he is fifty years old, his behavior at meetings is often **childish**." The second word has a more positive meaning: "There is a **childlike** innocence in Mary's eyes."

**cite, site, sight** When writing a research paper, students *cite* by identifying the source of a quotation or of other information. *Site* refers to a place in real or virtual space: "The proposed **site** of our college's off-campus center can be examined on our Web **site**." When used as a verb, *sight* means "to see" or "to spot." When used as a noun, *sight* means "vision."

**climactic, climatic** *Climactic* is the adjective form of *climax:* "The car chase was the movie's **climactic** scene." *Climatic* is the adjective form of *climate:* "Her job is to monitor **climatic** changes at the South Pole."

**complement, compliment, complementary, complimentary** *Complement* means "to complete" or "to fit with": "Uma's green handbag **complemented** her outfit." As a verb, *compliment* means "to praise," and as a noun, *compliment* means "a word of praise." Rarely used, *complementary* is the adjective form of *complement:* "The dress had a **complementary** belt." *Complimentary* means either "praising language" ("The boss was **complimentary** about our report") or "free of charge" ("The hotel room came with **complimentary** theater passes").

**conscience, conscious** The first word is a noun; it refers to a moral faculty: "Hitler lacked any semblance of a **conscience**." *Conscious* is an adjective, meaning "awake": "Was Ray **conscious** when he wrote his history paper?"

**contemptible, contemptuous** A person or an act that is *contemptible* is worthy of our contempt. A person who is *contemptuous* has contempt for someone or something: "Luisa was **contemptuous** of her boss, for his treatment of female employees was **contemptible**."

**continual, continuous** *Continual* means "habitual" or "normally repeated": "Rob's **continual** drinking was the reason Miranda left him." *Continuous* means "ongoing without interruption": "The pistons' pumping was **continuous**."

**could of** Avoid; use *could have* instead. See **of**.

**council, counsel, consul** A *council* is an administrative body: "The city **council** voted today on the zoning request." *Counsel* is advice: "I sought my grandfather's **counsel** on handling my debt." A *consul* is a civil servant stationed in another country: "As **consul**, she has worked at the embassy for nine years."

**couple** Be accurate. Do not use this term to refer to more than two.

**criteria, criterion** These terms derive from Latin. *Criterion* is the singular; *criteria* is the plural: "We focus on one **criterion** for promotion: productivity. To a lesser extent, however, we also consider other **criteria**, such as loyalty, punctuality, and effort."

**cute** Avoid this informal term for "attractive."

**data** A plural noun—use plural verbs and pronouns with *data*: "The **data were** [*not* **was**] insufficient.

**definite, very definite** The second of these terms is redundant. *Definite* suffices.

**desert, deserts, dessert** One travels on a camel through the *desert*. However, as a verb, *desert* means "to abandon": "They **deserted** their disabled aircraft and began walking across the **desert** in search of water and food." *Deserts* is a noun meaning "appropriate reward or punishment": "The killers got their just **deserts**." *Dessert* is a fruit or sweet eaten at the end of a meal.

**deviant, deviate** The first is a noun, the second a verb: "A **deviant** is one who **deviates** from social norms."

**device, devise** *Device*, a noun, refers to an instrument, machine, or tool. *Devise* is a verb meaning "to create or make": "Archimedes **devised** a **device** that used solar power to burn the sails of Roman ships."

**differ from, differ with** Use *differ from* to indicate dissimilarity: "Lemurs **differ from** meerkats." Use *differ with* to indicate disagreement: "Our local film critic **differed with** the New York critics' opinion of *The Matrix*."

**different from, different than** Use *different from:* "Pasta is **different from** risotto."

**discreet, discrete** *Discreet* means "judicious about revealing sensitive or private matters": "Senator Bing wishes his aide had been **discreet**." *Discrete* means "separate" or "distinct": "The park contains three **discrete** areas of interest: the zoological area, the botanical gardens, and the water park."

**disinterested, uninterested** These words are often used interchangeably, but their meanings are quite different. *Disinterested* means "unbiased" or "impartial": "The mediator was renowned for her professional **disinterest** when settling labor disputes." *Uninterested* means "not interested": "I am **uninterested** in modern sculpture; it does not move me."

**due to** Do not substitute *due to* for *because of*. "She lost her job **because of** [*not* **due to**] the recession." However, *due to* is permissible when used to describe the subject of a sentence. In such cases, it is used directly after a form of *to be*: "In the 1930s, the run on the banks was **due to** a massive loss in depositors' confidence."

**due to the fact that** Avoid this needless filler. Use *because* instead.

**each and every** Avoid this redundancy by using either *each* or *every,* not both.

**eachother, each other** Always spell as two words.

**economic, economical** *Economic* refers to the study of economics: "The president's **economic** advisors resigned after the new unemployment statistics were released." *Economical* means "frugal" or "thrifty": "Shopping at discount clubs is an **economical** way to provide for a large family."

**effect** See **affect, effect.**

**e.g.** Short for the Latin *exempli gratia*, which means "for example." Avoid using this abbreviation in most college writing, except in parentheses or in footnotes. In any case, always follow *e.g.* with a comma.

**elicit, illicit** *Elicit*, a verb, means "to draw forth": "The new rules for fraternities **elicited** the approval of the student newspaper." *Illicit*, an adjective, means "illegal": "The athlete was accused of using **illicit** drugs."

**emigrate, immigrate** A person *emigrates from* a country; a person *immigrates to* another country.

**eminent, imminent** Both are adjectives. *Eminent* means "important" or "prominent": "The **eminent** historian gave a fascinating public lecture." *Imminent* means "immediately going to happen": "The thunderstorm is **imminent**."

**enthused, enthusiastic** *Enthusiastic* is preferred in college writing.

**equally as** Avoid this redundancy. Use *as* by itself: "This pizza is **as good as** [*not* **equally as good as**] the one I had in New York."

**especially, specially** Use the first of these words in college writing; the second is colloquial.

**etc.** Short for the Latin *et cetera* ("and other things"). Avoid this abbreviation in most college writing, except in parentheses or in footnotes. Do not use it with *and,* for *and* is already part of the Latin term.

**eventhough, even though** Always spell as two words.

**everyone, every one** *Everyone* is an indefinite pronoun meaning "a person." *Every one* is a phrase meaning "all members of a group": "**Everyone** is eligible; **every one** of us should enter."

**except, accept** See **accept, except.**

**explicit, implicit** *Explicit* means "stated clearly or directly": "The directions were **explicit,** but Raymond managed to get in trouble anyway." *Implicit* is the opposite, meaning "suggested but not stated directly": "**Implicit** in my ninety-day review was a sense that the company is doing better as a whole."

**extant, extent** *Extant* is an adjective meaning "in existence" or "not extinct": "Scientists believe that only twenty **extant** reptile species are left in the area." *Extent* means "degree" or "amount": "Doctors removed the scar tissue to the **extent** possible."

**facilitate** Avoid this bureaucratic jargon; use *help* or *aid* instead.

**farther, further** Use *farther* to refer to actual distance: "It is **farther** to Detroit than it is to Chicago." Use *further* to mean "a greater degree" or "more": "After **further** debate, we decided to adopt Plan A."

**fewer, less** Use *fewer* to refer to countable things: "There are **fewer** cars on the lot now than there were this morning." Use *less* to refer to things that are normally measured, not counted: "There's **less** rice than usual in the dish."

**finalize** Avoid; use *finish* or *complete* instead.

**flaunt, flout** To *flaunt* is "to boast" or "to display ostentatiously." To *flout* is to "treat with contempt, sneer at, or disdain": "Avery does not hesitate to **flaunt** his wealth. Knowing he can pay any traffic fine, he **flouts** posted speed limits and parks wherever he likes."

**formally, formerly** *Formally* is the adverb form of *formal,* which indicates an adherence to particular rules, ceremonies, and conventions. Synonyms for *formerly* include *previously* and *in the past.*

**former, first; latter, last** Use *former* and *latter* to refer to one of two items; use *first* and *last* to refer to more than two items.

**get** Avoid using this word to mean "bother" or "affect": That music really **bothers** [*not* **gets**] me.

**goes** Avoid using this verb to mean "says."

**good and** This expression is informal. Instead, use *very* or *well*: "She returned from her vacation **well** [*not* **good and**] rested."

**good, well** *Good* is always an adjective: "This pasta is quite **good.**" *Well* is normally an adverb: "We played **well** together." Use *well* as an adjective only to refer to personal health: "Three months after his bout with pneumonia, Mr. Oshiro finally feels **well** again."

**got, gotten** *Got* is the past tense of the verb *to get; gotten* is its past participle. Don't confuse them: "Shortly after Maurizio **had gotten** [*not* **got**] promoted for the third time, he **got** an even better job offer and left the company."

**hanged, hung** *Hanged* is the past tense and past participle of the verb *to hang. Hanged* refers to killing by suspending from a height: "The prisoner **hanged** himself in his cell." *Hung* is also the past tense and past participle of *to hang,* but it means "to suspend" a thing or "to fasten" it on a wall or hook: "The portrait was **hung** in the living room."

**hardly** See **can't hardly.**

**highschool, high school** Always spell as two words unless you are quoting.

**hisself** Not a word—use *himself* instead.

**hopefully** Some writers avoid this form because its use can result in the omission of important information: "**Hopefully,** you will take the job." Who is doing the hoping in this sentence? A better alternative is "**I hope** you will take the job."

**how** Don't use *how* when you mean *that*: I learned **that** [*not* **how**] he had been arrested.

**i.e.** Short for the Latin *id est* ("that is"). Avoid using this abbreviation in most college writing. However, if you must use *i.e.,* follow it with a comma.

**if and when** Avoid this filler, which means "if."

**if, whether** *If* is used in sentences that express a condition. *Whether* is used to indicate an alternative: "**If** you lend me $10, I will accompany you to the movies tonight **whether** we go to the Bijou Theater or to the Star Cinemas."

**illicit, elicit** See **elicit, illicit.**

**immigrate, emigrate** See **emigrate, immigrate.**

**imminent, eminent** See **eminent, imminent.**

**impact** Use *impact* as a noun rather than a verb in college writing. When you need a verb, try *affect*: "Will the dip in the stock market **affect** our income? If so, what will be the **impact**?"

**implicit, explicit** See **explicit, implicit.**

**imply, infer** Use *imply* to mean "suggest"; use *infer* to mean "interpret" or "conclude": "Speakers **imply,** but listeners **infer.**"

**incidence, incidents** The first term refers to frequency or rate of occurrence. The second is the plural of a word that means "event," "occurrence," or "specific case": "The **incidence** of polio decreased dramatically after the Salk vaccine was introduced. There have been no **incidents** of the disease in this country for decades."

**incredible, incredulous** The first term means "unbelievable"; it relates to statements and phenomena. *Incredulous* describes people who are skeptical or unwilling to believe that a statement or phenomenon is true: "Naturally, I remained **incredulous** about his excuse for being late; considering the fact that he is an inveterate liar, his story about having two flat tires remains **incredible.**" Note that *incredible* is sometimes informally used to mean "unusual," "unique," or "spectacular." Avoid this usage in college writing: "Jason's 55-yard field-goal kick was **spectacular** [*not* **incredible**]."

**infact, in fact** Always spell as two words unless you are quoting.

**ingenious, ingenuous** Synonyms for *ingenious* include *intelligent, innovative,* and *inventive. Ingenuous,* on the other hand, means "innocent," "naïve," and "without guile": "Although Michael is **ingenious** at fixing cars, he is remarkably **ingenuous** when it comes to matters of the heart."

**in regards to** Avoid; use *in regard to* or *regarding* instead.

**inside of** Avoid this redundancy; use *inside* or *within.*

**inter-, intra-** *Inter* means "between"; *intra* means "within": "Susan has just competed in an **interstate** college field hockey tournament. She learned to play the game only last year, when she joined her college's **intramural** league."

**irregardless** Not a word—use *regardless* instead.

**is when, is where**  Students sometimes use these constructions when defining a term, as in this case: "Communism **is where** (or **is when**) the government owns the means of production." But *communism* is neither a time nor a place; it is an economic system. A better alternative is "Communism is an economic system in which the government owns the means of production." Note that in the second example, *communism,* a noun, is being defined by the noun *system,* not by the adverb *when* or *where.*

**its, it's**  *Its* is a possessive pronoun that means "belonging to it": "The new SUV has **its** virtues." *It's* is a contraction of *it is* or *it has:* "**It's** been three years since Sara took a vacation." Note that *its'* does not exist.

**kind of, sort of**  Avoid these informal terms.

**latter**  See **former, first; latter, last.**

**lay, lie**  *Lie* means "to recline": "I think that I will **lie** down for a while." *Lay* means "to put (something) in a lower position": "Jack **lays** the manual down on the desk." The past-tense form of *lie* is *lay:* "Alice **lay** down for a few minutes after supper." The past-tense form of *lay* is *laid:* "Rosa **laid** the packages down and searched for her car keys."

**leave, let**  *Leave* means "to depart"; don't use *leave* in place of *let,* which means "permit": "**Let** us go now," not "**Leave** us go now."

**lend, loan**  Never ask "Can you **loan** me a dollar?" *Lend* is a verb; *loan* is a noun: "Bankers **lend** money, but they make **loans.**" The correct wording of the question above is "Can you **lend** me a dollar?"

**less, fewer**  See **fewer, less.**

**let's us**  Avoid this redundancy; use *let's* instead.

**liable**  *Liable* means "obligated for" or "legally responsible for." Do not use it to mean "likely": "Susan is **likely** [*not* **liable**] to be promoted."

**lie, lay**  See **lay, lie.**

**like, as**  See **as, like.**

**lite**  Always spell as *light* unless you are quoting.

**loose, lose**  *Loose* means "not tight": "The nut holding the boiler plate was **loose.**" *Lose* means "to misplace" or "to be defeated": "We need to make sure not to **lose** the backup file."

**lots, lots of**  Avoid these informal constructions in formal writing. Instead, use *much, many,* and *a lot.*

**many, much**  *Many* is used with count nouns such as pounds, inches, people, and cars. *Much* is used with noncount nouns such as rice, string, and equipment: "**Much** water has passed under **many** bridges."

**may, can**  See **can, may.**

**may be, maybe**  Both terms mean "perhaps" or "possibly," but the first is a verb phrase, and the second is an adverb. Keep this distinction in mind: "**Maybe** the sun will shine; if not, the picnic **may be** postponed."

**media**  This noun is the plural of *medium.* It agrees with plural verbs and pronouns: "The **media are** [*not* **is**] divided on this issue; in fact, **they have** [*not* **it has**] many different approaches to the problem."

**might of**  Avoid; use *might have* instead. See **of.**

**most**  Don't use to mean *almost.*

**myself**  Correct when used as either a reflexive pronoun ("I pinched **myself**") or as an intensive pronoun ("I rebuilt this carburetor **myself**"). However, avoid using *myself* as part of a sentence's subject: "Rita and **I** [*not* **myself**] met with the college president yesterday."

**nice** This is an almost meaningless word because so many unrelated meanings have been attached to it: "likable," "kind," "good," "attractive," "polite," "friendly," "considerate," "suitable." In college writing, always choose a more specific alternative.

**nite** Always spell as *night* unless you are quoting.

**nohow, nowheres** Avoid—these are not words.

**nowhere near** Avoid—use *not nearly* instead: "Ten is **not nearly** [*not* **nowhere near**] enough."

**number, amount** See **amount, number.**

**of** Avoid using *of* to replace *have:* "I could **have** [*not* **of**] been a contender."

**off of** Avoid this redundancy; use *off* by itself: "Jason fell **off** the roof."

**oftentimes** *Often* works just as well and is less trouble to write.

**on account of** Avoid this wordy construction. Instead, use *because* or another synonym.

**orientate** British English uses *orientate;* American English uses *orient,* which means "to familiarize with" or "to place in a particular position": "Faculty advisors will **orient** students to the new regulations." "The church's large rose window was **oriented** south."

**outside of** Avoid this redundancy; use *outside.*

**passed, past** *Passed* is the past tense of the verb *pass:* "I **passed** the test" or "The former club president was glad she had **passed** her responsibilities on to her successor." *Past* means "former" or "previous" (when referring to time) or "beyond" (when referring to place or time): "We turned off the road just **past** the first bend; there a **past** president of our club had built a cabin."

**patience, patients** *Patience* is a virtue; *patients* are people under the care of doctors or dentists.

**percent, percentage** Use numbers with *percent* (9 **percent**), but use *percentage* when referring to a general concept: "A large **percentage** of voters skipped Tuesday's runoff election."

**persecute, prosecute** The first item means to "oppress" or "tyrannize": "In Russia, Jews have been **persecuted** since the time of the czars." The second term means to litigate or to bring charges against in a court of law: "Abigail was **prosecuted** for tax evasion."

**personal, personnel** *Personal* is an adjective that means "individual," "intimate," or "relating to 'person'": "Residents of Sunnyvale Nursing Home can make **personal** choices regarding room décor." *Personnel* is both a noun and an adjective. It refers to the employees or members of a business or organization: "**Personnel** at Acme Electrical Suppliers, including those who work in the **personnel** office, have voted to accept pay cuts."

**plenty** Do not use to mean "very": "This stew is **very** [*not* **plenty**] good, Mom."

**plus** Do not attempt to substitute *plus* for a coordinating conjunction: "It was late when we got home, **and** [*not* **plus**] the dishes still needed to be washed." *Plus* is a preposition: "Our tax owed **plus** the late penalty amounted to over eight hundred dollars."

**precede, proceed** *Precede* is a verb that means "to come before": "The bridesmaids **preceded** the bride by three steps." *Proceed* is a verb that means "to continue": "**Proceed** with your task, Wentworth."

**predominant, predominate** These words are not interchangeable. *Predominant,* the adjective form, is used to describe the leading or most important member of a group: "The **predominant** feeling is that the company president will be replaced very soon." *Predominate,* the verb form, indicates that one thing has more importance than others: "In the arts, modernist philosophy **predominated** during much of the twentieth century."

**presently** *Presently* means "very soon." Do not confuse it with *currently:* "Howard will be here **presently; currently**, he is in the restroom."

**principal, principle** As an adjective, **principal** means "dominant" or "most important": "The **principal** cause of the fire was an electrical short." As a noun, it refers to a school administrator ("the **principal** of Oakwood Elementary"), a leader of a company ("She is a **principal** [partner] at Jones & Jones"), or the base value of a loan or an investment ("drawing the interest but leaving the **principal** alone"). *Principle,* a noun, means "an axiom or theory" ("the **principle** of unintended consequences") or a moral belief ("Karen is a person of **principle**").

**proceed, precede** See **precede, proceed.**

**quiet, quite** The first is an adjective meaning the absence of sound; the second is an adverb meaning "very." Be careful not to confuse the spellings of these words.

**quite, rather** Overused as modifiers: "The airport was **quite** huge." "The hotel room was **rather** tiny." Neither *quite* nor *rather* helps here. In each case, the adjective is stronger when not afflicted by *quite* and *rather.*

**quotation, quote** Do not use *quote* as a noun: "My **quotation** [*not* **quote**] comes from a story by Flannery O'Connor." Remember also that text is not a quotation until you have borrowed it: O'Connor's **sentence** becomes your **quotation.**

**raise, rise** *Raise* is *transitive,* meaning that it must be used with a direct object: "The elderly farmer **raised** sunflowers." *Rise* is *intransitive,* meaning that it does not take an object: "The sun **rises** each day."

**rather, quite** See **quite, rather.**

**real, really** *Real* is an adjective that is frequently misused as an adverb. Use **really** instead: "You are **really** [*not* **real**] quiet today." However, **really** is often overused in a different way. How does "It is a **really** great film" improve upon "It is a great film"?

**reason is because** Avoid—use *reason that . . . is* instead. Instead of "The **reason** they postponed the game **is because** of bad weather," use "The **reason that** they postponed the game **is** bad weather."

**refer back** See **again, back.**

**respectfully, respectively** Use *respectfully* to mean "showing respect": "I **respectfully** ask that my interview be moved to next Friday." Use *respectively* to mean "in the order indicated": "On the exam, Robert, Tomoko, and Sarah made *A, A–,* and *B+,* **respectively.**"

**rise, raise** See **raise, rise.**

**sensual, sensuous** *Sensuous* relates to things that are pleasing to the senses: "A **sensuous** wind blew warm and fragrant breezes across the bay." *Sensual* relates to gratification of the physical senses, especially as they relate to sexuality: "In the Renaissance, painters felt free to depict the **sensual** qualities of the human form."

**set, sit** *Set* is a transitive verb (it takes an object) meaning "to place" or "to put"; *sit* is an intransitive verb (it doesn't take an object): "**Set** your luggage on the rack, and **sit** on the couch."

**shall, will** *Shall* was once used to indicate the future tense with the pronouns *I* and *we.* Today, *will* is almost universally used.

**should of** Avoid—use *should have* instead. See **of.**

**so** Don't use to mean "very": "It was **very** [*not* **so**] hot today." But note: "It was **so** hot today that I stayed inside all afternoon."

**some**  Don't use *some* as an intensifier: "Hurricane Hugo was a **terrible** [*not* **some**] storm."

**sometime, some time, sometimes**  *Sometime* is an adverb that means "at some indefinite point in time": "Matthew will be taking his college entrance exam **sometime** in the near future." *Some time* is a phrase made up of the noun *time* and the adjective *some:* "We hiked for **some time** before we reached the river." *Sometimes* is an adverb meaning "on some occasions": "**Sometimes** I stop at the Hungry Lion for a hamburger."

**somewheres**  Not a word—use *somewhere* instead.

**sort of, kind of**  See **kind of, sort of.**

**stationary, stationery**  Use *stationary* to mean "unmoving" or "fixed": "The sailboat has a **stationary** mast." Use *stationery* to mean writing paper and envelopes: "We bought this expensive paper at the **stationery** store."

**suppose to, supposed to**  The correct form is *supposed to.*

**sure, surely**  *Sure* is an adjective: "This investment is a **sure** thing." Do not use *sure* as an adverb; use *surely* instead: "The introduction to this proposal is **surely** stupid."

**than, then**  These words are frequently confused. Use *then* as an adverb signaling a time transition: "**Then** the concert ended." Use *than* as a comparative conjunction: "These pretzels are harder **than** the last batch we bought."

**their, there, they're**  These words are easily confused. *Their* is the possessive form of *they:* "They checked **their** bags at the curb." *There* can be either an adverb of location—"The exercise room is over **there** by the pool"—or an expletive, a word that delays the appearance of the subject—"**There** are many reasons for the boss's anger." *They're* is the contraction of *they are:* "**They're** going to Cancun for a vacation."

**theirselves**  Not a word—use *themselves* instead.

**through, thorough**  As a preposition, *through* means "by way of." As an adjective, it means "finished." *Thorough,* meaning "complete," is an adjective. Don't confuse the two by misspelling them.

**thru**  Always spell as *through* unless you are quoting.

**thusly**  Avoid—use *thus,* which is an adverb already and does not need the extra *ly.*

**till, until**  Both words mean the same thing. However, *till* is less formal.

**to, too, two**  These words are frequently confused. Use *to* either as a preposition—"Bill is going **to** Omaha"—or as part of an infinitive—"**To** look at museum paintings is one of Bill's great pleasures." Use *too* as an adverb meaning either "also" or "excessively": Sarah is **too** tired to go to the party; Andrea is **too.**" Use *two* to mean the number, either as a noun or an adjective: "Martin earned **two** degrees at the university."

**toward, towards**  In American English, *toward* is preferred.

**try and**  Avoid—use *try to* instead.

**uninterested, disinterested**  See **disinterested, uninterested.**

**unique**  Do not try to qualify *unique.* "Fairly unique" or "somewhat unique" are contradictions in terms. Something is either unique or it is not.

**usage**  Avoid unless referring to language choice: "His **usage** of old-fashioned words seems strained and affected." Otherwise, stick with *use:* "His **use** [*not* **usage**] of the car is limited to weekends."

**use to, used to**  *Used to* is correct.

**utilize, utilization**  Avoid this bureaucratic jargon; stick with *use* for both the verb and the noun: "We will **use** [*not* **utilize**] every means at our disposal."

**very definite**  This term is redundant; write *definite.*

**wander, wonder**  Don't confuse these. They mean very different things: *Wander* means to "roam." *Wonder* means to "think" or "consider."

**ways**  Avoid using this term to refer to distance: "Colorado is a long **way** [*not* **ways**] from here."

**were, where**  Don't forget the letter *h* in *where*.

**where**  Do not use to mean "that": "I heard on the radio **that** [*not* **where**] the big garden-supply store is going out of business."

**where . . . at**  Avoid colloquial expressions such as "Where is my car at?" Instead, write "Where is my car?"

**who, whom**  *Who* is a subject; *whom* is an object: "**Who** is the college loan officer?" "**Whom** did you speak with about your loan?"

**whose, who's**  These words are frequently confused. *Whose* is the possessive form of *who:* "**Whose** fishing rod is this?" *Who's* is the contraction of *who is:* "**Who's** out in the garden?"

**-wise**  This is a nonstandard noun ending. Don't write "**Math-wise**, I need a tutor." Instead, write "I need a tutor for math."

**would have, would of**  The correct form is *would have.*

**your, you're**  These words are frequently confused. *Your* is the possessive form of *you:* "Here are **your** tickets and itinerary, Karen." *You're* is the contraction of *you are:* "**You're** going to be late if you don't get started."

# APPENDIX
## Designing Documents

At some point in your life you have come across the stock listings that are published in daily newspapers. These devices list hundreds of stocks and provide the same information for each one: an abbreviated form of the company's name, the earnings per share, the stock price at the start of the trading day and then at the end of the day, and so on. This format is called a **table,** and it allows efficient display of a large amount of data.

Think of how difficult it would be to transmit this information if tables didn't exist: each stock would require its own sentence, and the reader would be forced to spend a great deal of time wading through unnecessary syntax to acquire the information that he or she needed.

Tables, along with **graphs** and **charts**, are a visually effective way of displaying information that would lose its "edge" if supplied in text format. The message of a visual can be instantly clear to the reader/viewer. Not all documents that you will produce in college and beyond will or should use visual devices. For example, a research paper for an English class follows a strict format supplied by the Modern Language Association that rarely involves the use of visual elements. However, as you go through your college classes and beyond, you'll probably find yourself producing documents that can be greatly enhanced by the use of visuals. As well, other forms of communication have visual connotations: e-mail messages, slideshows, and Web sites.

## TABLES

Typically, tables display numbers compared across categories, as in the following example:

|  | TABLE 1. AVERAGE NUMBER OF STUDENTS USING THE MCMILLAN AQUATIC CENTER IN MARCH–MAY 2007, BY DAY OF THE WEEK |  |  |  |  |  |  |
|---|---|---|---|---|---|---|---|
| March | 132 | 110 | 95 | 98 | 140 | 165 | 161 |
| April | 147 | 119 | 108 | 111 | 152 | 177 | 181 |
| May | 160 | 132 | 120 | 124 | 180 | 199 | 205 |
|  | M | Tu | W | Th | F | Sa | Su |

The reader/viewer sees the logic here: as the school week progresses, fewer students go swimming. Toward the weekend, the numbers sharply increase. Moreover, as the spring progresses toward summer, the numbers increase for each day of the week.

## GRAPHS AND CHARTS

This category covers many different types of visual devices, but three major ones are pie charts, bar graphs, and line graphs. **Pie charts** are used to show percentages or proportions. The following example displays average monthly expenses for a day-care center:

### Monthly Expenses by Type

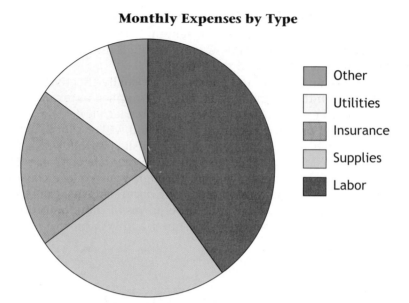

Note that the largest "slice"—Labor—has been displayed with the brightest color in order to reinforce its significance as an expense. Note also the category of Other is used to avoid having several tiny slices that would be hard to distinguish and hard to label.

**Bar graphs** can be used to display comparative numbers—achievements, for instance, as in the following example, which shows the unit sales for the five leading salespeople at a car dealership:

### Unit Sales for September

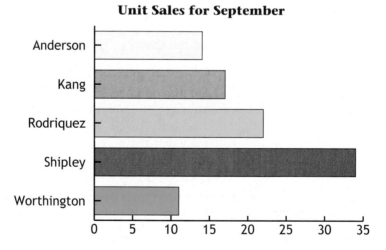

This chart would be used as a motivational tool—in other words, the exact numbers aren't important; Shipley's achievement is.

Line graphs are used to show trends, such as changes in revenues or profits over time. The following example contrasts 2007 revenues per month to 2006 revenues per month for a software company:

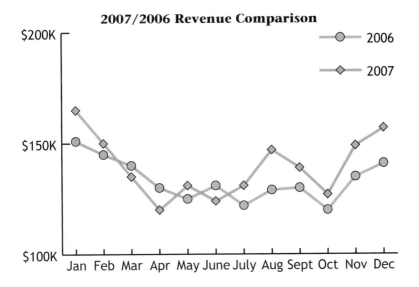

## GENERAL GUIDELINES FOR USING TABLES, CHARTS, AND GRAPHS

- Number your visuals by type. Tables are tables, but charts and graphs are called "figures." Therefore, a typical sequence might be Table 1, Figure 1, Table 2.
- Introduce your visuals; don't let them appear without explanation. For example, "Figure 1 displays sales trends for the first six months of this year." Also make sure that the visual *follows* its introduction.
- Check each visual against your text to ensure that one doesn't contradict the other.
- Don't use visuals unless they help your document. For example, a pie chart that shows two categories, one at 95% and the other at 5%, is probably not worth the trouble.

## E-MAIL DESIGN

The convenience of e-mail sometimes causes the sender to ignore the needs of the reader. Consider this example:

From: macdaddy413796@genericemail.com
Subject:
Date: 3/21/07
To: "Randall Coughlin"
Hey Dr Coughlkin I want to ask u abouyt the project due necxt week I missed class on fri and wanted to check w/u about my prop. if u rememeber I,m wanting to due setoids+highschool atheletes. I think that's what u and i agreed was ok. Get back to me beforer monday.

The only way to make this message more annoying would be to type it in all capital letters. The sender has a remarkable disregard for his or her reader. For one thing, Dr. Coughlin doesn't know who sent it to him. Second, the message is a run-together mishmash of ideas and bad writing. Notice how both the format (and the wording) can be improved:

From: macdaddy413796@genericemail.com
Subject: project topic
Date: 3/21/07
To: "Randall Coughlin"

Dr. Coughlin: I need to ask you about next week's project. Unfortunately, I missed class on Friday, and I want to check with you about my proposal.

When we last talked, I mentioned that I wanted to work on the issue of steroid use by high school athletes. I believe that you agreed that this is a suitable topic.

I'd like to work on my project this weekend. If at all possible, could you get back to me before Monday?

Thanks,
Matt McLarin
ENG 128

Note: in e-mail messages, the block format shown above—with a line space between paragraphs—works better than indented paragraphs because the indent can disappear when the message is received by the reader's e-mail system, which might be different from the sender's.

## SLIDESHOW DESIGN

Slideshows, such as those produced by Microsoft's PowerPoint, are immensely useful visual additions to oral presentations (see also Chapter 18). However, they can also be a hindrance, drawing too much attention to themselves and distracting the audience from the presentation itself. In some cases, the slideshow is overdeveloped, with text and graphics competing for attention with moving elements—a ball bouncing back and forth, for example, or virtual birds flying back and forth across the slide. In these instances, the audience will be concentrating on the image, not the speaker.

In many cases, the problem is caused by too much text on each slide. Keep in mind that the size of the room and the display method can vary widely. In other words, your slides might be displayed on a 24-inch television screen in a room that seats fifty people, or your slides might be shown on a theater-size screen in an auditorium. Plan accordingly, but keep in mind this simple directive: less is more. Don't crowd your slides. If you keep typing in a slide, the software will continue to reduce the point size to make the text fit. Spread your text out over several slides instead. The following is an example of a very crowded slide that will be hard to read for the people in the back row:

## Three Steps to a Successful Registration

- First, have a meeting with your advisor, and prepare a preferred schedule and a backup.

- Second, check with the Bursar's office for any "holds" upon your registration; if any exist, deal with them immediately.

- Third, register as early as you can; if you delay, the classes that you want may be filled up.

Instead, this slide can become three slides:

## A Successful Registration: Step One

- **Have a meeting with your advisor, and prepare a preferred schedule and a backup.**

### A Successful Registration: Step Two

- Check with the Bursar's office for any "holds" upon your registration; if any exist, deal with them immediately.

### A Successful Registration: Step Three

- Third, register as early as you can; if you delay, the classes that you want may be filled up.

# WEB SITE DESIGN

Many Web sites seem cluttered, with too much going on in the homepage image. However, the homepage is the first thing that the Web surfer sees when accessing your site, and it should be visually appealing, leading the user to want to enter.

A good example of a visually appealing homepage is that of the George Eastman House (www.eastmanhouse.org). Eastman, the founder of Kodak, built a mansion in Rochester, New York, that is now a museum devoted both to his career and to great photography. The homepage expertly displays these emphases.

## Text Credits

### Chapter 1
**p. 15** "Neat People vs. Sloppy People," by Suzanne Britt. From *Show and Tell*, Morning Owl Press, 1982. Reprinted by permission of the author.

### Chapter 2
**pp. 139-142** McGuane, Thomas. "Roanie." *Some Horses*. Lyons Press, 1999, pp. 123-135. Copyright © 1999 by Thomas McGuane, permission of The Wylie Agency. **pp. 144-146** From *The Woman Warrior: Memoirs of a Girlhood Among Ghosts*, by Maxine Hong Kingston. Copyright © 1975, 1976 by Maxine Hong Kingston. Used by permission of Alfred A. Knopf, a division of Random House, Inc. **pp. 147-150** Knef, Hildegard. Chapter 4, *The Gift Horse*. McGraw-Hill, 1971, pp. 24-28.

### Chapter 3
**pp. 176-178** Barry, Lynda. "The Sanctuary of School." *The New York Times*, January 5, 1992, Educational Life Section. **pp. 179-181** "Only Daughter" by Sandra Cisneros. Copyright © 1990 by Sandra Cisneros. First published in *Glamour*, November 1990. Reprinted by permission of Susan Bergholz Literary Services, New York, NY and Lamy, NM. All rights reserved. **pp. 183-185** Dillard, Annie. "The Chase." *An American Girlhood*. New York: HarperCollins, 1987, pp. 45-59. Reprinted by permission of HarperCollins Publishers.

### Chapter 7
**pp. 210-212** Staples, Brent. "Just Walk on By." *Ms.*, September 1986. Used by permission of the author. **pp. 214-218** From *Travels with Lizbeth*, by Lars Eighner. Copyright © 1993 by the author and reprinted by permission of St. Martin's Press, LLC. **pp. 219-224** Waters, Harry F. "Life According to TV." *Newsweek*, December 6, 1982. Reprinted by permission of Newsweek via PARS International.

### Chapter 8
**pp. 243-246** "Why Johnny Can't Fail" by Jerry Jesness. Reprinted with permission from July 1999 issue of *Reason* magazine. Copyright © 1999 by Reason Foundation, 3415 S. Sepulveda Blvd., Suite 400, Los Angeles, CA 90034, www.reason.com **pp. 248-250** *The Autobiography of Malcolm X*, by Malcolm X and Alex Haley. Copyright © 1964 by Alex Haley and Malcolm X. Copyright © 1965 by Alex Haley and Betty Shabazz. Used by permission of Random House, Inc. **pp. 252-254** "How Not to Use the Fax Machine" and "How Not to Use the Cellular Phone" from *How to Travel with a Salmon & Other Essays*, by Umberto Eco. Copyright © Gruppo Editoriale Fabbri, Bompiani, Sonzogno, Etas S.p.A., English translation by William Weaver, copyright © 1994 by Harcourt, Inc. Reprinted by permission of Houghton Mifflin Harcourt Publishing Company.

### Chapter 9
**pp. 277-279** "The Call of Busyness" by Barbara Ehrenreich from *The Years of Our Lives*, Pantheon, 1990, pp. 22-25. Reprinted by permission of International Creative Management, Inc. Copyright © 1990 by Barbara Ehrenreich. **pp. 281-282** "Drugs" by Gore Vidal. Copyright © 1970 by Gore Vidal, from *Homage to Daniel Shays: Collected Essays 1952-1972*, by Gore Vidal. Used by permission of Random House, Inc. **pp. 284-286** Rhodes, Richard. "Hollow Claims About Fantasy Violence." *New York Times*, September 17, 2000. Copyright © 2000 The New York Times. Reprinted by permission.

### Chapter 10
**pp. 312-313** Brady, Judy. "Why I Want a Wife." *Ms.*, Spring, 1972. Copyright © 1972 Judy Brady. **pp. 314-316** William Raspberry, "The Handicap of a Definition," *The Washington Post*, January 6, 1982. Copyright © 1982 The Washington Post. All rights reserved. Used by permission and protected by the copyright laws of the United States. The printing, copying, redistribution, or retransmission of the Material without express written permission is prohibited. **pp. 317-319** Dillard, Annie. "The Chase." *An American Girlhood*. New York: HarperCollins, 1987, pp. 222-225. Reprinted by permission of HarperCollins Publishers.

**Chapter 11**

**pp. 345-346** Fran Lebowitz, "The Sound of Music: Enough Already," *Metropolitan Life*, 1978. **pp. 348-349** Martin Luther King, Jr., "Three Types of Resistance to Oppression." Reprinted by arrangement with The Heirs to the Estate of Martin Luther King, Jr., c/o Writers House as agent for the proprietor New York, NY. Copyright © 1963 Dr. Martin Luther King, Jr.; copyright renewed 1991 Coretta Scott King. **pp. 351-355** Fussell, Paul. "Notes on Class." Abridged from *The Boy Scout Handbook and Other Observations*. Oxford University Press, 1982, pp. 46-60. By permission of Oxford University Press, Inc.

**Chapter 12**

**pp. 379-381** Mukherjee, Bharati. "Two Ways to Belong in America." *The New York Times*, September 22, 1996. **pp. 383-385** From *Me Talk Pretty One Day*, by David Sedaris. Copyright © 1999 by David Sedaris. By permission of Little, Brown and Company. **pp. 387-390** Barbara Mellix, "From Outside, In" originally appeared in *The Georgia Review*, Volume XLI, No. 2 (Summer 1987). Copyright © 1987 by The University of Georgia/ © 1987 by Barbara Mellix. Reprinted by permission of Barbara Mellix and The Georgia Review.

**Chapter 13**

**pp. 416-418** Minot, Walter S. "Students Who Push Burgers." *Christian Science Monitor*, November 22, 1988, p. 16. Reprint permission obtained via The Copyright Clearance Center. **pp. 419-421** Rivers, Caryl. "What Should Be Done About Rock Lyrics?" *Boston Globe*, 1985. Used by permission of the author. **pp. 423-424** Levin, Michael. "The Case for Torture." *Newsweek*, June 7, 1982. With permission from Michael Levin, Professor of Philosophy, City University of New York.

**Chapter 14**

**pp. 452-454** Scott Russell Sanders, "The Men We Carry In Our Minds." Copyright © 1984 by Scott Russell Sanders; first appeared in *Milkweed Chronicles*; from *The Paradise of Bombs*. Reprinted by permission of the author and the author's agents, Virginia Kidd Agency, Inc. **pp. 456-460** Bourdain, Anthony. "Don't Eat Before Reading This." *The New Yorker*, April 19, 1999, pp. 58-61. Used by permission of the author. **pp. 461-466** Elizabeth Kubler-Ross, "On the Fear of Death." Reprinted with permission of Scribner, an imprint of Simon & Schuster Adult Publishing Group, from *On Death and Dying*, by Elizabeth Kubler-Ross. Copyright © 1969 by Elizabeth Kubler-Ross; copyright renewed © 1997 by Elizabeth Kubler-Ross. All rights reserved.

**Chapter 20**

**p. 558** Libraries of Middlesex Automation Consortium. Used by permission. **p. 559** Libraries of Middlesex Automation Consortium. Used by permission. **p. 561** Reproduced with permission of the H.W. Wilson Company. **p. 564** Used with permission of EBSCO Publishing. **p. 568** Both screenshots used by permission of Google Marketing Department. **pp. 580 and 587 (same excerpt)** "A Hanging," from *Shooting an Elephant and Other Essays*, by George Orwell. Copyright © 1950 by Harcourt, Inc., and renewed 1979 by Sonia Brownell Orwell. Reprinted by permission of Harcourt, Inc.

**Chapter 21**

**p. 604** Slate.com and Washingtonpost.com Newsweek Interactive. All rights reserved. **p. 604** Copyright page of *Abroad: British Literary Traveling Between the Wars*, by Paul Fussell, Oxford University Press, 1980. By permission of Oxford University Press, Inc. **p. 605** Cover page of *Abroad: British Literary Traveling Between the Wars*, by Paul Fussell, Oxford University Press, 1980. By permission of Oxford University Press, Inc. **p. 606** Copyright © 1995 American Society of Criminology. All rights reserved. **p. 607** Copyright © 1995 American Society of Criminology. All rights reserved. **p. 632** Slate.com and Washingtonpost.com Newsweek Interactive. All rights reserved. **p. 633** Copyright page of *Abroad: British Literary Traveling Between the Wars*, by Paul Fussell, Oxford University Press, 1980. By permission of Oxford University Press, Inc. **p. 634** Cover page of *Abroad: British Literary Traveling Between the Wars*, by Paul Fussell, Oxford University Press, 1980. By permission of Oxford University Press, Inc. **p. 635** Copyright © 1995 American Society of Criminology. All rights reserved. **p. 636** Copyright © 1995 American Society of Criminology. All rights reserved.

**Chapter 22**

**p. 650** "The Answer is No," from *The Time and the Place and Other Stories* by Naguib Mahfouz. Copyright © 1991 by The American University in Cairo Press. Used by permission of Doubleday, a division of Random House, Inc.

# Abbreviations and Symbols for Revising and Editing Your Work

| | | | |
|---|---|---|---|
| adj | Problem with an adjective (28c–28e, pp. 753–756) | pl | Error in the plural form of a noun (32k, p. 821) |
| adv | Problem with an adverb (28c–28d, pp. 753–755) | red | Redundant (pp. 118–120; 32d, pp. 809–810) |
| art | Problem with article use (28g, pp. 757–760) | ref | Pronoun reference problem (27f–27g, pp. 737–742) |
| cap | Capitalization error (31a, pp. 795–800) | rep | Repetitious (p. 115; 32d, pp. 809–810) |
| case | Problem with pronoun case (27i–27m, pp. 744–748) | sexist | Sexist language (32e, pp. 810–813) |
| cl | Edit for clarity (pp. 807–808) | sl | Avoid slang (pp. 88–89; 32h, pp. 816–817) |
| cliché | Eliminate cliché (p. 122; 32f, pp. 813–815) | sm | Squinting modifier (28a, pp. 750–752) |
| com | Faulty comparison (25h, p. 714) | sp | Spelling error (32k, pp. 820–822) |
| coord | Faulty coordination (pp. 103–111) | split inf | Split infinitive (28f, pp. 756–757) |
| cs | Comma splice (pp. 105–106; 25d–25f, pp. 707–712) | sub | Faulty subordination (pp. 103–111) |
| | | s–v agr | Subject–verb agreement (26a–26i, pp. 717–726) |
| dict | Word choice problem (pp. 113–129; 32a–32c, pp. 807–808) | t shft | Tense shift (26j, pp. 726–727) |
| dm | Dangling modifier (28b, pp. 752–753) | trans | Transition needed (pp. 73–74) |
| fig | Problem with figurative language (pp. 121–123; 32f, pp. 813–815) | usage | Usage problem (33, pp. 823–835) |
| | | v shft | Voice shift (26k, p. 727) |
| frag | Fragment (p. 109; 25a–25c, pp. 700–707) | vb | Problem with verb form (23g–23j, pp. 678–684) |
| fs | Fused sentence (pp. 105–106; 25d–25f, pp. 707–712) | wordy | Wordy sentence (pp. 116–117, 126–127; 32d, pp. 809–810) |
| gr | Problem with sentence grammar (23, 24, pp. 663–698) | ʌ | Comma needed (29a–29g, pp. 762–772) |
| | | no ʌ | Unnecessary comma (29h, pp. 772–776) |
| hyph | Hyphen needed/not needed (31d, pp. 803–805) | . | Period (30a, pp. 778–779) |
| idiom | Problem with idiom (p. 125; 32j, pp. 818–820) | ; | Semicolon (30b, pp. 779–780) |
| inf | Language too informal (pp. 88–89; 32h–32i, pp. 816–818) | ? | Question mark (30c, pp. 780–782) |
| | | ! | Exclamation mark (30c, pp. 780–782) |
| ital | Problem with italics or underlining (31b, pp. 800–801) | : | Colon (30d, pp. 782–783) |
| | | — | Dash (30e, pp. 783–784) |
| jarg | Eliminate jargon (32g, pp. 815–816) | ( ) | Parentheses (30f, pp. 784–785) |
| log | Faulty logic (pp. 429–432) | [ ] | Brackets (30g, p. 785) |
| m shft | Mood shift (26l, pp. 727–729) | " " | Double quotation marks (30h, pp. 786–787) |
| mix | Mixed construction (25i, pp. 714–715) | ' ' | Single quotation marks (30i, p. 787) |
| mm | Misplaced modifier (28a, pp. 750–752) | ' | Apostrophe (30k, pp. 789–792) |
| num | Numbers and numerals (31c, pp. 801–802) | // | Parallelism needed (pp. 113–114) |
| | | ^ | Add a word or words |
| p agr | Pronoun–antecedent agreement (27a–27e, pp. 731–737) | X | Obvious error |
| | | ⌒ | Transpose words |
| p ref | Pronoun reference problem (27f–27g, pp. 737–742) | # | Add a space |
| | | ◡ | Close up space |
| p shft | Shift in person (27h, pp. 742–744) | ?? | Unclear |
| pred | Predication (verb) problem (23g–23j, pp. 678–684) | | |

**Powered by CATALYST (www.mhhe.com/writingtoday), *Writing Today* helps students throughout the writing process:**

# writing today

**:. CONTEXTS and OPTIONS for the REAL WORLD**

**2ᵉ**

## Donald Pharr | Santi Buscemi

Writing today is more than college papers and office memos. It is emails to customers, lecture notes on a laptop, and texting a friend. In every writing context—college, office, home—modern tools and technologies give you more options than ever before.

*Writing Today* will help students navigate among these options and succeed as writers. The new second edition includes:

- **New Chapter on Student Success:** *Writing Today* begins with a chapter helping students learn the skills they will need to thrive throughout college, written with both traditional and non-traditional students in mind.

- **New Chapter on Group Projects and Oral Presentations:** The second edition extends already robust coverage of collaborative work and oral presentations with Chapter 18, offering advice on teamwork and effective public speaking relevant to both the classroom and the workplace. New speaking assignments have also been added to all chapters.

- **New Chapters on Proposals and Evaluations:** Chapters 16 and 17, on proposals and evaluations, provide clear, organized instruction in these important writing tasks.

- **Increased Coverage of Visual Rhetoric:** Visual literacy and analysis has been further emphasized throughout the chapters of Part I: Approaches. In Part II: Structures, the authors have added new Modes and common patterns of development wit visual material.

- **Real World Vignettes:** One of *Writin* rhetorical strategies for writing with scenarios illustrate how the writing contexts beyond college.

- **Plenty of Models:** *Writing Today* pro draft as well as final form, along wit Barbara Ehrenreich, Sandra Cisneros, Dargis, and Anthony Bourdain.

**RENTAL**

**RETURN TO: KU CAMPUS STORE**
**DUE DATE: DECEMBER 11, 2015**

Writing Today

KUSSI PHARR 07/16
WRITING TODAY (P)

2 900073533222

*The* **McGraw·Hill** *Companies*

**McGraw Hill** **Higher Education**